LAW
AND
WAR
IN
SYRIA

A LEGAL ACCOUNT OF THE CURRENT CRISIS IN SYRIA

LAW AND WAR IN SYRIA

A LEGAL ACCOUNT OF THE CURRENT CRISIS IN SYRIA

W. VAN DER WOLF & C. TOFAN

Law and War in Syria; A legal account of the current crisis in Syria
W. van der Wolf & C. Tofan (eds.)

ISBN softcover: 978-90-5887-059-9

Published by:

International Courts Association
P.O. Box 31051
6503 CB Nijmegen
The Netherlands

E-Mail: info@eduscienceinternational.com

Produced and distributed by:
Wolf Productions
P.O. Box 313
5060 AH Oisterwijk
The Netherlands

Tel: +31 13 582 13 66
E-Mail: sales@wolfpublishers.nl

All rights reserved. No part of this publication may be reproduced, stored in a retrieval system, or transmitted in any form or by any means, electronic, mechanical, photocopying, recording or otherwise, without prior written permission of the publisher. Whilst the authors, editors and publisher have tried to ensure the accuracy of this publication, the publisher, authors and editors cannot accept responsibility for any errors, omissions, misstatements, or mistakes and accept no responsibility for the use of the information presented in this work.

© ICA 2013

Contents

I. INTRODUCTION

1.1. The Assads

The iron rule of the Assad dynasty over Syria's people is forty-two years old. It began in 1970 when then Defense Minister Hafez al-Assad carried out a bloody coup against his own party colleagues and appointed himself president. Hafez, the family patriarch and dictator for life, killed or jailed companions he perceived as his rivals, supported violent extremism whenever he found it useful, and plundered Syria's riches while arresting and torturing any dissenter. Over two generations of Assads, a brutal government in Damascus has been the main Mideast ally of an increasingly belligerent Iran. Bashar al-Assad, the son, has acted as the chief facilitator for Sunni extremist killers in Iraq over the past ten years. In Lebanon, Assad's father and son have wrought havoc since 1975, killing in turn Palestinians, Muslim Lebanese, Christian Lebanese, and whoever dared help the return of stability to a country torn asunder. They assassinated the most prominent Lebanese leaders who stood in their way, including Kamal Jumblat in 1977, Bashir Gemayel in 1982, and in all likelihood Rafik Hariri in 2005.[1]

Most tragically, the Assads never hesitated to commit mass murder against the Syrians. Hama's historic center was leveled to the ground in 1982, and the relentless siege, bombardment, and mass killing continues to this day a pattern of ruthless governance across the country. Both the future of the Middle East and the success of the formidable nonviolent mass movement in Tunisia, Egypt, Bahrain, and Yemen depend on what happens next in Damascus. If the dictatorship survives, if its main pillars are not brought to justice on the way to a democratic transition, Assad's continued rule will doom domestic and international peace in the region and beyond. Why? Because the nonviolent movement will find it hard to recover from this blow. Assad's regime itself will have its own noxious effect on peace. Yet more deeply, more world-historically, it will be harder - much harder - to argue to any brave young man or woman cleaving to nonviolence that this path, although potentially bloody in sacrifice, is the right form of resistance to tyranny.

The first days of 2013 brought new hope for peace to the Syrian people, but as far as we can see it was in vain. United Nations Secretary-General Ban Ki-moon was disappointed that a speech made by Syria's President Bashar al Assad on Sunday 6 January 2013 "does not contribute to a solution that could end

---

1   Operatives of self-proclaimed "Loyal to Assad's Syria" Hizbullah are now under indictment before the Special Tribunal of Lebanon for Hariri's murder, and scores of journalists and politicians along with hundreds of other innocent people have been assassinated, "disappeared," or randomly killed.

the terrible suffering of the Syrian people" he said[2]. "The speech rejected the most important element of the Geneva communiqué of 30 June 2012, namely a political transition and the establishment of a transitional governing body with full executive powers that would include representatives of all Syrians", he continued.

In his speech – made in the capital, Damascus, and his first public remarks in around six months – President al-Assad reportedly put forward a peace plan involving an army ceasefire which would follow a halt to operations by rebel groups, as well as a national reconciliation conference and a new constitution, amongst other points. He was also reported to have described opposition groups as "puppets" of Western countries.

Recent months have witnessed an escalation in the conflict, which is now in its 23rd month.

The so-called 'Geneva communiqué' was issued after a meeting in the Swiss city of the Action Group for Syria, and it layed out key steps in a process to end the violence in Syria. Amongst other items, it called for the establishment of a transitional governing body, with full executive powers and made up by members of the present Government and the opposition and other groups, as part of agreed principles and guidelines for a Syrian-led political transition.

The Action Group is made up of the Secretaries-General of the UN and the League of Arab States; the Foreign Ministers of the five permanent members of the Security Council – China, France, Russia, the United Kingdom and the United States – as well as the Turkish Foreign Minister; the High Representative of the European Union for Foreign Affairs and Security Policy; and the Foreign Ministers of Iraq, Kuwait and Qatar, in their respective roles related to the Arab League.

In December 2012 the UN Special Adviser on the Prevention of Genocide, Adama Dieng, warned of the increasing risk of sectarian violence in Syria, and called on all parties to the conflict to refrain from targeting individuals or groups based on religious or ethnic identity.[3]

According to UN estimates, the number of people in need of humanitarian assistance inside the country has quadrupled between March 2012 and December 2012, from one million to four million. UN humanitarian aid planning estimates that up to a million Syrian refugees will need help during

---

2 7 January 2013.
3 See appendix document 8.

the first half of 2013, with most of these located in Jordan, Iraq, Lebanon, Turkey and Egypt.[4]

1.2. How did it all start?

Protests asking for the release of political prisoners began mid-March 2011 and were immediately met by Syrian security forces who at first detained and attacked protestors with batons, and later opened gunfire, and deployed tanks and naval ships against civilians. Syrian President Bashar al-Assad refused to halt the violence and implement meaningful reforms demanded by protestors such as the lifting of emergency law, broader political representation and a freer media. Assad continued to deny responsibility for the attacks on protestors, placing the blame for the violence on armed groups and foreign conspirators instead. On 16 February 2012 President Assad called for a referendum to be held on 26 February that would end single party rule in Syria; however governments, such as the United States, analysts, and members of the opposition expressed reluctance that the promise of political reform would be upheld, and noted that conducting a referendum during such a crisis was not a necessary course of action to end the violence.

Massive human rights violations in Syria have been committed as Syrian security forces have responded to protestors with extreme violence. Evidence of systematic acts of brutality, including torture and arbitrary arrests, point to a clear policy by Syrian military and civilian leadership amounting to crimes against humanity. Under international law, commanders are responsible for the commission of international crimes by their subordinates if the commanders knew about the violations. In keeping with the norm of the Responsibility to Protect (R2P)[5], UN Member States, regional organizations and governments must urgently work together towards an end to the violence.[6]

---

4   The United Nations' World Food Programme (WFP) announced at a press conference on January 8th 2013 that it is unable to help 1 million Syrians who are going hungry. "This month, the agency aims to help 1.5 million of the 2.5 million Syrians that the Syrian Arab Red Crescent says need it" spokeswoman Elisabeth Byrs said. The lack of security and the agency's inability to use the Syrian port of Tartous for its shipment means that a large number of people in the some of the country's hardest hit areas will not get help. "Our main partner, the Red Cross, is overstretched and has no more capacity to expand further," Byrs said. She also said that the agency has temporarily pulled its staff out of its offices in the Syrian cities of Homs, Aleppo, Tartous and Qamisly due to the rising dangers in those areas. But in December, WFP was able to reach for the first time in many months some hard-to-reach areas near the Turkish border, she said.

5   On this principle see; W. van der Wolf (ed), R2P in International Law (to be published).

6   An interesting paper on these issues is: Humanitarian Intervention In Syria: The Legal Basis. Prepared By The Public International Law & Policy Group July 2012.

As the conflict wore on, demands grew more splintered and protestors began to organize. One of the main opposition groups, the Syrian National Council (SNC), is an umbrella organization that was formed by activists in Istanbul.

The SNC has received economic support from Turkey, who hosts an SNC office. The organization also met with the United Kingdom and United States. The SNC called for the Syrian government to be overthrown by a united opposition, rejected dialogue with Assad, and, though officially against military intervention, requested international protection of the population. In contrast, another main group, the National Co-ordination Committee (NCC) advocated for dialogue with the government, believing that toppling the Assad regime would lead to further chaos. These two groups signed an agreement to unite against the government. Another group, the Free Syrian Army[7], comprised of defected Syrian soldiers, executed retaliatory attacks against Syrian forces.

1.3. Death toll rising

Violence has nevertheless continued and the strength of the opposition, composed largely of defectors from the Syrian army, has grown. There are reports of violent attacks by both government forces and opposition groups. Now almost 2 years after the first violence started the U.N. Human Rights Office released the first days of 2013 a report that said that 59,648 people were killed between March 15, 2011, and November 30, 2012. That figure is considerably higher than those given out by Syrian rights groups and rebel organizations.[8] The preliminary analysis, which took five months to complete, was conducted using a combined list of 147,349 reported killings, fully identified by the first and last name of the victim, as well as the date and location of the death. Any reported killing that did not include at least these four elements was excluded from the list, which was compiled using datasets from seven different sources, including the Government.

Each reported death was compared to all the other reported deaths in order to identify duplicates. The analysis used manual classifications and a data mining technique called an 'alternating decision tree' to identify the duplicate records. After duplicates were removed, the combined dataset was reduced to 59,648 unique records of conflict-related deaths as of 30 November 2012.

At the press conference presenting the report the High Commissioner Navi Pillay said[9]:

---

7   See http://www.free-syrian-army.com/en/home/
8   Preliminary Statistical Analysis of Documentation of Killings in the Syrian Arab Republic, Megan Price, Je Klingner, and Patrick Ball, The Benetech Human Rights Program, 2 January 2013, report see document 1 in the Appendix.
9   http://www.ohchr.org/en/NewsEvents/Pages/Media.aspx

"Although this is the most detailed and wide-ranging analysis of casualty figures so far, this is by no means a definitive figure. We have not been able to verify the circumstances of each and every death, partly because of the nature of the conflict and partly because we have not been allowed inside Syria since the unrest began in March 2011. Once there is peace in Syria, further investigations will be necessary to discover precisely how many people have died, and in what circumstances, and who was responsible for all the crimes that have been committed. This analysis provides a very useful basis upon which future investigations can be built to enhance accountability and provide justice and reparations to victims' families. This massive loss of life could have been avoided if the Syrian government had chosen to take a different path than one of ruthless suppression of what were initially peaceful and legitimate protests by unarmed civilians. As the situation has continued to degenerate, increasing numbers have also been killed by anti-government armed groups, and there has been a proliferation of serious crimes including war crimes, and - most probably - crimes against humanity, by both sides. Cities, towns and villages have been, and are continuing to be, devastated by aerial attacks, shelling, tank fire, bomb attacks and street-to-street fighting. In addition, the increasingly sectarian nature of the conflict, highlighted in the recent update by the independent international Commission of Inquiry on Syria, means a swift end to the conflict will be all the more difficult to accomplish."

The analysts noted that 60,000 is likely to be an underestimate of the actual number of deaths, given that reports containing insufficient information were excluded from the list, and that a significant number of killings may not have been documented at all by any of the seven sources. The recording and collection of accurate and reliable data has grown increasingly challenging due to the conflict raging in many parts of the country.

The analysis - which the High Commissioner stressed is "a work in progress, not a final product" - shows a steady increase in the average number of documented deaths per month since the beginning of the conflict, from around 1,000 per month in the summer of 2011 to an average of more than 5,000 per month since July 2012. The greatest number of reported killings have occurred in Homs (12,560), rural Damascus (10,862) and Idlib (7,686), followed by Aleppo (6,188), Daraa (6,034) and Hama (5,080).

Over 76% of the victims documented so far are male, while 7.5% are female, according to the analysis. The gender of the victim is not clear in 16.4 percent of cases. The analysis was not able to differentiate clearly between combatants and non-combatants.

The High Commissioner continued:

> "While many details remain unclear, there can be no justification for the massive scale of the killing highlighted by this analysis. Unless there is a quick resolution to the conflict, I fear thousands more will die or suffer terrible injuries as a result of those who harbour the obstinate belief that something can be achieved by more bloodshed, more torture and more mindless destruction. Those people carrying out these serious crimes should understand that they will one day be brought to justice. The case against them will only be strengthened by adding more crimes to those already committed. The failure of the international community, in particular the Security Council, to take concrete actions to stop the blood-letting, shames us all. For almost two years now, my staff and the staff of the independent Commission of Inquiry have been interviewing Syrians inside and outside the country, listening to their stories and gathering evidence. We have been repeatedly asked: 'Where is the international community? Why aren't you acting to stop this slaughter?' We have no satisfactory answer to those questions. Collectively, we have fiddled at the edges while Syria burns."

The High Commissioner also called for serious preparations to restore law and order when the conflict comes to a halt:

> "We must not compound the existing disaster by failing to prepare for the inevitable – and very dangerous – instability that will occur when the conflict ends. Serious planning needs to get under way immediately, not just to provide humanitarian aid to all those who need it, but to protect all Syrian citizens from extra-judicial reprisals and acts of revenge and discrimination. Investment in a massive stabilization effort will cost far less than decades of instability and lawlessness such as those that have afflicted Afghanistan, Iraq, Somalia, the Democratic Republic of the Congo and several other states where the transition from dictatorship and conflict to democracy was given insufficient support. Given there has been no let-up in the conflict since the end of November, we can assume that more than 60,000 people have been killed by the beginning of 2013".

1.4. Syrian government use of excessive force against protestors

As already illustrated above the Syrian government's violent response to protests since mid-March has left many people dead. Thousands more have been wounded, arbitrarily arrested, tortured and disappeared as protestors and their families within and outside of Syria have been targeted. Under-Secretary-General B. Lynn Pascoe informed Security Council members on 27 April 2011

- already - that sources in Syria were "consistently reporting the use of artillery fire against unarmed civilians; door-to-door arrest campaigns; the shooting of medical personnel who attempt to aid the wounded; raids against hospitals, clinics and mosques and the purposeful destruction of medical supplies and arrest of medical personnel." Over ten thousand refugees fled the country since March, many to Lebanon and Turkey, as noted in the Office of the High Commissioner for Human Rights Commission of Inquiry's report to the General Assembly published on 23 November 2011.[10] Amnesty International stated in its 24 October report that wounded civilians seeking medical treatment in at least four hospitals faced torture and other forms of ill-treatment from security officials and medical staff.[11] Additionally, medical professionals attempting to help the wounded engaged in protests were threatened with arrest and torture. Human Rights Watch (HRW) reported as early as June that the attacks by the government reached the level of crimes against humanity in multiple cities across Syria, such as Daraa and Homs. Later on 15 December HRW named over 70 Syrian commanders who imposed a 'shoot to kill' policy against protestors, making clear that these crimes were knowingly committed against the civilian population. In January 2012, violence in Syria escalated as evidenced by reports of a "massacre" in the district of Karm al-Zeitoun on 26 January which resulted in the death of more than 74 Syrian citizens over two days. Further reports were released by HRW on 3 February stating that authorities had detained and tortured children with impunity.[12]

1.5. Access denied to monitoring and humanitarian groups

As President Bashar al-Assad deployed troops and tanks to meet protesters with deadly force, he compromised civilian access to necessities including food, water and medical supplies. The International Federation for Human Rights (FIDH) raised awareness of the forced humanitarian crisis in its 28 July 2011 report. President Assad blocked access to the country of most outside humanitarian and human rights groups, the OHCHR fact-finding mission and the OHCHR Commission of Inquiry. Information from within Syria on the state of the humanitarian crisis remained limited as a result of the refusal of entry for journalists as well as cracking down on internet and social media use.

Following weeks of negotiations, the Syrian government agreed on 19 December 2011 to allow an independent monitoring mission full freedom of movement within Syria as part of a peace initiative brokered by the League of Arab States. However, shortly after the mission began reports emerged stating that the Syrian government was obstructing monitors' access. Human Rights Watch reported on 27 December 2011 that Syrian security forces were

---

10 A/HRC/S-17/2/Add.1, 23 November 2011, paras. 31, 34, see document 2b in the Appendix.
11 See the list of NGO-reports in Annex 1 of this book.
12 Id.

moving detainees to more sensitive military sites where access to monitors would not be readily provided. HRW also reported that military personnel had in some cases been given police identification cards, violating the terms of the Arab League initiative for Syrian troop withdrawal. On 5 January 2012, Syrian activists claimed the Syrian government was deceiving observers, who had begun their mission on 26 December, by painting military vehicles to look like police cars and taking observers to areas loyal to the government.

1.6. The Kofi Annan plan

Clashes between government forces and the Syrian opposition continued throughout 2012 and did not stop at the end of the year, despite efforts by the international community to end the violence. The appointment of Kofi Annan as UN-Arab League Joint Special Envoy to Syria led to a 16 March 2012 presentation to the Security Council of a six-point plan, which included a ceasefire deadline of 10 April, the end of government troop movements towards population centers, the withdrawal of heavy weapons and troop withdrawal.

Here is a text of the proposal which calls on the Syrian authorities to:

(1) commit to work with the Envoy in an inclusive Syrian-led political process to address the legitimate aspirations and concerns of the Syrian people, and, to this end, commit to appoint an empowered interlocutor when invited to do so by the Envoy.

(2) commit to stop the fighting and achieve urgently an effective United Nations-supervised cessation of armed violence in all its forms by all parties to protect civilians and stabilize the country.

To this end, the Syrian government should immediately cease troop movements towards, and end the use of heavy weapons in, population centers, and begin pullback of military concentrations in and around population centers.

As these actions are being taken on the ground, the Syrian government should work with the Envoy to bring about a sustained cessation of armed violence in all its forms by all parties with an effective United Nations supervision mechanism.

Similar commitments would be sought by the Envoy from the opposition and all relevant elements to stop the fighting and work with him to bring about a sustained cessation of armed violence in all its forms by all parties with an effective United Nations supervision mechanism;

(3) ensure timely provision of humanitarian assistance to all areas affected by the fighting, and to this end, as immediate steps, to accept and implement a daily two-hour humanitarian pause and to coordinate exact time and modalities of the daily pause through an efficient mechanism, including at local level;

(4) intensify the pace and scale of release of arbitrarily detained persons, including especially vulnerable categories of persons, and persons involved in peaceful political activities, provide without delay through appropriate channels a list of all places in which such persons are being detained, immediately begin organizing access to such locations and through appropriate channels respond promptly to all written requests for information, access or release regarding such persons;

(5) ensure freedom of movement throughout the country for journalists and a non-discriminatory visa policy for them;

(6) respect freedom of association and the right to demonstrate peacefully as legally guaranteed.

Contrary to skepticism from the international community - including France and the United States - Syrian President Bashar al-Assad accepted Annan's proposal for the ceasefire. The Security Council, after being briefed by Annan on 2 April, issued a presidential statement on 5 April in support of the plan and calling on the government to follow through on its pledge, and on all parties to cease armed violence. Additional demands made by the Syrian government on 8 April - including a written ceasefire agreement and observer mission deployment occurring simultaneously with the ceasefire – were refused by the Syrian opposition; the armed opposition group Free Syrian Army warned they would resume attacks if the government did not adhere to ceasefire deadlines.

Despite the 10 April deadline – and complete ceasefire deadline of 12 April - set by Kofi Annan, attacks continued with no sign of troop withdrawal. According to Syrian National Council representatives in Geneva, over 1,000 civilians were killed in the first two weeks of April, with shelling and mortar fire in the northern village of Marea and the city of Homs on 10 April. Reports from Amnesty International and Human Rights Watch highlighted ongoing rights abuses, from the arrest of minors to extrajudicial executions.[13] The impact of the conflict began taking its toll on the countries bordering Syria, with over 24,000 Syrians occupying the Turkish refugee camp of Kilis, which reportedly came under fire from government forces on 9 April; meanwhile Lebanese

---

13 See Annex 1 in this book.

opposition leader Amin Gemayel has voiced concern that the fighting could spill over into Lebanon.

1.7. Reports of abuses during the conflict of NGO's

There have been numerous reports of abuses, mainly by state forces, during the Syrian conflict. The UN international commission of inquiry listed excessive use of force and extrajudicial executions, including orders to shoot without warning and to shoot to kill, as well as killings of soldiers refusing to carry out orders to shoot civilians.[14] Arbitrary detentions, enforced disappearances, torture and other forms of ill-treatment, sexual violence and violations of children's rights were further identified by the UN commission, leading it to express grave concern at this all amounting to crimes against humanity committed against the Syrian population.

International NGOs have also issued reports on abuses.[15] Human Rights Watch has also indicated its assessment of abuses by government forces as amounting to crimes against humanity.[16] It particularly identified the use of torture, including against children and in hospitals, as well as the use of sniper fire and mortars, and of banned antipersonnel and anti vehicle landmines along the borders with Turkey and Lebanon. Amnesty International has echoed such reports.

Over a hundred civilians, including women and children, were infamously killed in the Houla massacre on 25 May 2012, in an attack strongly condemned by the Human Rights Council[17] and by the Security Council.[18] By early June 2012, UN officials were confident in describing abuses in Syria as likely amounting to crimes against humanity. A new helicopter and tank attack in opposition-controlled Hama taking 220 civilian lives in mid-July 2012.

Reports of abuses by armed opposition groups have also emerged. Human Rights Watch has pointed to "kidnapping, detention, and torture of security force members, government supporters, and people identified as members of pro-government militias", as well as executions by armed opposition groups of security force members and civilians. The U.N. special representative for children and armed conflict has expressed concern that the Free Syrian Army was recruiting child soldiers.

---

14 See document 2b in the appendix of this book.
15 See Annex 1 in this book.
16 "We Live as in War" Crackdown on Protesters in the Governorate of Homs, HRW.
17 1 June 2012, press release on the opening of the Human Rights Council fourth special session on Syria, see Annex 2 of this book.
18 27 May 2012; Security Council Press Statement on Attacks in Syria, see Annex 3 of this book.

In April 2012, the Syrian Government forces were for the first time added to the Secretary-General's "list of shame" for the killing and maiming of children and attacks on schools and hospitals. The United Nations has also received reports of Syrian armed opposition using children as spies, porters and for other purposes in their operations.

Although the current security situation did not allow the Special Representative to meet the armed opposition in person, she contacted two armed opposition commanders to raise allegations of association of children with the opposition, and to deplore terror tactics by certain units which have taken the lives of innocent civilians, including children, over the past months. "Our eyes will stay on the opposition to see whether they are serious in the commitment made to protect girls and boys," Ms. Zerrougui stressed.

During her visit, the Special Representative also met with internally displaced and refugee children in Damascus, the Al-Yarmouk camp and Homswho are in desperate need of protection as well as food, medicine and shelter in the winter months to come.

> "The situation I witnessed in Syria is dire for children. The immediate end to the violence and an inclusive peace are the only viable options, if we are to preserve the future generation of Syria's children."[19]

The Security Council's resolutions 1612 (2005), 1882 (2009) and 1998 (2011)[20] on Children and Armed Conflict establish measures to end grave violations against children, through the creation of a monitoring and reporting mechanism, and the development of Action Plans to end violations by parties who have been listed in the Secretary-General's report for the commission of such violations.

---

19 OSRSG/181212
20 See document 3 in the Appendix of this book.

2. INTERNATIONAL RESPONSE TO THE CONFLICT

The violence in Syria has drawn increasing condemnation, with the United States and European Union imposing sanctions. A UN Security Council resolution based on Article 41 of the UN Charter was vetoed by China and Russia on 4 October 2011. A workplan to end the violence and protect citizens was announced by the League of Arab States on 2 November 2011, to which Syria formally agreed. However, the continued violence and non-implementation of the agreement led the League to suspend Syrian membership as well as to impose economic and political sanctions. The UN General Assembly has condemned the "continued widespread and systematic human rights violations by the Syrian authorities."[21]

Mr Kofi Annan was appointed as Joint Special Envoy of the United Nations and the League of Arab States in February 2012, with the mission of "bringing an end to all violence and human rights violations, and promoting a peaceful solution to the Syrian crisis."[22]

On 27 March 2012, it was announced that the Syrian Government had agreed to a six-point plan put forth by the Special Envoy[23]. The fragile ceasefire entered into effect on 12 April 2012 and UN observers began their monitoring work on 16 April 2012, despite reports of ongoing shellfire from government forces in Holms and other areas. In June 2012, the UN announced it was suspending its mission in Syria, due to its monitors' inability to conduct patrols and following reports of them being shot at.

On 30 June 2012, the UN-backed Action Group on Syria agreed on the necessary steps for the implementation of the six-point peace plan and for the country to transition toward stability. President Assad renewed his commitment to the plan in early July 2012. Meanwhile, members of the Syrian opposition, having previously criticised the UN peace plan, met in Cairo to discuss a political transition plan backed by the UN, Russia and the US.[24]

---

21 General Assembly, GA/11207/Rev.1, 16 February 2012, see Annex 5 in this book

22 See also A/RES/66/253 see document 9 of the appendix.

23 See infra.

24 Report of the United Nations High Commissioner for Human Rights on the situation of human rights in the Syrian Arab Republic (September 2011) See appendix document 2a. First report of the independent international commission of inquiry on the Syrian Arab Republic (November 2011) See appendix document 2b, Second report of the independent international commission of inquiry on the Syrian Arab Republic (February 2012) See appendix document 2c, Oral Update of the Independent International Commission of Inquiry on Syria see appendix document 2d, Third report of the independent international commission of inquiry on the Syrian Arab Republic (August 2012) See appendix document 2e and Periodic update of the Independent International Commission of Inquiry on the Syrian

The international community grew increasingly alarmed as the violence in Syria escalated. However, compared to the crisis in Libya, which saw widespread international support behind an early response, regional and international organizations proved more hesitant in responding to the political and humanitarian crisis in Syria. In the next paragraphs we will examine in some more detail the efforts of the various parties in the conflict to get to a solution of the current situation.

2.1. United Nations

2.1.1. Special Advisers on the Prevention of Genocide and R2P

The Special Adviser on the Prevention of Genocide acts as a catalyst to raise awareness of the causes and dynamics of genocide, to alert relevant actors where there is a risk of genocide, and to advocate and mobilize for appropriate action. The Special Adviser on the Responsibility to Protect leads the conceptual, political, institutional and operational development of the Responsibility to Protect. The mandates of the two Special Advisers are distinct but complementary. The efforts of their Office include alerting relevant actors to the risk of genocide, war crimes, ethnic cleansing and crimes against humanity, enhancing the capacity of the United Nations to prevent these crimes, including their incitement, and working with Member States, regional and sub-regional arrangements, and civil society to develop more effective means of response when they do occur.

Following reports of human rights violations by Syrian security forces in March 2011, the Office began to monitor the violent suppression of anti-government protests there. The alleged systematic and widespread attacks by police, military and other security forces appear to have primarily targeted the civilian population. In addition to the deaths of protestors, there have also been reports of mass arrests, arbitrary detentions, disappearances, and other grave human rights violations in towns where protests have taken place. Based on the available information, the Special Advisers consider that the scale and gravity of the violations may amount to crimes against humanity.

On 2 June 2011 and on 21 July 2011, the Special Advisers issued statements expressing concern at persistent reports of widespread and systematic human rights violations by Syrian security forces. They joined the international community in calling for an end to the violence, for an independent investigation of the alleged crimes and for the government to allow humanitarian access to affected areas. On 10 February 2012, Special Advisers Deng and Luck expressed concern at reports of growing tensions between different sectarian

---

Arab Republic, see document 2f in the appendix.

communities in Syria. They called on all parties to take immediate steps to ensure that the human rights of all individuals are respected and protected, regardless of their religious identity or political affiliation.[25]

On 15 March 2012, Special Advisers Deng and Luck expressed grave concern at the Syrian Government's increasingly violent assault against its population and deepening sectarian divisions. The Special Advisers stated that the lack of unified international response to protect the Syrian population has encouraged the Government to continue its course of action. Reiterating their calls for an end to the violence, the Special Advisers also called on the international community to take collective action to protect populations at risk of further atrocity crimes in Syria.

On 14 June 2012, Special Adviser Deng and Luck expressed alarm at widespread reports of mass killings as a result of attacks by Government artillery and tanks on residential neighbourhoods, as well as alleged attacks against civilians and civilian infrastructure by pro-government militia and other armed groups. They noted that these mass killings underscored the Syrian Government's manifest failure to protect its populations and called for all parties to immediately end all acts of violence and human rights violations against the Syrian population. The Special Advisers stated that the risk of further mass atrocity crimes was high, with increasing violence and deepening sectarian tensions, and called for immediate, decisive action.

2.1.2. Human Rights Council and Office of the High Commissioner for Human Rights (OHCHR)[26]

The Human Rights Council and OHCHR were seized of the situation in Syria early on and a Special Session of the Human Rights Council (HRC) was held on the crisis on 29 April. In a Resolution adopted during the session, the Council condemned the crackdown and called for the OHCHR to dispatch a fact-finding mission to investigate into human rights violations. The Mission, which was successfully launched on 15 March, released findings on 15 September that the widespread and systematic attacks against the Syrian population could amount to crimes against humanity, including murder, disappearance and torture as well as deprivation of liberty and persecution. The Report also called on the Syrian government to prevent impunity, allow the safe return of refugees, release all detainees, and facilitate further investigation by the OHCHR and the Human Rights Council.

---

25 See document 10 in the appendix to this book.
26 Due to the great amount of statements and reports issued by the OHCHR we had to sum-marize the work in this publication. In Annex 4 an overview of relevant documents is presented. In the Appendix to this book several reports and documents are reproduced.

From 22-23 August 2011, the HRC held a second Special Session on Syria to investigate the ongoing human rights violations, subsequently adopting a Resolution mandating an independent Commission of Inquiry to investigate human rights violations in Syria. The Commission's Report was released on 28 November[27], detailing extensive human rights violations occurring in Syria and expressing concern that crimes against humanity have been committed. On 19 September, High Commissioner Navi Pillay urged the Security Council to refer the case to the International Criminal Court, a recommendation she reiterated on 12 December as she warned that Syria was at risk of civil war.

As the crisis remained unresolved and the international community failed to take decisive action, Pillay stated on 8 February,

"At their 2005 Summit, World leaders unanimously agreed that each individual State has the responsibility to protect its population from crimes against humanity and other international crimes...They also agreed that when a State is manifestly failing to protect its population from serious international crimes, the international community as a whole has the responsibility to step in by taking protective action in a collective, timely and decisive manner...The virtual carte blanche now granted to the Syrian Government betrays the spirit and the word of this unanimous decision. It is depriving the population of the protection they so urgently need."

2.1.3. Security Council

The Security Council was a source of disappointment for many due to its consistent inability to form a consensus around the crisis. The Council released a presidential statement on 3 August that condemned the violence while reaffirming the Council's "strong commitment to the sovereignty (...) and territorial integrity of Syria."

All the while, the U.N. Security Council has struggled to respond. When the Syrian government began its crackdown against protesters in March 2011, the Security Council was preoccupied with events in Libya, where increasing violence against protesters led first to the Council's imposition of targeted sanctions and the referral of the situation to the International Criminal Court ("ICC"), followed by an authorization for the use of military force.[28] In contrast to the decisive and unified action on Libya, the Council's activities with respect to Syria have been faltering and divisive.

---

27 See appendix document 2b.
28 See S.C. Res. 1973, U.N. Doc. S/RES/1973 (Mar. 17, 2011); S.C. Res. 1970, U.N. Doc. S/RES/1970 (Feb. 26, 2011), see document 4 of the appendix of this book.

The Security Council first discussed the events in Syria during a meeting on Israeli-Palestinian negotiations in April 2011. The United States, United Kingdom, France, and Germany expressed concern about violence against the demonstrators, while the representative of Russia "deem[ed] unacceptable any external interference in Syrian affairs."[29] Later the same week, the Council held its first session devoted exclusively to Syria. Following a briefing by Under-Secretary-General for Political Affairs Lynn Pascoe that starkly described the deteriorating situation in Syria, delegates spoke out in greater number and with deeper urgency than during the previous meeting.[30] U.S. Permanent Representative Susan Rice, for example, stated that the United States "condemns in the strongest possible terms the abhorrent violence used by the Government of Syria,"[31] in contrast to the "deep concern" expressed earlier in the week.[32] South Africa, Germany, Brazil, and Bosnia added themselves to the voices condemning and urging an end to the violence,[33] and Russia, China, and India expressed their "concern" at the events taking place in Syria. Nonetheless, the Russia representative asserted that "the current situation in Syria (...) does not present a threat to international peace and security."[34] At that time, the United States and European countries were circulating a draft Security Council press statement calling on Syria's government to cease its use of force against the demonstrators, but it failed to gain the support of all Council members.[35] In the subsequent months, the United Kingdom and France also aimed to gather support for a resolution condemning the Syrian government's violent response, but because of anticipated resistance from Russia and China, the draft never was put to a vote.[36]

It was not until August, when the Security Council adopted a Presidential Statement, that the impasse was broken. The Statement, the Council's first collective act since the violence in Syria began, consisted of four main points.

- First, it voiced the Security Council's position on the events in Syria, expressing "grave concern over the deteriorating situation" and condemning the "widespread" human rights violations.

---

29 U.N. SCOR, 66th Sess., 6520th mtg. at 13, 15, 21, 27, U.N. Doc. S/PV.6520 (Apr. 21, 2011) [hereinafter Security Council 6520th Meeting].
30 See U.N. SCOR, 66th Sess., 6524th mtg. at 2, U.N. Doc. S/PV.6524 (Apr. 27, 2011) [hereinafter Security Council 6524th Meeting].
31 Id. at 4.
32 Security Council 6520th Meeting, *supra*, at 13.
33 *See* Security Council 6524th Meeting, *supr*, at 6–10.
34 Id. at 7.
35 See Neil MacFarquhar, Push in U.N. for Criticism of Syria Is Rejected, N.Y. Times, Apr. 28, 2011, at A12.
36 See Dan Bilefsky, New Move to Condemn Syria in U.N., N.Y. Times, June 9, 2011, at A10; Syria Crisis: UN Resolution Submitted by UK and France, BBC (June 9, 2011), http://www.bbc.co.uk/news/world-middle-east-13706317.

- Second, the Council called for an immediate end to the violence and unimpeded access for humanitarian workers and stated that "[t]hose responsible for the violence should be held accountable," without noting how that accountability process should take place.
- Third, the Council indicated its restraint, reaffirming its "strong commitment to the sovereignty, independence, and territorial integrity of Syria" and emphasizing the importance of a Syrian-led political process.
- Finally, the statement expressed the Council's intention to remain involved in the situation, requesting the Secretary-General to provide an update within one week. [37]

The Presidential Statement would mark the high point of agreement in the Council on Syria for the year.[38] In October, France, Portugal, and the United Kingdom tabled a draft resolution that repeated many of the points in the Presidential Statement, though in stronger terms.[39] The resolution initially had imposed sanctions as well, but it was watered down during negotiations preceding the vote so that it ultimately warned only of the Council's "intention (...) to consider its options," including measures under Article 41 of the U.N. Charter, thus hinting at the prospect of sanctions in the future.[40] Even despite these revisions, the resolution still was struck down by vetoes from both Russia and China. [41]

Looming over the Council's discussions of the resolution was ill will concerning Libya; governments that supported the no-fly zone believed they were misled into endorsing a far more expansive authorization of force to support the anti-Qaddafi rebels. In his explanation of vote, Russian Permanent Representative Vitaly Churkin described a clash between the resolution's sponsors' "philosophy of confrontation" and a logic of respect for sovereignty and nonintervention expressed by Russia and China, as well as Brazil, India, and South Africa, which abstained on the resolution.[42] Although the resolution did not suggest military confrontation, it was on the minds of the states opposing the resolution; Russia

---

37 See U.N. SCOR, 66th Sess., 6598th mtg. at 2, U.N. Doc. S/PV.6598 (Aug. 3, 2011).

38 Although the Statement was passed by consensus, Lebanon noted that it was "dissociat[ing] itself from the statement" in light of its belief that the statement "does not help to address the current situation in Libya," a move that appeared to reflect Lebanon's vulnerability to the Syrian regime. Id. at 2–3.

39 For example, the Presidential Statement "condemn[ed] violations of human rights, while the draft resolution "strongly condemn[ed]" them; and the Presidential Statement "call[ed] for" an immediate end to the violence, while the draft resolution "demand[ed]" it. Compare id. at 2, with France, Germany, Portugal and United Kingdom of Great Britain and Northern Ireland: Draft Resolution at 2, U.N. Doc. S/2011/612 (Oct. 4, 2011) [hereinafter October Draft Resolution].

40 October Draft Resolution, *supra* 13.

41 See U.N. SCOR, 66th Sess., 6627th mtg. at 2, U.N. Doc. S/PV.6627 (Oct. 4, 2011).

42 Id. at 3.

had tried and failed to secure an explicit statement in the draft on the non-acceptability of military intervention. Based on the events in Libya, Churkin said, the "alarming" omission of the suggested language "can only put us on our guard."[43] Russia was troubled also by the possibility that *any* resolution initiating Security Council involvement in the situation in Syria could be interpreted liberally, just as NATO's enforcement of the no-fly zone in Libya "morphed into the bombing of oil refineries, television stations and other civilian sites."[44] The Chinese representative did not refer to the ghost of Libya, but instead, in a statement milder in tone than that of Russia, emphasized the principle of noninterference in the internal affairs of states and noted China's belief the threat of sanctions would not help to resolve the situation in Syria. [45] This position was echoed by the representative of India, while Brazil more generally called for constructive engagement to resolve the crisis. [46]

The states that supported the resolution expressed their regret at the Council's failure to act and announced their intention to work through other channels to end the violence, bring those responsible to justice, and initiate some inclusive political process in Syria. U.S. Permanent Representative Susan Rice declared that the United States was "outraged" - but even this statement was measured, directing itself at the Council's collective failure, not at the obstruction by Russia and China.[47] In line with typical Council decorum, no state mentioned Russia and China by name when expressing disappointment at the resolution's demise.

This was in stark contrast to the anger voiced in February 2012 when the Council next attempted, and failed, to adopt a resolution to take action on Syria. The effort came on the heels of a new Arab League peace plan, which was discussed at the Council's January 31 meeting.[48] By that time, Morocco had put forward a resolution stating that the Council "[f]ully supports" the League's proposal; in the same paragraph, it specifically noted the Arab League's goals of forming a new national unity government, requiring that Assad step down and grant full authority to his deputy, and holding free elections under Arab and international supervision.[49] These three points generated significant

---

43 Id. at 4.

44 Id. at 4. South Africa also voiced its concern that the resolution was "part of a hidden agenda aimed at once again instating regime change." Id. at 11.

45 Id. at 5.

46 See id. at 6, 12.

47 Id. at 8 ("The United States is outraged that this Council has utterly failed to address an urgent moral challenge and a growing threat to regional peace and security.").

48 See U.N. SCOR, 67th Sess., 6710th mtg., U.N. Doc. S/PV.6710 (Jan. 31, 2012). At that meeting, most of the states supporting U.N. action in Syria were represented by their foreign minister rather than their U.N. representative.

49 See Draft of Security Council Resolution on Libya, 7(a)–(c), N.Y. Times, Jan. 31, 2012, http://www.nytimes.com/2012/02/01/world/middleeast/draft-of-security-council-resolution-on-

controversy and secured Russia's opposition. By the time the draft reached the floor of the Council, they had been removed, and the resolution being voted upon expressed only the Council's "full support" of the Arab League proposal without identifying the specific elements of the plan. In addition, the final draft was amended to specify that the political process should be "Syrian-led." [50]

Nonetheless, the resolution again fell victim to Russian and Chinese vetoes. In contrast to the October resolution, however, there were no abstentions; the remaining thirteen states voted in support of the resolution, thus disproving theories that the support of India and South Africa might persuade Russia to at least abstain. [51] Similar to its position on the October resolution, China again voiced concerns that the approach outlined in the resolution would complicate the situation in Syria rather than resolve it. [52] The Russian representative, more forcefully expressing opposition to the resolution, attacked the resolution's demand for "regime change" and the sponsors' refusal to include amendments that would call on the Syrian opposition to distance itself from violent extremist groups and to cease attacks on state institutions. [53] The language of the original resolution and its endorsement of the Arab League proposal appeared to taint the final version; delegates' hope that the deletion of the specific language would achieve consensus clearly was overly optimistic.

The statements made following the vote revealed deep disappointment and anger. In a rare citation of the names of states choosing to veto, the U.K. representative declared, "The United Kingdom is appalled by the decision of Russia and China to veto an otherwise consensus resolution." [54] Ambassador Rice stated that the United States was "disgusted." [55] The representative of Portugal described the vote as "[n]ot only (...) extremely disappointing," but also "simply unacceptable." [56] Such reactions were heard outside the Council

---

syria.html?pagewanted=all; see also Neil MacFarquhar, U.N. Tentatively Backs a Plan for Syria, N.Y. Times, Feb. 2, 2012, at A8.
50 Bahrain, Colombia, Egypt, France, Germany, Jordan, Kuwait, Libya, Morocco, Oman, Portugal, Qatar, Saudi Arabia, Togo, Tunisia, Turkey, United Arab Emirates, United Kingdom of Great Britain and Northern Ireland and United States of America: Draft resolution, 7, U.N. Doc. S/2012/77 (Feb. 4, 2012).
51 See U.N. SCOR, 67th Sess., 6711th mtg. at 2, U.N. Doc. S/PV.6711 (Feb. 4, 2012) [hereinafter Security Council 6711st Meeting]; Bill Varner, Brazil, India, S. Africa Planning Mission to Syria on Violence, Bloomberg (July 28, 2011), http://www.bloomberg.com/news/2011-07-28/brazil-india-s-africa-planning-mission-to-syria-on-violence.html. South Africa and India expressed their support for the Arab League process and also emphasized that the political process must be "led" and "owned" by the Syrian people. Security Council 6711th Meeting, supra, at 8, 11.
52 Security Council 6711th Meeting, supra at 9.
53 Id.
54 Id. at 6.
55 Id. at 5.
56 Id. at 6.

as well. U.N. High Commissioner for Human Rights Navi Pillay, for example, characterized the failure of the Council as a green light to the Assad regime, stating that it "appears to have fueled the Syrian Government's readiness to massacre its own people in an effort to crush dissent." [57] She even repeated these words several times the past weeks and was very outspoken when she presented the Preliminary Statistical Analysis of Documentation of Killings in the Syrian Arab Republic on the January 2, 2013. [58]

Since the vote in February, the Council has continued to hold meetings and has informally considered a new draft resolution. [59] Disputes remain over the Council's support for "regime change," and the Arab League has separately held meetings with Russian Foreign Minister Sergei Lavrov.

These intractable disagreements in the Security Council have served as a reminder of the organization's limits. When the Council agreed to take action on Libya it seemed possible that its often-clashing members were embarking on a new period of cooperation. The Council's unanimous vote to refer the situation in Libya to the ICC was the first referral adopted with no abstentions; the decision to impose a no-fly zone in Libya marked an occasion in which veto-wielding powers expressed reservations about the resolution before them, but chose not to block it. One year later, with disputes bitterly played out both within the Council chamber and outside of it, it appears that this consensus was merely a moment of unity in the Council's approach to the Arab Spring, an outlier rather than a new normal.

The Security Council's recent activities also expose new divisions in the body. China historically has given weight to the opinion of regional stakeholders; but whereas China stated that it "attache[d] great importance" to the support of the Arab League for a no-fly zone in Libya, [60] it has shown no deference to the body's recommendations with respect to Syria, and instead has aligned itself solely with Russia. By doing so, China has distanced itself not only from the Arab League, but also from South Africa and India, despite its traditional cooperation with the Non-Aligned Movement. This may signal a new "strategic understanding" between Moscow and Beijing, or it may relate more

---

57 UN Human Rights Chief Urges Action to Halt Escalating Violence in Syria, UN News Centre (Feb. 8, 2012), http://www.ohchr.org/en/NewsEvents/Pages/DisplayNews.aspx?NewsID=11804&LangID=E.

58 Preliminary Statistical Analysis of Documentation of Killings in the Syrian Arab Republic, Megan Price, Je Klingner, and Patrick Ball, The Benetech Human Rights Program, 2 January 2013. And her remarks http://www.ohchr.org/en/NewsEvents/Pages/Media.aspx See document 1 in the appendix to this book..

59 See Joe Lauria, US and Russia Clash over Syria, as Children Are Reported Killed in Homs, Wall St. J., Mar. 13, 2012, at A7.

60 U.N. SCOR, 66th Sess., 6498th mtg. at 10, U.N. Doc. S/PV.6498 (Mar. 17, 2011).

to China's own fears of dissidents within.[61] Irrespective of the source, as the Council's divisions have continued, and perhaps deepened, the Arab League has emerged as a central player in efforts to resolve the crisis.

Finally, the recent history of the Security Council shows the limits of the ideal of a responsibility to protect ("R2P"). There certainly have been some glimmers of hope: The Arab League suspended Syria from membership, prohibited travel by senior officials to Arab states, and froze Syria's assets; the United States and European Union have imposed diplomatic and economic sanctions; even the General Assembly adopted a resolution nearly identical to the one the Security Council rejected in February.[62] Each of these actions resonates with the R2P objective that states should respond when governments are unwilling to protect their own populations, but they cannot compare to the force of a Security Council-backed call for sanctions or a U.N.-imposed political process. While individual states may still be guided by a sense of a responsibility toward suffering populations, in the Security Council R2P's status is tenuous. "Libya has given R2P a bad name," said India's U.N. ambassador last year.[63] Even the relatively uncontroversial statement that governments have a responsibility to protect their own populations, which was included in Resolution 1973 on Libya, was notably absent from the Council's draft resolutions on Syria. As the principle confronts the machinery of the Security Council, they may be little hope for its survival.

2.1.4. General Assembly

The Third Committee (human rights) of the General Assembly (GA) passed a Resolution on 22 November that condemned the Syrian government's prolonged crackdown against protesters. A total of 122 states voted for the resolution, with 13 against and 41 abstentions. Introduced by Britain, France, and Germany, the resolution carried no legal weight, but called on the Syrian government to end all human rights abuses and urged Assad to immediately implement the Arab League's November peace plan. On 21 November, the Syrian envoy to the UN characterized the Resolution as declaring "diplomatic war" against the country. However, the vote at the GA was marked by strong regional support for the Resolution, with Bahrain, Jordan, Kuwait, Morocco, Qatar and Saudi Arabia – all co-sponsors of the Resolution – voting in favor. Russia and China abstained from voting, along with India and South Africa.

On 19 December, the GA adopted a second resolution calling for Syria to implement a peace plan brokered by the Arab League, which included allowing

---

61 See Minxin Pei, Why Beijing Votes with Moscow, Int'l Herald Trib., Feb. 8 2012, at 6.
62 See G.A. Res. 66/176, U.N. Doc. A/RES/66/176 (Feb. 23, 2012), see document 5 in the appendix..
63 Charles Homans, Just What Is a Just War?, For. Pol'y, Nov. 2011, at 34, 35.

observers into the country. The Resolution, which passed with 133 votes in favor, 11 against and 43 abstentions, also called on Syria to cooperate with the independent international commission of inquiry establish by the Human Rights Council.

The General Assembly was briefed by UN High Commissioner for Human Rights Navi Pillay in a meeting on Syria held on 13 February. Ms. Pillay again recalled her earlier statements urging the Security Council to refer the situation of Syria to the International Criminal Court so as to ensure that crimes do not go unpunished. On 16 February, a third resolution, circulated by Saudi Arabia, was passed in the GA with 137 votes in favor, 12 against and 17 abstentions. Based on the vetoed Security Council resolution text of 4 February, the resolution issued support for the League of Arab States' peace plan in Syria and stressed the importance of ensuring accountability, the need to end impunity and "hold to account those responsible for human rights violations, including those violations that may amount to crimes against humanity". The resolution further called for the Secretary-General to appoint a Special Envoy to the country.

2.1.5. United Nations-Arab League Joint Special Envoy to Syria

On 23 February 2012, Secretary-General Ban Ki-moon and Arab League chief Nabil Elaraby announced the appointment of Kofi Annan as UN-Arab League Joint Special Envoy to Syria, in accordance with GA Resolution A/RES/66/253. In a UN-Arab League statement on March 7 2012, former Palestinian Minister of Foreign Affairs Nasser Al Kidwa was announced as Deputy Joint Special Envoy, and was joined on 20 March by Jean-Marie Guéhenno, former UN Under-Secretary-General for Peacekeeping Operations. The Deputy Special Envoys are tasked to assist Annan in the exercise of his mandate.

In a meeting on 8 March 2012 in Cairo, the Arab League and Russia - in conjunction with Kofi Annan - ruled out military intervention, believing that it would only worsen the situation. Annan began talks with Syrian President Bashar al-Assad on 10 March, only to leave Syria without reaching a ceasefire agreement. Both Assad and the leader of Syria's main opposition group rejected dialogue, with the opposition saying negotiation was "unrealisitic" and advocating for military force.

Following a presentation in mid-March by Annan to the UN of a six-point proposal for ending the violence in Syria, the Security Council adopted a presidential statement on 22 March issuing support for the plan.[64]

---

64 See infra.

2.1.6. Under-Secretary General on Humanitarian Affairs

In response to escalating conflict, Secretary-General Ban Ki-moon called for Under-Secretary General on Humanitarian Affairs, Valerie Amos, to "visit Syria to assess the humanitarian situation and renew the call for urgent humanitarian access" a few times in 2012. On 7 February, the Under-Secretary General met with Syrian Foreign Minister Walid Muallim in Damascus, before visiting the neighborhood of Baba Amr in Homs, an area where fighting between government and opposition forces has been centered. In the summer she returned to Syria and she was shocked by the situation in the country:

"The end of the United Nations observer mission in Syria would not significantly impact humanitarian activities there, but more generous funding support was needed. According to the Syrian Government's own figures, 1.2 million people were sheltering in public buildings, and many more were staying with relatives and friends. Those who had fled, as well as their hosts, had urgent humanitarian needs due to the widening impact of the crisis on the economy and people's livelihoods, she said, adding that there were serious public health issues in the school buildings used as shelters. The most urgent and growing needs are for health care, shelter, food, water and sanitation. More than 820,000 people had been fed in July the Office of the United Nations High Commissioner for Refugees and the United Nations Population Fund (UNFPA) had distributed hygiene kits, blankets and other basic items to more than 60,000 people in the first two weeks of August. But it's not enough when we are dealing with the needs of an estimated 2.5 million people. Humanitarian activities faced problems in gaining access to people in need, particularly where there was intense fighting, but funding is also holding us back. All those engaged in the conflict should respect civilians and abide by international humanitarian law".[65]

2.2. Regional

2.2.1. The League of Arab States

The League of Arab States initially remained passive in its response to the Syrian government's crackdown, stressing that it would not take action itself in response to the crisis. The League issued a statement on 25 April 2011 that condemned the use of violence against protestors in Arab countries without highlighting Syria or proposing any measures to end human rights violations. Eventually, on 7 August, the League released a statement calling for a "serious dialogue" between Syrian authorities and protestors.

---

65 Press conference by under-secretary-general for humanitarian affairs on her recent visit to Syria, 22 august 2012.

As the conflict wore on, the League took a stronger position. On 10 September Secretary-General of the League Nabil El Araby met with President Assad and urged him to stop all violent attacks on civilians, reaching an agreement for the implementation of reforms. However it wasn't until 2 November that the Arab League secured Syria's agreement to implement a peace plan, which included a promise to halt violence, release prisoners, allow for media access and remove military presence from civilian areas. Even then, according to Amnesty International, over 100 civilians were killed in the week immediately after Assad agreed to the plan.

In response, the League suspended Syria's membership on 12 November, and in an unprecedented move, imposed economic sanctions on 27 November. On 19 December Syria signed a peace deal, agreeing to an Arab observer mission for an initial period of one month while explicitly ruling out intervention and protecting Syrian sovereignty. The initiative also included a ceasefire, the release of detainees and military withdrawal.

As the one-month mandate of the Arab League's observer mission in Syria came to a close, the League met on 22 January 2012 in Cairo to discuss the mission's future. Following the meeting, Arab leaders, in addition to extending the mission's mandate and providing additional equipment for observers, called on Syrian President Bashar al-Assad to cede power to his vice president and form a national unity government. This plan was immediately rejected by Syrian authorities who called the plan "flagrant interference" in Syrian affairs. Meanwhile, the monitoring mission launched by the Arab League in December 2011 suffered additional setbacks as Saudi Arabia and the Gulf States withdrew their support on 23 and 24 January respectively, citing Syria's failure to implement the peace plan. Though Arab leaders initially agreed to extend the mandate of the monitoring mission for another month on 27 January 2012[66], they later suspended the mission on 29 January due to "critical" worsening conditions. After the Security Council failed to reach a consensus on the Arab League's strengthened stance, resulting in a double veto of a resolution on 4 February, Arab leaders agreed on 12 February to open contact with Syrian opposition and ask the UN to form a joint peacekeeping force to halt the violence in Syria.

2.2.2. The Gulf Cooperation Council (GCC)

The GCC - Bahrain, Kuwait, Oman, Qatar, Saudi Arabia, and the United Arab Emirates – issued a statement on 7 February recalling their envoys and expelling Syrian ambassadors. The statement was a strong condemnation of the "mass slaughter against the unarmed Syrian people," and urged Arab leaders

66 See Annex 10.

to take "decisive measures in response to this dangerous escalation against the Syrian people."

2.2.3. The European Union (EU)

The European Council announced on 9 May 2011 that it would impose an arms embargo on Syria and a visa ban and asset freeze on 13 individuals identified as responsible for the conflict. The EU later imposed targeted economic sanctions, additional travel bans and asset freezes against Syrian government and military officials on 1 August. In a statement issued on the same day, EU High Representative Catherine Ashton reminded the Syrian government of "its responsibility to protect the population" and denounced attacks on civilians in Hama and other Syrian cities. The EU also adopted a ban on oil imports from Syria to increase pressure on the regime on 2 September, and continued to expand its economic sanctions on Syria for the duration of the conflict. On 23 January the European Union announced an expansion of economic sanctions to twenty-two more individuals. The EU gave its support on 13 February to the Arab League's call for a joint Arab-UN peacekeeping force.

2.2.4. Government responses

It is not possible to list all the reactions from around the world in this book. There have been more than 2000 messages, official remarks and complaints by states on various occassions. However we want to list some of the most remarkable remarks here.

Qatar was the first Arab state to recall its ambassador in Syria on 21 July 2011, with Saudi Arabia, Kuwait and Bahrain following suit on 8 August, and Tunisia and Morocco doing the same on 11 August and 17 November. Traditionally an ally of Syria's, Turkish Prime Minister Recep Tayyip Erdoğan, announced in a meeting with President Assad that Ankara had "run out of patience" with the situation on 9 August. Following several statements condemning the violence, Turkey imposed economic sanctions on Syria on 30 November. On 15 January 2012, a US news agency quoted Qatari leader Sheikh Hamad bin Khalifa Al Thani who suggested that Arab troops be sent to Syria to end the conflict. Syria immediately condemned Qatar's remark, warning it would jeopardize Syrian-Arab relations and promising to "stand firm" against any intervention. After Arab leaders affirmed on 23 January that they were not in favor of a military intervention, Qatar maintained its leadership role in responding to the crisis, briefing the Security Council alongside the Secretary-General of the Arab League on 27 January.

Outside the region, the United States reacted quickly by signing an executive order on 29 April 2011 imposing sanctions on three Syrian officials responsible for human rights violations, the Iranian Islamic Revolutionary Guard Corps for providing material support to the Syrian government for the suppression of civilians and the Syrian General Intelligence Directorate for participating in crackdowns on civilians. Additional sanctions were issued on 18 May targeting President Assad and six government aides, and Syrian oil imports were banned on 18 August. The US also joined several European nations, including UK, France and Germany, in calling for Assad to step down on 18 August 2011. Some governments recalled their ambassadors to Syria, including Italy on 2 August, Switzerland on 18 August, and France on 16 November. On 7 September French Foreign Minister Alain Juppé accused the Syrian government of committing crimes against humanity against the Syrian population.

Russia was criticized by many governments and civil society for its consistent support for Assad's government even as it deplored the ongoing violence. Russia has been a long-time arms exporter to Syria, and throughout the conflict worked to ensure both that the opposition's violence was internationally recognized and that Assad's sovereignty was protected, even in its 15 December 2011 draft resolution in the Security Council. Other states were similarly hesitant to condemn Assad, including the India, Brazil, South Africa Dialogue Forum (IBSA), which released a statement on 11 August 2011 calling for an immediate end to all violence and for all parties to exercise restraint. However, the statement did not call for further action to protect civilians and, in regards to the violent measures carried out by the Syrian government, merely noted that President Assad "acknowledged that some mistakes had been made by security forces." Russia's Permanent Representative to the UN, Vitaly Churkin, stated on 7 February 2012 that the international community should try to "put the parties at the table and to arrange dialogue among them in order to find a political solution without further bloodshed."

Following the second double veto in February, Member States remained seized of the situation, as evidenced by the U.S. government when Secretary of State Hillary Clinton called for the formation of a "friends of democratic Syria" on 5 February 2012. Echoing Clinton's remarks, the Prime Minister of Turkey announced on 7 February 2012 that Turkey would prepare "a new initiative with those countries that stand by the people, not the Syrian government." Since that date the situation remained difficult. The past months Turkey has asked its NATO allies to ensure the safety at their borders with Syria. NATO responded to that by sending for example (Dutch) Patriot rockets to the border with Syria in 2013.

3. LEGAL QUALIFICATION OF THE ARMED VIOLENCE IN SYRIA: A NON-INTERNATIONAL ARMED CONFLICT

The extent and sustained nature of armed violence, and the level of organization of the non-state armed groups fighting against the Syrian regime, mean that the situation across Syria is an armed conflict of a non-international character. A similar assessment has been made by the International Committee of the Red Cross (ICRC). Thus, hostilities between these parties wherever they may occur in Syria are subject to the rules of international humanitarian law. These rules impose limits on how the fighting can be conducted, with the aim of protecting the civilian population and persons not, or no longer, directly participating in the hostilities.

In June 2012, UN Under-Secretary-General for Peacekeeping Operations Herve Ladsous stated that the situation in Syria could be called a civil war. The same month, the second report by the Independent International Commission of Inquiry on Syria, which was set up by the UN Human Rights Council, was more conservative, stating that the violence in some areas "bears the characteristics of a non-international armed conflict."[67]

Previously, armed conflict had been limited to a relatively small and distinct number of areas. In early May 2012, the President of the ICRC declared that the violence in at least two places had reached the threshold of an armed conflict of a non-international character governed by international humanitarian law. Jakob Kellenberger said that conflict in Homs and the province of Idlib met the three criteria of a non-international armed conflict: intensity, duration, and the level of organisation of rebels fighting government forces.

According to the November 2011 report by the Independent International Commission of Inquiry on Syria:

> The commission is concerned that the armed violence in the Syrian Arab Republic risks rising to the level of an "internal armed conflict" under international law. Should this occur, international humanitarian law would apply. The commission recalls that the International Court of Justice has established that human rights law continues to apply in armed conflict, with the law of armed conflict applying as lex specialis in relation to the conduct of hostilities.

The Commission of Inquiry documented patterns of summary execution, arbitrary arrest, enforced disappearance, torture, including sexual violence, as

---

67 See documents 2a-2f of the Appendix.

well as violations of children's rights by the Syrian regime and was "gravely concerned that crimes against humanity have been committed in different locations in the Syrian Arab Republic."[68]

By February 2012, the Commission of Inquiry had reported that Syria was "on the brink" of a non-international armed conflict:

> International humanitarian law is applicable if the situation can be qualified as an armed conflict, which depends on the intensity of the violence and the level of organization of participating parties. While the commission is gravely concerned that the violence in certain areas may have reached the requisite level of intensity, it was unable to verify that the Free Syrian Army (FSA), local groups identifying themselves as such or other anti-Government armed groups had reached the necessary level of organization. [69]

In June 2012, the UN Secretary-General published a report on the situation of human rights in Syria, which stated, inter alia, the following:[70]

> Violence and killings, including during armed clashes, continued throughout the country. An increase in the use of explosive devices, inflicting loss of life among civilians, was also reported. Credible reports indicated that Government security and armed forces continued, unabated, to commit serious violations of human rights, including by the shelling of civilian areas and the use of lethal force against demonstrators, arbitrary arrests, torture and summary and extrajudicial execution of activists, defectors and opponents. Furthermore, ongoing violations by armed anti-Government forces continued to be reported, including cases of kidnapping and abduction, and the torture and killing of members of the security and armed forces and pro-Government elements.

3.1. How to end the war?

While there appears to be little appetite in the West for military intervention, there are many opposition groups within and outside Syria calling for increased international intervention to protect civilians from government forces or to assist in overthrowing the regime. To this should now be added the citizens whose security has been put into jeopardy by the increasing number of incursions by FSA units into densely populated neighbourhoods of Damascus and Aleppo. With the prospect of major civilian casualties being incurred in

---

68 Id.
69 Id.
70 See appendix document 6.

the intensifying battles, and with no negotiated end to the conflict in sight nor any prospect of outright military victory by either side, what options are open for the international community?

3.1.1. Options for non-military intervention

There are a number of non-military actions that can be escalated, but it is not clear how effective they are likely to be. The EU has imposed 17 rounds of sanctions on Syria since 2011, ranging from financial sanctions on key regime figures and security officials to an embargo on Syrian oil exports to EU states.[71]

The perception in Western capitals that sanctions are proving effective in the case of Iran means that they are seen as a useful policy option for Syria. Sanctions have also been an effective deterrent for regional third parties. In Lebanon, for example, despite the proximity of interests between the Hizbullah-led government and the Assad regime, both the banking sector and the government have been careful to respect them, for fear of knock-on sanctions being imposed on Lebanon in turn.

The Lebanese government passed on funding to the Special Tribunal for Lebanon (STL) because of its fear of the threat of sanctions.[72]

Syria is not very integrated into the international financial system, however. It operates a cash-based economy, heavily dependent on black and grey markets. Although there is a paucity of economic data, one participant noted it seemed likely that cash was coming through the borders from Iran and Iraq. If this were not so, the Syrian pound would have been expected to suffer a more severe collapse than it has. Oil exports are small in scale and cutting them off is unlikely to have had a big impact. Given the stalemate in the United Nations Security Council, it is also unlikely that the UN will be able to agree on the imposition of more far-reaching sanctions. Even if it does, it was argued that they would not be a 'game changer' given the regime's relative lack of dependence on the international banking system.

There may be other actions the international community can take to pursue a strategy of encouraging defections and capital flight, and these are doubtless being encouraged where the potential exists. The flight of Aleppo's business community has rapidly affected what was previously a relatively protected local

---

71 See Andrew Woodcock, 'EU agrees new sanctions on Syria', The Independent, 23 July 2012, http://www.independent.co.uk/news/world/middle-east/eu-agrees-new-syria-sanctions-7965984.html.

72 High-level Lebanese and Syrian security officials are suspected of being implicated in the assassination of Rafik Hariri in 2005, and the STL was formed in order to prosecute those responsible for the assassination.

economy. Scaling up the international support given to refugees and securing borders might also encourage the leakage of support from the Assad regime as well as hesitant Syrians if they knew they had somewhere safe to go. There may also be other ways of disrupting supply lines to the regime and its access to resources. In the complexity of the current situation, however, it is difficult to assess how outside assistance is benefiting or penalizing different actors in the conflict, especially now that the provision of heavy weaponry to the FSA risks intensifying the armed struggle in a number of areas.

3.1.2. Military intervention

Given the political and financial constraints as well as the current military commitments of NATO forces in Afghanistan, a fully-fledged ground invasion or a large-scale peacekeeping operation are unlikely to be options for Western military intervention in Syria. Other options that have been discussed include establishing a 'safe haven' along the Turkish border, which was proposed in September 2011 by the SNC. However, Turkey was not willing to police it without at least being sure of full international support, since establishing a buffer zone would pose a threat to Turkey's own security interests if the conflict were to migrate into the safe haven and from there across the Turkish border. Turkey was also looking for United Nations Security Council leadership and backing of the process, but this was not forthcoming.

Arming the resistance has also been a form of indirect military intervention. As the experience of Afghanistan in the 1980s demonstrated, it can have intensive effects, including unintended consequences for the sponsor countries. Until recently, only a small part of the Syrian opposition received any tangible support, and this was limited to light arms, which proved of limited utility when confronting the Syrian army's stock of heavy weaponry. There have been reports in August 2012 that Turkish support for training and the supply of weapons to FSA forces has been more organized than was hitherto publicly known. This, together with the sanctioning of CIA intelligence support to the FSA and the channelling of Qatari and Saudi funds and training to Islamist units within the FSA, points to the risk that the FSA will develop in directions not necessarily under the control of its sponsors. The more weaponry is dispersed within Syria, the more likely it is that local conflicts will also spread outside external control.

The ongoing debate in opposition circles as to the potentially negative consequences of uncontrolled foreign support for the FSA is a product of these fears as well as a contributing factor to the call for more direct external military intervention: the people who are being armed now will have to be disarmed later, and the experience of the post-Gaddafi situation in Libya suggests that it will prove difficult to bring them back under control of a civilian government in future.

If chemical weapons were to be used by the regime, then the political equation in the UN Security Council might well alter in favour of intervention. Syria is widely believed to have developed and deployed chemical weapons including blister and nerve agents. Although it has not yet signed the 1992 Chemical Weapons Convention, it did sign and ratify the 1925 Geneva Protocol banning the use of asphyxiating, poisonous or other gases, and of bacteriological methods of warfare, in 1968. The current civil war has led to increasing concern that the government may use chemical weapons against rebel forces and civilians. In response to such concerns, Jihad Makdissi, the Syrian foreign ministry spokesman, was reported in July as saying:

> No chemical or biological weapons will ever be used, and I repeat, will never be used (...) no matter what the developments inside Syria. All of these types of weapons are in storage and under security and the direct supervision of the Syrian armed forces and will never be used unless Syria is exposed to external aggression.[73]

3.1.2.1. Legal frameworks

If a military intervention were considered, the legal framework under which this would occur would need to be established. Most countries would be likely to want United Nations Security Council authorization before participating in a military intervention in Syria, although there are precedents for interventions without a United Nations Security Council resolution, such as Kosovo.

3.1.2.1.1. Kosovo

Is it lawful to use military intervention to protect another state's civilians without the authorization of a Security Council resolution? This issue arose at the time of the NATO intervention in relation to Kosovo in 1999. While most of the intervening states did not seek to justify their action under international law – although arguing that it was nonetheless legitimate and justifiable – the UK maintained that it had the legal right to use force since this was a case of 'overwhelming humanitarian necessity where, in the light of all the circumstances, a limited use of force is justifiable as the only way to avert a humanitarian catastrophe'. The UK House of Commons Foreign Affairs Committee concluded subsequently that the military action was of dubious legality, though morally justifiable.

---

73   Ian Black, 'Syria insists chemical weapons would only be used against outside forces', Guardian, 24 July 2012, http://www.guardian.co.uk/world/2012/jul/23/syria-chemical-weapons-own-goal.

Some analysts have maintained that the action was lawful because there were Security Council resolutions that either recognized the impending catastrophe in Kosovo or refused to condemn the NATO action after the event, but in international law such resolutions are not adequate to authorize the use of force.

3.1.2.1.2. 'Responsibility to Protect' (R2P) doctrine

The doctrine of Responsibility to Protect was accepted by the UN General Assembly in its 2005 resolution on the World Summit Outcome.[74] As elaborated in a report by the Secretary-General in 2009, it has three pillars: first, that the state itself has the responsibility to protect its own population from genocide, war crimes, ethnic cleansing and crimes against humanity; second, that the international community has the responsibility to provide assistance and capacity-building for the state to exercise this responsibility to protect; third, and in the last resort, the international community has the responsibility to take collective action 'through the Security Council, in accordance with the Charter, including Chapter VII, on a case-by-case basis and in cooperation with relevant regional organisations as appropriate, should peaceful means be inadequate and national authorities are manifestly failing to protect their populations.'[75]

R2P thus turns round the old debate about humanitarian intervention by insisting on a responsibility to protect, rather than a right to intervene. Although the concept was thus accepted by the General Assembly, it remains controversial in some parts of the world. The responsibilities of protection were mentioned in the Security Council resolution that authorized military intervention in Libya for the purpose of protecting civilians.[76] While the use of the concept was widely welcomed at the time, the perception that the later stages of the military operation went beyond protection of civilians and were used to overthrow the regime has been cited by some countries as a reason for refusing to agree to Security Council resolutions which could be interpreted as authorization for similar action in the future.

3.1.2.1.3. Criteria for intervention

Prudential criteria for the use of pillar 3 of R2P have been proposed: they include that the primary purpose of the proposed military action is to halt or avert the threat in question; that the operation is the last resort (and that there are no reasonably available peaceful alternatives); that the military operation is

---

74 A/Res/60/1, see document 7 in the appendix.

75 Id.

76 SCR 1973(2011), see document 4 in the appendix.

proportionate to the harm or threatened harm; and that an assessment of the balance of consequences indicates that overall more good than harm would be served by a military operation. While these criteria have not been adopted internationally, they are generally accepted as useful.

3.1.2.1.4. Consequences of arming the FSA

The recent judgment by the Special Court for Sierra Leone, when convicting former Liberian President Charles Taylor for war crimes and crimes against humanity, held that anyone who provides arms to government forces or to armed opposition groups who is aware of the substantial likelihood that they would be used to commit international crimes may themselves by guilty of aiding and abetting those crimes. This may be relevant in Syria given the possibility that reprisal massacres by opposition forces will take place, or have already taken place.

Giving arms to the FSA would be considered interference with Syrian state sovereignty as Bashar al-Assad's government remains the recognized entity in Syria. The decision to recognize or officially have dealings with a government is not a moral one, but is rather determined largely by the question of which entity has control over the state's territory. If states were prematurely to recognize the SNC, for example, as the representative of Syria this would constitute interference with state sovereignty. In Libya there were question marks over how quickly certain governments decided to recognize the Libyan National Transition Council (NTC) as the Libyan government. UN resolutions on the legitimacy of governments may also be taken into account by other states in deciding whether to recognize such governments in deciding whether a government should be recognized by other states.

3.1.3. Non-intervention

While careful consideration of the possible consequences of intervention is vital, it is equally important to examine the cost of inaction in order to be able to determine the 'balance of consequences'. The rapid turn of events since the killing of four (subsequently five) members of the inner circles of the Assad regime in a targeted bomb attack in July 2012 means that the Syrian regime now appears to have considerably fewer active supporters and the prevailing view is that most citizens would like to see a new government. However they are deterred by the uncertainty of what might follow on from regime collapse.

The international community has a growing sense that the costs of non-intervention (or a reliance only on covert intervention by a selfappointed coalition) could be high, with an increase in real or orchestrated sectarian violence, the risk of loss of control of chemical weapons or the regionalization of the conflict.

Keeping the regime in place means the pressure will still build up before potentially unleashing even greater problems than if intervention were to 'lift the lid' now. The longer the conflict continues in Syria, the more likely the rise in sectarianism, extremist and retaliatory violence and the advent of foreign fighters would be.

3.1.4. Sectarianism: a self-fulfilling prophecy

There is a difference between sectarianism on the ground and a sectarian interpretation of the conflict. In the latter respect, a number of external observers have depicted the conflict in a simplistic way, above all as a struggle between the minority Alawis (often wrongly depicted as Shia), from which the Assad family stems, and the Sunni majority of Syria.

The risk of this line of argument is that it reinforces the case for retaining a dictatorship in order to prevent sectarian violence from exploding. In reality, the regime does not come exclusively from the Alawi sect, just as the opposition is not exclusively anti-Alawi. From the outset, the main opposition narrative has been against sectarian interpretations of the conflict, the chief beneficiaries of which have been those seeking to influence the outcome of the conflict for or against a particular group, such as the Muslim Brotherhood.

In turn, arguments based on sectarianism have been heavily used in regime propaganda to make Syrian minorities afraid of potential alternatives to the Assad regime, which has a history of exploiting fears of sectarian violence. Syrian forces remained in Lebanon for 15 years after the end of the civil war there on the pretext that if they left Lebanon would explode into sectarian war. When they did leave, there were a number of incidents that seemed designed to stir up sectarian violence. The regime's use of sectarian narratives has had a number of regional consequences. Every time a story emerges about an FSA atrocity or about Al-Qaeda's presence in Syria,[77] it makes Shia communities across the region nervous. This situation is aggravated by a perception that the West is anti-Iranian, and that Saudi Arabia's involvement with the Syrian opposition is designed to counter Iranian and Shia influence in the region and has little to do with human rights. A diversity of views exists among Shia clerics in the Arab world, some of whom have been very critical of Assad (including Sheikh Nimr Al Nimr, an outspoken cleric who was arrested in Saudi Arabia

---

77 See, for example, the recent RAND blog by Seth G. Jones, 'Al Qaeda's war for Syria', 27 July 2012, citing intelligence source claims that 200 Al-Qaeda operatives are active in Syria: http://www.rand.org/blog/2012/07/al-qaedas-war-for-syria.html.

on 8 July 2012 after expressing his delight at the death of the Saudi interior minister).

There could be scope for clerical leaders from both sects to come together to call for the basic rights of Syrians to be respected and for the conflict to be 'de-sectarianized'. Given the instrumentalization of sectarian narratives by the regime and the potential for extremist groups to exploit the situation, it was emphasized that Syrian minorities do indeed have legitimate fears for their security. One participant raised the question of whether there might be further ways to limit the 'sectarianization' of the conflict, and noted that because regional actors all have an interest in the politics of sectarianism, it was a mistake to think that regional solutions to the conflict were necessarily the most legitimate: Saudi Arabia's involvement might be problematic in this respect, for example.

3.1.5. Who might intervene, when?

There are significant political, diplomatic and legal constraints on the possibility of military intervention in Syria, and it is not clear which actors might have the political will to take part in such an action. As noted above, most countries would prefer to have the backing of a United Nations Security Council resolution authorizing action, and this would be required for anything other than defensive operations.

The consistency of the principle of 'non-interference' defended by Russia and China at the United Nations Security Council means that a Security Council resolution directly sanctioning external intervention is unlikely to be achieved. Despite many months of diplomatic manoeuvres, most participants agreed that the Russians and Chinese were unlikely to change their position at the UN. After the experience of Iraq and Libya, they do not want to accept anything tabled under Chapter VII of the United Nations Charter because it might be used to justify an illegitimate 'regime change' operation.

However, as the prospect of a severely weakened Assad regime increases, a variety of diplomatic solutions are still being investigated, including in the invitation by the Saudi King Abdullah to Iranian President Mahmoud Ahmedinejad to attend the upcoming Organisation of Islamic Cooperation conference in Riyadh, and in discussions held between the British Prime Minister David Cameron and Russian President Vladimir Putin on the sidelines of the London Olympics in August 2012. However the need for 'favours' from Moscow should not be assumed, Russia might in fact be worried about its position in the Middle East as the Assad regime looked increasingly unlikely to last.

The West

It is unlikely that Western governments would intervene in Syria without a United Nations Security Council resolution. The lack of consensus in the United Nations Security Council was useful cover for Western governments that have too many other military commitments and would find it difficult to convince their publics. It is notable too, that NATO has kept a low profile over the conflict, with the Syrian attack on a Turkish plane in June 2012 only being referred by Turkey for discussion with its NATO allies, rather than the country invoking the collective right to self-defence (under Article 5 of the NATO treaty) that a more direct cross-border attack might have brought into play.[78]

If Washington decided to intervene, the lack of a United Nations Security Council resolution would not necessarily be a major obstacle, as the US is was seen as more likely to go ahead with actions that suit its national interest even if they are against international law. In the past presidential election year, however, the main aim of the White House in this area is to avoid becoming embroiled in prolonged actions. This would limit the range of possibilities to external air strikes in the event of overwhelming evidence that the regime's chemical weapons stocks were not secure, for example, or in actions in support of Israel's own defence and national security needs. Now Obama won the 2012 election it might change the position of the USA slightly. Active involvement in the crisis might become more relevant now the electoral influence is gone.

There is a significant degree of ambivalence in the West's stance on intervention: Western countries are now cautious about intervening directly in the Middle East because the idea has gained currency that their involvement in the region over the past decade does not constitute a positive track record. However, for many in the region, and especially in the Gulf, there is still a long-standing expectation that the West will take some action, whether or not this is seen as desirable.

Israel

Israel has not taken a public stance on whether Assad should go or not, but recent official statements about potentially launching a pre-emptive strike against Syria's chemical weapon supplies were interpreted as a message that Israel has intelligence about the location of chemical weapons and that it would intervene to keep them under control if its national security were to come under threat. Israel has also been strengthening its Arrow 2 ballistic missile shield in the broader regional context of Iran's nuclear weapons programme,

---

78 'Turkey goes to NATO over plane it says Syria downed in international airspace', Guardian, 24 June 2012, http://www.guardian.co.uk/world/2012/jun/24/turkey-plane-shot-down-syria.

amid renewed speculation that Israel might be contemplating a pre-emptive strike on Iranian nuclear facilities in coming months.[79]

Turkey

Turkey might be the most likely regional actor to intervene, commenting on recent official statements that Turkey would do so if the Syrian regime were to launch a 'Halabja-style' chemical weapon attack on Aleppo.15[80] However, Turkey has consistently maintained that the responsibility for protecting civilians is a UN-wide obligation, and that it is already providing assistance to Syrian refugees who have fled from northern Syrian to Turkey. Given the likely reluctance on the part of its military to enter Syrian territory, Turkey has restricted military movements to reinforcing its armed presence north of the border, and is unlikely to act alone.

The exception could arise from the new complexities of Kurdish politics emerging from the Syrian conflict: the Syrian Kurdish Democratic Union Party (PYD) now in control of a number of northern Syrian towns is closely linked to the Turkish Kurdish Workers Party (PKK) which has historically launched attacks against Turkish forces across Turkey's southeastern border. The threat of renewed PKK activism led Turkish Prime Minister Recep Tayyip Erdoğan to warn on 26 July, without directly naming the PKK:

> 'We will not allow a terrorist group to establish camps in northern Syria and threaten Turkey. If there is a step which needs to be taken against the terrorist group, we will definitely take this step.'[81]

The Turkish authorities face the most immediate challenges in managing the growing conflict on the country's southern border, but despite being increasingly robust in their statements that Assad should go, they have so far exercised restraint. However, Turkey might only intervene to protect its immediate national security interests, in the absence of a UN-sanctioned and more widely backed plan of joint military action, it would also be wary of appearing to act on behalf of Western states or at the West's bidding alone.

---

79 Dan Williams, 'Eye on Iran and Syria, Israel hardens missile shield', Reuters, 5 August 2012, http://news.yahoo.com/eye-iran-syria-israel-hardens-missile-shield-045906488--finance.html.

80 See Serkan Dimertas, 'Aleppo won't be another Halabja, Turkey says', Hurriyet, 31 July 2012, http://www.hurriyetdailynews.com/aleppo-to-see-no-new-halabja-turkeysays. aspx?pageI D=238&nID=26729&NewsCatID=338.

81 James Dorsey, 'Turkey and Syria: The Kurdish Dilemma', Huffington Post, 8 August 2012, http://www.huffingtonpost.com/james-dorsey/turkey-and-syria_b_1749637.html.

3.1.6. Balance of consequences

To conclude, there are three likely options for future intervention:
- an increase in the supply of arms to the FSA and an intensification of covert action;
- punitive air strikes triggered by a massacre in Aleppo;
- and an intensification of sanctions.

In the first two cases, the 'balance of consequences' is likely to escape the control of outside supporters of the FSA even if a clearer understanding of the dynamics on the ground emerges.

In contrast to the US-led military intervention in Iraq a decade ago, the US, UK and other European states are now facing a new set of realities in the Middle East. A newly assertive set of international and regional actors have put an effective block on Western governments taking the lead in decisionmaking over whether or not to intervene in Syria, even on humanitarian grounds alone. The experience of Libya has made Russia and China yet more suspicious that any United Nations Security Council mandate for humanitarian intervention in Syria could be used as a pretext for regime change.

There are also domestic considerations in the United States and Europe that have constrained official options, the euro and economic crises in Europe, and the lack of public and political support for intervention. All these factors weigh against Western states adopting more proactive measures in respect of Syria, at a time when (with the exception of limited US-led action) few states retain the military capacity to mount an operation in Syria while still actively engaged in Afghanistan.

Indirect intervention with Western support is already occurring, but in the absence of any real control over the consequences, external actions are unlikely to be decisive in bringing an end to Syria's descent into civil war – and if misjudged could even accelerate it.

The humanitarian imperative is nevertheless growing. With already close to 60000 dead in Syria and many more refugees, untenable strains are being placed on the neighbouring states of Jordan, Lebanon and Turkey in managing such population flows over the longer term. It was thus argued that part of the 'balance of consequences' also entailed considering intervention as a means of preventing further, larger-scale massacres, rather than waiting for them to occur before intervening.

4. APPLICABLE LAW

4.1. International humanitarian law

International humanitarian law (IHL), or the law of armed conflict, is the law that regulates the conduct of armed conflicts (jus in bello). It comprises the Geneva Conventions and the Hague Conventions, as well as subsequent treaties, case law, and customary international law. It defines the conduct and responsibilities of belligerent nations, neutral nations and individuals engaged in warfare, in relation to each other and to protected persons, usually meaning civilians.

Serious violations of international humanitarian law are called war crimes. International humanitarian law, jus in bello regulates the conduct of forces when engaged in war or armed conflict. It is distinct from jus ad bellum which regulates the conduct of engaging in war or armed conflict and includes crimes against peace and of war of aggression. Together the jus in bello and jus ad bellum comprise the two strands laws of war governing all aspects of international armed conflicts.

The law is mandatory for nations bound by the appropriate treaties. There are also other customary unwritten rules of war, many of which were explored at the Nuremberg War Trials. By extension, they also define both the permissive rights of these powers as well as prohibitions on their conduct when dealing with irregular forces and non-signatories.

International humanitarian law operates on a strict division between rules applicable in international armed conflict and those relevant to armed conflicts not of an international nature.

4.1.1. Codification of humanitarian norms

The Law of Geneva is directly inspired by the principle of humanity. It relates to those who are not participating in the conflict as well as military personnel hors de combat. It provides the legal basis for protection and humanitarian assistance carried out by impartial humanitarian organizations such as the International Committee of the Red Cross.

The Geneva Conventions are the result of a process that developed in a number of stages between 1864 and 1949 which focused on the protection of civilians and those who can no longer fight in an armed conflict. As a result of World War II, all four conventions were revised based on previous revisions and partly on some of the 1907 Hague Conventions and readopted by the international community in 1949. Later conferences have added provisions prohibiting certain methods of warfare and addressing issues of civil wars.

The Geneva Conventions are:

- First Geneva Convention "for the Amelioration of the Condition of the Wounded and Sick in Armed Forces in the Field" (first adopted in 1864, last revision in 1949)
- Second Geneva Convention "for the Amelioration of the Condition of Wounded, Sick and Shipwrecked Members of Armed Forces at Sea" (first adopted in 1949, successor of the 1907 Hague Convention X)
- Third Geneva Convention "relative to the Treatment of Prisoners of War" (first adopted in 1929, last revision in 1949)
- Fourth Geneva Convention "relative to the Protection of Civilian Persons in Time of War" (first adopted in 1949, based on parts of the 1907 Hague Convention IV)

In addition, there are three additional amendment protocols to the Geneva Convention:

- Protocol I (1977): Protocol Additional to the Geneva Conventions of 12 August 1949, and relating to the Protection of Victims of International Armed Conflicts.
- Protocol II (1977): Protocol Additional to the Geneva Conventions of 12 August 1949, and relating to the Protection of Victims of Non-International Armed Conflicts.
- Protocol III (2005): Protocol Additional to the Geneva Conventions of 12 August 1949, and relating to the Adoption of an Additional Distinctive Emblem.

While the Geneva Conventions of 1949 can be seen as the result of a process which began in 1864, today, they have "achieved universal participation this means that they apply to almost any international armed conflict.

There are some basic rules that emerged out of the International Humananitarian Law:

- Persons hors de combat (outside of combat) and those not taking part in hostilities shall be protected and treated humanely.
- It is forbidden to kill or injure an enemy who surrenders or who is hors de combat.
- The wounded and sick shall be cared for and protected by the party to the conflict which has them in its power. The emblem of the "Red Cross,"

or of the "Red Crescent," shall be required to be respected as the sign of protection.

- Captured combatants and civilians must be protected against acts of violence and reprisals. They shall have the right to correspond with their families and to receive relief.
- No one shall be subjected to torture, corporal punishment or cruel or degrading treatment.
- Parties to a conflict and members of their armed forces do not have an unlimited choice of methods and means of warfare.
- Parties to a conflict shall at all times distinguish between the civilian population and combatants. Attacks shall be directed solely against military objectives.

4.1.2. Non-international armed conflicts (NIAC)

Over the last few decades, there has been a considerable amount of practice insisting on the protection of international humanitarian law in this type of conflicts. This body of practice has had a significant influence on the formation of customary law applicable in non-international armed conflicts. Like Additional Protocol I, Additional Protocol II has had a far-reaching effect on this practice and, as a result, many of its provisions are now considered to be part of customary international law.

Examples of rules found to be customary and which have corresponding provisions in Additional Protocol II include:
- the prohibition of attacks on civilians;
- the obligation to respect and protect medical and religious personnel, medical units and transports;
- the obligation to protect medical duties;
- the prohibition of starvation;
- the prohibition of attacks on objects indispensable to the survival of the civilian population;
- the obligation to respect the fundamental guarantees of civilians and persons *hors de combat*;
- the obligation to search for and respect and protect the wounded, sick and shipwrecked;
- the obligation to search for and protect the dead;
- the obligation to protect persons deprived of their liberty;
- the prohibition of forced movement of civilians; and the specific protections afforded to women and children.

However, the most significant contribution of customary international humanitarian law to the regulation of internal armed conflicts is that it goes beyond the provisions of Additional Protocol II. Indeed, practice has created a substantial number of customary rules that are more detailed than the often rudimentary provisions in Additional Protocol II and has thus filled important gaps in the regulation of internal conflicts.

For example, Additional Protocol II contains only a rudimentary regulation of the conduct of hostilities. Article 13 provides that "the civilian population as such, as well as individual civilians, shall not be the object of attack (...) unless and for such time as they take a direct part in hostilities". Unlike Additional Protocol I, Additional Protocol II does not contain specific rules and definitions with respect to the principles of distinction and proportionality.

The gaps in the regulation of the conduct of hostilities in Additional Protocol II have, however, largely been filled through State practice, which has led to the creation of rules parallel to those in Additional Protocol I, but applicable as customary law to non-international armed conflicts. This covers the basic principles on the conduct of hostilities and includes rules on specifically protected persons and objects and specific methods of warfare.

Similarly, Additional Protocol II contains only a very general provision on humanitarian relief for civilian populations in need. Article 18(2) provides that "if the civilian population is suffering undue hardship owing to a lack of the supplies essential for its survival (...) relief actions for the civilian population which are of an exclusively humanitarian and impartial nature and which are conducted without any adverse distinction shall be undertaken".

Unlike Additional Protocol I, Additional Protocol II does not contain specific provisions requiring respect for and protection of humanitarian relief personnel and objects and obliging parties to the conflict to allow and facilitate rapid and unimpeded passage of humanitarian relief for civilians in need and to ensure the freedom of movement of authorized humanitarian relief personnel, although it can be argued that such requirements are implicit in Article 18(2) of the Protocol. These requirements have crystallized, however, into customary international law applicable in both international and non-international armed conflicts as a result of widespread, representative and virtually uniform practice to that effect.

In this respect it should be noted that while both Additional Protocols I and II require the consent of the parties concerned for relief actions to take place, most of the practice collected does not mention this requirement.

It is nonetheless self-evident that a humanitarian organization cannot operate without the consent of the party concerned. However, such consent must not be refused on arbitrary grounds. If it is established that a civilian population is threatened with starvation and a humanitarian organization which provides relief on an impartial and non-discriminatory basis is able to remedy the situation, a party is obliged to give consent. While consent may not be withheld for arbitrary reasons, practice recognizes that the party concerned may exercise control over the relief action and that humanitarian relief personnel must respect domestic law on access to territory and security requirements in force.

4.1.3. Fundamental guarantees

Fundamental guarantees apply to all civilians in the power of a party to the conflict and who do not or have ceased to take a direct part in hostilities, as well as to all persons who are *hors de combat*. These fundamental guarantees all have a firm basis in international humanitarian law applicable in both international and non-international armed conflicts. Some rules, however, were drafted so as to capture the essence of a range of detailed provisions relating to a specific subject, in particular the rules prohibiting uncompensated or abusive forced labour, enforced disappearances and arbitrary detention and the rule requiring respect for family life.

International human rights law continues to apply during armed conflicts, as expressly stated in the human rights treaties themselves, although some provisions may, subject to certain conditions, be derogated from in time of public emergency. The continued applicability of human rights law during armed conflict has been confirmed on numerous occasions in State practice and by human rights bodies and the International Court of Justice. Most recently, the Court, in its advisory opinion on the legal consequences of the construction of a wall in the occupied Palestinian territories, confirmed that "the protection offered by human rights conventions does not cease in case of armed conflict" and that while there may be rights that are exclusively matters of international humanitarian law or of human rights law, there are others that "may be matters of both these branches of international law."[82]

Applicable to all parties to the conflict, state and non-state actors:

*   Common Article 3 to the 1949 Geneva Conventions;
*   Additional Protocol II ; and
*   Customary international humanitarian law applicable to a Non-international armed conflict.

The threshold for the application of 1977 Additional Protocol II is higher than for common Article 3, but given the effective control of certain territory by non-state armed groups and their level of organisation, it is believed that this

---

82 International Court of Justice, Legal Consequences of the Construction of a Wall in the Occupied Palestinian Territory, Advisory Opinion, 9 July 2004, § 106.

threshold has been reached in. Syria is not, however, a party to 1977 Additional Protocol II so its provisions are not directly applicable.

4.2. International human rights law

International human rights law refers to the body of international law designed to promote and protect human rights at the international, regional and domestic levels. As a form of international law, international human rights law is primarily made up of treaties, agreements between states intended to have binding legal effect between the parties that have agreed to them; and customary international law, rules of law derived from the consistent conduct of states acting out of the belief that the law required them to act that way. Other international human rights instruments while not legally binding contribute to the implementation, understanding and development of international human rights law and have been recognised as a source of political obligation.

Enforcement of international human rights law can occur on either a domestic, regional or international level. States that ratify human rights treaties commit themselves to respecting those rights and ensuring that their domestic law is compatible with international legislation. When Domestic Law fails to provide a remedy for human rights abuses parties may be able to resort to regional or international mechanisms for enforcing human rights.

International Human rights law is closely related to, but distinct from international humanitarian law. Similar, because the substantive norms they contain are often similar or related – for example both provide a protection from torture. Distinct because they are regulated by legally distinct frameworks and usually operate in different contexts and regulate different relationships. Generally, human rights are understood to regulate the relationship between states and individuals in the context of ordinary life, while humanitarian law regulates the actions of a belligerent state and those parties it comes into contact with, both hostile and neutral, within the context of an armed conflict.

Syria is bound by both applicable treaty and customary human rights law.

• Non-state actors

There is increasing acceptance that armed non-state actors are also bound by at least customary norms of international human rights law. This would cover the armed groups in Syria. Thus, the UN Assistance Mission in Afghanistan stated in February 2012 that:

> While non-State actors in Afghanistan, including non-State armed groups, cannot formally become parties to international human rights

treaties, international human rights law increasingly recognizes that where non-State actors, such as the Taliban, exercise de facto control over territory, they are bound by international human rights obligations.[83]

4.3. International criminal law

International criminal law is a body of international law designed to prohibit certain categories of conduct commonly viewed as serious atrocities and to make perpetrators of such conduct criminally accountable for their perpetration. Principally, it deals with genocide, war crimes, crimes against humanity as well as the War of aggression.

Classical international law governs the relationships, rights, and responsibilities of states. Criminal law generally deals with prohibitions addressed to individuals, and penal sanctions for violation of those prohibition imposed by individual states. International criminal law comprises elements of both in that although its sources are those of international law, its consequences are penal sanctions imposed on individuals.

Syria is not a party to the Rome Statute, and therefore the International Criminal Court may not exercise jurisdiction over war crimes alleged to have been committed by on its territory unless the situation is referred to the Court by the UN Security Council.

The 1998 Statute of the International Criminal Court (Article 8(2) (c) and (e)) defines a list of acts that constitute war crimes in a NIAC. In the Tadić case, decided by the International Criminal Tribunal for the former Yugoslavia in 1999, the Tribunal ruled that serious violations of Common Article 3 involve individual criminal responsibility.

4.4. Core legal obligations

4.4.1. International humanitarian law

4.4.1.1. Common Article 3 to the 1949 Geneva Conventions

Common Article 3 obliges each party to a non-international armed conflict to treat humanely all persons "taking no active part in the hostilities", whether civilians or soldiers that have laid down their arms or who are hors de combat because of sickness, wounds, detention, or any other cause.

---

83 See UN Assistance Mission in Afghanistan (UNAMA), Annual report, February 2012 at p. iv..

Violence against such individuals, in particular murder, mutilation, torture, rape, or other cruel, humiliating or degrading treatment, is prohibited. Summary or arbitrary executions are also prohibited and sentences shall only be imposed after a fair trial. Hostages shall not be taken.

The extent to which Common Article 3 regulates directly the conduct of hostilities is disputed, although under customary international law the principles of distinction and proportionality are held to apply in a NIAC.

4.4.2. International human rights law

4.4.2.1. The right to life

According to Article 6 of the International Covenant on Civil and Political Rights (ICCPR):

> Every human being has the inherent right to life. This right shall be protected by law. No one shall be arbitrarily deprived of his life.

4.4.2.2. The rights to liberty and security

According to Article 9 of the ICCPR:

> 1. Everyone has the right to liberty and security of person. No one shall be subjected to arbitrary arrest or detention. No one shall be deprived of his liberty except on such grounds and in accordance with such procedure as are established by law.
> 2. Anyone who is arrested shall be informed, at the time of arrest, of the reasons for his arrest and shall be promptly informed of any charges against him.
> 3. Anyone arrested or detained on a criminal charge shall be brought promptly before a judge or other officer authorized by law to exercise judicial power and shall be entitled to trial within a reasonable time or to release. It shall not be the general rule that persons awaiting trial shall be detained in custody, but release may be subject to guarantees to appear for trial, at any other stage of the judicial proceedings, and, should occasion arise, for execution of the judgement.

4.4.2.3. The prohibition of torture

According to Article 7 of the ICCPR:

No one shall be subjected to torture or to cruel, inhuman or degrading treatment or punishment. In particular, no one shall be subjected without his free consent to medical or scientific experimentation.

According to Article 2 of the UN Convention against Torture and Other Cruel, Inhuman or Degrading Treatment or Punishment:

1. Each State Party shall take effective legislative, administrative, judicial or other measures to prevent acts of torture in any territory under its jurisdiction.
2. No exceptional circumstances whatsoever, whether a state of war or a threat or war, internal political instability or any other public emergency, may be invoked as a justification of torture.
3. An order from a superior officer or a public authority may not be invoked as a justification of torture.

4.4.2.4. The right to fair trial

According to Article 14 of the ICCPR:

1. All persons shall be equal before the courts and tribunals. In the determination of any criminal charge against him, or of his rights and obligations in a suit at law, everyone shall be entitled to a fair and public hearing by a competent, independent and impartial tribunal established by law. The press and the public may be excluded from all or part of a trial for reasons of morals, public order (ordre public) or national security in a democratic society, or when the interest of the private lives of the parties so requires, or to the extent strictly necessary in the opinion of the court in special circumstances where publicity would prejudice the interests of justice; but any judgement rendered in a criminal case or in a suit at law shall be made public except where the interest of juvenile persons otherwise requires or the proceedings concern matrimonial disputes or the guardianship of children.
2. Everyone charged with a criminal offence shall have the right to be presumed innocent until proved guilty according to law.
3. In the determination of any criminal charge against him, everyone shall be entitled to the following minimum guarantees, in full equality:
(a) To be informed promptly and in detail in a language which he understands of the nature and cause of the charge against him;

(b) To have adequate time and facilities for the preparation of his defence and to communicate with counsel of his own choosing;

(c) To be tried without undue delay;

4.4.2.5. Derogations

According to Article 4 of the ICCPR:

1. In time of public emergency which threatens the life of the nation and the existence of which is officially proclaimed, the States Parties to the present Covenant may take measures derogating from their obligations under the present Covenant to the extent strictly required by the exigencies of the situation, provided that such measures are not inconsistent with their other obligations under international law and do not involve discrimination solely on the ground of race, colour, sex, language, religion or social origin.

2. No derogation from articles 6, 7, 8 (paragraphs I and 2), 11, 15, 16 and 18 may be made under this provision.

3. Any State Party to the present Covenant availing itself of the right of derogation shall immediately inform the other States Parties to the present Covenant, through the intermediary of the Secretary-General of the United Nations, of the provisions from which it has derogated and of the reasons by which it was actuated. A further communication shall be made, through the same intermediary, on the date on which it terminates such derogation.

5. CONCLUSION

August 28, 1963 marks the day that Martin Luther King delivered out his worldwide knows speech "I have a dream". Now 50 years later the world has changed and we face second term of a black President of the USA. In his speech King focussed on the problems of those days in the USA. The current crisis in Syria is of course of different nature. It is the suppressor fighting the suppressed. But the dreams that the protestors must have had in 2011 when the revolt started must have been the same as King had when he delivered his speech. There is, and that is agreed worldwide, a lack of real democracy in Syria. This book is published and written in the midst of the crisis and thus does not contain the outcome. However, we found it important to list at least some of the developements so far and to provide the legal community, researchers and protestors with some basic information about the legal status and developments of the conflict.

We stand by the Syrian people in its courageous struggle for freedom, dignity and democracy. The use of force by the Syrian regime - but also by the newly founded forces of the oppostion - against civilians, including by heavy weapons and aerial bombardments, has reached unprecedented levels and can only exacerbate further the violence and endanger the stability of the whole region. We hope that the priorities should be to end oppression, stop all violence, deliver humanitarian aid for all those in need, prevent further regional instability and be prepared for the post-conflict period. However, with the hard winter ahead we fear for the lives of many refugees in and around Syria.

We have expressed concern about the protection of civilians, in particular vulnerable groups and religious communities. The intensification of violence and the recent series of terrorist attacks demonstrate the urgent need for a political transition that would meet the democratic aspirations of the Syrian people and bring stability in Syria.

But there is more. We hope that publications like these tribute to the universal movement to understand each other regardless the color of our skin, the religions we have. "Something" created this planet billions of years ago and it is our obligation to try to maintain peace in this beautiful world. Seeing the images on the TV of refugees, most profound the images of young children covered by dirt, not able to get education, in hunger and being the victim of some small group that want the power in their homeland, makes us realise that the words of King are still applicable to the people of the world. Even a more recent song of Michael Jackson tells in a few words what we should work for: "make this world a better place for you and for me". We hope that this book might add a little to the mutual understanding of people worldwide and that the crisis will be resolved without more lives to be lost.

We want to end this book with some words of Martin Luther King illustrating that we have the obligation to find a peaceful sollution in Syria in the foreseeable future:

> I have a dream that one day this nation will rise up and live out the true meaning of its creed: "We hold these truths to be self-evident, that all men are created equal."

> I have a dream that my four little children will one day live in a nation where they will not be judged by the color of their skin but by the content of their character.

> I have a dream today.

> Let freedom ring. And when this happens, and when we allow freedom ring -- when we let it ring from every village and every hamlet, from every state and every city, we will be able to speed up that day when all of God's children -- black men and white men, Jews and Gentiles, Protestants and Catholics -- will be able to join hands and sing in the words of the old Negro spiritual: "Free at last! Free at last! Thank God Almighty, we are free at last!"

ANNEXES

ANNEX 1: NGO reports

- "Syria: Indiscriminate attacks terrorize and displace civilians", Amnesty International, 19 September 2012
- "Syria: End Opposition Use of Torture, Executions", Human Rights Watch, 17 September 2012
- "Syria: Government Attacking Bread Lines", Human Rights Watch, 30 August 2012
- "Syria: all-out repression: Purging dissent in Aleppo, Syria", Amnesty International, 1 August 2012
- "Syria: Disturbing reports of summary killings by government and opposition forces", Amnesty International, 25 July 2012
- "Syria: Evidence of Cluster Munitions Use by Syrian Forces: Online Videos Appear to Show Remnants of the Weapons", Human Rights Watch, 12 July 2012
- "Syria: Torture Centers Revealed: For 27 Detention Sites: Locations, Commanders' Names, Torture Methods", Human Rights Watch, 3 July 2012
- "Torture Archipelago: Arbitrary Arrests, Torture, and Enforced Disappearances in Syria's Underground Prisons since March 2011", Human Rights Watch, 3 July 2012
- "Syria: Rights, Accountability Key to Transition Plan: Concrete Measures Needed to Rein in Security Services", Human Rights Watch, 30 June 2012
- "Syria: End Indiscriminate Shootings of Civilians Fleeing Country: Border Forces Appear to Shoot on Sight Syrians Fleeing to Jordan", Human Rights Watch, 27 June 2012
- "Syria: Sexual Assault in Detention: Security Forces Also Attacked Women and Girls in Raids on Homes", Human Rights Watch, 15 June 2012
- "Deadly Reprisals: Deliberate Killings and Other Abuses by Syria's Armed Forces", Amnesty International, 14 June 2012
- "Syria: Stop Grave Abuses of Children: Secretary General's Report Should Prompt Security Council Sanctions", Human Rights Watch, 11 June 2012
- "Isolate Syria's Arms Suppliers: Russian Arms Exporter Rosoboronexport Risks Complicity in Grave Abuses", Human Rights Watch, 3 June 2012
- ""They Burned My Heart": War Crimes in Northern Idlib during Peace Plan Negotiations", Human Rights Watch, 2 May 2012
- "In Cold Blood: Summary Executions by Syrian Security Forces and Pro-Government Militias", Human Rights Watch, 10 April 2012
- "Syria's Phase of Radicalisation", International Crisis Group, Middle East Briefing No. 33, 10 April 2012
- "Syria: Government Uses Homs Tactics on Border Town: Indiscriminate Shelling, Sniper Killings, Attacks on Fleeing Residents", Human Rights Watch, 22 March 2012
- "Syria: Armed Opposition Groups Committing Abuses End Kidnappings, Forced Confessions, and Executions", Human Rights Watch, 20 March 2012
- "Syria: Witnesses Describe Idlib Destruction, Killings: One Year On, Indiscriminate Attacks Inflicting Heavy Toll", Human Rights Watch, 15 March 2012
- "Syria: Army Planting Banned Landmines, Witnesses Describe Troops Placing Mines Near Turkey, Lebanon Borders", Human Rights Watch, 13 March 2012
- "Syria: New Amnesty International report on torture in Syria", Amnesty International, 7 March 2012
- "Now or Never: A Negotiated Transition for Syria", International Crisis Group, Middle East Briefing No. 32, 5 March 2012

- "Syria: Stop Torture of Children Security Forces Detain Juveniles, Occupy Schools", Human Rights Watch, 3 February 2012
- "By All Means Necessary!" Individual and Command Responsibility for Crimes against Humanity in Syria, Human Rights Watch, 15 December 2011
- "Uncharted Waters: Thinking Through Syria's Dynamics", International Crisis Group, Middle East Briefing No. 31, 24 November 2011
- Syria: Crimes Against Humanity in Homs", Human Rights Watch, 11 November 2011
- "Health Crisis: Syrian Government Targets the Wounded and Health Workers", Amnesty International, 25 October 2011 (see also press release here)
- "Deadly detention: Deaths in custody amid popular protest in Syria", Amnesty International, 31 August 2011
- "Popular Protest in North Africa and the Middle East (VII): The Syrian Regime's Slow-motion Suicide", Middle East/North Africa Report No. 109, 13 July 2011
- "Popular Protest in North Africa and the Middle East (VI): The Syrian People's Slow-motion Revolution", International Crisis Group, Middle East/North Africa Report No. 108, 6 July 2011
- "Crackdown in Syria: Terror in Tell Kalakh", Amnesty International, 6 July 2011
- ""We've Never Seen Such Horror," Crimes against Humanity by Syrian Security Forces", Human Rights Watch, 1 June 2011

Other human rights reports

- "A Wasted Decade: Human Rights in Syria during Bashar al-Assad's First Ten Years in Power", Human Rights Watch, 16 July 2010
- "'Your son is not here': Disappearances from Syria's Saydnaya Military Prison", Amnesty International, 5 July 2010
- "Group Denial: Repression of Kurdish Political and Cultural Rights in Syria", Human Rights Watch, 26 November 2009

ANNEX 2:
Human Rights Council opens
fourth special session on Syria

Human Rights Council

MORNING 1 June 2012

The Human Rights Council this morning opened a Special Session to examine the deteriorating human rights situation in Syria and the recent killings in El Houleh.

The session was convened after the Council received a request from Qatar, Turkey, United States, Saudi Arabia, Kuwait, Denmark and the European Union, backed by 17 other Member States and supported by 33 observer States. This is the fourth Special Session the Council has convened on the situation in Syria in the past 14 months. The Council held the first Special Session on the human rights situation in Syria on 29 April 2011 and the second on 22 August 2011. The third special session, held on 2 December 2011, resulted in a resolution establishing a mandate of a Special Rapporteur on the situation of human rights in Syria, to begin once the Independent International Commission of Inquiry to Syria (formed as a result of a resolution passed in the second Special Session held on 22 and 23 August 2011) ended.

Navi Pillay, United Nations High Commissioner for Human Rights, in a statement read out on her behalf, said last week's killing of 108 civilians at El Houleh in Syria, including 49 children and 34 women, may amount to crimes against humanity. The High Commissioner urged the international community to make all efforts to end impunity and ensure accountability for the perpetrators of the atrocities. Ms. Pillay regretted that despite the Council's repeated calls for cooperation the Commission of Inquiry still had not been granted access to Syria. Those who ordered, assisted, or failed to stop attacks on civilians were individually criminally liable for their actions. Other States had a duty to do all they could to prevent and prosecute perpetrators of international crimes. Ms. Pillay urged the Security Council to consider referring the case of Syria to the International Criminal Court.

The Council was also addressed in a videotaped message by Christof Heyns, Special Rapporteur on extrajudicial, summary or arbitrary executions, delivering a statement on behalf of all Special Procedures mandate-holders of the United Nations Human Rights Council, who deplored the alarmingly deterioration in the situation in Syria and condemned in the strongest possible terms the series of attacks on residential areas, in particular the recent massacres of civilians in the village of El Houleh which reportedly involved Government forces and militias. The mandate holders expressed particular shock at the death of numerous young children. The mandate holders agreed there were indications that crimes against humanity, and possibly other crimes under international law, had been committed in Syria, and the recent tragic events constituted an additional reason for the Security Council to refer the situation to the International Criminal Court.

Speaking as the concerned country, Syria condemned in the strongest terms the killing of innocent people in a brutal and horrendous massacre, and said groups of armed terrorists had attacked the area and perpetrated the massacre. The Syrian Government had established an inter-ministerial commission to find out the truth and bring the perpetrators to justice; the Government had also closely collaborated with the team of international monitors in Syria. It was despicable that some of the States sponsoring the current Special Session could make the request when they had publicly supported the armed terrorist groups in Syria, filling ships with Israeli-made weapons or training terrorists on their soil before dispatching them to Syria to carry out killings. While Syria was committed to implementing the plan of the Joint Special Envoy, which would spare the region serious consequences, some of the sponsors of the current Special Session had condemned the Joint Special Representative as sterile.

In the general debate all States condemned the killings in El Houleh, with many describing the murder of more than 100 people, including 49 children, as a "heinous act" and others calling it a "crime against humanity". States demanded that the Syrian Government cooperate with the Joint Special Envoy Kofi Annan and the Human Rights Council Commission of Inquiry, and several speakers said the United Nations Security Council must immediately refer the situation to the International Criminal Court. Some States said the events in El Houleh must not be used as a pretext for foreign intervention, which would hold serious consequences for world peace. One State resolutely opposed any form of international intervention and regime change. Others emphasized that the international community should fulfil its humanitarian responsibility and put an end to bloodshed, violence, and violations of human rights.

Speaking during this morning's debate were representatives of Denmark speaking on behalf of the European Union and other States, Sweden speaking on behalf of Denmark, Finland, Iceland and Norway, Venezuela speaking on behalf of Bolivia, Cuba, Ecuador and Nicaragua, Saudi Arabia, Italy, Kuwait, United States, Uruguay, Qatar, Chile, China, Spain, Thailand, Hungary, Switzerland, Angola, Indonesia and Peru.

The Council will next meet this afternoon at 2.30 p.m. to continue the Special Session, hear more statements from States and representatives of non-governmental organizations, and to consider and vote on the proposed draft resolution before closing the Special Session. Documentation relating to the Special Session is available on the Human Rights Council webpage.

Opening Statements

LAURA DUPUY LASSERRE (Uruguay), President of the Human Rights Council, said the request for a Special Session on "the deteriorating human rights situation in the Syrian Arab Republic and the recent killings in El Houleh" was received on Wednesday, 30 May at 11 a.m. The request for the Special Session was supported by the following Member States of the Council: Austria, Belgium, Chile, Costa Rica, Czech Republic, Djibouti, Guatemala, Hungary, Italy, Jordan, Kuwait, Maldives, Mexico, Norway, Peru, Poland, Qatar, Republic of Moldova, Romania, Saudi Arabia, Spain, Switzerland, United States, and Uruguay. The request was also supported by the following observer States: Australia, Bahrain, Brazil, Bulgaria, Canada, Croatia, Cyprus, Denmark, Estonia, Finland, France, Germany, Greece, Honduras, Ireland, Japan, Latvia, Lithuania, Luxembourg, Malta, Monaco, Morocco, Netherlands, New Zealand, Portugal, Republic of Korea, Slovakia, Slovenia, Sweden, Tunisia, Turkey, United Arab Emirates, and the United Kingdom.

MARCIA KRAN, Officer-in-Charge of the Office of the High Commissioner for Human Rights, delivering a statement on behalf of NAVI PILLAY, United Nations High Commissioner for Human Rights, expressed concern that for the fourth time the Council was compelled to convene a Special Session to discuss the situation in Syria and was appalled by the atrocities committed in El Houleh. Preliminary investigations indicated that the attacks possibly directed at the civilian population had resulted in the killings of 108 people, including 49 children and 34 women. According to preliminary reports, the Syrian military allegedly unleashed a barrage of heavy weapons on the El Houleh area, including artillery and tank fire, which continued until 2 a.m. on Saturday, 26 May. Some reports suggested that pro-government Shabiha paramilitary groups also entered the villages and may bear responsibility for dozens of killings. These acts may amount to crimes against humanity and other international crimes, and may be indicative of a pattern of widespread or systematic attacks against civilian populations that had been perpetrated with impunity. The Government of Syria had stated that its military was acting only in self-defence, and that it sought to protect the civilian population; that three members of the armed forces were killed and 16 soldiers were injured as a result of the armed clashes in El Houleh. The Government of Syria had also said that an inter-ministerial committee had been established to investigate these events. Nevertheless, there was a need for prompt, independent and impartial international investigations into all serious human rights violations in Syria, including those that had occurred in El Houleh.

Ms. Pillay regretted that despite the Council's repeated calls on Syria to cooperate fully with the Commission of Inquiry, the Commission still had not been granted access to Syria. Ms. Pillay took note of the Security Council's call on the United Nations Supervision Mission in Syria to continue its investigations into the El Houleh killings; and urged the Government of Syria to cooperate fully with UNSMIS. The Commission of Inquiry had continued to gather information and investigate human rights violations committed in Syria and, on 24 May, the Commission published a periodic update based on two field missions it conducted in March and April. It reported that gross violations and abuses continued unabated in an increasingly militarized context despite the ceasefire announced on 12 April in Syria. In addition, on 30 May, UNSMIS reported the discovery of 13 bodies in the area of Assukar in Dier EL-Zour, with their hands tied behind their backs and some of whom appeared to have been shot at close range.

Ms. Pillay reiterated a call to the Government of Syria to grant the Commission of Inquiry full and unimpeded access to the country so as to carry out investigations into all human rights violations and to assume its responsibility to protect the civilian population in the country. Those who ordered, assisted, or failed to stop attacks on civilians were individually criminally liable for their actions. Other States had a duty to do all they could to prevent and prosecute perpetrators of international crimes. Once again, Ms. Pillay urged the Security Council to consider referring the case of Syria to the International Criminal Court. The Joint Special Envoy's six-point plan sought to pave the way for a peaceful solution to the Syrian crisis, in particular by ending all violence and human rights violations. It was vital that the Government of Syria immediately and comprehensively implement this plan; and it was equally vital that all parties desisted from all forms of violence. Ms. Pillay urged the international community to throw its weight behind the Joint Envoy's six-point plan and called for the conduct of immediate investigations into the El Houleh events, as well as into other human rights violations committed in Syria.

CHRISTOF HEYNS, Special Rapporteur on extrajudicial, summary or arbitrary executions, delivering a statement on behalf of all Special Procedures mandate-holders of the United Nations Human Rights Council by video conference, said the Special Procedures deplored the fact that since the last Special Session and after more than one year of widespread violence, the situation in Syria had alarmingly deteriorated. The killings which occurred over the past few days had again alerted them to the imperative for immediate action from the highest level, in particular President Assad. The mandate holders condemned in the strongest possible terms the series of attacks on residential areas, in particular the recent massacres of civilians in the village of El Houleh which reportedly involved Government forces and militias. The mandate holders expressed particular shock at the death of numerous young children and recalled the State's obligations to protect every individual's right to life, including children, under the International Covenant on Civil and Political Rights and the Convention on the Rights of the Child. It was noted that the Government had appointed an inter-ministerial committee to investigate the events in El Houleh: the mandate holders stressed that that investigation should be prompt, independent and thorough so as to shed light on the circumstances of the killings, and to ensure that perpetrators were held to account.

The recent attacks occurred in contradiction to the commitments of the Joint Special Envoy's six-point plan. Reprisals had reportedly been carried out against protestors, political and human rights activists, or persons suspected of anti-Government activities. That had led to arbitrary arrests and detentions, enforced disappearances, ill-treatment including of minors in interrogation and detention facilities, and sexual violence in places of detention against men, women and children. As reported by humanitarian agencies, livelihoods and access to medical care, food, and water had been affected across the country, and dramatically so in conflict affected areas. Ensuring unhindered access to humanitarian assistance, including to internally displaced persons, must be a priority for all parties and be provided irrespective of other efforts to resolve the crisis. Reports of interference with and even deliberate destruction preventing access to adequate food, water and in particular medical care and assistance were of great concern and would, if confirmed, represent further egregious human rights violations.

All available information indicated that crimes against humanity, and possibly other crimes under international law had been committed in Syria, and the Special Procedure mandate holders considered that recent tragic events constituted an additional reason for the Security Council to refer the situation to the International Criminal Court.

As a matter of urgency, the Syrian Government and all parties were urged to take immediate measures to ensure that no more human rights violations were committed and to prevent further civilian losses. All parties must refrain from violence.

Statement from Syria as the Concerned Country

Syria, speaking as the concerned country, said that Syria had witnessed one of the most horrendous massacres and condemned in strongest terms the killing of innocent people in a brutal massacre. Groups of armed terrorists numbering from 600 to 800 persons had attacked the area and perpetrated this massacre by employing different kinds of mortar shells and weaponry to kill peaceful civilians. Hours after these events, the Syrian Government announced the establishment of an interministerial commission to find out the truth and bring the perpetrators to justice; the Government had also closely collaborated with the team of international monitors in Syria. Yesterday a preliminary report included important conclusions: the main motive for these murders had been to ignite sectarian strife in an area made up of a multi-sectarian social fabric that had lived in peace and neighbourly relations. The committee concluded that there were no traces of artillery shelling on the bodies of the victims, an allegation made by the representative of the High Commissioner; the committee also affirmed that the killings had occurred at close range and the investigations suggested the participation of several non-Syrian nationals. The intention of the attacks had been to create an area outside the control of the State close to the Lebanese border.

It was now something familiar for armed gangs and terrorist groups to carry out these attacks before the meetings of the Security Council with the purpose of bringing Special Sessions against Syria and condemning resolutions such as the current draft resolution today. The resolution's paragraphs were full of hatred that showed the despair and lack of orientation of those drafting it. Syria regretted the fact that honest States had associated themselves with these resolutions which harmed the Council. It was despicable that some of the States sponsoring the current Special Session could make this request, revealed publicly through their statements where they had voiced their support through the media and millions of dollars from oil revenue to those groups in Syria and filling ships with Israeli made weapons or hosting and training terrorists on their soil and then dispatching them to Syria to carry out killings.

The United States was the first instigator for the convening of the meeting and had not hidden its support for the armed opposition and encouraged them not to surrender. Those who instigated this meeting had as their objective more bloodshed of Syrian blood and to ignite strife. Those States sponsoring the holding of this session were hastily making judgements, overlooking the real murders, bypassing the principles of justice, and casting doubt on the role being played by United Nations monitors and the plan of the Joint Special Envoy. The investigation would show the responsibility of those who had carried out the killings and those instigators behind them and this evidence would be presented to the world. While Syria was committed to implementing the plan of the Joint Special Envoy, which would spare the region serious consequences, some of the sponsors of the current Special Session had condemned the Joint Special Representative as sterile. They ignored everything Israel committed, including the settlements, conferring a Jewish character to Jerusalem. If the Syrian Government thought that those who sponsored this Special Session were interested in defending the innocent in Syria, the Government would have been the first to adopt a resolution condemning the bloodshed, but the real objective was flimsy political trading targeting Syria. Syria had reaffirmed several times its responsibility to protect its people against violence and terror and would do everything possible according to law and international commitments to protect the Syrian people and to emerge from the crises. Those who intended to help Syria on these objectives should stop the media war. Everyone should realise that the solution in Syria would never be through arms, but rather through a positive debate among those who would forgo violence.

Discussion

Denmark, speaking on behalf of the European Union and other States, said the lives of more than 100 people, including 49 children, had been indiscriminately taken in heinous acts perpetrated by the Syrian regime against its own population in El Houleh. All violence must be brought to an end immediately. The European Union would continue to impose sanctions on the Syrian regime as long as the repression continued and encouraged partners to do the same. It pledged full support to the Syrian people who were proudly standing up for their rights to freedom and democracy. It was high time that they should be rewarded for their outstanding efforts in the pursuit of peace and dignity.

Sweden, speaking on behalf of the Nordic countries, Denmark, Finland, Iceland and Norway, said they condemned in the strongest possible terms the continuous atrocities in Syria, including the killings of civilians and the most appalling recent example of the killings and brutal executions of children in El-Houleh. The Syrian Government must cooperate with the Joint Special Envoy Kofi Annan and the Human Rights Council Commission of Inquiry.
Venezuela, speaking on behalf of Bolivia, Cuba, Ecuador and Nicaragua, condemned in the strongest possible terms the murders in El Houleh and called for a far-reaching inquiry into those crimes. However, those events must not be used as a pretext for foreign intervention, which would hold serious consequences for world peace. Bolivia, Cuba, Ecuador, Nicaragua and Venezuela feared a repetition in Syria of the same scenario seen in Libya. The Government had shown willingness to implement reform and Kofi Annan's peace plan. The countries rejected the draft resolution as it interfered in the internal affairs of Syria.

Saudi Arabia said that the Council had convened the Special Session to discuss human rights violations following the unfortunate recent events in El Houleh. The Council of Ministers of the Kingdom of Saudi Arabia had strongly condemned these events and the targeting of women and children, as well as the ongoing violence in Syria. The statement also emphasized that the international community should fulfil its humanitarian responsibility and put an end to bloodshed, violence, and violations of human rights. The Syrian people's aspiration for progress and reform should be listened to. Saudi Arabia further condemned torture and mutilation that children and women had been subjected to and stressed that the perpetrators should be brought to justice.

Italy strongly condemned the atrocities allegedly perpetrated by the Syrian army and security forces in El Houleh and echoed the call by the High Commissioner for a prompt international investigation in order to establish individual accountability. Impunity was no longer tolerable. Italy reiterated in the strongest terms the call on the Syrian authorities to immediately stop the bloodshed and to fulfil the duty to protect their people. Unimpeded access to Syria must be granted to international humanitarian agencies. In coordination with other European Union partners, targeted sanctions had been adopted against those more directly involved in the most serious human rights violations.

Kuwait said that the Syrian people were exposed to grave violations of their fundamental rights and notably the right to life. Kuwait stressed the importance of implementing the Council's resolution which demanded accountability for those responsible for human rights violations. Kuwait emphasized the importance of maintaining the territorial integrity and independence of Syria and believed that the failure of the plan of the Joint Special Representative could lead to disastrous consequences on Syria and the region.

United States condemned in the strongest possible terms the heinous summary executions committed at close range of families in their own homes, including over 30 children younger than 10, after a vicious assault by tanks and artillery, weapons only the Syrian regime possessed. Syrians bravely risked their lives daily to broadcast to the world the horrendous and brutal campaign of killing that the Assad Government was waging against the Syrian people. Assad's brutal rule would ultimately come to an end.

Uruguay said the attacks in Syria were not just a violation of international law by the Syrian Government but also a shattering of the efforts undertaken by the United Nations and Arab League Joint Special Envoy Kofi Annan. The Syrian Government must give unhampered access to humanitarian agencies, allow an uninterrupted dialogue with the Syrian people, and follow the Six Point Plan.

Qatar said the hideous massacre of children by the Syrian regime in El Houleh was a flagrant violation of childhood and humanity. The Syrian Government had taken no measures to put an end to the bloodshed. It must immediately end all acts of violence and open safe humanitarian corridors. The souls of the innocent women and children of the El Houleh massacre would be calling upon the Council to pass a resolution.

Chile called on all sides to halt the violence indiscriminately affecting the lives of people and expressed its solidarity with the families of the victims. Chile condemned the massacre in El Houleh and the violations committed in the previous months, and called for the implementation of the plan of the Joint Special Envoy. Chile supported the draft resolution mechanism to investigate recent events. The protection of human dignity was unavoidable and States should continue with their diplomatic efforts to stop the slaughter, ensure humanitarian access, and create the conditions that allowed Syrian people to decide on their own future.

China said that China was deeply shocked by the events in El Houleh and condemned the killing of innocent women and children. It was necessary to implement a comprehensive ceasefire preventing further violence. The Syrian Government and all parties should effectively implement the plan of the Joint Special Envoy and Security Council resolutions. It should also support the work of the United Nations supervision mission in Syria. China resolutely opposed any form of international intervention and regime change. A political dialogue process should begin without prejudging the outcome.

Spain expressed concern about the Syrian Government's systematic non-compliance with the international obligations arising from Security Council resolutions. As the independent commission of inquiry confirmed, the Syrian Government had neglected its most basic human rights obligations vis-à-vis its people. Spain urged Syria to facilitate the access of humanitarian assistance; stressed that the international community should stand united; and urged States which had not done so to join consensus. The regime should take effective steps to put an end to the spiralling of violence, ensure that massive human rights violations did not go unpunished, and urged all delegations to adopt the resolution without a vote.

Thailand strongly condemned the violence in El Houleh, especially against children, and supported the current investigation by the United Nations Supervision Mission in Syria and the Syrian authorities. The deteriorating situation in Syria was a serious concern and reports of continuing violence by both the Syrian authorities and other parties were worrisome. Humanitarian assistance should be given access without delay.

Hungary said the escalation of violence and the deteriorating human rights situation in Syria, clearly demonstrated by the murder of more than 100 individuals, including children, in El Houlah, was unacceptable. The international community must not remain idle in the face of such atrocities. The Syrian Government must immediately end the violence, support the mission of United Nations observers, and fully implement Kofi Annan's six-point plan.

Switzerland strongly condemned the appalling massacre in El Houleh and it could constitute a war crime or even a crime against humanity and must be established. The facts already known seemed to suggest that the Syrian authorities carry substantial responsibility. The Security Council must immediately refer the situation to the International Criminal Court. The credibility of the United Nations was at stake, together with its Member States it had a duty to act now.

Angola joined the international community in expressing deep concern for the deterioration of the situation in Syria, as well as the attacks in Damascus, Aleppo and El Houleh. Angola stressed the importance of complying with the plan of the Joint Special Envoy and called on all parties to put an end to violence and allow access for humanitarian agencies; and the need for an independent inquiry that was impartial and with the support of the United Nations supervision mission, and to ensure that such acts would not happen again. Angola urged parties to show restraint and engage in dialogue.

Indonesia shared the deepest concern of the international community at the worsening situation in Syria and welcomed the United Nations engagement to seek peaceful and agreed solutions for all parties in Syria. It called upon the Syrian Government and other parties to cease the use of force and to build trust. The commitment of all parties to shy away from violence was imperative for an inclusive democratic transition; Indonesia urged Syria to cooperate with the United Nations human rights machinery and to fulfil its commitments to promote and protect the human rights of its people.

Peru said that the Council could not remain silent in the face of the situation in Syria and effective measures should be adopted to protect the lives of people in Syria. Peru condemned the use of force against civilians and reiterated its call to ensure that human rights were in full effect and that the violence came to an end. It was essential to ensure effective access of humanitarian assistance in areas affected by conflict. The plan of the Joint Special Envoy should be complied with and Peru appealed to the Government to protect life and respect for its people and find a peaceful solution to this crisis.

ANNEX 3:
Security Council Press Statement on Attacks in Syria

27 May 2012

The following Security Council press statement was issued today by Council President Agshin Mehdiyev (Azerbaijan):

The members of the Security Council condemned in the strongest possible terms the killings, confirmed by United Nations observers, of dozens of men, women and children and the wounding of hundreds more in the village of El-Houleh, near Homs, in attacks that involved a series of Government artillery and tank shellings on a residential neighbourhood. The members of the Security Council also condemned the killing of civilians by shooting at close range and by severe physical abuse. The members of the Security Council extended their profound sympathies and sincere condolences to the families of the victims, and underscored their grave concern about the situation of civilians in Syria.

Such outrageous use of force against civilian population constitutes a violation of applicable international law and of the commitments of the Syrian Government under United Nations Security Council resolutions 2042 (2012) and 2043 (2012) to cease violence in all its forms, including the cessation of use of heavy weapons in population centres. The members of the Security Council reiterated that all violence in all its forms by all parties must cease. Those responsible for acts of violence must be held accountable. The members of the Security Council requested the Secretary-General, with the involvement of UNSMIS [United Nations Supervision Mission in Syria], to continue to investigate these attacks and report the findings to the Security Council.

The members of the Security Council demanded that the Government of Syria immediately cease the use of heavy weapons in population centres and immediately pull back its troops and its heavy weapons from in and around population centres and return them to their barracks.

The members of the Security Council reaffirmed their strong commitment to the sovereignty, independence, unity and territorial integrity of Syria, and to the purposes and principles of the Charter.

The members of the Security Council reiterated their full support to the efforts of the Joint Special Envoy for the implementation of his six-point plan in its entirety and requested him to convey in the clearest terms to the Syrian parties, and in particular the Syrian Government, the demands of the Security Council.

ANNEX 4:
OHCHR involvement in the crisis

- HRC 20th 19/11/2012 A/HRC/20/37/Corr.1 Situation of human rights in the Syrian Arab Republic: implementation of Human Rights Council resolution 19/22 - Report of the Secretary-General - Corrigendum
- HRC 21st 15/11/2012 A/HRC/21/32/Corr.1 Situation of human rights in the Syrian Arab Republic: implementation of Human Rights Council resolution 19/22 - Report of the Secretary-General - Corrigendum
- HRC 21st 17/10/2012 A/HRC/RES/21/26 Situation of human rights in the Syrian Arab Republic
- HRC 21st 25/09/2012 A/HRC/21/32 Situation of human rights in the Syrian Arab Republic: implementation of Human Rights Council resolution 19/22 - Report of the Secretary-General
- HRC 21st 24/09/2012 A/HRC/21/L.32 Situation of human rights in the Syrian Arab Republic
- HRC 21st 19/09/2012 A/HRC/21/G/6 Note verbale dated 14 September 2012 from the Permanent Mission of the Syrian Arab Republic to the United Nations Office and other international organizations in Geneva addressed to the Office of the United Nations High Commissioner for Human Rights
- HRC 21st 19/09/2012 A/HRC/21/G/5 Note verbale dated 14 September 2012 from the Permanent Mission of the Syrian Arab Republic to the United Nations Office and other international organizations in Geneva addressed to the Office of the United Nations High Commissioner for Human Rights
- HRC 21st 19/09/2012 A/HRC/21/G/3 Note verbale dated 6 August 2012 from the Permanent Mission of the Syrian Arab Republic to the United Nations Office and other international organizations in Geneva addressed to the Office of the United Nations High Commissioner for Human Rights
- HRC 21st 18/09/2012 A/HRC/21/G/7 Note verbale dated 14 September 2012 from the Permanent Mission of the Syrian Arab Republic to the United Nations Office at Geneva addressed to the Office of the United Nations High Commissioner for Human Rights
- HRC 21st 11/09/2012 A/HRC/21/NGO/121 Joint written statement submitted by the General Arab Women Federation (GAWF). The situation in Syrian Arab Republic
- HRC 21st 09/09/2012 A/HRC/21/G/2/Corr.1 Note verbale dated 31 May 2012 from the Permanent Mission of the Syrian Arab Republic to the United Nations Office and other international organizations in Geneva addressed to the Office of the United Nations High Commissioner for Human Rights
- HRC 21st 07/09/2012 A/HRC/21/NGO/88 Written statement submitted by the Cairo Institute for Human Rights Studies (CIHRS). Human rights violations and conflict increasing in Lebanon as conflict from Syria spills-over into country
- HRC 21st 07/09/2012 A/HRC/21/NGO/108 Written statement submitted by the Syriac Universal Alliance (SUA). The indigenous Aramean (Syriac) Christians of Iraq, Turkey and Syria: The final solution?
- HRC 21st 07/09/2012 A/HRC/21/G/2 Note verbale dated 31 May 2012 from the Permanent Mission of the Syrian Arab Republic to the United Nations Office and other international organizations in Geneva addressed to the Office of the United Nations High Commissioner for Human Rights

- HRC 21st 16/08/2012 A/HRC/21/50 Report of the independent international commission of inquiry on the Syrian Arab Republic
- GA 67th 25/07/2012 A/67/181 Human rights and unilateral coercive measures - Report of the Secretary-General
- HRC 20th 16/07/2012 A/HRC/RES/20/22 Situation of human rights in the Syrian Arab Republic
- HRC 12/07/2012 A/HRC/WGAD/2012/9 Opinions adopted by the Working Group on Arbitrary Detention at its sixty-third session, 30 April–4 May 2012 - No. 9/2012 (Syrian Arab Republic)
- HRC 20th 03/07/2012 A/HRC/20/L.22 Situation of human rights in the Syrian Arab Republic
- HRC 20th 26/06/2012 A/HRC/20/G/6 Note verbale dated 6 June 2012 from the Permanent Mission of the Syrian Arab Republic to the United Nations Office and Other International Organizations in Geneva addressed to the Office of the United Nations High Commissioner for Human Rights
- HRC 20th 22/06/2012 A/HRC/20/37 Situation of human rights in the Syrian Arab Republic: implementation of Human Rights Council resolution 19/22 - Report of the Secretary-General A
- HRC 20th 18/06/2012 A/HRC/20/22/Add.4 Report of the Special Rapporteur on extrajudicial, summary or arbitrary executions, Christof Heyns - Addendum - Observations on communications transmitted to Governments and replies received
- HRC 20th 15/06/2012 A/HRC/20/G/4 Note verbale dated 30 May 2012 from the Permanent Mission of the Syrian Arab Republic to the United Nations Office and Other International Organizations in Geneva addressed to the Office of the United Nations High Commissioner for Human Rights
- HRC 20th 15/06/2012 A/HRC/20/G/3 Note verbale dated 24 May 2012 from the Permanent Mission of the Syrian Arab Republic to the United Nations Office and Other International Organizations in Geneva addressed to the Office of the United Nations High Commissioner for Human Rights
- HRC 20th 15/06/2012 A/HRC/20/G/2 Note verbale dated 23 May 2012 from the Permanent Mission of the Syrian Arab Republic to the United Nations Office and Other International Organizations in Geneva addressed to the Office of the United Nations High Commissioner for Human Rights
- HRC 20th 06/06/2012 A/HRC/20/NGO/18 Joint written statement submitted by the General Arab Women Federation. The situation in the Syrian Arab Republic
- HRC 19th SS 04/06/2012 A/HRC/RES/S-19/1 The deteriorating situation of human rights in the Syrian Arab Republic, and the recent killings in El-Houleh
- HRC 19th SS 01/06/2012 A/HRC/S-19/NGO/2 Written statement submitted by Amnesty International. Syria. The UN Human Rights Council must prompt action across the UN to end the violence and ensure accountability
- HRC 19th SS 01/06/2012 A/HRC/S-19/L.1 The deteriorating situation of human rights in the Syrian Arab Republic, and the recent killings in El-Houleh
- HRC 19th SS 31/05/2012 A/HRC/S-19/NGO/1 Written statement submitted by the Arab NGO Network for Development. Severe and gross human rights violations in Syria continue requiring bold action from the United Nations
- HRC 19th SS 31/05/2012 A/HRC/S-19/1 Letter dated 30 May 2012 from the Permanent Representatives of Denmark, Kuwait, Qatar, Saudi Arabia and Turkey, the Ambassador of the European Union to the United Nations Office at Geneva and the Ambassador of the United States of America to the Human Rights Council addressed to the President of the Human Rights Council

- HRC 19th 10/04/2012 A/HRC/RES/19/22 Situation of human rights in the Syrian Arab Republic
- HRC 19th 10/04/2012 A/HRC/RES/19/17 Israeli settlements in the Occupied Palestinian Territory, including East Jerusalem, and in the occupied Syrian Golan
- HRC 19th 10/04/2012 A/HRC/RES/19/14 Human rights in the occupied Syrian Golan
- HRC 19th 10/04/2012 A/HRC/RES/19/1 The escalating grave human rights violations and deteriorating humanitarian situation in the Syrian Arab Republic
- HRC 19th 04/04/2012 A/HRC/DEC/19/109 Outcome of the Universal Periodic Review: Syrian Arab Republic
- HRC 19th 22/03/2012 A/HRC/19/L.38/Rev.1 Situation of human rights in the Syrian Arab Republic
- HRC 19th 19/03/2012 A/HRC/19/L.38 Situation of human rights in the Syrian Arab Republic
- HRC 19th 12/03/2012 A/HRC/19/G/7 Note verbale dated 1 March 2012 from the Permanent Mission of Uganda to the United Nations Office and other international organizations in Geneva addressed to the secretariat of the Human Rights Council
- HRC 19th 08/03/2012 A/HRC/19/G/5 Note verbale dated 31 January 2012 from the Permanent Mission of the Syrian Arab Republic to the United Nations Office and other international organizations at Geneva addressed to the Office of the United Nations High Commissioner for Human Rights
- HRC 19th 08/03/2012 A/HRC/19/G/4 Note verbale dated 10 February 2012 from the Permanent Mission of the Syrian Arab Republic to the United Nations Office and other international organizations in Geneva addressed to the Office of the United Nations High Commissioner for Human Rights
- HRC 19th 08/03/2012 A/HRC/19/80 Report of the Secretary-General on the implementation of Human Rights Council resolution S-18/1 A
- HRC 19th 06/03/2012 A/HRC/19/11/Add.1 Report of the Working Group on the Universal Periodic Review - Syrian Arab Republic - Addendum - Views on conclusions and/or recommendations, voluntary commitments and replies presented by the State under review
- HRC 29/02/2012 A/HRC/WGAD/2011/39 Opinions adopted by the Working Group on Arbitrary Detention at its sixty-first session, 29 August–2 September 2011 - Opinion No. 39/2011 (Syrian Arab Republic)
- HRC 29/02/2012 A/HRC/WGAD/2011/38 Opinions adopted by the Working Group on Arbitrary Detention at its sixty-first session, 29 August–2 September 2011 - No. 38/2011 (Syrian Arab Republic)
- HRC 29/02/2012 A/HRC/WGAD/2011/37 Opinions adopted by the Working Group on Arbitrary Detention at its sixty-first session, 29 August–2 September 2011 - No. 37/2011 (Syrian Arab Republic)
- HRC 19th 29/02/2012 A/HRC/19/L.1/Rev.1 The escalating grave human rights violations and the deteriorating humanitarian situation in the Syrian Arab Republic
- HRC 19th 29/02/2012 A/HRC/19/61/Add.4 Report of the Special Rapporteur on torture and other cruel, inhuman or degrading treatment or punishment, Juan E. Méndez - Addendum - Observations on communications transmitted to Governments and replies received
- HRC 19th 29/02/2012 A/HRC/19/46/Add.1 Human rights in the occupied Syrian Golan - Report of the Secretary-General - Addendum - Information received from Member States

- HRC 28/02/2012 A/HRC/WGAD/2011/26 Opinions adopted by the Working Group on Arbitrary Detention at its sixty-first session, 29 August–2 September 2011 - No. 26/2011 (Syrian Arab Republic)
- HRC 27/02/2012 A/HRC/WGAD/2011/1 Opinions adopted by the Working Group on Arbitrary Detention at its sixtieth session, 2–6 May 2011 - No. 1/2011 (Syrian Arab Republic)
- HRC 19th 27/02/2012 A/HRC/19/L.1 The escalating grave human rights violations and the deteriorating humanitarian situation in the Syrian Arab Republic
- HRC 24/02/2012 A/HRC/WGAD/2010/27 Opinions adopted by the Working Group on Arbitrary Detention at its fifty-ninth session, 18–26 November 2010 - No. 27/2010 (Syrian Arab Republic)
- HRC 24/02/2012 A/HRC/WGAD/2010/24 Opinions adopted by the Working Group on Arbitrary Detention at its fifty-ninth session, 18–26 November 2010 - No. 24/2010 (Syrian Arab Republic)
- GA 66th 23/02/2012 A/RES/66/176 Situation of human rights in the Syrian Arab Republic
- HRC 19th 23/02/2012 A/HRC/19/NGO/94 Joint written statement submitted by CIVICUS World Alliance for Citizen Participation. Human rights conditions in Syria
- HRC 19th 23/02/2012 A/HRC/19/NGO/82 Written statement submitted by the Cairo Institute for Human Rights Studies. Torture with impunity in the context of the Arab uprisings
- HRC 19th 23/02/2012 A/HRC/19/55/Add.2 Report of the Special Rapporteur on the situation of human rights defenders, Margaret Sekaggya - Addendum - Observations on communications transmitted to Governments and replies received
- HRC 19th 22/02/2012 A/HRC/19/69 Report of the independent international commission of inquiry on the Syrian Arab Republic
- GA 66th 21/02/2012 A/RES/66/253 The situation in the Syrian Arab Republic
- HRC 19th 15/02/2012 A/HRC/19/G/2 Note verbale dated 27 December 2011 from the Permanent Mission of the Syrian Arab Republic to the United Nations Office at Geneva addressed to the President of the Human Rights Council
- HRC 18th SS 31/01/2012 A/HRC/S-18/2 Report of the Human Rights Council on its eighteenth special session
- HRC 19th 24/01/2012 A/HRC/19/11 Report of the Working Group on the Universal Periodic Review - Syrian Arab Republic
- HRC 19th 19/12/2011 A/HRC/19/46 Human rights in the occupied Syrian Golan - Report of the Secretary-General
- HRC 19th 16/12/2011 A/HRC/19/79 Report of the High Commissioner on the implementation of Human Rights Council resolution S-17/1
- HRC 18th SS 05/12/2011 A/HRC/RES/S-18/1 The human rights situation in the Syrian Arab Republic
- HRC 18th SS 02/12/2011 A/HRC/S-18/NGO/2 Written statement submitted by Amnesty International, a non-governmental organization in special consultative status
- HRC 18th SS 30/11/2011 A/HRC/S-18/L.1 The human rights situation in the Syrian Arab Republic
- HRC 18th SS 30/11/2011 A/HRC/S-18/1 Letter dated 30 November 2011 from the Permanent Representative of the European Union to the United Nations Office in Geneva and the Permanent Representative of Poland to the United Nations Office in Geneva addressed to the President of the Human Rights Council

- HRC 17th SS 23/11/2011 A/HRC/S-17/2/Add.1 Report of the independent international commission of inquiry on the Syrian Arab Republic
- HRC 18th 16/09/2011 A/HRC/18/G/1 Note verbale dated 4 July 2011 from the Permanent Mission of the Syrian Arab Republic to the United Nations Office and other international organizations in Geneva addressed to the President of the Human Rights Council
- HRC 18th 15/09/2011 A/HRC/18/53 Report of the United Nations High Commissioner for Human Rights on the situation of human rights in the Syrian Arab Republic
- HRC 18th 12/09/2011 A/HRC/18/NGO/73 Written statement submitted by the Cairo Institute for Human Rights Studies - CIHRS, a non-governmental organization in special consultative status
- HRC 18th 12/09/2011 A/HRC/18/NGO/72 Written statement submitted by the Cairo Institute for Human Rights Studies – CIHRS, a non-governmental organization in special consultative status
- HRC 18th 06/09/2011 A/HRC/18/NGO/20 Written statement submitted by the Jammu and Kashmir Council for Human Rights (JKCHR), a non-governmental organization in special consultative status
- HRC 12th WG UPR 05/09/2011 A/HRC/WG.6/12/SYR/2 Compilation prepared by the Office of the High Commissioner for Human Rights in accordance with paragraph 15 (b) of the annex to Human Rights Council resolution 5/1 - Syrian Arab Republic
- HRC 12th WG UPR 02/09/2011 A/HRC/WG.6/12/SYR/1 National report submitted in accordance with paragraph 15 (a) of the annex to Human Rights Council resolution 5/1 - Syrian Arab Republic
- HRC 17th SS 18/08/2011 A/HRC/S-17/L.1 Grave human rights violations in the Syrian Arab Republic
- HRC 17th SS 18/08/2011 A/HRC/S-17/1 Letter dated 17 August 2011 from the Permanent Observer of the European Union to the United Nations Office at Geneva and the chargé d'affaires a.i. Deputy Permanent Representative of Poland to the United Nations Office at Geneva addressed to the President of the Human Rights Council
- HRC 12th WG UPR 25/07/2011 A/HRC/WG.6/12/SYR/3 Summary prepared by the Office of the High Commissioner for Human Rights in accordance with paragraph 15 (c) of the annex to Human Rights Council resolution 5/1 - Syrian Arab Republic
- GA 66th 20/07/2011 A/66/161 Human rights and cultural diversity - Report of the Secretary-General
- HRC 16th 02/06/2011 A/HRC/16/47/Add.1 Report of the Working Group on Arbitrary Detention - Addendum - Opinions adopted by the Working Group on Arbitrary Detention
- HRC 17th 27/05/2011 A/HRC/17/27/Add.1 Report of the Special Rapporteur on the promotion and protection of the right to freedom of opinion and expression, Frank La Rue - Addendum - Summary of cases transmitted to Governments and replies received
- HRC 17th 25/05/2011 A/HRC/17/NGO/46 Written statement submitted by the Cairo Institute for Human Rights Studies (CIHRS), a non-governmental organization in special consultative status
- HRC 17th 19/05/2011 A/HRC/17/NGO/5 Written statement submitted by Pax Christi International, International Catholic Peace Movement, a non-governmental organization in special consultative status

- HRC 17th 18/05/2011 A/HRC/17/26/Add.1 Report of the Special Rapporteur on violence against women, its causes and consequences, Rashida Manjoo - Addendum - Communications to and from Governments
- HRC 17th 16/05/2011 A/HRC/17/25/Add.1 Report of the Special Rapporteur on the right of everyone to the enjoyment of the highest attainable standard of physical and mental health, Anand Grover - Addendum - Summary of communications sent and replies received from States and other actors
- HRC 17th 13/05/2011 A/HRC/17/40/Add.1 Report of the Special Rapporteur on contemporary forms of racism, racial discrimination, xenophobia and related intolerance, Githu Muigai - Addendum - Summary of cases transmitted to governments and replies received
- HRC 16th SS 04/05/2011 A/HRC/RES/S-16/1 The current human rights situation in the Syrian Arab Republic in the context of recent events
- HRC 16th SS 28/04/2011 A/HRC/S-16/NGO/2 Written statement submitted by United Nations Watch, a non-governmental organization in special consultative status
- HRC 16th SS 28/04/2011 A/HRC/S-16/NGO/1 Written statement submitted by Amnesty International, a non-governmental organization in special consultative status
- HRC 16th SS 28/04/2011 A/HRC/S-16/L.1 Situation of human rights in the Syrian Arab Republic
- HRC 16th 13/04/2011 A/HRC/RES/16/31 Israeli settlements in the Occupied Palestinian Territory, including East Jerusalem, and in the occupied Syrian Golan
- HRC 16th 13/04/2011 A/HRC/RES/16/17 Human rights in the occupied Syrian Golan
- HRC 16th 22/03/2011 A/HRC/16/G/12 Note verbale dated 18 March 2011 from the Permanent Mission of the Syrian Arab Republic addressed to the Office of the United Nations High Commissioner for Human Rights
- HRC 17th 21/03/2011 A/HRC/17/25/Add.3 Report of the Special Rapporteur on the right of everyone to the enjoyment of the highest attainable standard of physical and mental health, Anand Grover - Addendum - Mission to the Syrian Arab Republic
- HRC 16th 21/03/2011 A/HRC/16/L.30 Israeli settlements in the Occupied Palestinian Territory, including East Jerusalem, and in the occupied Syrian Golan
- HRC 16th 17/03/2011 A/HRC/16/L.2 Human rights in the occupied Syrian Golan
- HRC 16th 07/03/2011 A/HRC/16/44/Add.3 Report submitted by the Special Rapporteur on the situation of human rights defenders, Margaret Sekaggya - Addendum - Responses to the questionnaire on risks and challenges faced by women human rights defenders and those working on women's rights and gender issues A
- HRC 16th 01/03/2011 A/HRC/16/52/Add.1 Report of the Special Rapporteur on torture and other cruel, inhuman or degrading treatment or punishment, Juan E. Méndez - Addendum - Summary of information, including individual cases, transmitted to Governments and replies received
- HRC 16th 28/02/2011 A/HRC/16/44/Add.1 Report of the Special Rapporteur on the situation of human rights defenders, Margaret Sekaggya - Addendum - Summary of cases transmitted to Governments and replies received
- HRC 16th 22/02/2011 A/HRC/16/NGO/7 Written statement submitted by the Khiam Rehabilitation Center for Victims of Torture, a nongovernmental organization in special consultative status
- HRC 16th 14/02/2011 A/HRC/16/51/Add.1 Report of the Special Rapporteur on the promotion and protection of human rights and fundamental freedoms while

countering terrorism, Martin Scheinin - Addendum - Communications to and from Governments (From 1 January to 31 December 2011)

- HRC 16th 14/02/2011 A/HRC/16/42/Add.1 Report of the Special Rapporteur on adequate housing as a component of the right to an adequate standard of living, and on the right to non-discrimination in this context, Raquel Rolnik - Addendum - Summary of communications sent and replies received from Governments and other actors
- HRC 16th 27/01/2011 A/HRC/16/49/Add.2 Report of the Special Rapporteur on the right to food, Olivier De Schutter - Addendum - Mission to the Syrian Arab Republic

ANNEX 5:

General Assembly, GA/11207/Rev.1, 16 February 2012

Plenary

97th Meeting (PM)

General Assembly Adopts Resolution Strongly Condemning 'Widespread and Systematic'

Human Rights Violations by Syrian Authorities

Text Passes by 137 Votes in Favour to 12 against, with 17 Abstentions

Strongly condemning continued widespread and systematic human rights violations by the Syrian authorities, the General Assembly today voted overwhelmingly to call on both the Government and allied forces and armed groups "to stop all violence or reprisals immediately".

Adopting an Arab-backed resolution by a recorded vote of 137 in favour to 12 against, with 17 abstentions, the Assembly expressed grave concern at the deteriorating situation in Syria, and condemned a raft of violations carried out by the authorities, such as the use of force against civilians, the killing and persecution of protestors and journalists, and sexual violence and ill-treatment, including against children. (For voting results, see Annex)

The Assembly called on Syria to abide by its obligations under international law, and demanded that the Government, in line with the 2 November 2011 Action Plan of the League of Arab States, and its decisions of 22 January and 12 February 2012, without delay, stop all violence and protect its people, release all those detained during the unrest, withdraw all armed forces from cities and towns, guarantee peaceful demonstrations and allow unhindered access for Arab League monitors and international media.

The language of the resolution closely mirrored that of a text vetoed by China and the Russian Federation in the Security Council two weeks earlier. (See Press Release SC/10536) The Assembly's action also followed a special briefing on Monday by Navi Pillay, United Nations High Commissioner for Human Rights, who expressed outrage at the bloody 11-month crackdown on opposition protesters. She warned that the Council's failure to take action had emboldened the Syrian Government to launch an all-out assault to crush dissent, most evident in its "appalling" siege of the city of Homs. (See Press Release GA/11206)

By other terms of the text adopted today, the Assembly expressed its full support for the Arab League's decision to facilitate a Syrian-led political transition to a democratic, pluralistic political system, including through a "serious political dialogue between the [Syrian Government] and the whole spectrum of the Syrian opposition". Reaffirming its strong commitment to Syria's sovereignty, independence, unity and territorial integrity, it further reaffirmed that all Member States "should refrain in their international relations from the threat or use of force against the territorial integrity or political independence of any State".

The measure requested Secretary-General Ban Ki-moon and all relevant United Nations bodies to support the Arab League's ongoing efforts to resolve the crisis peacefully, including through good offices and the appointment of a Special Envoy. The Secretary-General was also requested to report to the Assembly within 15 days on the status of the resolution. Ahead of the action, the Secretariat announced that approval of those elements of the text would incur $900,000 in additional budgetary resources for an initial six months of the 2012-2013 biennium.

Egypt's representative, presenting the draft resolution on behalf of the Arab Group, described the situation in Syria as "critical" and demanded that the Government immediately end the bloodshed. He said the text was based on the principle of peaceful settlement of disputes, which was at the core of efforts to resolve the Syrian conflict. Stressing that the Arab League's efforts enjoyed unprecedented worldwide acceptance, he expressed hope that today's vote would show that the international community was speaking with "one voice" on events in Syria.

Syria's representative took the floor immediately thereafter in response to the points raised by his Egyptian counterpart, and said that the Government was responding in an accelerated manner to demands for reform. A new Constitution providing for the establishment of a modern democratic State would be put to a referendum on 26 February, as part of "extremely important" developments, in line with popular demands by the majority and the opposition. A comprehensive dialogue had been called for among all those who wished to maintain Syria's stability and to end the violence.

However, Member States must stop encouraging the violent groups in Syria, he emphasized, declaring that no State would tolerate the presence of armed terrorists on its territory. Unfortunately, certain countries were supporting such armed groups, even as they claimed to be anxious to save Syrian lives. "Stop adding fuel to the fire," he said, pointing out that the resolution's failure to call on the opposition to dissociate itself from armed groups "says everything" about the intention of the text's co-sponsors, as did its failure to condemn terrorist acts. Asking whether anyone had thought about the aftermath, he warned: "This step will not only bring disaster to Syria, but to all international relations."

Speaking after the vote, in a statement directed largely at the Arab League, he said that a "Trojan horse" had been unmasked today, as the Western co-sponsors of the resolution had paved the way to internationalizing the situation. It was clear that the League - "broken politically and morally" - had been kidnapped by the Gulf Cooperation Council countries, he added.

Most other delegations hailed the resolution's strong calls for an end to the violence and for the Syrian Government to protect civilians. Many reiterated their firm belief that the Arab League's Action Plan, which proposed a negotiated solution among all Syrian factions, was the best path out of the crisis. Other speakers expressed grave concern about reports of massive human rights violations in Syria, and said that ending them must be the international community's main priority. Costa Rica's representative, who voted in favour of the resolution, emphasized that impunity must not be tolerated and, if necessary, the situation should be referred to the International Criminal Court.

At the same time, several speakers echoed the concerns raised by the representative of the Democratic People's Republic of Korea, who voted against the text and roundly denounced "attempts by imperial Powers and their allies" to trigger regime change in Syria, "even at the cost of further bloodshed". The text represented an intervention in the internal affairs of an independent State, he added. He was also among those who commended the Russian Federation's efforts to produce a more balanced text, by placing demands on opposition forces to disassociate themselves from armed groups, expressing support for that country's peace initiatives in Damascus.

China's representative expressed support for the Arab League's position that the violence must stop immediately and that civilians must be protected. Yet, the international community should respect Syria's sovereignty and territorial integrity fully, he stressed, adding that actions taken by the United Nations should not complicate matters, but be helpful in easing tensions, facilitating political dialogue and resolving differences.

In other action, the Assembly decided that the Marshall Islands, Sudan and the Federated States of Micronesia had all made the payments necessary to reduce their arrears under Article 19 of the United Nations Charter. Under that Article, a Member State in arrears cannot vote in the General Assembly "if the amount of the arrears equals or exceeds the amount of the contributions due from it for the preceding two years".

Also speaking in explanation of position were representatives of Venezuela, Grenada, Russian Federation, Serbia, Pakistan, Ukraine, Iran, Bolivia, Argentina, India, Singapore, Viet Nam, Chile, Bangladesh and Egypt.

The General Assembly will reconvene at a time and date to be announced.

Background

Meeting this afternoon to consider matters relating to the prevention of armed conflict, the General Assembly was expected to take action on a draft resolution on the situation in the Syrian Arab Republic (document A/66/L.36).

Procedural Matters

The representative of Syria, recalling the Assembly's previous meeting on the report of the Human Rights Council, said his delegation had informed Member States at the time that the earlier meeting contravened the rules of procedure, and had called on the Assembly President to obtain a legal opinion on the matter. It had been announced during that meeting that a draft resolution on Syria would be presented to the Assembly, but today it was meeting under the item "Prevention of armed conflict". It was "pathetic" that the Syrian issue was being addressed under at least three different agenda items, he said, adding that there was clearly confusion over the matter. The Assembly's legitimacy was at stake, he said, asking the President to provide the rules of procedure governing the current meeting.

GARY FRANCIS QUINLAN (Australia), Assembly Vice-President, responded by saying it was his understanding that the Assembly President could convene a meeting at any time, under any agenda item, to consider a draft resolution presented to Member States.

The representative of Yemen said his delegation had been surprised by reference to Article 19 of the United Nations Charter.

Action on Draft Resolution

OSAMA ABDELKHALEK MAHMOUD (Egypt), introducing the draft resolution the situation in the Syrian Arab Republic (document A/66/L.36) on behalf of the Arab Group, said the Assembly was meeting as that country faced "critical circumstances". The major escalation of violence there had been condemned by the League of Arab States, the Arab Group, the United Nations and the wider international community. Demanding that the Syrian Government end the bloodshed, he said the matter was at the very top of the Arab League's agenda. That regional body had called for an immediate and faithful implementation of the Arab Action Plan as the only way to meet the aspirations of the Syrian people, he said, stressing the primacy of the Arab solution, under the "Arab roof", and its rejection of military intervention.

The draft before the Assembly was based on the principle of peaceful settlement of disputes, which was at the core of efforts to resolve the Syrian conflict, he continued. It reaffirmed Syria's territorial integrity and supported the aims set out in the decisions and resolutions of the Arab League. Stressing that those efforts enjoyed unprecedented worldwide acceptance, he said more than 70 Member States were co-sponsoring the draft, and it was to be hoped that today's vote would show that the international community was speaking with one voice on events taking place in Syria. Hopefully, the vote would also show broad and commanding support for the Arab Action Plan, he added, calling on all Member States to stand shoulder to shoulder with each other and the Syrian people by voting in favour of the text.

Following that statement, the Secretariat announced that approval of the text, which requested the Secretary-General and all relevant bodies to support the Arab League's efforts, including through good offices and by appointing a Special Envoy, would incur additional budgetary resources in the amount of $900,000 for an initial six months in the 2012-2013 biennium. Those requirements would be met through the use of commitment authority granted to the Secretary-General as related to the maintenance of international peace and security.

Speaking in explanation of position, the representative of Syria said his country continued to respond in an accelerated manner to demands for reform, in response to all the points raised by Egypt's representative in presenting the draft resolution. A new Constitution providing for the establishment of a modern democratic State would be put to a referendum on 26 February, as part of "extremely important" developments that responded to popular demands by the majority and the opposition. A comprehensive dialogue had been called for among all those who wished to maintain Syria's stability and prestige and to end the violence. He called on all Member States to encourage the opposition to take part in that dialogue and not to impede participation by others.

In addition, he called on Member States to stop encouraging the violent groups in Syria. No country could tolerate the presence of armed terrorist groups on its territory, he emphasized. Neither would it tolerate attacks against its officials, people and institutions. Unfortunately, certain countries were supporting the armed groups, even though they claimed to be anxious to save Syrian lives. They had also cut relations with Syria without justification, which showed that they did not wish to promote peaceful reform. He called on them to stop adding fuel to the fire, pointing out that the draft resolution's failure to call on the opposition to dissociate themselves from armed groups "said everything" about the intention of the text's co-sponsors, as did their failure to condemn terrorist acts. They had paid no heed to Syria's plans for reforms, he added.

The Arab League, in its resolution supported by today's draft, had decided to provide all forms of support to the opposition, opening the door to the funding and arming of violent groups for terrorist acts, he said. The League was providing support to countries that had long wanted to undermine Syria, and Member States should instead help Syria's Government and people to face the challenges of extremism and terrorism, which had been documented, but not well publicized. Adopting the draft resolution would only lead to a worsening of the crisis by encouraging extremism, he warned, appealing to all Member States to vote against the text lest they increase the chaos in Syria. Asking whether anyone had thought about the aftermath, he warned: "This step will not only bring disaster to Syria, but to all international relations." It would also play into the hands of Israel and help its efforts to defeat the aspirations of Palestinians and other people under occupation in the region.

The representative of Venezuela, affirming the fundamental importance of sovereignty, independence, unity and territorial integrity, denounced the attempt by imperial powers and their allies to trigger regime change in Syria, even at the cost of further bloodshed, reproducing the dire consequences of the Libyan situation. Those Powers sought to occupy Syria, to foment a coup against its legitimate authorities and to turn the country into a protectorate. The draft resolution, with its mentoring and monitoring mechanisms, represented an intervention in the internal affairs of an independent State, he said. The text also attacked the Government for human rights abuses while hiding the heinous crimes committed by terrorist groups against civilians, as well as attacks with varied weaponry against public officials and facilities.

He went on to note that the draft ignored the Government's initiatives to promote inclusive political dialogue and its call for a referendum on a new Constitution, which were the best options for moving forward. The draft denied the Syrian State's right to protect its population and ensure internal peace and security, he said, adding that it did not call for opposition groups to dissociate themselves from groups engaged in violence. Commending the Russian Federation's efforts for a more balanced text, he supported that country's peace initiatives in Damascus as well its efforts, with China, to prevent the Security Council from being used to violate Syria's sovereignty. "It is not desirable that the logic of war, which imperialists intend to impose on Syria and the world, prevails," he said. Instead, the Assembly should be concerned about recognition of a Palestinian State, the end of Israeli rights violations and ending the blockade on Cuba.

The representative of the Democratic People's Republic of Korea said that any issue relating to a Member State must be discussed in line with the principles of territorial integrity and State sovereignty. As a full-fledged member of the United Nations, Syria was no exception to that rule, he said, emphasizing that all violence in Syria must stop. The issues in that country should be settled in the best interest of its people. The country's fate and future should be in their hands and they alone should lead the process towards a peaceful negotiated solution, which should be reached without outside influence. The Democratic People's Republic of Korea would vote against the text, he said.

The representative of Grenada offered condolences to the families of all those who had lost loved ones in Syria and stressed that the United Nations must act - and be seen to act - in line with the tenets of its founding Charter. Grenada was proceeding with the understanding that the draft resolution would "do only what the text says" - provide diplomatic support to Syria, the Arab League and the Secretary-General in order to help the Government and people of Syria to end all bloodshed, while finding an agreed solution. It also understood that the Assembly was not voting on or for a text that could in any way be interpreted as a basis for the removal of the Government, military intervention or any act against the spirit and letter of the Charter, she said. With that understanding, Grenada would vote in favour of the draft resolution, she added.

The Assembly then adopted the resolution by a recorded vote of 137 in favour to 12 against, with 17 abstentions. (See Annex)

The representatives of Burundi, Kyrgyzstan and Comoros informed the Secretariat that they had been unable to cast their votes properly.

The representative of the Russian Federation said he had opposed the resolution because it clearly did not meet the criteria for ending the violence in Syria. The Russian delegation had proposed to place reasonable demands on opposition forces to disassociate themselves from armed groups and to demand that those groups themselves stop their attacks, he said, noting that those amendments had not been accepted. The Russian Federation would continue to work with all those striving for regional stability, he stressed.

The representative of China said his Government had closely followed developments in Syria and was deeply worried about the escalating crisis that had caused civilian casualties and affected peace and security in the wider Middle East. China condemned all acts of violence against innocent civilians and urged the Syrian Government as well as all political factions to "immediately and fully" end all acts of violence and quickly restore order. It also called on the political factions in Syria to express their political aspirations through non-violent means under the rule of law.

He went on to urge all parties concerned immediately to launch an inclusive political dialogue, without preconditions, hold a referendum on the new draft Constitution, as well as early parliamentary elections, and establish a national unity Government that included all factions. "We understand the concern of Arab countries and the League of Arab States on seeking a quick resolution to this issue," he said, expressing support for their position that the violence must stop immediately and that civilians must be protected. Emphasizing that the international community should respect Syria's sovereignty and territorial integrity fully, he said: "We do not approve of armed intervention or forcing a so-called regime change in Syria."

Neither did China believe that sanctions or the threat of such measures would be helpful in achieving an appropriate solution, he continued. The actions of the United Nations and the wider international community should be helpful in easing tensions, facilitating political dialogue and resolving differences. Instead of complicating matters, such actions should promote the maintenance of peace and stability in the Middle East, he said, adding that he had voted in accordance with those principles. As a friend of the Arab people, China had always followed the purposes and principles of the Charter and would continue to work with the international community to resolve the situation in Syria.

The representative of Serbia said he had voted in favour of the text, adding that all international efforts should aim solely for an end to the suffering of the Syrian people. At the same time, Serbia would have wished that the proposals and amendments put forward by some delegations had been considered and evaluated. In particular, the resolution would have been enriched by some of the changes submitted by the Russian Federation, which were "truly constructive", he said, adding that they could have led to the consensus adoption of the text. He expressed hope that the international community would nevertheless take notice of those proposed amendments as the diplomatic process progressed. "Their content cannot be avoided, and sooner or later will need to be addressed," he said.

The representative of Pakistan said he supported the Arab League position and had voted in favour of the resolution, but condemned the use of violence on all sides. An immediate end to violence and killing, as well as a peaceful resolution were aims upon which all Member States agreed. In that light, Pakistan had been stressing the need for consensus on the Syrian situation, he said, noting that there could have been better efforts in the Assembly and the Security Council to reach consensus and to fully assure delegations that there was no intention to carry out a hostile intervention. Reiterating his call for the Syrian people to be respected, he said they must be allowed to resolve their crisis, and he reaffirmed the absolute importance of respecting the sovereignty, territorial integrity and independence of all States.

The representative of Costa Rica expressed his delegation's deepest concern about the gruesome human rights violations being carried out in Syria. The international community could not remain silent, he stressed, calling on the Syrian authorities to definitively end attacks against civilians and other human rights violations. Condemning reports of sexual violence, including that perpetrated against girls and boys, he said all international stakeholders should work towards a swift and peaceful solution to the crisis, in line with the Arab League's Plan of Action. The Human Rights Council had been playing its role of promoting a peaceful solution and, with the appropriate tools already at its disposal, it should move to create the position of Special Rapporteur on the situation in Syria, he said, calling attention to that Council's report on the very serious acts - pointing to possible crimes against humanity - being carried out in Syria.

Expressing concern that the Security Council had been unable to act on the matter, he said it had been prevented from acting by the use of a veto. The Council required deep reform, chiefly so that such measures could not be used to stymie action in the face of the worst international crimes, he emphasized. Stakeholders might disagree on certain matters, but the international community must speak resoundingly when human rights violations and acts of violence against civilians were committed. The international community should explore all avenues to reach a solution and ensure that those who had committed grave crimes were held responsible, including through referring the Syrian issue to the International Criminal Court. Finally, he said the "voices of change cannot be silenced with violence", and called for a solution that met the legitimate aspirations of the Syrian people.

The representative of Ukraine said that the Arab League's peaceful efforts for a negotiated settlement deserved the Assembly's support. Ukraine's Ministry of Foreign Affairs had issued a statement last week in which it had expressed grave concern at the escalating violence in Syria, "which threatens to grow into a full-scale civil war, with unpredictable consequences in the entire Middle East". Ukraine urged all parties in Syria to cease the violence and begin a dialogue, with the aim of finding a mutually acceptable and effective way to resolve their differences.

The representative of Iran said he had voted against the resolution, in line with his delegation's position that the Syrian people's legitimate demands must be addressed through a peaceful and domestically led political process and without foreign intervention in the country's internal affairs, which would only worsen the crisis and have ramifications on the region as a whole. He regretted, in addition, that the Assembly's consideration of the Syrian crisis had not followed proper procedure, including the vote under the agenda item "prevention of armed conflict", which did not apply.

It was even more regrettable, he continued, that the resolution's co-sponsors had chosen not to accommodate any amendments that might have made it more balanced, comprehensive and suited to the real situation on the ground. In that light, it was necessary to be clear and steadfast in condemning any act of violence and terrorism, in any form and manifestation, he emphasized. As long as armed groups continued to resort to violence, the crisis would continue, serving the interests of the Zionist regime. All States must work together in a practical manner to assist a peaceful resolution of the crisis.

The representative of Bolivia, stating that he had voted against the resolution, asked the Assembly to consider exactly what was happening in Syria. With the many possibilities and few answers, it was clear that no one really knew exactly what the real situation was. All that was known was that there was a recognized opposition and a Government that was prepared to undertake meaningful reforms. Indeed, Syria's representative had twice informed the Assembly that such reforms, including constitutional changes, had been agreed and were under way. Saying he understood that such reforms were a work in progress, he added that Bolivia knew the dangers of a political vacuum, which could lead to destabilization of the entire region.

He said there were two possible ways in which the Syrian situation could end, the first being "the way of Libya", in which the United Nations had facilitated a "recipe for intervention" to justify regime change through a Security Council resolution. That text had actually promoted further destabilization and civil unrest, he pointed out, warning: "I fear we have not learned our lessons from that situation." He added: "Last year, it was the Security Council and this year it appears to be the General Assembly." Bolivia seriously hoped that that was not the case, but had voted against the resolution just the same. The other possible ending was through a peaceful resolution, as had occurred in Egypt and Tunisia, he said. In those cases, efforts had been channelled towards democracy and changes of Government borne by the will of the people, not foreign intervention. Hopefully, the winds of the "Arab Spring" would blow in Syria's direction and stir peaceful change, he said, adding that, had the amendments put forward by the Russian Federation been integrated into the resolution, it would have been adopted by consensus.

The representative of Argentina said he had voted in favour of the resolution and emphasized the utmost importance of ensuring the protection and promotion of human rights in Syria. It was necessary to preserve the fundamental rights of free association and expression, he said, adding that the crisis in Syria should be resolved through dialogue and democratic negotiations involving all sectors of society.

The representative of India noted that his country had condemned all violence in Syria, no matter by whom it was committed, and had been supporting a peaceful, inclusive and nationally led political resolution of the crisis. India had voted in favour of the resolution, in accordance with its support for the Arab League's efforts for such a political resolution. Regrettably, however, there had been exceptions to established General Assembly procedures during the week, he said, expressing a wish that there had been greater readiness from all quarters to negotiate a text with a view to reaching consensus.

He went on to note that the resolution expressly reaffirmed that all countries should refrain from the threat or use of force against the territorial integrity or political independence of any State. It condemned all violence, irrespective of its origin, and called for serious political dialogue under the Arab League. The country's leadership was a matter for the Syrian people to decide, he stressed, calling on all opposition forces to engage peacefully in constructive dialogue with the authorities. In that connection, he noted the Syrian leadership's decision to hold a referendum and multi-party elections, expressing hope that that decision would create an environment of peace and facilitate a political process.

The representative of Singapore said he had voted in favour of the resolution because it was not a politically motivated text, but instead dealt with a unique emergency in an appropriate manner. He joined with all in calling on all stakeholders to end violence and resolve the situation peacefully.

The representative of Viet Nam, affirming his country's concern about developments in Syria, joined the call for all parties in Syria to exercise self-restraint, end the violence and find a political solution through a domestically led constructive dialogue and national reconciliation, in conformity with the people's aspirations. He also underlined the importance of respecting the principles of sovereignty, territorial integrity and independence of States. Viet Nam supported efforts by the international community, including the Arab League, to contribute constructively to the restoration of stability and the promotion of national reconciliation in Syria, he said.

The representative of Chile said he had voted in favour of the text, adding that the Assembly had raised its voice to "energetically" condemn the "grave and massive" violations of human rights under way in Syria. Serious acts, such as torture, sexual violence and arbitrary detention, including those highlighted by the High Commissioner for Human Rights in her briefing earlier in the week, must be denounced and those responsible brought to justice, he emphasized. All parties in Syria must open a true dialogue, and the authorities must allow access to those in need, he added.

The representative of Bangladesh said he had voted in favour of the resolution. Despite its principled position of abstaining when texts targeted human rights situations in specific countries, Bangladesh had voted in favour of today's resolution to end the shedding of the Syrian people's blood, he said. The Assembly's decision earlier in the week to consider the report of the Human Rights Council had contravened its rules of procedure, he said, expressing hope that no precedent would result from that action. The resolution had been drafted in line with the aims of the Arab League Action Plan, but Bangladesh would have hoped for the inclusion of the amendments submitted by the Russian Federation, he said, emphasizing that any actions taken in Syria must be in line with the aspirations of its people and lead towards a peaceful resolution.

The representative of Egypt then made a general statement, saying that the international community had made its views known through its overwhelming support for the resolution. It had reaffirmed the need for a peaceful solution to the Syrian crisis and sent a clear message to the Government to listen to the voice of the Syrian people and implement the decisions of the Arab League. The situation was deteriorating and all should now focus on ending the violence and meeting the people's aspirations in order to avoid a worse situation, which would have effects in the region and lead to a humanitarian crisis. Egypt would continue to work with the League in that effort, he pledged.

The representative of Syria also made a general statement, saying that a "Trojan horse" had been unmasked today as the resolution's Western co-sponsors had paved the way to internationalizing the situation. It was clear that the Arab League had been kidnapped by the Gulf Cooperation Council countries, he added. Syria had left the Arab League temporarily; it was broken, politically and morally, he said, congratulating it on its new alliance with Israel. Syria no longer wanted the League to stand by it following its shameful actions, but it did want them to save whatever face it had left and cease the plotting against other Arab States.

He went on to warn that the wealth of all the Gulf Cooperation Council countries would be squandered on losing causes and the price would be borne by all Arabs, who would be used as fuel to obtain the objectives of Israel and the West. Had the co-sponsors retained any credibility, they would have accepted the Russian amendments and worked to counter support for armed groups in Syria. In addition, the United Nations was betraying its own principles, and if that continued, the Organization would collapse, destroying the normative efforts of the past 66 years, he said. That would be the end result of intervention in the internal affairs of others.

ANNEX

Vote on Situation in Syria

The draft resolution on the situation in Syria (document A/66/L.36) was adopted by a recorded vote of 137 in favour to 12 against, with 17 abstentions, as follows:

In favour: Afghanistan, Albania, Andorra, Antigua and Barbuda, Argentina, Australia, Austria, Azerbaijan, Bahamas, Bahrain, Bangladesh, Barbados, Belgium, Belize, Benin, Bhutan, Bosnia and Herzegovina, Botswana, Brazil, Brunei Darussalam, Bulgaria, Burkina Faso, Canada, Central African Republic, Chad, Chile, Colombia, Congo, Costa Rica, Côte d'Ivoire, Croatia, Cyprus, Czech Republic, Democratic Republic of the Congo, Denmark, Djibouti, Egypt, El Salvador, Estonia, Finland, France, Georgia, Germany, Ghana, Greece, Grenada, Guatemala, Guinea, Guyana, Haiti, Honduras, Hungary, Iceland, India, Indonesia, Iraq, Ireland, Israel, Italy, Jamaica, Japan, Jordan, Kazakhstan, Kenya, Kuwait, Latvia, Lesotho, Liberia, Libya, Liechtenstein, Lithuania, Luxembourg, Malawi, Malaysia, Maldives, Malta, Marshall Islands, Mauritania, Mauritius, Mexico, Micronesia (Federated States of), Monaco, Mongolia, Montenegro, Morocco, Mozambique, Nauru, Netherlands, New Zealand, Niger, Nigeria, Norway, Oman, Pakistan, Panama, Papua New Guinea, Paraguay, Peru, Poland, Portugal, Qatar, Republic of Korea, Republic of Moldova, Romania, Rwanda, Saint Kitts and Nevis, Saint Lucia, Samoa, San Marino, Saudi Arabia, Senegal, Serbia, Seychelles, Singapore, Slovakia, Slovenia, Solomon Islands, Somalia, South Africa, South Sudan, Spain, Sudan, Sweden, Switzerland, Thailand, The former Yugoslav Republic of Macedonia, Timor-Leste, Togo, Trinidad and Tobago, Tunisia, Turkey, Ukraine, United Arab Emirates, United Kingdom, United States, Uruguay, Zambia.

Against: Belarus, Bolivia, China, Cuba, Democratic People's Republic of Korea, Ecuador, Iran, Nicaragua, Russian Federation, Syria, Venezuela, Zimbabwe.

Abstain: Algeria, Angola, Armenia, Cameroon, Comoros, Fiji, Lebanon, Myanmar, Namibia, Nepal, Saint Vincent and the Grenadines, Sri Lanka, Suriname, Tuvalu, Uganda, United Republic of Tanzania, Viet Nam.

Absent: Burundi, Cambodia, Cape Verde, Dominica, Dominican Republic, Equatorial Guinea, Eritrea, Ethiopia, Gabon, Gambia, Guinea-Bissau, Kiribati, Kyrgyzstan, Lao People's Democratic Republic, Madagascar, Mali, Palau, Philippines, Sao Tome and Principe, Sierra Leone, Swaziland, Tajikistan, Tonga, Turkmenistan, Uzbekistan, Vanuatu, Yemen.

ANNEX 6:

Security Council Resolution 2042 regarding Syria, 14 April 2012

The Security Council,

Recalling its presidential statements of 3 August 2011, 21 March 2012 and 5 April 2012, and also recalling all relevant resolutions of the General Assembly,

Reaffirming its support to the Joint Special Envoy for the United Nations and the League of Arab States, Kofi Annan, and his work, following General Assembly resolution A/RES/66/253 of 16 February 2012 and relevant resolutions of the League of Arab States,

Reaffirming its strong commitment to the sovereignty, independence, unity and territorial integrity of Syria, and to the purposes and principles of the Charter,

Condemning the widespread violations of human rights by the Syrian authorities, as well as any human rights abuses by armed groups, recalling that those responsible shall be held accountable, and expressing its profound regret at the death of many thousands of people in Syria,

Noting the Syrian Government's commitment on 25 March 2012 to implement the six-point proposal of the Joint Special Envoy of the United Nations and the League of Arab States, and to implement urgently and visibly its commitments, as it agreed to do in its communication to the Envoy of 1 April 2012, to (a) cease troop movements towards population centres, (b) cease all use of heavy weapons in such centres, and (c) begin pullback of military concentrations in and around population centres, and to implement these in their entirety by no later than 10 April 2012, and noting also the Syrian opposition's expressed commitment to respect the cessation of violence, provided the Government does so,

Noting the Envoy's assessment that, as of 12 April 2012, the parties appeared to be observing a cessation of fire and that the Syrian Government had started to implement its commitments, and supporting the Envoy's call for an immediate and visible implementation by the Syrian Government of all elements of the Envoy's six-point proposal in their entirety to achieve a sustained cessation of armed violence in all its forms by all parties,

1. Reaffirms its full support for and calls for the urgent, comprehensive, and immediate implementation of all elements of the Envoy's six-point proposal (annex) aimed at bringing an immediate end to all violence and human rights violations, securing humanitarian access and facilitating a Syrian-led political transition leading to a democratic, plural political system, in which citizens are equal regardless of their affiliations, ethnicities or beliefs, including through commencing a comprehensive political dialogue between the Syrian Government and the whole spectrum of the Syrian opposition;

2. Calls upon the Syrian Government to implement visibly its commitments in their entirety, as it agreed to do in its communication to the Envoy of 1 April 2012, to (a) cease troop movements towards population centres, (b) cease all use of heavy weapons

in such centres, and (c) begin pullback of military concentrations in and around population centres;

3. Underlines the importance attached by the Envoy to the withdrawal of all Syrian Government troops and heavy weapons from population centres to their barracks to facilitate a sustained cessation of violence;

4. Calls upon all parties in Syria, including the opposition, immediately to cease all armed violence in all its forms;

5. Expresses its intention, subject to a sustained cessation of armed violence in all its forms by all parties, to establish immediately, after consultations between the Secretary-General and the Syrian Government, a United Nations supervision mission in Syria to monitor a cessation of armed violence in all its forms by all parties and relevant aspects of the Envoy's six-point proposal, on the basis of a formal proposal from the Secretary-General, which the Security Council requests to receive not later than 18 April 2012;

6. Calls upon the Syrian Government to ensure the effective operation of the mission, including its advance team, by: facilitating the expeditious and unhindered deployment of its personnel and capabilities as required to fulfil its mandate; ensuring its full, unimpeded and immediate freedom of movement and access as necessary to fulfil its mandate; allowing its unobstructed communications; and allowing it to freely and privately communicate with individuals throughout Syria without retaliation against any person as a result of interaction with the mission;

7. Decides to authorize an advance team of up to 30 unarmed military observers to liaise with the parties and to begin to report on the implementation of a full cessation of armed violence in all its forms by all parties, pending the deployment of the mission referred to in paragraph 5 and calls upon the Syrian Government and all other parties to ensure that the advance team is able to carry out its functions according to the terms set forth in paragraph 6;

8. Calls upon the parties to guarantee the safety of the advance team without prejudice to its freedom of movement and access, and stresses that the primary responsibility in this regard lies with the Syrian authorities;

9. Requests the Secretary-General to report immediately to the Security Council any obstructions to the effective operation of the team by any party;

10. Reiterates its call for the Syrian authorities to allow immediate, full and unimpeded access of humanitarian personnel to all populations in need of assistance, in accordance with international law and guiding principles of humanitarian assistance and calls upon all parties in Syria, in particular the Syrian authorities, to cooperate fully with the United Nations and relevant humanitarian organizations to facilitate the provision of humanitarian assistance;

11. Requests the Secretary-General to report to the Council on the implementation of this resolution by 19 April 2012;

12. Expresses its intention to assess the implementation of this resolution and to consider further steps as appropriate;

13. Decides to remain seized of the matter.

Resolution Annex

Six-Point Proposal of the Joint Special Envoy of the United Nations and the League of Arab States

(1) commit to work with the Envoy in an inclusive Syrian-led political process to address the legitimate aspirations and concerns of the Syrian people, and, to this end, commit to appoint an empowered interlocutor when invited to do so by the Envoy;

(2) commit to stop the fighting and achieve urgently an effective United Nations supervised cessation of armed violence in all its forms by all parties to protect civilians and stabilize the country;

To this end, the Syrian Government should immediately cease troop movements towards, and end the use of heavy weapons in, population centres, and begin pullback of military concentrations in and around population centres;

As these actions are being taken on the ground, the Syrian Government should work with the Envoy to bring about a sustained cessation of armed violence in all its forms by all parties with an effective United Nations supervision mechanism.

Similar commitments would be sought by the Envoy from the opposition and all relevant elements to stop the fighting and work with him to bring about a sustained cessation of armed violence in all its forms by all parties with an effective United Nations supervision mechanism;

(3) ensure timely provision of humanitarian assistance to all areas affected by the fighting, and to this end, as immediate steps, to accept and implement a daily two hour humanitarian pause and to coordinate exact time and modalities of the daily pause through an efficient mechanism, including at local level;

(4) intensify the pace and scale of release of arbitrarily detained persons, including especially vulnerable categories of persons, and persons involved in peaceful political activities, provide without delay through appropriate channels a list of all places in which such persons are being detained, immediately begin organizing access to such locations and through appropriate channels respond promptly to all written requests for information, access or release regarding such persons;

(5) ensure freedom of movement throughout the country for journalists and a non-discriminatory visa policy for them;

(6) respect freedom of association and the right to demonstrate peacefully as legally guaranteed."

Statements

MARK LYALL GRANT (United Kingdom) welcomed the adoption of the resolution, but expressed regret that it had come about only after the Syrian people had suffered more than one year of brutality at the hands of their Government, resulting in more than 10,000 deaths. Reiterating support for Mr. Annan's work and the full implementation of his six-point plan, he said: "A narrow window now exists to improve the situation on the ground," adding that it provided the rationale for deploying the advance group. However, that was only a first step, he said, emphasizing that the Syrian Government must now meet all its commitments under the six-point plan, and ensure that the monitoring group had full freedom to accomplish its mandate. Opposition groups must also cooperate and not give the Government any excuse to renew military action, he added.

VITALY CHURKIN (Russian Federation) said the degree of suffering and the possibility of further destruction had put the Syrian situation "front and centre". The Russian Federation had consistently warned against external interference, while supporting a political process to end the violence, and today's resolution was consistent with that effort, as it included requirements of both parties. Noting that the text had become more balanced through long negotiations, he said the observer team, which would include one Russian member, must be deployed in strict accordance with the resolution. The Council, meanwhile, also awaited a detailed proposal from the Secretary-General for a more extensive mission, and it was essential that all Syrian parties quickly refrain from violence, abide fully with the six-point plan and begin a peaceful negotiating process.

PETER WITTIG (Germany), noting that the resolution just adopted was the first since the start of violent repression by the Syrian regime, welcomed the Council's unity of action, which had come "deplorably late, but hopefully not too late". The cessation of violence had largely held, but new reports of attacks by regime forces were now coming in. Indeed, too many promises by Damascus had not been met; it had yet to make the fundamental change of course demanded by Joint Special Envoy Annan, including a halt to military forward movement and the return of heavy weapons to the barracks. Violence would only truly end when those conditions were met, he said, adding that arbitrary detentions, torture, sexual violence and violence against children must also end immediately.

Applauding the opposition's halting of all its activities, he said the swift deployment of the advance team would be essential to the cessation of all violence. However, conditions for the deployment of observers must be in place, and the mission must be able to implement its mandate quickly. Too often, United Nations missions had turned into "pawns in technical games", and that must not be allowed to happen again. The Council must send the message that any such impediments would come at a high price. He emphasized that no observer mission on the ground could replace the will of the parties to end the violence and reach a peaceful settlement, and that accountability for the crimes committed must be an essential element of the transition process. "There cannot be a return to the status quo."

LI BAODONG (China) said his country had always maintained that the sovereignty, territorial integrity, choices and will of the Syrian people must be respected, and that the conflict must be resolved in a peaceful manner. Urging all parties to honour strictly their commitment to end all forms of violence and allow for an inclusive political process to begin, he said the Joint Special Envoy's solution was a way forward, and China appreciated and supported his efforts. China further called on the international community to guard against words or deeds that might stand in the mission's way, he said, adding that its deployment, with the consent of the Syrian Government and aimed at swiftly kicking off the task of supervision and the cessation of violence, would help implement the six-point plan and launch the transition process at an early date.

MOHAMED LOULICHKI (Morocco) said the adoption of the resolution was a practical translation of the efforts of the United Nations and the League of Arab States, and of the good-faith efforts of their Joint Special Envoy to implement General Assembly resolution 66/253, the Council presidential statement of 5 April, and the relevant resolutions of the League of Arab States. Since becoming a member of the council, Morocco had been involved in all efforts aimed at allowing the Council to speak with one voice as the only option to influence events in Syria. In that respect, today's resolution was an important landmark that hopefully would represent a decisive Council position.

He recalled that the Arab League, at its recent summit, had expressed, support for Mr. Annan's work to achieve a swift and lasting peace as well as the immediate implementation of his six-point plan, thereby allowing for a political solution and a response to the legitimate aspirations of the Syrian people. Morocco hoped that the deployment and actual work of the advance team would begin as soon as possible in order to verify the end of all violence and to create an environment suitable for an observer mission. Today, the Council had also reaffirmed its support for Syria's sovereignty and territorial integrity, in line with the principles of the United Nations Charter.

RAZA BASHIR TARAR (Pakistan) said the resolution was an important step towards a peaceful resolution of the situation in Syria, with full recognition of its sovereignty and territorial integrity. Strongly backing Mr. Annan's work, he said it had shown the effectiveness of combining preventive diplomacy with mediation. All sides should cooperate with the Joint Special Envoy and pursue a peaceful settlement of the crisis, he said.

NÉSTOR OSORIO (Colombia) said the resolution was first and foremost a call upon the Syrian Government for a cessation of violence after more than a year of atrocities. Colombia fully supported the full implementation of Mr. Annan's plan, particularly measures that would lead to dialogue and a lasting political resolution.

GÉRARD ARAUD (France) said he hoped the resolution would be a turning point that, in the short term, ended the violence, which had, in fact, de-escalated in the past days, though today's attacks on the population of Homs had led to doubts. "We will judge the Syrian regime by its acts and nothing else," he said, pointing out that the de-escalation had only come after much repression, for which there must be criminal accountability. In all areas of the plan, the Government must meet its commitments fully, he emphasized. An end to violence meant an end to all torture, arbitrary detentions, forced disappearances and other human rights violations committed by the regime for more than 13 months.

In order for the monitoring mission to succeed, it was critical that the regime pull back its troops and heavy weaponry from population centres, he continued. The aim was not just to freeze the situation on the ground, but to lead to steps that would allow the realization of the Syrian people's aspirations through a peaceful political solution. He welcomed the unity regained by the Council today and paid tribute to Mr. Annan's work, while noting that the consensus among members was fragile and the country still teetered on the edge of civil war. He called on all of them to remain united and be prepared to take actions that would lead to a lasting end to the violence.

HARDEEP SINGH PURI (India) said his country had consistently supported all efforts to end the crisis through an inclusive, Syrian-led political process that met the legitimate aspirations of the people. It was a matter of satisfaction that Joint Special Envoy Annan's efforts had resulted in a cessation of violence, he said, welcoming that development as well as the Syrian Government's commitment to the six-point plan. India expected the opposition also to adhere to the relevant parts of the plan, he said, expressing hope that all parties, including the opposition, would implement their responsibilities regarding the advance mission to be deployed. Noting the Government's support for an inclusive and Syrian-led political process, he urged it to maintain that support in order to end the crisis without further bloodshed. It was also necessary that all countries in the region and beyond show their support for the Joint Special Envoy's plan, he added.

KODJO MENAN (Togo) recalled that Council had previously not managed to speak with one voice on Syria. Today, in deciding to authorize a limited monitoring team to facilitate the complete and immediate implementation of the Joint Special Envoy's six-point plan, it had sent a message in unison. Togo firmly supported implementation of the resolution by all parties, and pledged its support for Mr. Annan and his team. "For a long time now, all Syrians have been awaiting this type of action from the Council," he said, adding that the resolution should pave the way for the initiation of a political process that would allow all Syrians to make a contribution in building a free and prosperous nation.

AGSHIN MEHDIYEV (Azerbaijan) said his delegation had from the outset expressed its full support for the Joint Special Enjoy and his six-point proposal. The Council had also supported Mr. Annan's mission from its inception, and the resolution today was another example of its unanimity. It was important that the resolution reaffirmed the Council's commitment to Syria's sovereignty, independence, unity and territorial integrity, he said, adding that he had voted in favour of the resolution in the hope that its adoption would lead to the end of human suffering in Syria.

JOSÉ FILIPE MORAES CABRAL (Portugal) said the resolution was a first step that had come tragically late, and much more must be done to avoid a civil war in Syria. Calling on the Government to cooperate fully with Special Envoy Annan and immediately implement his full six-point plan, including the pull-back of troops, he said all parties must guarantee freedom of movement for the monitoring mission and its advance party. Those responsible for human rights violations must be held accountable, he emphasized, calling for an end to armed violence in all its forms, and for a credible, Syrian-led political process.

BASO SANGQU (South Africa) also called for an end to all violence to and expressed support for Mr. Annan's plan, calling on all sides to implement fully all their commitments. South Africa welcomed the steps already taken and called on all sides to guarantee the safety and access of the monitoring mission and its advance team. He underlined the importance of respecting Syria's sovereignty and territorial integrity, and of helping the country work for a peaceful resolution of the crisis.

GERT ROSENTHAL (Guatemala) said his country had always held that the violence in Syria must cease immediately and that "the only way" out was a process of political dialogue, led by Syrians that would result in the reforms that the country's people demanded. Guatemala's support of the resolution not only pursued those aims, but implied its total support for the Joint Special Envoy's initiative, while also reflecting its continuing support for the Arab League's search for a peaceful outcome to the Syrian situation, he said.

Council President SUSAN RICE (United States), speaking in her national capacity, said that after more than a year of brutal violence by the Assad regime, after some 10,000 deaths, 45,000 people driven out of Syria and many more out of their homes, after the "grotesque destruction" of towns and neighbourhoods, the Government had finally said that it was ready to "step back from its murderous policies". The Council, for its part, had said today that it would judge the Government by its actions and not by its words. It had taken a step towards fulfilling its responsibilities, she said, adding that it was "about time". A fragile calm appeared to be prevailing and would hopefully continue, she said.

Nonetheless, "we are under no illusions", she stressed. Two days of calm after a year of violent rampage hardly proved that the regime was serious about its commitments. More deaths had been reported just today and such renewed violence cast serious doubts, yet again, on the cessation of violence. The opposition had honourably sought to expand the fragile calm, barely responding to those actions by the regime, which must meet all its commitments, not just the bare minimum. "And it must do so now," she emphasized.

The Arab League had proposed a way forward to end the violence and meet the aspirations of the Syrian people, but the regime had responded with broken promises and an outrageous escalation of violence, she said. That horrific cycle had lasted way too long, and the Syrian people must be allowed to exercise their rights and freedoms peacefully and without fear. Commending the opposition again for the restraint it had shown during the ceasefire, she urged the Government to honour its commitments "that are clear to everyone".

The resolution just adopted established the Council's intention to launch a larger mission if it was clear that that ceasefire was holding and that the Government was cooperating, she said. On the other hand, any Government obstruction of its work would raise serious concerns about moving forward. The United States expressed its appreciation for the Joint Special Envoy and its commitment to his plan, which aimed for legitimate and stable governance in Syria, she said. "The opportunity is there, the burden is now on the Syrian Government to seize it."

BASHAR JA'AFARI (Syria), recalling the recent killings of a son of the Imam of Syria and a university professor, said the authorities had arrested two young men who had confessed to the crimes. Each had been promised $800 for every crime they committed. That was an answer to those who questioned the existence of armed gangs in Syria, he said, stressing the importance of urging them to end their violence, as some had indeed done today. Syria would spare no effort to ensure the success of Mr. Annan's mission and end the crisis, which threatened the country's stability.

He went on to say that the Syrian Government had taken serious measures to comply with Mr. Annan's plan, declaring its intention to end armed confrontations and providing frequent updates on its efforts in that regard to Mr. Annan, in addition to accepting a monitoring mission. However, the mission must act within the limits of Syrian sovereignty, which "represented a red line that cannot be crossed under any condition". Meanwhile, there had been an increase in terrorist acts as well as threats to use a refugee crisis as an excuse for imposing buffer zones and foreign military intervention.

Some delegations did not hold armed gangs to account for their violence, even though some 50 violations had been recorded since the declaration of the ceasefire, he said, adding that he found it "puzzling" that those who claimed to care about human rights did not care about violations committed by armed gangs, including kidnapping, torture, recruitment of child soldiers and the use of civilians as human shields. Accounts of such atrocities had been documented, and Mr. Annan must obtain guarantees from the armed gangs that they would abide by his plan. Certain States must also stop encouraging them to continue the violence and avoid national dialogue.

Describing the recent conference in Istanbul as an attempt to undermine Mr. Annan's mission, he said some participants had proposed that Gulf countries fund the armed groups, offering $100 million to "feed the flames" of the crisis. What did it mean when some States said they supported Mr. Annan's mission while engaging in such actions? he asked. The States encouraging further armed opposition must be held to account, and those supporting sanctions must be held responsible for the additional suffering in Syria, he emphasized, noting that a settling of regional scores in the current crisis exacerbated factionalism and could cause a much greater conflagration.

Syria was ready to continue cooperating with Mr. Annan, he said, expressing hope that the Joint Special Envoy would not allow any party to escape its commitments. While today's resolution was not balanced, it was in Syria's interest to cooperate with measures aimed at restoring stability. Those who had voted in favour of the resolution could help by ending sanctions and taking other measures that would help the Syrian people, instead of arming Israel. "The time for violence is gone," he said. "The time for stewardship over us is gone as well," he added, referring to the upcoming anniversary of the end of the French mandate over Syria.

* *** *

---

* The 6750th Meeting was closed.

ANNEX 7:

Security Council Resolution 2043, 21 April 2012

The Security Council,

Recalling its Resolution 2042 (2012), as well as its Presidential Statements of 3 August 2011, 21 March 2012 and 5 April 2012, and also recalling all relevant resolutions of the General Assembly,

Reaffirming its support to the Joint Special Envoy for the United Nations and the League of Arab States, Kofi Annan, and his work, following General Assembly resolution A/RES/66/253 of 16 February 2012 and relevant resolutions of the League of Arab States,

Reaffirming its strong commitment to the sovereignty, independence, unity and territorial integrity of Syria, and to the purposes and principles of the Charter,

Condemning the widespread violations of human rights by the Syrian authorities, as well as any human rights abuses by armed groups, recalling that those responsible shall be held accountable, and expressing its profound regret at the death of many thousands of people in Syria,

Expressing its appreciation of the significant efforts that have been made by the States bordering Syria to assist Syrians who have fled across Syria's borders as a consequence of the violence, and requesting UNHCR to provide assistance as requested by member states receiving these displaced persons,

Expressing also its appreciation of the humanitarian assistance that has been provided to Syria by other States,

Noting the Syrian government's commitment on 25 March 2012 to implement the six-point proposal of the Joint Special Envoy of the United Nations and the League of Arab States, and to implement urgently and visibly its commitments, as it agreed to do in its communication to the Envoy of 1 April 2012, to (a) cease troop movements towards population centres, (b) cease all use of heavy weapons in such centres, and (c) begin pullback of military concentrations in and around population centres, and to implement these in their entirety by no later than 10 April 2012, and noting also the Syrian opposition's expressed commitment to respect the cessation of violence, provided the government does so,

Expressing concern over ongoing violence and reports of casualties which have escalated again in recent days, following the Envoy's assessment of 12 April 2012 that the parties appeared to be observing a cessation of fire and that the Syrian government had started to implement its commitments, and noting that the cessation of armed violence in all its forms is therefore clearly incomplete,

Supporting the Envoy's call for an immediate and visible implementation by the Syrian government of all elements of the Envoy's six-point proposal in their entirety to achieve a sustained cessation of armed violence in all its forms by all parties,

Taking note of the assessment by the Secretary-General that a United Nations monitoring mission deployed quickly when the conditions are conducive with a clear mandate, the requisite capacities, and the appropriate conditions of operation would greatly contribute to observing and upholding the commitment of the parties to a cessation of armed violence in all its forms and to supporting the implementation of the six-point plan,

Noting the 19 April 2012 Preliminary Understanding (S/2012/250) agreed between the Syrian Arab Republic and the United Nations which provides a basis for a protocol governing the Advance Team and, upon its deployment, the UN supervision mechanism,

Having considered the Secretary-General's letter addressed to the President of Security Council(S/2012/238),

1. Reaffirms its full support for and calls for the urgent, comprehensive, and immediate implementation of all elements of the Envoy's six-point proposal as annexed to resolution 2042 (2012) aimed at bringing an immediate end to all violence and human rights violations, securing humanitarian access and facilitating a Syrian-led political transition leading to a democratic, plural political system, in which citizens are equal regardless of their affiliations, ethnicities or beliefs, including through commencing a comprehensive political dialogue between the Syrian government and the whole spectrum of the Syrian opposition;

2. Calls upon the Syrian government to implement visibly its commitments in their entirety, as it agreed to do in the Preliminary Understanding and as stipulated in resolution 2042 (2012), to (a) cease troop movements towards population centres, (b) cease all use of heavy weapons in such centres, (c) complete pullback of military concentrations in and around population centres, as well as to withdraw its troops and heavy weapons from population centres to their barracks or temporary deployment places to facilitate a sustained cessation of violence;

3. Calls upon all parties in Syria, including the opposition, immediately to cease all armed violence in all its forms;

4. Calls upon the Syrian armed opposition groups and relevant elements to respect relevant provisions of the Preliminary Understanding;

5. Decides to establish for an initial period of 90 days a United Nations Supervision Mission in Syria (UNSMIS) under the command of a Chief Military Observer, comprising an initial deployment of up to 300 unarmed military observers as well as an appropriate civilian component as required by the Mission to fulfil its mandate, and decides further that the Mission shall be deployed expeditiously subject to assessment by the Secretary-General of relevant developments on the ground, including the consolidation of the cessation of violence;

6. Decides also that the mandate of the Mission shall be to monitor a cessation of armed violence in all its forms by all parties and to monitor and support the full implementation of the Envoy's six-point proposal;

7. Requests that the Secretary-General and the Syrian government without delay conclude a Status of Mission Agreement (SOMA), taking into consideration General As-

sembly resolution 58/82 on the scope of legal protection under the Convention on the Safety of United Nations and Associated Personnel, and notes the agreement between the Syrian government and the United Nations that, pending the conclusion of such an agreement, the model SOFA agreement of 9 October 1990 (A/45/594) shall apply provisionally;

8. Calls upon the Syrian government to ensure the effective operation of UNSMIS by: facilitating the expeditious and unhindered deployment of its personnel and capabilities as required to fulfil its mandate; ensuring its full, unimpeded, and immediate freedom of movement and access as necessary to fulfil its mandate, underlining in this regard the need for the Syrian government and the United Nations to agree rapidly on appropriate air transportation assets for UNSMIS; allowing its unobstructed communications; and allowing it to freely and privately communicate with individuals throughout Syria without retaliation against any person as a result of interaction with UNSMIS;

9. Calls upon the parties to guarantee the safety of UNSMIS personnel without prejudice to its freedom of movement and access, and stresses that the primary responsibility in this regard lies with the Syrian authorities;

10. Requests the Secretary-General to report immediately to the Security Council any obstructions to the effective operation of UNSMIS by any party;

11. Reiterates its call for the Syrian authorities to allow immediate, full and unimpeded access of humanitarian personnel to all populations in need of assistance, in accordance with international law and guiding principles of humanitarian assistance and calls upon all parties in Syria, in particular the Syrian authorities, to cooperate fully with the United Nations and relevant humanitarian organizations to facilitate the provision of humanitarian assistance;

12. Invites all Member States to consider making appropriate contributions to UNSMIS as requested by the Secretary-General;

13. Requests the Secretary-General to report to the Council on the implementation of this resolution within 15 days of its adoption and every 15 days thereafter, and also to submit, as necessary, to the Council proposals for possible adjustments to the UNSMIS mandate;

14. Expresses its intention to assess the implementation of this resolution and to consider further steps as appropriate;

15. Decides to remain seized of the matter. Unanimously adopting resolution 2042 (2012), the Council also authorized a team of up to 30 unarmed military observers "to liaise with the parties and to begin to report on the implementation of a full cessation of armed violence in all its forms by all parties". It underlined the importance of pulling back military forces and urgently implementing in full the six-point plan proposed by Kofi Annan, Joint Special Envoy of the United Nations and the League of Arab States.

ANNEX 8:

General Assembly, GA/SHC/4033, 22 November 2011

Sixty-sixth General Assembly
Third Committee

THIRD COMMITTEE APPROVES RESOLUTION CONDEMNING HUMAN RIGHTS VIOLATIONS IN SYRIA,

BY VOTE OF 122 IN FAVOUR TO 13 AGAINST, WITH 41 ABSTENTIONS

Also Approves 9 Other Texts on Range of Issues, Including Social Development, Disabilities and Development Goals, Child Rights, Palestinian Self-Determination

Strongly condemning the continued grave and systematic human rights violations by the Syrian authorities, the General Assembly would call for Syria to immediately put an end to all human rights violations, to protect their population and to fully comply with their obligations under international human rights law by a text approved by the Third Committee (Social, Humanitarian and Cultural) today, at the conclusion of its current session.

Following the defeat - by a vote of 20 in favour to 118 against, with 29 abstentions - of a "no action" motion on that text, the Committee approved the draft resolution on Syria by a vote of 122 in favour to 13 against, with 41 abstentions.

The five-paragraph draft would have the Assembly call on Syrian authorities to implement the Plan of Action of the League of Arab States in its entirety without further delay. In that regard, it would invite the Secretary-General, in accordance with his functions, to provide support, if requested, to the League's observer mission in the Syria, consistent with its decisions of 12 and 16 November 2011.

By further terms, the Syrian authorities would also be called on to comply with Human Rights Council resolutions S-16/1 and S-17/1, including by cooperating fully and effectively with the independent international commission of inquiry.

Speaking on behalf of the text's 61 co-sponsors, the representative of the United Kingdom said the draft was a "one-off" response to the ongoing and widespread human rights violations that had existed in Syria since March. The draft did not create any new mechanisms or procedures, he stressed, while underscoring that its approval would send a strong signal to Syria and its people that the ongoing human rights violations unfolding there must come to an end.

Saying that "sedition, political hegemony and sabotage" lay behind the proposed text, Syria's representative - who also called for the "no action" motion with support from Nicaragua and Venezuela - argued that consideration of human rights situations should be undertaken in the Human Rights Council, not the Third Committee.

He acknowledged that, like all Member States, Syria had some solvable problems. But, its comprehensive reform process, across many socio-political and economic walks of life, must be national in nature, and not follow from politically motivated United Nations texts. Moreover, the text was both unbalanced and adversarial. Among other things, it made no mention of the armed groups abusing the security of Syrian citizens, as well as the safety of public and private properties.

Pointing to its invitation to Syria to cooperate with and fully implement the Arab League's Plan of Action, he said his Government had not only signed the initiative, but received the Arab Committee charged with following up on it and participated in a joint meeting with that Committee's members. It had also accepted the draft protocol for the dispatch of Arab monitors to observe the full implementation of the Plan of Action.

During action on the text, several delegations echoed concerns over the text's political motivations. Speaking on behalf of the Non-Aligned Movement, Cuba's delegate said the draft was a clear exploitation of the topic of human rights and violated the principles of impartiality and non-selectivity. She cautioned that its approval would have a negative impact on the international human rights machinery.

Expressing similar alarm, Venezuela's representative suggested such country-specific texts were part of the geopolitical power game and were a vehicle for satisfying neo-colonial desires for others' resources. Far from contributing to the resolution of the issue, the draft text undermined efforts being promoted internationally.

In contrast, Egypt's representative said his country's vote in favour of the resolution reaffirmed its governmental and popular support for the pursuit by all peoples in the Arab region and beyond to realizing their aspirations for a better future. The recently added preambular paragraph 8 included clear language reaffirming the commitment of all Members States to refrain in their international relations from the use or the threat of force against the territorial integrity or political independence of any State. Consequently, the text could not be interpreted as an invitation for foreign intervention.

(...)

Background

(...)

Next, the Committee took up the draft resolution on the situation of human rights in Syria (document A/C.3/66/L.57/Rev.1), which was presented by the representative of the United Kingdom. On behalf of the 61 co-sponsors, he said the resolution had been tabled in response to the ongoing and widespread human rights violations that had existed in Syria since March, despite calls from the United Nations and the League of Arab States to cease those violations. Further, Syria had failed to implement the Plan of Action it had agreed to with the Arab League.

He stressed that the current draft text was a "one-off" response to the situation in Syria. It drew attention to the Plan of Action of the League of Arab States and highlighted the continuing violence and human rights violations in Syria. It also called for cooperation by Syria with the international commission of inquiry established by the Human Rights Council. It did not create any new mechanisms or procedures, but was a unique response to the events taking place on the ground. He hoped all Member States would support the resolution, thereby sending a strong signal to Syria and its people that the ongoing human rights violations must come to an end.

Cuba's representative, on behalf of the Non-Aligned Movement, reiterated the position expressed at the Movement's meeting of Heads of State and Government in Bali in 2011. Paragraph 95 of the Bali outcome document emphasized the role of the Human Rights Council as the body to review human rights situations in countries around the world, through its Universal Periodic Review mechanism. The Bali document also expressed profound concern regarding the selectivity of adopting resolutions on countries in the General Assembly.

She stressed that the current draft text was a clear exploitation of the topic of human rights and had clear political motivations behind it, violating the principles of impartiality and non-selectivity. Moreover, the draft would have a negative impact on the international human rights machinery. For those reasons, the Non-Aligned Movement called on all Member States to vote against the draft text.

Syria's representative, adding his voice to that of Cuba's delegate and subscribing to her statement, said he had taken the floor to call for a "no action" motion as it was known in the English language – the language of Shakespeare. Consideration of human rights situations should be undertaken in the Human Rights Council, not the Third Committee. Noting that Syria had completed the Universal Periodic Review, he said it had accepted a large number of recommendations, thus confirming the Government's commitment to protecting human rights.

He said Syria took pride in the fact that its written history extended over a 10,000-year period and that it had been a haven for the three divine religions. It had taken principled positions in support of States whose internal affairs had been interfered with. Syria had also voted in favour of granting independence to countries colonized by European and Western States. Indeed, Syria had always supported those States that sought help in critical situations, while many others were behaving cowardly on account of political pressure.

Like all Member States, Syria had some solvable problems, he said. It was in need of pressing ahead in implementing a comprehensive reform process across many socio-political and economic walks of life. Invoking the provisions of the Charter and international law, he argued that that reform must be national in nature, and not follow from politically motivated United Nations texts. Nor should it take the form of launching a diplomatic, political and media war and some of the text's co-sponsors should cease their media campaigns of incitement. Those States should encourage armed groups to put down their weapons, cease any engagement in violence and participate in a national dialogue.

He went on to say that the actions by some of those States constituted part of the problem. How could human rights in Syria be reformed at the time when the co-sponsors imposed economic sanctions against Syria? How could they claim to be helping Syrian citizens while they withheld electricity from Syria? How could they host meetings of the armed opposition groups, allowing them to issue declarations? He noted that last week, on one single day, 90 persons had been assassinated. Of those 90, 79 had been among the ranks of the Syrian army and the Armed Forces and those losses constituted deep wounds for Syria.

For its part, Syria had hoped to see the same enthusiasm by the draft's co-sponsors for supporting the Palestinian people, he said. Yet, ethical short-comings and short-sightedness by some had prevailed. None of the fact-finding missions established by the United Nations to address the situation in Palestine had been carried out. Only half of the partition resolution had been implemented, while the other half was forgotten.

He emphasized that accusing certain States of human rights violations was a politicization, as well as an unethical enterprise, on the part of the Third Committee. He called on States to examine their conscience, including by keeping apprised of the facts separately from exaggeration and politicization. He rejected the projects of sedition, political hegemony and sabotage. Former colonial powers would not be allowed to interfere in internal affairs anew. For all those reasons, he urged States to vote in favour of a "no action" motion.

Noting this call for a "no action" vote, the Chair invited two representatives to speak in favour of that motion.

Nicaragua's representative said her delegation was truly concerned about the proliferation of resolutions targeting certain countries. Those were not about operation and objectivity, but selectivity and double standards. Those States that were concerned about the situation of human rights in other countries should first examine the situation in their own countries. If they still felt it was morally appropriate to address the situation in other countries, they should do so through the Human Rights Council and its Universal Periodic Review mechanism. She noted that country-specific resolutions, which were only aimed at developing countries, did nothing to further the cause of human rights. Thus, Nicaragua supported the "no action" motion and called on all developing nations to do so, as well.

Venezuela's delegate also endorsed the "no action" motion, underlining her country's principled opposition to resolutions targeting specific countries. The draft in the Third Committee and the plenary of the General Assembly was unjustified and should be immediately suspended. The text undermined the principles of dialogue, cooperation and non-selectivity, among others. Far from contributing to the resolution of the issue, the draft text undermined the efforts being promoted internationally. Action on it was undertaken by superpowers who proclaimed themselves defenders of human rights, even though reality revealed their hypocrisy.

The Chair then invited two representatives to speak against the "no action" motion.

The representative of Saudi Arabia said the situation in Syria could not be ignored. His Government had, on a number of occasions, attempted to call on the Syrian authorities to work towards ending the violence there and to undertake true dialogue and reform. Those appeals had not met with a favourable response, however, and given the situation facing the Syrian people, Saudi Arabia had worked to put in place a plan to end the violence without foreign intervention. That plan sought to help Syrians live in peace and dignity. While it had been accepted by Syria, obstacles to its implementation remained in place.

He confirmed that Saudi Arabia was aware of the honourable role played by Syria throughout history. Yet, the international community must send a message to the Syrian people; otherwise the people would conclude they were being ignored and that was unacceptable for the United Nations. Stressing that the resolution was about a State in a certain situation, he appealed for States to vote against the "no action" motion, particularly since it supported the Arab League's Plan of Action.

France's representative noted that the current draft text responded to a single, unique situation. It was needed because Syria had rejected the Arab League's Plan of Action and the number of those being killed increased daily. He noted that the text reflected the efforts by regional countries, which sought to promote human rights in Syria. France would vote against the "no action" motion and urged all States to do likewise.

As the Committee moved to take action on the "no action" motion, the Chair reminded them that a "yes" vote meant they supported the motion, while a "no" vote meant they did not. The Committee then rejected the "no action" motion by a vote of 20 in favour to 118 against, with 29 abstentions.

The Committee then turned to the draft text as orally corrected.

Syria's representative said one of his colleagues had just said his Government supported the cessation of violence by all parties – armed parties – in Syria. That was a position agreed to by Syrian authorities. However, the draft text was devoid of that point. It had no balance and took an adversarial position. That colleague's country hosted a satellite facility that constantly incited the Syrian street, with a view to fuelling sedition there. While he felt sorry for mentioning that fact, he stressed that he would refrain from mentioning the country out of respect for Arab traditions.

Underlining the principle of non-interference in internal affairs, he noted that it was enshrined in the United Nations Charter. Syria was surprised that the co-sponsors cited the Charter, despite their own violations of that document. Also strange was the invitation to Syria to cooperate with and fully implement the Arab League's Plan of Action, since Syria itself had not only signed the initiative, but received the Arab Committee charged with following up on it and participated in a joint meeting with that committee's members. It had also accepted the draft protocol for the dispatch of Arab monitors to observe the full implementation of the Plan of Action.

Further stressing that the draft did not mention the armed groups that abused the security of Syrian citizens and the safety of public and private properties, he said all countries would resist such groups. Some of the text's co-sponsors still insisted on the non-presence of those groups in the text because they were fully responsible for sponsoring those groups, both by arming and financing them. While the draft text had been presented by three European States, it was no secret that the United States was the mastermind behind it. The text had nothing to do with human rights, but with the United States' agenda against Syria.

He also noted that he had provided to the Secretary-General, the President of the Security Council and the Chair of the Counter-Terrorism Committee a list of the names of the terrorists who had smuggled arms across the Syrian border. Syria had also provided to the Secretary-General and the Security Council semi-periodic updates on reforms in Syria, including the establishment of national verification committees and the release of innocent detainees. Despite that transparency, none of the supplied information had been included in the draft text, which turned a blind eye to the situation.

Regretful of that fact, Syria noted that the co-sponsors themselves had a black record in the field of human rights. Some of the European States, as well as the United States, invaded other States and imposed sanctions against sovereign States in the developing world, preventing them from achieving their right to development. The United States, France, United Kingdom, Germany and Canada had also punished the Palestinian people simply because they exercised their rights in a democratic process.

He stressed that the actions by some co-sponsors – which aimed to divert the focus on the Israeli occupation - constituted a "wrong reading" that would turn the clock back to an era of ignorance. Syria would not go along with them. In that regard, he noted that some States had said they would curtail their assistance to the Palestinian people if they presented their application for membership to the United Nations. Indeed, the United States had withdrawn support to the United Nations Educational, Scientific and Cultural Organization (UNESCO) for accepting Palestinian membership.

He called on all States to stop participating in the conspiracy, as embodied in the words of the spokesperson of the United States State Department, who advised the "terrorists" not to surrender their arms as part of the amnesty offered by the Syrian Government. The promotion, by some of the text's co-sponsors, of the demands of the radical opposition to overthrow Syria's authorities was a coup attempt supported from abroad, not a reform process. Moreover, what was promoted as the "Arab Spring" was a new version of the Sykes-Picot colonial convention to build a "new Middle East" that was supposed to be led by Israel, and was based on a new fragmentation of the region's countries on a sectarian, ethnic and religious basis.

Arguing that the draft text would not control Syria's decision to move forward in the reform process, he said the current manoeuvres would not prevent Syrian authorities from protecting their country and its people from foreign ambitions. Thus, Syria called for a recorded vote on the draft resolution and urged all States to vote against it.

Kuwait's representative asked that her State be added to the list of co-sponsors to the draft resolution.

Speaking in explanation of vote before the vote, the representative of Iran said it was the principled position of his country, as a member of the Non-Aligned Movement and Organisation of Islamic Cooperation, to oppose country-specific resolutions in the Third Committee. While there were relevant United Nations mechanisms for the same purpose, the Third Committee would not be the right and competent place to address the issue. The Government of Syria had presented its country reports to the 12-nation Universal Periodic Review working group, in a professional environment. Unfortunately, the Third Committee was "beating the very familiar wrong drum" of the Human Rights Commission, which had not been in harmony with the promotion and protection of human rights. By rejecting the resolution, the Committee could denounce mischief-making by the sponsors. Equality and sovereign rights of the State were the condition for cooperation among all States; therefore, his delegation would vote against the draft text.

The representative of Venezuela, aligning with the statement of the Non-Aligned Movement, said her delegation rejected the individual condemnation of States through use of their human rights situations, which had become part of the geopolitical power-game. It was not a human rights issue, but merely a way to satisfy neo-colonial desires for the resources of other countries. Some powers were trying to convict other countries, using the noble principles of human rights for the sole purpose of satisfying their interests in domination. Venezuela applauded the efforts of Syria to establish dialogue with the opposition. Diplomacy was for peace, not war. It was time for dialogue, not violence. Venezuela would be voting against the resolution, and urged all delegations to do the same.

Cuba's representative said those harmful and selective practices of double standards in human rights issues had been the cause of the dissolution of the Human Rights Commission five years ago. International cooperation based on the principles of objectivity, unconditionality and non-selectivity was the only way to protect human rights. Unfortunately, that was not the purpose of the text. It represented clear political motivations, and that was why Cuba would be voting against the draft resolution.

The representative of the Democratic People's Republic of Korea said his delegation was strongly concerned about continued country-specific resolutions. The resolution was politically motivated and aimed at overthrowing the political and social system in Syria, under the guise of human rights. Yesterday, his own country, along with Iran and Myanmar, had been targeted in country-specific resolutions, and today Syria was targeted. If the practice of country-specific resolutions continued, no one knew which country would be selected tomorrow. His delegation strongly opposed the draft resolution and would be voting against it.

The Committee then approved the draft resolution on the situation of human rights in Syria by a vote of 122 in favour to 13 against, with 41 abstentions.

By that text, the Assembly would strongly condemn the continued grave and systematic human rights violations by the Syrian authorities, such as arbitrary executions, excessive use of force and the persecution and killing of protesters and human rights defenders, arbitrary detention, enforced disappearances, and torture and ill treatment of detainees, including children. It would call on the Syrian authorities to immediately put an end to all human rights violations, to protect their population and to fully comply with their obligations under international human rights law, and call for an immediate end to all violence in Syria.

Further to the text, the Assembly would call on Syrian authorities to implement the Plan of Action of the League of Arab States in its entirety without further delay. It would invite the Secretary-General, in accordance with his functions, to provide support, if requested, to the League of Arab States observer mission in Syria, consistent with the League's decisions of 12 and 16 November 2011. Finally, it would call upon the Syrian authorities to comply with Human Rights Council resolutions S-16/1 and S-17/1, including by cooperating fully and effectively with the independent international commission of inquiry.

Speaking in explanation of vote after the vote, Ukraine's representative said it had voted in favour of the draft resolution under the understanding that its second operative paragraph calling for an end of violence referred to all parties in the confrontation.

China's representative said his country always believed constructive dialogue was the only right way to approach human rights, while country-specific resolutions were not a constructive way to end differences. At the same time, it called on Syria to end violence and install order as soon as possible, and endorsed the Arab plan. For those reasons, China had voted in favour of the "no action" motion and abstained on the draft resolution.

The representative of Viet Nam said his delegation had voted against the draft resolution under its principled position of not supporting country-specific resolutions. At the same time, it noted concern about the situation in Syria and called upon all parties there to put an end to violence, put an end to the conflict and engage in constructive dialogue.

Malaysia's representative said his delegation had abstained from the vote, and took note that Syria had taken steps to engage with the international community, including its participation in the Universal Periodic Review process. Malaysia was a firm believer in the non-confrontation approach on all matters, including human rights, and supported sovereignty and territorial integrity. Human rights should not be politicized, including through selective targeting of countries. The Government of Syria had a positive role to play in the process, and the best approach of the international community was respectful dialogue.

The representative of Israel expressed support for the draft resolution. The Syrian delegate's "cynical attacks" on his country today were just an effort to divert attention from the matter at hand and he would not bother with a response, he said. Israel stood ready to engage with its neighbours in the region to promote peace and stability.

Egypt's representative said his delegation had voted in favour of the text in reaffirmation of its governmental and popular support to the pursuit by all peoples in the Arab region and beyond to the realization of their aspirations for a better future. Its favourable vote took into account several important considerations, starting with Egypt's support, based on its own revolution of 25 January 2011, for the demands by the Syrian people for fundamental reforms that would enable them to live in freedom, dignity and democracy, to achieve better living standards and to ensure the full respect of the rule of law, human rights and fundamental freedoms.

He further noted that the draft resolution had been improved over the past few days, making it more consistent with the leading Arab position adopted by the Council of the League of Arab States at the level of Foreign Ministers at its two meetings on 12 and 16 November. Thus, the draft was based on the full and immediate implementation of the Plan of Action proposed by the Arab League, which, among other things, called for the immediate cessation of military actions and the dispatch of an observer mission to Syria. At the same time, it was based on ensuring the honest implementation of the two Human Rights Council resolutions 16/1 of 29 April and 17/1 of 22 August, including guaranteeing Syria's cooperation with the independent fact-finding mission.

Finally, the text preserved the unity of Syria and its territorial integrity and could not be interpreted as an invitation for foreign intervention. Indeed, the recently added preambular paragraph 8 included clear language reaffirming the commitment of all Members States to refrain in their international relations from the use or the threat of force against the territorial integrity or political independence of any State. In a clear assertion of the importance of reaching a comprehensive political settlement for the deteriorating situation in Syria, it also stressed that States would refrain from acting in any other manner inconsistent with the purpose of the United Nations.

The representative of the Russian Federation said his country had consistently opposed unilateral country-specific resolutions. History showed such texts were ineffective. States themselves were responsible for the protection and promotion of human rights and it fell to the international community to provide technical assistance. While national dialogue was needed, the efforts of the Syrian authorities should not be overlooked. Further, the opposition groups should not boycott those efforts. The Russian Federation believed it was inadmissible to use force or intervention in Syria. The human rights situation in any country could be a source of concern for the international community. However, those issues should in no instance be used as an excuse for interference.

Singapore's representative said his Government maintained a principled opposition to country-specific resolutions. However, its abstention should not be taken as pronouncing a position on the human rights situation in Syria, nor the mistreatment of citizens. He called on all States to promote and protect human rights and fundamental freedoms.

Thailand's representative said her delegation registered serious concern for current violence in Syria and its sincere hope for the return of peace there. It also hoped the recommendations resulting from the Universal Periodic Review would be implemented. Nevertheless, Thailand had abstained in today's vote on the basis of its opposition to country-specific texts.

The representative of Costa Rica said his country had voted in favour of the resolution on the basis of its concern about the situation in Syria. He recalled that the Human Rights Council, which had the necessary tools to look into certain cases that concerned the international community, was the ideal forum for looking into such matters. Costa Rica would not co-sponsor the current draft and supported the Universal Periodic Review, as well as the Human Rights Council as the optimal body for protecting human rights. However, the international community must not abdicate its responsibility for denouncing human rights violations and address them specifically, as had been done today.

Ecuador's representative regretted the politicization in the Third Committee, which was not the forum to deal with human rights situations. That was why his Government had supported the "no action" motion and subscribed to the statement made by Cuba on behalf of the Non-Aligned Movement. Ecuador adhered to equality and non-selectivity in considering human rights and believed that specific countries should not be targeted. Further, all States should abstain from making threats concerning territorial integrity. Only dialogue would enable effective resolution. For those reasons, Ecuador had voted against the draft text.

(...)

ANNEX 9:

GA/11198, 19 December 2011

The General Assembly today adopted 63 resolutions and 9 decisions recommended by its Third Committee (Social, Humanitarian and Cultural), including a text that strongly condemned "continued grave and systematic" human rights violations in Syria and called for an immediate end to all violence in that country.

The resolution on Syria - which was tabled late in the session, in the Committee - was adopted by a recorded vote of 133 in favour to 11 against, with 43 abstentions. (See Annex XV)

By its terms, the Assembly called on the Syrian authorities to immediately put an end to all such violations, to protect their population and to fully comply with their obligations under international human rights law. It also called on them to implement the Plan of Action of the League of Arab States in its entirety without further delay and to comply with Human Rights Council resolutions S-16/1 and S-17/1, including by cooperating fully and effectively with the independent international commission of inquiry.

The representative of Germany, the text's main co-sponsor, noted that despite repeated calls from the international community, Syria's crackdown against widespread civil protests continued unabated, with evidence of ongoing attacks on victims, including a "shoot to kill" policy and the widespread use of torture. According to the High Commissioner for Human Rights (OHCHR), the number of people killed likely exceeded 5,000 to date, including many children. Syrian officials continued to refuse access to the United Nations commission of inquiry and had not implemented Arab League's Plan of Action. The resolution, with significant backing from Arab States, "supports the voice of the Arab region."

Syria's representative rejected the text as part of the part of a "political, diplomatic and media war" being waged against his country and denounced its selective approach, suggesting that some of the text's co-authors were attempting to destroy his Government via military intervention on the basis of civilian protection. Syria had affirmed - and reaffirmed today - that the only solution to the current crisis was national dialogue, reform and meeting the legitimate aspirations of its people.

Arguing that that dialogue should be undertaken with an honest investigation of the events taking place, he called on United Nations Member States to support an inclusive national Syrian dialogue. He also noted that his delegation had submitted to a number of United Nations officials and agencies fully documented information on confessions made by armed terrorists that confirmed the violence committed against civilians. Despite that transparency, however, the draft reflected none of that information.

Acting today without a vote, the Assembly also adopted a third Optional Protocol to the Convention on the Rights of the Child on a communications procedure, which would allow the Committee overseeing the Convention's implementation to receive and examine individual complaints from children and to organize country visits to investigate cases of grave and systematic violations of children's rights. Recommending that it be opened for ratification in 2012, the Assembly stipulated that the Optional Protocol would enter into force following its tenth ratification.

(...)

Background

The General Assembly met today to consider the reports of its Third Committee (Social, Humanitarian and Cultural).

(...)

Report of the Human Rights Council

The Committee's report on the Report of the Human Rights Council (document A/66/457) contains three draft resolutions and one draft decision.

Draft resolution I on the Report of the Human Rights Council, approved by a recorded vote of 95 in favour to 4 against (Belarus, Democratic Republic of the Congo, Democratic People's Republic of Korea and Syria), with 60 abstentions, on 15 November, would have the Assembly note that report, as well as its addendum and its recommendations. (Press Release GA/SHC/4029)

Draft resolution II on the United Nations Declaration on Human Rights Education and Training, approved without a vote on 17 November, would have the Assembly adopt that Declaration, which was annexed to the present resolution. Inviting Governments, agencies and organizations of the United Nations system, and intergovernmental and non-governmental organizations to intensify their efforts to disseminate the Declaration and to promote universal respect and understanding thereof, the Assembly would also request the Secretary-General to include the text of the Declaration in the next edition of Human Rights: A Compilation of International Instruments. (Press Release GA/SHC/4030)

Draft resolution III on the Optional Protocol to the Convention on the Rights of the Child on a communications procedure, approved without a vote on 15 November, would have the Assembly adopt that Optional Protocol as contained in the text's annex. Further recommending that the Optional Protocol be opened for signature at a signing ceremony to be held in 2012, it would request the Secretary-General and the United Nations High Commissioner for Human Rights (OHCHR) to provide the necessary assistance. (Press Release GA/SHC/4029)

(...)

The Assembly then took up Addendum 3 to the Committee's report on the promotion and protection of human rights (document A/66/462/Add.3), which contains four draft resolutions on human rights situations and reports of special rapporteurs and representatives.

Speaking in explanation of vote before the vote, the representative of Iran said the creation of the Human Rights Council had inspired new hopes and desires for sound and decent solutions to the maladies of its predecessor, the Commission on Human Rights. That was especially true relating to the Commission's selective approach to human rights situations in different countries. Likewise, Iran considered the current Council to be a focal point for human rights situations around the world devoid of confrontation and selectivity.

In that context, he reaffirmed that the rationale behind creating the Universal Periodic Review was to ensure universality and non-selectively in the Council's work. Its performance would allow the United Nations human rights machinery to function beyond the manipulation of a few States. However, it was deplorable that a handful of States still did so through the submission of country-specific resolutions.

Stressing that Iran had always manifested its sincere commitment to the promotion and protection human rights at all levels, he said its activities in that regard emanated from its religious obligation, the provisions of its Constitution and its obligations under international human rights instruments. Accordingly, Iran was cooperating with the Universal Periodic Review mechanism. Its third periodic report was considered by the Human Rights Committee on 17 and 18 October 2011 with the active participation of a high-ranking delegation dispatched from Iran. Further, Iran was a member of a number of core human rights treaties, and among other things, had submitted and defended two reports and was at the last stage of preparing its third report for the Committee on the Rights of the Child.

He reiterated his Government's position that, if Canada was really concerned about human rights, it was certainly on the very wrong track. He would not accuse them by raising the situation of minority groups in that country, as well as racial profiling as a systematic practice and excessive use of force by Canadian authorities. Nor did he choose to refer to the human rights situation in the United States, including the reaction of Government authorities to recent peaceful protests around the country or the cruel practices regarding detainees held in Guantanamo.

Rather, he stressed that all countries should work together to promote human rights since "naming and shaming" tactics, the adoption of country-specific resolutions and the manipulation of United Nations human rights mechanisms would not lead to mutually beneficial situations. Against the backdrop, Iran requested all delegations to vote in favour the no-action motion his country was proposing.

Syria's representative said all distinguished diplomats knew that the international framework was based on non-interference in the internal affairs of any country. That principle was enshrined in Article 2, paragraph 7 of the United Nations Charter, among other cornerstone documents. While firmly convinced of the importance of protecting of human rights, his Government was highly surprised by the authors and proponents of the draft resolution, who were claiming to promote and protect human rights in Syria, since they themselves had argued against protecting the rights of those Syrians living under Israeli occupation in the Syrian Golan.

Clearly, those States exploited human rights issues to conspire against the territorial integrity and independence of some countries and the text on Syria was part of the political, diplomatic and media war being conducted against it. Among other things, that war sought to promote the Israeli theory of "Judaization", which was being waged to deny the rights of the Palestinian people. The striking proof of that political manoeuvring and duplicity was that those States themselves had imposed economic sanctions against Syria, as well as its media and television channels. Why? Clearly it was because those television channels were systematically broadcasting confessions made by terrorist groups and elements belonging to armed groups. Those confessions testified to the transfer of arms across international borders and that armed groups were receiving arms and funds from neighbouring countries and using them to commit terrible crimes. Could the authors of the resolution explain the link between the promotion and protection of human rights, on one hand, and the bombings of pipelines and railways and other acts, including attacks against civilians, in Syria, on the other?

Today, Syria was all the more indignant about the selective approach because the text's main authors had a sad history regarding human rights, he said. The United States continued to threaten people and countries through the imposition of sanctions. He also asked how other countries could support the draft resolution at a time when their authorities were depriving their own people of a minimum guarantee of human rights, including the right to elections, freedom of religion, as well as women's rights. Some of those States did not even have a constitutional guarantee for basic human rights, he noted.

Syria had submitted to a number of United Nations officials and agencies fully documented information on the confessions made by armed terrorists that confirmed the violence committed against civilians. It had also conveyed information on the reforms being undertaken by Syria. But, despite that transparency, the draft reflected none of that information. It seemed that some of the text's co-authors were attempting to destroy Syria via military intervention on the grounds of civilian protection. Last week's briefing of the Security Council by the High Commissioner for Human Rights had been sentimental, individual and non-professional. The High Commissioner had attributed full responsibility for the events unfolding in Syria to its Government. Going beyond its mandate, her Office went so far as to call for the transfer of the Syria dossier to the International Criminal Court. But, it had closed its eyes to the actions of terrorist groups and the billions of dollars transferred for the State's destabilization.

He noted that Syria had affirmed - and reaffirmed today - that the only solution to the current crisis was national dialogue, reform and meeting the legitimate aspirations of its people. That dialogue should be undertaken with an honest investigation of the events taking place. Thus, he called on United Nations Member States to support an inclusive national Syrian dialogue and to abstain from considering non-professional reports, which harmed the integrity and credibility of the Organization.

He also asked where the Security Council and the High Commissioner were when the rights of Syrians in the occupied Syrian Golan were being violated. For decades, the Council had failed to carry out its duty to act against expansionist policies by Israel. Moreover, he asked why members of Salafist groups were being held in Guantanamo, while others were being encouraged to become active in Syria. His Government, therefore, called for a recorded vote on the draft resolutions related to Syria and called on all States to vote against it.

The representative of Germany recalled that the Third Committee had adopted the resolution before the Assembly by a vote of 122 in favour to 13 against with 41 abstentions. Those "unprecedented and clear results" were meant to send a strong signal to Syria that it must immediately stop the violence and the systematic human rights violations being perpetrated against its own people. Despite that message, the crackdown had continued unabated, he said. There was evidence of ongoing attacks on victims, including a "shoot to kill" policy and the widespread use of torture. According to the High Commissioner for Human Rights, the number of people killed likely exceeded 5,000 to date, including many children.

Despite the repeated calls of the international community, the Syrian officials continued to refuse access to the United Nations commission of inquiry and had not implemented the plan of action of the League of Arab States.

The draft resolution before the Assembly, of which Germany was a main co-sponsor and which enjoyed significant support from the Arab States in the region, was a "unique and ad hoc response to events taking place on the ground in [Syria] as we speak", he said. It called, among other things, for the immediate and full implementation of the plan of action, which "supports the voice of the Arab region". It was also important to note that the resolution did not establish any new mechanisms. As the situation in Syria continued to deteriorate, he concluded, the General Assembly - as the main and universal body of the United Nations - should reaffirm the message sent by its Third Committee.

(...)

ANNEX XV

Vote on Syria

The draft resolution on the situation of human rights in Syria (document A/66/462/Add.3) was adopted by a recorded vote of 133 in favour to 11 against, with 43 abstentions, as follows:

In favour: Afghanistan, Albania, Andorra, Antigua and Barbuda, Argentina, Australia, Austria, Azerbaijan, Bahamas, Bahrain, Barbados, Belgium, Belize, Benin, Bosnia and Herzegovina, Botswana, Brazil, Bulgaria, Burkina Faso, Burundi, Cambodia, Canada, Cape Verde, Central African Republic, Chile, Colombia, Comoros, Congo, Costa Rica, Côte d'Ivoire, Croatia, Cyprus, Czech Republic, Denmark, Dominican Republic, Egypt, El Salvador, Estonia, Ethiopia, Finland, France, Georgia, Germany, Greece, Grenada, Guatemala, Guinea, Guinea-Bissau, Guyana, Haiti, Honduras, Hungary, Iceland, Indonesia, Iraq, Ireland, Israel, Italy, Jamaica, Japan, Jordan, Kazakhstan, Kiribati, Kuwait, Kyrgyzstan, Latvia, Liberia, Libya, Liechtenstein, Lithuania, Luxembourg, Madagascar, Malawi, Maldives, Malta, Marshall Islands, Mauritius, Mexico, Micronesia (Federated States of), Monaco, Mongolia, Montenegro, Morocco, Nauru, Netherlands, New Zealand, Nigeria, Norway, Oman, Palau, Panama, Papua New Guinea, Paraguay, Peru, Poland, Portugal, Qatar, Republic of Korea, Republic of Moldova, Romania, Rwanda, Saint Lucia, Samoa, San Marino, Sao Tome and Principe, Saudi Arabia, Senegal, Serbia, Seychelles, Sierra Leone, Slovakia, Slovenia, Solomon Islands, South Sudan, Spain, Sudan, Sweden, Switzerland, Thailand, The former Yugoslav Republic of Macedonia, Timor-Leste, Togo, Tonga, Trinidad and Tobago, Tunisia, Turkey, Tuvalu, Ukraine, United Arab Emirates, United Kingdom, United States, Uruguay, Vanuatu.

Against: Belarus, Cuba, Democratic People's Republic of Korea, Ecuador, Iran, Myanmar, Nicaragua, Syria, Uzbekistan, Venezuela, Zimbabwe.

Abstain: Algeria, Angola, Armenia, Bangladesh, Bhutan, Bolivia, Brunei Darussalam, Cameroon, Chad, China, Djibouti, Dominica, Fiji, Gambia, Ghana, India, Kenya, Lao People's Democratic Republic, Lebanon, Lesotho, Malaysia, Mali, Mauritania, Mozambique, Nepal, Niger, Pakistan, Philippines, Russian Federation, Saint Kitts and Nevis, Saint Vincent and the Grenadines, Singapore, Somalia, South Africa, Sri Lanka, Swaziland, Tajikistan, Turkmenistan, Uganda, United Republic of Tanzania, Viet Nam, Yemen, Zambia.

Absent: Democratic Republic of the Congo, Equatorial Guinea, Eritrea, Gabon, Namibia, Suriname.

* *** *

ANNEX 10:

League of Arab States Observer Mission to Syria

Report of the Head of the League of Arab States Observer Mission to Syria for the period from 24 December 2011 to 18 January 2012

In the name of God, the Merciful, the Compassionate

"We offered the trust to the heavens and the earth and the mountains, but they refused to carry it, and were afraid of it; and man carried it. Surely he is sinful, very foolish" [Qur'an 33:72]

I. Legal bases

1.   By resolution 7436 of 2 November 2011, the Council of the League of Arab States adopted the Arab plan of action annexed thereto, welcomed the Syrian Government's agreement to the plan, and emphasized the need for the Syrian Government to commit to the full and immediate implementation of its provisions.

2.   On 16 November 2011, the Council of the League of Arab States adopted resolution 7439 approving the draft protocol of the Legal Centre and the mandate of the League of Arab States Observer Mission to Syria, namely to verify implementation of the provisions of the Arab plan of action to resolve the Syrian crisis and protect Syrian civilians. The resolution requested the Secretary-General of the League of Arab States to take such steps as he deemed appropriate to appoint the Head of the League of Arab States Observer Mission and to make contact with the Syrian Government with a view to signing the Protocol.

3.   By resolution 7441 of 24 November 2011, the Council of the League of Arab States requested the Secretary-General of the League to deploy the Observer Mission to the Syrian Arab Republic in order to fulfil its mandate under the protocol immediately on its signature.

4.   The Syrian Arab Republic and the General Secretariat of the League of Arab States signed the protocol on 19 December 2011. The protocol provided for the establishment and deployment to the Syrian Arab Republic of a Mission comprising civilian and military experts from Arab countries and Arab non-governmental human rights organizations. Paragraph 5 stated that the Mission should transmit regular reports on the results of its work to the Secretary-General of the League of Arab State and the Syrian Government for submission — via the Arab Ministerial Committee on the Situation in Syria — to the Council of the League at the ministerial level for its consideration and appropriate action.

5.   On 20 December 2011, the Council of the League approved the appointment of General Muhammad Ahmad Mustafa Al-Dabi from the Republic of the Sudan as Head of the Observer Mission.

II. Formation of the Mission

6.   The General Secretariat requested Member States and relevant Arab organizations to transmit the names of its candidates for the Mission. On that basis, 166 monitors from 13 Arab countries and six relevant Arab organizations have thus far been appointed.

III. Visit of the advance delegation of the General Secretariat to Syria

7.   In preparation for the Mission, an advance delegation of the General Secretariat visited the Syrian Arab Republic on 22 December 2011 to discuss the logistical preparations for the Mission.

8.   In accordance with the protocol, the Syrian Government confirmed its readiness to facilitate the Mission in every way by allowing the free and safe movement of all of the observers throughout Syria, and by refraining from hindering the work of the Mission on security or administrative grounds. The Syrian Government side also affirmed its commitment to ensuring that the Mission could freely conduct the necessary meetings; to provide full protection for the observers, taking into consideration the responsibility of the Mission if it were to insist on visiting areas despite the warning of the security services; and to allow the entry to Syria of journalists and Arab and international media in accordance with the rules and regulations in force in the country.

VI. Arrival and preliminary visits of the Head of Mission

9.   The Head of the Mission, General Muhammad Ahmad Mustafa Al-Dabi, arrived in the Syrian Arab Republic on the evening of Saturday 24 December 2011. He held a series of meetings with the Minister for Foreign Affairs, Mr. Walid Al-Moualem, and with Syrian Government officials, who stated that they stood

27/01/12   2   McAULEY
259.12D   12-21687

prepared to cooperate fully with the Mission and to endeavour to ensure its success, overcoming any obstacles that may arise. The necessary logistical and security arrangements were agreed.

10.   The Syrian side stated that there were certain areas that the security protection detail would not be able to enter with the observers for fear of the citizens' reaction. The Head of the Mission replied that that situation would enable the Mission to engage with citizens and opposition parties without government monitoring, thereby removing the citizens' fear of repercussions as a result of communicating with the Mission.

11.   The Head of the Mission completed the technical field preparations and secured the necessary transportation and communication devices in order to start work. He met with the observers who arrived successively in Syria and briefed them on their duties and the bases of their work under the protocol. The observers took a special oath for the Mission which had been drafted by the Head.

12.   On 27 December 2011, the Head of the Mission and ten observers conducted a preliminary visit to the city of Homs, one of the epicentres of tension, which has seen acts of violence and armed confrontation between the Army and the Syrian opposition. Some security barriers separating districts remain in place.

13.   Immediately on arriving in Homs, the Head of the Mission met with the Governor of the city, who explained that there had been an escalation in violence perpetrated by armed groups in the city. There had been instances of kidnapping and sabotage of Government and civilian facilities. Food was in short supply owing to the blockade imposed by armed groups, which were believed to include some 3000 individuals. The Governor further stated that all attempts by religious figures and city notables to calm the situation had failed. He made enquiries regarding the possibility of addressing the issue of soldiers and vehicles blocked inside Baba Amr.

14.   The Mission visited the residential districts of Baba Amr, Karam Al-Zaytun, Al-Khalidiyya and Al-Ghuta without guards. It met with a number of opposition citizens who described the state of fear, blockade and acts of violence to which they had been subjected by Government forces. At a time of intense exchanges of gunfire among the sides, the Mission witnessed the effects of the destruction wrought on outlying districts. The Mission witnessed an intense exchange of gunfire between the Army and opposition in Baba Amr. It saw four military vehicles in surrounding areas, and therefore had to return to the Governorate headquarters. It was agreed with the Governor that five members of the Mission would remain in Homs until the following day to conduct field work and meet with the greatest possible number of citizens.

15.   Immediately on returning from Homs, the Head of the Mission met with the Government and insisted that it withdraw military vehicles from the city, put an end to acts of violence, protect civilians, lift the blockade and provide food. He further called for the two sides to exchange the bodies of those killed.

16.   At that meeting, the Syrian side agreed to withdraw all military presence from the city and residential areas except for three army vehicles that were not working and had been surrounded, and one that had been taken from the Army by armed groups. The Syrian side requested the Mission's assistance to recover and remove those vehicles in exchange for the release of four individuals, the exchange of five bodies from each side, the entry of basic foods for families in the city, and the entry of sanitation vehicles to remove garbage. It was agreed at the end of the meeting that the Mission would conduct another visit to Homs on the following day in the company of General Hassan Sharif, the security coordinator for the Government side.

17.   During that visit, the Mission was introduced to one of the leading figures in the opposition, who acted as media representative of the National Council. An extensive discussion took place regarding the offer of the Syrian Government and the best way to implement the agreement. As a result, the military vehicles were returned and removed; the bodies of those killed were exchanged; trucks entered the city with food; and three detainees and two women were released and returned to their families in the presence of the Mission, thereby calming the situation inside the city.

18.   Five days after the monitors were deployed to five zones, the Ministerial Committee requested that the Head of the Mission report on the Mission's work. He travelled to Cairo and gave an oral presentation to the members of the Committee at their meeting of 8 January 2012. It was decided that the work of the Mission should continue and that the Head of the Mission should submit a report at the end of the period determined in the protocol, on 19 January 2012. After the Head's return to Damascus to resume his duties, the Mission faced difficulties from Government loyalists and opposition alike, particularly as a result of statements and media coverage in the wake of the Committee meeting. That did not, however, affect the work of the Mission or its full and smooth deployment across the country.

19.   Following its arrival, and to this date, the Mission has received numerous letters from the Syrian committee responsible for coordination with the Mission. The letters refer to the material and human losses sustained by Government institutions and offices as a result of what is described as sabotage. They assert that all of the States' vital services have been affected.

V.   Deployment of the Observer Mission to Syria

20.   The observers were divided into 15 zones covering 20 cities and districts across Syria according to the time frame set out below. The variation in dates was a result of shortcomings in administrative and technical preparations, such as the arrival of cars and personnel. Care was taken to ensure even distribution of observers. Each unit comprised some ten observers of different Arab nationalities. The groups were deployed to Syrian governorates and towns as follows:

- On 29 December 2011, six groups travelled to Damascus, Homs, Rif Homs, Idlib, Deraa and Hama.

- On 4 January 2012, a group travelled to Aleppo.

- On 9 January 2012, two groups went to Deir Al-Zor and Latakia. However, both returned to Damascus on 10 January 2012 owing to attacks that led to the injury of two of the monitors in Latakia and material damage to the cars.

- On 10 January 2012, a group travelled to Qamishli and Hasaka.

- On 12 January 2012, a group travelled to Outer Damascus.

- On 13 January 2012, four groups travelled to Suwaida, Bu Kamal, Deir Al-Zor, Palmyra (Tadmur), Sukhna, Banyas and Tartous.

- On 15 January 2012, two groups travelled to Latakia, Raqqa and Madinat Al-Thawra.

Annex 1. List of observers, their nationalities and their distribution.

21.   The observers were provided with the following:

- A map of the region;

- A code of conduct for observers;

- The duties of the group leaders;

- The duties of the observers;

- Necessary equipment such as computers, cameras and communication devices.

22.   An operations room was established at the offices of the League of Arab States in Damascus. The office is open 24 hours a day and is directly linked to the League of Arab States operations room in Cairo and to the groups deployed across Syria. The room receives daily reports from the field teams and conveys special instructions for monitoring. Owing to the volume of work, an additional operations room was opened at the Mission headquarters in Damascus with the task of allocating individuals and assigning committees on follow-up, detainees, the media and financial affairs. It coordinates with the main operations room at the offices of the League of Arab States.

23.   In Latakia and Deir Al-Zor, the Mission faced difficulties from Government loyalists. In Latakia, thousands surrounded the Mission's cars, chanting slogans in favour of the President and against the Mission. The situation became out of control and monitors were attacked. Two sustained light injuries and an armoured car was completely crushed. In order to address the matter, the Head of Mission contacted the Syrian committee responsible for coordination with the Mission. Nevertheless, the Head of the Mission ordered the immediate return of the two groups to Damascus. He met the Minister for Foreign Affairs and made a strongly-worded formal protest. The Syrian side strongly condemned the incident and extended a formal apology, explaining that the events were not in any sense deliberate. In order to emphasize the point, the Syrian Deputy Minister for Foreign Affairs met with the members of the Latakia team and stated that the Syrian Government would address the shortcoming immediately and guarantee the safety and security of observers everywhere. He apologized to them for the unfortunate and unintentional incidents. The members were then assigned to new zones after four days' rest.

VI.   Implementation of the Mission's mandate under the protocol

117

24.   The Head of the Mission stresses that this assessment in terms of the provisions of the protocol summarizes the findings of the groups as relayed by group leaders at their meeting with the Head of the Mission on 17 January 2012.

A.   Monitoring and observation of the cessation of all violence by all sides in cities and residential areas

25.   On being assigned to their zones and starting work, the observers witnessed acts of violence perpetrated by Government forces and an exchange of gunfire with armed elements in Homs and Hama. As a result of the Mission's insistence on a complete end to violence and the withdrawal of Army vehicles and equipment, this problem has receded. The most recent reports of the Mission point to a considerable calming of the situation and restraint on the part of those forces.

26.   In Homs and Dera'a, the Mission observed armed groups committing acts of violence against Government forces, resulting in death and injury among their ranks. In certain situations, Government forces responded to attacks against their personnel with force. The observers noted that some of the armed groups were using flares and armour-piercing projectiles.

27.   In Homs, Idlib and Hama, the Observer Mission witnessed acts of violence being committed against Government forces and civilians that resulted in several deaths and injuries. Examples of those acts include the bombing of a civilian bus, killing eight persons and injuring others, including women and children, and the bombing of a train carrying diesel oil. In another incident in Homs, a police bus was blown up, killing two police officers. A fuel pipeline and some small bridges were also bombed.

28.   The Mission noted that many parties falsely reported that explosions or violence had occurred in several locations. When the observers went to those locations, they found that those reports were unfounded.

29.   The Mission also noted that, according to its teams in the field, the media exaggerated the nature of the incidents and the number of persons killed in incidents and protests in certain towns.

B.   Verifying that Syrian security services and so-called *shabiha* gangs do not obstruct peaceful demonstrations

30.   According to their latest reports and their briefings to the Head of the Mission on 17 January 2012 in preparation for this report, group team leaders witnessed peaceful demonstrations by both Government supporters and the opposition in several places. None of those demonstrations were disrupted, except for some minor clashes with the Mission and between loyalists and opposition. These have not resulted in fatalities since the last presentation before the Arab Ministerial Committee on the Situation in Syria at its meeting of 8 January 2012.

31.   The reports and briefings of groups leaders state that citizens belonging to the opposition surround the Mission on its arrival and use the gathering as a barrier from the security services. However, such incidents have gradually decreased.

32.   The Mission has received requests from opposition supporters in Homs and Deraa that it should stay on-site and not leave, something that may be attributable to fear of attack after the Mission's departure.

C.   Verifying the release of those detained in the current incidents

33.   The Mission received reports from parties outside Syria indicating that the number of detainees was 16,237. It also received information from the opposition inside the country that the number of detainees was 12,005. In validating those figures, the teams in the field discovered that there were discrepancies between the lists, that information was missing and inaccurate, and that names were repeated. The Mission is communicating with the concerned Government agencies to confirm those numbers.

34.   The Mission has delivered to the Syrian Government all of the lists received from the Syrian opposition inside and outside Syria. In accordance with the protocol, it has demanded the release of the detainees.

35.   On 15 January 2012, President Bashar Al-Assad issued a legislative decree granting a general amnesty for crimes perpetrated in the context of the events from 15 March 2011 through to the issuance of the decree. In implementation of the amnesty, the relevant Government authorities have been periodically releasing detainees in the various regions so long as they are not wanted in connection with other crimes. The Mission

27/01/12   5   McAULEY
259.12D   12-21687

has been supervising the releases and is monitoring the process with the Government's full and active coordination.

36.   On 19 January 2012, the Syrian government stated that 3569 detainees had been released from military and civil prosecution services. The Mission verified that 1669 of those detained had thus far been released. It continues to follow up the issue with the Government and the opposition, emphasizing to the Government side that the detainees should be released in the presence of observers so that the event can be documented.

37. The Mission has validated the following figures for the total number of detainees that the Syrian government thus far claims to have released:

- Before the amnesty: 4,035

- After the amnesty: 3,569.

    The Government has therefore claimed that a total of 7,604 detainees have been released.

38.   The Mission has verified the correct number of detainees released and arrived at the following figures:

- Before the amnesty: 3,483

- After the amnesty: 1,669

    The total number of confirmed releases is therefore 5152. The Mission is continuing to monitor the process and communicate with the Syrian Government for the release of the remaining detainees.

D.   Confirming the withdrawal of the military presence from residential neighbourhoods in which demonstrations and protests occurred or are occurring

39.   Based on the reports of the field-team leaders and the meeting held on 17 January 2012 with all team leaders, the Mission confirmed that all military vehicles, tanks and heavy weapons had been withdrawn from cities and residential neighbourhoods. Although there are still some security measures in place in the form of earthen berms and barriers in front of important buildings and in squares, they do not affect citizens. It should be noted that the Syrian Minister of Defence, in a meeting with the Head of the Mission that took place on 5 January 2012, affirmed his readiness to accompany the Head of the Mission to all sites and cities designated by the latter and from which the Mission suspects that the military presence had not yet been withdrawn, with a view to issuing field orders and rectifying any violation immediately.

40.   Armoured vehicles (personnel carriers) are present at some barriers. One of those barriers is located in Homs and some others in Madaya, Zabadani and Rif Damascus. The presence of those vehicles was reported and they were subsequently withdrawn from Homs. It has been confirmed that the residents of Zabadani and Madaya reached a bilateral agreement with the Government that led to the removal of those barriers and vehicles.

E.   Confirming the accreditation by the Syrian Government of Arab and international media organizations and that those organizations are allowed to move freely in all parts of Syria

41.   Speaking on behalf of his Government, the Syrian Minister of Information confirmed that, from the beginning of December 2011 to 15 January 2012, the Government had accredited 147 Arab and foreign media organizations. Some 112 of those organizations entered Syrian territory, joining the 90 other accredited organizations operating in Syria through their full-time correspondents.

42.   The Mission followed up on this issue. It identified 36 Arab and foreign media organizations and several journalists located in a number of Syrian cities. It also received complaints that the Syrian Government had granted some media organizations authorization to operate for four days only, which was insufficient time, according to those organizations. In addition to preventing them from entering the country until they had specified their destinations, journalists were required obtain further authorization once they had entered the country and were prevented from going to certain areas. The Syrian Government confirmed that it grants media organizations operating permits that are valid for 10 days, with the possibility of renewal.

43.   Reports and information from some sectors [teams] indicate that the Government places restrictions on the movement of media organizations in opposition areas. In many cases, those restrictions caused journalists to trail the Mission in order to do their work.

44.   In Homs, a French journalist who worked for the France 2 channel was killed and a Belgian journalist was injured. The Government and opposition accused each other of being responsible for the incident, and both sides issued statements of condemnation. The Government formed an investigative committee in order to determine the cause of the incident. It should be noted that Mission reports from Homs indicate that the French journalist was killed by opposition mortar shells.

Annex 2. A list of media organizations identified and a list of media organizations that entered Syria, according to the official information.

VII.   Obstacles encountered by the Mission

A.   Monitors

45.   Some of the experts nominated were not capable of taking on such a responsibility and did not have prior experience in this field.

46.   Some of the observers did not grasp the amount of responsibility that was being placed on them and the importance of giving priority to Arab interests over personal interests.

47.   In the course of field work, some observers were unable to deal with difficult circumstances, which are at the core of their duties. Monitors must have certain traits and the specializations required for such work.

48.   A number of the observers are elderly, and some of them suffer from health conditions that prevent them from performing their duties.

49.   Twenty-two observers declined to complete the mission for personal reasons. Some observers offered unfounded reasons, which were not accepted by the Head of the Mission, while others had a personal agenda.

Annex 3. List of the names of observers who declined to complete the Mission.

50.   Some observers reneged on their duties and broke the oath they had taken. They made contact with officials from their countries and gave them exaggerated accounts of events. Those officials consequently developed a bleak and unfounded picture of the situation.

51.   Some of the observers in the various zones are demanding housing similar to their counterparts in Damascus or financial reimbursement equivalent to the difference in accommodation rates resulting from the difference in hotel standards or accommodation in Damascus. These issues do not warrant comment.

52.   Some observers are afraid to perform their duties owing to the violent incidents that have occurred in certain locations. The unavailability of armoured cars at all the sites and the lack of bulletproof vests have negatively affected some observers' ability to carry out their duties.

Comments of the Head of the Mission concerning the observers

53.   Some of the observers, unfortunately, believed that their journey to Syria was for amusement, and were therefore surprised by the reality of the situation. They did not expect to be assigned to teams or to have to remain at stations outside the capital or to face the difficulties that they encountered.

54.   Some of the observers were not familiar with the region and its geography. The unavailability of armoured vehicles and protective vests had a negative effect on the spirits of some observers.

55.   Some of the observers experienced hostility both from the Syrian opposition and loyalists. This hostility also had a negative effect on their spirits.

56.   Despite the foregoing comments, the performance of many of the observers was outstanding and praiseworthy. Those who underperformed will improve with experience and guidance.

B.   Security restrictions

57.   Although it welcomed the Mission and its Head and repeatedly emphasized that it would not impose any security restrictions that could obstruct the movement of the Mission, the Government deliberately attempted to limit the observers' ability to travel extensively in various regions. The Government also attempted to focus the attention of the Mission on issues in which it is interested. The Mission resisted those attempts and responded to them in a manner that allowed it to fulfil its mandate and overcome the obstacles that stood in the way of its work.

C.   Communication equipment

58.   The Mission communicates with the various groups by mobile phones and facsimile machines connected to the local Syrian telephone network. Occasional cuts in service prevent the Mission from communicating with the groups.

59.   The Mission was equipped with 10 Thuraya satellite phones. Such devices are hard to use inside buildings owing of the difficulty in obtain a satellite signal. As a result, ordinary phones and fax machines, which are not considered secure communications equipment, were used to send daily reports, instead.

60.   The communication equipment the Qatari observers brought with them was held at the Jordanian border, despite demands made by the Head of the Mission to the Syrian authorities to permit entry of that equipment. That notwithstanding, the amount of equipment would not have been enough to meet the needs of all sites and station.

61.   The Mission does not have portable two-way radios for communication between team members. The Chinese Embassy provided 10 such radios as a gift to the Mission. They were used in three sectors only.

62.   Internet service is unavailable in some regions, and in other areas it is intermittent, including in the capital.

63.   There are no cameras attached to the vehicles used by the Mission, which would facilitate observers' work in dangerous areas.

D.   Transportation

64.   The Mission has 38 cars at its disposal (23 armoured and 15 non-armoured), including 28 four-wheel drive vehicles and 10 sedans. It should be noted that the Mission's mandate requires the used of armoured four-wheel drive vehicles, given the nature of the Mission. The number of such vehicles currently available does not satisfy the needs of the Mission, particularly for transportation into trouble spots.

65.   When it was first deployed, the Mission rented several cars from local sources for use in monitoring operations. However, owing to some acts of violence directed against the field teams, the rental companies recalled those vehicles and their drivers out of fear for their safety.

66.   The Mission encountered difficulties in hiring drivers because the opposition groups refused to allowf local drivers to enter their areas because they believed the drivers were members of the security services, which forces the observers to drive the vehicles themselves.

67.   Some of the observers demanded to use vehicles sent by their countries, a demand that was denied by the Head of the Mission, who allocated the vehicles according to the needs of each zone.

Annex 4. List showing the number, types and distribution of vehicles and the countries that provided them.

E.   The media

68.   Since it began its work, the Mission has been the target of a vicious media campaign. Some media outlets have published unfounded statements, which they attributed to the Head of the Mission. They have also grossly exaggerated events, thereby distorting the truth.

69.   Such contrived reports have helped to increase tensions among the Syrian people and undermined the observers' work. Some media organizations were exploited in order to defame the Mission and its Head and cause the Mission to fail.

VIII.   Basic needs of the Mission, should its mandate be renewed

- 100 additional young observers, preferably military personnel

- 30 armoured vehicles

- Light protective vests

- Vehicle-mounted photographic equipment

- Modern communications equipment

- Binoculars, ordinary and night-vision

IX.   Evaluation:

70.   The purpose of the Protocol is to protect Syrian citizens through the commitment of the Syrian Government to stop acts of violence, release detainees and withdraw all military presence from cities and residential neighbourhoods. This phase must lead to dialogue among the Syrian sides and the launching of a parallel political process. Otherwise, the duration of this Mission will be extended without achieving the desired results on the ground.

71.   The Mission determined that there is an armed entity that is not mentioned in the protocol. This development on the ground can undoubtedly be attributed to the excessive use of force by Syrian Government forces in response to protests that occurred before the deployment of the Mission demanding the fall of the regime. In some zones, this armed entity reacted by attacking Syrian security forces and citizens, causing the Government to respond with further violence. In the end, innocent citizens pay the price for those actions with life and limb.

72.   The Mission noted that the opposition had welcomed it and its members since their deployment to Syria. The citizens were reassured by the Mission's presence and came forward to present their demands, although the opposition had previously been afraid to do so publicly owing to their fear of being arrested once again, as they had been prior to the Mission's arrival in Syria. However, this was not case in the period that followed the last Ministerial Committee statement, although the situation is gradually improving.

73.   The Mission noted that the Government strived to help it succeed in its task and remove any barriers that might stand in its way. The Government also facilitated meetings with all parties. No restrictions were placed on the movement of the Mission and its ability to interview Syrian citizens, both those who opposed the Government and those loyal to it.

74.   In some cities, the Mission sensed the extreme tension, oppression and injustice from which the Syrian people are suffering. However, the citizens believe the crisis should be resolved peacefully through Arab mediation alone, without international intervention. Doing so would allow them to live in peace and complete the reform process and bring about the change they desire. The Mission was informed by the opposition, particularly in Dar'a, Homs, Hama and Idlib, that some of its members had taken up arms in response to the suffering of the Syrian people as a result of the regime's oppression and tyranny; corruption, which affects all sectors of society; the use of torture by the security agencies; and human rights violations.

75.   Recently, there have been incidents that could widen the gap and increase bitterness between the parties. These incidents can have grave consequences and lead to the loss of life and property. Such incidents include the bombing of buildings, trains carrying fuel, vehicles carrying diesel oil and explosions targeting the police, members of the media and fuel pipelines. Some of those attacks have been carried out by the Free Syrian Army and some by other armed opposition groups.

76.   The Mission has adhered scrupulously to its mandate, as set out in the Protocol. It has observed daily realities on the ground with complete neutrality and independence, thereby ensuring transparency and integrity in its monitoring of the situation, despite the difficulties the Mission encountered and the inappropriate actions of some individuals.

77.   Under the Protocol, the Mission's mandate is one month. This does not allow adequate time for administrative preparations, let alone for the Mission to carry out its task. To date, the Mission has actually operated for 23 days. This amount of time is definitely not sufficient, particularly in view of the number of items the Mission must investigate. The Mission needs to remain on the ground for a longer period of time, which would allow it to experience citizens' daily living conditions and monitor all events. It should be noted that similar previous operations lasted for several months or, in some cases, several years.

78.   Arab and foreign audiences of certain media organizations have questioned the Mission's credibility because those organizations use the media to distort the facts. It will be difficult to overcome this problem unless there is political and media support for the Mission and its mandate. It is only natural that some negative incidents should occur as it conducts its activities because such incidents occur as a matter of course in similar missions.

79.   The Mission arrived in Syria after the imposition of sanctions aimed at compelling to implement what was agreed to in the Protocol. Despite that, the Mission was welcomed by the opposition, loyalists and the Government. Nonetheless, questions remains as to how the Mission should fulfil its mandate. It should be noted that the mandate established for the Mission in the Protocol was changed in response to developments on the ground and the reactions thereto. Some of those were violent reactions by entities that were not mentioned

in the Protocol. All of these developments necessitated an expansion of and a change in the Mission's mandate. The most important point in this regard is the commitment of *all sides* to cease all acts of violence, thereby allowing the Mission to complete its tasks and, ultimately, lay the groundwork for the political process.

80.   Should there be agreement to extend its mandate, then the Mission must be provided with communications equipment, means of transportation and all the equipment it requires to carry out its mandate on the ground.

81.   On the other hand, ending the Mission's work after such a short period will reverse any progress, even if partial, that has thus far been made. This could perhaps lead to chaos on the ground because all the parties involved in the crisis thus remain unprepared for the political process required to resolve the Syrian crisis.

82.   Since its establishment, attitudes towards the Mission have been characterized by insincerity or, more broadly speaking, a lack of seriousness. Before it began carrying out its mandate and even before its members had arrived, the Mission was the target of a vicious campaign directed against the League of Arab States and the Head of the Mission, a campaign that increased in intensity after the observers' deployment. The Mission still lack the political and media support it needs in order to fulfil its mandate. Should its mandate be extended, the goals set out in the Protocol will not be achieved unless such support is provided and the Mission receives the backing it needs to ensure the success of the Arab solution.

X.   Recommendations:

83.   In view of the above and of the success achieved in executing the provision of the Protocol, which the Syrian Government pledged to implement, I recommend the following:

• The Mission must be provided with administrative and logistic support in order allow it to carry out its tasks. The Mission must also be give the media and political support required to create an appropriate environment that will enable it to fulfil its mandate in the required manner.

• The political process must be accelerated and a national dialogue must be launched. That dialogue should run in parallel with the Mission's work in order to create an environment of confidence that would contributes to the Mission's success and prevent a needless extension of its presence in Syria.

(*Signed*) Muhammad Ahmad Mustafa **Al-Dabi**
Head of the Mission

Annexes

1. List of observers, their nationalities and their distribution.

2. List of media organizations identified and a list of media organizations that entered Syria, according to the official information.

3. List of the names of observers who declined to complete the Mission.

4. List showing the number, types and distribution of vehicles and the countries that provided them.

———————————

Translated from Arabic

League of Arab States Observer Mission to Syria

Annex I

Names of the observers of the League of Arab States Observer Mission to Syria

No.	Name	Nationality	Field team	Remarks
1	Mr. Abdulaziz Saya'a	Algeria	Tartous and Banyas (leader)	
2	Mr. Zerdani Meziane	Algeria	Tartous and Banyas	
3	Col. Jawad Kazem Ja'afar Jassem	Iraq	Tartous and Banyas	
4	Col. Ismail Husayn 'Uwaysh Muhsin Al-Zaidi	Iraq	Tartous and Banyas	
5	Mr. Said Belabad	Algeria	Tartous and Banyas	
6	Mr. Said Sultan Muhammad Ben Sulayman	United Arab Emirates	Qamishli and Hasaka (leader)	
7	Mr. Fethi Belhaj	Tunisia	Qamishli and Hasaka (deputy)	Permanent Arab Committee for Human Rights, Paris
8	Mr. Ahmed Mana'a	Tunisia	Qamishli and Hasaka	Permanent Arab Committee for Human Rights, Paris
9	Mr. Khalid Nasir Muhammad Al-Suwaidi	United Arab Emirates	Qamishli and Hasaka	
10	Mr. Ali Raja'a Ali Al-Saheli	Saudi Arabia	Qamishli and Hasaka	
11	Mr. Muhammad Ahmed Ali Al-Ma'ashi	Saudi Arabia	Qamishli and Hasaka	
12	Mr. Abulrahman Hamud Al-Qadib	Saudi Arabia	Qamishli and Hasaka	
13	Brig. Abbas Wannas 'Abbud	Iraq	Qamishli and Hasaka	
14	Col. Abdulrahman Jassem Hilal Jassem Al-Ameri	Iraq	Qamishli and Hasaka	
15	Brig. Sabah Kazem Ghanem Amer Al-Saidi	Iraq	Qamishli and Hasaka	
16	Brig. Adwar Al-Fur'an	Jordan	Suwaida (leader)	

17	Brig. Khadr Qalih Hattab Muhammad Al-Sudani	Iraq	Suwaida	
18	Col. Maj. Mahmud Al-Muwali	Jordan	Suwaida	
19	Maj. Fawzi Al-Sahmiyet	Jordan	Suwaida	
20	Mr. Adel Ibrahim Hassan	Sudan	Suwaida	
21	Brig. Abbas Hassan 'Aydan Abdul Khaqalji	Iraq	Suwaida	
22	Mr. Khalid Ali Al-Bawsit	Bahrain	Tadmur and Sukhna (leader)	
23	Mr. Abdulaziz Al-Bu Rashid	Bahrain	Tadmur and Sukhna	
24	Ambassador Rashid Lounas	Algeria	Tadmur and Sukhna	
25	Mr. Ashika Bashir	Algeria	Tadmur and Sukhna	
26	Mr. Said Saif Al-Shamsi	United Arab Emirates	Tadmur and Sukhna	
27	Mr. Ali Rashid Ali Al-Husni	United Arab Emirates	Tadmur and Sukhna	
28	Mr. Ahmed Farhan Thabit	Iraq	Aleppo	
29	Mr. Mazen Fakhir 'Aliwi	Iraq	Aleppo	
30	Mr. Mustafa Al-Mawhad Mustafa	Morocco	Aleppo	
31	Col. Sadiq Al-'Awran	Jordan	Aleppo	
32	Mr. Al-Arbi Mkharek	Morocco	Aleppo	
33	Mr. El Hassan Zahid	Moroco	Aleppo	
34	Mr. Abullatif Al-Jabali	Tunisia	Idlib (leader)	
35	Mr. Mustafa Al-Hasan Taha	Egypt	Idlib	Permanent Arab Committee for Human Rights, Paris
36	Mr. Al-Bukhari Walid Ahmadi	Mauritania	Idlib	
37	Ms. Nun Ja'afar Yunus	Sudan	Idlib	
38	Mr. Abulqasim 'Uthman Said	Sudan	Idlib	
39	Mr. 'Umar Ahmad Abbas	Sudan	Idlib	
40	Mr. Mohammed Yarqi	Algeria	Deraa (leader)	
41	Mr. Muhammad Mahmud Walid Bubakr	Mauritania	Deraa	
42	Mr. Beltut 'Ashur	Algeria	Deraa	
43	Mr. Rafa'at Merghani Abbas	Sudan	Deraa	Arab Organization for Human Rights
44	Mr. Hashim Hasan Ali	Iraq	Deraa	
45	Mr. Al-Sharif 'Awwad Rahmat	Sudan	Deraa	
46	Mr. Muhammad Nafi'ullah Walid	Mauritania	Deraa	

		Al-Ni'ma			
47	Col. Maj. Ahmad Salim Al-Kharafi	Kuwait	Deir Al-Zor and Bu Kamal (leader)	
48	Mr. Issa Sultan Al-Sulayti	Bahrain	Deir Al-Zor and Bu Kamal	
49	Mr. Husayn Salman Mattar	Bahrain	Deir Al-Zor and Bu Kamal	
50	Col. Khader Jabbar Kayan Khalifa Al-Ka'abi	Iraq	Deir Al-Zor and Bu Kamal	
51	Mr. Munib Ja'afar Salih Kasid Al-Maliki	Iraq	Deir Al-Zor and Bu Kamal	
52	Brig. Nidal Muzhir Muhammad Abdullah Al-Rukabi	Iraq	Deir Al-Zor and Bu Kamal	
53	Lt. Col. Salim Muhammad Al-Hajiri	Kuwait	Deir Al-Zor and Bu Kamal	
54	Lt. Col. Khalid Nasir Al-Radhan	Kuwait	Deir Al-Zor and Bu Kamal	
55	Brig. Kazem Jawad Yasir Abdulrida Al-Adili	Iraq	Deir Al-Zor and Bu Kamal	
56	Mr. Ja'afar Kubayda	Sudan	Damascus (leader)	
57	Mr. Juraybi Mihraz	Algeria	Damascus	
58	Mr. Mikati Ali	Algeria	Damascus	
59	Mr Ibrahim Fadl Al-Mawna	Sudan	Damascus	
60	Mr. Muhammad Khalil	Morocco	Damascus	
61	Mr. Muhammad Abduljalil Abdullah Al-Ansari	United Arab Emirates	Damascus	
62	Mr. Lahsan Tahami	Algeria	Damascus	
63	Mr. Abdullah Al-Tahir	Sudan	Homs (a) (leader)	
64	Mr. Salah Abdulkarim Said Abdullah	Iraq	Homs (a)	
65	Mr. Zaki Koko Khalid Al-Jak	Sudan	Homs (a)	
66	Mr. Al-Jili Al-Bashir	Sudan	Homs (a)	
67	Mr. Al-Sadiq Al-Fadil	Sudan	Homs (a)	
68	Brig. Ihsan Ali Bu'aywi Ali Al-'Anuz	Iraq	Homs (a)	
69	Mr. Aid Abdullah Iyad Al-'Utaybi	Saudi Arabia	Homs (a)	
70	Maj. 'As'ad Abu 'Ata	Jordan	Homs (a)	
71	Mr. Umar Sulayman Khayr Abbas	Iraq	Homs (b) (leader)	
72	Mr. Zaid Muhammad Abdullatif Muhammad Ali	Iraq	Homs (b)	
73	Mr. Salih Walid Said Mahmud	Mauritania	Homs (b)	
74	Mr. Muhammad Hassan Said	Iraq	Homs (b)	

	Muhammad			
75	Mr. Muhammad Al-Bashir Walid Saidi Hammadi	Mauritania	Homs (b)	Arab Organization for Human Rights
76	Mr. Islam Muhammad Abu Al-Aynayn Sultan	Egypt	Homs (b)	Arab Organization for Human Rights
77	Mr. Mustafa Sulih	Morocco	Homs (b)	Permanent Arab Committee for Human Rights, Paris
78	Mr. Muhammad Husayn Idris	Sudan	Homs (b)	
79	Maj. Muhammad Salim ‘Ata Al-Salim	Jordan	Homs (b)	
80	Mr. Salih Ahmad Muhammad Al-Ghamidi	Saudi Arabia	Homs (b)	
81	Brig. Sulayman Hassan Karim Al-Siyahi	Iraq	Homs (b)	
82	Gen. Ali Hassan Hussein Habib Al Habib	Iraq	Latakia (leader)	
83	Col. Akram Husayn Tahir	Sudan	Latakia (deputy)	
84	Gen. Hassan Ali Mali Wali Al-‘Ubaydi	Iraq	Latakia	
85	Gen. Muhammad Sa‘ud Munji Atya Zayni	Iraq	Latakia	
86	Mr. Said Mursi	Egypt	Latakia	
87	Mr. Ali Muhammad Abdullah Al-Shahhi	United Arab Emirates	Latakia	
88	Mr. Khalid Muhammad Ali Al-Shahhi	United Arab Emirates	Latakia	
89	Mr. Muhammad Khalifa Ali Al-Kutbi	United Arab Emirates	Latakia	
90	Mr. Abulqadir Azaria Bin Ahmad	Morocco	Latakia	
91	Mr. Al-Karimani Muwali Muhammad	Morocco	Latakia	
92	Gen. Sadiq Ja‘afar Hawsan Al-Wa’ili	Iraq	Raqqa and Madinat Al-Thawra (leader)	
93	Mr. Mubarak Said Musafir Al-Khayili	United Arab Emirates	Raqqa and Madinat Al-Thawra	
94	Gen. Sattar Jabbar Zamil Al-Sa‘idi	Iraq	Raqqa and	

			Madinat Al-Thawra	
95	Mr. Muhammad Said Al-Kutbi	United Arab Emirates	Raqqa and Madinat Al-Thawra	
96	Lt. Col. Muhammad Nasir Al-Humaynan	Kuwait	Raqqa and Madinat Al-Thawra	
97	Maj. Dr. Huquqi Yusuf Ya'qub Al-Kandari	Kuwait	Raqqa and Madinat Al-Thawra	
98	Mr. Khadr Husayn Salih	Iraq	Raqqa and Madinat Al-Thawra	
99	Mr. Safa' Husayn Ibrahim Radi Al-A'raji	Iraq	Raqqa and Madinat Al-Thawra	
100	Mr. Hadi Rashid Khalid	Qatar	Damascus countryside (leader)	
101	Mr. Muhammad Hamad Jarullah	Qatar	Damascus countryside	
102	Mr. Muhammad Naji' 'Awwad	Qatar	Damascus countryside	
103	Mr. Hassan Ali Rashid	Qatar	Damascus countryside	
104	Mr. Muhammad Sayf Muhammad	Qatar	Damascus countryside	
105	Mr. Hamad Tawim Muhammad	Qatar	Damascus countryside	
106	Mr. Said Ahmad Yati Al-Falasi	United Arab Emirates	Damascus countryside	
107	Mr. Ali Sultan Al-Suraydi	United Arab Emirates	Damascus countryside	
108	Maj. Muhammad 'Ubayd Al-'Anzi	Kuwait	Damascus countryside	
109	Mr. Nawaf Mubarak Sayf	Qatar	Damascus countryside	
110	Mr. Dayfullah Hasan Abdullah	Qatar	Damascus countryside	
111	Mr. Abdullah Sultan Abdullah	Qatar	Damascus countryside	
112	Mr. Muhammad Abdulman'am Shadhili Al-Shadhili	Egypt	Hama (leader)	
113	Mr. Ghanem Mahya Al-Harbi	Saudi Arabia	Hama	

27/01/12
259.12D

McAULEY
12-21687

114	Mr. Muhammad Abdulaziz Mana'a Al-Dusri	Saudi Arabia	Hama	
115	Mr. Ahmad Al-Nu'aymi	Bahrain	Hama	
116	Mr. Sami Jalil Salim	Iraq	Hama	
117	Mr. Ali 'Auda	Iraq	Hama	
118	Mr. Fawaz Mukhlid Musafir Al-Mutayri	Saudi Arabia	Hama	
119	Mr. Jassim Muhammad Habib 'Issa	Iraq	Hama	
120	Mr. Abdulrahim Shalabi	Egypt	Consultative team	
121	H. E. Nazih 'Umarayn	Jordan	Consultative team	
122	Brig. Muhammad Ahmad Zaza	Jordan	Coordination of operations	
123	Mr. Abdullah Said 'Abbud Al-Asri	Saudi Arabia	Operations control	
124	Mr. Razzaq Abd Ali Muhammad Al-Tali	Iraq	Committee on detainees	
125	Dr. Khalfan Sultan Hamad Al-Kindi	United Arab Emirates	Committee on detainees	
126	Mr. Mazen Ibrahim Al-Tamimi	Bahrain	Committee on detainees	
127	Mr. Ahmad Abdullatif	Sudan	Committee on detainees	
128	Mr. Tariq Al-Mawmani	Jordan	Public information	
129	Mr. Al-Shadhili Hamid	Sudan	Public information	
130	Mr. Abdulrahman Ben 'Umar	Morocco	Advisers	
131	Mr. Tali' Al-Sa'ud Abdullah Al-Atlasi	Morocco	Advisor on public information	
132	Mr. Abdulillah Muhammad Hassun Haydar Al-Khafaji	Iraq	Transportation	
133	Mr. Hamad Rashid Jabir	Qatar	Administrative support	
134	Mr. Salih Faraj Muhammad	Qatar	Administrative support	
135	Mr. Khalid Salim Salih Al-Saidi	United Arab Emirates	Medical support	
136	Mr. Afifi Abdullatif Muhammad	Sudan	Chief, operations room	
137	Mr. Khalid Bin Rabi'an	Saudi Arabia	Operations control	
138	Mr. Adel Ahmad Sultan	United Arab	Operations control	

		Emirates		
139	Mr. Farijat Bushu'ayb	Morocco	Operations supervisor	
140	Mr. Fahd Muhammad Ali	Qatar	Communications control	
141	Mr. Ali Muhammad Ali	Qatar	Damascus countryside	
142	Ms. Ilham Al-Shajali	Yemen	Team office	League of Arab States
143	Mr. Sidi 'Uthman Walid Al-Sheikh	Mauritania	Team office	
144	Mr. Maslah Salih Maslah Al-'Utaybi	Saudi Arabia	Team office	

Annex II

Extent of compliance with paragraph 5 regarding the media

With regard to the media, the protocol states that the Mission should verify that the Syrian Government gives accreditation to Arab and international media and allows them free and unfettered movement throughout Syria.

The Mission teams have followed up the issue. They observed that members of the media were exercising their profession in various regions. They noted some complaints made by members of the media, who said that the Syrian Government had given them four days in which to work in the country, a time frame that they considered insufficient. In view of the complaints, and after the Head of the Mission referred the matter to the Syrian side, the Government agreed to increase the time frame to ten days including the initial four. The media were thus able to work freely with the Mission teams.

While the Mission was present, there was only one killing. The victim was the French journalist Gilles Jacquier, a correspondent for the channel France II, who was walking through Homs. Each side blamed the other for his death and issued statements condemning it. The Government formed a committee to investigate the incident, in which a Belgian journalist was also wounded.

With regard to the decision whether or not to grant entry, the Syrian President Bashar Al-Assad stated in his speech of 10 January 2012 that the media were selectively allowed to operate in Syria. However, he did not define the criteria in use. Government figures have indicated that the decision whether or not to grant entry is based on the journalist's position regarding Syria and the events taking place in the country. They stated that only two channels had been barred, namely Al-Jazeera and Al-Arabiya, which the Government believes to be targeting Syria and its system of government.

In regions where media access is difficult, the events are being relayed through high-technology devices incompatible with television, such as mobile phones and simple cameras that give a poor picture on satellite television.

According to the latest information, the Mission teams have observed 44 media outlets and a number of freelance journalists. The Minister of Information, Mr. Adnan Mahmud, stated that 147 Arab and international media outlets had been accredited between the start of December 2011 and 15 January 2012, of which 112 had entered the country, in addition to 90 media outlets that were already based in Syria and had permanent correspondents.

The media outlets observed covering the events in Syria are as follows.

I.   Monitoring by teams of observers

	Name	Date of monitoring	Place
1.	Algerian delegation	31/12/2011	Daraa/Damascus
2.	Dubai Network	3/1/2012	Damascus
3.	BBC Arabic Network	5/1/2012	Outskirts of Damascus
4.	German television	7/1/2012	Damascus
5.	Iranian television	7/1/2012	Damascus
6.	German television	7/1/2012	Damascus
7.	Chinese media delegation (14 media organizations)	7/1/2012	Damascus
8.	Russian television - RT	7/1/2012	Damascus

9.	TSR	8/1/2012	Damascus
10.	CNN	8/1/2012	Damascus
11.	RTL	8/1/2012	Damascus
12.	Associated Press Agency	8/1/2012	Damascus
13.	France 2 Network	9/1/2012	Homs
14.	Italian journalist	9/1/2012	Homs
15.	Lebanese journalist	9/1/2012	Homs
16.	Japanese television	10/1/2012	Daraa
17.	Al-Kawthar Iranian television network	10/1/2012	Damascus
18.	Iraqi network	12/1/2012	Damascus
19.	Canadian media delegation	12/1/2012	Damascus
20.	CBS Network - America	13/1/2012	Damascus
21.	Voice of America Radio	13/1/2012	Damascus
22.	Financial Times	15/1/2012	Damascus
23.	Belgian journalist and writer	15/1/2012	Lattakia
24.	Indonesian media delegation	16/1/2012	Aleppo

II.   Arab and foreign media that entered Syria since the signing of the Protocol   between 19/12/2011 and 16/1/2012, according to official reports:

	Name	Date of entry	Remarks
1.	Chinese media delegation made up of 14 journalists from different Chinese media outlets	19/12/2011	Monitored by team of observers
2.	Japanese TBS Network and Japanese journalist Yuta Furukawa	19/12/2011	
3.	Xinhua Chinese News Agency	20/12/2011	
4.	Agence France Presse French News Agency	20/12/2011	
5.	Yomiuri Japanese newspaper and Japanese journalist Tao Shigeki	26/12/2011	Monitored by team of observers
6.	Belgian journalist Pierre Piccinin	27/12/2011	Monitored by team of observers
7.	New TV - Firas Hatoum, Sa`d al-Din Al-Rifa`i and Ali Sha`ban	27/12/2011	
8.	Algerian National Television	30/12/2011	Monitored by team of observers - part of Algerian delegation
9.	Algerian National Radio	30/12/2011	Part of Algerian delegation
10.	Algerian News Agency	30/12/2011	Part of Algerian delegation
11.	Mainichi Japanese newspaper and Japanese journalist Hiroaki Wada	1/1/2012	
12.	TBS Japanese broadcasting network	3/1/2012	Monitored by team of observers
13.	Italian official television	3/1/2012	
14.	French journalist Hervé Degal	3/1/2012	

15.	BBC News Arabic network	3/1/2012	Monitored by team of observers
16.	Asahi Shimbun Japanese newspaper	3/1/2012	
17.	RTL German television and Austrian journalist Antonia Rados	4/1/2012	Monitored by team of observers
18.	ORF Austrian broadcasting network and correspondent Fritz Orter	4/1/2012	
19.	Aftenposten Norwegian newspaper and Norwegian journalist Jørgen Lohne	5/1/2012	Monitored by team of observers
20.	Milli Gazete Turkish newspaper	5/1/2012	Monitored by team of observers (Turkish media delegation)
21.	TV5 Turkish network	5/1/2012	Part of the delegation
22.	Milliyet Turkish newspaper	5/1/2012	" "
23.	İhlas Turkish news agency	5/1/2012	" "
24.	Vatan Turkish newspaper	5/1/2012	" "
25.	Akşam Turkish newspaper	5/1/2012	" "
26.	Vakit Turkish newspaper	5/1/2012	" "
27.	Yeni Şafak Turkish newspaper	5/1/2012	" "
28.	Today's Zaman English-language Turkish newspaper	5/1/2012	" "
29.	KON Turkish television network	5/1/2012	" "
30.	Hürriyet Turkish newspaper	5/1/2012	" "
31.	Star Turkish newspaper	5/1/2012	" "
32.	Turk online news site	5/1/2012	" "
33.	STV Turkish television network	5/1/2012	" "
34.	Yeni Asya Turkish newspaper	5/1/2012	" "
35.	Bugün Turkish newspaper	5/1/2012	" "
36.	Sözcü Turkish newspaper	5/1/2012	" "
37.	Cumhuriyet Turkish newspaper	5/1/2012	" "
38.	Guardian British newspaper and British journalist Ian Black	5/1/2012	Monitored by team of observers
39.	NHK Japanese Government television and Japanese journalist Yujiru Fuori	6/1/2012	Monitored by team of observers
40.	Russian media delegation and journalist Dimitri	6/1/2012	
41.	FR2 French television	7/1/2012	Monitored by team of observers
42.	Hebdo Swiss newspaper	7/1/2012	
43.	Lebanese New TV network and correspondent Firas Hatoum	7/1/2012	Monitored by team of observers
44.	CNN network: British journalist Dominic Robertson	8/1/2012	Monitored by team of observers
45.	Spanish official television and journalist Oscar Fernando Gómez	8/1/2012	
46.	British journalist Elizabeth Cocker	8/1/2012	
47.	Russian journalist Boris Dolgov	8/1/2012	
48.	Polish journalist Marcin Domagala	8/1/2012	

49.	Polish journalist Kornel Sawinski	8/1/2012	
50.	VRT Belgian radio network	8/1/2012	
51.	Newspaper of the Republic of Egypt and journalist Sayyid Husayn Abdul`al	8/1/2012	
52.	Sole 24 Italian newspaper and journalist Alberto Negri	9/1/2012	Monitored by team of observers
53.	Italian-Arab Centre and Lebanese journalist Talal Khreis	9/1/2012	Monitored by team of observers
54.	La Vie French magazine	10/1/2012	
55.	Bild Zeitung German newspaper and journalist	10/1/2012	
56.	EFE official Spanish news agency and journalist Javier Rodríguez	10/1/2012	Monitored by team of observers
57.	CBC Canadian broadcasting network and Canadian journalist Susan Ormiston	10/1/2012	Monitored by team of observers
58.	VRT Belgian television and journalist Rudi Vranckx	10/1/2012	
59.	American CBS News network and British journalist Elizabeth Palmer	11/1/2012	
60.	Iranian journalist Mostafa Afzalzadeh	11/1/2012	
61.	British Broadcasting Corporation (BBC) News, International news department and journalist Timothy Whewell	11/1/2012	
62.	Czech TV: Jan Molacek and Martin Bobin	12/1/2012	Monitored by team of observers
63.	Asahi Shimbun Japanese newspaper, editor	13/1/2012	Monitored by team of observers
64.	Sky News network and British journalist Jeremy Thompson	13/1/2012	Monitored by team of observers
65.	Voice of America radio and television network: American journalist Elizabeth Arrott	13/1/2012	Monitored by team of observers
66.	Financial Times newspaper and British journalist Abigail Fielding-Smith	14/1/2012	Monitored by team of observers
67.	Los Angeles Times newspaper and journalist Alexandra Zavis	14/1/2012	Monitored by team of observers

List of Arab and international media representatives who have entered Syria since the start of December 2011

1.   The United States channel ABC News: Barbara Jill Waters on 3 December.

2.   Delegation of various French media outlets including the journalist Richard Labévière, working from the Institut Français du Proche Orient (IFPO); Professor Eric Denec, a teacher at IFPO; and Saida Ben Hbeibes, on 3 December.

3.   The Egyptian journalist Sana Al-Said, on 10 December.

4.   Abduh Maghribi, editor of the Egyptian newspaper Al-Anba Al-Duwaliyya on 10 December.

5.   Muhammad Al-Fawwal, deputy editor of the newspaper Al-Gumhuriyya, on 10 December.

6.   Ilham Al-Maliji, press journalist and analyst, 10 December.

7.   Muhammad Mahmud Al-Sayyid of the newspaper Al-Ahram, 10 December.

8.   Nura Khalaf, deputy editor of the magazine Hurriyyati, 10 December.

9.   Muhammad Said Galal, deputy editor of Akhbar Al-Yawm (Egypt), 10 December.

10.   Muhsin Abdulaziz of Al-Ahram, 10 December.

11.   Laarbi Usama Al-Dalil, head of the international section, Al-Ahram, 10 December.

12.   Ayman Al-Sisi, Al-Ahram, 10 December.

13.   Yasir Mishali, deputy editor of Ruz Al-Yusif, 10 December.

14.   Rami Al-Maliji of the newspaper Al-Yawm Al-Sabi`, 10 December.

15.   Shadiya Ahmad Al-Husri of the Kuwaiti newspaper Al-Ra'y, 10 December.

16.   Lenka Ardnašova, editor of the Slovak newspaper Extra Plus, 11 December.

17.   Robert Kolisek of the State publication Tasar, 11 December.

18.   Peter Durkovic, a journalist specializing in the Middle East, 11 December.

19.   Filip Fosfić, editor for Slovak television, 11 December.

20.   Martin Kubala of the Slovak channel JOV, 11 December.

21.   Josef Durica, editor of a weekly magazine, 11 December.

22.   Andrea Emkova, a journalist who publishes in the State media, 11 December.

23.   German radio and television, 12 December.

24.   Makoto Sasaki of the Japanese network Fuji, 13 December.

25.   Joerg Ambruster, Friedre Meissner and Heiko Viehl of the German television channel ARD, 15 December.

26.   Dietmar Ossenberg of the German television channel ZDF, 15 December.

27.   Takeshi Tsuchiya of the Japanese news agency Kyodo , on 15 December.

28.   Giuseppe Bonavolontà of the Italian television channel RAI, 16 December.

29.   Sara Firth of the English-language channel Russia Today, 17 December.

30.   Mariana Belenkaya of the Arabic-language Russian channel Rusiya Al-Yawm, 17 December.

31.   Annalisa Rapanà of the Italian news agency ANSA, 18 December.

The Chinese delegation is composed of 14 journalists from various news outlets and entered the region on 19 December:

32.   Zhou Hu, correspondent for Travel News Weekly.

33.   Tao Haibin, editor of Global Travel Magazine.

34.   Li Wei, editor of Wings of China Magazine.

35.   Liu Qiang, editor of Wings of China Magazine.

36.   Lin Haidong, editor of Wang Jia Travel.

37.   Zau Yinghao, editor of Wang Jia Travel.

38.   Zau Qi, editor of Shanghai Media Group.

39.   Jin Song, editor of Shanghai Media Group.

40.   Bao Gang, editor of Shanghai Media Group.

41.   Yu Meug, editor of Century Business Herald.

42.   Ruan Yuhong, editor of the website Blashe

43.   Ho Yanguang, editor of China Youth Daily.

44.   Qiu Xiaoyu, editor of Chinese international radio.

45.   Bao Limin, editor of Youth Reference News.

46.   Yuta Furukawa of the Japanese channel TBS, on 19 December.

47.   Zheng Kaijun, Li Muzi and Li Jia of the Chinese news agency Xinhua, on 20 December.

48.   The French news agency AFP on 20 December.

49.   Pierre Piccinin, Belgian author and journalist, entered the region on 27 December.

50.   Tao Shigeki of the Japanese newspaper Yomiuri, 26 December.

51.   Firas Hatoum, Sa`duddin Al-Rifa`i and Ali Sha`ban of the channel Al-Jadid, 27 December,

52.   Algerian national television, on 30 December.

53.   Algerian national radio, 30 December.

54.   Algerian news agency, 30 December.

55.   Hiroaki Wada of the Japanese newspaper Mainichi, 1 January 2012.

56.   The Japanese channel TBS, 3 January.

57.   Italian State television, 3 January.

58.   Hervé Degal, French journalist, 3 January.

59.   BBC News Arabic, 3 January.

60.   Correspondents for the Japanese newspaper Asahi Shimbun, 3 January.

61.   The Austrian journalist Antonia Rados for the German television channel RTL, 4 January.

62.   Fritz Orter of the Austrian radio and television network ORF, 4 January.

63.   Jørgen Lohne of the Norwegian newspaper Aftenposten, 5 January.

64.   The Turkish newspaper Milli Gazete, 5 January.

65.   The Turkish channel TV5, 5 January.

66.   The Turkish newspaper Milliyet, 5 January.

67.   The Turkish news agency İhlas, 5 January.

68.   The Turkish newspaper Vatan, 5 January.

69.   The Turkish newspaper Akşam, 5 January.

70.   The Turkish newspaper Vakit, 5 January.

71.   The newspaper Yeni Şafak, 5 January.

72.   The Turkish English-language newspaper Today's Zaman, 5 January.

73.   The Turkish television channel KON, 5 January.

74.   The Turkish newspaper Hürriyet, 5 January.

75.   The Turkish newspaper Star, 5 January.

76.   The Turkish website Haber Türk, 5 January.

77.   The Turkish channel STV, 5 January 2011.

78.   The Turkish newspaper Yeni Asya, 5 January.

79.   The Turkish newspaper Bugün, 5 January.

80.   The Turkish newspaper Sözgü, 5 January.

81.   The Turkish newspaper Cumhuriyet, 5 January.

82.   Ian Black of the UK newspaper The Guardian, 5 January.

83.   Yujiru Futori of the Japanese State television NHK, 6 January.

84.   The journalist Dimitri of the Russian press delegation, 6 January.

85.   The British journalist Dominic Robertson of CNN, 8 January.

86.   Oscar Fernando Gómez of Spanish State television, 8 January.

87.   The French television channel FR2, 7 January.

88.   The Swiss publication Hebdo, 7 January.

89.   Firas Hatoum of the Lebanese channel Al-Jadid, 7 January.

90.   The British journalist Elizabeth Cocker, 8 January.

91.   The Russian journalist Boris Dolgov, 8 January.

92.   The Polish journalist Marcin Domalaga, 8 January.

93.   The Polish journalist Mateusz Piskorski, 8 January.

94.   The Polish journalist Kornel Sawinski, 8 January.

95.   The Belgian radio VRT, 8 January.

96.   Sayyid Husayn Abdul`al of the Egyptian newspaper Al-Gumhuriyya, 8 January.

97.   Alberto Negri of the Italian newspaper Il Sole 24 Ore, 9 January.

98.   The Lebanese journalist Talal Khreis of the Italian-Arab Centre, 9 January.

99.   The French magazine La Vie, 10 January.

100.   Julian Reichelt of the German newspaper Bild Zeitung, 10 January.

101.   Javier Rodríguez of the Spanish State news agency EFE, 10 January.

102.   Susan Ormiston of the Canadian radio and television network CBC, 10 January.

103.   Rudi Vranckx of the Belgian television channel VRT, 10 January.

104.   Elizabeth Palmer of the US channel CBS News, 11 January.

105.   The Iranian journalist Mostafa Afzalzadeh, 11 January.

106.   Tim Whewell of BBC News, international section, 11 January.

107.   Jan Molacek and Martin Bubin of Czech television, 12 January.

108.   The editor of the Japanese newspaper Asahi Shimbun, 13 January.

109.   The British journalist Jeremy Thompson of the channel Sky News, 13 January.

110.   Elizabeth Arrot of Voice of America radio and television, 13 January.

111.   Abigail Fielding-Smith of the British newspaper Financial Times, 14 January.

112.   Alexandra Zavis of the newspaper Los Angeles Times, 14 January.

List of Arab and international media granted accreditation for the region since 1 January who have yet to enter the country:

1.   Kazuhide Iketaki of the Japanese agency Jiji Press, 26 December 2011.

2.   Kazayuki Bandok, Head of office and correspondent for the newspaper Hokkaido Shimbun, accompanied by the Egyptian journalist Mahmud `Id Mahmud, 26 December.

3.   Enrique Rubio of the Spanish agency EFE, 27 December.

4.   Salwa Al-Khatib, correspondent for Press TV, 9 December.

5.   Jon Anderson, correspondent for the magazine The New Yorker, 28 December.

6.   Jeremy Bowen of the BBC, 9 December.

7.   Roel Maria Geeraedts of the Dutch channel RTL4, 27 December.

8.   Paul Jørgensen of the Norwegian channel TV2, 28 December.

9.   William Spindle of the Wall Street Journal, 27 December.

10.   Hristo Petrov of the independent news agency Trinity M, 27 December.

11.   The Algerian newspaper Al-Khabar, 24 December.

12.   The US television channel NBC, 26 December.

13.   Vidal Dominguez of the Cuban station Radio Habana, 9 December.

14.   Tomas Avenarius of the German newspaper Süddeutsche Zeitung, 9 December.

15.   The Argentinean journalist Karen Marón, who is currently working for French international radio and the Colombian press, 26 December.

16.   Fausto Biloslavo of the newspaper Il Giornale, 28 December.

17.   Turutumita Wakishi Tumura of the Japanese television channel Nippon, 1 January 2012.

18.   The Arabic-language Russian channel Rusiya Al-Yawm, 1 January.

19.   The English-language channel Russia Today, 1 January.

20.   The Spanish-language Russian station, 1 January.

21.   The American author Charles M. Glass, 7 January.

22.   Alexandra Zavis of the Los Angeles Times, 7 January.

23.   Alice Fordham of the Washington Post, 7 January.

24.   Arwa Damon of CNN, 7 January.

25.   The American journalist Ayman Mohyeldin of NBC News Cairo, 8 January.

26.   The journalist Jorg Armbruster of the German channel ARD.

27.   The American journalist Kareem Fahim of the New York Times, 8 January.

28.   The British journalist and academic James Harkin, 8 January.

29.   The Chinese journalist Li Lianxing of the newspaper China Daily, 12 January.

30.   Karim Al-Jawhari of the Austrian channel ORF, 12 January.

31.   Toshihiro Fuji of the Japanese channel NHK, 12 January.

32.   Wang Chu of the Chinese news agency Xinhua, 12 January.

33.   Abigail Fielding-Smith of the Financial Times, 12 January.

34.   Claudie Abi Hanna of the Lebanese channel Al-Hurra, 12 January.

35.   Michael Robert Peel of the Financial Times, 12 January 2012.

36.   Jan Eikelboom of Dutch television, 12 January.

37.   Ahmad Jadullah Hasan Salem and Maryam Qar`uni of the agency Roberts, 13 January.

Annex III

Names of observers who withdrew from the League of Arab States Observer Mission

	Name	Nationality	Field team	Comments	Comments
1	Muhammad Husayn Umar	Djibouti	Homs A	Qatar Charity	Departed
2	Anwar Abdulmalik	Algeria	Homs A		Departed
3	Muhammad bin Yusuf Al-Nafati	Tunisia	Idlib		Departed
4	Ahmad Abdullah Muhamamd Abdullah	Egypt	Idlib		Departed
5	Abdulhamid Al-Wali	Morocco			Departed
6	Jamal Hamid Barakat	Egypt	Hama	Arab Human Rights Organization	Departed
7	Nabil Abdulmuhsin Hasan Al-Shalabi	Egypt	Hama	Arab Human Rights Organization	Departed
8	Haidi Ali Muhammad Al-Tayyib	Egypt	Hama	Arab Human Rights Organization	Departed
9	Ibrahim Abdullah Al-Sulayman	Saudi Arabia	Hama	Arab Human Rights Organization	Departed
10	Karim Abdulmuhsin Hasan Al-Shalabi	Egypt	Homs A	Arab Human Rights Organization	Departed
11	Manina bint Muhammad Salim	Mauritania	Deraa	Arab Human Rights Organization	Departed
12	Hisham Bnay`ish	Morocco	Damascus		Departed
13	Isam Abdulrahman	Sudan	Damascus		Departed
14	Muhammad Salim	United Arab	Deraa		Departed

	Muhammad Rashid Al-Ka`bi	Emirates			
15	Yahya Abdulmuhsin Al-`Itabi	Iraq	Deraa	Arab Human Rights Organization	Left without the Mission's permission and at his own expense
16	Isam Mansur Muhammad Miqdad	Jordan	Coordinator	Arab Committee on Human Rights	Departed
17	Muhammad Uthman Al-Sudairi	Tunisia	Aleppo		Departed
18	Sabr Al-Rawashida	Jordan	Aleppo		Departed
19	Jalal bin Ibrahim Al-Sanusi	Tunisia	Idlib		Departed
20	Muhammad bin Husayn bin Yusuf	Tunisia	Idlib		Departed
21	Muhammad Salah Ali Shawar	Egypt	Idlib	Egyptian National Council on Human Rights	Departed
22	Hadi Al-Yami	Saudi Arabia	Committee on detainees	Arab Committee on Human Rights	Special leave for five days

27/01/12
259.12D

McAULEY
12-21687

Vehicle fleet
League of Arab States Observer Mission to Syria

N o.	Country	Land Cruiser		Mercedes		Nissan		Cadillac		Tot al	Rema rks
		Armou red	Regu lar	Armou red	Regu lar	Armou red	Regul ar	Armou red	Regu lar		
1	Iraq	7	-	10	-	-	-	-	-	17	23 armour ed
2	Qatar	-	5	-	-	-	4 (Toyo ta)	1	-	10	15 g armour ed
3	Saudi Arabi a	5	-	-	-	-	-	-	-	5	
4	Unite d Arab Emira tes	-	-	-	-	-	6	-	-	6	
Total armoured vehicles		12	5	10	-	-	10	1	-	38	

Appendix IV
Vehicles used by the League of Arab States Observer Mission to Syria

No.	Country	Make	Plate number	Regular/ armoured	Type	Sector	Remarks
1	Qatar	Land Cruiser	2192	Regular	4 x 4	Deraa	
2	Qatar	Land Cruiser	2193	Regular	4 x 4	Homs (b)	
3	Qatar	Land Cruiser	2194	Regular	4 x 4	Banyas	
4	Qatar	Land Cruiser	2195	Regular	4 x 4	Hama	
5	Qatar	Land Cruiser	2196	Regular	4 x 4	Idlib	
6	Qatar	Land Cruiser	2197	Regular	4 x 4	Suwaida	
7	Qatar	Land Cruiser	2198	Regular	4 x 4	Damascus	Ready for deploy
8	Qatar	Land Cruiser	2199	Regular	4 x 4	Qamishli	
9	Qatar	Land Cruiser	2201	Regular	4 x 4	Damascus	Ready for deploy
10	Qatar	Cadillad	2212	Armoured	4 x 4	Damascus countryside	
11	Saudi Arabia	GMS	2231	Armoured	4 x 4	Homs	
12	Saudi Arabia	GMS	2232	Armoured	4 x 4	Homs	
13	Saudi Arabia	GMS	2233	Armoured	4 x 4	Qamishli	
14	Saudi Arabia	GMS	2234	Armoured	4 x 4	Hama	
15	Saudi Arabia	GMS	2235	Armoured	4 x 4	Tadmur	
16	United Arab Emirates	Nissan	2214	Regular	4 x 4	Latakia	Inoperable
17	United Arab Emirates	Nissan	2215	Regular	4 x 4	Latakia	
18	United Arab Emirates	Nissan	2216	Regular	4 x 4	Qamishli	
19	United Arab Emirates	Nissan	2217	Regular	4 x 4	Latakia	Inoperable
20	United Arab Emirates	Nissan	2222	Regular	4 x 4	Tadmur	
21	United Arab Emirates	Nissan	2223	Regular	4 x 4	Latakia	
22	Iraq	Mercedes	2202	Armoured	Station wagon	Homs (a)	
23	Iraq	Mercedes	2203	Armoured	Station wagon	Damascus countryside	
24	Iraq	Mercedes	2204	Armoured	Station wagon	Aleppo	
25	Iraq	Mercedes	2205	Armoured	Station wagon	Homs (a)	
26	Iraq	Mercedes	2206	Armoured	Station wagon	Suwaida	
27	Iraq	Mercedes	2207	Armoured	Station wagon	Deraa	
28	Iraq	Mercedes	2208	Armoured	Station wagon	Deir Al-Zor	
29	Iraq	Mercedes	2209	Armoured	Station	Banyas	

						wagon		
30	Iraq	Mercedes	2210	Armoured	Station wagon	With the team	
31	Iraq	Mercedes	2211	Armoured	Station wagon	Homs (b)	
32	Iraq	Land Cruiser	2224	Armoured	4 x 4	Latakia	
33	Iraq	Land Cruiser	2225	Armoured	4 x 4	Damascus	Undergoing maintenance
34	Iraq	Land Cruiser	2226	Armoured	4 x 4	Idlib	
35	Iraq	Land Cruiser	2227	Armoured	4 x 4	Raqqa and Al-Thawra	
36	Iraq	Land Cruiser	2228	Armoured	4 x 4	Raqqa and Al-Thawra	
37	Iraq	Land Cruiser	2229	Armoured	4 x 4	Deir Al-Zor	
38	Iraq	Land Cruiser	2230	Armoured	4 x 4	Raqqa and Al-Thawra	

Preliminary Statistical Analysis of Documentation of Killings in the Syrian Arab Republic

Executive Summary

This report presents findings integrated from six databases built by Syrian human rights monitors and one database collected by the Syrian government. The databases collect information about conflict-related violent deaths — killings —- that have been reported in the Syrian Arab Republic between March 2011 and November 2012. Although conflict conditions make it difficult to identify an accurate record of events, governmental and non-governmental monitors are persevering in gathering information about killings through a variety of sources and venues. The purpose of the report is to explore the state of documentation, the quantitative relationship of the sources to each other, and to highlight how understanding of the conflict may be affected due to variations in documentation practices.

This report examines only the killings that are fully identified by the name of the victim, as well as the date and location of death. Reported killings that are missing any of this information were excluded from this study. This report finds that when the fully identified records were combined and duplicates identified, the seven databases collected here identified **59,648** unique killings.

It should be noted that this count is not the number of conflict-related killings in the Syrian Arab Republic. The statistics may include a small number of undetected duplicates among the unique killings, thus, this count may be slightly too high. More significantly, there is an unknown number of killings which have not yet been documented by any of these seven projects. As each additional dataset has been added over the past few months, previously undocumented deaths have been reported. The statistics presented in this report should be considered minimum bounds.

This report provides comparative statistical analyses of all seven datasets, including patterns of documented killings over time, as well as by geography, sex and age of the victims (in Section 2). A detailed analysis of how the datasets overlap with each other is presented in Section 3; the overlap analysis helps explain how the various data sources each capture distinct aspects of the total universe of killings.

Methodology

This report begins with 147,349 records of reported killings of fully identified victims from seven datasets. Many of these records are duplicates.
An expert whose native language is Syrian Arabic and who is fluent in English reviewed 8,280 pairs of reported deaths. He classified the reports as
either referring to the same victim or to different victims. Benetech used
the expert's classifications with a computer algorithm called an Alternating
Decision Tree to build a model to classify the remaining records as either
matches or non-matches. The resulting records were merged into a combined dataset which, with duplicates removed, includes 59,648 records of
documented killings (more detail on matching is available in Appendices A.1
and A.2).

1   Documented Killings

This report presents an analysis of killings that have been reported in the
Syrian Arab Republic between March 2011 and November 2012, based on
seven datasets: 1) the Violations Documentation Centre[1] (VDC), the documentation arm of the Local Coordination Committees; 2) the Syrian Network for Human Rights[2] (SNHR); 3) the Syrian Revolution General Council (SRGC), which was combined with the SNHR (see below); 4) the Syria
Shuhada Website [3] (SS); 5) the March 15 Group (15Mar); 6) the Syrian
Observatory for Human Rights[4] (SOHR); and 7) the Syrian government
(GoSY). For brevity, each list will be referred to by its acronym in the
tables and figures throughout this report.

Benetech is aware of other organizations collecting data on killings in the
Syrian Arab Republic, for example the Strategic Research and Communication Centre[5] and Syria Tracker[6], among others. Unfortunately, Benetech
has not yet been able to obtain copies of data from these sources.

The first step in this analysis involves close examination of each individual record in each dataset in order to identify multiple records that refer to

---

[1] http://www.vdc-sy.org/
[2] http://www.syrianhr.org/
[3] http://syrianshuhada.com/
[4] www.syriahr.com, www.syriahr.net
[5] http://www.strescom.org/
[6] https://syriatracker.crowdmap.com/

the same death. Sometimes these records occur within a single dataset (duplicate records) and other times they occur in multiple datasets (matched records). See Appendix A for a description of this process.

Each dataset covered slightly different periods of time (see Section 2 for more detailed descriptions of each individual dataset) so this comparison of records was conducted over three time periods. For March 2011-December 2011, Benetech examined March 15, GoSY, SOHR, SS, VDC, and SNHR. The March 15 group stopped collecting data in December 2011, so records from this source were only included in the first ten months of analyses. Similarly, the government data only extended until March 2012, so for the period of January 2012-March 2012 Benetech examined GoSY, SOHR, SS, VDC, and SNHR. Finally, the four remaining datasets (SOHR, SS, VDC, and SNHR) include records through November 2012.

Benetech also examined data from the Syrian Revolution General Council (SRGC). Data from this group covered the period from March 2011 to January 2012. Benetech learned that the Syrian Network for Human Rights was a spin-off of the Syrian Revolution General Council, so the records of these two groups were compared before comparing them with March 15, GoSY, SOHR, SS, and VDC. From the time period covered by SRGC, 90.2% of killings recorded by SRGC were also recorded by SNHR. Considering the high level of overlap, the contextual knowledge that SNHR was originally a part of SRGC, and the fact that SNHR's dataset covers a longer period of time, Benetech chose to combine the SNHR and SRGC datasets into a single dataset, referred to in the following sections as only SNHR.

This comparison of records has only been possible for records with sufficient identifying information - the name of the victim, plus the date and location of death. Each dataset considered in this study included a number of records which lacked this information. Table 1 lists the number of records from each dataset included in the analyses presented in this report (those with sufficient identifying information) and the number of records excluded from these analyses (those lacking sufficient identifying information).

It is worth noting that none of the included counts in Table 1 match the total number of documented killings — 59,648 — because each dataset contains records that none of the other groups documented, duplicates within the dataset, as well as records that are common to two or more datasets.

Table 1: Number of Records Included and Excluded in Analyses

Dataset	Identifiable Records	Unidentifiable Records
GoSY	2,539	10
March 15	4,195	165
SOHR	29,521	232
SS	33,617	9,769
SRGC	6,206	369
SNHR	33,151	5,397
VDC	38,120	1,984

Based on a comparison of records from March 15, SOHR, GoSY, SS, VDC, and SNHR (combined with SRGC), Benetech found that the seven datasets document a total of 59,648 unique records of killings between March 2011 and November 2012. Of those documented killings, 76.1% are male victims, 7.5% are female victims, and 16.4% of records do not indicate the sex of the victim.

2 Descriptive Statistics for Individual Datasets

Prior to matching and comparing specific records across datasets, Benetech examined summary statistics for each individual dataset. This section presents those basic summary statistics. It must be noted that the analyses presented in this section describe only identifiable victims documented by each individual dataset; unobserved and unidentifiable killings are not considered. Therefore the analysis is affected by selection bias, that is, differences between what can be seen in the analysis and the true patterns that result from patterns in common among the unobserved killings. Selection bias is an inevitable outcome when certain events are more or less likely to be observed and recorded based on the characteristics of both the event and the data collection organization. For example, one group may have better contacts within a certain ethnic group or region, whereas another may have access to government personnel records. Another group may have excellent sources one week and be unable to contact these sources at other times. And of course, there are also violent events that occur, but are not reported to any source, either because only the perpetrators survived the event, or because surviving witnesses were unable or chose not to report the incident. Individual datasets are useful for case studies and as inputs to aggregated analyses (like the ones presented in the following sections), but on their own they are not suitable for drawing conclusions about statistical patterns.

Nonetheless, analysis of the individual datasets explores what has been seen. This analysis is called "descriptive" because it describes the data. Although this may not provide much insight into the unobserved true patterns, descriptive analysis shows what the datasets have in common, and how they differ.

These descriptive statistics only include records of identifiable victims. Records of identifiable victims include the victim's name, plus date and location of death. The full identifying information is essential for the record comparisons required to match records across different datasets. Records lacking the complete information are considered 'anonymous' and were excluded from the integration and analysis. The anonymous records describe victims of violence in the Syrian Arab Republic who deserve to be acknowledged. However, they cannot be included in the analysis as observed victims because it is impossible to determine if the records with partial information refer to killings also described by other records. That is, anonymous records cannot be matched or de-deduplicated. Records with partial information provide hints about the existence of killings which have not been fully documented; a full accounting of the undocumented killings will require more information and additional data analysis.

Figure 1 shows the frequency of reported killings by week for each dataset. Four datasets, SOHR, VDC, SNHR, and SS indicate roughly comparable patterns of violence over time (as also indicated in Figures 13–16 in Section 3). Note though that VDC reports more killings than SNHR and SOHR; VDC, SNHR, and SOHR report more killings than SS. The patterns of violence recorded by the remaining two datasets, March 15 and GoSY, look quite different. The pattern shown by March 15 approximately tracks SOHR, VDC, SNHR, and SS, but the similarity is difficult to see in these graphs because March 15 documents so many fewer cases. The variation in 2011 in SOHR, VDC, SNHR, and SS is much smaller than the variation in 2012. Because March 15 stopped documenting killings in December 2011, its pattern seems different. Data from the Syrian government includes very few records after March 2012 and shows a February 2012 peak that is not found in the other datasets.

Although four of the datasets (SOHR, VDC, SNHR, SS) indicate a substantial increase in documented killings over time, it is important to note that these are recorded killings and this increase may reflect an overall in-

crease in violence or an increase in documentation efforts and therefore in
records of violence. Alternatively, it may be that documentation has weakened over time, which would mean that violence has increased even more
than shown in Figure 1. Because this report includes only the fully-identified
reported deaths, it is impossible to rigorously distinguish between these alternatives.

Figure 1: Distribution of Reported Death Dates by Week

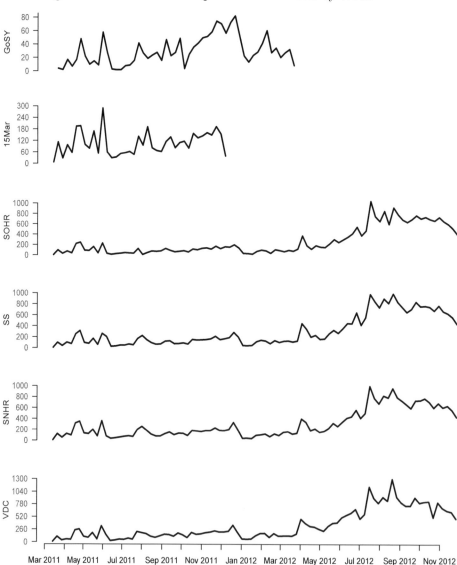

Figure 2 compares patterns of violence over geographic area across all six datasets. As in Figure 1, SOHR, SS, SNHR, and VDC indicate comparable patterns. All four groups record the highest number of killings in Homs, followed by Rural Damascus and Idlib, Aleppo, Daraa.

March 15 and the GoSY dataset also report the highest number of recorded killings in Homs. However, March 15 reports the next highest number of recorded killings in Daraa, Hamaa, Idlib, and Damascus. The government dataset reports the highest number of recorded killings in Homs, followed by Idlib, Hama, Rural Damascus, Daraa, and Aleppo. However, the pattern in the GoSY data may be distorted: Benetech cannot be certain, but it seems that in some cases, the location recorded in the GoSY dataset corresponds to the governorate of birth of the victim, rather than the location of the death, as it is recorded in most of the other datasets. This may account for differing patterns of violence recorded by governorate in the GoSY dataset as compared to the others. There is the possibility of similar location confusion in the SOHR data, however this dataset included an additional variable which indicated location of death if it differed from location of birth.

Figure 2: Distribution of Recorded Deaths by Governate

Distribution of Recorded Deaths by Governate

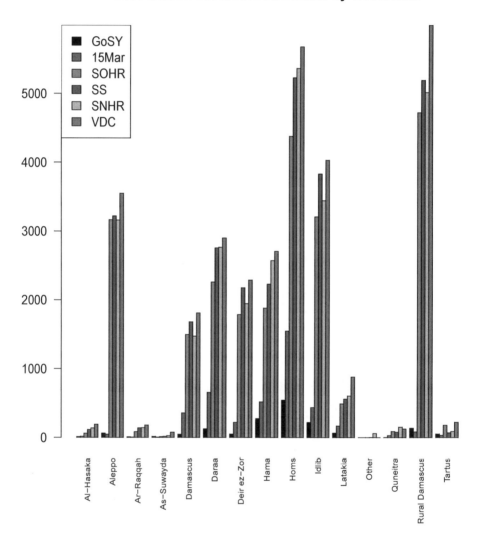

All six datasets include information about the sex (Table 2) and age of victims (Figure 3). There seems to be general agreement across the datasets that the vast majority of victims are male, however March 15 and SOHR contain the most missing information with regard to sex.

Table 2: Sex			
Dataset	Female	Male	Unknown
GoSY	0	2,534	0
March 15	109	2,407	1,667
SOHR	2,517	21,357	5228
SS	3,012	30,476	0
SNHR	3,032	26,096	3,740
VDC	3,398	34,498	4

As indicated in Figure 3, these six datasets indicate a similar *reported* age distribution pattern; the majority of victims for whom age is reported are under 40 years old. While the March 15 data has relatively few children less than ten years old, the SOHR, SS, SNHR, and VDC datasets show substantial numbers of young children. It could be that more children have been affected in 2012, after the March 15 group stopped their documentation efforts. However, many records are missing indication of age. Consider the histograms in Figure 3. With the exception of GoSY, the remaining datasets are all missing information on age for over 70% of records. The records without ages could have substantially different ages than the records with reported ages. For example, the age of very young people and very old people is often relevant to their identity. "He was only four years old" or "he was over seventy years old" are common phrases, but there is no comparable salience for an adult's age. It may be that most or all of the records with missing age data are in fact adults, which would make most distributions look more like the GoSY or 15 March patterns. The high proportion of missing age data prevents us from drawing conclusions about the true distribution of the age of victims reported to each group.

Figure 3: Age Distribution

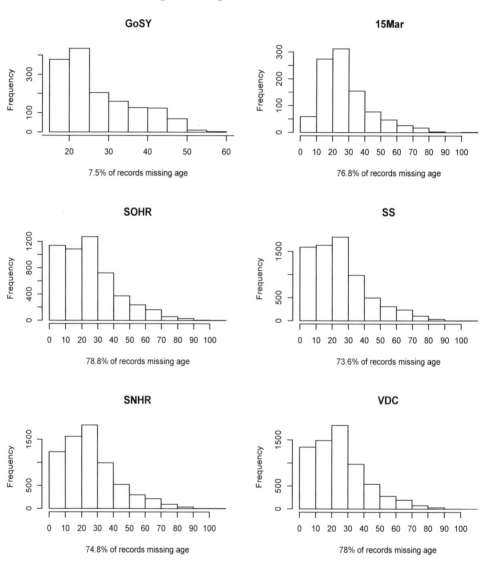

3   Data Overlaps

Once records have been matched and deduplicated, it is possible to compare each pair of datasets (VDC and SS, SS and SNHR, etc.) according to the number of records they have in common, relative to the number of records documented by each dataset alone. Since each data source includes records from slightly different periods of time, the following sections describe comparisons of pairs of datasets organized according to the periods of time they cover.

Figures 4–16 show this overlap analysis over time and space (each panel is a single governorate, that is, a Syrian province; six governorates were selected to display as examples) for each combination of pairs from the datasets listed in the previous section. The light and dark blue portions of each bar indicate records in a single dataset and the pink portions indicate identical records shared by both groups.

For March–December 2011 datasets were compared over three to four month periods - from March to May, June to August, and September to December. Comparisons for 2012 were conducted for each individual month.

3.1   March 2011-December 2011

Figures 4–7 show that the March 15 group shares roughly the same proportion of records of killings with VDC, SS, SOHR, and SNHR. In three of these Figures, VDC, SS, and SNHR appear to document the majority of killings in five of the six governorates displayed (the lighter blue portions of the bars in each Figure, indicating killings recorded only by VDC, SS, or SNHR). Exceptions to this pattern are Damascus, where March 15 appears to be documenting the majority of recorded killings (the darker blue portions of the bars in the Damascus section of each Figure) and in Daraa between March and May. This pattern mostly holds for the overlap between March 15 and SOHR as well (Figure 7), however SOHR also appears to document fewer deaths in Hama than the other groups, resulting in roughly comparable numbers of deaths recorded in Hama by March 15 alone and by SOHR alone, with relatively few overlapping records. It is worth further investigation to determine if March 15 had sources of information in Damascus and Daraa that were not available to the other groups and if these other groups had sources of information in Hama not available to March 15 and SOHR.

In general, the records of killings documented by March 15 appear to be somewhat different from those documented by VDC, SS, SOHR, and SNHR. This can also be seen in Section 2 in terms of the period of time covered by March 15, the number of killings recorded, and the number of records in each governorate. In all of these attributes March 15 differs somewhat from VDC, SS, SOHR, and SNHR; Benetech underlines the complementary importance of the March 15 data for understanding 2011.

Figure 4: Distribution of Records between March 15 and VDC

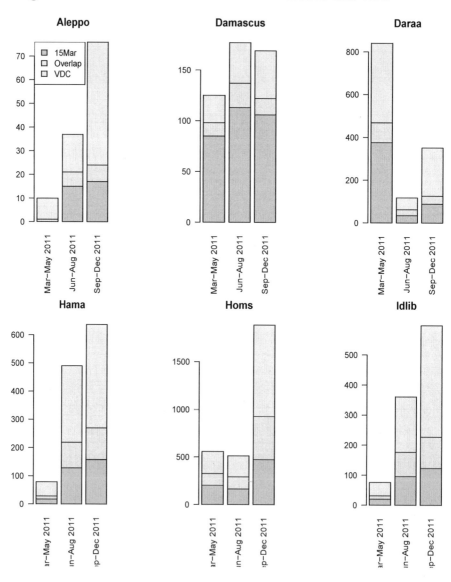

Figure 5: Distribution of Records between March 15 and SS

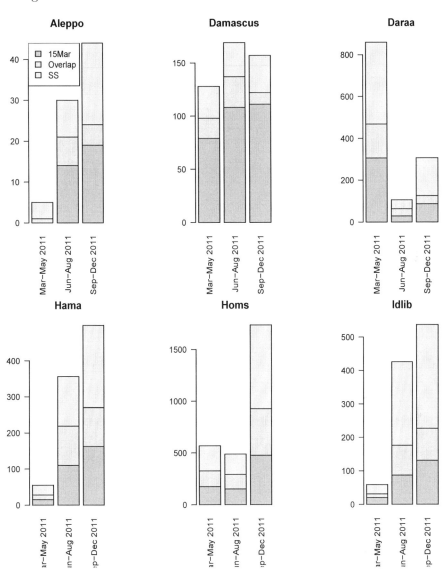

Figure 6: Distribution of Records between March 15 and SNHR

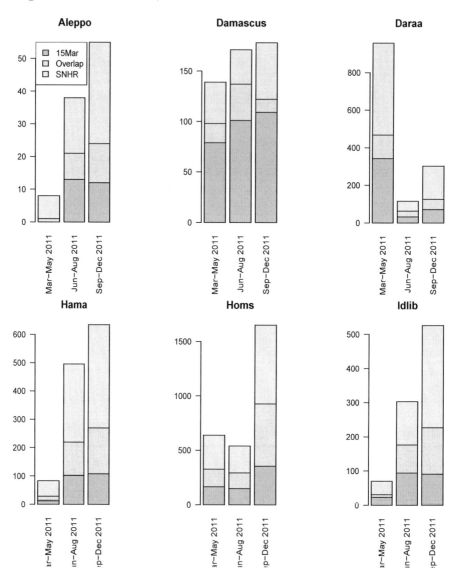

Figure 7: Distribution of Records between March 15 and SOHR

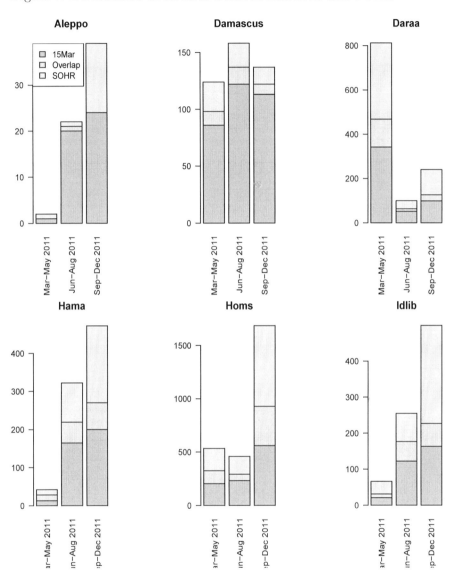

In contrast, Figure 8 indicates virtually zero records shared between March 15 and GoSY - very little pink sections, indicating overlapping records, are visible in Figure 8. This is a pattern seen again in the following section comparing GoSY and SS, SOHR, VDC, and SNHR. Additionally, with the exception of the last four months of 2011 in Aleppo, Damascus, Hama,

Homs, and Idlib, GoSY appears to record very few documented killings (the small light blue portions of each bar in Figure 8).

Figure 8: Distribution of Records between March 15 and GoSY

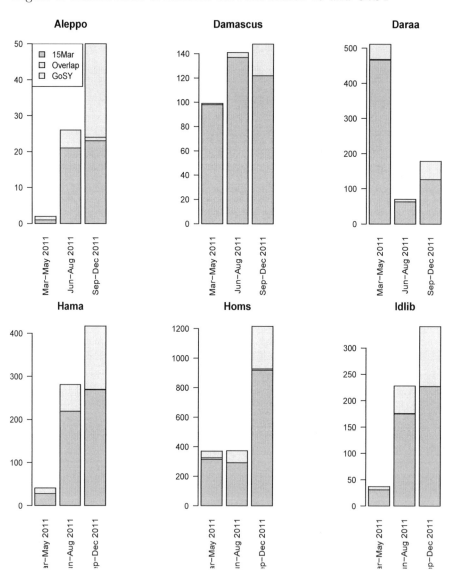

3.2 March 2011-March 2012

Five of the datasets (GoSY, SS, SOHR, SNHR, and VDC) include records for one year, from March 2011 to March 2012. Figures 9–12 show these comparisons. As in Figure 8 we see that the government data source shares very few records in common with the other data sources. Figure 9 demonstrates this most dramatically, with virtually no visible pink sections in any of the bar charts, indicating records in common between GoSY and SS.

Figures 10 and 11 show a slightly higher number of records shared between GoSY and SNHR and GoSY and SOHR (as compared to GoSY and March 15 or GoSY and SS) with notable overlaps (pink sections) in Aleppo, Damascus, Hama, and Homs. As with the comparison of March 15 and GoSY in Figure 8, overall the GoSY dataset records a much smaller number of documented killings than the other datasets (see in Figures 9 – 11). The dark blue portions of the bars in Figures 9–11 are quite small, indicating few killings documented only by GoSY. This can also be seen in the descriptive summary of GoSY in Section 2 - this dataset includes far fewer records than any of the other datasets.

Lastly, Figure 12 shows that although VDC also has relatively few records in common with GoSY, compared to March 15, SS, SNHR, and SOHR, VDC has the most overlap with GoSY. Figure 12 shows noticeable overlap (pink sections of bars) between the two groups in Aleppo, Damascus, and Hama, with slightly smaller overlap sections in Daraa, Homs, and Idlib.

Figure 9: Distribution of Records between GoSY and SS

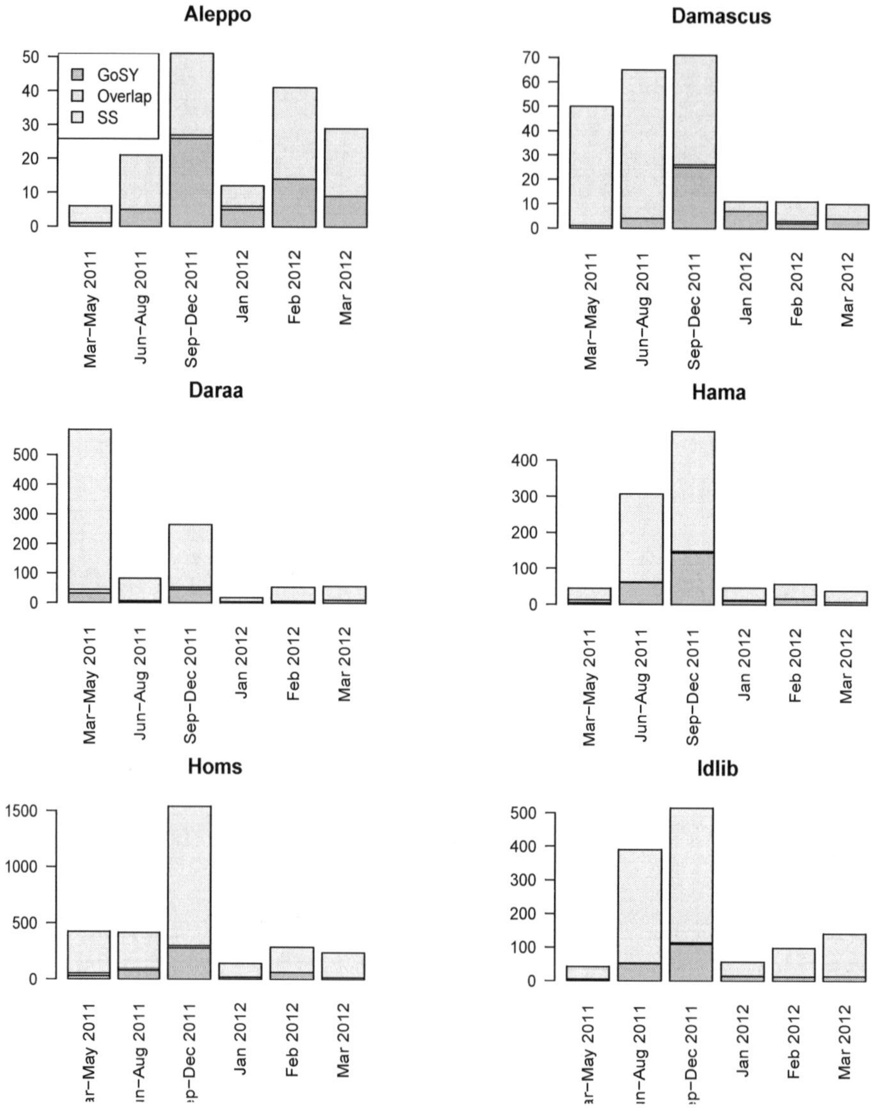

Figure 10: Distribution of Records between GoSY and SNHR

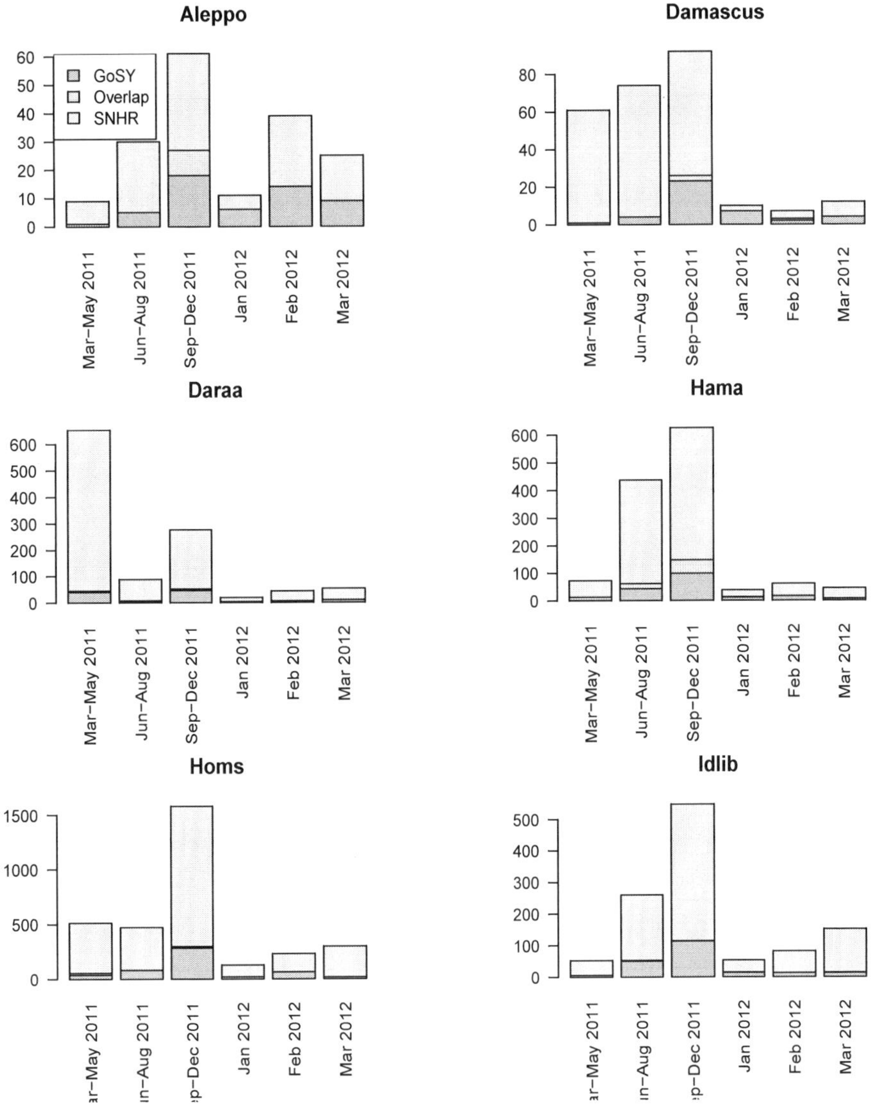

Figure 11: Distribution of Records between GoSY and SOHR

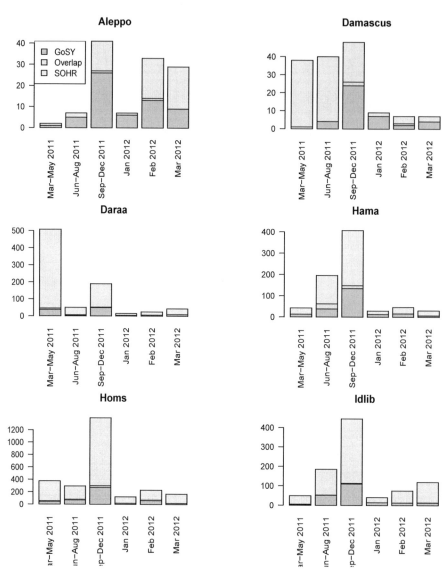

Figure 12: Distribution of Records between GoSY and VDC

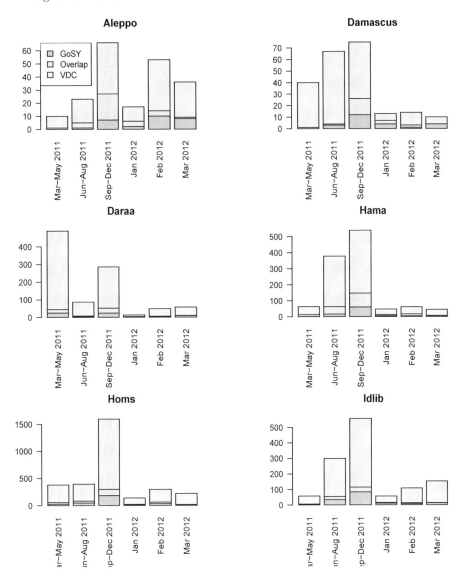

These analyses present two possibilities in terms of the GoSY data. It is possible that the records included in the GoSY data are inaccurate, although there is no reason to believe this is the case. Alternatively, if the GoSY records are accurate, and we have no reason to believe they are not, they appear to be covering a different 'universe' from the other data sources.

That is, it may be that the GoSY dataset primarily includes records not included in any of the other five datasets, and it largely excludes records included in one or more of the other five datasets. This may indicate that the GoSY dataset has access to different sources, or has different criteria for recording a death, or is in some other way documenting a different universe of violence than the other five datasets.

3.3 March 2011-November 2012

Four datasets (SOHR, SS, SNHR, and VDC) cover the entire time period under study (March 2011 - November 2012). As Figures 13–16 show, there is broad agreement between these four datasets and this agreement appears to increase over time. In most governorates, the size of the pink portion of the bar graph, indicating records in common between each pair of datasets, increases over time. In general, these four data sources appear increasingly to be sharing sources documenting killings in the Syrian Arab Republic.

However, there are notable exceptions to this broad overlap, and these are worth highlighting as they may point to times or locations when one group had access to information that another group lacked. For example, Figure 13 indicates both SNHR (light blue) and VDC (dark blue) were documenting killings unrecorded by the other group in Daraa between March and May 2011. A similar pattern can be seen between SS and SOHR in Figure 15 - there is a notable lack of overlapping records, as compared to records documented by only one of the groups, in Daraa between March and May 2011, Hama between June and December 2011, Homs between September and December 2011 and Idlib between June and December 2011. Such reflections may help each group to further improve their documentation efforts.

Figure 13: Distribution of Records between VDC and SNHR

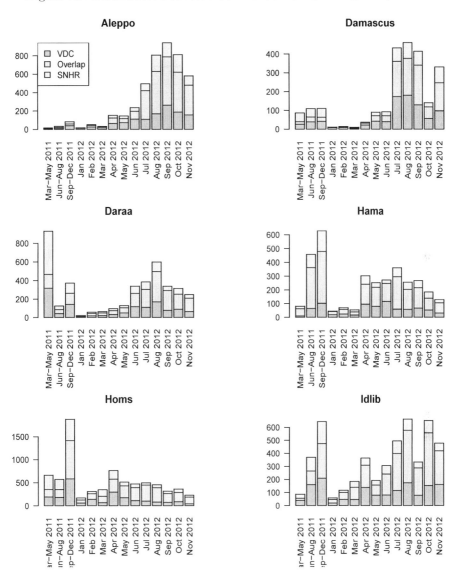

Figure 14: Distribution of Records between VDC and SS

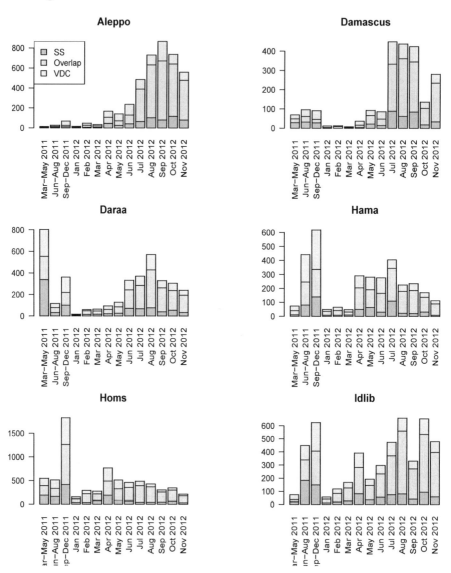

Figure 15: Distribution of Records between SOHR and SS

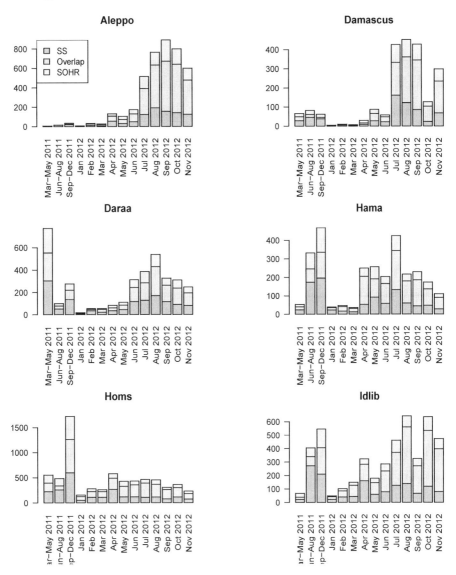

Figure 16: Distribution of Records between SNHR and SS

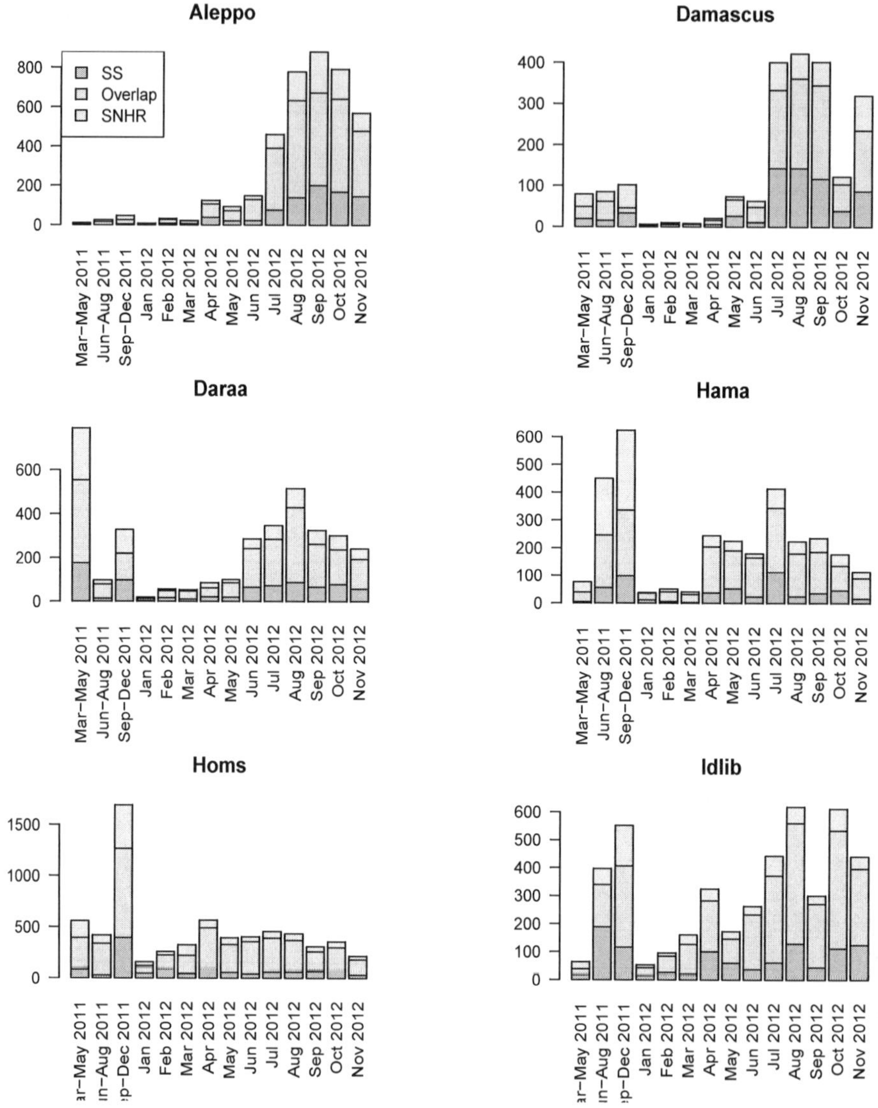

3.4 Patterns of Overlap over Time

This report began with a warning that despite the enormous efforts by the data collecting groups, many killings in the Syrian Arab Republic are still undocumented. One way to imagine that is to consider that in any particular month, some killings are documented by four groups, other killings are documented by three groups, others by two groups, and some killings are reported by only one group. The question this observation raises is: how many killings are reported by zero groups?

Figure 17: Documented Killings by Month and by Number of Sources per Killing

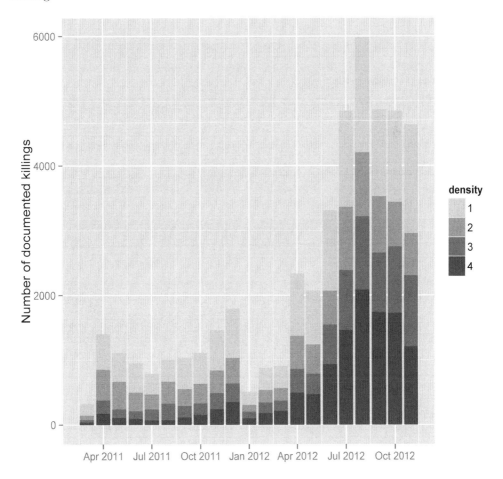

One way to visualize the intensity of reporting is shown in Figure 17 . This graph includes only the killings documented by the four datasets that cover the entire period (SS, VDC, SOHR, and SNHR). In a very informal

sense, as more killings are documented by all four groups, the intuition is that there are fewer undocumented killings. By contrast, when a greater proportion of killings are documented by only one group, the intuition is that there are probably relatively more killings that have not been documented at all. The key observation from Figure 17 is that in all months, at least some killings are reported by only one group (represented by the light pink part at the top of each bar). It is therefore very likely that there are substantial numbers of killings undocumented by these four groups; in practice, many killings may be undocumented by any project. Comparing October and November 2012, note that a higher proportion of killings were documented by four projects in October than in November; similarly, a higher proportion of killings were documented by one project in November than in October. The implication is that there may be more undocumented deaths in November than in October; the true estimate is affected by many additional factors which limit the scope of this simple comparison. In a subsequent report, Benetech will address the question of undocumented killings directly through statistical modeling.

By comparing pairs of datasets over time and space, and by considering the density of overlap over time (and in the future, over space), an analyst can get a better sense of the state of data collection in the Syrian Arab Republic. Statistical modeling and estimation could provide insights about the total magnitude and true pattern of all killings, including those that have not been documented. These comparisons can be used to help individual groups improve their data collection. At a conference in Brussels in early July 2012, hosted by the Euro-Mediterranean Human Rights Network[7], Benetech heard repeatedly that monitoring groups are eager to coordinate their documentation efforts. Benetech is optimistic that most monitoring groups will welcome comparative information like that presented in this report.

---

[7]http://www.euromedrights.org/en/

A   Matching

As mentioned in Section 1, to use the records described in this report, they must be linked together, identifying the records which refer to the same people. This is challenging, since each data source records slightly different information (as indicated by Section 2), not to mention each data source is working to overcome the difficulties inherent in collecting complete, accurate information in the midst of a conflict.

A.1   Non-technical matching overview

The linking together of records within each system is called de-duplication, and identifying the same death across different sources is called record linkage. Both are performed together, by starting with a single list of all records with sufficient information, including sex, age or date of birth, name, and date and location of death.

The records were divided in three groups, called partitions. The first includes data from seven sources (SOHR, SS, VDC, 15 March, SNHR, SRGC, and GoSY) during March to December 2011. The second partition includes six sources (SOHR, SS, VDC, SNHR, SRGC, GoSY) for January to March 2012. The third partition includes four sources (SOHR, SS, VDC, SNHR) for April to November 2012.

From the full list, all possible pairs of records are generated. There are hundreds of millions of possible pairs, and this is much more data than can be processed. To reduce the number of candidate pairs (that is, the set of pairs from which the computer algorithm is identifying plausible pairs) Benetech limits pairs to plausible pairs of records by excluding records that cannot plausibly represent the same person. Rejection rules include differences between records that preclude them from being considered a candidate pair, such as records with different sex, with locations of death that are geographically distant, or with dates that are widely separated in time. The remaining pairs are called candidate pairs: there are 3.8 million candidate pairs in the first partition, 3.0 million in the second partition, and 11.5 million candidate pairs in the third partition.

In the next step, Benetech generated numeric comparisons among all the candidate pairs and all the training set pairs, which is a way to summarize how 'similar' records are in terms of variable name spellings, date of death, date of birth, and location of death. Many different comparisons are done with each field. For example, two dates could be equal; they could vary by a certain number of days; they could be the same date with the month and day fields interchanged; in this project, Benetech considered eighteen comparisons among pairs of records. Then a 'training set' was generated which included a list of both plausible pairs and records identified as non-matches by the rejection rules. A human being (a Syrian expert, in this case) reviewed the training set and classified pairs as referring to the same person (a match) or to different people (a non-match). This data was used to teach the computer how to classify all the pairs as matches or non-matches. The expert examined 8,280 pairs of records for this step in the matching process.

From the numeric comparisons on the training set, Benetech calculated a model which predicts which pairs of records refer to the same person and which refer to different people. The model is calculated from the training set and applied to all the millions of candidate pairs.

With a set of all the pairs identified by the model as matches, the matched pairs are combined into groups of records which all refer to the same person. This process is called clustering. Lastly, the records in each cluster are merged into a single record containing the most precise information available from each of the individual records.

A.2   Matching technical details

Matching databases using partial information has a long history - first formulated by Dunn (1946) and Newcombe et al. (1959), and approached theoretically by Fellegi and Sunter (1969).[8] Specifically, Benetech used the iterated procedure described in Sarawagi and Bhamidipaty (2002). As described in the previous section, the data were divided into three partitions so that different combinations of sources could be matched in each partition. The expert reviewed a total of 8,280 pairs of records drawn from the

---

[8]See the reviews of the problem, called variously "record linkage,", "matching," and "database deduplication" in Winkler (2006) and Herzog et al. (2007). A key method is approximate string distance, see Levenshtein (1966).

various sources (called the "training pairs"). He classified the training pairs as either referring to the same person or to different people. Using the training pairs, Benetech generated a computer model called an Alternating Decision Tree (ADT).[9] Benetech implemented a method for transliterating and comparing names written in Arabic and Latin script developed by Freeman et al. (2006). The model classified all the possible pairs of records from all seven datasets as referring to the same person (a *match*) or to different people (a *non-match*). When tested against the examples, averaged across the partitions, the model classified 92% of the training pairs accurately. In a stratified 10-fold cross-validation, the kappa statistics for the three partitions were 0.78, 0.77, and 0.79, respectively. The pairs were organized into larger groups of records that refer to the same person by a method called "clustering." Benetech used a Hierarchical Agglomerative Clustering algorithm (Manning et al., 2008). Records in each cluster were merged to preserve the most specific information in the group.

References

Dunn, H. L. (1946). Record Linkage. *American Journal of Public Health*, 36(12):1412–1416.

Fellegi, I. P. and Sunter, A. B. (1969). A Theory for Record Linkage. *Journal of the American Statistical Association*, 64(328):1183–1210.

Freeman, A. T., Condon, S. L., , and Ackerman, C. M. (2006). Cross Linguistic Name Matching in English and Arabic: A "One to Many Mapping" Extension of the Levenshtein Edit Distance Algorithm. In *Proceedings of the Human Language Technology Conference of the North American Chapter of the ACL*, pages 471–478.

Freund, Y. and Mason, L. (1999). The Alternating Decision Tree Learning Algorithm. In *Sixteenth International Conference on Machine Learning, Slovenia*.

---

[9] For an overview of machine learning techniques for classification and clustering, as well as a description of the software Benetech used for classification, the Weka software, version 3-7-4 (Hall et al., 2009), see Witten et al. (2011). The ADTree software is documented at http://weka.sourceforge.net/doc/weka/classifiers/trees/ADTree.html. The algorithm for ADT was first described by Freund and Mason (1999) and optimized by Pfahringer et al. (1996).

Hall, M., Frank, E., Holmes, G., Pfahringer, B., Reutemann, P., and Witten, I. H. (2009). The WEKA Data Mining Software: An Update. *SIGKDD Explorations Newsletter*, 11:10–18.

Herzog, T. N., Scheuren, F. J., and Winkler, W. E. (2007). *Data Quality and Record Linkage Techniques*. Springer.

Levenshtein, V. I. (1966). Binary Codes Capable of Correcting Deletions, Insertions, and Reversals. *Soviet Physics Doklady*, 10(8):707–710.

Manning, C. D., Raghavan, P., and Schutze, H. (2008). *Introduction to Information Retrieval*. Cambridge.

Newcombe, H. B., Kennedy, J. M., Axford, S. J., and James, A. P. (1959). Automatic Linkage of Vital Records. *Science*, 130(3381):954–959.

Pfahringer, B., Holmes, G., and Kirkby, R. (1996). Optimizing the Induction of Alternating Decision Trees. In *Fifth Pacific-Asia Conference on Advances in Knowledge Discovery and Data Mining*.

Sarawagi, S. and Bhamidipaty, A. (2002). Interactive Deduplication Using Active Learning. In *KDD '02: Proceedings of the Eighth ACM SIGKDD International Conference on Knowledge Discovery and Data Mining*, pages 269–278. ACM Press.

Winkler, W. E. (2006). Overview of Record Linkage and Current Research Directions. Technical Report RRS2006/02, Statistical Research Division, U.S. Census Bureau.

Witten, I., Frank, E., and Hall, M. (2011). *Data Mining: Practical Machine Learning Tools and Techniques*. Morgan Kaufman.

About the Benetech Human Rights Program

The Benetech Human Rights Program has more than 20 years of experience applying statistical analysis to data about human rights violations. Our expertise has been sought by nine Truth and Reconciliation Commissions, by UN missions and official human rights bodies, by international and domestic criminal tribunals, and by many non-governmental human rights organizations. We have conducted projects in El Salvador, Ethiopia,

Guatemala, Haiti, South Africa, Kosovo, Sierra Leone, Sri Lanka, Timor-Leste, Colombia, Perú, Liberia, and the DR Congo, among others; and provided extensive guidance on data processing and analysis methodologies to non-governmental organizations and partner groups in many countries throughout the world. With our partners, we make scientifically-defensible arguments based on rigorous evidence.[10]

This project was commissioned by the United Nations Office of the High Commissioner for Human Rights (OHCHR). Additional funding was provided by the Sigrid Rausing Trust, the Oak Foundation, and a private, anonymous US-based foundation donor through their core support to the Benetech Initiative.

The materials contained herein represent the opinions of the authors and editors and should not be construed to be the view of the Benetech Initiative, any of Benetech's constituent projects, the Benetech Board of Directors, the donors to Benetech or to this project, or of OHCHR.

---

[10](http://www.benetech.org, http://www.hrdag.org).

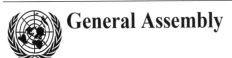

United Nations

General Assembly

A/HRC/18/53

Distr.: General
15 September 2011

Original: English

DOCUMENT 2a

Human Rights Council
Eighteenth session
Agenda item 4
Human rights situations that require the Council's attention   ·

Report of the United Nations High Commissioner for Human Rights on the situation of human rights in the Syrian Arab Republic·**

Summary

The present report has been prepared by the Office of the United Nations High Commissioner for Human Rights pursuant to Human Rights Council resolution S-16/1, in which the Council requested the High Commissioner to dispatch urgently a mission to the Syrian Arab Republic to investigate all alleged violations of international human rights law and to establish the facts and circumstances of such violations and of the crimes perpetrated, with a view to avoiding impunity and ensuring full accountability.

---

*   Late submission.
** For reasons of length, the footnotes in and the annexes to the present report are circulated as received, in the languages of submission only.

Contents

I. Introduction

A. Background

1. Mandate

1.   The fact-finding mission for the Syrian Arab Republic was established by the Human Rights Council in its resolution S-16/1, at the special session convened by the Council in the light of the widespread anti-Government protests in the Syrian Arab Republic and the grave deterioration of the human rights situation.

2.   In resolution S-16/1, the Council called upon the Government of the Syrian Arab Republic to cooperate fully with the mission, including by granting access to its staff. It also condemned the use of lethal violence against peaceful protestors by the Syrian authorities and urged, inter alia, that no reprisals be taken against those taking part in demonstrations, and that the Government launch a credible and impartial investigation and prosecute those responsible for attacks on peaceful protestors.

3.   The Council requested the Office of the United Nations High Commissioner for Human Rights (OHCHR) to dispatch urgently a mission to the Syrian Arab Republic to investigate all alleged violations of international human rights law and to establish the facts and circumstances of such violations and of the crimes perpetrated, with a view to avoiding impunity and ensuring full accountability.

4.   In resolution S-16/1, the Council requested the High Commissioner to provide a preliminary report and an oral update on the situation of human rights in the Syrian Arab Republic at its seventeenth session. It also requested her to submit a follow-up report to the Council at its eighteenth session and, at that session, to organize an interactive dialogue on the situation of human rights in the Syrian Arab Republic. The present report, submitted pursuant to those requests, covers the events in the Syrian Arab Republic since 15 March 2011.

5.   Following the sixteenth special session, the High Commissioner established a mission consisting of 13 members and headed by the Deputy High Commissioner.[1] The mission began its work on 23 May 2011.

2. Dialogue with the Government of the Syrian Arab Republic

6.   In a note verbale dated 6 May 2011, the High Commissioner formally requested the Government of the Syrian Arab Republic to cooperate with the mission. Having received no response from the Government on this matter, the High Commissioner reiterated her request for access to the country in another note verbale, on 20 May 2011, in a meeting with the Permanent Representative of the Syrian Arab Republic to the United Nations Office at Geneva on 7 June 2011, and in a letter to the Prime Minister Adel Safar, on 15 July 2011, to which was annexed a series of questions and requests for information on issues relating to detentions and the administration of justice; torture and ill-treatment; investigations into incidents of killings; and reform measures (annex I).

7.   At the time of writing, the Government of the Syrian Arab Republic had not responded to the requests for access. OHCHR received five notes verbales from the

---

[1] The members of the mission included officials with substantive, technical and administrative expertise in the relevant fields, including human rights investigation, public order issues, forensic expertise and country knowledge.

Permanent Representative of the Syrian Arab Republic to the United Nations Office at Geneva, the contents of which are referred to in this report where relevant (annexes II–VI).[2] On 5 August 2011, OHCHR received a letter from the Government in response to its letter to Prime Minister Safar (annex V). On 16 August, the Permanent Mission addressed a note verbale to the High Commissioner (annex VI).

B. Methodology

8.   The present report covers events in the Syrian Arab Republic from 15 March to 15 July 2011. The mandate took into account the time constraints placed on the mission to complete its work in accordance with the schedule specified by the Human Rights Council.

9.   The failure of the Government of the Syrian Arab Republic to cooperate with OHCHR with regard to access to the country significantly hampered the work of the mission. The present report does not therefore cover all major geographical areas where protests took place, nor is it exhaustive in documenting the many relevant incidents that occurred in the period covered by the mission's mandate. It addresses only the most serious violations.

10.   In June 2011, the mission conducted three field investigations outside the Syrian Arab Republic where reliable and credible information could be obtained from a range of sources, including thousands of Syrian nationals who had fled the country in the preceding weeks. The mission interviewed a total of 180 people in four countries, some of whom were in the Syrian Arab Republic at the time of the interviews. In developing its methodology and implementing its mandate, the mission was guided by the overall concern for protection of victims and witnesses, and took the measures necessary to ensure the confidentiality of their accounts.[3]

11.   The findings in the present report are based primarily on an analysis of first-hand information obtained through interviews conducted with victims and witnesses, consisting of civilians and military personnel, including military defectors, some of whom had refused to follow orders to shoot civilians. The findings are also based on an examination of victims of torture or other forms of ill-treatment whose injuries were still visible, and on the analysis by the mission's forensic physician of the medical reports of wounded persons in hospitals and refugee camps outside the Syrian Arab Republic, most of whom bore firearms injuries. The mission also studied information received through written communications.[4] The mission assessed the credibility of accounts on the basis of consistency among witnesses and the existence of other corroborative accounts. The mission also interviewed witnesses regarding instances in which civilians may have used violence against security personnel or others.

12.   The mission also examined more than 50 videos and numerous photographic images relating to apparent human rights violations, documented in the present report, which were

---

[2]   OHCHR had also received a note verbale dated 15 April 2011 containing references to reforms announced by the Government.

[3]   Interaction with the media was limited to statements issued by the High Commissioner in response to further deterioration in the situation in the Syrian Arab Republic, including on 9 and 15 June 2011. The Deputy High Commissioner gave media interviews in connection with the issuance of the aforementioned preliminary report on 15 June 2011.

[4]   A public call for submissions was posted on the OHCHR website inviting the submission of written communications by individuals. During the period covered by its mandate, the mission received 135 communications, most of which were from Syrian human rights groups or individual activists, addressing issues relating to killings, arrests and torture.

obtained from both private sources and the media. It reviewed information compiled by national and international non-governmental organizations, the media and other information in the public domain. In addition, the mission considered public statements made by Government officials or submitted to OHCHR in the form of notes verbales.

13.   In interpreting its mandate and examining the facts obtained through its investigations, the mission applied an international legal framework. During its investigations, the mission compiled a list of 50 alleged perpetrators at various levels of Government and its agencies in connection with incidents documented herein. This information remains confidential but may be presented by OHCHR in the context of future investigations and possible indictments by a competent prosecutor.

C. Legal framework

1. International human rights law

14.   The Syrian Arab Republic is party to most of the core international human rights treaties, and has made international voluntary pledges, including to "continue working to raise promotion and protection of all human rights and fundamental freedoms".[5] Four of the international instruments ratified by the State and which apply to the events described in the present report are particularly relevant: the International Covenant on Civil and Political Human Rights; the International Covenant of Economic, Social and Cultural Human Rights; the Convention on the Rights of the Child; and the Convention against Torture and Other Cruel, Inhuman or Degrading Treatment or Punishment. The Syrian Arab Republic is not a party to the International Convention for the Protection of All Persons from Enforced Disappearance, although it is bound by the provisions of the International Covenant on Civil and Political Human Rights that also prohibit enforced disappearances.

2. International criminal law

15.   The Syrian Arab Republic signed the Rome Statute of the International Criminal Court on 29 November 2000, but it has yet not ratified it. The Rome Statute establishes four categories of international crimes: war crimes; crimes against humanity; genocide; and the crime of aggression. In the present context, crimes against humanity are particularly relevant to the events in the country since mid-March 2011, in particular the provisions referring to murder, torture, enforced disappearances, persecution, imprisonment or other severe deprivation of physical liberty, and other inhumane acts. Despite non-ratification, the Syrian Arab Republic is still obliged to refrain from acts that would "defeat the objects and purpose of [the] treaty" according to the Vienna Convention on the Law of Treaties (art. 18), to which the State acceded in 1970.

3. Domestic law

16.   While the Constitution of 1973 sets out basic freedoms that reflect international standards, Syrian domestic law cannot be adequately relied on because it violates constitutional guarantees and encourages impunity on two fronts.

17.   First, the Penal Code (Law 148/1949, as amended) sets out various crimes that are broadly defined and may result in the violation of freedom of expression and association, among others. These include "spreading false or exaggerated information with the aim of harming the State", "publishing mendacious information liable to weaken the nation's moral" (arts. 285-286) and "belonging to a secret society that aims to change the State's

---

[5] A/65/784, annex.

political and social structure" (art. 306). While the Code of Criminal Procedure required suspects to be brought before a judicial authority within 24 hours of arrest or released,[6] on 21 April 2011 it was amended to allow for suspects to be held for up to seven days pending investigation and the interrogation of suspects for certain crimes, renewable for up to a maximum of 60 days.[7]

18.   Moreover, the State of Emergency Law[8] provided for the detention of suspects for crimes that are not defined by this or other laws, including "crimes committed against State security and public order" and "crimes committed against public authorities".[9] The Law permitted Government agencies to "monitor all types of letters, phone calls, newspapers... and all forms of expression", to "impose restrictions on the freedom of persons...[to hold] meetings", to "evacuate or isolate certain areas" and to "seize any property or real estate".[10] It also allowed the security forces to hold suspects in preventive detention without judicial oversight for indefinite periods. It should be noted in this respect that, on 21 April 2011, the Syrian authorities lifted the State of Emergency Law and abolished the Supreme State Security Court,[11] even though the law itself remains in force.

19.   Secondly, the security and intelligence agencies, responsible for reported atrocities committed over time and particularly since March 2011, continue to enjoy immunity from prosecution under laws that remain in force under Legislative Decrees Nos. 14/1969 and 69/2008.

D.   Context of protests: political and human rights background

20.   The Constitution of the Syrian Arab Republic confers on the executive authorities sweeping powers that cannot be challenged effectively by the legislature and the judiciary. The President of the Republic selects and dismisses ministers and the Prime Minister; appoints Supreme Court justices; appoints higher civil servants, security and intelligence personnel; dissolves at will the unicameral People's Assembly (parliament); and enjoys parallel legislative privileges allowing him to bypass the Assembly. The executive authorities control most other institutions, including schools, universities, social and health services, student and trade unions, professional organizations and the media.[12] Even though

---

[6] Code of Criminal Procedure, Law No. 112 of 1950 as amended, arts. 104 (1) and (2). The detaining authority violating this provision may be prosecuted for the crime of deprivation of personal liberty (Code of Criminal Procedure, art. 105), punishable by imprisonment for one to three years (Penal Code, art. 358).

[7] Legislative Decree No. 55/2011, amending article 17 of the Code of Criminal Procedure.

[8] Legislative Decree No. 51 of 22 December 1962 introduced the State of Emergency Law, which came into force on 8 March 1963. Article 1 of the Law declared that "a state of emergency may be declared in wartime, in the event of a war-threatening situation or in the event that security or public order in the territories of [the Syrian Arab Republic] or in part thereof is subjected to danger because of internal riots or public disasters". The abolition of the Law, effective upon the adoption of Legislative Decree No. 161 on 21 April 2011, had been one of the protestors' key demands.

[9] State of Emergency Law, art. 6. Other offences include "crimes violating public trust" and "crimes that constitute an overall hazard".

[10] Article 4 (d). The Government laid siege to Dar'a and other cities and towns after the lifting of the emergency law was announced.

[11] Legislative Decree No. 47/1968 established the Supreme State Security Court, which operated outside the framework of the judicial system and whose verdicts were not subject to appeal. It was abolished by Legislative Decree No. 53/2011.

[12] With a few exceptions, "civil society organizations" are also run by individuals close to the ruling group, as is part of the private sector.

the Constitution[13] reflects the predominance of some Baathist military and security officers and their families, members of the ruling group frequently sideline formal hierarchies through informal chains of command. The presidential family and most of the officers belong to the Alawite minority, which, prior to urbanization, was concentrated in the north-west of the country.

21.   Since the 1990s in particular, the Government has been in an alliance of sorts with businesses that were among the principal beneficiaries of economic reforms that emphasized private sector growth. Economic liberalization and growth led to a growing gap between rich and poor, despite the rhetoric about a "social market economy". This was compounded by cuts in social services and subsidies, severe droughts, the rise in global food prices and the negative effects of the recent global financial crisis on remittances received from Syrians working abroad. Structural shortcomings of the economy were never seriously addressed by the Government.

22.   For over four decades, the situation in the country has been characterized by gross human rights violations under the cloak of emergency legislation, in force since 1963. Syrians suffered arbitrary arrests and illegal detentions, prolonged detention without trial or unfair trials before exceptional or military courts, torture and ill-treatment resulting in deaths in custody, forced disappearances and summary executions.[14] The rights to freedom of expression, association and assembly have been systematically violated. The brutality of the country's security forces is notorious, and a number of the security and intelligence agencies act as independent entities and are involved in matters beyond their official functions. They enjoy immunity from prosecution by law (see paragraph 19 above).

23.   When Bashar Al Assad succeeded his father as President in July 2000, hopes were raised that a series of reforms outlined in his inaugural speech, delivered on 17 July 2000, might result in greater political freedoms and civil rights. Debate on possible reforms was tolerated to a limited extent, but was short-lived and the crackdown on political and human rights activists resumed. Promised reforms did not materialize over the next decade.[15] Some of these proposals were resurrected after protests that erupted in March 2011 galvanized anti-Government sentiment nationally and developed into a significant threat to the State.

24.   Economic grievances were particularly strong in traditionally poor areas, including the north-eastern and border areas, such as Dar'a. They also reinforced long-standing issues of discrimination and neglect suffered by specific ethnic and religious groups, notably the Kurds, who inhabit the north-east and who, until March 2011, were deprived of basic civil, economic and social rights.[16] Sunnis often consider themselves marginalized by rulers, who are overwhelmingly Alawites. Various alliances between the rulers and Sunni entrepreneurs

---

[13]   Promulgated by the previous President Hafez Al Assad, father of the current President.

[14]   These violations have been extensively documented over the years by international non-governmental organizations, including Amnesty International and Human Rights Watch, and by the own monitoring mechanisms of the United Nations, including treaty bodies and special procedures of the Human Rights Council. A number of Syrian human rights groups have also documented many of these violations, including the Syrian Committee for Human Rights.

[15]   See "Popular Protest in North Africa and the Middle East (VI): The Syrian People's Slow-motion Revolution", International Crisis Group, Middle East/North Africa Report No.108, 6 July 2011; and "Popular Protest in North Africa and the Middle East (VII): The Syrian Regime's Slow-motion Suicide", Middle East/North Africa Report No.109, 13 July 2011.

[16]   Kurds living in the Syrian Arab Republic have been deprived of Syrian nationality since 1962, as have their descendants. Their statelessness has given rise to other problems relating to personal status and an inability to seek employment in the public sector. They have also been denied basic social and cultural rights. See CRC/C/15/Add.212.

and local notables notwithstanding, resentment is all the stronger given that Sunnis account for some 70 to 75 per cent of the population, and the Alawites 10 per cent.

25.   Initial protests in Dar'a and elsewhere were local responses to specific abuses of power by Syrian officials against the general backdrop of growing economic and political discontent. The partly successful uprisings in other countries in the Middle East provided inspiration and hope, but the non-participatory and highly repressive nature of the Government made it that much harder for people to voice their grievances. Syrians still remember the shelling of Hama in 1982 by security forces, which led to the killing of between 5,000 and 10,000 people.[17] In the absence of legalized opposition parties and independent organizations, discontent was channelled through informal networks and in semi-private contexts. Electronic means of communication and social media also played an important role despite the authorities' efforts to shut them down. Opposition conferences held in June and July 2011 in Antalya and Istanbul, Turkey, revealed tensions between different groups both inside and outside the country. The convening of another conference by key opposition figures in Damascus, in late June 2011, tolerated by the authorities, was contested by some of the younger activists within local coordination committees.

26.   Over several weeks, cautious protests that began in marginalized regions developed into a countrywide uprising. The spread of protests and growing demands – for dignity and reforms, then for the departure of the President – seemed to reflect the failure of a policy combining harsh repression with tardy political concessions.

27. The lifting of the state of emergency was immediately followed by the shooting of peaceful protestors, which continued even as the Government-sponsored national dialogue conference was being held in July 2011; the conference was thus boycotted by the opposition.

E.   Military and security forces implicated in human rights violations since mid-March 2011

28.   Both the armed forces and the security forces have been involved in the suppression of peaceful protests and related violations across the Syrian Arab Republic. The civilian police have also been deployed in urban areas for the purposes of crowd control. In addition, an Alawite civilian militia known as the *Shabbiha* participated in the commission of abuses against civilians.[18] According to multiple accounts obtained by the mission, foreign fighters had been present and active during operations in several locations.[19]

1.   Armed forces

29.   All three corps of the Syrian army[20] are said to have been deployed as support for the security forces in quelling protests since mid-March 2011[21] and to have participated in attacks on anti-Government protests. Witness accounts indicate that the armed forces

---

[17] See *Syria Unmasked: The Suppression of Human Rights by the Asad Regime*, Human Rights Watch, Yale University Press, 1991, pp. 19-21.

[18] There are conflicting accounts regarding the origin of the word *Shabbiha*.

[19] Witnesses claimed that, during raids on mosques and other public places, they heard a foreign language being spoken by some of the armed groups fighting alongside Syrian security forces. Some witnesses did not recognize the language, while others thought it may have been Farsi.

[20] According to the International Institute for Strategic Studies, the Syrian army is estimated at 220,000, including conscripts, with an additional 280,000 reserves. These figures exclude the Air Force, Air Defence and the Navy.

[21] Including the Fourth Armoured Division of the First Corps.

actively participated in the killing of unarmed civilians and in imposing sieges on cities and towns, and were also complicit in the perpetration of collective punishments.

2. Security forces

30.	The agencies identified by the majority of witnesses interviewed by the mission as having played the key role in suppressing peaceful protests since mid-March 2011 are the General Security Directorate (*Idarat Al Mukhabarat Al Amma*), the Political Security Branch (*Shubat Al Amn Al Siyassi*), the Military Intelligence Branch (*Shubat Al Mukhabarat Al Askariyya*) and the Air Force Intelligence Branch (*Shubat Al Mukhabarat Al Jawwiyya*). Security and intelligence agencies are pervasive and are present at all administrative levels of the State.[22] Typically, each agency has a branch in each governorate and a division in each city; some also have units in villages or smaller towns. Many of the victims and witnesses interviewed by the mission identified the heads of the security and intelligence branches in their governorates or cities as having ordered the human rights abuses committed, including summary executions, arbitrary arrests and torture.[23]

3. National Police Force

31.	The civil police personnel of the Ministry of the Interior are divided into several forces, including the riot police, who were deployed to quell protests and demonstrations.[24] They were often on the front lines, usually equipped with shields and helmets with visors and armed with Kalashnikovs, batons and tear gas canisters. During some of the earlier protests, riot police used water cannon and tear gas to disperse crowds.

4. Civilian militias

32.	The *Shabbiha*, led by the security forces, participated in operations against civilian protestors. They are members of the Alawite minority in the Syrian Arab Republic and are closely linked to the ruling Assad family, many of them having belonged to the earlier Defence Brigades (*Saraya Al Difa*).[25] Numerous victims or witnesses stated that members of the *Shabbiha* took part in the crackdown against unarmed civilians in locations including

---

[22]	Two of the main agencies – Military Intelligence and Air Force Intelligence – are nominally part of the Ministry of Defence, and their responsibilities relate to affairs of the Army, and the Air Force and Air Defences, respectively. The Political Security Branch is part of the Ministry of the Interior, and is said to have within its jurisdiction matters relating to political parties, opposition groups, students and State employees, including the police force. The General Security Directorate (formerly known as State Security or *Amn Al Dawla*) is a separate institution that falls outside the framework of any ministry, and its formal responsibilities focus on crimes affecting the internal and external security of the State.

[23]	At the time of writing, the heads of these four agencies were among a number of Syrian officials and others subject to sanctions imposed by the European Union or the Government of the United States of America, or both. See "U.S. Sanctions on Syrian President, Six Senior Officials", U.S. Department of Treasury press release, 18 May 2011; and Council Regulation (EU) No. 442/2011 of 9 May 2011 concerning restrictive measures in view of the situation in Syria, and Council Decision 2011/273/CFSP of 9 May 2011 concerning restrictive measures against Syria, *Official Journal of the European Union*, vol. 54, 10 May 2011.

[24]	Each governorate has its own Police Command, except for Damascus, where there is an additional Police Command for the capital.

[25]	The Defence Brigades were security forces under the command of the late President's brother, Rif'at Al Assad. They were responsible for gross violations of human rights, particularly during the 1980s, including the killing of thousands of civilians and detainees. The members of the *Shabbiha* are generally dressed in civilian clothes and armed with Kalashnikovs or various light weaponry, as well as batons, and are typically identifiable by their shaved heads, thick beards and tattooed arms.

Dar'a, Damascus, Aleppo, Baniyas, Jisr Al Shughour and Ma'arrat an Nu'man, and in widespread looting of homes and commercial property.

II. Facts

33.   At the time of writing, the mission had received more than 1,900 names and details of persons killed in the Syrian Arab Republic since mid-March 2011; all are said to be civilians.[26] According to the Government, "hundreds of public order officers and personnel died and thousand others were injured" in protests during the same period (see annex V).

A.   Details of events since mid-March 2011

1.   Dar'a Governorate

34.   The city of Dar'a, which has a population of approximately 80,000 and is situated in the south-west, near the border with Jordan, witnessed the country's first large-scale protests, triggered by the continued detention of a group of youths and children arrested in February 2011, accused of having written anti-Government slogans on walls. In mid-March, their relatives approached Syrian officials in the city to plead for their release,[27] but they were both rebuffed and insulted. In response, a demonstration was held on 18 March following Friday prayers at the Omari Mosque in Dar'a Al Balad, the old part of the city. Witnesses claimed that security forces, positioned in the square facing the Mosque, sought to quell the protest by firing tear gas, then used live ammunition, killing at least four people. The following day, security forces opened fire on a large group of mourners who had taken part in the funeral procession of the four victims, killing another two.

35.   In the early hours of 23 March, security forces stormed the Omari Mosque, where some 60 protestors were spending the night in tents erected in the courtyard of the Mosque.[28] According to witnesses, security forces shot live ammunition in the direction of the tents, killing at least six people. The next day, several of the mourners who had taken part in the funeral procession for those killed the previous day were also shot dead. On 15 April, several people were killed and others injured when security forces shot demonstrators gathered near the Omari Mosque and the Political Security headquarters.

36.   On 25 April, the army and security forces launched a large-scale military operation, putting Dar'a under siege. Tanks were stationed around the city entrances as the armed forces erected checkpoints and banned movement into and out of the city. A curfew was imposed, electricity and water supplies were cut off, and all means of communication shut down. The security forces then moved through Dar'a Al Balad, conducting house-to-house searches for wanted persons or arresting men at random. Hundreds of people were arrested. Many were routinely beaten during arrest and subsequently tortured while held in Dar'a or Damascus. The siege in its initial form lasted at least two weeks, causing acute shortages of food and water and denying the residents access to medical treatment.

---

[26]   This information is compiled by local coordinating committees active within the Syrian Arab Republic in documenting the names and details of victims. The mission is unable to verify independently this information.

[27]   The officials included the Governor of Dar'a, Faisal Kulthoum, and the head of the local Political Security branch, "Atif Najib".

[28]   The Omari Mosque quickly became the focal point for protests, which began following noon prayers on a daily basis. It was also used as a base for a makeshift medical facility providing treatment and shelter for the injured.

37.　Following these developments, numerous protests were staged elsewhere in the governorate, with inhabitants of nearby villages and towns marching towards Dar'a to demand an end to the siege. One of the largest demonstrations was held on 29 April, when thousands of people headed for Dar'a. Security forces opened fire on the demonstrators, killing at least 60 people, according to multiple witness accounts.

2.　Damascus and Rif Dimashq[29]

38.　The majority of incidents involving violent dispersal of demonstrators and widespread arrests took place in towns and villages in the governorate of Rif Dimashq, including Dumah, Al Tal, Darayya, Dmair and Madaya. Similar incidents took place in several suburbs of Damascus, such as Harasta and Zamalka. In the capital, the heavy security presence militated against larger gatherings, but a number of demonstrations were held nevertheless, followed by waves of arrests.[30]

39.　On 15 March, security forces made a number of arrests during a demonstration in the Souq Al Hamidiyya marketplace in Damascus. The following day, security forces arrested 16 demonstrators who were among some 150 protestors gathered outside the Ministry of the Interior. During another protest, on 18 March, several demonstrators were beaten and arrested as they gathered outside the Omayyad Mosque.

40.　On 25 March, in Dumah, north-west of Damascus, security forces started shooting randomly at civilians as they left a local mosque to begin a protest, reportedly killing 11 demonstrators. Witnesses claimed that the four main security and intelligence agencies (see paragraph 30 above) participated in the operation, and that snipers who were positioned on rooftops targeted the protestors.

41.　On 1 April, around 300 people marched from a mosque in Zamalka, a suburb east of Damascus, and gathered peacefully in a central square. They were soon surrounded by an estimated 500 security personnel, many of whom were dressed in civilian clothes and who proceeded to attack them with electric batons. On 22 April, a demonstration of some 70 people in Damascus in support of the people of Dar'a was violently dispersed by security forces and 30 of the participants arrested. On the same day, a demonstration in Barzeh Al Balad, a suburb in northern Damascus, was repressed violently as security forces, including snipers, reportedly shot at demonstrators.

42.　From 29 April to 2 May, Madaya, a resort town some 40 kilometres north-west of Damascus, was kept under siege. Witnesses described a large military campaign in which more than 2,000 soldiers were deployed to secure the town and set up checkpoints on its outskirts. Security forces as well as the Fourth Armoured Division of the First Corps were present, accompanied by ambulances from the Syrian Red Crescent. After cutting off all means of communication, security forces carried out widespread arrests in the town during house-to-house searches. Scores were arrested either randomly or on the basis of lists of wanted persons. According to witnesses, the detainees were beaten as they were made to

---

[29]　Rif Dimashq, literally "Damascus countryside", is a separate governorate to the capital. It lies south of the governorate of Homs, and is divided into nine districts.

[30]　On 16 February, a spontaneous demonstration took place in the Al Hariqa market in Damascus after a young man was beaten by a police officer. In protest, some 2,000 demonstrators gathered at the scene and refused to disperse until the Minister for the Interior arrived and gave assurances that he would personally investigate the case.

board buses. Most were reportedly transferred to a detention facility in Kafr Sousseh, a south-western suburb of Damascus.[31]

3. Homs Governorate

43.   On 18 March, demonstrations began in Homs, the country's third largest city with a population of 1,500,000, the majority of which are Sunni Muslims, with a Christian minority. Multiple witnesses claimed that security forces identified as the "Anti-Terrorism Unit" of Air Force Intelligence sought to disperse the crowds by shooting in the air and using tear gas. According to one eyewitness, more than 40 protestors were arrested during the demonstration. The ensuing days witnessed several smaller demonstrations in various parts of the city, together with an increased use of live ammunition by security forces and mass arrests to quell protests. On 25 March, thousands of demonstrators took to the streets, some of them heading towards the Officers' Club, where security forces were stationed. Eyewitnesses reported that security forces and the *Shabbiha* fired live ammunition at protestors, while snipers targeted other civilians from rooftops.[32]

44.   On 17 April, 17 demonstrators were reportedly killed after thousands gathered in the city centre, partly in response to the death in custody of a tribal leader a few days earlier. One eyewitness stated that the security forces gave no warning before targeting the protestors, and that he saw a teenager next to him get shot. Several thousand protestors participated in demonstrations the following day to mourn those deaths. The Syrian authorities stated that three army officers, including a brigadier general, together with his two sons and a nephew, were killed by Salafist groups (see annex IV).

45.   On 5 May, the Syrian army was deployed to Bab Amr in Homs Governorate, to quell what was described as an insurrection by Salafist armed groups.[33] According to a witness, the whole area was surrounded and orders were given to break into all houses and kill all members of armed gangs.[34] Dozens of people were reportedly killed in the operation, during which soldiers also received orders to plant weapons at a local mosque.[35] The following day, the division was ordered to besiege the town of Talbisa in preparation for a similar security operation to "cleanse" the area of armed gangs using tanks, armoured vehicles and troops. During the operation, three officers and 20 civilians were reportedly killed.

46.   A large-scale military operation was launched on 25 May in the town of Ar Rastan, where "armed gangs" were still allegedly operating, and demonstrators had reportedly

---

[31] Some of those detained were later released after being brought before an investigative judge, who ordered their release. Some of the accusations levelled against them included "demeaning the dignity of the country", "disrupting the peace of the nation" and "weakening the spirit of the nation".

[32] One eyewitness claimed that the *Shabbiha* had been brought in to support security forces in larger demonstrations. They reportedly targeted demonstrators, directly causing a significant number of casualties. The same account details how the *Shabbiha* prevented the transport of those killed by ambulances, but instead removed them to an unknown location. Fire-fighter trucks then cleaned the bloodstains using water cannon.

[33] According to the witness statements, the orders received referred to a Salafist insurrection.

[34] In order to cover the whole area, the division broke into groups, each composed of roughly 100 soldiers. Each group was accompanied by six to eight members of the *Shabbiha*, to undertake what was described as the "dirty work". The witness claimed that the soldiers were given no information on how members of the armed gangs could be identified.

[35] Witnesses claimed that, as the troops were pulling back from Bab Amr, they broke into the mosque in the area, reportedly killing the imam and then planting arms there. They added that the security forces then arranged for the arms cache to be filmed by Syrian television and for it to be reported that armed gangs had hidden weapons in the mosque.

toppled the statue of the late President Assad. Highly consistent accounts given by witnesses described the events there. The armed forces surrounded the town, controlling all points of access with tanks and armoured vehicles to prevent the entry of food and medical supplies.[36] The town was divided into two operational zones. Inside each zone, rows of soldiers pushed through the different areas, preceded by officers. Behind each unit there were groups of six to eight *Shabbiha* members, allegedly ready to shoot any soldier who looked back or refused to obey orders. Soldiers broke into homes and looted, shooting indiscriminately at cars and passers-by, and damaging property. Many of the inhabitants of Ar Rastan fled to nearby fields to hide, but were pursued, and numerous people were killed. Several of the witness accounts also referred to the killing of army officers by unidentified sniper fire during the operation.[37]

4.   Hama Governorate

47.   On 22 April, eight people were believed to have been killed in Hama, a city located north of Damascus with a population of some 700,000, in the first known instance of security forces firing at demonstrators with live ammunition in the city. A larger demonstration on 27 May involving thousands of people took place without any reported casualties, although elsewhere in the Governorate, mass arrests, indiscriminate shooting and looting by security forces were reported. For example, on 12 April, the village of Al Bayda (south-east of the city of Al Ladhiqiyya but part of the Governorate of Hama) was the scene of destruction and looting as a military operation was launched to rid it of "terrorist gangs". It resulted in the arrest of some 400 inhabitants, some of whom were beaten and humiliated upon arrest. According to witnesses, the armed forces deployed from Baniyas to Al Bayda received orders to shoot indiscriminately upon entering the village, said to be under the control of "terrorist groups". Security forces also took part. Video footage examined by the mission showed scores of civilians rounded up and made to lie on the ground. Some were beaten, including one man who had a bullet wound in his back. All were then taken to an unknown destination. They were eventually released following protests by their families, apparently bearing injuries consistent with the infliction of torture.

48.   On 3 June, some 50,000 protestors gathered in the Al Asi square in the centre of Hama. Security was extensive in the vicinity of the square to prevent protestors from entering. A security officer gestured to the protestors, warning them not to approach the security perimeter. A few protestors managed to get through and handed flowers to some of the security officers as a gesture of peace and the rejection of violence. As they turned back, security forces fired on the protestors, who ran or threw themselves to the ground. At the same time, numerous security officers, identified by witnesses as Military Intelligence personnel, descended from vans and took up position in the vicinity of the square and the surrounding buildings.[38] Other accounts confirmed that snipers, dressed in black and stationed on top of the Baath party building, started shooting at demonstrators from the opposite direction. In the aftermath of the shooting, witnesses described a chaotic scene in which demonstrators removed some of the injured on motorcycles where available, while others had to be left behind. A heavy security presence in the area, coupled with sniper fire,

---

[36]   The scale and intensity of the campaign was markedly greater than in earlier operations. Witnesses reported that they had been told that Ar Rastan was "infested with armed groups".

[37]   According to Human Rights Watch, 41 people were killed during the operations in Ar Rastan. Accounts from eyewitnesses suggest that the figures may be significantly higher. The military operation lasted until 2 June, but was most intense during the first 48 hours.

[38]   Some witnesses reported that security personnel were hiding in a nearby orphan's shelter, and that they attacked demonstrators as they approached the square. Many described this incident as a trap in which demonstrators were confined to narrow alleyways with no means of escape.

prevented the transport of the wounded to hospitals for treatment. In one incident, between 20 and 25 demonstrators reportedly bled to death in the Um Al Hassan garden area as no one could reach them.[39] Dozens of demonstrators were reportedly killed, while others who were wounded were said to have died owing to the lack of adequate or timely medical attention.[40]

49.   According to many accounts, the heightened tensions in Hama after 3 June led the security forces to withdraw from the streets to avoid any further friction with protestors.[41] In the ensuing weeks, tens and sometimes hundreds of thousands of demonstrators took to the streets in Hama (an estimated 200,000 people participated in a demonstration in the city on 24 June) with no visible security presence. This relative calm was broken by a series of night raids on homes that began on 3 July.[42] Among those targeted were activists and organizers of demonstrations in the Hader and Al Sabouniyah neighbourhoods. Witnesses confirmed that security forces raided homes and arrested individuals on the basis of lists of names, and looted and damaged property at the same time. According to multiple accounts, at least 22 civilians were killed in the period leading up to 8 July during search and arrest operations.

5.   Idlib Governorate

50.   The largest demonstrations in Idlib Governorate took place in the towns of Jisr Al Shughour and Ma'arrat an Nu'man. Protests were also organized from the surrounding villages into the towns.[43] The section below describes incidents reported in Al Mastuma, Saraqeb, Jisr Al Shughour and Ma'arrat an Nu'man.[44] Most of the incidents involved the killing of peaceful demonstrators by security forces using live ammunition.[45]

51.   On 20 May, demonstrators heading for the town of Ariha were met with security forces based at a Baath party youth camp in the village of Al Mastuma, several kilometres south of Idlib. Witnesses described a peaceful march by demonstrators carrying olive branches, who were however fired upon with live ammunition without warning. Some of the estimated 20 security personnel had hidden behind trees, while others were positioned on rooftops.[46] An estimated 200 people were injured and 30 killed, some of whom were reportedly "finished off" with knives as they lay on the ground. Some of the witnesses assisted in collecting the bodies and taking the injured to hospital, adding that they were turned away at the hospital in Ariha. One witness claimed that he attended the funeral of a demonstrator who had the word *Maher* – in reference to Maher Al Assad, brother of the President – carved into his stomach.

---

[39] Eyewitnesses reported having found the bodies of the demonstrators in the Um Al Hassan garden area with pools of blood around them, suggesting they had bled to death.

[40] Some of the injured reportedly refused to go to public hospitals because they feared that they would be arrested by security officers stationed there.

[41] To this end, security forces removed a statue of former President Al Assad from the city centre, both to avoid further clashes and to prevent it being attacked and toppled by protestors.

[42] The security forces carrying out the arrests were believed to belong to Political Security and Military Intelligence.

[43] A number of predominantly Alawite villages in the area did not participate in the protests.

[44] Details of incidents reported in Ariha, Sallet Al Zuhour and other locations researched by OHCHR are not given in the present report.

[45] Several of those injured were examined by the mission's forensic physician during a field visit to Turkey.

[46] Some of the personnel wore dark green military uniforms, while others were dressed in black. The latter had shaved heads and long beards and, according to witnesses, looked "foreign".

52.   On 10 June, military forces were deployed to Idlib Governorate to, according to the accounts of several soldiers who took part, regain control of several towns and villages from "armed groups" linked to "the Muslim Brotherhood" and "Salafist groups".[47] A witness claimed that the forces, equipped with modern weaponry and more than 100 vehicles, including tanks, arrived that evening in the town of Saraqeb, south of Idlib city.[48] Demonstrators were seen chanting "freedom, freedom"; some of them were children who tried to climb on top of the military vehicles. Others called on the soldiers to go back and not to kill them. The witness claimed that he overheard a captain receiving instructions from a superior officer to "spray them with bullets", and that several soldiers approached their superiors because they were facing unarmed civilians, including women and children. The officer stated that the orders were to shoot to kill and those who refused would themselves be killed.[49]

53.   Some of the most serious events witnessed in Idlib Governorate took place in Jisr Al Shughour, between Aleppo and Al Ladhiqiyya, some 20 kilometres from the border with Turkey. Protests that began on 18 March passed without incident until 30 April, when, according to witnesses, some 38 to 40 people from the town were arrested during house raids. They were released following a large demonstration on 2 May, and subsequently walked through the streets without their shirts to show injuries sustained under torture. On 13 May, the Baath party building in the town was torched by unidentified persons during a demonstration, in which helicopters were seen overhead firing at the demonstrators.[50] The demonstration was held in response to an earlier incident involving the killing of 11 people and the wounding of three others travelling in a van heading to Jisr Al Shughour from Homs.[51]

54.   On 3 June, a crowd of 30,000 protestors marched through Jisr Al Shughour. According to witnesses, security personnel used tear gas and fired in the air to disperse the crowd. The following day, some 20,000 people gathered at a public garden in the town,

---

[47] Witnesses referred to a "blockade of information", that ordinary rank and file soldiers had no idea what was happening when they were deployed, and that they had not been allowed leave for several months and were confined to their barracks in between operations.

[48] The witness reported that he had been told that "terrorists had infiltrated Syria and the population needed help to resist these groups who were committing acts of violence".

[49] According to the witness, at this stage, shooting broke out among the soldiers themselves and he fled. He had to run towards the demonstrators, since the *Shabbiha* were positioned behind the lines with instructions to shoot anyone who deserted or refused to obey orders. Another witness to the same events added that, after the operations, checkpoints were set up on the Idlib road and that he witnessed military personnel killing at point blank range three car passengers at one such checkpoint. The witness also noted during this incident the presence of *Shabbiha* members, claiming that they had shaved heads and long beards. He reported that others spoke in a foreign language or in broken Arabic. Upon deciding to leave the army, he learned that seven others who had attempted the same had been killed.

[50] It remains unclear who was responsible for setting the building on fire. Some witnesses claimed demonstrators were responsible, while others said it was Ba'ath Party officials themselves who set fire to the premises as they vacated it. Video footage of the incident appears to support the latter version.

[51] On 8 May, a van carrying 17 passengers returning from Lebanon and heading to Jisr Al Shughour was attacked near Homs. The van was fired upon from two directions as it became trapped between two checkpoints. The army reportedly claimed that the van failed to stop at the first checkpoint and alerted soldiers manning the second. Photographs obtained by the mission show the vehicle riddled with bullet holes. According to the victims' relatives, the bodies of those killed were returned to them some 10 days later, and that they were pressured into signing documents stating that the attack had been carried out by "terrorists". In its note verbale of 5 August 2011 (annex V), the Government denied these allegations.

near the post office, for the funeral of Basel Al Masri, a protestor killed the previous evening. Al Masri was found dead with three bullet wounds, and a friend with him at the time was injured. After the funeral, one of the participants, Hassan Malesh, was killed while making a speech from a platform in the middle of the crowd. According to witnesses, he was shot dead by snipers positioned on the roof of the nearby post office.[52] This was quickly followed by more shooting with live ammunition from the direction of the post office and adjacent security buildings. Witnesses claimed that helicopters were also used in the operation to fire on the crowds. The mission obtained the names of 14 people killed on that day. One witness stated that he took seven bodies in his car to his home village and placed them in the refrigerator of a vegetable shop, as the hospitals were controlled by security forces. According to a witness, 17 soldiers who refused orders were killed by a senior security official. Some witnesses told the mission that the official was later killed, together with several other Alawite security personnel, following their capture by protestors, while others said he had been killed by a soldier. The mission was not able to investigate these accounts further. There were more killings the following day, when security and military personnel fired on demonstrators heading for Jisr Al Shughour in an area called Sahl Al Ghab.[53]

55.   On 6 June, the Minister of Interior, Muhammad Ibrahim Al Sha'ar, announced on national television that the authorities intended to act decisively against "any armed attack" in Jisr Al Shughour. Shortly thereafter, many of the town's residents headed towards the border with Turkey, fearing reprisals and further violence by the security forces.[54] A witness reported that two army brigades advanced towards Jisr Al Shughour on 8 June to lay siege, and were stationed at the town's sugar factory.[55] Jisr Al Shughour was virtually deserted when the army entered it on 13 June, together with selected media and invited guests to witness what the authorities described as an operation to liberate the town from armed gangs.[56]

56.   The town of Ma'arrat Al Nu'man, located on the highway connecting Aleppo and Hama, witnessed a number of protests during which security forces used live ammunition against unarmed civilians. Regular demonstrations were held by residents of the town and nearby villages, initially in support of the people of Dar'a. Witnesses stated that, initially, the demonstrations were held without any killings, despite the presence of security forces. In one instance, water cannon were used to disperse demonstrators, and *Shabbiha* members dressed in civilian clothes beat up some of the participants. On 13 May, security forces attempted to disperse demonstrators gathered on the highway outside the town, using tear gas. According to witnesses, when this failed to halt the advance, security forces fired live

---

[52] Some witnesses stated that the basement of the post office had been used by security personnel for the interrogation of suspects.

[53] Other witnesses claimed that, at that stage, armed clashes broke out between the group of soldiers, who attempted to flee, and the security forces. The witnesses added that two helicopters providing backup began firing at both the civilians and the fleeing soldiers. Some of the civilians managed to flee to Jisr Al Shughour safely. The mission interviewed one of the civilians wounded after the helicopters began shooting at the crowd, and another civilian who was injured as he made his way to Jisr Al Shughour.

[54] Military and security forces had reportedly gathered some 20 kilometres outside the town.

[55] According to other witnesses, the sugar factory was used in that period as the headquarters for armed forces deployed from other areas, as well as for the interrogation, detention and torture of suspects. Several sources also reported that four girls were raped at that location, although the mission was unable to corroborate these accounts.

[56] On 6 June, Syrian television reported that members of security forces had been killed in several attacks, including during an ambush by "armed gangs" operating in Jisr Al Shughour, where clashes took place at a security centre and other Government buildings were set alight.

ammunition at the demonstrators. One of the witnesses, who was injured while trying to help others, said he was taken to a private hospital, because many feared that the State-run hospitals were unsafe. Others were treated in private homes.

57. Further violence erupted during a larger demonstration on 20 May, when tear gas, hand grenades and live ammunition were used to quell the protest. In addition, snipers also fired on the crowd from positions on several buildings, including the Al Masri Mosque. Witnesses claimed that the armed forces and special police forces took part in this operation, and that *Shabbiha* members were also present to shoot anyone who disobeyed orders.[57] The security forces erected roadblocks, which were later used to trap demonstrators. In turn, demonstrators burned tyres and erected makeshift roadblocks to try to prevent the security forces from advancing.[58] In one incident, a witness who had been injured said a soldier tried to help him by gesturing him to leave, but he was seen by another soldier, who came up behind him and shot him in the head. Protestors nearby tried to pull the soldier away to safety to save him, but other soldiers approached and wrenched the body away as protestors threw stones at them. The injured witness escaped and was taken to a clinic in a village, where he said many wounded people had arrived from Al Mastuma. Others with more serious injuries requiring surgery were taken across the border to Turkey. The public hospital in Ma'arrat an Nu'man was closed during that period.

58. Two other large demonstrations were held in Ma'arrat an Nu'man, on 3 and 10 June. Thousands gathered in the street, and in both instances witnesses claimed that security forces fired live ammunition at the demonstrators without warning or instructions to disperse.[59] In addition to sniper fire, tanks were brought in; one witness saw firing from one or more of the five helicopters she counted. According to witness accounts, security forces reportedly shot dead some of the injured at point blank range as they lay on the ground. The injured had to be transferred to other locations outside the town, as most believed they would come to more harm in public hospitals controlled by security forces.

6. Other governorates

59. Baniyas in Tartus Governorate witnessed its first demonstration on 18 March, when protestors gathered outside the Rahman Mosque and headed for the city centre. The police and local sheikhs noted down a list of the protestors' grievances, but a week later, on 25 March, violence erupted, leading to casualties. According to witnesses, water cannon were used by security forces to disperse a crowd outside the Abu Bakr Mosque. Security forces, together with *Shabbiha* members and snipers, began shooting at people as they emerged from the mosque. At least three were killed and others were wounded. Three of the *Shabbiha* members were reportedly subsequently killed, when their car was intercepted by a group of demonstrators and torched. Other incidents involving the killing or wounding of civilians occurred during demonstrations held in April. On 7 May, military forces were deployed to Baniyas to lay siege to the city, accompanied by tanks and helicopters.

60. In the city of Al Ladhiqiyah (capital of Al Ladhiqiyah Governorate, located on the Mediterranean coast in the north-west of the Syrian Arab Republic), two demonstrations

---

[57] One witness gave an account of the killing of a soldier by a *Shabbiha* member.

[58] Several witnesses identified a key security official, who was reportedly responsible for much of the violent reaction towards demonstrators. Other witnesses identified the same person in the context of killings in Jisr Al Shughour on 4 June.

[59] Witnesses described the forces as dressed in both army and police uniforms. Many also referred to *Shabbiha* members dressed in black civilian clothes. Others said "foreigners" were present, also wearing black.

were held, on 18 and 25 March, without any confrontation with security forces.[60] During a demonstration on 26 March, security forces fired at demonstrators when they tried to topple a statue of the President.[61] Witnesses said *Shabbiha* members fought alongside the security forces, reportedly attacking some of the demonstrators with knives. A demonstration on 8 April was described as particularly bloody, although witnesses were unable to say how many demonstrators were killed or injured. They claimed that, after the shooting stopped, garbage trucks were brought in by the security forces to pick bodies up off the streets.

61.   The demonstrations in Aleppo began on 15 March, but have been largely confined to student demonstrations in the city's university. Several such demonstrations were held in April and May, mostly at night. According to witness accounts, some demonstrations were broken up by military and security forces in combination with other groups said to have been "recruited" for this purpose.[62] One of the larger demonstrations took place on 30 June, when over 400 students were said to have been arrested.

62.   In the governorate of Dayr Az Zawr, located in the east of Syria and sharing a border with Iraq, smaller demonstrations were first organized in mid-March, but grew larger over several weeks. According to witness accounts, security and intelligence personnel regularly filmed the protestors for the purposes of identification, and numerous arrests were made. In the demonstrations held on 20 April and 27 May, during which snipers were positioned on rooftops, witnesses said demonstrators were dispersed with tear gas and shots in the air.

63.   The governorate of Al Hasakah, a predominantly Kurdish region located in the north-east and sharing borders with both Turkey and Iraq, witnessed demonstrations in a number of locations, including in the cities of Al Hasakah, Al Qamishli, Ra's al 'Ayn and Amouda. The demonstrations, which were relatively small, called for basic civil and political rights for the Kurdish minority in the Syrian Arab Republic. According to witnesses, the security forces refrained from using lethal force in this region, but infiltrated some of the protests to identify activists. A small number were arrested but later released, apparently after signing documents in which they pledged not to participate in future demonstrations.

B.   Response of the Government

64.   The Government of the Syrian Arab Republic has addressed five notes verbales to OHCHR in relation to the mandate of the mission. Although the Government has continued to cooperate with OHCHR, it did not grant the mission access to the country.

65.   On 30 March, President Assad announced his intention to introduce a raft of reforms, including the lifting of emergency laws, the abolition of the Supreme State Security Court and amnesties for certain prisoners and detainees. The proposed reforms included legislation to regulate the right to peaceful assembly and the establishment of political parties, as well as the establishment of committees to draft electoral and

---

[60] According to nine witnesses who later fled to Turkey, on 18 March, , the demonstrators walked towards Al Shaikh Daher square carrying olive branches. There were no clashes with security forces, but some altercations took place with scores of Alawite residents who tried to prevent the demonstrators from reaching the square.

[61] Witnessed stated that some of the forces firing at them were dressed in military uniform, others in civilian clothes, and others in black fatigues.

[62] In one instance, witnesses claimed that armed groups belonging to a local clan referred to in the accounts as *baltajiyya* (literally "axe carriers", but closer in meaning to "thugs") took part in breaking up protests and intimidating the demonstrators. The mission was unable to further investigate this claim.

information laws. At least two new laws have since been promulgated, and a decree was issued in April to regulate the status of Syrian Kurds.[63] In a note verbale dated 9 June 2011 (see annex II), the Government pointed out that, in early June, a decision was taken to establish a committee for national dialogue. In the same note verbale, it announced that a judicial committee had been established to investigate and bring to justice all perpetrators of crimes against protestors and security personnel in Dar'a on 31 March 2011. It also stated that the mandate of the committee had been recently extended to investigate all crimes committed against civilians, as well as security and army personnel, throughout the country.

66.   At various times, Syrian officials, including President Assad (such as during an address to Damascus University on 20 June 2011), acknowledged the legitimacy of certain demands by protestors, drawing a distinction between those with legitimate demands and those aiming to destabilize the country. In its note verbale dated 27 June 2011 (see annex IV), the Government claimed that those aiming to destabilize the country had used legitimate protests as a cover for acts of sabotage. The Government maintained that these groups had attacked "a large number of innocent civilians and security forces" and were seeking to create "sectarian rifts" and "overthrow the regime and establish Salafist emirates". According to the Government, 260 members of the armed and security forces had been killed and a further 8,000 injured in the period up to late June 2011.

67.   In its note verbale dated 5 August 2011 (see annex V), the Ministry of Foreign Affairs responded to questions by OHCHR and provided information pertaining to, inter alia, existing criminal legislation; laws granting full citizenship rights to Kurds; the adoption of parliamentary decrees to end the state of emergency; the granting of a general amnesty, which, according to the Government, has led to the release of 10,433 detainees; and the adoption of new electoral laws. The Ministry also referred to the conduct of Syrian authorities, and provided figures of cases of torture before the Syrian courts. In the same note, it claimed that the Government had established a commission to investigate allegations of crimes in the context of the ongoing events in the Syrian Arab Republic. The commission was established pursuant to decision No. L/905 of 31 March 2011 issued by the Deputy President of the Judiciary Council. The commission comprises, inter alia, the Attorney General of the Syrian Arab Republic, as Chairperson; the Head of the Judicial Inspection Department; the First Prosecutor of Damascus; and the First Investigative Judge of Damascus. The commission has been mandated to investigate into the circumstances leading to the death of a number of civilians and military personnel in Dar'a and Latakia. According to the information given in the note verbale, the commission has gathered statements from a number of witnesses in Dar'a and investigated individual allegations. Those investigated have included the former Governor of Dar'a and members of the security forces. In reference to the matter of mass graves, the Ministry noted that some armed "terrorist groups" had attacked a police station in Jisr Al Shughour with live ammunition, killing all police personnel. According to the Ministry, the corpses were then removed by bulldozers, piled up and buried in mass graves.

68.   OHCHR shared the report of the mission with the Permanent Mission of the Syrian Arab Republic on 10 August for comments. The Permanent Mission addressed a note verbale to OHCHR on 16 August (see annex VI), in which it pointed out that the Government abided by international human rights law and had embarked on a series of thorough reforms. It added that those who provided information to the mission in refugee camps had breached Syrian law and therefore could not be considered reliable sources. The

---

[63] Legislative Decree No. 49, adopted on 7 April 2011. Article 1 states that individuals registered as foreigners in the Al Hasakah Governorate shall be granted Syrian nationality.

Government criticized the role of the media in distorting the facts, and claimed that the reference to a "repressive minority" in the report was unacceptable. It also claimed that this particular reference demonstrated the biased approach of the mission. According to the note verbale, the reference to 1,900 people killed in the country was correct. However, it added that the figure included police and security officers, as well as victims of terrorist armed groups. The Government also explained that 120 police officers had been brutally killed in Jisr-el Shoughour by armed groups.

III. Patterns of violations

69.   The mission found a pattern of human rights violations constituting widespread or systematic attacks against the civilian population, which may amount to crimes against humanity, as provided for in article 7 of the Rome Statute of the International Criminal Court.

A.   Murder and disappearances

70.   Following the widespread killing of civilians by Government-controlled security forces, the Syrian Arab Republic has grossly violated the non-derogable right to life, enshrined in article 6 of the International Covenant on Civil and Political Rights.

71.   The mission gathered corroborative eyewitness statements on numerous summary executions, including 353 named victims. In addition, the mission found corroborative accounts indicating that members of the security forces posed as civilians in order to cause unrest and to depict an inaccurate view of events. Civilians were often able to distinguish themselves from members of the security forces, who wore colour-coded armbands.[64] Several types of security forces and the army were deployed to the demonstrations, but were clearly not trained in crowd control.

72.   While violent incidents have been caused by a minority of civilians in some demonstrations,[65] the disproportionate use of force by military and security forces are a violation of the State's international human rights obligations.

73.   Reports from a wide variety of sources assert that the demonstrations were mostly peaceful. Civilians of all ages participated in protests and often carried olive branches or bared their chests to show that they were unarmed. Government-controlled media channels reported these events inaccurately, in most cases attributing disturbances to "terrorist" elements.[66] Most killings reported were due to live ammunition fired by security forces, the military and *Shabbiha* members using Kalashnikovs and other guns.[67] Reports from witnesses indicate that there was a widespread modus operandi to kill civilians by using (a) forces on the ground; (b) snipers on rooftops; and (c) air power.

---

[64] According to some reports, various security units would even at times shoot at each other.

[65] For example, the mission received uncorroborated accounts from Baniyas and Jisr Al Shughour of the killing of security or other officials by demonstrators or unidentified persons.

[66] For example, there are corroborated reports that security forces planted weapons in the Omari Mosque in the city of Dar'a after clearing it and murdering civilians, then blamed innocent demonstrators. For the version of the Syrian Arab News Agency (DARA), see www.sana.sy/eng/337/2011/04/27/343519.htm.

[67] In several incidents documented by the mission, *Shabbiha* members used knives or bayonets to kill protestors.

74.   Consistent with an apparent shoot-to-kill policy, most of the bullet wounds found in victims were in the head, chest and general upper body area. Interviews were conducted with a number of former soldiers who had deserted the army, the police and different branches of the security forces. They claimed that they had received clear orders to use live ammunition against protestors.[68] Those who refused to shoot civilians were shot from behind by other security officers and *Shabbiha* units. An analysis by the mission's public order expert of video footage showing security operations revealed the lack of training in riot control by most of the forces deployed against civilians. This was compounded by weaponry that facilitated the excessive use of force against civilians.

75.   On the ground, officers often fired indiscriminately at civilians, at close range and without warning.[69] Many children and women were killed. In only a few demonstrations were non-lethal methods used: tear gas, water cannon and the firing of live ammunition into the air. Some of the demonstrations involved the indiscriminate use of rapid and intense ammunition fire at the same time as, or shortly after, the use of tear gas. Corroborative reports from different regions indicate that soldiers deserted after being ordered to fire on peaceful civilians.[70]

76.   Witnesses attested to the use of tanks, heavy machine guns mounted on anti-personnel carriers and helicopters in urban areas. Security forces also used rocket-propelled grenades and grenade launchers mounted on AK47s against civilians in other areas.

77.   Summary executions were also reported outside the context of demonstrations. For example, on 1 May, in Dar'a, it is alleged that some 26 men were blindfolded and summarily shot at the football stadium, which had been transformed into the local security forces headquarters. Executions were also reported during the sieges of cities and house-to-house searches.[71]

78.   Given that it was not permitted to visit the country, the mission was unable to verify repeated allegations that civilians were routinely and summarily executed in hospital (or make-shift hospital) beds by security forces. However, it was widely reported that forces conducted regular raids in hospitals to search for and kill injured demonstrators. The mission observed a high and consistent degree of fear among civilians of going to hospitals, with many preferring to remain untreated rather than risk being captured and killed.

79.   There was a clear pattern of snipers shooting at demonstrators,[72] including reports that officers were specially trained to deal with civilian demonstrations. Buildings where snipers were positioned included premises belonging to the security forces, Government or Baath party buildings, and mosques. In most cases, no warnings were given before opening fire. In some instances, snipers apparently even targeted people trying to evacuate the wounded.

---

[68]   Witness stated that the orders at Saraqeb, and near the camp of the Youth of the Baath Party in Al Mastuma, were given on 20 May 2011, when security forces opened fire at demonstrators as soon as they arrived, killing more than 40 people.

[69]   Early on when the protests began, instances were reported of attempted negotiation by security or military personnel seeking to disperse the crowds. In most cases, such attempts were brief. As the situation on the ground worsened, such tactics gave way to direct attacks with live ammunition.

[70]   Many of these soldiers were shot dead immediately upon breaking ranks during demonstrations, and some were killed or treated inhumanely for being suspected of disloyalty towards the Government.

[71]   Including at Dar'a, Al Ladhiqiyah, Hamah and Jisr Al Shughour.

[72]   For example, in Dar'a, Jisr Al Shughour, Banias, Al Ladhiqiyya and Duma.

80.   Civilians were shot at by security officers from helicopters, deployed to various demonstrations.[73] No warnings were given before opening fire.

81.   Victims and witnesses reported widespread attempts to cover up killings by the security forces, including the use of mass graves.[74] In Al Ladhiqiyah, on 8 April, garbage trucks were seen collecting dead bodies. Civilians stored murdered victims in makeshift refrigerators during the sieges.[75] There were several reports, however, of security forces killing injured victims by putting them into refrigerated cells in hospital morgues.[76]

82.   The Syrian Arab Republic has violated its obligations under the International Covenant on Civil and Political Rights relating to enforced disappearances, particularly articles 2, 6, 7, 9, 10 and 14, and other articles relating to freedom. Many civilians, including children, have disappeared. Some bodies were returned to their families, many bearing marks of torture. The fate and whereabouts of hundreds of detainees remain unknown. Meanwhile, the mission continues to receive reports of enforced disappearances.

B.   Torture

83.   Of the 180 witness accounts taken by the mission, 98 revealed torture and other inhuman and degrading treatment of civilians by military and security forces, which violate the State's obligations under the Convention against Torture. A clear widespread or systematic policy appears to have been in place whereby security forces targeted people suspected of participating in demonstrations, with a view to intimidating and terrorizing them as a way to quell protests.[77] Torture and ill-treatment were commonly used to obtain false statements from detainees. Many reports spoke of security forces breaking into homes and beating civilians, including women and children. After mass arrests, security forces and *Shabbiha* members transported detainees in buses and trucks to secret detention centres or public stadiums, where the victims were then inhumanely treated or tortured.[78] Many victims were repeatedly subjected to torture upon their transfer from one detention facility to another.[79] Former detainees cited cases of death in custody as a result of torture. Others referred to the torture of children.[80] Security agents often forced family members of the deceased to sign a document stating that the person had been killed by armed gangs.

84.   The mission documented numerous methods of torture, most of which are known to have been used in the Syrian Arab Republic over many years. They include severe beatings, electric shocks, suspension for long periods by the limbs, psychological torture and routine

---

[73] Including Jisr a-Shughour and Ma'arrat Al Nu'man, in Idlib Governorate.

[74] The locations of alleged mass graves will not be disclosed until they can be secured or properly exhumed.

[75] For example, in Dar'a, bodies that could not be buried during the siege were stored in a refrigerated food truck.

[76] One of the cases reported to the mission took place in Dar'a.

[77] In Dar'a, Nawa, Al Yaduda, Jisr Al Shughour, Madaya, Homs, and Hama, among others.

[78] Detention centres cited in accounts and located in or around Damascus include Kafr Soussah, Al Mezze, Adra and Al Qaboun; other cited detention facilities were in Idlib and Homs. Most appeared to be under the jurisdiction of one of the security agencies, including Air Force Intelligence, Military Security and Political Security. Victims were often immobilized on the ground by security agents, who stepped upon their faces and tied their hands, as well being inhumanely treated during their transfer to detention centres.

[79] Some people were taken to up to four detention centres, where they were abused.

[80] These cases included that of Hamza Al Khatib, aged 13, from Dar'a, who died in custody. It its note verbale of 14 June 2011, the Government denied this allegation.

humiliation.[81] The mission photographed witnesses who bore injuries consistent with the torture alleged. The mission's forensic physician examined other victims who were hospitalized after fleeing the country. Victims of arbitrary arrests declared that they had been beaten and humiliated with insults referring to their religious, democratic or political beliefs. Many victims reported abuse such as "You want freedom, this is your freedom" during torture or beatings.

C. Deprivation of liberty

85.   The Syrian Arab Republic has also violated the right to liberty as enshrined in article 9 of the International Covenant on Civil and Political Rights through the widespread practice of arbitrary, unlawful arrests and subsequent unlawful detention aimed in large part at intimidating protestors, including women, children and the elderly.[82]

86.   Statements point to two categories of detainees. Firstly, individuals suspected of being Government opponents (including activists and protest organizers) arrested during sweeping raids that appeared to be both speculative and unwarranted. Secondly, detainees arrested during operations to collectively punish inhabitants of cities and towns that the authorities perceived to be recalcitrant or centres of democratic activism. Arrests appeared to be random and widespread.[83] Medics and human rights activists were also targeted. Several witnesses who fled the country reported that members of their families had been arrested in lieu of the person being sought.

87.   Witnesses who had been detained claimed that they had been denied fair trial provisions, such as access to a lawyer or any form of legal recourse.[84] They were not informed of the reason for their arrest or allowed to contact their families. They were constantly moved from one detention centre to another without notice, and often tortured or inhumanely treated in each facility. Scores of civilians were collectively brought before investigative judges, often bearing the signs of torture or beatings, or had ad hoc hearings in their cells with military personnel, without knowing the charges against them. In addition, there was no appeal process. Many detainees were forced to sign or fingerprint documents while blindfolded, not knowing what the documents contained. Others had to sign pledges declaring that they would no longer take part in demonstrations.

---

[81] In some cases, male detainees were forced to remain naked for long periods in their cells, or while being otherwise tortured or under interrogation. The mission received a number of reports of sexual assault or rape of women and girls during raids on homes. The mission was unable to corroborate these accounts.

[82] Targeted and mass arbitrary arrests and unlawful detention were reported in, inter alia, Aleppo, Baniyas, Damascus (city and outskirts), Dar'a (city and outskirts), Jisr Al Shughour and Al Ladhiqiyah. During the siege on Dar'a, it was reported that hundreds of people were arbitrarily arrested on a daily basis. Witnesses told the mission that, given the very large number of detainees, school yards and sports fields had been transformed into makeshift detention areas.

[83] Most of those interviewed by the mission were not privy to the whereabouts of their detained family and friends.

[84] See the International Covenant on Civil and Political Rights, article 14, and the United Nations Standard Minimum Rules for Non-custodial Measures (The Tokyo Rules), General Assembly resolution 45/110, annex.

D. Persecution

88.   The mission received disturbing reports that many discriminatory and abusive remarks about religion and/or ethnicity were made during arrest and detention, and when detainees were tortured.

89.   A number of towns and cities[85] were blockaded by heavy artillery and military vehicles, including tanks and mortars, in violation of articles 10 and 11 of the International Covenant on Economic, Social and Cultural Rights. Water tanks were targeted, leaving civilians without water. Restriction of movement was imposed on civilians in a highly disproportionate manner to any threat that may have existed. Those who left their homes to find food were often killed or injured, including children shot by snipers. People were stopped at checkpoints by security personnel, who would not allow them to pass, and subject them to physical and verbal abuse. In addition, power was cut off by the security forces while cities and towns were under siege, as were means of communication. Public hospitals were sometimes closed ahead of a military operation,[86] or staff told the injured that there was no room.[87] In other instances, public hospitals refused to treat injured victims, the doctors apparently being under threat from security forces or cooperating with them. People were forced to assemble makeshift hospitals that were unable to give adequate medical attention to victims.[88] There were numerous instances of the targeting of civilians attempting to assist the wounded by moving them to safer areas or taking them to hospital. Ambulances or other vehicles used by demonstrators were also targeted.

90.   Children have not only been targeted by security forces, but also repeatedly subject to the same human rights and criminal violations as adults, including torture, with no consideration for their vulnerable status. The fact that Syrian forces have tortured or killed children on several occasions – even targeted by snipers – in what are clearly not isolated incidents is a cause for grave concern.

91.   Lastly, the mission received disturbing reports that many discriminatory and abusive remarks about religion and/or ethnicity were made to detainees.

IV. Recommendations

92.   **Bearing in mind the findings of the mission, the response provided by the Government of the Syrian Arab Republic and the international community to date, and the ongoing situation on the ground, the High Commissioner recalls the fact that States unanimously agreed at the 2005 summit that each individual State has the responsibility to protect its population from crimes against humanity and other international crimes. This responsibility entails the prevention of such crimes, including their incitement, through appropriate and necessary means. When a State is manifestly failing to protect its population from serious international crimes, the international community has the responsibility to step in by taking protective action in a collective, timely and decisive manner.**

---

[85] Cities and towns under siege included Dar'a, Baniyas and Madaya.

[86] Such as in Ma'arrat an Nu'man.

[87] In one incident in Jisr Al Shughour, security forces said that they could "solve a space problem", then proceeded to murder wounded civilians.

[88] Such as the makeshift hospital set up in the Omari Mosque in Dar'a.

93.   In particular, the High Commissioner recommends that the Government of the Syrian Arab Republic:

(a)   Put an immediate end to gross human rights violations, including the excessive use of force against demonstrators and the killing of protestors, torture and ill-treatment of detainees and enforced disappearances, and halt all violations of economic, social and cultural rights;

(b)   Take immediate steps to end impunity, including by abolishing legislation that grants security and intelligence personnel virtual immunity from prosecution;

(c)   Ensure the immediate and unconditional release of detainees held on the basis of their participation in peaceful demonstrations, and other political prisoners;

(d)   Ensure the safe and voluntary return of refugees and internally displaced persons to their areas of origin in the Syrian Arab Republic;

(e)   Allow safe and unrestricted access to international and national journalists to investigate and report on the situation in the Syrian Arab Republic, without hindrance;

(f)   Take immediate measures to ensure full and unhindered access for humanitarian workers to provide aid and assistance to those in need;

(g)   Allow OHCHR immediate access to the Syrian Arab Republic to conduct investigations into all human rights abuses, irrespective of alleged perpetrator, in the context of protests since mid-March 2011;

(h)   Invite the special procedures of the Human Rights Council, in particular the Special Rapporteur on extrajudicial, summary or arbitrary executions, the Special Rapporteur on torture and other cruel, inhuman or degrading treatment or punishment, and the Working Group on Arbitrary Detention, to visit the Syrian Arab Republic to monitor and report on the human rights situation.

94.   The High Commissioner also recommends that the Human Rights Council:

(a)   Ensure that the situation of human rights in the Syrian Arab Republic remains on the agenda of the Council through the establishment of appropriate monitoring and investigating mechanisms, including the possibility of extending the mandate of the fact-finding mission, as well as through periodic reporting;

(b)   Urge the Syrian Arab Republic to cooperate with OHCHR and the special procedures, including by granting them unfettered access to the country;

(c)   Urge the Security Council to remain seized of and to address, in the strongest terms, the killing of peaceful protestors and other civilians in the Syrian Arab Republic through the use of excessive force and other grave human right violations, to call for an immediate cessation of attacks against the civilian population, and to consider referring the situation in the Syrian Arab Republic to the International Criminal Court.

95.   The High Commissioner further recommends that the League of Arab States continue to be actively engaged in calling for concerted action for the protection of human rights in the Syrian Arab Republic.

Annexes

Annex I

Letter dated 15 July 2011 from the United Nations High Commissioner for Human Rights addressed to the Prime Minister of the Syrian Arab Republic

NATIONS UNIES
HAUT COMMISSARIAT AUX DROITS DE L'HOMME

UNITED NATIONS
HIGH COMMISSIONER FOR HUMAN RIGHTS

Télégrammes: UNATIONS. GENEVE
Télex. 41 29 62
Téléphone: (41-22) 928 9257
Téléfax (41-22) 928 9018
Internet: www.ohchr.org

Palais des
Nations
CH-1211
GENEVE 10

REFERENCE

15 July 2011

Excellency,

I write further to resolution S-16/1 adopted by the United Nations Human Rights Council in a special session on human rights in the Syrian Arab Republic on 29 April 2011. As you will be aware, this resolution requested my Office to urgently dispatch a fact-finding mission to investigate all alleged violations of international human rights law and to establish the facts and circumstances of such violations and of the crimes perpetrated, with a view to avoiding impunity and ensuring full accountability.

Through a Note Verbale dated 6 May 2011, my Office formally requested Your Excellency's Government to cooperate with this mission, in particular by ensuring full access to the country. Having received no response from Your Excellency's Government on this matter, I reiterated my request for access to the country through a Note Verbale dated 20 May 2011 and again on 7 June 2011 through a meeting between the Deputy High Commissioner, Ms. Kyung-wha Kang, and Your Excellency's Permanent Representative to the United Nations Office in Geneva, H.E. Mr. Faysal Khabbaz Hamoui. I regret that the Syrian Government has to date remained silent on this matter, and once again I renew my request for access for the fact-finding mission.

I take this opportunity to stress that the material currently before my Office reflects a dire human rights situation and remains a matter of the gravest concern. Facts suggesting a pattern of widespread and systematic attacks against civilians and consequential breaches of the most fundamental rights documented by OHCHR require thorough investigation and full accountability with respect to the perpetrators. In my view, the credibility of the Syrian Government's statements on the nature of the on-going protests and the individuals or groups reportedly responsible for those abuses rests in substantial part on its willingness to allow independent investigation on the ground.

H.E. Mr. Adel Safar
Prime Minister
DAMASCUS

I have noted the series of reforms announced to date, and I welcome the information received from Your Excellency's Government on these and certain other issues. Allow me to stress however that the value of political and other reforms lies in their practical implementation, and reform plans also require transparent monitoring mechanisms to ensure sound and timely translation into effective change. More importantly, the promulgation of laws and decrees aimed at introducing greater political and civil rights cannot be accompanied by a progressively deteriorating human rights situation and commission of the gravest human rights violations.

Resolution S-16/1 also requested my Office to provide a follow-up report the Human Rights Council at its 18th Session, containing substantive information documented by the fact-finding mission. While the refusal of Your Excellency's Government to date to grant access has hampered the mission's work, it has nevertheless documented egregious violations of human rights committed since March 2011. These include summary executions, excessive use of force in quelling peaceful protests, arbitrary detentions, torture and ill-treatment, violations of the rights to freedom of assembly, expression, association and movement, and violations of the rights to food and health, including medical treatment to injured persons. This information will form the basis of the follow-up report, which will be made public in September.

In this context, and alongside my request for the mission to be granted access to the country, my Office wishes to raise with the Syrian Government a range of issues that have emerged in the course of the mission's work and requests further information, as detailed in the Annex attached to this letter. I would appreciate receiving the responses of Your Excellency's Government to these enquiries by 5 August 2011 in order to enable my Office to reflect the position of Your Excellency's Government on these issues in its report.

Please accept, Excellency, the assurances of my highest consideration.

Navanethem Pillay
High Commissioner for Human Rights

Questions submitted by the Office of the High Commissioner for Human Rights (OHCHR) to the Government of Syria, 15 July 2011.

A. Rights of individuals deprived of their liberty and the administration of justice: OHCHR would appreciate receiving the following information regarding legislative reforms announced by the Syrian Government:

1. The text of the decision announced by President Bashar al-Assad on 19 April 2011 to abrogate the 1963 State of Emergency Law and to abolish the High State Security Court. We wish to receive information regarding the legal measures taken to implement this decision, including the text of the relevant laws and their current status, including the date of their publication in the Official Gazette.

2. The text of Legislative Decree No. 61/2011 announcing a general amnesty for crimes committed before 31 May 2011, and Legislative Decree No. 72/2011 extending the scope of the amnesty to crimes committed before 20 June 2011. OHCHR would appreciate receiving information on how the amnesty laws have been implemented across the country, information about any committees (other than medical committees) which may have been set up to consider individual cases and their terms of reference, any existing appeal process for prisoners against a negative decision, and data showing how many prisoners and detainees have been released in each category. We would appreciate receiving the texts of other legislative decrees referred to in the amnesty law.[1] Additionally, Legislative Decree No. 61/2011 is also said to cover "all members of the Muslim Brotherhood party and other detainees belonging to political movements".[2] OHCHR wishes to receive details on which other political movements are covered under the amnesty law, and how many such detainees have been released to date and their presumed political affiliation.

3. Given the abrogation of emergency legislation on 19 April 2011, we wish to receive clarification as to the legal basis for the arrest and continued detention of individuals who have been apprehended in the context of protests and other incidents since 15 March 2011. If the purpose of the lifting of emergency laws is to afford basic rights to persons deprived of their liberty, and to curtail the exceptional powers granted to security and intelligence personnel, then it follows that other legislation is being applied in these cases. We would appreciate receiving information on current arrest and detention procedures being followed by the security forces since 19 April.

4. In its efforts to determine the fate and whereabouts of the significant numbers of persons detained or missing it has recorded since mid-March 2011, OHCHR requests information on the places of detention used by each of the security and intelligence agencies, together with information on individuals held there in connection with protests.[3]

---

[1] These are: Law 49/1980; Legislative Decree 37/1966 as amended; Legislative Decree 13/1974; and Legislative Decree 59/2008.

[2] Note Verbale to OHCHR dated 8 June 2011 from the Permanent Mission of Syria in Geneva.

[3] This should include names, dates of arrest, place of detention, reason for arrest and the arresting authority.

B. Torture and ill-treatment and deaths in custody

1. OHCHR refers to a Note Verbale received from the Permanent Mission of Syria in Geneva, dated 14 June 2011, containing a summary of the official investigation into the death of the child Hamza al-Khatib on 29 April 2011. We wish to receive additional information on this investigation, including the following: copy of Administrative Order 913 dated 30 May 2011 establishing an investigative committee under Ministry of Interior jurisdiction; copies of all documents prepared on this case by officials on duty at Tishreen Military Hospital during the period of Hamza al-Khatib's hospitalization and death, including copies of photographs taken of the body on 30 April 2011; copy of the report of a three-person committee which prepared a comparative study between the aforementioned photographs and others taken of the body on 24 May 2011 at the National Hospital in Daraa; copy of the report prepared by the Office of the General Prosecution in Damascus relating to the procedures followed in the criminal and judicial investigations relating to the case; and copies of all documentation, including photographs, prepared on this case by medical and judicial personnel at the National Hospital in Daraa. We also request an explanation as to why there was a delay of one month before an investigation into the death of the child was established, and information on the whereabouts and condition of the body between his death on 29 April and its handing over to his family on 24 May 2011.

2. OHCHR would appreciate receiving information regarding the procedures and laws currently in force for the investigation of cases involving the torture or ill-treatment of detainees and other persons deprived of their liberty, including cases resulting in death in custody. It would be useful to receive official data from the relevant ministries and the judiciary regarding the nature and number of such investigations since January 2011, the procedures followed in these cases, and details on cases which resulted in the prosecution of officials found guilty of such crimes. These should include cases where named individuals were declared by officials to be responsible for killings and other crimes, and whose "confessions" were broadcast on Syrian television. Additional information on any provisions under Syrian law for the compensation of victims of torture and their families would also be useful.

C. Investigations into killings of civilians and security personnel, and mass graves: several communications received by OHCHR from the Permanent Mission of Syria in Geneva contained references to a judicial committee and on-going investigations into incidents involving the killing of civilians and military personnel. There have also been a number of statements by Syrian officials regarding the discovery of mass graves, responsibility for which was attributed to "armed gangs". OHCHR would appreciate receiving the following information:

1. In early June, OHCHR was informed that a judicial committee was established to "investigate and bring to justice all perpetrator[s] of crimes against protestors and security personnel in Dara'a [o]n 31/3/2011", and that "the mandate of this committee was recently extended to investigate all crimes committed against civilians and security and army personnel in all parts of Syria".[4] We would appreciate receiving the texts of the decision to establish this committee in the first instance and to subsequently extend its mandate, and details of any

---

[4] Note Verbale to OHCHR dated 6 June 2011 from the Permanent Mission of Syria in Geneva.

investigations it has conducted to date, together with the relevant findings. OHCHR notes the establishment of a complaints procedure which is accessible electronically, and which refers to a 'Judicial Private Investigation Commission'.[5] In this regard, we request information on the composition and competence of its members, its terms of reference, and information on the nature and volume of complaints received to date. In particular, given the reference to" bringing perpetrators to justice", we wish to receive clarification as to the nature of the judicial powers of this committee. Does the committee have powers of enforcement or is it limited to making recommendations? What legislation is being used to formally charge any perpetrators with specific crimes, and which courts will be competent to hear such cases? Which laws will regulate the rights of the defendants and any appeals procedures?

2. At various times since the current protests began, Syrian officials have made references to the discovery of mass graves said to contain the remains of security personnel killed by "armed gangs". This included an announcement on 12 June, upon the entry of Syrian forces to the town of Jisr al-Shughour, of one such site said to contain the remains of some ten security personnel.[6] OHCHR wishes to receive details of the locations and contents of all sites of purported mass graves, and the procedures followed in the exhumation of these sites and the ensuing forensic examinations. Copies of official reports of any such investigations are particularly important. We also wish to be informed of the procedures followed in the related criminal investigations to determine culpability and identify the perpetrators, and the results of such investigations.

D. Conduct of law enforcement officials: Since mid-March 2011, several Syrian Government officials have publicly stated that orders were issued to law enforcement personnel, including the security forces, not to shoot at unarmed demonstrators.[7] Further, that the police have "strict instructions not to assault or harass the demonstrators", and that "security personnel have exercised maximum restraint while trying to control the situation".[8] OHCHR requests the following information and clarifications:

1. What instructions were issued to law enforcement personnel assigned to deal with crowd control since protests began in mid-March 2011? Who issued these orders and to whom?

2. Were these orders issued orally or in writing? If they were oral instructions, we wish to receive details of these orders and how they were communicated to the relevant commanders. We also wish to receive copies of any written orders and information on how they were disseminated and to whom. Additionally, what procedures are in place to ensure that orders on crowd control mechanisms are implemented, and what disciplinary measures are in place to deal with breaches of these orders?

---

[5] Referred to in Note Verbale to OHCHR dated 6 June 2011 from the Permanent Mission of Syria in Geneva (www.pir.gov.sy).

[6] There were also references to "three mass graves dug by the armed groups and fundamentalist forces" having been discovered by the Syrian authorities (Note Verbale to OHCHR dated 27 June 2011 from the Permanent Mission of Syria in Geneva).

[7] Note Verbale to OHCHR dated 15 April 2011 from the Permanent Mission of Syria in Geneva.

[8] Note Verbale to OHCHR dated 27 June 2011 from the Permanent Mission of Syria in Geneva.

3. Were these or other orders also issued to members and commanders of the Syrian armed forces, who also participated in a number of incidents since March 2011? We would appreciate receiving details of any oral or written orders issued in this regard. We also seek clarification of laws and procedures governing the role and conduct of specialised military agencies, including Air Force Intelligence (al-Mukhabarat al-Jawwiyya) and Military Security (al-Amn al-'Askari).

4. How many security agencies are authorized to deal with public order issues, and particularly with peaceful assemblies or demonstrations? Which law enforcement agencies, including security and intelligence agencies, participated in crowd control operations since March 2011?

5. Is there a crowd control strategy for managing demonstrations and peaceful assemblies, and is it integrated in an overall strategy for dealing with public order issues?

6. What decision-making criteria are available, if any, to assist in applying legitimate and reasonable tactical options that are proportional to crowd behaviour? What level of law enforcement officials take such decisions, in particular with regard to the use of lethal weapons?

7. Under what circumstances does Syrian law permit law enforcement officials to carry and use firearms? What types of firearms and ammunition are permitted for use in the context of demonstrations and peaceful assembly?

8. What procedures are followed by commanders to communicate to crowds the intent to use force, and to ensure that adequate time is given for such warnings to be observed?

9. What procedures are integrated into operations plans for crowd control to facilitate the movement of ambulances and to ensure adequate medical services for emergency cases?

10. OHCHR would appreciate receiving copies of the relevant Syrian laws governing the conduct of law enforcement officials generally, including amendments to the Police Service Regulations (Law 1962/1930), and the Syrian Penal Code (Law 148/1949).[9] Of particular relevance is information on legislative amendments currently in force relating to the use of force, including non-lethal incapacitating weapons.

11. We also seek clarification of any other laws and procedures governing the role and conduct of specialised security and intelligence agencies, including the General Intelligence Directorate (Idarat al-Mukhabarat al-'Amma) and Political Security (al-Amn al-Siyassi). What is the current status of Legislative Decree No. 14/1969, which provided immunity from prosecution for employees of General Intelligence except by order of the Director, and Legislative Decree No. 69/2008, which extended this immunity to members of other security forces except by order of the Armed Forces General Command?[10] Are there cases where such immunity was waived? What other mechanisms or laws are available to ensure that abuses of powers by law enforcement personnel are prosecuted as criminal offences under the law?

---

[9] Selected articles of the Syrian Penal Code and the Police Service Regulations were accessed on the Syrian Ministry of Interior website.
(http://www.syriamoi.gov.sy/portal/index.php?page=show&ex=2&dir=docs&ex=2&ser=2&lang=1&cat=71).
[10] Legislative Decree No. 14 of 15/01/1969 establishing the General Intelligence Directorate; and Legislative Decree No. 69 of 30/09/2008 amending the Military Penal Code.

E. Political and other reforms announced by the Syrian Government, OHCHR would appreciate receiving the latest information regarding the implementation of these measures:

1. The text of the new law regulating the right to peaceful assembly, which the Syrian authorities said had been issued on 21 April 2011.[11] We would appreciate clarification of the current status of this law, and what procedures and consultations were followed in its preparation.

2. Information regarding the decision taken on 11 May 2011 to establish a National Committee of Legal Experts to draw up a new law on elections.[12] We would appreciate receiving the text of this decision, details of the composition of this committee, the terms of reference of its mandate, its progress to date and an indication on the proposed timeline for the issuance of the law.

3. Information regarding the decision taken on 24 May 2011 to establish a National Committee to draw up a new information law.[13] We would appreciate receiving the text of this decision, details of the composition of this committee, the terms of reference of its mandate, its progress to date and an indication as to whether the draft law may be drafted within the two-month deadline proposed by the Syrian authorities.

4. Information regarding the decision taken on 5 June 2011 to establish a committee to draw up a new law on political parties.[14] We would appreciate receiving the text of this decision, details of the composition of this committee, the terms of reference of its mandate, its progress to date and an indication as to whether the draft law may be drafted within the one-month deadline proposed by the Syrian authorities.

5. Information regarding the decision taken on 1 June 2011 to establish a Committee for National Dialogue.[15] We would appreciate receiving the text of this decision, details of the composition of this committee, the terms of reference of its mandate and its progress to date.

6. Text of the decree issued by President Bashar al-Assad in early April concerning the issue of the 1962 Census and the status of stateless members of the Kurdish community in Syria. According to Syrian officials, "beneficiaries of this decree were given the full rights of citizens".[16] OHCHR wishes to receive information on how the provisions of this decree have been implemented to date.

END

---

[11] Note Verbale to OHCHR dated 6 June 2011 from the Permanent Mission of Syria in Geneva.
[12] Ibid
[13] Ibid
[14] Ibid.
[15] Ibid.
[16] Note Verbale to OHCHR dated 15 April 2011 from the Permanent Mission of Syria in Geneva.

Annex II

Note verbale dated 6 June 2011 from the Permanent Mission of the Syrian Arab Republic addressed to the Office of the United Nations High Commissioner for Human Rights

MISSION PERMANENTE
DE LA
RÉPUBLIQUE ARABE SYRIENNE
GENÈVE

اَلْجُمْهُورِيَّةُ الْعَرَبِيَّةُ السُّورِيَّةُ

الْبَعْثَةُ الدَّائِمَةُ لَدَى مَكْتَبِ الْأُمَمِ الْمُتَّحِدَةِ

جِنِيفْ

N° ٢٩٠/11

Geneva, 6 June 2011

The Permanent Mission of the Syrian Arab Republic to the United Nations Office and other International Organizations in Geneva presents its compliments to the High Commissioner for Human Rights, and the honour to inform of the latest steps of political reform in the Syrian Arab Republic.

As The High Commissioner already knows, Syria has lifted the state of emergency, and has abolished the High State Security Court early in April 2011, in addition to setting up a judicial Committee to investigate and bring to justice all perpetrator of crimes against protestors and security personnel in Dara'a in 31/3/2011.

New more advanced steps were taken since that date within the continuing reform process the Syrian authorities have taken upon themselves. These steps also serve to meet legitimate requests for reform by national movements within Syria. They have been accompanied with a number of other steps for social and economic reform that seek to further improve the human rights situation of the Syrian citizens in accordance with Syria's international commitments including human rights commitments. However, this verbal note will discuss the political reforms underway at the time being, bearing in mind that other steps are still anticipated, including the results of the Committee set up for combating corruption and increasing transparency. The Committee is expected to present the results of its work to the Prime Minister today, or tomorrow at the latest.

The other latest steps for political reforms are as follows:

1- A new law regulating the right to peaceful assembly was issued on the 21st of April 2011, in accordance with the belief that the right to peaceful assembly is one of the basic human rights enshrined in the Syrian Constitution. It serves to reconcile the constitutional human right to peaceful assembly of all citizens while protecting the security of the nation, the citizens, and public and private property. This law was formulated in accordance with the highest international standards.

2- H.E. the President has issued an unprecedented General amnesty for all crimes committed before the 31st of May 2011. This amnesty has special relevance in pardoning all those arrested for belonging to illegal political parties. The decree comes within the spirit of social forgiveness and national cohesion in the state.

3-   A presidential decision has also been issued on the 1st of June 2011 to establish a **committee for national dialogue**. The Committee includes law professors, economists, politicians from a number of political parties, and other experts. H.E. the president met with the Committee on the 2nd of June and discussed with its members the importance of national dialogue to overcome the current situation of political and social turmoil. The Committee will formulate the bases for the dialogue in a comprehensive, and an all inclusive way to allow all national movements to present, freely, their points of view on the future of the political economic and social life in Syria.

4-   On the 11th of May 2011 H.E. the Prime Minister Mr. Adel Safar has set up a national committee of competent legal experts to formulate a **new law on elections**. The committee presented the draft text to the Prime Minister later that month. The text was put up for public comments and amendments. The text is available for comments on the website:

http://www.youropinion.gov.sy/Tasharukia/projectdetail.asp?law_id=46

5-   On the 24th of May, H.E. the Prime Minister set up a national committee consisting of a large number of journalists, including members of the internet media, writers and scholars, to formulate a **new information law** to restructure the information sector in all its forms in Syria in accordance with the most contemporary applicable laws in the world, and with accordance with Syria's commitments in this domain. The committee has 2 months, maximum, to present the draft of the new law.

6-   On the 5th of June, H.E. the Prime Minister Mr. Adel Safar established a committee of wise men and women, including those with high expertise and competence, to formulate a **new law to regulate the formation and the functioning of political parties in Syria**. The Committee has already started its work, and will present a draft law to the Prime Minister within a month at the latest.

As with the elections law, the initial draft will be put forward to the public, including on the formal website to be created for this goal, to enrich the draft and collect suggestions before the law takes its final form.

7-   Another development worth noting is related to the above mentioned decision to establish a **judicial committee to investigate all crimes committed against demonstrators and security personnel** in the city of Dara'a on the 31st of March 2011. The mandate of this committee was recently extended to investigate all crimes committed against civilians and security and army personnel in all parts of Syria. Plaintiffs in these crimes would not have to travel to Damascus to present their complaints. They can present them to the public prosecutors in their cities. Furthermore, the Ministry has set up a hotline, and a separate website to receive all such complaints at the address: www.jpic.gov.sy

The Permanent Mission of the Syrian Arab Republic avails itself of this opportunity to renew to the High Commissioner for Human Rights, the assurances of its highest consideration.

The High Commissioner for Human Rights
Palais Wilson
Geneva- Switzerland

Annex III

Note verbale dated 14 June 2011 from the Permanent Mission of the Syrian Arab Republic addressed to the Office of the United Nations High Commissioner for Human Rights

Mission Permanente
De La
République Arabe Syrienne
Genève

الجمهورية العربية السورية
البعثة الدائمة لدى مكتب الأمم المتحدة
جنيف

Nº 311 /11

Geneva, 14ᵗʰ of June 2011

The Permanent Mission of the Syrian Arab Republic to the United Nations Office and other International Organizations in Geneva presents its compliments to the Office of the High Commissioner for Human Rights, and has the honour to submit here with the report of the committee of inquiry subject of allegations concerning the case of the child Hamza Al Khatib and 3 CDs describing the situation in Syria.

The Permanent Mission of the Syrian Arab Republic avails itself of this opportunity to renew to the Office of the High Commissioner for Human Rights the assurances of its highest consideration.

Encl. ment.

OHCHR REGISTRY

14 JUN 2011

Recto ... MENA
H.C.
(SPD)

*Office of the High Commissioner for
Human Rights
Palais Wilson*

217

إشارة إلى حملة التضليل المفبركة التي قامت بها الدوائر المتربصة بـسوريا وأجهـزة الإعـلام التابعة لها حول وفاة الطفل حمزة الخطيب ، وتنفيذاً لتوجيهات السيد رئيس الجمهورية، وصـدور الأمر الإداري رقم ٩١٣/ص بتاريخ ٢٠١١/٥/٣٠م، المتضمن لتشكيل لجنة برئاسة الـسيد معـاون وزيـر الداخلية، وعضوية كل من :

- مدير إدارة الأمن الجنائي.
- النائب العام العسكري.
- قائد الشرطة العسكرية.
- رئيس فرع التحقيق بإدارة الأمن الجنائي.

والتي مهمتها التحقيق بموضوع الادعاءات المتعلقة بوقوع أعمال عنف وشدة وتعذيب على جثة الطفل حمزة الخطيب.

* مباشرة قامت اللجنة بالإجراءات التالية بغية الوصول للحقيقة:

١- الانتقال بكامل أعضائها إلى مشفى تشرين العسكري، وعاينت الصور الـضوئية المـأخوذة للجثة بعد الوفاة مباشرة، وكانت ست صور ملونة ومعرفة وتدون رقم ٢٣ على كل منهـا، وكانت الصور بوضعيات مختلفة، وسبب تعريفها برقم ٢٣ كون الجثة كانت مجهولة الهوية، ويجري تنظيم التحقيقات اللازمة حسب الأصول.

٢- طلبت نسخة عن محضر الكشف على جثة المتوفى المعدة من قبل اللجنة الطبية الثلاثية التي شكلت لهذه الغاية من القاضي المناوب بتاريخ ٢٠١١/٤/٣٠.

٣- وكلفت اللجنة الطبية الثلاثية بإعداد دراسة مقارنة بين الصور الضوئية المأخوذة لجثة الحدث المتوفى حمزة بمشفى تشرين العسكري بتاريخ ٢٠١١/٤/٣٠ مع الصور الضوئية المـأخوذة لنفس الجثة بتاريخ ٢٠١١/٥/٢٤ بالمشفى الوطني في درعا وتنفيذاً لهـذا التكليـف قـدمت اللجنة الدراسية المقارنة بالتقرير مؤلف من صفحتين حيث تبين لها مجموعة فروقات.

٤ – كما اطلعت اللجنة على تقرير معاون رئيس النيابة العامة بدمشق الذي يبين فيه الإجراءات التحقيقية القضائية التي قام بها حيال جثة الحدث المتوفى حمزة الخطيب.

٥ – استدعت اللجنة بتاريخ ٢٠١١/٦/١ الطبيب الشرعي في المجلس الوطني الذي أجرى الخبرة والكشف على جثة الحدث المتوفى حمزة الخطيب وصولاً لحقيقة علمية ساطعة لا يتسرب إليها الشك أو الريبة واستدعت أيضاً أعضاء اللجنة الطبية الثلاثية الذين قاموا بالكشف على نفس جثة الحدث، وتم إجراء المقابلة بينهم جميعاً واتهموا موضوع سبب الخطورة والمقابلة والغاية من هذا الاجتماع وبالتلاقي الشفوي العلمي والطبي والنفسي أقرر بإجماع الأطباء الأن حالة العضو التناسلي للطفل لم تكن حالة بتر بشكل جازم وذلك لوجود التغيرات التفسخية مع احتمال أن هذا الضياع المادي الذي لوء هذه حدث في سياق التشميع أو أثناء نقل الجثة أو احتكاك في هذه الناحية".

٦ – ومنعاً للتأويل أحضرت اللجنة بيان قيد مدني فردي للمتوفى حمزة الخطيب من أمين السجل المدني الذي يتبع له.

* بعد القيام بالإجراءات المذكورة أعلاه (تم إيجازها) استخلصت اللجنة وبالإجماع النتائج التالية:

أ – وصلت الجثة إلى مشفى التدريب العسكري بدمشق بتاريخ ٢٠١١/٤/٢٩ في ساعة متأخرة من الليل ويتوفر في إجراء الكشف الطبي والقضائي عليها أصولاً على وقت تصدير من وصولها بشكل فني وقانوني متكامل.

ب – لا يوجد من آثار الشدة والعنف سوى آثار المرامي النارية الموصوفة بمحضر الكشف.

ج – أن سبب الوفاة هو الإصابة يلتزيف شديد ناجم عن الإصابة بمرامي نارية ثلاث:

١ – مرمي ناري بدخوله وخروجه في العضد السفلي الأيسر بداية ثم دخل ثانية في الصدر الجانب الأيسر وخرج من منتصف القص.

٢ – مرمي ناري بدخوله في الخاصرة اليمنى وخروجه في الظهر الأيمن الوحشي.

٣ – مرمي ناري بدخوله في الثلث السفلي للعضد الأيمن، مسافة الإطلاق لجميع المرامي بعيدة: مئة وواحد كبد أنثى.

– الإطلاق من قبل الغير وهن عدة مصادر أو من مصدر واحد بوضعية الحركة أيضاً وحسب رأس المستوى الأطباي.

– لقد سببت المرامي النارية بنزيفها ضخورية صندوقية بطنية وبعائية نازفة بشدة أدت إلى الوفاة.

– الوفاة ناجمة عن المرامي النارية وما نجم عليها.

د- إن حالة العضو التناسلي للطفل لم تكن حالة بتر بالشكل جازم وذلك لوجود التغيرات التفسخية مع احتمال أن هذا الضياع المادي الذي نوه عنه حدث في سياق التفسخ أو أثناء نقل الجثة أو احتكاك في هذه الناحية.

هـ- ثبوت فضاحة والد الحدث المتوفى حمزة الخطيب بأن جثة ولده سليمة وخالية من العيب، وبهذه الفناعة نبعث من أرضية الحوار بينه وبين أعضاء اللجنة من جهة وفسق الثبوتيات الرسمية القضائية والصور الضوئية والتقرير الخبري الطبية الثلاثية والدراسة المقارنة بين الصور المأخوذة في درعا والصور المأخوذة في دمشق من جهة أخرى.

و- ثبوت وجود جهات معادية ولجأت أشخاصاً لنقل صور مغايرة للحقيقة أو متلاعب بها فنياً لتحقيق مآرب دنيئة يجب متابعتها من الجهات المعنية لوصلاً لمعرفتها والقبض على ناقلي للك الصور وملتقطيها عامة وفيما يتعلق بهذه الواقعة خاصة.

وخلصت اللجنة إلى النتيجة التالية:

"ثبت بالدليل العلمي والفني والقضائي عدم وجود آثار لأعمال شدّ أو صلب أو تعذيب على جثة الحدث المتوفى حمزة الخطيب لا بحياته ولا بعد وفاته سوى آثار المراسي الباردة التي أصيب بها."

[Unofficial translation]

Note verbale dated 14 June 2011 from the Permanent Mission of the Syrian Arab Republic addressed to the Office of the United Nations High Commissioner for Human Rights

Geneva, 14 June 2011

In relation to the campaign conducted by circuits hostile to Syria, a misleading media campaign related to the death of the boy Hamza Al Khateeb, and in response to the presidential decision, an administrative order number 913/S was issued in May 30th, 2011, stipulating the creation of a committee presided by the Deputy of the Minister of Interior, and consists of the following members:

The Director of Criminal Security

The Military Prosecutor

The Commander of Military Police

And the Criminal Investigations Security branch director

The mission of this committee consists of investigating claims of acts of violence and torture on the cadaver of the child Hamza Al Khateeb.

Immediately, the committee took the following steps with the intention to reach the truth about this issue:

1.   All committee members moved to the Teshreen Military Hospital, to view 6 colored photos, each of them carry the number 23, because there was no identification of the cadaver at the moment the photos were taken. It portrayed the cadaver in several different positions. The photos were included in the investigation file according to regulation procedures.

2.   Committee members viewed a copy of the forensic file that was established by a committee of three medical doctors created by the Judge on duty on April 30th, 2011.

3.   The committee which was composed of three medical doctors was mandated to make a comparative study of the photos taken of the boy Hamza Al Khateeb in Teshreen Military Hospital on April 4th, 2011, compared to the photos taken in the National Hospital in Darra on May, 24th, 2011, the medical committee presented a 2-page report about the subject.

4.   The committee also viewed the report established by Deputy General Prosecutor of Damascus, explaining the investigative judiciary measures taken during examination of the cadaver of Hamza Al Khateeb.

5.   June 1st, 2011, the committee called on forensic doctor who had performed examination on the cadaver of Hamza Al Khateeb at the National Hospital in Darra and established a report, aimed at understanding the scientific facts that would not leave any room for doubt. The three members of the committee of medical doctors –mentioned above- who have examined the cadaver were also called, they held a meeting and discussed the situation from technical, medical and scientific view points, and reached a conclusion specifying that an amputation of the boy's penis had not occurred. The physical loss might have taken place during an advanced stage of decomposition of the body, or with skin friction at the area during the transportation of the cadaver, which explains the situation.

6.   To avoid errant interpretations, the committee included an official birth certificate that belonged to the deceased.

Following the measures briefly described above, the committee unanimously reached the following conclusions:

(a)   The cadaver arrived to Teshreen Military Hospital in Damascus late at night on April 29th, 2011. Its forensic examination took place according to regulations. A short time after its arrival, examination of the cadaver was conducted in a comprehensive scientific, technical and lawful manner.

(b)   The cadaver did not carry signs of

(c)   The cause of death is severe internal bleeding due to bullets in three locations:

1.   Perforation caused by bullet entry at the lower part of the left upper arm, re-entered the chest from the left side, and exited at the middle of the sternum.

2.   Perforation caused by bullet entry at waist's right area, exited at the lower side of the back area.

3.   Perforation caused by bullet entry and exit in the right upper arm. All three bullets were shot from a distance no less than one meter away from the victim.

Shooting originated from one or several third party sources. Shooter(s) were moving at the time of shooting, they were on the same height.

(d)   No confirmation of penis amputation at this point, especially with the manifest degradation in the state of the cadaver, and the possibility of this material loss taking place while the cadaver was transported.

(e)   Evidence stated by Mr. Ali Al Khateeb, father of the victim, declaring that his son's cadaver is intact and not tampered with. He ultimately formulated his conviction in presence of committee members. The conviction of Ali Al Khateeb is based on facts discussed with the medical committee members, in addition to viewing official judicial documents, photos, medical experts' report and the comparative illustration of cadaver photos taken in Daraa, and Damascus.

(f)   It is proven that hostile third party have commissioned certain persons to influence information about facts, and to apply digital manipulation on photos of the cadaver of Hamza Al Khateeb. The concerned authorities are following up on these facts in order to put their hands on manipulated photos and their authors in general and particularly in relation to this case.

The committee concludes the following:

Scientific, medical and judicial evidence has proven the cadaver of the boy Hamza Al Khateeb does not sustain traces of acts of violence or torture, not in post mortem, nor when he was alive, except perforations of bullet shots from fire arms.

Annex IV

Note verbale dated 27 June 2011 from the Permanent Mission of the Syrian Arab Republic addressed to the United Nations High Commissioner for Human Rights

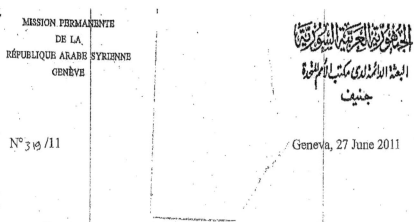

N° 3ı9 /11   Geneva, 27 June 2011

The Permanent Mission of the Syrian Arab Republic to the United Nations Office and other International Organizations in Geneva presents its compliments to the High Commissioner for Human Rights, and with reference to the preliminary report issued by the High commissioner on the 14th of June 2011 regarding the situation of Human Rights in the Syrian Arab Republic as mandated by the Human Rights Council resolution S-16/1 of 29/4/2011, has the honour to inform the High Commissioner of its shock at the unrealistic approach used by the High Commissioner towards the situation of human rights in Syria.

The report relied on media reports, as is evident from the footnotes of the report itself, and on unverified allegations to make serious human rights accusations against Syria. The report was prepared with a premeditated goal. It is biased and unprofessional. Despite that, and since the Syrian Arab Republic is keen on clarifying all the facts, and since it wishes to continue the dialogue with the High Commissioner to promote and protect human rights in accordance with her mandate and with respect to the Syrian sovereignty, the Syrian Arab Republic would therefore kindly inform the High Commissioner of the following:

1-   In his speech of 20/6/2011, H.E. the president of the Syrian Arab Republic, clarified the comprehensive national plan for political, economic and administrative reform that is being conducted within a clearly defined and short timeframe. It seeks to meet all the demands of the Syrian people which became clear through the number of meetings H.E. the president had with different social groups over a 2 month period, including the trend to conduct substantial amendments to the constitution, or even replace it with a new constitution.

2-   The right to peaceful assembly is enshrined in the Syrian Arab Republic in accordance with the constitution and the national and international commitments of Syria. Even though the High Commissioner was informed of the decree no: 54 of 21/4/2011 that regulated the right to peaceful assembly as a basic human right guaranteed by the constitution of the Syrian Arab Republic, yet she refrained from presenting it in her report, for reasons well known by now, and chose to present it as an 'intention'.

3-   The citizens of the Syria called for a number of legitimate demands for reform. The government is working to implement them within the law and in a manner to respect the law and serve the interests of the people. The High Commissioner was officially informed, through a number of verbal notes, of the steps that were taken in this context such as: lifting the state of emergency, abolishing the state security court, issuing a new law for peaceful assembly, a first in Syria and is in accordance with the highest international standards. In addition to other measures to combat corruption, and meet the public demands in issues related to the every day life of citizens. Many more reforms are underway. Yet none of this found its way to this report.

4-   The Syrian government has become certain that there are foreign regional and international forces, acting to destabilize security and stability in Syria through exploiting legitimate demonstrations and calls for reform. It also became evident that there are armed groups that do not want reform, but want to overthrow the regime and establish salafist emirates. And instead of retreating in the face of reform measures undertaken by the Syrian leadership, they answered by seeking sectarian rifts and by escalating attacks against innocent civilians and against army posts. They also answered with destroying security enforcing forces headquarters, killing their personnel and mutilating their corpses (as was the case of the brigadier- general Abdu Khidr Tilawi and his three children), forcing schools to shut their doors. Furthermore three mass graves dug by the armed groups and fundamentalist forces were discovered. Members of the diplomatic corps in Damascus, international Organizations, and the international media witnessed the last one.

5-   In the city of Talbise in the governorate of Homs, for example, armed men cut off the international highway for long hours and attacked policemen who had strict instructions not to assault or harass the demonstrators. This led to a number of casualties, which in turn led to the intervention of the army. In Jisr al-Shughur the armed groups have gained control of the city and terrified the residents. This made them call for the military intervention to protect them from the armed groups.

6-   The armed groups that raise havoc in Syria killed a large number of innocent civilians and security personnel. Security personnel have exercised maximum restraint while trying to control the situation. This led the armed groups to exploit the situation and increase their attacks on civilians (as per our verbal note to the High Commissioner no:213/11 dated 15/4/2011). However, the High Commissioner chose to ignore all this information and to ignore the horrific violations of human rights such as extrajudicial killings, abductions, torture and other crimes committed by those groups. She made no reference to these crimes in any way, and aligned herself with one side and established herself as its defender.

7- What happened in Syria lately, and what is still going on, is not related in any way to peaceful demonstration. Rather, we are up against acts of destruction, and terrorizing people. This has largely affected the markets, the national economy and tourism. It also affected the feeling of security by Syrians, a feeling Syria takes pride in.

8- The fundamentalist leadership outside Syria mainly guides the protests, in synchronization with issuing many 'fatwa's' outside Syria calling for resisting the authority through abusing Friday prayers to incite violence, to destroy, to kill, and extend the sphere of chaos. A number of phone calls of those who have incited violence have been intercepted. And even though they were aired on a number of the media channels (including some of which the High Commissioner cited in her report) the High Commissioner refrained from referring to these cases. Collaborators of that leadership inside Syria, and a number of Jihadi Salafist groups and paid men, attacked the army, the police and the security. What is going on now is a repetition of what Syria witnessed in the 1980s but with modern tools. At the time, Syria paid the price of terrorist activities dearly with its best scientist, intellectuals, and sons. For this reason, the state has to take measures to protect its citizens, the private and public establishments, and protect its economy from this haemorrhage. It is unacceptable for the state to stand by watching while the electricity stations, TV. buildings, land registries, schools and hospitals are burnt down, and ambulances, paramedics, telephone and telecommunication centres are targeted, as was the case in Jisr al-Shughur, where representatives of the foreign embassies and UN agencies made a first hand evaluation at the situation.

9- This was accompanied with an unprecedented incitement campaign against Syria in a number of media outlets. A number of satellite channels lately aired photos and videos of people injured or killed during the protests. It was later proved that they were clips from other countries or even totally fabricated. A number of satellite channels aired the way these clips were fabricated and produced to present events from outside Syria as happening in Syria. Reuters, other news agencies and television channels apologized for airing misinformation or information from events in other countries. Unfortunately, the High Commissioner chose not to mention this, neither did she refer to the information and videos sent to her by the Mission in the Verbal Note of 14/6/2011. She chose to close her ears to any neutral or objective voice.

10- The Syrian Laws, as in other countries, demand that journalists wishing to enter its territory, to do so in a legitimate and legal way, and not through presenting wrong information and invalid documents. It is surprising to single out the case of the Al Jazeera reporter as a proof to what the High Commissioner called 'deportation of foreign journalists'. This journalist entered Syria with an expired passport and irregular documents. This is illegal and no country in the world would accept it.

11- The High Commissioner refrained from mentioning 260 deaths from members of the security and the army. Some were killed while they were outside working hours. As for the injured from army and the security, they have reached 8.000 casualties.

12- In an effort to protect its borders, Syria discovered a large number of smuggled weapon shipments and arms supplies used by the armed groups to strike at security and order in Syria using foreign finance. No country in the world accepts this. It is a matter of national security. Those groups were tracked down, and a number of them were arrested, while others fled outside the country. The national TV aired their confessions, showing the foreign involvement in supporting them financially and logistically. They also confessed to the large amounts of money they received for the crimes they committed, and which cannot be justified under any human rights bill. It is worth noting that the weapons being used currently by the armed groups against the civilians, the security and army are advanced weapons. They range from machine guns to RBGs, bombs, other weapons and advanced communication systems that are not compatible with allegation of peaceful protest, and show a high level of training and prior preparations for acts of violence and killings.

13- In addition to all above, the report contained a number of fallacies. The Mission of the Syrian Arab Republic would like to hereby present some:

a- In paragraph 6 of the report the High Commissioner alleged that *'helicopter machine guns were also said to have been used during a military assault on the town of Jisr al-Shughur'*. This is not true. One helicopter was used in an exploratory mission to find out what was happening on the ground due to the siege imposed by the armed groups on security headquarters in the city. That helicopter never took part in any military activities.

b- The allegation in paragraph 7 that *'while women and children were among those detained, human rights defenders, political activists, and journalists were particularly targeted'*, is a reprehensible allegation that serves only to smear the image of Syria, a campaign that is being conducted by media outlets. It is a fact that there are many Syrians who express their different views through all media outlets, and from within Syria, without being harmed in any way.

c- The High Commissioner referred in paragraph 8 of her report to the case of Syrian Child Hamza alkhatib, as presented in the media. she ignored the ad hoc committee set up in Syria to investigate the death of the child and the affirmative conclusions it reached on the circumstances of his death, including the lack of traces of torture on his body. The High commissioner was informed of this in the Missions' verbal note no: 311/11 dated 14/6/2011.

d- Paragraphs 9 and 10 of the report, claimed that *the Syrian authorities violated the freedoms of assembly, expression and movement.* There is no better proof of this fallacy than the declaration of the Syrian authorities, at the highest levels, that they respects peaceful assemblies and that they are making every effort to study and meet the demands of the protestors.

14- The Mission rejects the use of the term *'Syrian Government claims 120 security personnel in attacks'* in the city of Jisr Alshugour. At the time when she did not use the term to refer to media and NGO reports. In fact she used terms such as 'reliable sources' while quoting those reports. This proves she intends to adopt a one sided approach and align herself with this side, refusing to deal in an impartial manner with all that is presented to her by the Syrian Government. This in turn sheds doubts on carrying out her mandate impartially and objectively.

15- Syria reiterate that it is proceeding in the road to reform as announced by H.E. the President, and its persistence in meeting the legitimate demands of its citizens and protecting their lives and properties, and stresses that it will not allow terrorism and fundamentalism to claim the lives of Syrian citizens.

16- The Syrian Arab Republic expects the High Commissioner to carry out her work in an impartial and objective manner with the aim of protecting victims of human rights violations, and promote and protect human rights within her mandate and without politicization. The position taken by the High Commissioner, through relying on misinformation, does wrong to the Syrian people, and to the blood of the innocent casualties. This puts the High Commissioner in a position as if take part in the hatred campaign against Syria launched by other organizations, in order to undermine the Syrian peoples national interests.

Finally, the Syrian Arab Republic reiterates its readiness to cooperate with the High Commissioner for Human Rights and her office, to promote and protect human rights, in a framework of impartiality, objectivity, non-politicization and without adopting one point of view against another, and within the mandate of the High Commissioner, and within respect to the sovereignty of the Syrian Arab Republic and its freedom to make its political choices within its national and international human rights commitments.

The Permanent Mission of the Syrian Arab Republic avails itself of this opportunity to renew to the High Commissioner for Human Rights, the assurances of its highest consideration.

The High Commissioner for Human Rights
Palais Wilson
Geneva- Switzerland

Cc: - The Deputy High Commissioner for Human Rights
    - The MENA Unit at the OHCHR

Annex V

**Note verbale dated 5 August 2011 from the Permanent
Mission of the Syrian Arab Republic addressed to the United
Nations High Commissioner for Human Rights**

MISSION PERMANENTE
DE LA
RÉPUBLIQUE ARABE SYRIENNE
GENÈVE

N° 395/11

Geneva, 5th August 2011

The Permanent Mission of the Syrian Arab Republic to the United Nations Office and other International Organizations in Geneva presents its compliments to The High Commissioner for Human Rights, and in reference to the High Commissioner Note Verbal dated 15 July 2011 which included the letter addressed to H.E Dr. Adel Safar prime Minister of The Syrian Arab Republic, has the honour to attach herewith the answers to the questions attached to above mentioned letter. The related documents and CDs will be sent next week.

The Permanent Mission of the Syrian Arab Republic avails itself of this opportunity to renew to the High Commissioner for Human Rights the assurances of its highest consideration.

United Nations
High Commissioner for Human Rights
Palais des Nations
CH'1211 GENEVE 10

OHCHR REGISTRY

– 5 AOUT 2011

Recipients : ...MENA......

Rue de Lausanne 72 (3e étage), 1202 Genève   Tel: +41 22 79 2 45 60   Fax: +41 22 738 42 75

231

الجمهورية العربية السورية

وزارة الخارجية والمغتربين

رد حكومة الجمهورية العربية السورية على الأسئلة الموجهة إلى
السيد رئيس مجلس الوزراء من المفوضية السامية لحقوق الإنسان
حول الأوضاع في سورية

أولاً: تعبر حكومة الجمهورية العربية السورية مجدداً عن استمرارها في التعاون مع
المفوضية العليا لحقوق الإنسان وتؤكد إصرارها الدائم على كشف وتقديم كافة الحقائق
التي يتم السؤال عنها وذلك بعيداً عن ما يتم تلفيقه وتقديمه للمفوضية السامية من
وقائع كاذبة ومطبوعات ملفقة تقدمها لها بعض المصادر والجهات التي تتركز أهدافها
على تشويه سمعة الجمهورية العربية السورية، وتشيع من أجل الوصول إلى هذه
الأهداف كافة الوسائل البعيدة عن الأخلاق الإنسانية والشرائع والأعراف.

ثانياً: إن حكومة الجمهورية العربية السورية تود التأكيد على مجموعة المبادئ التي
تسير على هديها في التعامل والمعالجة لكافة الأمور المطروحة للنقاش وفقاً للنقاط
الآتية:

إن حق التعبير عن الرأي بحرية مصان بموجب دستور الجمهورية العربية السورية،
ويجب على الحكومة حمايته وتعزيز ممارسته وتطوير الثقافة الخاصة به ليكون إيجابياً
مفيداً للمجتمع ككل.

إن الحق بالتظاهر السلمي مصان أيضاً بموجب دستور الجمهورية العربية السورية، وقد صدر مؤخراً قانون ينظم ممارسة هذا الحق وفقاً للمعايير المعمول والمتعارف بها دولياً وبما ينسجم ويتطابق مع ما هو مطبق في معظم دول العالم.

إن القوانين السورية النافذة تعاقب على أي ضرب من ضروب الشدة أو التعذيب بنصوص صارمة .

إن القوانين السورية النافذة تعاقب على أي نوع من أنواع حجز الحرية خارج نطاق القانون سواء قام به أشخاص تابعون للسلطات العامة أو أفراد عاديون.

إن الدفاع عن حقوق الإنسان وحمايتها وتعزيزها هو أحد أهم المرتكزات التي تقوم عليها سياسة حكومة الجمهورية العربية السورية في الداخل والخارج.

إن مكافحة الفساد هي عملية مستمرة وتعمل حكومة الجمهورية العربية السورية على متابعتها وتعزيزها وسن التشريعات التي تواكب آليات معالجة هذه الظاهرة بما ينسجم مع قوانين الدول الرائدة في هذا المجال.

حكومة الجمهورية العربية السورية تعمل بشكل حثيث على تطوير العمل السياسي في سورية من كافة النواحي وقد اتخذت من القرارات والخطوات الواسعة في هذا المجال بما يؤكد على عزمها هذا.

إن الحوار الوطني الشامل بين كافة أطياف المجتمع السوري هو السبيل الأمثل للإصلاح والتطوير من أجل الوصول إلى الأهداف المرجوة في الارتقاء نحو الأفضل في المجالات السياسية والتشريعية والاجتماعية والاقتصادية.

سيادة القانون والقضاء هما من أهم المرتكزات التي تقوم عليها عملية الإصلاح الشامل بهدف تحقيق أرقى معايير العدالة الاجتماعية بين أفراد المجتمع السوري.

ومن خلال ما سبق بيانه فإننا نؤكد أن السلطات السورية المختصة ومنذ بداية الأحداث في شهر آذار ٢٠١١ تعاملت مع المظاهرات السلمية التي نادى أصحابها مطالب وأهداف تتعلق بالإصلاح ومكافحة الفساد بصورة حضارية تعكس طبيعة وجوهر العلاقة القائمة بين المجتمع والدولة، وكانت تقوم بتأمين هذه التظاهرات إلى حين انتهائها وعودة المشاركين فيها كل إلى منزله، لكن هذا الأمر لم يرق لجهات وأطراف داخلية وخارجية هدفها الرئيس زعزعة الاستقرار الذي تعيشه سورية حيث لحظت تظهر على أرض الواقع جماعات إرهابية مسلحة تقوم بالاعتداء على المتظاهرين السلميين وإرهابهم وقتلهم، وصارت هذه

المجموعات الإرهابية تنشط إما عن طريق الانخراط ابتداءً ضمن صفوف المتظاهرين حيث كان بحمل أفرادها العصي والسيوف والسكاكين ويبادرون إلى التهييج والقيام بالأعمال التخريبية، انطلاقاً من داخل المظاهرات فيحرقون السيارات ويخربون الممتلكات والإدارات والمباني للعامة والخاصة، أو كان الأفراد المسلحين بأسلحة حربية من هذه المجموعات يقومون بإطلاق النار بشكل مباشر على المتظاهرين أو على قوات حفظ النظام بقصد قتل أكبر عدد من الناس، والسبب هو كون هؤلاء يتظاهرون بشكل سلمي وتحت حماية السلطات العامة التي كانت تؤمن لهم تجمعهم حفاظاً على الأمن العام، أما الهدف الحقيقي والأساسي للجماعات الإرهابية فهو التشويه سمعة السلطات العامة في سورية عبر تصويرها بأنها تقوم بعملية قمع دموي للمتظاهرين، كل ذلك ترافق مع حملة إعلامية خارجية مضللة ضد سورية تواكبت مع مجموعة من الفتاوى التكفيرية التي أطلقها عدد ممن يعتبرون أنفسهم رجال دين أخذوا يحرضون على القتل وسفك الدماء تحت ستار الدين وبما يتطابق بشكل تام مع فكر ونهج التنظيمات الإرهابية التكفيرية التي تنتشر في الكثير من دول العالم وتسعى إلى تخريب المجتمعات والدول التي تنشط فيها، فأخذت الخلايا الإرهابية النائمة تنشط وتظهر إلى العلن مستفيدة من التمويل الخارجي الهائل الذي يقدم لها ومن وسائل الاتصال الحديثة والأسلحة الحربية المتنوعة التي تم تهريبها وإدخالها لصالحها عبر الحدود بوسائل غير مشروعة وصارت بعض الجوامع تستخدم كمستودعات للأسلحة الحربية والذخائر وهذا ما كان عليه حال المسجد العمري في درعا وبعض المساجد الأخرى في نفس المحافظة وفي محافظات أخرى من سورية التي أقدم القائمين عليها على تغطية هذه الأعمال وتنسيقها ضمن نطاق انحرافهم الفكري والديني ودعوتهم للقتل، واستقطابهم وتحريرهم ببعض ضعاف النفوس للعمل، ضمن نطاق أعمال القتل والتخريب والإرهاب ضد أفراد الشرطة والجيش وضد المتظاهرين السلميين على حد سواء، حيث وصل عدد الشهداء الذين قتلهم الإرهابيون من أفراد الشرطة والجيش إلى المئات من الضباط والعناصر ووصل عدد المصابين بطلقات نارية أو بطعنات السيوف والسكاكين أو بالضرب المبرح إلى الآلاف إضافة إلى ما قام به هؤلاء الإرهابيون من تمثيل بجثث ضحاياهم من أفراد الشرطة والجيش.

أما بالنسبة لكل من أوقف لقيامه بأعمال غير مشروعة فقد تمت إحالته إلى الجهات القضائية وفقاً لأحكام قانون أصول المحاكمات الجزائية السوري وبما ينسجم بشكل تام مع ما صدر من تشريعات لجهة رفع حالة الطوارئ بحيث لم يعد هناك مجال في سورية لأي توقيف، عرفي بل تتم إحالة المشتبه فيهم خلال أربع

وعشرين ساعة إلى النيابة العامة المختصة ويصبحون تحت عهدة وولاية للقضاء السوري، وفي معظم الحالات التي أحيلت إلى القضاء تم إخلاء سبيل الأشخاص المشتبه فيهم فوراً، أما من قاموا بارتكاب أعمال التخريب أو الإحراق أو القتل فإن السلطات القضائية المختصة تقوم بملاحقتهم قضائياً وفقاً لأحكام القانون ومن ثبت براءته يتم إعلان هذه البراءة بحكم قضائي، أما من يثبت للقضاء أنه ارتكب هذه الجرائم فتتم معاقبته وفقاً لنصوص قانون العقوبات السوري.

ثالثاً: أما فيما يتعلق بمجموعة الأسئلة التي يطرحها مكتب المفوض السامي لحقوق الإنسان على حكومة الجمهورية العربية السورية بتاريخ ٢٠١١/٧/١٥ فنورد لكم الإجابات عليها وفقاً لما يلي:

١- بتاريخ ٢٠١١/٤/٢١ صدرت ثلاثة مراسيم تشريعية، من المرسوم التشريعي رقم (١٦١) المتضمن إنهاء العمل بحالة الطوارئ، والمرسوم التشريعي رقم (٥٣) المتضمن إلغاء محكمة أمن الدولة العليا المحدثة بالمرسوم التشريعي رقم (٤٧) تاريخ ١٩٦٨/٣/٢٨، وإحالة جميع الدعاوى المنظورة لدى المحكمة المذكورة والنيابة العامة فيها بحالتها الحاضرة إلى مرجعها القضائي المختص وفق ما للنص عليه قواعد قانون أصول المحاكمات الجزائية، والمرسوم التشريعي رقم (٥٥) المتضمن تعديل المادة (١٧) من قانون أصول المحاكمات الجزائية بحيث تختص الضابطة العدلية أو المفوضون بمهامها باستقصاء بعض الجرائم المنصوص عليها في قانون العقوبات العام (الجرائم الواقعة على أمن الدولة والسلامة العامة) وجمع أدلتها، والاستماع إلى المشتبه بهم فيها على ألا تتجاوز مدة التحفظ عليهم سبعة أيام قابلة للتجديد من النائب العام وفقاً لمعطيات كل ملف على حده، وعلى ألا تزيد هذه المدة عن ستين يوماً، وفقاً لأحكام قانون أصول المحاكمات الجزائية فإنه يتوجب على الضابطة العدلية تقديم المشتبه فيه إلى القضاء فور انتهاء مهلة السبعة أيام إلا إذا كان يوجد موجبات قانونية أو واقعية مستمدة من ماهية التحقيقات تستدعي تمديد هذه المهلة لأكثر من سبعة أيام وعند ذلك تستطيع الضابطة العدلية إطلاع النائب العام المختص على سير التحقيقات وطلب مهلة إضافية للتحفظ على المشتبه فيه لمتابعة التحقيق في القضية وجمع أدلتها وللنائب العام في هذه الحالة الصلاحية في تمديد المهلة أو إعطاء الأمر للضابطة العدلية بتقديم المشتبه فيه فوراً إلى القضاء.

وبالعودة إلى ما ورد حول هذه الموضوع من أسئلة نفيدكم أنه بمجرد إنهاء حالة الطوارئ لم يعد يوجد في سورية أي مجال لأي توقيف عرفي بالنسبة للجرائم الواقعة على أمن الدولة أو السلامة العامة وأصبحت

النصوص الواردة في قانون أصول المحاكمات الجزائية هي الوحيدة واجبة التطبيق في التوقيف الاحتياطي

وآلياته ومبرراته، وهذه النصوص تمنع بأي حال توقيف المشتبه فيهم من قبل الضابطة العدلية احتياطياً

لأكثر من أربع وعشرين ساعة لتتم تقديمهم فوراً إلى النيابة العامة المختصة، ويصبحوا تحت عهدة

وولاية القضاء، وقد أباحت هذه النصوص تمديد المهلة المذكورة لكن بأمر وموافقة النائب العام المختص

حسب ماهية ومآل التحقيقات، وذلك بالنسبة لكافة الجرائم المنصوص عليها في القوانين السورية النافذة

باستثناء الآليات والمدد المتعلقة بالجرائم الواقعة على أمن الدولة والسلامة العامة التي سبق لنا ذكرها أما

عن الإجراءات القانونية التي تم اتخاذها لتنفيذ المرسوم التشريعي المتضمن إلغاء محكمة أمن الدولة العليا

فقد تمت إحالة كافة الدعاوى التي كانت المنظورة أمامها حين إلغائها إلى المحاكم المختصة حسب قواعد

الاختصاص المكاني المنصوص عليها في قانون أصول المحاكمات الجزائية وتم نقل كافة الأشخاص الذين

كانت تجري محاكمتهم أمامها إلى السجون التي تتبع محاكم المحافظات لتتم محاكمتهم وفقاً لأحكام قانوني

العقوبات وأصول المحاكمات الجزائية النافذين في سوريا.

٢- بالنسبة لكيفية تنفيذ العفو العام فإن النيابة العامة المختصة في كل منطقة أو محافظة تقوم بتنفيذ

أحكام العفو العام وفقاً لمضمون المرسوم التشريعي الصادر بهذا الصدد ووفقاً لأحكام قانوني العقوبات

وأصول المحاكمات الجزائية بحيث يتم فور صدور العفو العام إحصاء الموقوفين المشمولين بأحكامه من

خلال سجلات المحاكم والنيابات العامة وسجلات السجون ويصدر النائب العام المختص قراره بإطلاق سراح

الموقوفين فوراً بالنسبة لمن يشمل العفو العام كامل عقوبتهم، أما الذين شمل العفو جزءاً من عقوبتهم فيتم

ترك أمر إطلاق سراحهم للقضاة للتحقيق أو الحكام الجنائية المختصة التي تنظر في قضاياهم ويتم أخذ

مفاعيل العفو العام بعين الاعتبار لدى إصدار الأحكام بحقهم بحيث تقرر المحكمة في الحكم الذي يصدر

عنها إسقاط الجزء المشمول بالعفو من العقوبة النهائية.

٣- لم يتم تشكيل أية لجان (عدا الطبية) للنظر في الحالات الفردية المتعلقة بالاستفادة من أحكام العفو

العام لكن أي سجين يستطيع تقديم طلباته إلى المحكمة المختصة أو إلى النائب العام المختص ليتم النظر

فيها ومعالجتها وفقاً لأحكام القانون.

ب- بالنسبة لأعداد السجناء الذين أطلق سراحهم تنفيذاً للعفو العام فنوردها لكم وفقاً للقوائم التالية:.

زقم المرسوم	تاريخ صدوره	عدد المشمولين بأحكامه	
المرسوم التشريعي رقم 34	2011/3/7	المحافظة	العدد
		دمشق	138
		حلب	244
		ريف دمشق	4195
		إدلب	97
		حمص	57
		حماة	185
		اللاذقية	52
		طرطوس	37
		درعا	52
		السويداء	11
		دير الزور	46
		الحسكة	57
		الرقة	56
		المجموع	5227
المرسوم التشريعي رقم 61	2011/5/31	المحافظة	العدد
		دمشق	323
		حلب	66
		ريف دمشق	1431
		إدلب	65
		حمص	168
		حماة	61
		اللاذقية	83

		2011/6/20	المرسوم التشريعي رقم 72
160	طرطوس		
45	درعا		
26	السويداء		
50	دير الزور		
46	الحسكة		
160	الرقة		
2684	المجموع		

العدد	المحافظة		
196	دمشق		
103	حلب		
344	ريف دمشق		
32	إدلب		
30	حمص		
59	حماة		
1600	اللاذقية		
13	طرطوس		
12	درعا		
55	السويداء		
31	دير الزور		
27	الحسكة		
20	الرقة		
2522	المجموع		

وبالتالي فإن عدد من ضمنهم العفو من الموقوفين الذين أطلق سراحهم فور صدور المراسيم التشريعية المشار إليها أعلاه يبلغ (١٠،٤٣٣) شخصاً، مع التنويه بأن الإحصائية المتقدمة لا تشمل إلا من أطلق سراحه فوراً بموجب مراسيم العفو. ومن ثم فإنها لا تشمل المخالفات، أو الجنح المنصوصة، كما أنها لا تشمل الدعاوى قيد النظر في الجنايات التي يستفيد أصحابها من العفو عند الحكم فهناك عدد كبير ممن استفاد من العفو جزئياً كالاستفادة من نصف العقوبة، أو ربعها، ولا تشمل أيضاً المتوارين عن الأنظار إلا إذا سلموا أنفسهم خلال المدد المحددة في مرسوم العفو، وهنا لابد من الإشارة إلى أن مرسومي العفو المذكورين لم يشملا أيضاً بعض الجرائم كالخيانة والإرهاب والتجسس والاغتصاب والاتجار بالأسلحة والمخدرات ويعد هذين المرسومين الأكثر اتساعاً وشمولية مقارنة بجميع قوانين ومراسيم العفو السابقة، كما لابد من الإشارة إلى أن العفو العام الصادر بتاريخ ٢٠١١/٥/٣١ شمل كافة أعضاء وقيادات التنظيمات والجمعيات السياسية غير المرخصة باستثناء تلك التي تتخذ من وسائل الإرهاب عنصراً جوهرياً في نشاطها من أجل تحقيق أهدافها، لكن حكومة الجمهورية العربية السورية ومن خلال إصرارها وسعيها الحثيث باتجاه إطلاق الحوار الوطني الشامل بين كافة أطياف المجتمع السوري وبين كافة القوى السورية بادرت إلى تشميل كافة المنتمين إلى تنظيم جماعة الإخوان المسلمين بالعفو العام وعن كامل العقوبة على الرغم من أن التنظيم المذكور اتخذ من وسائل الإرهاب والتخريب والقتل عنصراً جوهرياً إن لم يكن وحيداً من أجل تحقيق أهدافه في سورية وعلى مدى عقود طويلة مضت، كما تم بنفس الاتجاه والهدف إطلاق سراح عدد من الموقوفين المنتمين لحزب العمل الشيوعي، وصدرت القرارات بتسهيل عودة المسؤولين بالعفو إلى الفطر، كما تم إلغاء الموافقات الأمنية في كافة معاملات المواطنين السوريين.

٥- بعد رفع حالة الطوارئ فإن الأساس القانوني للتوقيف بالنسبة لأية مشتبه فيه بأية جريمة منصوص عليها في القوانين السورية النافذة: هو ما ورد من نصوص في قانون أصول المحاكمات الجزائية، كما أسلفنا بيانه سابقاً وهذا يشمل حالات التوقيف على خلفية القيام بأعمال الشغب والتخريب والإرهاب كما يحصل حالياً في سورية ويتم تسميته احتجاجات سلمية، أما بالنسبة للتظاهر السلمي فلم يتم إلقاء القبض على أي محتج أو متظاهر سلمي لجأ إلى التظاهر الاحتجاج أو التظاهر وفقاً لأحكام القانون، إلا أنه في حالات محدودة للغاية جرى إلقاء القبض على من يتظاهر بصورة مخالفة لأحكام المرسوم التشريعي رقم

(٥٤) تاريخ ٢٠١١/٤/٢١ الذي ينظم حق التظاهر السلمي، وفي هذه الحالة غالباً ما يطلق القضاء سراح الموقوفين فوراً أو خلال خمسة أيام على أبعد تقدير في حال التظاهر. أما في الحالات التي لا يكون فيها التظاهر سلمياً فإن أحكام قانون العقوبات الصادر بالمرسوم التشريعي رقم (١٤٨) لعام ١٩٤٩ هي التي يطبقها القضاء في ضوء ظروف كل قضية على حدة. ذلك أن سورية تواجه في الغالب الأعم من الحالات والوقائع التي تحصل على الأرض عصابات إرهابية مسلحة، مزودة بأحدث الأسلحة وأكثرها تقنية، في إطار من العنف المنظم الذي تناهضه القوانين والأعراف الدولية والقوانين الداخلية على حد سواء، وفي ظل فبركة وتضليل إعلامي غير مسبوق، إذ لا يعقل أن تسمح أية دولة ذات سيادة بقيام تمرد إرهابي مسلح على أراضيها وبطال وبقتل كافة مواطنيها من المدنيين أو العسكريين دون أن تلقي القبض في وجه القائمين به وتقديمهم إلى العدالة لينالوا عقابهم أمام القضاء الوطني خاصة وأن أعمال التخريب والإرهاب والإحراق لنصيب على أبنية الخدمة العامة في الدولة.

٦- إن الإجراءات القانونية التي اتبعتها، وتتبعها كافة قوى الأمن الداخلي في سورية بعد رفع حالة الطوارئ تخضع جميعها لما ورد في قانون أصول المحاكمات الجزائية في التوقيف والاعتقال فكل القوى الأمنية والشرطية وفقاً لأحكام للمادة رقم /٨/ من القانون المذكور تعبر من الضابطة العدلية التي تساعد النائب العام في مهامه وأفراد هذه الضابطة مكلفون وفقاً للنص للمادة رقم /٦/ من نفس القانون باستقصاء الجرائم وجمع أدلتها والقبض على فاعليها وإحالتهم على المحاكم الموكول إليها أمر معاقبتهم، ولا توجد لدينا أي موقوف خارج نطاق القانون على خلفية مظاهرات أو احتجاجات سلمية، أما إذا كان من يستخدم السلاح والعنف والإرهاب في مواجهة الدولة هو المقصود بهذا التساؤل فإن هذا أمر مختلف غاية الاختلاف، ومع ذلك فإننا على استعداد حتى بالنسبة لمن ارتكب عملاً إرهابياً موالاتكم بما يطلب بشأنه، على أن تكون لدينا أسماء ومعطيات محددة ودقيقة، وليس مجرد كلام غير مستند إلى أي دليل معقول.

٧- فيما يتعلق بمقتل حمزة الخطيب لنفيدكم بأن المذكور لدى مقتله كان يشارك مع مجموعة إرهابية تخريبية مسلحة في الهجوم على ضاحية سكنية في محافظة درعا، وكان يحمل بيده سلاح حاد قاطع وأصيب بعدة طلقات نارية من مسافة قريبة جداً مما يشير إلى أن مطلقي الرصاص الذين أصابوه هم رفاقه من المخربين، وأرفق تقريراً مفصلاً حول الكشف الطبي والتحقيقات القانونية التي جرت على جثته.

٨ـ إن قانون العقوبات السوري يحوي النصوص القانونية الواضحة والصريحة التي تعاقب على أي ضرب

من ضروب الشدة أو التعذيب بحق أي موقوف، كما تعاقب على حجز الحرية بعقوبات صارمة ونجيبكم

حول تساؤلاتكم عن هذا الموضوع وفق التفصيل التالي:

١ـ الحرية الشخصية حق مقدس كفلها الدستور والقانون، ولا يجوز احتجاز أحد دون توجيه تهمة إليه

حسب الأصول القانونية، وإلا كان ذلك حجز حرية غير مشروع ومعاقب عليه، فالمادة (357) من قانون

العقوبات تنص على أن : "كل من أوقف أو حبس شخصاً في غير الحالات التي ينص عليها القانون يعاقب

بالأشغال الشاقة المؤقتة "، وتنص المادة (358) على الحبس من سنة إلى ثلاث سنوات لمديري وحراس

السجون، والمعاهد التأديبية، أو الإصلاحية، وكل من اضطلع بصلاحياتهم من الموظفين إذا قبلوا شخصاً

دون مذكرة قضائية، أو قرار، أو استبقوه إلى أبعد من الأجل، وأي شخص يتم توقيفه وفقاً للقانون

السوري يتم إعلامه بأسباب هذا التوقيف، والجرم الذي استوجب إصداره، ولوعه، والمادة القانونية التي

تعاقب عليه، ويبلغ المدعى عليه مذكرات الدعوة، والإحضار، والتوقيف، ويترك له صورة عنها، وللقاضي

التحقيق في دعاوى الجناية والجنحة أن يكلفي بإصدار مذكرة دعوة، على أن يبدلها بعد لاستجواب المدعى

عليه بمذكرة توقيف إذا اقتضى التحقيق ذلك.

وإذا أوقف المدعى عليه بموجب مذكرة إحضار، وظل في النظارة أكثر من أربع وعشرين ساعة دون أن

يستجوب أو يساق إلى النائب العام اعتبر توقيفه عملاً تعسفياً، ولحق الموظف المسؤول بجريمة حجز

الحرية الشخصية المنصوص عليها في المادة (358) من قانون العقوبات.

٢ـ تعاقب المادة (391) من قانون العقوبات على التعذيب بأبسط صوره يجعل مرتكبه عرضة للعقاب، فقد

جاء نص هذه المادة على النحو الآتي:

" من سام شخصاً ضروباً من الشدة لا يجيزها القانون رغبة منه في الحصول على إقرار عن جريمة أو

على معلومات بشأنها عوقب بالحبس من ثلاثة أشهر إلى ثلاث سنوات. وإذا أفضت أعمال العنف عليه إلى

مرض أو جراح كان أدنى العقاب الحبس سنة".

فالنص القانوني يستخدم عبارة "من سام شخصاً ضروباً من الشدة..."، أي أنه يشمل أبسط صور التعذيب

وحالاته.

241

وجدير الذكر أن الجمهورية العربية السورية قد انضمت إلى الاتفاقية الدولية لمناهضة التعذيب، وقد ناقشت تقريرها بتاريخ ٣ - ٤/٥/٢٠١٠، ووافت اللجنة المعنية بكل ما هو مطلوب.

والجمهورية العربية السورية ملتزمة بكل ما تضمنته الاتفاقية لمناهضة التعذيب وغيره من ضروب المعاملة القاسية أو اللاإنسانية أو المهينة من أحكام، ذلك أنه من المستقر دستورياً وقضائياً وفقهياً في سورية، ومنذ أمد بعيد، أن المعاهدة التي تستكمل إجراءات التصديق الدستورية تتقدم على أي نص تشريعي نافذ، وتعامل على أنها جزء من التشريع الوطني، وإذا كانت متعارضة مع نص نافذ قبلها تعد معدلة له، وتتقدم عليه.

ويستخلص من نصوص الدستور السوري الدائم لعام 1973، ولا سيما المادتان (71) و(104) أنه أعطى المعاهدات قيمة مساوية للقانون الداخلي عندما يتم إبرام معاهدة، وإقرارها بشكل صحيح، ووفقاً لأحكام الدستور، فإذا خالفت الاتفاقية الدولية القانون نافذاً، وكانت سليمة من حيث إقرارها وإبرامها، ومن حيث نفاذها، فإنها تكون ذات قيمة مساوية للقانون الداخلي.

وخلاصة القول إن ما أثير لجهة الادعاءات المتعلقة باستخدام التعذيب بصورة اعتيادية من قبل موظفي إنفاذ القانون، والصحفيين، أو بتحريض منهم، ولا سيما في مواقع الاحتجاز، إنما هو قول مرسل لا يؤيده أي دليل قانوني أو مادي. وبعد صدور المرسوم رقم (161) بتاريخ 2011/4/21 المتضمن إنهاء حالة الطوارئ، والمرسوم التشريعي رقم (55) الصادر بتاريخ 2011/4/21، لم يعد بالإمكان الحديث عن أي احتجاز تعسفي أو مخالف للقانون لدى أي جهة كانت.

ولبيان فيما يلي على سبيل المثال جدولاً بأعداد الدعاوى المنظورة حالياً أما م القضاء في قضايا تتعلق بالادعاء بالتعذيب:

عدد الدعاوى	الجهة المنظور أمامها الدعوى
1	عدلية دمشق
5	عدلية ريف دمشق
1	عدلية حلب
1	عدلية اللاذقية

2	عدلية دير الزور
1	عدلية حماة
لا يوجد	عدلية إدلب
لا يوجد	عدلية الرقة
لا يوجد	عدلية الحسكة
لا يوجد	عدلية حمص
لا يوجد	عدلية طرطوس
لا يوجد	عدلية درعا
لا يوجد	عدلية السويداء
12	المجموع

أما الجهة التي تتولى التحقيق فإنه القضاء في معرض الدعاوى المرفوعة إليه، أو هي في معرض الدفع في قضية قائمة بتعرض المتهم للتعذيب، مع ملاحظة أنه غالباً ما يدفع المتهم حد عثوره أمام القضاء بتعرضه للتعذيب في معرض التحقيق معه بالجرم المسند إليه كي يستفيد من عثر بعفيه من العقاب، ويبطل إجراءات التحقيق معه، لأن الإقرار المنتزع تحت التعذيب لا يعتد به أمام القضاء، ولا يصلح لوحده دليلاً لإدانة المتهم.

ولا مجال على الإطلاق لاعتماد إقرار ملتزع بالإكراه، والإقرار على هذا النحو لا قيمة له إن لم تكن هناك أدلة لتؤيده. وقد بينت الهيئة العامة لمحكمة النقض (وهي أعلى مرجع قضائي، وتلتزم سائر القضاة بما تصدره من اجتهادات لأن لها منزلة القواعد القانونية، ومن يخالف اجتهادها يعد مرتكباً لخطأ مهني جسيم)، بأن الاعتراف الذي يبني به المتهم في ضبط الشرطة لا يؤخذ به إلا إذا تأيد بدليل آخر (قرار الهيئة العامة لمحكمة النقض رقم 293 في الدعوى رقم أساس 538 لعام 2005). وأن الاعتراف أمام رجال الضابطة العدلية ويمكن الرجوع عنه، ولا يصلح دليلاً للإدانة إذا لم تؤيده قرينة، أو دليل (القرار رقم 400 في الدعوى رقم أساس 97 لعام 2005). والاعتراف الوارد بضبط الأمن وحده ليس كافياً للحكم، وأن إهمال الدفوع الجوهرية، والأدلة المتوفرة في الدعوى، وعدم مناقشتها، يشكل خطأ مهنياً جسيماً (القرار

رقم 52 في الدعوى رقم أساس 259 لعام 2006). كما ذهبت الهيئة العامة لمحكمة النقض إلى أنه في الجرم الجنائي الوصف لا تعتمد الأقوال المنتزعة بالإكراه لدى رجال الأمن كدليل وحيد في إثبات الإدانة، ما لم تؤكد بأدلة أخرى، ويكون ضبط الشرطة والأقوال الفورية معلومات أساسية للسير في التحقيق، والوصول إلى الحقيقة، وإن عدم الأخذ بهذه الأقوال، لا يشكل خطأ مهنياً جسيماً (القرار رقم 222 في الدعوى رقم أساس 1097 لعام 2006).

أما عن تعويض ضحايا التعذيب فإن القوانين السورية النافذة تبيح لكل من يدعي تعرضه لسوء المعاملة أو التعذيب أن يطالب المسؤول عن ذلك بالتعويض فإذا ثبت للمحكمة التي تنظر دعواه أنه تعرض للتعذيب على يد أي جهة كان لها أن تحكم لصالح من يطالب بالتعويض بمبالغ مالية تناسب الضرر المادي والمعنوي الذي تعرض له، كل ذلك ضمن نطاق التعويض عن العمل غير المشروع إذ أن كل عمل غير مشروع يلزم من ارتكبه بالتعويض وفقاً لقواعد المسؤولية عن الأعمال الشخصية المنصوص عليها في مواد القانون المدني السوري.

9 – لم نسجل لدينا أي حالة تتعلق بوفاة تمت بالسجن جراء التعذيب، وفي حال توفر لديكم معلومات محددة بشأن أعمال من هذا القبيل يرجى موافاتنا بها.

10 – بالنسبة لأسئلتكم حول لجنة التحقيق القضائية التي شكلت للنظر والتحقيق في الجرائم التي تحصل لنتيجة الأحداث الجارية لنفيدكم بما يلي:

شكلت لجنة قضائية بموجب القرار الصادر عن نائب رئيس مجلس القضاء الأعلى برقم (905/ل) تاريخ 2011/3/31، وذلك على النحو الآتي:

- القاضي تيسير قلا عواد/ النائب العام للجمهورية ... رئيساً
- القاضي محمد ديب المقطرن/ رئيس إدارة التفتيش القضائي ... عضواً
- القاضي حسان السعيد/ المحامي العام الأول بدمشق ... عضواً
- القاضي أحمد السيد/ قاضي التحقيق الأول بدمشق ... عضواً

ومهمتها التحقيق بصورة فورية في جميع القضايا التي أودت بحياة عدد من المواطنين المدنيين والعسكريين في محافظتي درعا واللاذقية.

244

وبناء طلبه قامت اللجنة في يوم صدور القرار القاضي بتشكيلها، أي بتاريخ 2011/3/31 بالانتقال إلى محافظة درعا والاستماع إلى عدد من الشهود، وذوي المتوفين، كما قامت بالاستعانة بقضاة التحقيق والنيابة العامة في المحافظة المذكورة في الكشف على جثث المتوفين، وسماع أقوال ذويهم. كما جرى الاستماع إلى أقوال عدد من المصابين، وتم استجواب محافظ درعا السابق، وعدد من المسؤولين الأمنيين في المحافظة، وقد اتخذت اللجنة قراراً بمنع سفر كل من محافظ درعا ورئيس فرع الأمن السياسي السابق...

بتاريخ 2011/4/2 توجهت اللجنة القضائية إلى محافظة اللاذقية، وقد استعانت بقضاة التحقيق والنيابة العامة في المحافظة، وضبط أقوال ذوي المتوفين، وسماع العديد من الشهود، وسماع المصابين في المشافي...

بتاريخ 2011/4/5 انتقلت اللجنة إلى مدينة دوما (في ريف دمشق) وباشرت لتحقيقاتها في المجمع القضائي بدوما، وتم الاستماع إلى ذوي المتوفين والمصابين وعدد من الشهود...

وبتاريخ 2011/4/19 أصدر السيد نائب رئيس مجلس القضاء الأعلى القرار رقم (1092/ل) المتضمن إعادة تشكيل اللجنة القضائية لتصبح على النحو الآتي:

- القاضي محمد ديب المقطرن/ رئيس إدارة التفتيش القضائي   رئيساً
- القاضي حسان أسعيد/ المحامي العام الأول بدمشق   عضواً
- القاضي محمد رضوان حجة/ قاضي الإحالة الثالث في ريف دمشق   عضواً
- القاضي أحمد السيد/ قاضي التحقيق الأول بدمشق   عضواً

بتاريخ 2011/4/21 انتقلت اللجنة إلى محافظة طرطوس وتم الاجتماع بالمحامي العام ورئيس النيابة العامة، والاطلاع منهما على واقع الأحداث في المحافظة.

وبتاريخ 2011/4/23 انتقلت اللجنة إلى مدينة بانياس (محافظة طرطوس) وهناك باشرت عملها مستعينة بقضاة التحقيق والنيابة العامة، وتم الاستماع إلى ذوي المتوفين، والشهود. وفي اليوم التالي انتقلت اللجنة إلى بلدة "البيضاء" التابعة لمدينة بانياس، وتم الالتقاء ببعض الأهالي، وإطلاعهم على مهمة اللجنة، والطلب إليهم إعلام من لديه معلومات تتعلق بالأحداث بوجوب مراجعة اللجنة في مدينة بانياس، وفي هذه الأثناء لحظت اللجنة بعض التصرفات المخلة بالنظام العام من قبل بعض الأهالي الذين ثم يرغبوا بالتعاون مع اللجنة.

LAW AND WAR IN SYRIA

بتاريخ 2011/5/11 أصدر السيد نائب رئيس مجلس القضاء الأعلى القرار رقم (1421/ل) المتضمن تعديل المادة (3) من القرار رقم (905/ل) بتاريخ 2011/3/31 بحيث تصبح مهمة اللجنة "إجراء التحقيقات الفورية في جميع القضايا التي أودت بحياة عدد من المواطنين المدنيين والعسكريين أو إصابتهم، وجميع الجرائم الأخرى الناجمة عنها أو المرتبطة بها، وذلك في جميع المحافظات، وتلقي الشكاوى بهذا الخصوص. ويعتبر كل من المحامي العام وقاضيي التحقيق الأول وأقدم رئيس نيابة عامة في كل محافظة بمثابة لجنة فرعية تتبع لجنة التحقيق القضائية وتباشر مهماتها في نطاق المحافظة وترفع نتائج أعمالها إليها.

تم تحديد مقر خاص للجنة في مدينة دمشق، وتم الإعلان عنه، وعن أرقام الهواتف، وعن المواقع الإلكتروني في جميع وسائل الإعلام المرئية والمسموعة والمقروءة لتلقي الشكاوى من المواطنين أو استقبالهم في مقر اللجنة. وبالفعل باشرت اللجنة عملها في المكان المحدد، كما أن اللجان الفرعية تتابع عملها في جميع المحافظات بشكل متواصل حتى تاريخه...

11- بالنسبة للمقابر الجماعية في جسر الشغور: قامت مجموعات إرهابية مسلحة مؤلفة من مئات العناصر بالهجوم على أحد مقرات قوى حفظ النظام في جسر الشغور مستخدمة مختلف أنواع الأسلحة والذخائف حيث سيطرت على المبنى من حيث النتيجة وقتلت كافة العناصر الذين كانوا فيه ومثلت بجثثهم وبعد ذلك قام عناصر هذه الجماعات الإرهابية بتجميع عشرات الجثث ممن تم قتلهم ورميهم فوق بعضهم البعض في عدة أماكن بواسطة الجرافات، ومن ثم رمي التراب والأنقاض فوق جثثهم، كل ذلك تم خلال قيام هذه المجموعات بالسيطرة على المدينة المذكورة وترويع سكانها وإجبارهم على النزوح والهرب من منازلهم والاتجاه إلى الأراضي التركية حيث كانت مخيمات اللجوء معدة سلفاً بغية استغلال ذلك إعلامياً عبر عملية التضليل والكذب الإعلامي التي تتم إدارتها ضد حكومة الجمهورية العربية السورية عبر تصوير هؤلاء المواطنين الهاربين من إرهاب الجماعات المسلحة بأنهم لجأوا إلى الأراضي التركية خوفاً من الجيش السوري، وبعد إعادة السيطرة على مدينة جسر الشغور من قبل الدولة وإلقاء القبض على بعض عناصر التنظيمات الإرهابية قام هؤلاء المقبوض عليهم بدلالة السلطات المختصة على الأمكنة التي قاموا بدفن جثث ضحاياهم من رجال الشرطة والأمن العام فيها، حيث تم نبش هذه المقابر الجماعية بحضور وسائل الإعلام وعدد كبير من أعضاء البعثات الدبلوماسية المعتمدين في سورية، نرفق لكم نسخة

246

عن شريط تصويري مسجل لذلك، وتفيدكم بأن الملف القضائي المتعلق بالأحداث المذكورة هو قيد الإنجاز لدى القضاء المختص في محافظة إدلب التي تتبع لها مدينة جسر الشغور.

٢-١٢- أما بالنسبة لموضوع تعامل السلطات السورية المختصة مع الحشود فلابد لنا أولاً من إيراد النصوص القانونية المتعلقة بذلك.

أ- المرسوم التشريعي رقم /٥٤/ لعام ٢٠١١ المتعلق بتنظيم التظاهر السلمي في سورية والذي تتوافق نصوص مواده مع ما هو وارد في تشريعات معظم دول العالم بهذا الشأن لجهة اعتبار التظاهر السلمي أحد الحقوق الأساسية للإنسان، وآليات الترخيص للتظاهر والجهة التي تصدر هذا الترخيص والمرجع القضائي المختص بالنظر في الطعن بقرار عدم الموافقة على ترخيص المظاهرة إضافة إلى النصوص العقابية التي تتضمن تجريم أعمال التظاهر أو الشغب غير المرخص والعقاب عليها.

ب- مواد قانون العقوبات السوري التي تجرم وتعاقب تظاهرات وتجمعات الشغب، وهي المواد من رقم /٣٣٥/ إلى /٣٣٩/ وفيما يلي نصها:

- المادة ٣٣٥: من كان في اجتماع ليس له طابع الاجتماع الخاص، سواء من حيث غايته أو شرطه أو عدد المدعوين إليه أو الذين يتألف منهم أو من مكان انعقاده أو كان في مكان عام أو بمحل مباح للجمهور أو معرض لأنظاره فجهر بصياح أو بأناشيد الشغب أو أبرز شارة من الشارات في حالات يضطرب معها معها الأمن العام أو أقدم على أية تظاهرة شغب أخرى يعاقب بالحبس من شهر إلى سنة وبالغرامة مائة ليرة.

- المادة ٣٣٦: كل حشد أو موكب على الطرق العامة أو في مكان مباح للجمهور يعد تجمعاً للشغب ويعاقب بالحبس من شهر إلى سنة:

إذا تألف من ثلاثة أشخاص أو أكثر يقصد اقتراف جناية أو جنحة وكان أحدهم على الأقل مسلحاً.

إذا تألف من سبعة أشخاص على الأقل بقصد الاحتجاج على قرار أو تدبير اتخذتهما السلطات العامة بقصد الضغط عليها.

إذا أربى عدد الأشخاص على العشرين وظهروا بمظهر من شأنه أن يعكر الطمأنينة العامة:

LAW AND WAR IN SYRIA

المادة ٢٣٧: -

١ - إذا تجمع الناس على هذه الصورة أنذرهم بالتفرق أحد ممثلي السلطة الإدارية أو ضباط من الضابطة العدلية.

٢ - ويعفى من العقوبة المفروضة آنفا الذين يتصرفون قبل الإنذار المسلط أو يمتثلون في الحال لإنذارها دون أن يستعملوا أسلحتهم أو يرتكبوا أية جريمة أخرى.

المادة ٢٣٨: -

١ - إذا لم يتفرق المجتمعون بغير القوة كانت العقوبة الحبس من شهرين إلى سنتين.

٢ - ومن استعمل السلاح عوقب بالحبس من سنة إلى ثلاث سنوات فضلاً عن أية عقوبة أشد قد يستحقها.

المادة ٢٣٩: يمكن الحكم بالمنع من الحقوق المدنية ويمنع الإقامة ويطرد من البلاد وفاقا للمواد من ٦ - ٨٢ - ٨٨ في الحين المنصوص عليها في الفصول ٢ إلى ٥ من هذا الباب.

ومن خلال ما سبق بيانه ووصفه في الفقرات السابقة لتظاهرات وتجمعات الشغب والتخريب وما قامت به الجماعات الإرهابية المسلحة من قتل وترويع للمواطنين ومن تدمير وإحراق لمؤسسات الدولة وأبنية إداراتها العامة لنؤكد بأن قوى الأمن الداخلي المختصة تعاملت وما زالت تتعامل مع أية تظاهرة سلمية حتى ولو كانت غير مرخصة عن طريق تأمين الحماية لهذه المظاهرة وكفالة للمواطنين المشاركين فيها إلى حين تفرقهم من تلقاء أنفسهم وذهاب كل منهم إلى منزله، أما عندما تخرج المظاهرة عن النطاق السلمي ويدخل المشاركين فيها ضمن نطاق أعمال تخريب المباني العامة وإحراقها فيتم مواجهتهم بالقوة العددية المتناسبة ودون استخدام أية أسلحة حربية من قبل عناصر قوات حفظ النظام كذلك الأمر عندما يخرج من بين المتظاهرين بعض العناصر المسلحة التي تبادر لإطلاق النار على عناصر حفظ النظام وعلى المتظاهرين أنفسهم لإثارة البلبلة والذعر وتشويه صورة السلطات العامة أمام المواطنين فإن قوات حفظ النظام وحفاظا منها إلى أرواح المواطنين تبادر إلى الابتعاد عن منطقة الشغب والتظاهر حتى لا يؤدي اشتباكها مع المسلحين إلى إصابة المتظاهرين الآخرين، ولا يسمح بأي حال من الأحوال باستخدام السلاح إلا في حالات الاشتباكات المسلحة مع المجموعات الإرهابية وضمن نطاق الدفاع عن النفس فقط أو في الحالات التي يقوم فيها عناصر هذه المجموعات بأعمال الترهيب أو القتل الجماعي للمواطنين الآخرين في مناطق تواجدهم. وفي جميع الأحوال فإن الاستراتيجية الوحيدة المطبقة في سورية لجهة ضبط الحشود

248

والتعامل مع التظاهرات سلمية كانت وهي نادرة جداً أم غير سلمية وهي السائدة منذ بدء الأحداث هي ضبط النفس إلى أبعد الحدود وأقصاها وقد أدت هذه الاستراتيجية التي اقترنت بأوامر صارمة لجهة عدم استخدام الأسلحة حتى مع التظاهرات التخريبية إلى قتل المئات من عناصر وضباط قوات حفظ النظام وإصابة الآلاف منهم بجروح خطيرة أصيبوا بها بسبب استخدام المجموعات التخريبية والإرهابية للأسلحة الحربية والسيوف والخناجر، وإن أي عنصر أو ضابط من قوات حفظ النظام يخرق هذه الأوامر أو يتجاوز على الصلاحيات الممنوحة له يتعرض للعقوبات الصارمة المنصوص عليها في هذا الصدد بالقوانين الجزائية السورية النافذة، ولا يوجد أية حصانة لأحد أو لأية جهة في هذا المجال، أما عن إسعاف المصابين وتأمين الخدمات الطبية لهم فإن الجهات المختصة ضمن هذا المجال تقوم بإسعاف الجميع

وتأمين الرعاية الطبية اللازمة لهم سواء كانوا من المتظاهرين أو من الإرهابيين أو من عناصر حفظ النظام وينفس السوية والأداء للجميع، وتعزيزاً لهذه الإجراءات فقد صدرت التعليمات لقوات حفظ النظام بعدم توقيف أي مصاب تم إسعافه إلى أية مشفى أو مستوصف طبي مهما كانت فعاليته الجرمية خلال أعمال الشغب التي أصيب خلالها.

١٣- إن عملية الرصد والتفتيش التي تمارس من قبل وزارة العدل ومن قبل وزارة الداخلية على مختلف السجون هي عملية دائمة ومتواصلة، وتتم بشكلٍ منهجي وفعّال، وفي جميع الأوقات، وقد أورد قانون أصول المحاكمات الجزائية النصوص الواجبة حول ذلك في المواد من /٤٢١/ إلى /٤٢٥/ منه وفقاً لما يلي:

المادة ٤٢١: تنظيم السجون ومحال التوقيف بمرسوم يتخذ في مجلس الوزراء.

المادة ٤٢٢: يتفقد قاضي التحقيق وقاضي الصلح مرة واحدة في الشهر ورؤساء المحاكم الجزائية مرة واحدة عن ثلاثة أشهر على الأقل الأشخاص الموجودين في محال التوقيف والسجون.

المادة ٤٢٣: لرؤساء المحاكم الجزائية وقضاة التحقيق وقضاة الصلح أن يأمروا حراس محال التوقيف والسجون التابعين لمحكمتهم بإجراء التدابير التي يقتضيها التحقيق والمحاكمة.

المادة ٤٢٤: على كل من علم بتوقيف أحد الناس في أمكنة غير التي أعدتها الحكومة للحبس والتوقيف أن يخبر بذلك النائب العام أو معاونه أو قاضي الصلح.

المادة ٤٢٥:

١- عندما يبلغ الموظفون المذكورون في المادة السابقة مثل هذا الخبر عليهم أن يتوجهوا في الحال إلى المحل الحاصل فيه التوقيف وأن يطلقوا سراح من كان موقوفاً بصورة غير قانونية.

٢- وإذا تبين لهم سبب قانوني موجب للتوقيف أرسلوا الموقوف في الحال إلى النائب العام أو القاضي الصالح العائد إليه الأمر.

٣- وعليهم أن ينظموا محضر بالوقائع.

٤- إذا أهملوا العمل بما تقدم عدوا شركاء في جريمة حجز الحرية الشخصية وجرت الملاحقة بحقهم بهذه الصفة.

١٤- بالنسبة لموضوع المواطنين السوريين من أصل كردي فقد صدر المرسوم التشريعي رقم /٤٩/ تاريخ ٢٠١١/٤/٧ الذي نص على منحهم لجنسية العربية السورية وبالتالي يستطيع أي منهم الحصول على الجنسية ويظهر بالتالي مواطناً سورياً يتمتع بكافة حقوق وواجبات المواطن السوري على كافة الأصعدة وبكل المجالات وقد وصل عدد الذين حصلوا على الجنسية إلى الآلاف منهم.

١٥أ- بالنسبة للقوانين التي يجري العمل على إصدارها حالياً ضمن نطاق عملية الإصلاح الجارية في سورية فقد أقر مجلس الوزراء قانوني الانتخابات والأحزاب السياسية تمهيداً لصدورهما ولود أن نعرض عليكم ما تم القيام به في إطار إصدار قانون الانتخابات العامة من خطوات بهدف إطلاعكم على المراحل التي يسير بها إصدار أي من التشريعات الحديثة في سورية لكي تكون مواكبة عن أفضل النصوص القانونية المعمول بها في معظم دول العالم وفقاً لما يلي:

أصدر السيد رئيس مجلس الوزراء القرار رقم (٦١٨٦) تاريخ ٢٠١١/٥/٨، المتضمن تشكيل لجنة مهمتها إعداد مشروع قانون جديد للانتخابات العامة يتوافق وأفضل المعايير العالمية المتعارف عليها على أن تنجز اللجنة مهمتها خلال أسبوعين...

وتضم اللجنة:

- د. نجم الأحمد — معاون وزير العدل
- حسن جلالي — معاون وزير الداخلية
- محمود صالح — المستشار القانوني في رئاسة مجلس الوزراء

أستاذ في كلية الحقوق بجامعة دمشق	د. محمد يوسف الحسين	-
أستاذ في كلية الحقوق بجامعة دمشق	د. جميلة شربجي	-
أستاذ في كلية الحقوق بجامعة دمشق	د. محمد خير العكام	-
المستشار في وزارة الإدارة المحلية	فوزي محاملة	-
مدير المجالس في وزارة الإدارة المحلية.	خالد كامل	-

واستناداً إلى القرار المشار إليه أعلاه تبين الآتي:

- عكفت اللجنة موضوع القرار أعلاه على عقد اجتماعات يومية متتالية إلى أن أنهت مشروع القانون.

- اطلعت اللجنة على القوانين النافذة في دول عديدة منها: فرنسا- بلجيكا- مصر - الجزائر - الأردن-

العراق - فلسطين...

- كما اطلعت اللجنة على القوانين والأنظمة السورية سواء النافذة، أو ما كان نافذاً قبل هذه القوانين.

- استعانت اللجنة بآراء ومقترحات عدد كبير من المختصين ورجال القانون (أساتذة جامعات- قضاة-

محامون...)، ومن مختلف التخصصات والشرائح العمرية، وقد كان لخبرتهم وآرائهم دوراً في إثراء

مشروع القانون.

- انتهت اللجنة من عملها قبل الموعد المحدد بيوم واحد.

- عرض مشروع القانون على موقع "التشاركية" التابع لرئاسة مجلس الوزراء، وعلى المواقع الإلكترونية

لوزارات العدل، والداخلية، والإدارة المحلية، وكان عدد الزيارات قد تجاوز (٣٤,٠٠٠) زيارة، وكان عدد

الآراء المسجلة نحو (٣٤٠٠) ملاحظة.

- تمت دراسة جميع الملاحظات الواردة، والأخذ بجميع الملاحظات الموضوعية التي تسهم في إثراء

مشروع القانون، كما أسهم البرنامج الإنمائي للأمم المتحدة UNDP بملاحظات قيمة تم الأخذ بها جميعها.

ولعل أهم ما تضمنه مشروع القانون لجهة الالتزام بالمعايير العالمية:

قانون الانتخابات واحد:

تضمن مشروع القانون جمعاً للأحكام الموضوعية المتعلقة بانتخاب أعضاء مجلسي الشعب ومجالس الإدارة

المحلية في قانون واحد، أسوة بما عليه الحال في غالبية دول العالم.

الأهداف:

251

وكان الهدف المبتغى هو تنظيم الأحكام الموضوعية المتعلقة بهذه الانتخابات، وتأمين سلامة العملية الانتخابية، وحق المرشحين في مراقبتها، وتضمين مشروع القانون نصوصاً تضمن معاقبة المعتدين بالعملية الانتخابية وبإرادة الناخبين، إضافة إلى تأمين تمثيل الشرائح الاجتماعية الأوسع في المجتمع...

وجود إدارة انتخابية مستقلة ومتكاملة عضوياً وفقاً للمعايير الدولية:

ذلك أن نزاهة الانتخابات من الناحية العملية إنما تكمن في كيفية تنظيمها وتنفيذها على أرض الواقع، مما يقتضي وجود جهة محايدة لضمان تطبيق الضوابط القانونية فلا يجوز لأحد أن يكون طرفاً في منافسة ما وحكماً فيها، وبمعنى آخر لا يجوز لمن تكون له مصلحة مباشرة أو غير مباشرة في نتيجة الانتخاب القيام بتنظيمها أو إدارتها، لذلك كان الحرص في مشروع القانون على أن يتولى القضاء عملية الإشراف على الانتخابات وإدارتها، فكانت اللجنة العليا للانتخابات التي تتولى هذه المهمة، كما أن اللجنة الفرعية القرعية في كل محافظة هي لجنة قضائية، ولم يترك للسلطة التنفيذية إلا جانباً بسيطاً من الأمور الإدارية.

لجان انتخابية مستقلة:

ولأن المعايير الدولية تقتضي أن تكون الإدارة الانتخابية مستقلة ومتكاملة عضوياً، فإن مشروع القانون كان قد أفرد نصوصاً واضحة تتعلق بتشكيل لجان انتخابية مستقلة وحيادية تكون مسؤولة عن تنظيم وإدارة العملية الانتخابية بمختلف مراحلها ومستوياتها، وقد جرى تحديد الاختصاصات والمسؤوليات على نحو يعكس أعلى مستويات المصداقية والنزاهة في العملية الانتخابية.

الدوائر الانتخابية:

أخذاً بالمفاهيم السياسية والدستورية المتعلقة بفلسفة التمثيل سواء في المجالس النيابية (مجلس الشعب) أو المجالس المحلية فقد كان الحرص في مشروع القانون على أن تكون الدوائر الانتخابية بالنسبة لانتخابات مجلس الشعب دوائر كبيرة نسبياً لأن عضو مجلس الشعب لا يمثل رقعة جغرافية محددة، وإنما هو ممثل للشعب بأكمله، بينما كانت الدوائر الانتخابية بالنسبة للانتخابات المحلية دوائر صغيرة تتناسب ومفهوم التمثيل المحلي.

شروط الترشيح:

ثم رفع الحد الأعلى للمدة الزمنية المتعلقة بالمتجنس من (٥) إلى (١٠) سنوات. وقد استثنى مشروع القانون الذين اكتسبوا الجنسية السورية بموجب المرسوم رقم (٤٩) لعام ٢٠١١ (المتعلق بمعالجة مشكلة إحصاء ١٩٦٢)، إذ يحق لهم الترشح فوراً دون الانتظار لمرور عشر سنوات:

الدعاية الانتخابية:

نظم مشروع القانون موضوع الدعاية الانتخابية متيحاً إمكانية الوصول إلى مختلف وسائل الإعلام، بحيث تتاح فرصة معقولة للمتنافسين في الانتخابات بأن يعلنوا عن برامجهم الانتخابية.

مراقبة العملية الانتخابية:

أتاح مشروع القانون للمرشحين أو من يمثلهم قانوناً حق الرقابة على العملية الانتخابية بهدف التأكد من سير الانتخابات بنزاهة بعيداً عن أي تزوير أو تلاعب، وتشمل هذه الرقابة عمل اللجان، والانتخاب، وفرز الأصوات، وكافة الأمور المتعلقة بالعملية الانتخابية إلى حين إعلان النتائج.

الجرائم الانتخابية:

تم إفراد فصل خاص في مشروع القانون فيه عرض مفصل ومسهب لكل فعل أو امتناع عن فعل من شأنه أن يشكل جرماً انتخابياً، وذلك على نحو من شأنه خلق جو من الأمان القانوني. وفي مشروع القانون جرى تحديد نطاق الجرائم الانتخابية بشكل دقيق، وجرّمت الأعمال التي من شأنها الاعتداء على سير مكونات العملية الانتخابية.

المنازعات الانتخابية:

حرص مشروع القانون على وجود مراجع مختصة يمكن للناخب أو المرشح اللجوء إليها بشكل مباشر لعرض طعنه في أمر من الأمور المتعلقة بالعملية الانتخابية، بدءاً مسح أجنحة الانتخاب، وكذلك لجنة الترشيح، واللجان الفرعية، وانتهاء بإمكانية الطعن بالنتائج الانتخابية في صيغتها النهائية أمام المراجع القضائية المختصة. وفي جميع هذه المراحل حددت آجال زمنية قصيرة إن لجهة الطعن أو البت فيه، وذلك بما لا يؤثر على سير العملية الانتخابية وبما يضمن حقوق الطاعنين في آن معاً.

• تم تشكيل لجنة وزارية لمراجعة القانون في صيغته النهائية.

• أقر مجلس الوزراء مشروع القانون تمهيداً لصدوره.

١٦ـ لترفق ربطاً كافة النصوص التشريعية ومشاريع القوانين التي لوهنا عنها في معرض إجاباتنا هذه، وتسعة أقراص ليزرية (CD) تتضمن تقليداً لوجريمة مقتل حمزة الخطيب وفقاً لشهادات ذويه، إضافة لموضوع المقابر الجماعية بجسر الشغور وأصل التخريب والإرهاب في بعض المحافظات، واعترافات بعض أعضاء المجموعات الإرهابية المسلحة بما قاموا به من أعمال إجرامية.

رابعاً: أخيراً فإن حكومة الجمهورية العربية السورية تؤكد مجدداً سعيها الدائم إلى استمرار التعاون معكم في كافة مجالات عملكم وتقديم العون لكم في مهامكم والإجابة على تساؤلاتكم من أجل الوصول إلى الحقيقة في كافة المواضيع التي نتواصل معكم بشأنها، حتى تتمكنوا من اتخاذ قراراتكم وآرائكم حولها بشكل عادل وحيادي بعيداً عن الوقائع الملفقة التي تقدمها لكم بعض المصادر من أجل الظهور أمامكم بمظهر الدفاع عمن حقوق الإنسان غير لتشويه سمعة الجمهورية العربية السورية بهدف الوصول إلى أهداف غير مشروعة، ولابد من الإشارة لكم بأن عملية الإصلاح التشريعي والسياسي مازالت مستمرة في سورية بخطوات واسعة وفيما يتوافق مع المعايير والأسس الراسخة في الدستور السوري وتتطابق مع المعايير المعمول بها دولياً، إضافة إلى الاستفادة في تلك من التفاعل الايجابي والمثمر والمستمر القائم فيما بيننا.

[Unofficial translation]

Note verbale dated 5 August 2011 from the Permanent Mission of the Syrian Arab Republic addressed to the United Nations High Commissioner for Human Rights

Geneva, 5 August 2011

First: The government of the Syrian Arab Republic expresses its continued interest to cooperate with the United Nations High Commissioner for Human Rights, and confirms its persistence in uncovering and exposing facts about the questions raised. The Government will do so to exclude all fabricated claims, made up lies and false information that are being submitted to the High Commissioner from sources with questionable objectives and methods that are immoral, inhuman, unlawful methods aimed at discrediting Syria.

Second: The Government of the Syrian Arab Republic re-affirms the basic principles guiding its logic in dealing with matters to be discussed; it is according to the following points:

The Constitution of the Syrian Arab Republic guarantees freedom of expression. The Government has the responsibility to protect and promote the practice of the right of freedom of expression, and to develop a nurturing environment aimed at cultivating this basic right for its citizens in order to achieve a positive outcome for the Syrian society.

The right to peaceful demonstrations is also secured by the constitution of the Syrian Arab Republic. A law regulating the exercise of this right in accordance with internationally recognized standards has been recently issued.

Syrian laws contain texts clearly aimed at reinforcing reprehension for committing acts of torture, or distress of any kind.

Syrian laws provide for punishment for acts resulting in depravation of freedom or illegal imprisonment, whether carried out by private individuals or by persons affiliated with the authorities.

One of the main pillars of the policy adopted by the Syrian Government is to defend, protect and advance human rights in the country and abroad.

Fighting corruption is an ongoing process, and the Government of the Syrian Arab Republic is determined to pursue and advance legislations complementing the mechanisms addressing this phenomenon. In this area, we are in line with the laws adopted by leading countries.

The government of the Syrian Arab Republic is actively working on developing political activism in Syria; it has proven its intention by proceeding to making important decisions and taking comprehensive steps in this regard.

A comprehensive national dialogue among all segments of the Syrian society is the best approach to achieve reform and development in subjects related to politics, legislations, society and economy.

In order to achieve the highest standards of social justice for all individuals in the society, it is decided that the rule of law and the judiciary are the two most important pillars upon which the overall reform process shall be built.

Based on the above, and since the beginning of the events in March 2011, we confirm that the concerned Syrian authorities have accompanied and protected peaceful demonstrations, and made sure everybody went back home safe; demonstrations where protestors had legitimate claims and aspirations aimed at reform and stopping corruption, those who had chosen a civilized manner of conduct, reflecting the nature and essence of the relationship between individuals in a society and the state. The way things worked out did not satisfy third parties inside the country and abroad, whose sole aim is to destabilize the Syrian society. Armed terrorist groups emerged; started assaulting, terrorizing and murdering peaceful demonstrators. Members of terrorist groups operate by engaging in demonstrations; they carry sticks, swords and knives, and start to agitate the crowds, set cars on fire and sabotage public and private properties. They also shoot fire arms on protestors and security forces alike, aiming to kill as many as possible. The reason terrorists attack protestors is because they demonstrate under protection of authorities. In reality, the main goal of these groups is to discredit authorities in Syria and portray the Government as if it is employing brutal force to repress protestors. Their actions are accompanied by a misleading press campaign against Syria, a campaign conducted by foreign media to coincide with few "fatwas" uttered by the so-called Muslim clergymen. "Fatwas" incite violence, murder and bloodshed justified by fake religious reasoning. This is the same methodology and expiatory logic adopted by terrorist organizations in other parts of the world, while always seeking to destroy the societies where they operate. Benefiting from substantial external funding, dormant terrorist cells were reactivated, expressing themselves in public, using contemporary means of communication, and weapons smuggled through the Syrian borders. They use mosques to stock ammunition and weapons, a scenario that took place in the case of Al-Omari mosque and few other mosques in Dar'a and other provinces in the country. These actions are also facilitated by mosque attendants, who aided, covered up and coordinated invitations to kill, while propagating their perverse religious ideologies among gullible individuals to produce actions of murder, sabotage and terror against police agents and armed forces as well as among peaceful demonstrators, the number of deaths reached hundreds among armed forces of all ranks, as well as thousands of injured, victims of gunshots or stabbing wounds or those who were severely beaten, in addition to terrorists maiming cadavers of police agents and military personnel.

With respect to the recent abolition of the State of Emergency Law, individuals who are arrested for committing illegal actions are transferred, according to the Syrian code of criminal procedures, to specialized instances in the judiciary system. Arrests in Syria are no longer taking place under the State of Emergency Law. All arrested individuals are transferred to public prosecutors within 24 hours of their initial arrest to become in court custody. In most cases transferred suspects are immediately released except those who have committed acts of murder, setting fire to or sabotaging properties and are prosecuted by the competent judicial authority in accordance with the Law. Those who are proven innocent, will be declared as such by the court. Those who are proven guilty of the mentioned crimes will be judged and punished according to directives provided by the Syrian penal code.

Third: answers presented by the Syrian government to 15 July 2011 questions asked by the Office of the High Commissioner for Human Rights:

1.   Three legislative Decrees were issued on 15 July 2011. Legislative decree number (161), stipulating the abolition of the State of Emergency Law. Legislative decree number (53), stipulating the abolition of the Supreme State Security Court -which was established on 28 March 1968 by legislative decree number (47)- and the transfer of all cases in deliberation before the Supreme State Security Court onto the relevant judicial authorities, according to Syria's criminal justice regulations, and in light of the legislative decree number (55) containing the amendment of Article (17) of Criminal Procedures Code, to allow the competent law enforcement and related bodies to investigate crimes described in the general penal code, crimes touching on state security, and public safety matters. These investigations should not exceed seven days, during which evidence would be collected and suspects would be heard. The reservation period of seven days is renewable for a maximum

of 60 days by order of attorney general on a case by case basis. According to code of criminal justice regulations, law enforcement officials are bound to bring suspects to a judge at the end of seven days. In the absence of realistic or legal obligations, specific to a single investigation, it is permitted to keep suspects beyond the period of seven days. The public prosecutor needs to be informed of details of the investigation and, if necessary, could be asked for an additional detention period for further questioning and collection of evidence. He could then accept or refuse the demand for extension, in which case, the suspect will be immediately referred to a court of law.

To sum up what was stated in relation to the points in question, we would like to convey that the abolition if the State of Emergency Law will result in no emergency arrests related to public safety or national security crimes taking place in Syria. Only texts mentioned in the criminal justice code will be applied to mechanisms and justifications of pre-trial detention. Generally speaking, those regulations prohibit arresting suspects for over 24 hours before they are presented to court to become in the custody of law, the regulations in question allow for extension of detention period after the approval of the attorney general and in accordance with the nature and outcome of investigations. This applies to most crimes mentioned under the Syrian law. Exceptions include detention periods and detention mechanisms related to crimes affecting national security or public safety. As for the legal procedures used in implementing the abolition of the State of Emergency Law, all cases currently deliberated before the Supreme State Security Court are transferred to relevant judicial authorities according to criminal justice regulations. Suspects in these cases are also transferred to their respective provinces to stand in courts with relevant competencies, to be judged according to procedures dictated by the Syrian penal code.

2.   Concerning general amnesty implementation, it is up to respective prosecution authorities in every region and province in Syria to execute rules of general amnesty according to the content of the legislative decree issued in this regard, and the directives provided by the Syrian penal code and regulations of criminal courts. Immediately following the issuing of the general amnesty decree, detainees who will be granted amnesty will be considered; records of their cases in prisons, court registers and public persecution offices will be opened; and the attorney general will issue appropriate decisions for immediate release (for those to whom general amnesty applies for the whole period of their sentences). As for those who are partially included in general amnesty decree, their release will be decided by investigation judges and the competent criminal courts deliberating their cases, courts make their final decisions, while taking into consideration the effect of general amnesty on the relevant portion of detainees' sentences.

3.   Except for a medical committee, no other committee was formed to study individual cases of detainees who could be included in the general amnesty decree. Prisoners are invited to submit requests to consider their cases according to the law by the public prosecutor and competent courts.

4.   A list describing the numbers of prisoners included in the general amnesty decree:

decree number	issue date	Number of individuals included	
Legislative decree number 34	3 July 2011	province	number
		Damascus	138
		Aleppo	244
		Damascus country side	4'195
		Idlib	97
		Homs	57
		Hama	185

decree number	issue date	Number of individuals included	
		Latakkia	52
		Tartus	37
		Daraa	52
		Swaida	11
		Dair Al Zor	46
		Hasaka	57
		Raqa	56
		total	**5'227**

Legislative decree number 61	31 May 2011	province	number
		Damascus	323
		Aleppo	66
		Damascus country side	1'431
		Idlib	65
		Homs	168
		Hama	61
		Latakkia	38
		Tartus	160
		Daraa	45
		Swaida	26
		Dair Al Zor	50
		Hasaka	46
		Raqa	160
		total	**2'684**

Legislative decree number 72	20 June 2011	province	number
		Damascus	196
		Aleppo	103
		Damascus countryside	344
		Idlib	32
		Homs	30
		Hama	59
		Latakkia	1'600
		Tartus	13
		Daraa	12
		Swaida	55
		Dair Al Zor	31
		Hasaka	27
		Raqa	20
		total	**2'522**

Thus, 10,433 detainees are included in the amnesty decrees issued and were immediately released according to the list mentioned above. Consequently, this does not include detainees for violations and misdemeanors, or pending cases of crimes for which detainees might benefit from partial amnesty coverage at the moment of sentencing. They could get amnesty for half or quarter of the sentence. In addition, this does not include those evading justice unless they surrender within the periods specifies by the decrees. It should also be noted that crimes of treason, espionage, terrorism and rape are not included in this amnesty. Those two decrees are most comprehensive and extensive when compared to all previous decrees related to amnesty in the country. It is noteworthy that the general amnesty decree issued on 31 May 2011 has included all leaders and members of illegitimate political organizations and associations with the exception of terrorist organizations using means of terror to reach their objectives. The Government of the Syrian Arab Republic in its plan to include all parties of the Syrian society in a comprehensive national dialogue has included members of the Muslim Brotherhood Party in its general amnesty, despite the fact that the party in question had used, for decades, terror, murder and destruction as principal means – among others- to achieve its goals in the country. Detainees of the Communist Labor Party have received the same amnesty. Decisions to facilitate return to Syria for those who are included in this amnesty are issued and all procedures related to security clearances for Syrian citizens are lifted.

5.   Following abolition of the State of Emergency Law, as it was mentioned previously, criminal court procedures under the Syrian judicial law remain the basis for arresting crime suspects. This includes detainees arrested for participating in riots, sabotage and terrorism in the so-called peaceful demonstrations currently taking place in Syria. When it comes to peaceful protestors, who are demonstrating according to the rules of the law, no arrests were conducted except for few cases where demonstrators have broken rules related to the legislative decree number (54) of 21 April 2011, regulating citizens' peaceful demonstration rights, detainees are immediately released, while recidivists are released in five days of their arrest. When demonstrations are not peaceful, regulations provided by the Syrian penal code as mentioned in the legislative decree number (148) of the year 1949 will be applied by the judiciary instances on a case by case basis. Syria is often subject to activities of terrorist groups, who are equipped with the latest weapons and technologies. They propagate organized violence which is in opposition to international laws and Syrian laws alike and they are supported by unprecedented misleading mass media campaign. It is unreasonable for any sovereign state to be asked not to respond to insurgents' terrorist attacks reaching its citizens, both military and civilians, and sabotaging public service buildings, or not to bring those criminals to justice.

6.   Legal procedures adopted by law enforcement bodies in Syria following the abolition of the State of Emergency Law and applied to situations of arrests and detentions conform to legislations dictated by Syria's criminal code. All security forces and police follow article 8 of the law in question which constitutes the basis for the work of the attorney general. The members of law enforcement bodies are charged, according to Article number 6 of the same law, with investigating, collecting evidence, arresting criminals and bringing them to court to be judged. We have no detainees unlawfully arrested with regards to peaceful demonstrations. If your question concerns individuals who have used weapons or terrorist acts against the state, it is an entirely different matter. Yet even for those who have committed terrorist acts, we are ready to cooperate. We need to receive specific names and information to be able to deliver documents concerning the persons in question. We cannot respond to claims which lack the basis of reasonable evidence.

7.   Concerning Hamza Al-khateeb, we inform you that this person was participating in a terrorist attack on a residential suburb in the Dara'a province the moment he was killed. He

A/HRC/18/53

carried a sharp weapon in his hand, he received few shots from a short distance, most probably by his fellow terrorists. We will attach a detailed report including procedures and results of judicial investigations and medical exams performed on his cadaver.

8.   Syrian penal code contains clear texts in relation to committing acts of violence or torture on detainees, including severe punishment for conducting unlawful imprisonment. Related to this point, following, is our answer in details:

(a)   Personal freedom is a sacred right guaranteed by the Constitution and the law. Detaining individuals without proper charges formulated according to judicial regulations is prohibited. It equals unlawful imprisonment and is punishable by the law. Article number (357) of the penal code states that conducting unlawful detention or imprisonment is punishable by a temporary hard labor sentence. Article (358) states that a punishment of three years of imprisonment is applied to prison guards, managers of disciplinary institutions and their staff when they accept to receive detainees without proper legal warrant, or court decision, or when they keep detainees beyond the legal term of sentences. When a Syrian citizen is arrested, he is informed of the legal reason for his arrest, the crime he is accused of and the article of law which will determine his punishment. He is also given copies of files containing information of invitation to interrogation. A magistrate examining felony or misdemeanor cases has the authority to issue an invitation for interrogation that will eventually be substituted by an arrest warrant after interrogation of the suspect, when it applies. When a defendant is detained for over 24 hours without being interrogated or brought to the attorney general, his detention is considered to be an unlawful arbitrary act. Whoever is responsible for this situation will be persecuted according to article number (358) of the penal code for unlawful imprisonment.

(b)   Article number (391) of the penal code stipulates punishment for conducting any kind of torture, according to the following text:

He who conducts illegal torture acts in order to get someone to admit a crime, or deliver information related to a crime, will receive a punishment of imprisonment for 3 months to 3 years. If acts of torture committed led to illness or injury of the person tortured, a minimum punishment by the law is one year of imprisonment. The expression used in the text of this law singles out "the slightest forms of torture".

It should also be mentioned that the Syrian Arab Republic has joined the International Convention Against Torture and has presented its report on 3-4 May 2010 and relevant documents to the Committee.

The Syrian Arab Republic is committed to all the principles of the International Convention Against Torture and supports measures taken against torture and other cruel, inhuman or degrading treatment. In Syria, it is agreed that from constitutional, jurisprudential and legislative view points, when a treaty completes its ratification procedure of constitutional precedence over any legislative text in force, it is treated equally to any national legislation. When it is inconsistent with the text in question, it will rule over the existing text, as it will be considered as an improvement.

When we sum up the 1973 permanent Syrian constitution, especially the two articles number (71) and (104), we realize that it gives treaties a value equal to domestic Syrian laws. This means that when a treaty is concluded and properly approved by constitutional rules, even when it contradicts with an enforced domestic law, it will have an equal value to it.

Having said that, allegations that torture is performed routinely by Syrian law enforcement officers or that authorities tacitly encourage torture during interrogations of suspects in places of detention are untrue, it has no legal or material evidence. Following Abolition of the State of Emergency Law, decree number (161) on 21 April 212011, and decree number (55) on 21 April 2011, the possibility of maintaining allegations of the existence of arbitrary detention or abuse of the law in any of our law enforcement institutions is no longer plausible.

Here is a list containing the numbers of cases of allegations of torture performed on detainees:

courts	Number of cases
Damascus Court	1
Damascus countryside court	5
Aleppo Court	1
Lattakia Court	1
Dair Al Zor Court	2
Hama Court	1
Idlib Court	none
Raqqa Court	none
Hasaka Court	none
Homs Court	none
Tartus Court	none
Dara Court	none
Swaida Court	none
total	**12**

Authorities conduct investigations in these cases under the judiciary system as they are usually cases involving suspects which accuse interrogators of torture in order to get less punishment for their crimes. If it proven that torture has been used, the investigation will be considered invalid. Confessions proven to be under torture are also invalid.

No valid confession can be obtained by torture. Yet, when this happens, it has no value without additional supporting evidence.

The general authority of the Cassation Court, which is the highest judicial authority, produces jurisprudence rules that have the status of legal rules. For fear of making a serious professional error, jurisprudence of the Cassation Court is respected by all judges. Cassation Court declared that the mention of a confession made by an accused of a crime in a police report is invalid, unless it is supported by additional evidence (The general authority of the Cassation Court, decision number 293, in the court case number 538 of the year 2005). It also stipulates that confessions in presence of law enforcement agents are revocable, it is not considered as legal proof of crime unless supported by additional evidence (Decision number 400, in the court case number 97 of 2005). A confession mentioned in a police document is not a basis for judgment and neglecting essential motives and other evidence pieces or refraining from discussing these elements is considered to be a serious professional error (Decision number 52, in the court case number 259 of 2006). Information obtained by force in police stations, although it might appear to be important for the investigation taking place, and might help to uncover the truth, is legally invalid, unless supported by additional pieces of evidence. Not taking into consideration information obtained by force is not regarded as a serious professional error (Decision number 222, in the court case number 1097 of the year 2006).

Torture victims are authorized to claim compensational measures. Compensation is adapted to the extent of proven physical and moral damages, and is decided by courts on a case by case basis. It is mentioned in the law that individuals who commit unlawful acts leading to physical and moral damages are liable. According to Syria's civil code they are legally responsible for compensating their victims.

9.   We have no records involving death as a result of torture during detention. Please provide us with your information related to this question, if you have any.

10.   To answer to your question concerning the Committee of Judicial Inquiry established to examine and investigate crimes that occurred as a result of the ongoing events in Syria: A judicial committee was created following decision of vice-president of the Supreme Judicial Council, decision number (905/L) of March 31st, 2011 with the following:

- President: Judge Tayseer Qala Awwad / Syrian Republic General Prosecutor

- Member: Judge Mohamed Deeb Al Maqtaran / President of the Judicial Inspection Department

- Member: Judge Hassan Al Saeed / Attorney General of Damascus

- Member: Judge Ahmad Al Saeed / First Investigation Judge in Damascus

The mission of this committee is to immediately investigate cases of murder of a number of citizens in the Dara'a and Lattakia provinces.

On 31 March 2011, the day the committee was created, all its members moved to Dara'a province and proceeded to hearing witnesses, victims' family members, and people injured in the events, also, in collaboration with 'investigation judges and prosecutors from Dara'a. They have also examined cadavers of victims. The former mayor of Dara'a and a number of high ranking security services individuals were heard. The committee issued a decision regarding the former mayor and the former president of Dara'a Branch of political security office; they were both banned from leaving the country. On 2 April 2011, members of the judicial committee moved to Lattakia, collaborated with investigation judges and prosecutors, heard and included statements of victims' family members, witnesses and injured citizens in hospitals.

On 5 April 2011, committee members moved to Duma (Damascus Countryside) to start its investigation at the judicial center of Duma. Victims' family members, witnesses and injured citizens were heard...

On 19 April 2011, Vice Chief Justice issued decision number (1092/L), restructuring the judicial committee as follows:

- President: Judge Mohamed Deeb Al Maqtaran/ President of the Judicial Inspection Department

- Member: Judge Hassan Al Saeed/ Attorney General of Damascus

- Member: Mohamed Radwan Hijja / Third Referral Judge in Damascus Countryside

- Member: Judge Ahmad Al Saeed / First Investigation Judge in Damascus

On 21 April 2011, Committee members moved to Tartus, met with attorney general and the general prosecutor, they were informed of facts related to the events taking place in the province.

On 23 April 2011, Committee members moved to Banyas, proceed their work in collaboration with investigation judges and the general prosecutor. Victims' family members, witnesses and injured citizens were heard. The next day, the committee members moved to the village of Baida near Banyas. There they met with residents of the village, explained the mission of this committee and asked residents to give any information they might have about the recent events and cooperate with the Judiciary. Committee members observed at this point some acts of disturbance of the public order generated by citizens who refused to cooperate with the committee.

On 5 May 2011, the Deputy Chief Justice issued decision number (1421/L), altering article number (3) of decision number (905/L) of 31 March 2011. The description of committee's mission becomes "Taking on immediate investigations of the cases of murder against citizens among civilian and military personnel, or the cases of their injury, and all crimes related or resulted from it, this mission applies to all provinces of Syria, and the committee is authorized to receive complaints with this regard. All attorneys general, first investigation judge and the chief prosecutor general, who have the most seniority in every province, are to be considered members of subcommittees initiating investigations in their respective provinces and reporting to the main investigation committee.

To facilitate receiving of citizens, or their complaints, a physical location in Damascus with telephone, fax numbers and email address was chosen. Its contact information was published in all media. Today, the investigation committee operates from that location, while subcommittees work in their respective provinces.

11.   In the subject of mass graves in Jisr al-Shughur: using different kinds of weapons and fire arms, hundreds of armed terrorists attacked a law enforcement office in Jisr al-Shughur. The terrorist group took control of the building, murdered all personnel working at that time, maimed and dragged their bodies by bulldozers to form piles of dead bodies in different locations. Piles were then covered with dirt and debris. This incident took place while terrorist groups took over the city of Jisr al-Shughur, terrorized its inhabitants and forced them to leave their houses and take refuge at the Turkish border, where tents were erected waiting for them. This incident was exploited by a massive misleading campaign conducted by media hostile to the Government of the Syrian Arab Republic. It portrayed refugees running away from armed terrorist groups as if they were running from attacks perpetuated by the Syrian army. When army forces eventually took control of the city, they arrested some members of the terrorist groups who indicated locations of mass graves that contained bodies of police and security services personnel. The bodies were dug out in presence of a number of press and media and members of accredited diplomatic missions in the country. Attached please find a visual record related to this incident. As for the judicial file, it is being completed by the competent judiciary department in the province of Idlib, administrative location of the city of Jisr al-Shughur.

12.   In the claims related to the way crowds were treated by the Syrian authorities, we need to mention legislative texts related to the subject:

(a)   Legislative decree number (54) of the year 2011, related to regulating peaceful demonstrations in Syria - mainly considering the right to demonstrate peacefully as one of the basic human rights- is a decree in compliance with most world states' legislations in this regard, it regulates mechanisms of exercising the right to peaceful demonstrations, designates authority departments responsible for issuing permissions of peaceful demonstrations, it names a judicial authority reference to appeal decisions refusing to grant permit to demonstrate. It also contains texts related to forms of legal punishment when demonstrations do not abide by this decree or in case of riots.

(b)   Syrian penal code articles related to prohibiting people's demonstrations and gatherings, articles number 335 and 339 as follows:

• **Article number 335:** All persons present in a gathering which is not of a private nature in its purpose or final objective, in relation to the number of individuals invited or present, or in relation to the location of the meeting, if it is in a public location or a location of a possible public access or a location visible by the public, when the person utters a riot calls or song, or displays an emblem that carries the potential of disturbing public security, or if the person participates in any other riot, is punishable by the law with a month to a year imprisonment and a 100 Syrian pounds fine.

• **Article number 336:** All rallies, or procession on public roads, or in location with public access is considered as a riot, and participants are punishable by the law with a sentence for one month to a year imprisonment.

This applies to three or more people, with the intent to commit a felony or a misdemeanor, and if at least one of them carries a weapon.

It applies to a gathering of seven or more people, with the intention to pressure the government into changing decisions or measures by means of public protesting.

It also applies to a gathering of around 20 people, who adopt an appearance that might disturb public peace.

• Article number 337:

1-   When people gather as described above, a law enforcement representative warns them and asks them to disperse.

2-   Participants who walk away before the warning of law enforcement representatives takes place are exempt from punishment adopted in these cases. It also applies to participants who immediately respond to law enforcement representative's warning and never use their weapons nor commit other misdemeanors.

• Article number 338:

1-   If force has to be used to disperse a gathering, legal punishment is of two months to two years imprisonment for participants.

2-   Those who use weapons, get a one to three years imprisonment sentence, in addition to a more severe punishment they might deserve.

• Article number 339:

1-   According to articles number 65, 82 and 88, related to misdemeanors mentioned in paragraphs 2 to 5 of this chapter, a possible sentencing could reach stripping participants of their civil rights, or a prohibition of residency within the country, or they might be expelled outside Syria.

Despite the description of riots contained in the previous paragraphs, illegal gatherings, demonstrations, sabotage and horrors committed by armed terrorist groups against citizens, in addition to setting fire to governmental institutions and public service buildings, our Law enforcement agents continue to escort all peaceful demonstrations, whether it had obtained permission to demonstrate or not, they protect protestors participating in any peaceful demonstration, they accompany all peaceful participants throughout the whole period of a demonstration, and only leave when demonstrators willingly disperse, and everyone goes back home safely. But when a demonstration deviates toward adopting manifestations of violence, sabotage and setting fire to public service buildings, they are faced with an adequate number of unarmed law enforcement agents with a mission to control the situation. In this case when few individuals initiate shooting at the police as well as other protestors in order to create confusion and discredit the Syrian general authorities, law enforcement agents usually move away from the demonstration to avoid clashes with terrorists, in order to prevent more fire arm shootings that might hurt protestors. Law enforcement agents are not allowed to use fire arms under any circumstances, except to react in self defense while fighting terrorist groups, or when these groups terrorize and mass-murder other citizens in locations where law enforcement agents happen to be. The Strategy followed by law enforcement agents in dealing with the few peaceful demonstrations and the bigger number of riots since the begging of events in Syria is to adopt unlimited self control. This strategy, paired with strict orders not to use fire arms – even with riots- has resulted in murders of hundreds of officers and law enforcement agents, and thousands were injured by fire arms, swards and knifes used by terrorists. There is no immunity for officers and other law enforcement members who break orders, or exceed the power granted to them, in doing so, they expose themselves to severe punishments according to the penal code. In the subject of rescuing the injured and provide them with the appropriate medical attention, the competent medical emergency bodies equally perform services destined to all citizens in need of medical attention, whether they are peaceful protestors, terrorists or law enforcement agents, In support of this policy. Orders are to refrain from arresting any injured person who is transported to a hospital, regardless of this person's extent of criminal actions conducted during demonstrations during which he was injured.

13.   The Ministry of Justice in Syria conducts a continuous, methodological and effective operation of monitoring and inspection of all Syrian prisons. This procedure complies with regulations of penal courts mentioned in article (421) to (425) as follows:

Article **421**: regulating prisons and detention places in a decree issued by the Council of Ministers.

Article **422**: both the judge of peace and the investigation judge are asked to inspect all detainees once a month, as for penal courts presidents, they need to do it once every three months.

Article **423**: Penal courts presidents, investigation judges and the judges of peace are authorized to give prison guards orders to undertake measures related to investigations and court cases.

Article **424**: Every person with information about a detention location other than those allowed by the government is asked to communicate this information to the attorney general, vice attorney general, or to the justice of peace.

Article **425**:

1-   When the attorney general, or vice attorney general, or the justice of peace get informed about such illegal detention locations, they are asked to immediately go and release any detainee that might be on location.

2-   It they discern a legal reason for this person's detention; the detainee should be transferred to the custody of the general attorney or the judge of peace immediately.

3-   A record of the situation should be established.

4- If they neglect to perform the points previously mentioned, they will be persecuted as they will be considered partners in the crime of unlawful imprisonment.

14. In the subject of Syrian citizens of Kurdish origin, a legislative decree number (49) dated 7 April 2011 was issued: Kurds of Syria could apply for citizenship. They will be granted citizenship and will benefit in all levels and in all areas from all civic rights – and duties- of full Syrian citizenship. Thousands of Kurds of Syria have been granted Syrian citizenship since.

15. In the subject of the ongoing reform process, new laws are on the way to being issued, the new general election law, and the parties law are approved by the Council of Ministers, we would like to share the steps taken so far in developing the new general election law to illustrate how any of the new legislations in Syria is structured in compliance with the best laws in action anywhere else in the world:

Syria's prime minister has issued decision number (6186) dated May 8th, 2011, including the creation of a committee to prepare a project of the new general election law in compliance with the highest known standards, the committee was given two weeks to complete its mission... committee's members are:

- Dr. Najm Al Ahmad – Deputy of Minister of Justice

- Hassan Jalali – Deputy Minister of interior

- Mahmoud Saleh – Legal Advisor at the Council of Ministers Presidency

- Dr. Mohamed Yousef Al Hussain – Professor, University of Damascus, Law School

- Dr. Jamilah Shurbaji – Professor, University of Damascus, Law School

- Dr. Mohamed Khair Al Akkam – Professor, University of Damascus, Law School

- Fawzi Mahasneh – advisor, Ministry of Local Administrations

- Khaled Kamel – Director of Councils, Ministry of Local Administrations

Based on the above decision, note the following:

- The committee met daily until the project of the law was completed.

- The committee viewed different states laws, like France, Belgium, Egypt, Algeria, Jordan, Iraq and Palestine.

- The committee viewed Syrian laws both inactive and the active ones.

- The committee heard a number of professionals in Law (College professors, judges, lawyers) with different expertise and ages, their contributions and opinions had a great influence on the project of law.

- The committee completed its mission one day ahead of the scheduled time.

- the project of law was published in the official website of the Council of Ministers, and individual ministries websites (Ministry of Justice, Ministry of Interior, Ministry of Local Administrations), visits to all these websites exceeded 34'000, 3'400 of them left written comments.

- All comments were viewed, and some were taken into consideration because they showed the kind of objectivity the project of law could benefit from, the UNDP project's contribution was valuable, all the observations submitted by UNDP were taken into consideration.

To illustrate commitment to global standards, these are the essentials of what the project of law included.

A unique election law:

As it is the case in other countries, the project of law includes all substantive provisions to regulate the process of electing members of the Parliament and members of Local Administrations Councils in one Law.

Goals:

To organize substantive provisions aimed to regulate the process of elections, and to provide a safe electoral process, and to ensure candidates' right to monitor elections. The bill also included terms related to punishment of abusers, and vote manipulators, in addition to securing all essential social segments' representations.

To create an independent electoral management, with integrity, in compliance with international standards: Securing integrity of elections is achieved through the process of implementing regulations on the ground; this requires the presence of an impartial third party in charge of ensuring the legal application of regulations, thus, in no way a party should be competitor and arbitrator. Likewise, those who organize and manage elections should hold no special interests related to the outcome of elections. This led the bill to appoint the judiciary to supervise elections' management, a Supreme Commission for Elections will be charged with this task, and provinces sub-committees will be formed by the juridical. The Executive authorities were left with fewer administrative tasks.

Independent Electoral Commissions:

According to international standards which require an independent electoral management with integrity, the project of law singled out the texts referring to the composition of independent, impartial Electoral Commissions, responsible for organizing and managing the electoral process in all its stages, on all levels. In this regard, competencies and responsibilities that reflect the higher levels of credibility and integrity in the electoral process were identified.

Electoral Districts:

Thinking the concepts of the philosophy of representation in both assemblies from a political and constitutional view points, whether in Parliament or in Local Councils, we were careful to describe larger constituencies for parliamentary elections, for the members of Parliament usually don't represent specific geographic areas, they are representatives of all the people. As for Local Administrations elections, smaller constituencies were described in order to fit with local representations concept.

Nomination conditions:

Nominated candidates need to have obtained Syrian citizenship for a minimum of 10 years (previously 5 years) except those who were included in the decree number 49 of the year 2011 (related to the year 1962 problematic population census) as they can be immediately nominated regardless of the 10 years citizenship condition.

Election campaigns:

In the project of law, election campaigns are regulated in a way allowing candidates to access various media in order to have a reasonable possibility for communicating their individual programs to the public.

Monitoring electoral process :

Throughout all phases of the electoral process, starting from committees' work, to election, vote counting and all the details related to the electoral process, and ending with announcing elections' results, the bill grants candidates and their representatives the right to monitor election process, to make sure of its integrity, and confirm the absence of fraud and manipulation.

Electoral crimes:

In order to reassure all parties involved, a special chapter in the project of law was designed to single out possible offenses related to elections. Every action or absence of action under this possibility was described, the scope of electoral crimes accurately determined, including criminalizing acts aiming to harm the components of the electoral process.

Electoral disputes:

The Project of law referrers to specific bodies with competencies to be put in the service of both candidates and voters, where they can directly address legal complaints related to the electoral process. They have the possibility to challenge election or nomination committees, as well as subcommittees, or election results in its final form before the competent judicial authorities. In all these cases, short deadlines were set for both appeals and the decisions made by authorities, in a way to avoid affecting the electoral process, while ensuring protection of the rights of all parties involved.

- A ministerial committee was established to review the finalized the Law project.

- The project of law was approved by the Council of Ministers, and is being prepared for its release.

16.	Please find attached legislative texts and the bills mentioned in this document, in addition to 9 CDs including a refutation of the crime of killing Hamza Al Khatib according to his family, in addition to the subject of mass graves in Jisr Al Shughur, and acts of sabotage and terrorism in some provinces, and the confessions of some members of armed terrorist groups describing how they have committed their crimes.

Forth: In conclusion, the government of the Syrian Arab Republic reaffirms its commitment to cooperate with you on all levels, to answer your questions and to help with your mission in order to reach the truth about the issues of your inquiry in order for you to form a just and impartial opinion away from the influence of biased sources, who portray themselves as human rights defenders but whose sole intent is to discredit Syria in order to serve their own unlawful goals.

We are taking steps in our ongoing legislative and political reform, in concordance with standards and principles established by the Syrian constitution and in conformity with internationally established norms. We also capitalize on our interaction with you, and hope it will remain positive, fruitful and exiting.

Annex VI

Note verbale dated 16 August 2011 from the Permanent Mission of the Syrian Arab Republic addressed to the Office of the United Nations High Commissioner for Human Rights

Mission Permanente
De La
République Arabe Syrienne
Genève

الجمهورية العربية السورية
البعثة الدائمة لدى مكتب الأمم المتحدة
جنيف

N° 435/11

Geneva, the 16ᵗʰ of August 2011

The Permanent Mission of the Syrian Arab Republic to the United Nations Office and other International Organizations in Geneva presents its compliments to the Office of the High Commissioner for Human Rights, and in reference to its communication dated 10 August 2011 which included the report of the Office of the High Commissioner for Human Rights Mission to Syria, has the honour to convoy to the Office of the High Commissioner the response of the Syrian Government to this report.

The Permanent Mission of the Syrian Arab Republic avails itself of this opportunity to renew to the High Commissioner for Human Rights the assurances of its highest consideration.

United Nations
The Office of the High Commissioner for Human Rights
Palais des Nations
CH 1211 Genève 10

إضافة إلى المعلومات التي سبق للجمهورية العربية السورية وأن و/التقدم بها، والتي تتضمن عرضاً
كاملاً لحقيقة الأحداث في سورية، تقدم فيما يلي المعلومات التالية استكمالاً لما سبق لتقديمه وتوضيحاً لما ورد
في تقرير المفوضة من مغالطات:

- كانت الحكومة السورية قد قدمت ردودها على أسئلة المفوضة السامية حول الأحداث الجارية في سورية
وما اتخذته السلطات السورية من إجراءات لمعالجة المسائل التي نتجت عن هذه الأحداث قبل الالتهام من الموعد
المحدد لتضمين الرد السوري على هذه الأجوبة في التقرير الذي ستقدمه المفوضة إلى مجلس حقوق الإنسان حول
الأوضاع في سورية. ومن المؤسف أن تقرير المفوضة الحالي لم يتضمن موقف سورية من الأحداث، والذي تم
شرحه بشكل واف في تلك الردود، وأن عدم تضمين المعلومات الواردة من الحكومة السورية واعتماد المفوضة
السامية على المصادر المغرضة فقط تخلق حالة من عدم الثقة وعدم المصداقية في مهنية عمل المفوضة خصوصاً
وأن سورية قدمت كل ما لديها من معلومات موثقة حول المواضيع المثارة.

- اعتمد التقرير على مصدر واحد هو بعض من السوريين المساعدين في الخارج والمطلوبين للعدالة بعد
ـــــ القيام بجرائم مسلحة روعت الناس وفرت إلى الخارج وهي أقرب إلى ـ~ قائمة على دليل أو مستند قانوني وتعبر
عن وجهة نظر أحادية الجانب ليست لها مصداقية يمكن الركون إليها، فعلى سبيل المثال فإن ما تحدث عنه هؤلاء
عن فرار آلاف السوريين خارج القطر هو قول يفتقر إلى المصداقية، كما جرى أن نحو عشرة الآف شخص قد
نصبت لهم الخيام على الحدود التركية قبل شهر من وقوع الأحداث، وقد هجرة مدنهم وقراهم قبل أي تواجد أمني
أو عسكري هرباً من العصابات المسلحة، وبينما أعادت السلطات المختصة الأمن والاستقرار إلى المنطقة عاد
أكثر من عشرة آلاف من هؤلاء إلى مدنهم وقراهم، وهم يعيشون الآن حياة هادئة ومستقرة، ولم يبق في الخارج إلا
من استخدام السلاح والعنف المنظم.

- ورد في الإطار القانوني لتقرير المفوضية تناقضاً صارخاً ففي جانب منه أشار التقرير إلى التزام
سورية بالعديد من الاتفاقيات والمواثيق الدولية. وفي جانب آخر تحدث عن الانتهاكات سورية لهذه الاتفاقيات. وهذا
الجانب الأخير مناف للحقيقة، لأن اعتقال كل من يخالف القوانين والأنظمة وتقديمه للعدالة أصولاً لا يعد خرقاً أو
انتهاكات لتلك الاتفاقيات الدولية أو القوانين الوطنية.

- لا توجد في سورية. كما ورد في التقرير - أقلية تستغل السلطة وتقمع المتظاهرين، إلا أن تأثر معدو
التقرير وانحيازهم لشهادات من تمت مقابلتهم ممن يطلقون على أنفسهم شهود عيان وهم في الحقيقة بغالبيتهم فارون
من وجه العدالة لما اقترفوه من جرائم، الأمر الذي ينأى بالتقرير عن المصداقية. إن التدخل السافر من قبل معدي
التقرير لإضعاف النسيج الوطني السوري ووصفها بأغلبيته أو أقليته هو وصفة لتخريب سورية ناهيك عن كونه
أصلاً غير مقبول (طلاق)؟

يتحدث التقرير كذلك عن ضحايا وشهود عيان من مدنيين وعسكريين معتمداً على معلومات وردت عبر
تقارير صحفية، ومع أن التقارير الصحفية ليست مرجعاً يمكن الاستناد إليه في إعداد تقارير دولية في مواجهة
الدول فإن التقرير لم يوضح ما إذا كان هؤلاء ضحايا بالفعل وشهود لهم مصداقيتهم أم أنهم طرف في المعادلة
وجزء ممنهج من العنف المنظم. كما أن رفض المعلومات التي توفرها الحكومة يعني أن مفوضية حقوق الإنسان لا
تتعامل مع دول بل مع تنظيمات وجهات معادية لسورية كمصدر لمعلوماتها. وفي هذا إضعاف لدور الدول
ومصداقيتها.

والقول المتقدم ينصرف أيضاً على مقاطع الفيديو الواردة من منظمات غير حكومية أو المنشورة عبر
وسائل إعلام كانت جزءاً من الحملة التضليلية والتحريضية في مواجهة سورية ولعبت دوراً في تحريض السوريين
على الاقتتال الطائفي فيما بينهم متجاهلة حقيقة أن هنالك مئات الفظائع المصورة التي تثبت بشاعة الجرائم التي
أقدمت عليها المجموعات الإرهابية المسلحة من قتل واغتصاب وتقطيع للأوصال ومقابر جماعية ومجازر لم ترتكب

271

بحق العسكريين ومدنيين من قبل هذه الجماعات، وفي كثير من الأحيان كانت بعض وسائل الإعلام تضخم الأمور حول ما يجري في سوريا في سبيل نشر أخبار كاذبة ومفبركة جرى فضحها عبر وسائل الإعلام السورية، ومن ذلك إعلام معلومات معاكسة لحقيقة الأمور أو عرض صور لمظاهرات جرت في دول أخرى على أنها جرت في سوريا، وهناك عشرات المقاطع المصورة التي تثبت هذا الأمر بشكل واضح لا لبس فيه ولا غموض كما قد أرسلناها إلى المفوضية.

إن سوريا ملتزمة بتطبيق القانون الدولي وهي طرف في معظم الاتفاقيات والبروتوكولات الخاصة بحقوق الإنسان متقدمة بذلك على العديد من دول العالم وهيأت سلسلة متتالية من الإصلاحات الهادفة إلى إحداث تغيير شامل في سوريا نحو مستقبل أفضل، ملغية حالة الطوارئ في وقت كانت بحاجة فيه إلى الإبقاء عليها لأن ما جرى في سوريا على الأرض من قبل العصابات الإجرامية المسلحة يفوق حدود للتصور والتوقعات لجهة الفوضى والاضطراب والعنف المؤيد في بعض من الأحيان دوليا وإقليميا وهو ما يشكل تدخلا سافرا في الشؤون السورية الداخلية من قبل بعض الدول خلافا للقانون الدولي والأعراف والمواثيق الدولية. كما ألغت الحكومة محكمة أمن الدولة العليا وتشكيل لجان إصلاحية أنجزت مهماتها بما يعزز رؤى التنمية والتطوير في سوريا وتبعا لذلك صدرت ثلاثة مراسيم تشريعية تتعلق بسلح عفو عام وشامل عن الجرائم جرائم الخيانة والتجسس والإرهاب والاغتصاب وهي المرسوم التشريعي رقم ٣٤ تاريخ ٢٠١١/٢/٧ والمرسوم التشريعي رقم ٦١ تاريخ ٢٠١١/٥/٣١ والمرسوم التشريعي رقم ٧٢ تاريخ ٢٠١١/٦/٢٠ وكان حصيلة الموقوفين ممن شملتهم هذه المراسيم وأطلق سراحهم فورا تصل إلى ١٠٤٣٢ شخصا مع التنويه بأن هذا الرقم لا يشمل المخالفات والجنح المشمولة التي تعد بعشرات الألاف استفاد أصحابها من هذه المراسيم كما لا يشمل الدعاوى قيد النظر في الجنائيات حيث طال العفو نصف العقوبة الجنائية إلا عند صدور الحكم فضلا عن عدد كبير ممن يطالبهم العفو جزئيا.

وثقافة منا بأن الحوار الوطني الشامل بين أطياف المجتمع السوري كافة هو السبيل الأمثل للإصلاح والتطوير من أجل الوصول إلى الأهداف المرجوة في الارتقاء نحو الأفضل في المجالات السياسية والتشريعية والاجتماعية والاقتصادية، فقد صدر عن القرار الجمهوري بتاريخ ٢٠١١/٦/٢ القاضي بتشكيل هيئة مهمتها وضع أسس لحوار وطني وتحديد آلية عمله وبرنامجه الزمني.

وقد دعت هيئة الحوار الوطني إلى لقاء تشاوري في الفترة ما بين ١٠ إلى ١٢ تموز ٢٠١١ ضم مجموعة من رجال السياسة والفكر والمجتمع والناشطين الشباني ومختلف الأطياف الشعبية والتوجهات السياسية في الوطن للتدارس والتشاور، من أجل الخروج بتصورات ومقترحات الموصول بالحوار الوطني إلى النتيجة المتوخاة. وبلقاء اللقاء التشاوري لطبيعة المرحلة الدقيقة التي تمر بها للبلاد والمعالجات السياسية والاقتصادية والاجتماعية المطلوبة مع استشراف الآفاق المستقبلية والاهتمام بالقضايا المعيشية للمواطنين. وقد خلص المجتمعون على توصيات عديدة منها:

- إن الحوار هو الطريق الوحيد الذي يوصل البلاد إلى إنهاء الأزمة.
- ضرورة إعلاء قيمة حقوق الإنسان وصونها وفق أرقى المعايير الدستورية والاعتيادية والعصرية والتوصية بإنشاء مجلس أعلى لحقوق الإنسان في سوريا.
- وبضرورة الإفراج الفوري على جميع المعتقلين السياسيين ومعتقلي الرأي الذين لم يرتكبوا جرائم يعاقبها عليها القانون.

ومن القوانين الإصلاحية الأخرى:

١. المرسوم التشريعي رقم ٥٥ تاريخ ٢٠١١/٤/٢١ المتضمن اختصاصات الضابطة العدلية في بعض من الجرائم جمع لجهة أدلتها والاستماع إلى المشتبه بهم فيها ومدة التوقيف.

٢. المرسوم التشريعي رقم ٥٤ تاريخ ٢٠١١/٤/٢١ المتعلق بتنظيم حق التظاهر السلمي بوصفه حقا من حقوق الإنسان الأساسية التي كلفها دستور الجمهورية العربية السورية.

٣. المرسوم التشريعي رقم ٥٣ تاريخ ٢٠١١/٤/٢١ المتضمن إلغاء محكمة أمن الدولة العليا.

٤. المرسوم التشريعي رقم ٤٩ تاريخ ٢٠١١/٤/٧ المتضمن منح المسجلين في سجلات أجانب الحسكة من الأكراد الجنسية العربية السورية.

٥ـ المرسوم التشريعي رقم ٤٦ تاريخ ٢٠١١/٤/٣ المتعلق بتشميل المتقاعدين في الدولة والقطاع العام والمنظمات الشعبية من الموظفين والعسكريين بالتأمين الصحي.

٦ـ المرسوم التشريعي رقم ٤٣ تاريخ ٢٠١١/٣/٢٤ المتعلق بالتملك في المناطق الحدودية.

٧ـ المرسوم التشريعي رقم ٤٠ تاريخ ٢٠١١/٣/٢٤ المتضمن زيادة الرواتب والأجور للعاملين المدنيين والعسكريين في الدولة.

٨ـ المرسوم التشريعي رقم ٦٢ تاريخ ٢٠١١/٦/٥ المتعلق بتثبيت العمال المؤقتين.

٩ـ المرسوم التشريعي رقم ٨٤ تاريخ ٢٠١١/٧/١٣ المتعلق بالتنمية الاجتماعية.

١٠ـ المرسوم التشريعي رقم /١٠٠/ تاريخ ٢٠١١/٨/٦ المتضمن قانون الأحزاب.

١١ـ المرسوم التشريعي رقم /١٠١/ تاريخ ٢٠١١/٨/٦ المتضمن قانون الانتخابات العامة.

وقد أنجزت الحكومة قانون الإدارة المحلية وقانون الإعلام اللذان سيصدران خلال أيام معدودة كما صدرت العديد من المراسيم التنظيمية ومدها على سبيل المثال مراسيم تتعلق بمنح دورات إضافية للطلاب في جميع مراحل التعليم، وإحداث شركات جديدة وكليات جديدة في مختلف الجامعات.

كما شكلت الحكومة العديد من اللجان من كبار المختصين ومن ذلك:

١ـ لجنة للتحقيق في الجرائم المرتكبة بحق المدنيين والعسكريين وجميع الجرائم ذات الصلة المرتبطة بالأحداث التي تشهدها سورية.

٢ـ لجنة لوضع الرؤى والتصورات المتعلقة بالفساد لجهة بيان أسبابه والعوامل المؤدية إليه وكيفية الوقاية منه وآليات تعزيز مبدأ المراقبة.

٣ـ لجنة لوضع قانون الإعلام.

٤ـ لجنة للإصلاح القضائي.

٥ـ لجنة للإصلاح الإداري.

٦ـ لجنة للحوار الوطني.

وغير ذلك العديد من المراسيم التشريعية والتنظيمية والقرارات الإستراتيجية مما لم تشر إليه المفوضية في التقرير.

ـ إن تحميل الأجهزة المسؤولية كاملة عن الأحداث في سورية هو أمر يجافي الحقيقة والمنطق ويتطرق إلى المواضيع من وجهة نظر أحادية الجانب ومن واجب الأجهزة الأمنية في أية دولة من دول العالم تحقيق الأمن والاستقرار للمواطنين، وإعادة الهدوء والأمان وحماية الممتلكات العامة والخاصة، علماً بأن الغالبية العظمى ممن سقط في الأحداث هم من رجال الجيش والشرطة والأمن على أيدي العصابات المسلحة، وخلافاً ما تم الاعتداء على هؤلاء في أماكن عملهم أو أثناء وجودهم لحماية المتظاهرين، إلا أنهم كانوا هم والمتظاهرين على حد سواء عرضة لإطلاق النار من مسلحين مثلمين تجاهلهم تقرير المفوضية كلياً.

ـ ومن المغالطات أيضاً الحديث عن إصلاحات اقتصادية ملوقعة في الوقت الذي تشهد فيه تقارير المنظمات والمؤسسات الدولية التي ساهمت في برامج إصلاحية عديدة بسورية وأكدت بأن الإصلاح الاقتصادي الذي حصل في سورية غير مسبوق في دول المنطقة لجهة اعتماد معايير اقتصادية جديدة منها:

ـ اقتصاد السوق الاجتماعي.

ـ الانفتاح الاقتصادي على مختلف دول العالم.

والذي انعكس بوضوح في رفع مستوى المعيشة وقلص من مستويات الفقر وحد من الفوارق التنموية بين مناطق سورية، وتركز هذا الأمر تقارير بعثات صندوق النقد الدولي إلى سورية.

فضلاً عن عشرات المراسيم التشريعية التي دفعت بعجلة الإصلاح الاقتصادي في سورية قدماً مع التنويه بأن قوة الاقتصاد السوري لا تتحدد في منطقة بذاتها إنما لكل منطقة جغرافية قوتها الاقتصادية الخاصة بها.

ـ ليس صحيحاً بأن الأكراد ظلوا مبعدين عن السلطة والحياة المدنية حتى عام ٢٠١١ فما جرى بآذار ٢٠١١ هو منح عشرات الآلاف ملهم الجنسية السورية، وهو أمر لم تفعله أية دولة أخرى إزاء أجانب مقيمين على

أراضيها، وقد ظل السوريون من أصل كردي طوال تاريخ سورية بتقلدون أعلى المناصب السياسية والمدنية والعسكرية، ويمكن بيان ذلك بشكل مفصل إذا رغبت المفوضية بذلك.

.. من الغريب أن يقال أن قيام المظاهرات في درعا سببه استغلال السلطة بينما كان معلناً في بدء المظاهرات أن المطالبة بإصلاحات محددة، كما أن تقرير المفوضية يشير لاحقاً إلى أن الشرارة الأولى قد انطلقت من درعا بعد سجن مجموعة من الأطفال و هذا يعني تناقضاً فاضحاً طالما تكرر في صفحات هذا التقرير، وذلك قبل أن تستغل العصابات المسلحة هذا الحراك العفوي لتمعن في إطلاق النار على المدنيين والعسكريين مع التنويه بأن محافظة درعا تضم عدد كبير من المسؤولين في الدولة و هو ما يمكن أيضاً إثباته مفصلاً إذا رغبت المفوضية بذلك.

.. إن مصطلح الشبيحة الذي يرد في التقرير هو مصطلح مختلق من قبل المليشيات المسلحة وبعض وسائل الإعلام المفضلة التي روجوها في تقاريرها بهدف تأجيج الفتنة بين شرائح المجتمع، إنما في بعض من المناطق التي استباحتها المجموعات الإرهابية المسلحة ويسبب الفراغ الأمني الذي حصل مؤقتاً في تلك المناطق قلم الأهالي بتشكيل لجان شعبية سلمية ليس لديها أي نوع من أنواع الأسلحة تعمل على حراسة الممتلكات العامة والخاصة.

.. صحيح أن هناك نحو ١٩٠٠ شهيد إلا أنه ليس صحيحاً أن جميع هؤلاء من المدنيين بل أن القسم الأكبر منهم هم من رجال الجيش والشرطة والمواطنين الذين ذهبوا ضحية أعمال القتل التي أقدمت عليها الجماعات الإرهابية المسلحة.

.. فيما يتعلق بمدينة حماة لم يعمد الجيش على اجتياحها فهو جيش سورية الوطني وليس جيشاً أجنبياً بل تعاون مع القوى الأمنية لتخليص المدينة المعتدلة من المسلحين والمتطرفين الإرهابيين الذين حولوها إلى مدينة أشباح بعد ترويع سكانها واضطرارهم لمغادرتها حفاظاً على أرواحهم و هذا ما خلق ارتياحا لدى الأهالي بدخول الجيش الذي أعاد الهدوء و الحياة الطبيعية. وهذا ينطبق على العديد من البلدات التي حاول المجرمون تثبيت حالة الرعب والخوف فيها، وقد لجأت الدولة إلى الاعتماد على قوات الجيش لأنه لا توجد لديها قوة شرطة مختصة لمقاومة الشغب والتمرد والإرهاب ولم يستخدم الجيش أياً من معداته الثقيلة لإيذاء المواطنين بل لحماية نفسه من المسلحين والإرهابيين.

.. حينما تحدث التقرير عن جسر الشغور أشار إلى ٣٠ قتيل ومائتي جريح متجاهلاً تماماً حقيقة أن الإرهابيين المسلحين قد قتلوا بوحشية قتل مليئها جميع عناصر الأمن الموجودين وفي المنطقة والبالغ عدده ١٢٠/ عنصراً ودفنوهم في مقابر جماعية جرى الكشف عنها بمعرفة بعض من الإرهابيين الذين القي القبض عليهم وبحضور ومرأى عدد كبير من الدبلوماسيين والصحافة العالمية.

.. مع التنويه بأنه لم يلقى القبض على أي متظاهر سلمي، وخلافاً ما يتم الإفراج عن المتظاهرين بشكل مخالف للقانون من قبل القضاء خلال خمسة أيام على الأكثر، وإذا كان هناك معتقلين سلميين على خلفية المظاهرات فلم يرجوا موافاتنا بأسمائهم أما الادعاء بالتعذيب فهو إدعاء عار عن الصحة تماماً ومبالغ به وذلك فأن عدد الحالات الموضوعة أمام القضاء هو ١٢ حالة كنا قد بيناها سابقاً في الكتاب السابق المرسل للمفوضية.

.. لا توجد أية أوامر بإطلاق النار ضد المتظاهرين السلميين إنما على العكس من ذلك الأوامر هي عدم حمل السلاح أثناء مواكبة المظاهرات السلمية.

.. لم تستخدم الأسلحة الثقيلة والمدرعات في أية مواجهة مع العصابات المسلحة وكل ما ورد في التقارير كان مضللاً وغير صحيح ويهدف إلى تشويه سمعة سورية ومناورتها للاقتصاص منها لأهداف سياسية أصبحت معروفة العالم.

- إن الحكومة مصممة وجادة في عدم جواز استخدام أو تهريب أي مواطن سوري للتعذيب، ولجنة التحقيق القضائية الخاصة اتخذت خطوات مباشرة لمقاضاة كل من يثبت انتهاكه لحقوق الإنسان وكل من يثبت تورطه في اغتيال المدنيين والعسكريين على حد سواء.

- أما بشأن عودة المهجرين فليس هناك أي عقبة تحول دون عودتهم ويقدم لكل من يعود كامل التسهيلات اللازمة، وقد سمحت للصحفيين بدخول المناطق الساخنة.

- أما بالنسبة للسماح لمنظمات حقوق الإنسان بالدخول إلى سورية وإجراء تحقيقات عن حقوق الإنسان فإنه أمر تقدره الدولة وفقاً لاعتبارات السيادة الوطنية وفي الوقت الذي تراه مناسباً.

- ومن الناحية الإجرائية نجد أن تقرير اللجنة يخرج عن الإطار القانوني الذي وضعه القرار S-16/1 في جوانب عدة أهمها:

١. تقدير اسم اللجنة "لجنة تقصي حقائق" وذلك في محتوى التقرير وفي الفقرة الأولى منه.

٢. عدم الالتزام بمنطوق القرار S-16/1 حول "قيام اللجنة بتحقيق وتقديم تقرير محايد وذو مصداقية".

٣. تم تكييف الإطار القانوني للانتهاكات التي ارتكبها هؤلاء وفقاً للفقرتين ١٥ و١٧ من التقرير باعتبار أنه يمكن أن ترتقي بعض هذه الخروقات لمستوى "جرائم ضد الإنسانية". إذ يعتبر هذا التكييف خروجاً عن ولاية اللجنة التي تنحصر بجمع المعلومات وليس التوصيف القانوني للخروقات.

٤. تقديم توصية إلى مجلس الأمن الدولي في حين تكمن علاقة المفوضية مع مجلس حقوق الإنسان.

٥. تقديم توصية لجامعة الدول العربية وكأنها إحدى المؤسسات التي تتبع المفوضية.

- إن سورية إذا تقدر عالياً الدور المسند إلى المفوضية السامية لحقوق الإنسان، والمهمات المنوطة بها ترجو أن تلتزم المفوضية جانب الحياد وأن تأخذ جميع الرؤى ووجهات نظر الأطراف جميعها، وتحللها بموضوعية ودون انحياز إلا للجوانب الإنسانية، وأن تكون جهة محايدة مستقلة لا تضع رؤى وتصورات مسبقة دون تدقيق أو تحليل، وإن بيد الحكومة السورية مندوبة إليها من أجل تعاون مثمر يضع الأمور في نصابها للصحيح، علماً بأن الحكومة الآن بشأن إعداد ملفات قضائية متكاملة ستتقدم بها إلى المفوضية وغيرها من الجهات الدولية المستقلة والمختصة تثبت تورط دول ومجموعات وأفراد في تأجيج الأوضاع الداخلية. والفتنة الطائفية ودعم العصابات الإرهابية المسلحة بما يقوض دعائم الاستقرار الداخلي وأوصدة الوطنية، والتدخل السافر في الشؤون الداخلية الدولة وتقديم الدعم المادي والمعنوي للعصابات الإجرامية التي استباحت البلاد وقتلت المدنيين والعسكريين وخلقت حالة من الفوضى والاضطراب والعنف المنظم.

نتائج عمل اللجنة المكلفة بموضوع حمزة الخطيب

بناءً على الأمر الإداري رقم ٩١٣/ص تاريخ ٣٠ /٥/٢٠١١ المتضمن تشكيل لجنة برئاسة اللواء عبد
الكريم سليمان معاون وزير الداخلية وعضوية كل من :
ـــ العميد محمد درويشة، مدير إدارة الأمن الجنائي؛
ـــ السيد محمد كنجو، النائب العام العسكري.
ـــ السيد عبد العزيز الشلال، قائد الشرطة العسكرية.
ـــ السيد رائد جازم، رئيس فرع التحقيق بغدارة الأمن الجنائي.
مهمتها: التحقيق بموضوع الإدعاءات المتعلقة بوقوع أعمال عنف وشدة وتعذيب على جثة الطفل حمزة
الخطيب.

لجمعت اللجنة بكامل قوامها في مكتب رئيسها يوم الثلاثاء الواقع في ٣١/٥/٢٠١١ الساعة الثامنة
صباحاً، وبالمداولة تقرر القيام بالإجراءات التالية بغية الوصول للحقيقة.

١ـ انتقلت اللجنة بكامل قوامها إلى مشفى تشرين العسكري ـ قسم الطب الشرعي وفي القسم المذكور
وبناءً على تكليف منها أحضرت الصور الضوئية المأخوذة لجثة المتوفى الحدث حمزة الخطيب، وباختصار
تبين أنها ستة صور ملونة لهذا الحدث المتوفى مثبته على كرتون متوى بلون ابيض تحمل رقم متسلسل ٢٠٢
/٧٥٧ صادرة عن الشرطة العسكرية الأدلة القضائية/ قسم التصوير الجنائي ومعركة هذه الصور بتدوين رقم
٢٣ على كل منها، وهذه الصور بوضعيات مختلفة وبجيب تعريفها برقم ٢٣ كون الجثة كانت مجهولة الهوية،
ويعد الاطلاع على الصور جرى ضمنها للتحقيقات القائمة لدينا حسب الأصول.

٢ـ طلبت نسخة عن محضر الكشف على جثة المتوفى الحدث حمزة الخطيب المعدة من قبل اللجنة
الطبية الثلاثية والمؤلفة من السادة الأطباء : أكرم الشمار ـ حسام احمد ـ اسماعيل كبول، وبلمشار الخبرة
تبين لنا أنها مؤلفة من أربعة صفحات مطبوعة والتي جاء فيها بالحرف الواحد:

لتقرير خبرة طبية شرعية ثلاثية حول وفاة المولفان حمزة الخطيب

الوصف الظاهري:
ـ الجثة تعود لفتى /حدث/ في العقد الثاني من العمر بدين جداً محتمل البلوغ سمطي البشرة شعر رأسه
اسود بطول ٤ سم .
ـ العينان مسليتان والحدقتان متسعتان بشكل كامل وبتناظر في الجانبين.

الجثة تبدي صمتاً مزرقاً وزرقة رمية جثوية متوضعة في الأقسام الخلفية غير الاستنادية من الجذع والأطراف.

– الجثة ملطخة بالدماء وتبدي سحجات متكلمة سطحية خفيفة في مستوى الجبهة اليمنى والأجفان والخد الأيمن وهي ناجمة عن سقوط أثناء الاحتضار وليس لها علاقة بالوفاة.

– يلاحظ أن الجثة لا تتناسب مع السن المتوفى وتبدي طولن في قياسات الجذع وعرضه وزيادة في حجم الثديين، صغر في حجم الخصيتين وكيس الصفن وصغار في حجم القضيب وغؤور للقضيب داخل الصفن.

– كما يلاحظ غياب كامل للإشعار من الوجه والشاربين وتحت الإبطين وناحية العانة.

وتبدي الجثة الإصابات التالية:

~~~~~~

(الداخلي) للعضد الأيسر.
ثم دخل دخولاً ثانياً إلى البدن في الصدر الجانبي المتوسط وخروج خروجاً بـ ١٠ سم.

٢ – مرمى ناري دخل في الخاصرة اليمنى العلوية وخرج في الظهر السفلي الأيمن الوحشي.

٣ – مرمى ناري دخوله وخروجه في مستوى الثلث للعضد الأيمن.

ولا تبدي الجثة:

أية آثار لعنف أو شدة أو مقاومة أو ضرب أو تعذيب من كدمات، سحجات ظفرية، جروح قاطعة طعنية أو وخزية، كسور عظمية أو تجلوع منفصلية أو فوهات لمرامي نارية أخرى سوى ما سبق ذكره بالتفصيل أعلاه.

<u>المناقشة :</u>

لقد مني المتوفي حمزة بثلاثة مرامي نارية أحدها كان له دخولين وخروجين حيث أنه دخل في العضد الأيسر وخرج من العضد ودخل ثانية في الصدر الجانبي الأيسر وخرج من الصدر المتوسط الأمامي بين الجامتين.

والمرمى الآخر دخل من الخاصرة اليمنى وخرج من الظهر الأيمن قرب النهاية السفلية للأضلاع.

ومرمى دخل وخرج في الثلث السفلي للعضد الأيمن.

– إن المرامي النارية الثلاث بنت حوافها في الدخول والخروج متماة حمراء وبدت حواف الدخول للداخل والخروج للخارج كما ظهر الطوق السحجي على فوهات الدخول ولم يظهر على فوهات الخروج وهي علامة هامة لتمييز الدخول عن الخروج.

– إن الصفات والموجودات التي أوردناها سابقاً بفوهات الدخول والخروج إنما هي علامة على أنها حياتية أي حدثت للمتوفى حمزة وهو على قيد الحياة.

ـــ إن ما يميز هذه الفوهات أنها واسعة نوعاً ما وهذا يدل بأن المرمى لم يدخل البدن بشكل مباشر وإنما اصطدم قبل بدخوله المتشوه جزئياً أو أن الدخول بشكل جانبي لبدث لفوهات أكبر من الطبيعي قليلاً.

ـــ لقد لاحظنا أن المرامي لإصابت المغدور في مواقع متعددة في العضد الأيسر وواحد في الجذع (الخاصرة) وآخر في العضد الأيسر وأن توزع المرامي يدل بأنه قد أصيب من قبل رامي بوضعية الحركة للرامي والمغدور أو أصيب من أكثر من مصدر.

ـــ إن المرميين اللذين أصابا الفتى في صدره وخاصرته هما مرميان قاتلان فوراً وأن المرمي الذي أصاب العضد الأيمن فهو ليس قاتلاً بأثره.

ـــ إن المرامي النارية سببت أذيات : ـــ عظمية

ـــ حشوية صدرية .

ـــ حشوية بطنية.

أدت إلى النزيف والوفاة.

ـــ إن الإطلاق هو من قبل الغير والرامي كان لحظة الإطلاق في نفس المستوى الأفقي للمغدور.

ـــ مسافة الإطلاق بعيدة للمرامي الثلاث وهي أكثر من متر ولحد كحد أدنى.

النتيجة :

وفاة بنزيف شديد ناجم عن إصابة بمرامي نارية ثلاث.

أ ـــ مرمي ناري دخوله وخروجه في العضد السفلي الأيسر بداية ثم دخل ثانية في الصدر الجانبي الأيسر وخرج من منتصف القص.

٢ ـــ مرمي ناري دخوله في الخاصرة اليمنى وخروجه في الظهر الأيمن الوحشي.

٣ ـــ مرمي ناري دخوله وخروجه في الثلثا السفلي للعضد الأيمن مسافة الإطلاق لجميع المرامي بعيدة ، متر واحد كحد أدنى.

الإطلاق من قبل الغير ومن عدة مصادر أو رامي واحد بوضعية الحركة والمغدور كان بوضعية الحركة أيضاً وفي نفس المستوى الأفقي .

لقد سببت المرامي أذيات بالنزعة حشوية صدرية بطنية وعائية نازفة بشدة أدت للوفاة .

والوفاة ناجمة عن المرامي النارية وما نجم عنها.

٣ كلفت اللجنة الطبية الثلاثية المذكورة بالبند رقم ٢ بإعداد دراسة مقاربة بين الصور الضوئية المأخوذة لجثة الحدث المتوفى حمزة بمشفى تشرين العسكري في الكائن بدمشق بتاريخ ٢٠١١/٤/٣٠ مع الصور الضوئية المأخوذة لنفس الجثة بتاريخ ٢٠١١/٥/٢٤ بالمشفى الوطني بدرعا ، وتنفيذاً لهذا التكليف قامت اللجنة بالدراسة المقاربة بتقرير مؤلف من صفحتين جاء فيه بالحرف الواحد ما يلي:

لدى معاينة الصور الضوئية المأخوذة لجثة المتوفى حمزة الخطيب بتاريخ الوفاة بدمشق وذلك بتاريخ ٢٠١١/٤/٣٠ ومقارنتها مع الصور الضوئية المأخوذة له بتاريخ ٢٤ / ٥ / ٢٠١١ في مشفى درعا الوطني، تبين لدا الفرو قات التالية:

المميزات	في مشفى درعا الوطني	في مشفى تشرين العسكري
١	انتفاخ شديد واسوداد وتورم في مستوى الأجفان والأنف والشفتين وهي تفسخيه بعد الموت	سحجات خفيفة وهي سحجات متكدمة حياتية. والجثة ملطخة بالدماء ولا يوجد وذمات.
٢	لون أخضر محمر ومناطق مسودة تقع في ناحية الخد الأيمن والصدر العلوي والأطراف وهي استخديه بعد الموت.	لا يوجد لون أخضر أو مناطق مسودة
٣	انتفاخ شديد في مستوى الصفن مع تلون كيس الصفن بالأخضر المسود وأيضاً في الفخذين والبطن وهي تفسخيه بعد الموت	لا يوجد انتفاخ في مستوى الصفن أو تلون لكيس الصفن باللون الأخضر المسود.
٤	سلاخات جلدية أكثرها وضوحاً في مستوى اليدين والعنق وهي تفسخيه بعد الموت	لا يوجد سلاخات جلدية
٥	ظهور الشبكة الوعائية في مستوى الطرفين السفليين والصدر بشكل واضح ويلون يميل للبنى وهي تفسخيه بعد الموت	لا يوجد شبكة وعائية وعائية ظاهرة على جثة المتوفى
٦	آثار سوائل نتلة في مستوى سطح الجثة بشكل كامل وهي تفسخيه بعد الموت	لا توجد آثار لسوائل
٧	ظهور حشفة القضيب بلون أسود مع انسلاخ جلدي في قاعدة الصفن عن التلاقي مع جذور القضيب وظهور النسيج تحت الجلد أصفر وهي تفسخيه بعد الموت ولا يوجد ما يؤكد وجود القطع على الصور.	بقت الخصيتان صغيرتين وفي مكانهما الطبيعي والقضيب صغير الحجم وظاهر في كيس الصفن ولا يظهر منه إلا الحشفة الواضحة بلون أحمر زهري مع قرحة الاحليل الصغيرة في منتصف الحشفة بسبب السمنة دونما علامات لانسلاخات
٨	ظهور فوهات المراسي النارية مسودة بفعل التفسخ الرمي والدماء بلون أسود غامق	ظهور فوهات المراسي النارية بلون أحمر قاني والدماء حمراء قانية تحيط بفوهة المراسي النارية وتنتشر على سطح الجسم في المناطق المخفضة من الجسم

المناقشة للفروقات الظاهرة على المقارنة بين الصور المأخوذة للجثة في مشفى تشرين بدمشق بتاريخ ٢٠١١/٤/٣٠ والصور المأخوذة للجثة في مشفى درعا الوطني بتاريخ ٢٠١١/٥/٢٤:

ــ إن ما ظهر في الصور المأخوذة في المشفى الوطني بدرعا هو عبارة عن تبدلات حدثت بفعل التفسخ الرمي بسبب تقادم الزمن على الجثة ما بين لحظة حدوث الوفاة وتاريخ تسليمها إلى مشفى درعا الوطني، وهي تبدلات فيزيولوجية طبيعية تحدث على كل الجثث بعد حدوث الوفاة بفترات زمنية. ونتيجة لفعل الجراثيم الهوائية واللاهوائية وهذا كله يؤدي إلى حدوث انتفاخ في الأجواف بفعل انطلاق الغازات التفسخية وحدوث انسلاخات جلدية بمجرد ملامسة الجثة وخروج سوائل مثلة من الفوهات ومن الجلد وفي مراحل متقدمة من الزمن سوف يؤدي ذلك إلى انحلال في النسيج العضلي وجسيم الأحشاء ولا يبقى سوى الهيكل العظمي من الجثة كلما تقادم الزمن مع العلم أن هذه الخدمية الفيزيولوجية تتبع كما هو معروف في الطلب الشرعي للظروف التي وجدت فيها الجثة من ناحية حرارة الجو، مكان وجود الجثة، مع العلم أنه في الحالة التي أمامنا فإن الجثة كانت موجودة في البراد ويتبرد (س٥) تحت الصفر وهذا سيؤخر حدوث التفسخ الرمي ويجعله بطيئاً إلا أن ذلك لا يمنع من حدوثه وهذا ما حصل في حالتنا هذه والذي أدى إلى ظهور الفوارق بين الوصف للجثة في مشفى تشرين وفي مشفى درعا الوطني.

ثـ كلفت اللجنة معاون رئيس النيابة العامة بدمشق بتقديم تقرير يبين فيه الإجراءات التحقيقية القضائية التي قام بها حيال جثة الحدث المتوفي حمزة الخطيب فقدم تقريره مطبوعاً موقعاً من قبله مؤلفاً من صفحة واحدة والتي جاء فيه بالحرف الواحد:

في ساعة متأخرة من ليل الجمعة الموافق ٢٠١١/٤/٢٩ تم إعلامنا من مشفى تشرين العسكري بوجود جثة مجهولة الهوية في قسم الطلب الشرعي واردة إليهم من محافظة درعا، وعلى الفور وكوني قاضي الجرائم المشهودة، توجهت برفقة كاتب الضبط والطبيب الشرعي السيد مبسلن وقمنا بإجراء الكشف الطبي والقضائي عليها، وتحديد سبب الوفاة، والتي تبين أنها ناجمة عن المراسي النارية التي تعرضت لها، وقام مصور الأدلة الجنائية بتصويرها بدقة، وقمنا بإعطائها رقم ٢٣/ ولم نشاهد أي آثار شدة أو عنف أو ضرب أو تعذيب أو كسور عليها، واستمر الكشف حتى صباح يوم السبت الموافق ٢٠١١/٤/٣٠.

ولم نكتف بذلك، قمنا بتكليف لجنة طبية ثلاثية لحدث خبرة وتحديد سبب الوفاة بدقة، وهي مؤلفة من الطبيب أكرم الشعار والطبيب حسام أحمد والطبيب إسماعيل كبولان ــ وتم إيداعها في براد مشفى تشرين العسكري ــ قسم الطلب الشرعي، لبصار تسليمها لذويها بعد التعرف عليها، وفعلاً بتاريخ ٢٠١١/٥/٢١ حوالي الساعة الخامسة مساءً تم تسليم الجثة رقم ٢٣/ التي يبين فيما بعد أنها عائدة للفتى حمزة علي الخطيب وتم تلقيها من مشفى

تشرين العسكري برفقة دورية من الشرطة العسكرية ووصلت بعد حوالي ساعة ونصف إلى برّد مشفى درعا الوطني دون علمنا بماذا حصل بعد ذلك.

٥- استدعت اللجنة بتاريخ ٢٠١١/٦/١ الطبيب الشرعي إسماعيل أبو ديبوت الموظف بالمشفى الوطني - قسم الطب الشرعي باعتباره هو من أجرى الخبرة والكشف على جثة الحدث المتوفي حمزة الخطيب ووصولاً لحقيقة عملية ساطعة قاطعة لا يتسرب إليها الشك أو الريب، واستدعت أيضاً أعضاء اللجنة الطبية الثلاثية الذين قاموا بالكشف على جثة نفس الشخص والذين سبق ذكرهم أعلاه، وتم إجراء المقابلة بينهم جميعاً وأفهموا موضوع سبب الحضور والمقابلة والغاية من هذا الاجتماع، وبالنقاش الشفوي العلمي والطبي والفني أعلن الطبيب الشرعي إسماعيل أبو ديبوت:

" نحن الطبيب الشرعي إسماعيل أبو ديبوت طبيب شرعي في محافظة درعا.

بعد الاطلاع على تقرير اللجنة الطبية الثلاثية الذي قامت بتاريخ ٢٠١١/٤/٢٩ بفحص جثة المرحوم حمزة الخطيب وكذلك الصور الضوئية المجراة ٢٠١١/٤/٢٩ في دمشق والصور الضوئية المجراة بتاريخ ٢٠١١/٥/٢٤ في درعا.

وبعد مقابلة الزملاء أعضاء اللجنة الطبية الثلاثية : الدكتور أكرم الشبار والدكتور حسام أحمد والدكتور إسماعيل كيوان وتقرير المقاربة بين الصور المأخوذة لنفس الشخص في دمشق وهي درعا من قبل اللجنة الثلاثية أفيد بما يلي:

أنه كتب في تقريري المؤرخ بتاريخ ٢٠١١/٥/٢٤ أن هناك بثر في القضيب غير حياتي (أي أنه لم يحدث أثناء الحياة وإنما قد حدث بعد الموت وأن الجثة وقت الفحص كانت تبدي تفسخاً حتى في الناحية التناسلية لوجود انتفاخ في كيس الصفن وظهور اللون الأزرق، وحدوث انسلاخات جلدية، ولذا أقر بأن الحالة لم تكن حالة بثر بشكل جازم وذلك لوجود التغيرات التفسخية السابقة مع احتمال أن هذا الضياع المادي الذي بوهث عنه حدث في سياق التفسخ أو أثناء نقل الجثة أو احتكاك في هذا الناحية وهذه تعبيري"

وبعد أن انتهى بتدوين التقرير بخطة قدمه إلى اللجنة قمت بدراسته ومشاهدته بالاسم والتوقيع لكامل قوام اللجنة كني بأخذ القيمة الرسمية والقوة الثبوتية وبعد ذلك جرى ضم هذا التقرير إلى التحقيقات الجارية حسب الأصول.

٦- تم استدعاء المدعو علي الخطيب والد الحدث المتوفي حمزة الخطيب بتاريخ ٢٠١١/٦/١ وبالمناقشة معه أكد أنه على قناعة بأن جثة ولده سليمة وليس لأحد مصلحة بالعبث بها وولد هذه القناعة بعد اطلاعه على محضر الكشف الطبي والقضائي الجاري على جثة ولده من اللجنة الطبية الثلاثية والصور الضوئية المأخوذة على الجثة بدمشق لكنه رجا اللجنة بأن لا يكون حضوره وقناعته خوفاً على نفسه من القتل من قبل المتطرفين في درعا، ونزولاً عند رغبته قررت اللجنة صرف النظر على ضبط أقواله ..

٧- منعا للتأويل أحضرت اللجنة ديوان قيد مدني فردي للمتوفي حمزة الخطيب من أمين السجل المدني الذي يتبع له والذي جاء فيه (الاسم: حمزة - النسبة: الخطيب - اسم الأب: علي - اسم الأم: سميرة - الأمانة: درعا - محل وتاريخ القيد: الجيزة ١٩٩٨/٥/٦ اليوم السادس من شهر أيار لعام ألف وتسعمائة وثمانٍ وتسعون

وتسعين ميلادي ــ الدين والمذهب: إسلام ــ الرقم الوطني /١٢٠١٠١١٨٩٨٣/ ــ الجنس: ذكر ــ تاريخ القيد :
١٩٩٨/٥/٢٧ ـ الوضع العائلي: خازب ـ متسلسل الاسم: ٨٣).

وبعد القيام بهذه الإجراءات المذكورة أعلاه استخلصت اللجنة وبالإجماع النتائج التالية:
١ــ وصلت الجثة إلى مشفى تشرين العسكري بدمشق بتاريخ ٢٠١١/٤/٢٩ في ساعة متأخرة من الليل وبوشر
في إجراء الكشف الطبي والقضائي عليها أصولا عقب وقت قصير من وصولها بشكل فني وعلمي وقانوني
متكامل.
٢ــ لا يوجد من أثار الشدة والعنف سوى أثار المرامي النارية الموصوفة بمحضر الكشف.
٣ــ إن سبب الوفاة هو الإصابة بنزف شديد ناجم عن الإصابة بمرامي نارية ثلاث:

أ ــ مرمى ناري دخوله في العضد العظمي الأيسر بدايته ثم دخل في العضد الجانبي الأيسر وخروجه من
منتصف القص.
ب ــ مرمى ناري دخوله في الخاصرة اليمنى وخروجه في الظهر الأيمن الوحشي.
ج ــ مرمى ناري دخوله وخروجه في الثلث السفلي للعضد الأيمن مسافة الإطلاق لجميع المرامي
بعيدة: متر واحد كحد أدنى.

الإطلاق من قبل الغير ومن عدة مصادر أو من رامي واحد بوضعية الحركة والمغدور كان بوضعية
الحركة أيضاً وفي نفس المستوى الأفقي:
لقد سببت المرامي أذيات بليغة عضوية صدرية بطنية وعائية بشدة أدت للوفاة.
والوفاة ناجمة عن المرامي النارية وما نجم عنها.

٤ــ لا يوجد بتر للعضو الذكري وإنما حصل التباس من قبل الطبيب الشرعي إسماعيل أبو ديوب الذي قام
بالكشف على الجثة بدرعا بتاريخ ٢٠١١/٥/٢٤. وصوب قراره في تقريره المعد بهذا التاريخ على ضوء
المعطيات الفنية والعلمية والطبية والدراسة المقارنة التي أجرتها اللجنة الطبية الثلاثية بدمشق بين الصور
الضوئية المأخوذة للجثة بدمشق وبين الصور الضوئية المأخوذة للجثة في درعا والمتعاقبة الجيارية مع الأطباء
الشرعيين الثلاثة الذين قاموا بالكشف على الجثة بتاريخ ٢٠١١/٤/٣٠.
٥ــ ثبوت قناعة المدعو علي الخطيب والد الحدث المتوفى حمزة الخطيب بأن جثة ولده سليمة وخالية من
العبث وأبدى صراحة هذا القناعة أمام أعضاء اللجنة والتمس عدم تدوين إفادته أو رأيه هذا بشكل خطي خوفاً
على نفسه من الجماعات المتطرفة في درعا والتي قد تتقدم على قتله إذا علمت بأنه حضر وبدّل قناعته بما أشيع
عن بتر العضو الذكري لابنه بوسائل الأعلام المغرضة، وهذا القناعة نبعت من أرضية الحوار بينه وبين
أعضاء اللجنة من جهة والتقويات الرسمية القضائية والصور الضوئية وتقرير الخبرة الطبية الثلاثية والدراسة
المقارنة بين الصور المأخوذة في درعا والصور المأخوذة في دمشق من جهة أخرى.

٦ ـــ ثبوت وجود جهات معادية وأبحت أشخاصاً لنقل صور مغايرة للحقيقة أو متلاعب بها فنياً للتحقيق مآرب دنيئة يجب متابعتها من الجهات المعنية توصلاً لمعرفتها والقبض على تلك الصور ومبتدعيها عامة وفيما يتعلق بهذه الواقعة خاصة.

الخلاصة :

ـــ ثبت بالدليل العلمي والفني والقضائي عدم وجود أثار لأعمال شدة أو عنف أو تعذيب على جثة الحدث المتوفى حمزة الخطيب لا بحياته ولا بعد وفاته سوى أثار التشريح التشريحية التي أصيب بها.

ـــ كما ثبت عدم وجود بتر للعضو الذكري لهذه الجثة أيضاً.

ــــــــــــــــــــــــــــــــــــ يرجى الاطلاع ، ـــــــــــــــــــــــــــــــــــــ

[Unofficial translation]

Note verbale dated 16 August 2011 from the Permanent Mission of the Syrian Arab Republic addressed to the Office of the United Nations High Commissioner for Human Rights Geneva

16 August 2011

In addition to information previously delivered by the Syrian Arab Republic, which includes a comprehensive account of the events currently taking place in Syria, we submit this complementary information intended to clarify and rectify the erroneous believes mentioned in the UN High Commission report.

The Syrian government had promptly delivered its response to the High Commission's questions concerning the events taking place, and fully explained the measures taken to resolve the issues raised with regards to the situation in Syria. The Syrian government response was delivered prior to the date the High Commission was to present its report to the Human Rights Council. It is regrettable that the presented report did not include the position of the Syrian government, and was solely based on unreliable sources. When the High Commission chooses to be unprofessional in dealing with this matter, it creates an environment of distrust, especially that the Syrian report included all documented information the Syrian government possesses concerning the points raised in the High Commission's report.

The High Commission report was based on a one-sided source of information which is the opposition based abroad, they are few individuals who were outlawed for committing crimes related to using arms and spreading terror amongst the Syrian people. What they claim, without any proof, is untrue and has no basis in the law; it only expresses personal view points with no credibility. For example, the incident describing thousands of Syrian civilians fleeing the country lacks credibility, what really happened is that tents were erected at the Turkish border and prepared to receive ten thousand people a month even before the incident had taken place. The fleeing Syrian citizens have deserted their towns and villages before any military or security forces presence took place, they fled armed groups that have infested their areas, but when authorities restored safety, ten thousands of them returned, and today, they run a peaceful life in their towns and villages. Only those who used arms and organized terror against the population remain outside of the country.

- The high Commission report contains an obvious legal contradiction, in one part it mentions how Syria complies with international Laws, in another part it claims Syria breaking international Laws, which is untrue; when the Syrian government takes on arresting, detaining and presenting to justice those who violate the law, it is not considered breaking international laws on the part of the Syrian government.

- In Syria -as it was incorrectly mentioned in the High Commission report- there is no minority that uses power to repress protestors, in fact, it shows how representatives of the High Commission have chosen a biased approach to collect information from individuals who portrayed themselves as eyewitnesses, while they are in reality a group of outlaws who have committed crimes, which makes them completely unreliable as a source of information. The description of certain groups as "minority" or "majority" by representatives of the High Commission is an outrageous interference in our national internal makeup, a recipe for disaster and a call to destroy Syria, it is totally unaccepted.

- While the High Commission has based its report on press information, despite the fact that press information should not be considered as a reliable source, especially when it is used to create reports addressed to states! Besides civilian and military victims, the report mentions eyewitnesses, although, the report did not support those individuals' credibility, nor clarify whether they are real victims and eyewitnesses? or, are they taking part in the equation and the methodic spread of organized terror? In disregarding information provided by the Syrian government, the High Commission implies its reliance on information offered by organizations considered to be hostile toward Syria, which leads to weakening the state's role and its credibility.

- This also applies to videos provided by nongovernmental organizations, presented by different media in the frame of a misleading campaign against Syria, destined to incite sectarian violence among Syrian citizens. In fact, these videos represent evidence of ugly crimes carried on by armed terrorist groups, crimes of murder, rape, dismemberment, massive graves and genocides that were perpetuated against both civilians and the armed forces by terrorists. The Syrian media has shown how certain international media had spread lies and amplified what is happening in Syria, they either have presented information contrary to the truth, or shown videos of demonstrations taking place in countries other than Syria. We have sent tens of examples of these videos to the High Commission, clearly showing manipulations of that kind.

- Contrary to few other states, Syria is committed to apply International Law. Syria, who takes part in most agreements and protocols related to human rights, is today declaring a series of consecutive reform measures destined to implementing a comprehensive change toward a better future of Syria, starting by the abolition of the State of Emergency Law, at a time when it is most needed, while groups of armed terrorists are surpassing all our predictions in spreading terror, violence and chaos, they, in some cases, are supported by regional and international third parties, which in itself, constitutes a blatant meddling in Syria's internal affairs by certain states, which, in turn is a contradiction with international law, charters and conventions.

In addition, Syria had put an end to the Supreme State Security Court, and proceeded to creating reform committees that had accomplished its mission in view of achieving progress and development in Syria. This effort had resulted in three legislative decrees; decree number 34 (March, 7th, 2011), a general amnesty covering all crimes except treason, espionage, terrorism and rape, decree number 61 (May, 31st, 2011) and decree number 72 (June, 20th, 2011). As a result, 10'433 detainees were released immediately, this number does not include tens of thousands of minor violations and misdemeanors whose actors benefit from these decrees, this is in addition to criminal lawsuits underway, for which the general amnesty covers half of the sentence unless a verdict is pronounced, and many other cases that fall partially under the general amnesty.

We are convinced that a comprehensive national dialog is the best way to achieve development and reform in the political, legislative, social and economic areas. A presidential decree was issued on June 2nd, 2011 stipulating the creation of an official body with the mission to establish the basis of our national dialog, to describe its mechanisms and specify its timetable. Between June 10th and 12th, the national dialog committee invited intellectuals, politicians and young activists, a full spectrum of the Syrian society and its different political orientations, to participate in a dialog intended to reach a vision and produce recommendations. Participants discussed the nature of the delicate phase Syria is going through, explored future possibilities and contemplated citizens' daily life concerns. Here are some of the recommendations issued following the meeting:

- Dialog is the only choice to end the crisis.

- Confirms the necessity of focusing on the value of human rights, to use means of constitutional, humanistic and contemporary standards in order to protect human rights, also a recommends the creation of a Syrian high council for human rights.

- Advises an immediate release of all political, and opinion prisoners in Syria, who did not commit crimes punishable by the law.

Some of the other reform laws:

1- Legislative decree number 55 (April, 21st, 2011) related to law enforcement in few particular kinds of crimes, it concerns procedures of collecting evidence, hearing suspects and respecting temporary detention period.

2- Legislative decree number 54 (April, 21st, 2011) related to managing citizens' right to organize peaceful demonstrations, which is already mentioned in the Syrian constitution as a basic human right.

3- Legislative decree number 43 (April, 21st, 2011) related to the abolition of the Supreme State Security Court.

4- Legislative decree number 49 (April, 7th, 2011) related to granting Syrian citizenship documents to the Kurdish populations registered as foreigners in Al Hasaka.

5- Legislative decree number 46 (April, 3rd, 2011) related to including under health insurance coverage both civilian and armed forces retirees, those who were employed by the government, public sector or public organizations.

6- Legislative decree number 43 (March, 24th, 2011) related to property acquisition in border areas.

7- Legislative decree number 40 (March, 24th, 2011) related to salary increase for civilian and armed forces' governmental employees.

8- Legislative decree number 62 (June, 5th, 2011) related to substituting workers' short term contracts by long term contracts.

9- Legislative decree number 84 (July, 13th, 2011) related to social development.

10- Legislative decree number 100 (August, 6th, 2011) related to multiple parties law.

11- Legislative decree number 101 (August, 6th, 2011) related to the general elections law.

The government had also completed working on two laws, the first concerns the media, the second is related to local administrations, they will be issued in the next few days. Additionally, we issued many regulatory decrees related to offering students more study cycles, and creating enterprises and new colleges in all Syria's universities.

The Syrian government is also creating a number of committees involving senior professionals and experts to work on the following questions:

1- Committee investigating crimes committed against civilians and the armed forces, and other crimes related to the currently events taking place in Syria.

2- Committee exploring the reasons and elements taking part in the system of corruption, with the mission to describe mechanisms of prevention of corruption and promote values of integrity.

3- Committee to establish a media law.

4- Committee for judicial reform.

5- Committee for administrative reform.

6- Committee for national dialog.

And many other legislative and regulatory decrees and strategic decisions that have failed to be brought up in the High Commission report.

• Blaming Syria's security services as a sole responsible for what's happening in Syria is irrational, incorrect and expresses a unilateral perspective. It is the duty of state's security services to protect private and public property, and to achieve a calm, safe and stable environment for its citizens, taking into consideration that the vast majority of this crisis's victims are police, armed forces and security service agents who were murdered by groups of armed terrorists. They were attacked at their places of work or while protecting peaceful demonstrators, everybody was exposed to fire attacks of masked individuals, a segment that was completely overlooked by the High Commission report.

• Another erroneous belief included in the High Commission report is the mention of how Syrian economic reform is being put on hold. On the other hand, in the reports delivered by many of the international organizations participating in development programs in the country, there is a mention of how the economic reform lead by Syria went beyond anything that has been done in the neighboring states.

Some of the adopted contemporary economy standards were noticeable in the following areas:

1– Social market economy.

2– Adopting liberal economy and exchange with all world countries.

These new measures in economy had reflected on elevating lifestyle, decreasing poverty and diminishing the development gap among the different areas in Syria. This was mentioned in reports issued by consecutive International Monetary Fund's missions to Syria.

All this and tens of legislative decrees that gave a boost to Syria's economic reform, while taking into account that the Syrian economy is not bound to a specific geographic area, each part of Syria has its own advantages related to the economy.

• The idea that the Kurdish population of Syria is excluded from power, or from Syria's civic life until 2011 is far from the truth. What really took place in March 2011 is that tens of thousands of Kurds were granted Syrian citizenships, a gesture no other country had made toward its alien residents. The Kurds of Syria have occupied high political, military and civic positions; we can produce detailed count of this claim at the demand of the High Commission.

• Despite the fact that protestors in Daraa had specific reform demands since the beginning of the uprising, peculiarly, the report referred to the origin of Daraa's demonstrations as being a popular uprising against power abuse by local authorities. Later on, the High Commission report also mentioned that Daraa's events started after the detention of a group of children, this is one of the contradictions repeatedly appeared in the High Commission report. The event took place before armed terrorist groups have grasped the occasion of Daraa's people's spontaneous movement to attack civilians and armed forces with fire arms, in addition to the fact that, many of Daraa's sons occupy high governmental positions. We are pleased to present evidence of the facts we advance at the demand of the High Commission.

- The term "Shabbiha", made use of in the report, is an expression created and exploited by terrorist groups and some biased media; they propagated the expression in their press reports with the intention to create discord among the different segments of the Syrian society. Due to security vacuum, terrorist groups succeeded in taking over some areas, yet, unarmed citizens were able to organize themselves in people's committees, defending private and public properties against criminals.

- The number of martyrs is truly 1900, but not all of them are civilians; armed forces and police agents make up the largest part of victims of terrorist groups.

- Concerning the city of Hama, the Syrian army did not occupy the city; it is the national Syrian army, not some foreign army! What it did was to cooperate with security forces to rid the city from armed groups, extremists and terrorists who turned Hama into a ghost city by terrorizing its citizens, and pushing them to flee the city in fear for their lives. Citizens of Hama were relieved to see that the army took control over, and returned calm and normality to their city. The same thing happened in several other towns where terrorist groups tried to maintain a state of horror. The government chose to make use of its armed forces for lack of specialized police forces capable of dealing with riots, rebellion and terrorism; the army did not use heavy weaponry to harm civilians, but rather to protect itself from armed terrorist groups.

- The report has also mentioned 30 dead, and 200 wounded when reporting events at Jissr Al Shughur, ignoring the reality, which is the number of victims in the area had reached 120 among members of the security forces, who were brutally murdered and tossed in mass graves later discovered -when some terrorists were arrested- in the presence of a number of diplomats and foreign press representatives.

- There was no arrest of peaceful demonstrators. Detainees among demonstrators are released, contrary to the law, within five days of their arrest, if there are any peaceful demonstrators among our detainees, please send us their names.

Accusing authorities of torture is exaggerated and utterly untrue, only 12 cases of that kind are presented to courts, they are all mentioned in our earlier response to the High Commission.

- There were no orders to fire on peaceful protestors, if anything; orders were given not to carry weapons, while accompanying peaceful demonstrations.

- No heavy weaponry or helicopters were used while facing armed terrorist groups. All what the report included in relation to this fact is misleading, contrary to the truth, and clearly intended to discredit Syria, and to harass the state for obvious political reasons known to everybody.

- The Syrian government is seriously determined to oppose to torture used against Syrian citizen. A special judicial commission of inquiry is taking direct measures to bring to justice individuals who are found guilty with violating human rights, or who were involved in murdering civilians and armed forces.

- Concerning refugees, they will face no obstacle at their return, we will facilitate their homecoming, and we also allow members of the press to cover events in turbulent areas.

- Permission to enter the country and proceed with its investigations of human rights will be granted to human rights organizations by the Syrian state in accordance with considerations related to national sovereignty, in a time the state determines as suitable.

- In terms of procedures, we find the High Commission's report deviating from the usual legal framework set up by the resolution S-16/1 in many aspects, including:

  1- Changing the "Mission" name into "Fact Finding Mission" in the report title, as well as the first paragraph.

  2- Non-compliance with the logic of resolution S-16/1 requiring the Commission to investigate and present an impartial, reliable report.

  3- In paragraph 15 and 17 of the report, some of the violations were described as potential crimes against humanity, this description does not fall under the High Commission's jurisdiction, and has no place to appear in this report. The High Commission's mission stops at collecting information and does not extend to attributing legal designations to the mentioned violations.

  4- The High Commission has presented its recommendations to UN Security Council, while, in fact, its relation is limited to the Human Rights Council.

  5- The High Commission has presented its recommendations to the Arab League, is acting as if the Arab League is under authority of the Human Rights Council.

- With the high estimation Syria has with regards to the Human Rights Council, and its missions, Syria expects the Council to keep its impartial position, and to take into account the different existing view points, to objectively analyze it away from prejudice, especially with respect to humanitarian aspects. We implore the High Commission to remain independent, and not allow pre determined perceptions and lack of scrutiny to take over its judgment. The Syrian government is extending a helping hand to the High Commission in proposing a fruitful cooperation aiming to set matters in their right places. Syria is in the process of preparing comprehensive judicial documents, which will be presented to the High Commission and other competent international bodies, clearly showing the involvement of individuals, groups and states in fueling internal unrest and sectarian friction, while supporting armed terrorist groups' work in destroying stability and the national unity of Syria. In addition to interfering with internal affairs of Syria, and offering financial and moral support to criminal gangs ravaging the country and murdering both civilians and armed forces personnel and bringing about chaos, confusion and organized violence.

The committee in charge of Hamza Al Khateeb's issue

Investigation's outcome

Based on administrative order number 913/s dated May 30th 2011 related to naming a committee with major general AbdulKareem Sulaiman, Deputy Minister of Interior as president, and the following members:

- Director of Criminal Security, Mr. Mohamed Darwisha

- Military Prosecutor, Mr. Mohamed Kanjo

- Commander of Military Police, Mr. AbdelAziz Al Shallal

- Criminal Investigations Security branch director, Mr. Raed Jazem

The mission of this committee consists of investigating claims of acts of violence and torture performed on the cadaver of the child Hamza Al Khateeb.

All members of the committee met in its president's office at 8 am on Tuesday, May 5th, 2011, and decided, after deliberations, to take the following measures in order to reach the truth about this issue:

1.   All committee members took a trip to the Teshreen Military Hospital, and visited its forensic department, viewed 6 colored photos on thick white photography paper, produced by the military police, judicial evidence, of the criminology photo department, and numbered 202/757, each of them carry the number 23, the photos are taken of the cadaver of a minor, Hamza Al Khateeb, it portrayed the cadaver in several different positions, and were marked with the number 23, because there was no identification of the cadaver at the moment the photos were taken. The photos were included in the file of investigation according to regulated procedures.

2.   A copy of the forensic file was viewed, the file was established by three medical doctors, Dr. Akram Al Shaar, Dr. Essam Ahmad, Dr. Ismael Kiwan. The 4 pages of this report included the following, verbatim:

Report of forensic expertiseconcerning the death of citzen Hamza Al Khteeb

Description of appearance:

- The cadaver belongs to a minor/boy in his teens, overweight, medium height, light brown skin color, black hair 4 centimeter long.

- Honey colored eyes, pupils completely dilated, symmetrical.

- The cadaver shows blue color in the back parts of torso and extremities.

- The cadaver is soiled with blood, and shows abrasions and light superficial bruises in the right side of the front, eyelids and right cheek; it is caused by falling while dying, and has no connection to the cause of death.

- It is noted that the cadaver appearance is not in concordance with the age of the dead person, it shows big proportions of torso, width and height, and increased mammal glands size, small size testicles, scrotum and penis, the penis appears to be buried in the scrotum.

- It is also noted that the cadaver did not carry hair in the face, mustache, armpits and pubic areas.

The cadaver shows the following injuries:

1.   Perforations caused by bullet entry into the lower lateral part of the left upper arm, exit at the lower-third- part of the inner left upper arm, re-entered the chest from the side, and exited in 10 centimeters.

2.   Perforations caused by bullet entry at the top right waist area, exited at the lower lateral back area.

3.   Perforations caused by bullet entry and exit in the right upper arm.

The cadaver does not show:

There are no signs of violence or sprain, or resisting violence, no beating marks, no traces of torture, like bruises and fingernail abrasions, it does not show wounds with sharp objects, nor traces poking, no bone fracturing or dislocation of articulations, nor bullets wounds other than what is previously detailed.

Discussion:

- The deceased Hamza Al Khateeb had received 3 bullet wounds, the first one had two entrances and two exits perforations, entering at the left upper arm, exiting, and re-entering at the left side of the chest, exiting in the front part of the chest, between the nipples. The second entered in the right side of the waist area and exited in the back close the last rib on the right. The third entered and exited in the lower third of his right upper arm.

- All three bullets caused perforations with edges pointing inside the body at the entry locations, pointing outside when exiting the body, abrasion traces were formed around bullets' entry locations, they were absent for bullets' exit locations, which is an important evidence of bullets entry and exit locations.

- Bullet wounds occurred while the person of Hamza was alive.

- The perforation created by entry of bullets is relatively big and deformed, which leads us to think it had possibly gone through some kind of an obstacle before it hit the body of the victim, or had entered the body in an angle.

- The bullets hit the body in different areas, left and right upper arms and torso; this indicates that both shooter and deceased were moving around, or, the possibility of having more than one shooter.

- The two bullets in the boy's chest and waist might have caused instant death, while the right upper arm wound is not deadly.

- Bullets have caused damage in bones and internal chest and abdomen organs, and were the direct cause of internal bleeding and death.

- Shooting originated form a third party, the shooter was at the same height of the victim at the moment of shooting.

- Shooting occurred from a distance of more than one meter away from the victim.

Conclusion:

- Death is due to severe internal bleeding resulted from wounds of three bullets.

- Perforations are caused by bullet entry and exit at the lower part of the left upper arm, re-entered the chest from the side, and exited at the middle of the sternum.

- Perforations are caused by bullet entry at the top right waist area, exited at the lower back area.

- Perforation are caused by bullet entry and exit in the right upper arm.

- Shooting has originated from one or several third party sources. Shooter(s), as well as the victim might have been moving at the time of shooting.

- The bullets have damaged internal chest and abdomen organs and caused severe bleeding ended in death.

Death is a result of the damages caused by bullets shots from a fire arm.

4.   The committee formed of three doctors (names mentioned above) was mandated to prepare a comparative study of Hamza Al Khateebs' cadaver photos taken at the Teshreen Military Hospital in Damascus on April 30th 2011, to be compared with the same cadaver photos taken at the National Hospital in Daraa on May 24th 2011, the Committee produced a 2 pages report related to its mandate as follows:

When examining photos taken at the Teshreen Military Hospital in Damascus on April 30th 2011, and comparing it with the cadaver photos taken at the National Hospital in Daraa on May 24th 2011 we found the following distinctions:

differences	The National Hospital in Daraa	Teshreen Military Hospital, Damascus
1	Black color, swelling in eyelids, nose, lips, signs of post mortem decomposition process.	Light abrasions of bruises happened when the person was alive; the body is soiled with blood, no signs of swelling.
2	Flushed green color and blackened areas in the right cheek, upper chest and extremities, all due to post mortem decomposition process.	No green color or blackened areas on the body.
3	Severe swelling with green tint of the testicles area, lower abdomen and top of the thighs, due to post mortem decomposition process.	No swelling or black green coloring of testicles area.
4	Scored skin, especially in the neck and hands areas, due to post mortem decomposition process.	No scored skin.
5	Visible parts of the vascular system, tinted with brown color on the legs, due to post mortem decomposition process.	No apparent vascular system elements on the surface of the body of the deceased.
6	Traces of fetid liquids completely covering the surface of the cadaver, a sign of post mortem decomposition process.	No traces of liquid.
7	Glans appear in a black color with testicles scored skin at the basis of the penis, subcutaneous tissue is colored in yellow, a sign of post mortem decomposition process. Nothing in the photos suggests amputation.	Testicles, in their normal location, appear to be small, the penis is small and buried in the scrotum, the only visible part is glans with reddish pink color, a little opening of urethra in the center, this appearance is related to his overweight, no signs of scored skin.
8	Perforations of bullets entry blackened with blood, a sign of post mortem decomposition process.	Perforations of bullets entry and blood are of red color, also light red color blood is spread in different areas on the surface of the cadaver.

To discuss dissimilarities appeared in the cadaver's photos taken in Teshreen Hospital in Damascus on April 30th, 2011, compared to photos taken in the National Hospitel in Daraa on May 24th, 2011:

- What emerged from the photos taken in the National Hospitel in Daraa on May 24th, 2011 are the changes of the state of the cadaver due to the process of decomposition that was taking place between the moment of death and the time the cadaver was delivered to the National Hospital in Daraa. These are normal physiological shifts that generally occur with time after death takes place, they are related to different bacteria in the air and elsewhere producing gas and leading to enlargement of cadavers' cavities, and characterized by skin becoming easy to shred just by simple friction, and body orifices producing rotten liquids, muscles tissue and internal organs start to decay with time, leaving only a skeleton. According to forensics this process is conform to the circumstances and temperature of the place where the cadaver was found, despite the fact that in this particular case, the cadaver was kept refrigerated at minus 5 Celsius, which had contributed in slowing down the process without completely stopping it, that explains the discrepancies in cadaver description between Teshreen Hospital in Damascus on April 30th, 2011, and the National Hospitel in Daraa on May 24th, 2011.

5.   The committee mandated Deputy Public Prosecution in Damascus to present a report explaining the judicial procedures of investigations he ran in relation to the cadaver of deceased Hamza al Khateeb. A report of one page signed by the Deputy Public Prosecution was presented as follows:

In a late hour on Friday night, April 29th, 2011, we were informed by Teshreen Military Hospital about the existence in their forensic department of a cadaver with no identity, the cadaver arrived from Daraa. As judge of crimes, I immediately went to Teshreen Military Hospital, accompanied by a clerk and a forensic expert, Dr. Seles Waqqaf, we all examined the cadaver from a medical and judicial view points in order to determine the cause of death, lately appeared to be bullets from a fire arms. Forensic photographer took detailed photos of the cadaver, we attributed the number 23 to it, the cadaver did not bear traces of acts of violence or beating or torture or broken bones. Our examination of the cadaver continued until the morning of Saturday, April 30th, 2011.

In addition, we mandated a committee of three experienced medical doctors, Dr. Akram Al Shaar, Dr. Issam Ahmad and Dr. Ismael Kiwan, to determine the exact cause of death. The cadaver was confined to a refrigerator in the morgue of Teshreen Military Hospital, Department of Forensics. It would be delivered to the family as soon as we identify the deceased, which later took place when the cadaver number 23, turned out to belong to the boy Hamza Al Khateeb, was moved from Teshreen Military Hospital on May 21st, 2011, 5 pm, to a refrigerator in the National Hospital in Daraa. It took an hour and a half trip to get there. We have no information as to what happened next.

6.   The committee called Dr. Ismael Abu Nabut, employed by the National Hospital, forensic department on June 1st, 2011, as he was the person who had examined the cadaver of the boy Hamza Al Khateeb, in order to get the accurate scientific facts beyond any doubts, the three members of the committee of medical doctors –mentioned above- who examined the cadaver were also called, they held a meeting and discussed the situation from a technical, medical and scientific view points, and reached a description that was formulated by forensic Dr. Abu Nabut as follows:

"We, Dr. Ismael Abu Nabut, forensic doctor of the province of Daraa, hereby declare, after viewing the report presented by the committee of three medical doctors dated April 29th, 2011, in the matter of examining the cadaver of the deceased Hamza Al Khateeb, in addition to seeing photos of the cadaver taken in Damascus on April, 4th, 2011, and photos taken in Daraa on May 24th, 2011.

Following a meeting with my colleagues, members of the medical committee, Dr. Akram al shaar, Dr. Issam Ahmad and Dr. Ismael Kiwan, and the viewing of comparative documents related to the photos taken by them of the same cadaver in Damascus and in Daraa, I declare the following:

It was mentioned in my report dated May 24th, 2011, the existence of a post mortem amputation on the penis, and that the cadaver had presented at the time of examination, general signs of decomposition, also in its reproductive areas, which was apparent in swelling of the scrotum, and blue coloring and skin abrasions. I support the possibility that an amputation might have not occurred, and this physical loss might have taken place during the advancing stage of decomposition previously described, or with skin friction at the area during transport of the cadaver. This is my conclusion of expertise"

When he finished hand writing this report, it was presented to all committee members, who equally signed it, this report has full power of an official document, and later was combined with the rest of investigation documents accordingly.

7.   Mr. Ali Al Khateeb, father of the deceased, was called on June 1st, 2011, he willingly declared, after discussing the matter, that his son's body was intact, and that no one has any interest in tampering with the cadaver, he formulated this opinion after viewing records related to medical and judicial examinations of the cadaver, records established by the committee of three medical doctors, in addition to viewing the photos taken in Damascus. He implored the committee to omit his presence and convictions from the official records, for fear of vengeance by extremists in Daraa. The committee decided to respect his wishes by not mentioning his statement in the official records.

8.   To limit erroneous interpretations, the committee used Hamza Al Khateeb's official birth certificate, issued by secretary of the civil registry, which included the following information:

Name: Hamza. Family name: al Khateeb. Father name: Ali. Mother name: Samira. Registry: Daraa. Place and Date of registration: Al Jeeza, June 5th, 1998. Religion and Denomination: Islam. National Number: 12010118983. Sex: male. Date of Birth: May 27th, 2011. Marital Status: single. Name Serial: 83.

Following the above mentioned procedures, the committee unanimously declares:

1.   The cadaver arrived late at night on April 29th, 2011, to Teshreen Military Hospital in Damascus, a forensic examination of the cadaver took place according to regulations, short time after its arrival, examination was conducted in a comprehensive, scientific, technical and lawful manner.

2.   The cadaver did not carry signs of violence except the perforations caused by fire arms previously described.

3.   The cause of death is severe internal bleeding due to bullets wounds in three occasions:

(a)   Perforations caused by bullet entry at the lower part of the left upper arm, re-entered the chest from the left side, and exited at the middle of the sternum.

(b)   Perforation caused by bullet entry at waist's right area, exited at the lower side of the back area.

(c)   Perforation caused by bullet entry and exit in the right upper arm. All three bullets were shot from a distance no less than one meter away from the victim.

Shooting originated from one or several third party sources. Shooter(s), as well as the victim might have been moving at the time of shooting, they were on the same height. Bullets have damaged internal chest and abdomen organs and caused severe bleeding ended in death.

Death is the result of the damages caused by bullet shots from a fire arm.

4.   No amputation of penis was observed, Dr. Ismael Abu Nabut had misjudged the situation in an earlier examination in Daraa on May, 24th, 2011, and later rectified his declaration in today's report. The alteration of his statement is based on comparative technical and medical evidence presented in the photos taken in Damascus and Daraa, and discussed with a committee of three medical doctors who examined the cadaver on April 30th, 2011 in Damascus.

5.   Evidence of conviction of Mr. Ali Al Khateeb, father of the victim, declaring that his son's cadaver is intact, not tampered with. He ultimately formulated his conviction in presence of committee members, and asked to keep his statement out of the written report for fear for his life of Daraa's extremist groups retaliation, in case they discover that he had altered his convictions about the rumors spread by biased press and mass media concerning the amputation of his son's penis. This new conviction of Ali Al Khateeb is based on discussing facts with committee members, in addition to viewing official judicial documents, photos, medical experts' report and the comparative illustration of cadaver photos taken in Daraa, and Damascus.

6.   It is proven that hostile third parties have commissioned certain persons to influence information about facts, and to apply digital manipulations on photos of the cadaver of Hamza Al Khateeb. The concerned authorities are following up on these facts in order to put their hands on the manipulated photos and their authors in general and particularly in relation to this case.

<u>Conclusion:</u>

- Scientific, medical and judicial evidences have proven the cadaver of the boy Hamza Al Khateeb does not sustain traces of acts of violence or torture, not in post mortem, nor when he was alive. Except for perforations of bullet shots from fire arms.

- It is also proven that Hamza Al khateeb's cadaver did not undergo an amputation of penis.

Annex VII

Chronology

Chronology of the events in Syria from 15 March, 2011 until 20 July, 2011:

15 March – The "Day of Dignity": Dozens of protesters convene in Damascus and Aleppo. Activists call for the abolition of the state of emergency, in existence since 1963, the implementation of reforms and the release of political prisoners.

23 March –The Syrian president dismisses the Governor of Dar'a against the backdrop of the latest protests in the city.

24 March – The Syrian president orders the creation of a committee to raise living standards and explores the lifting of the emergency law.

25 March – Friday of Glory (جمعة العزة): thousands participate in demonstrations in Dar'a during a funeral procession.

31 March –The Syrian President orders an investigation into the recent killings in Dar'a and the establishment of a panel to examine the nationalization of Syrian Kurds.

1 April – "Friday of Martyrs" (جمعة الشهداء): reports indicate that Dar'a is isolated by security forces and the army.

12 April – Banias is reported to be "under siege" by security forces. Electricity and phone lines are cut off and food shortages are reported.

April 16: The Syrian President gives a televised speech pledging to lift the emergency law and instate further reforms.

21 April: A number of presidential decrees are issued lifting the emergency law, abolishing the Higher State Security Court and regulating the right to peaceful assembly.

25 April – The army deploys to Da'ra, where electricity and water are reportedly cut off and medical supplies and blood stocks are running low.

28 April – 233 members of Syria's ruling Baath party in Dar'a announce their resignation in protest over the deadly crackdown on protesters. The UN Security Council fails to agree on a statement condemning the violence in Syria.

29 April – "Friday of Rage" (جمعة الغضب): the US imposes a series of new sanctions on Syria's intelligence agency and two relatives of President Assad. The Human Rights Council convenes a Special Session and adopts resolution S-16/1 on the situation in Syria where the High Commissioner also calls for the dispatch of an OHCHR Fact Finding mission to the country.

6 May – "Friday of Defiance" (جمعة التحدي): thousands of protesters gather in many cities including Banias, Homs, Edleb, al-Qamishli and the Damascus suburbs of Zabadani and Saqba.

10 May – The European Union imposes sanctions (including asset freezes, an arms embargo and travel bans) on Syria, naming 13 high-ranking officials on its list. Syria renounces its candidacy for a seat in the Human Rights Council.

11 May –The Syrian Prime Minister announces that the government has established a committee to prepare a new law on parliamentary elections.

18 May – Al Jazeera reports, that their correspondent, Dorothy Parvaz is released after having disappeared for three weeks upon arrival in Damascus. The US expands its sanctions on Syria to include President Assad and six other Syrian officials.

23 May –EU restrictions against Syria are expanded to include President Assad and nine other senior members of the government. Restrictions include a ban from travelling to the EU and freeze on the officials' assets.

27 May – "Home Protector's Friday" (جمعة حماة الديار): protests take place in Latakia, Homs, Hama, Qamishli, Deir az-Zour and Damascus.

31 May –Dozens of tanks surround the towns of Rastan and Talbiseh. President Assad issues an amnesty on all political crimes committed before May 31, 2011.

1 June – Members of the Syrian opposition meet during a three-day conference in Antalya, Turkey.

3 June – "Freedom Children Friday" (جمعة أطفال الحرية): more than 50,000 demonstrators gather in the centre of Hama amid heavy security presence.

5 June –Official governmental sources report that armed terrorist groups have attacked state buildings and police centers in the town of Jisr al-Shughour in the Idlib province.

6 June – The Syrian Official News Agency (SANA) reports that armed gangs have killed 120 policemen in an ambush in the town of Jisr al-Shughour.

9 June –Russia and China announce that they will oppose a US-backed UN Security Council resolution on Syria.

12 June: The Syrian army takes control of the town of Jisr al-Shughour. The government stated that it is trying to restore order after 120 security personnel were killed in the town.

16 June: The OHCHR presents its preliminary report on the situation in Syria at the Human Rights Council's seventeenth session. In the report the High Commissioner, Navi Pillay, expresses grave concern about the deterioration of the human rights situation in Syria and renews calls for allowing access to the Fact-Finding mission in the country.

17 June: According to the UNHCR, the number of refugees in Turkey fleeing from north-western Syria is at 9'600.

20 June : The Syrian President addresses the nation in a one-hour speech at the Damascus University in which he promises to initiate a process of "national dialogue" and a series of economic and political reforms.

21 June: The Syrian state news agency (SANA) reports that Syrian President has ordered a new general amnesty for all crimes committed in the country until 20 June. Syrian authorities organize a tour around Jisr al-Shughour for diplomats.

22 June: Syrian Foreign Minister Walid al-Muallem states that al-Qaeda might be behind some of the violence in the country.

24 June: "Friday of Lost Legitimacy" (جمعة فقدان الشرعية): according to the Turkish foreign ministry, the number of Syrians sheltered in Turkey reached 11,739. The EU expands its sanctions to include three Iranian Officials.

27 June: Around 200 regime critics and intellectuals meet in Damascus to discuss strategies for peaceful transition to democracy in Syria.

1 July: "Friday of Departure" (جمعة الرحيل): large-scale demonstrations are reported in various parts of the country. There are reportedly a million demonstrators in Hama, making it the largest single demonstration so far since the unrest began.

7 July: Secretary-General Ban Ki-moon calls on the Syrian authorities to "stop their bloody crack-down on protesters" and to allow access to the United Nations to assess the Human Rights situation in the country.

8 July: "Friday of No Dialogue" (جمعة اللاحوار): hundreds of thousands attend a demonstration in the city of Hama, which according to some estimates reached 500'000. The French and British ambassadors to Syria visit the city. The Syrian government condemns the visit.

11 July: Supporters of the Syrian president attack the French and US embassies. The US secretary of state condemns these attacks and states that President Assad had "lost legitimacy."

12 July: Secretary-General Ban Ki-moon and the Security Council condemn the attacks against the British and French embassies in the Syrian capital Damascus.

15 July: "Detainees' Freedom Friday" (جمعة اسرى الحرية): hundreds of thousands demonstrate in various parts of the country including Hama, Aleppo and Damascus.

20 July: Secretary-General Ban Ki-moon calls on the Syrian government "to stop repression immediately" and urges all sides to refrain from violence.

Annex VIII

Map of the Syrian Arab Republic

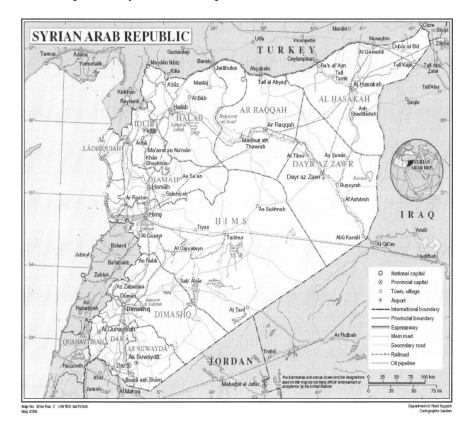

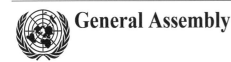

United Nations

General Assembly

A/HRC/S-17/2/Add.1

Distr.: General
23 November 2011

Original: English

DOCUMENT 2b

Human Rights Council
Seventeenth special session

Report of the independent international commission of inquiry on the Syrian Arab Republic*

Summary

    The deteriorating situation in the Syrian Arab Republic prompted the Human Rights Council to establish an independent international commission of inquiry to investigate alleged violations of human rights since March 2011. From the end of September until mid-November 2011, the commission held meetings with Member States from all regional groups, regional organizations, including the League of Arab States and the Organization of Islamic Cooperation, non-governmental organizations, human rights defenders, journalists and experts. It interviewed 223 victims and witnesses of alleged human rights violations, including civilians and defectors from the military and the security forces. In the present report, the commission documents patterns of summary execution, arbitrary arrest, enforced disappearance, torture, including sexual violence, as well as violations of children's rights.

    The substantial body of evidence gathered by the commission indicates that these gross violations of human rights have been committed by Syrian military and security forces since the beginning of the protests in March 2011. The commission is gravely concerned that crimes against humanity have been committed in different locations in the Syrian Arab Republic during the period under review. It calls upon the Government of the Syrian Arab Republic to put an immediate end to the ongoing gross human rights violations, to initiate independent and impartial investigations of these violations and to bring perpetrators to justice. The commission also addresses specific recommendations to opposition groups, the Human Rights Council, regional organizations and States Members of the United Nations.

    The commission deeply regrets that, despite many requests, the Government failed to engage in dialogue and to grant the commission access to the country. The Government informed the commission that it would examine the possibility of cooperating with the commission once the work of its own independent special legal commission was completed. The commission reiterates its call for immediate and unhindered access to the Syrian Arab Republic.

---

* The annexes to the present report are reproduced as received, in the language of submission only.

Contents

I.   Introduction

A.   Establishment of the commission of inquiry

1.   At its seventeenth special session, the Human Rights Council considered the report of the fact-finding mission submitted by the Office of the United Nations High Commissioner for Human Rights (OHCHR) pursuant to Council resolution S-16/1.[1] In the light of the mission's findings, including that patterns of human rights violations may amount to crimes against humanity, and the deteriorating human rights situation in the Syrian Arab Republic, the Council decided to establish an independent international commission of inquiry.

2.   On 12 September 2011, the President of the Human Rights Council appointed three high-level experts as members of the commission: Paulo Pinheiro (Chairperson), Yakin Ertürk and Karen Koning AbuZayd. A secretariat of the commission, with a broad range of expertise in the field of human rights investigations and international law, was provided by OHCHR.

3.   The Human Rights Council requested the commission to make its report public before the end of November 2011. The commission will present a written update to the Council at its nineteenth session, in March 2012. The present report is submitted pursuant to the request of the Council.

B.   Mandate and terms of reference

4.   The Human Rights Council, in its resolution S-17/1, mandated the commission to investigate all alleged violations of international human rights law since March 2011 in the Syrian Arab Republic, to establish the facts and circumstances that may amount to such violations and of the crimes perpetrated and, where possible, to identify those responsible with a view of ensuring that perpetrators of violations, including those that may constitute crimes against humanity, are held accountable. The commission adopted its terms of reference (annex I) in the light of its mandate.

5.   The commissioners agreed that the first component of the mandate ("to establish facts and circumstances") required the commission to act as a fact-finding body. As such, the standard of proof used was one of "reasonable suspicion". This standard was met when the commission obtained a reliable body of evidence, consistent with other information, indicating the occurrence of a particular incident or event. This is a lower standard of proof than that applied in a criminal proceeding.

6.   In order to fulfil the second component of the mandate ("to identify those responsible"), the commission understood that it had to collect a reliable body of material to indicate which individuals might be responsible for human rights violations. The commission received information on the alleged responsibility of a number of individuals for violations committed in the Syrian Arab Republic from March 2011 to the time of drafting of the present report.

---

[1] A/HRC/18/53.

C. Methods of work

7.   First-hand information was collected through interviews with victims and witnesses of events in the Syrian Arab Republic. The interviewing process began in Geneva on 26 September 2011. Overall, 223 victims and/or witnesses, including personnel who defected from the military and the security forces, were interviewed.

8.   A public call was made to all interested persons and organizations to submit relevant information and documentation that would help the commission implement its mandate. It held meetings with Member States from all regional groups, regional organizations, including the League of Arab States and the Organization of Islamic Cooperation, non-governmental organizations, human rights defenders, journalists and experts. Reports, scholarly analyses and media accounts, as well as audio and visual material, were also duly considered.

9.   The information collected is stored in a secure database governed by United Nations rules on confidentiality.

10.   The protection of victims and witnesses lies at the heart of the methodology of human rights investigations. While the collected information remains confidential, the commission is deeply concerned about the possibility of reprisals against individuals who cooperated with it, and against their relatives in the Syrian Arab Republic. It is also concerned about the protection of those individuals who openly spoke to the media in an attempt to counter the news blockade imposed by the Government.

D. Cooperation of the Government

11.   The Human Rights Council called upon the Government of the Syrian Arab Republic to cooperate fully with the commission. The commission addressed letters on 29 September (annex II), 19 October (annex IV), 27 October (annex V), and 4 November 2011 (annex VI) requesting to visit the country. The Chairperson of the commission conveyed in person similar requests to representatives of the Syrian Arab Republic in Brazil and in the United States of America. The commission solicited meetings with the Permanent Representative of the Syrian Arab Republic in Geneva, as well as with the Head of the Syrian delegation attending the universal periodic review of the Council. In a letter dated 12 October 2011, the Government stated that an independent special legal commission had been established to investigate all cases pertaining to the events that had taken place since March 2011 (annex III). The Government would therefore examine the possibility of cooperating with the commission once its own commission had concluded its work.

12.   In its letter dated 27 October 2011, the commission reiterated its invitation to the members of the independent special legal commission and relevant Syrian officials to visit Geneva in November. A questionnaire was annexed to the letter with a view of engaging the Government of the Syrian Arab Republic in a dialogue (annex V).

13.   The commission deeply regrets not having had access to the Syrian Arab Republic.

II. Context

A. Political background

14.   Syria gained independence in April 1946 as a parliamentary republic. The post-independence period was marked by several military coups and coup attempts. A state of emergency, from 1963 to April 2011, effectively suspended most constitutional protections

for citizens. Hafez Al Assad became President in 1971 following a military coup. Bashar Al Assad succeeded his father in 2000. Under their rule, the Baath party came to dominate and control all aspects of political and social life.

15.   The Syrian Arab Republic has a population of 22 million, of whom 74 per cent Sunni Muslim, 10 per cent Alawite, 3 per cent other Shia Muslim, 10 per cent Christian and 3 per cent Druze. Major ethnic minorities include Kurdish, Assyrian, Armenian, Turkmen and Circassian populations. The Al Assad family belongs to the Alawite religious community. While comprising only 10 per cent of the population, Alawites today make up the majority in the key positions of the State apparatus, including the officer corps of the armed forces, the Republican Guard and the Fourth Division.

16.   In 1982, severe human rights violations occurred in the context of an uprising by the Muslim Brotherhood in the city of Hama. In an attack by Syrian forces, several neighbourhoods of the city were shelled and destroyed, and between 10,000 and 25,000 people are estimated to have been killed, most of them civilians. These documented mass killings and numerous violations of human rights remain unpunished.

17.   During the past four decades, suspected opponents of the Government have suffered torture, detention and long prison sentences imposed under vaguely defined crimes relating to political activity. Surveillance and suppression has been conducted by an extensive apparatus of intelligence, the *mukhabarat*. Decades of tight control of freedom of expression, as well as surveillance and persecution of opponents, have severely limited political life and the constitution of an autonomous civil society.

B.   Military and security forces

18.   The Syrian Arab Armed Forces comprise the Army, the Navy and the Air Force. They are responsible for defending the national territory and protecting the State from internal threats. Numbering around 300,000, the armed forces are organized into three corps with a total of 12 divisions: seven armoured, three mechanized, one Republican Guard and the Special Forces. Elite units include the 10,000-man Republican Guard, under the President's control, tasked to counter any threat from dissident military forces, and the 20,000-man Fourth Division, which is commanded by Maher Al Assad, the President's brother.

19.   The State security apparatus is reported to be large and effective, with a multitude of security forces and intelligence agencies that have overlapping missions. They play a powerful role in Syrian society, monitoring and repressing opposition to the Government. The internal security apparatus includes police forces under the Ministry of the Interior, Syrian Military Intelligence, Air Force Intelligence, the National Security Bureau, the Political Security Directorate and the General Intelligence Directorate. The latter consists of 25,000 members formally under the Ministry of the Interior but reporting directly to the President and his inner circle. It includes Internal Security (also known as the State Security Service), External Security and the Palestine Division.

20.   The militia includes the *Shabbiha,* which is composed of an estimated 10,000 civilians, who are armed by the Government and are widely used to crush anti-Government demonstrations alongside national security forces; and the People's Army, a Baath party militia with an estimated 100,000 reservists, designed to provide additional security and protection in cities in times of war.

C.   National legal framework

21.   The 1973 Constitution of the Syrian Arab Republic enshrines a number of fundamental human rights, such as the equality of citizens before the law, the rights to freedom of expression and peaceful assembly and the right not to be subjected to torture or humiliating treatment. Article 8 states that the Baath party is the leading political party. The President is the supreme commander of the armed forces. He may declare war and general mobilization, and conclude peace with the approval of the People's Assembly;[2] he may also declare and terminate a state of emergency pursuant to the law.[3] The President issues all necessary decisions and orders for the exercise of his authority and can delegate certain powers.[4] Article 113 provides the President with the power to take necessary measures to address grave emergencies.

22.   Legislative Decrees 14/1969 and 69/2008 give immunity to members of the security forces. While the Constitution guarantees the independence of judges, membership in the Baath party is a precondition for judicial and prosecutor positions. The President presides over the Higher Council of the Judiciary, which administers the judicial system. He also sits on the Supreme Constitutional Court and appoints its other four members.

D.   International legal obligations

23.   The Syrian Arab Republic is party to most major international human rights treaties, including the International Covenant on Economic, Social and Cultural Right, the International Covenant on Civil and Political Rights, the Convention on the Elimination of All Forms of Racial Discrimination, the Convention on the Elimination of All Forms of Discrimination against Women, the Convention against Torture and Other Cruel, Inhuman or Degrading Treatment or Punishment, the Convention on the Rights of the Child and the Optional Protocol thereto on the involvement of children in armed conflict, and the Convention on the Prevention and Punishment of the Crime of Genocide.

24.   As a State party to the above treaties, the Syrian Arab Republic is bound to respect, protect, promote and fulfil the human rights of all persons within its jurisdiction. This includes the responsibility of the State to provide victims with an effective remedy, including reparation, and to undertake prompt and impartial investigations.[5]

25.   Derogations from human rights provisions are foreseen only in certain human rights treaties and are exclusively permitted under specific circumstances. The Syrian Arab Republic has never notified the Secretary-General of any state of emergency and subsequent derogations made to its obligations under the International Covenant on Civil and Political Rights. Non-derogable provisions include, but are not limited to, the right to life, the prohibition of torture or cruel, inhuman or degrading punishment, and freedom of thought, conscience and religion. The commission furthermore recalls that article 2(2) of the Convention against Torture states that "no exceptional circumstances whatsoever, whether a state of war or a threat of war, internal political instability or any other public emergency, may be invoked as a justification of torture."

---

[2] Art. 100.

[3] Art. 101.

[4] Art. 103.

[5] Human Rights Committee, general comment No. 31 (CCPR/C/21/Rev.1/Add.13); Basic Principles and Guidelines on the Right to a Remedy and Reparation for Victims of Gross Violations of International Human Rights Law and Serious Violations of International Humanitarian Law (General Assembly resolution 60/147, annex).

26.   United Nations treaty bodies and special procedures have raised a number of concerns with regard to serious violations of human rights in the Syrian Arab Republic in recent years. In 2010, the Committee against Torture expressed concern at the lack of judicial independence and arbitrary procedures that resulted in the systematic violation of the right to fair trials. The Committee also reported widespread, routine and consistent torture of prisoners in detention.[6] In 2011, concerns were also raised with regard to the number of enforced disappearances by the Working Group on Enforced or Involuntary Disappearances.[7] The widespread harassment of human rights defenders, including restrictions on their freedom of movement, violations of the freedom of expression and the right to assembly were also addressed by various treaty bodies.

III.   Events and human rights violations since March 2011

A.   Sequence of events

27.   In February 2011, limited protests broke out around issues such as rural poverty, corruption, freedom of expression, democratic rights and the release of political prisoners. Subsequent protests called for respect for human rights, and demanded far-reaching economic, legal and political reforms. By mid-March, peaceful protests erupted in Dar'a in response to the detention and torture of a group of children accused of painting anti-Government graffiti on public buildings. Following the suppression by State forces of peaceful protests, including firing at a funeral procession, civilian marches in support of Dar'a spread to a number of cities, including some suburbs of Al Ladhiqiyah, Baniyas, Damascus, Dayr Az Zawr, Homs, Hama and Idlib.

28.   On 25 April, Syrian armed forces undertook the first wide-scale military operation in Dar'a. Since then, protests have continued across the country, with an increasingly violent response by State forces. Other major military operations were carried out in different locations. On 8 November, OHCHR estimated that at least 3,500 civilians had been killed by State forces since March 2011. Thousands are also reported to have been detained, tortured and ill-treated. Homs, Hama and Dar'a reportedly suffered the highest number of casualties.

29.   Numerous defections from military and security forces have occurred since the onset of the protests, and have, by many accounts, increased in recent months. An unknown number of defectors have organized themselves into the "Free Syrian Army", which has claimed responsibility for armed attacks against both military and security forces (although there is no reliable information on the size, structure, capability and operations of this body). Colonel Riad Al Asaad, who declared his defection in July, is said to be in charge of the Free Syrian Army.

30.   From the start of the protests, the Government has claimed to be the target of attacks by armed gangs and terrorists, some of whom it accused of being funded by foreign sources. On 30 March 2011, in his national address, President Al Assad asserted that the Syrian Arab Republic was "facing a great conspiracy" at the hands of "imperialist forces". He stated that conspirators had spread false information, incited sectarian tension and used violence. He contended that they were supported inside the country by media groups and others.

---

[6]   CAT/C/SYR/CO/1, paras. 7 and 12.

[7]   A/HRC/16/48.

31.   In April, the President announced several steps towards political and legal reform. These steps included the formation of a new Government,[8] the lifting of the state of emergency,[9] the abolition of the Supreme State Security Court,[10] the granting of general amnesties[11] and new regulations on the right of citizens to participate in peaceful demonstrations.[12]

32.   On 2 June, the President announced the establishment of the National Dialogue Commission, responsible for preparing consultations as part of a transitional process towards a multiparty democracy. Several leading opposition figures boycotted the meeting because of the continued violence used against protesters.

33.   On 6 June, the President stated that members of the military and security forces, as well as innocent people, had been killed in acts of sabotage and terror. While admitting that the State should work tirelessly to meet the demands of its people, he affirmed that among those demanding change was a small group of criminals and religious extremists attempting to spread chaos. The Government news agency increasingly reported armed attacks against State forces in cities, including Homs, Hama, Idlib and Talkalakh.

34.   The Government has since announced a number of policy initiatives as part of the reform process, including Decree No. 100 of 3 August, promulgating a new law on political parties, and Decree No. 101 of 3 August, promulgating a general law on elections.[13] Local elections were announced for 12 December,[14] and a new law on the media was introduced on 2 September.[15] On 16 October, the President established a national committee tasked with preparing a draft constitution, which would be subject to a referendum within four months.[16]

35.   On 3 August, the Security Council issued a presidential statement condemning the ongoing violence against protesters by Syrian forces and calling on restraint from all sides. It also called on the Syrian Arab Republic to implement political reforms and to cooperate with OHCHR.[17] On 4 October, China and the Russian Federation vetoed a draft resolution of the Security Council,[18] in which the Council recommended possible measures against the Syrian Arab Republic under Article 41 of the Charter of the United Nations.

36.   A number of States and regional organizations have imposed sanctions on the Syrian Arab Republic.

37.   On 7 October, the Government of the Syrian Arab Republic reiterated that the country was being subjected to a series of criminal attacks by armed terrorist groups and an unprecedented media campaign of lies and allegations, supported by certain western States. According to the Government, the groups involved had committed offences against the Syrian people, including acts of theft, murder and vandalism, and they were exploiting peaceful demonstrations to create anarchy. The Government also claimed that 1,100 members of State forces had been killed by terrorists and armed gangs.[19] It pointed out that,

---

[8]   Decree No. 146 of 14 April 2011.
[9]   Decree No. 161 of 21 April 2011.
[10]   Decree No. 53 of 21 April 2011.
[11]   Decrees No. 34, 61 and 72 of 2011.
[12]   Decree No. 53 of 21 April 2011.
[13]   A/HRC/WG.6/12/SYR/1, para. 98.
[14]   SANA news agency, 6 October 2011
[15]   See A/HRC/WG.6/12/SYR/1, para. 49, referring to Decree No. 108, 2011.
[16]   Presidential Decree No. 33, 2011, SANA News Agency, 16 October 2011.
[17]   Statement by the President of the Security Council of 3 August 2011 (S/PRST/2011/16).
[18]   6627th meeting of the Security Council, 4 October 2011, meeting record S/PV. 6627.
[19]   A/HRC/19/11, para. 102.

while many protests had been conducted in full legality, others had been held without notification and disrupted public order.

38.	On 2 November, the Council of the League of Arab States announced that the Syrian Arab Republic had agreed on a workplan to end violence and protect citizens. The Government also pledged to release all those detained in relation to the recent events, to remove armed elements from cities and inhabited areas, and to give the specialized organizations of the League and Arab and international media access to the country. The Council mandated a ministerial committee of the League to oversee and report on the implementation of the workplan. According to the Government, 553 detainees were released pursuant to the agreement. Continued violence and the non-implementation of the agreement prompted the League, on 12 November, to adopt a resolution suspending Syrian activities within the organization. The resolution also imposed economic and political sanctions on the country, and reiterated the previous demand that the Syrian Arab Republic withdraw its armed forces from cities and residential areas. The League urged its Member States to recall their ambassadors from Damascus. The measures came into force on 16 November. On 15 November, 1,180 prisoners were also released.

39.	In November, military and security forces carried out operations in Homs, Dar'a, Hama, Dayr Az Zawr and Rif Damascus, targeting public assemblies and funeral processions. In Homs, the operations were conducted in the residential areas of Alqaseer, Bab Amr, Bab Al Sibaa, Bab Hood and Karm Al Zaitoon. According to eyewitnesses, tanks deployed in and around the city frequently fired at residential buildings. It is estimated that, in a three-week period until 13 November, 260 civilians were killed. According to information received, a small number of defectors claiming to be part of the Free Syrian Army engaged in operations against State forces, killing and injuring members of military and security forces.

40.	On 20 November, in an interview published by *The Sunday Times*, President Al Assad explained that his Government did not have a policy to treat the public harshly; its aim was to fight militants to restore stability and protect civilians. He added that any "mistakes" committed by officials would be addressed by the independent special legal commission.

## B.	Excessive use of force and extrajudicial executions

41.	According to individual testimonies, including those of defectors who have acknowledged their role in policing and quelling the protests, State forces shot indiscriminately at unarmed protestors. Most were shot in the upper body, including in the head. Defectors from military and security forces told the commission that they had received orders to shoot at unarmed protesters without warning. In some instances, however, commanders of operations ordered protesters to disperse and issued warnings prior to opening fire. In some cases, non-lethal means were used prior to or at the same time as live ammunition.

42.	The commission received several testimonies indicating that military and security forces and *Shabbiha* militias had planned and conducted joint operations with "shoot to kill" orders to crush demonstrations. Such operations were conducted in the centre of Al Ladhiqiyah around Sheikh Daher Square in early April, and also in the Ramel suburb of Al Ladhiqiyah on 13 and 14 August. During the latter incident, at least 20 people, including children, were reportedly killed. In other incidents, officers ordered their personnel to attack protesters without warning, hitting them with batons.

43.	A defector described to the commission the rationale for deployment and the orders that were given to his army battalion on 1 May:

Our commanding officer told us that there were armed conspirators and terrorists attacking civilians and burning Government buildings. We went into Telbisa on that day. We did not see any armed group. The protestors called for freedom. They carried olive branches and marched with their children. We were ordered to either disperse the crowd or eliminate everybody, including children. The orders were to fire in the air and immediately after to shoot at people. No time was allowed between one action and the other. We opened fire; I was there. We used machine guns and other weapons. There were many people on the ground, injured or killed.

44.   The rationale for the use of force and orders to open fire on demonstrators were echoed in numerous testimonies of other former soldiers who had been dispatched to different locations and at different times. For example, on 29 April, thousands of people walked from nearby villages to the town of Dar'a to bring food, water and medicine to the local population. When they reached the Sayda residence complex, they were ambushed by security forces. More than 40 people were reportedly killed, including women and children.

45.   The commission is aware of acts of violence committed by some demonstrators. However, it notes that the majority of civilians were killed in the context of peaceful demonstrations. Accounts collected by the commission, including those of defectors, indicated that protesters were largely unarmed and determined to claim their rights and express their discontent peacefully.

46.   Snipers were responsible for many casualties. On some occasions, snipers appeared to be targeting leaders of the march and those using loudspeakers or carrying cameras and mobile phones. The commission heard several accounts of how those who were trying to rescue the wounded and collect the bodies of demonstrators also came under sniper fire. The commission documented several cases in Dar'a, Hama and Al Ladhiqiyah.

47.   Checkpoints and roadblocks were set up to prevent people from moving freely and joining demonstrations, especially on Fridays. Defectors who were deployed at checkpoints told the commission about "black lists" with names of people wanted by the authorities. They were given instructions to search for weapons and, in some cases, given orders to shoot. A soldier who manned two checkpoints in the Dar'a governorate, from April to August, was given orders "to search everybody and if any demonstrators try to pass through, to fire at them".

48.   Several defectors witnessed the killing of their comrades who refused to execute orders to fire at civilians. A number of conscripts were allegedly killed by security forces on 25 April in Dar'a during a large-scale military operation. The soldiers in the first row were given orders to aim directly at residential areas, but chose to fire in the air to avoid civilian casualties. Security forces posted behind shot them for refusing orders, thus killing dozens of conscripts.

49.   Civilians bore the brunt of the violence as cities were blockaded and curfews imposed. The commission heard many testimonies describing how those who ventured outside their homes were shot by snipers. Many of the reported cases occurred in Dar'a, Jisr Al Shughour and Homs. A lawyer told how security forces took positions in old Dar'a during the operation in April. Snipers were deployed on the hospital rooftop and other buildings. "They targeted anyone who moved", he said. Two of his cousins were killed on the street by snipers.

50.   A number of cases was documented of injured people who were taken to military hospitals, where they were beaten and tortured during interrogation. Torture and killings reportedly took place in the Homs Military Hospital by security forces dressed as doctors and allegedly acting with the complicity of medical personnel. As people became afraid of going to public hospitals, makeshift clinics were set up in mosques and private houses,

which also became targets. This was the case of the Omari Mosque in Dar'a, which was raided on 23 March. Several of the injured and some medical personnel were killed there.

51.   According to the Government, global media inaccurately reported the use of weapons against civilians to discredit the Syrian Arab Republic. Security forces were deployed to the demonstrations to keep the peace, but many of them were killed, including unarmed police officers. For instance, in the city of Homs, 12 police officers were reportedly murdered. The Government claimed that security forces were not usually armed when policing demonstrations. It also claimed that the information on the use of tanks was false, and that they were used solely for rescuing overwhelmed police officers who had no means of defending themselves.

C.   Arbitrary detentions, enforced disappearances, torture and other forms of ill-treatment

1.   Arbitrary detentions

52.   According to many accounts gathered, arbitrary arrests and unlawful detentions were widespread and occurred at an alarming rate in places such as Homs, Hama, Jisr Al-Shughour, Dar'a and in Rif Dimashq, regarded as supportive of the protest movement.

53.   Arrests have been conducted mainly in the context of wide-scale military operations targeting specific areas or during demonstrations. Various victims consistently stated that they had been physically or verbally assaulted during the arrest process before being held for various periods of time without due process and routinely subjected to torture.

54.   One of the reportedly largest-scale arbitrary arrest campaigns took place in the city of Baniyas on 7 May. According to various eyewitness accounts, the army swept through the villages surrounding the city using tanks, armoured vehicles and soldiers. Security and military forces broke into houses and reportedly arrested more than 500 people, including women and children. A similar incident was reported in Jisr Al-Shughour in the early hours of 14 May. Following a large demonstration on the previous day, members of the security forces arrested more than 400 people during night raids. Some 400 people, including women and children, were detained in the Ramel suburb of Al Ladhiqiyah on 13 and 14 August.

55.   Other arrests targeted activists who participated or helped to organize demonstrations and whose names appeared on security forces' lists. Families and acquaintances of wanted individuals were detained by security forces as a measure of intimidation and retribution.

56.   A number of journalists and web activists claimed they had been detained and tortured for reporting on demonstrations.

57.   Many of the defectors interviewed indicated that soldiers suspected of sympathizing with or aiding demonstrators were immediately detained. A conscript explained how he witnessed the torture of many defectors inside a prison.

58.   Accounts obtained from victims and defectors described arbitrary arrest and conditions of detention in grave terms. Some were detained in the offices of security forces or in prisons, while others were transferred to open stadiums, schools and, in some cases, hospitals. Most of those arrested were blindfolded and handcuffed, and denied food and medical assistance. Several people reported that scores were detained, beaten and tortured in the stadium in Al Ladhiqiyah in August.

2. Enforced disappearances

59.   Allegations of enforced disappearances were received. Although it is impossible to assess the exact scale of the phenomenon, many reports put the number of the missing and unaccounted for in the thousands. A witness described the abduction of his brother-in-law in September in the Dar'a governorate. His family has heard nothing about him since. He stated that his aunt and uncle had gone to look for him in both Dar'a and Damascus. "The authorities refused to give them any information. In the course of a telephone conversation with an acquaintance in the security services, my uncle was advised to forget about his son."

60.   Another witness stated that, on 24 July, members of the military security came to arrest one of his cousins in their family home in Dar'a. Five days later his father and brother went to the military security quarters to ask about him. "We were given the run around. There was no further news of my cousin," the interviewee concluded.

3. Torture and other forms of ill-treatment

61.   Numerous victims of torture and other forms of ill-treatment were interviewed. Many were subjected to severe beatings with batons and cables. They also endured prolonged stress position for hours or even days in a row, electroshocks and deprivation of food, water and sleep. Detainees were often put in overcrowded cells and forced to take turns to sleep. Many were blindfolded and sometimes handcuffed, then forced to thumb-sign written confessions of crimes that, at best, were read to them by an officer. Several witnesses and victims interviewed emphasized that they were tortured whether they confessed or not.

62.   Children were also tortured, some to death. Two well-known cases are those of Thamir Al Sharee, aged 14, and Hamza Al Katheeb, aged 13, from the town of Sayda in the Dar'a governorate. They were seized and allegedly taken to an Air Force Intelligence facility in Damascus in April. They did not return home alive. The injuries described in the post-mortem report of Thamir Al Sharee are consistent with torture. A witness, himself a victim of torture, claimed to have seen Thamir Al Sharee on 3 May. The witness stated that "the boy was lying on the floor and was completely blue. He was bleeding profusely from his ear, eyes and nose. He was shouting and calling for his mother and father for help. He fainted after being hit with a rifle butt on the head."

63.   Torture has been described as rampant at detention facilities of the Air Force Intelligence Branch in the Mazzeh airport near Damascus. Other facilities where torture was reported to have taken place are the facilities of Air Force Intelligence in Bab Tuma, in Homs; the Maza Al Jabal prison of the Republican Guard; the Political Security Branch detention facility in Al Ladhiqiyah; and the Altala'a military base, which hosts the central command centre for police, military and intelligence operations in Idlib governorate.

64.   Defectors were tortured because they attempted to spare civilians either surreptitiously or by openly refusing to obey orders. A defector showed scars on his arms compatible with electroshock marks and about 30 stitches on his scalp. He stated:

> On Friday 12 August, we received orders to go to the Omar al Khattab Mosque, in Duma (Damascus governorate), where about 150 people had gathered. We opened fire. A number of people were killed. I tried to aim high. Later, I realized that security forces had been taking pictures of us. I was pictured firing in the air. I was interrogated. I was accused of being a secret agent. Members of the Republican Guard beat me every hour for two days, and they tortured me with electroshocks.

65.   Several methods of torture, including sexual torture, were used by the military and the security forces in detention facilities across the country. Torture victims had scars and

bore other visible marks. Detainees were also subjected to psychological torture, including sexual threats against them and their families and by being forced to worship President Al Assad instead of their god.

D.   Sexual violence

66.   Several testimonies reported the practice of sexual torture used on male detainees. Men were routinely made to undress and remain naked. Several former detainees testified reported beatings of genitals, forced oral sex, electroshocks and cigarette burns to the anus in detention facilities, including those of the Air Force Intelligence in Damascus, the Military Intelligence in Jisr Al Shughour, the Military Intelligence and the Political Security in Idlib and Al Ladhiqiyah and the intelligence detention facilities in Tartus. Several of the detainees were repeatedly threatened that they would be raped in front of their family and that their wives and daughters would also be raped.

67.   Testimonies were received from several men who stated they had been anally raped with batons and that they had witnessed the rape of boys. One man stated that he witnessed a 15-year-old boy being raped in front of his father. A 40-year-old man saw the rape of an 11-year-old boy by three security services officers. He stated: "I have never been so afraid in my whole life. And then they turned to me and said; you are next." The interviewee was unable to continue his testimony. One 20-year-old university student told the commission that he was subjected to sexual violence in detention, adding that "if my father had been present and seen me, I would have had to commit suicide". Another man confided while crying, "I don't feel like a man any more".

68.   Several women testified that they were threatened and insulted during house raids by the military and security forces. Women felt dishonoured by the removal of their head scarves and the handling of their underwear during raids of their homes, which often occurred at night. Defectors from the military and the security forces indicated that they had been present in places of detention where women were sexually assaulted; the commission, however, received limited evidence to that effect. This may be due in part to the stigma that victims would endure if they came forward.

E.   Violations of children's rights

69.   The information collected indicates that children have suffered serious violations and that State forces have shown little or no recognition of the rights of children in the actions taken to quell dissent.

70.   Witnesses informed the commission that children (mostly boys) were killed or injured by beatings or shooting during demonstrations in several locations across the country, including Sayda, Dar'a, Idlib, Hama, Homs, Sarmeen Al Ladhiqiyah and Dayr Az Zawr. Reliable sources indicated that 256 children had been killed by State forces as at 9 November. The commission spoke with several children who had witnessed the killing of adults and of other children, and also met a 2-year-old girl whose mother was killed by the Syrian military in August while trying to cross the border. The commission saw several children whose mental health was seriously affected by their traumatic experience.

71.   One military defector stated that he decided to defect after witnessing the shooting of a 2-year-old girl in Al Ladhiqiyah on 13 August by an officer who affirmed that he did not want her to grow into a demonstrator. A 15-year-old boy interviewed was shot in the leg in Homs on 15 August while returning home from the mosque. The neighbours tried to take him to hospital, but checkpoints by security forces blocked access to it.

72.   Numerous accounts from former detainees indicated the presence of children, some younger than 10, in detention centres in various locations run by the military and security forces. Torture was reportedly applied equally to adults and children. Several former detainees informed the commission that young boys were tortured at the Air Force Intelligence detention facilities in and around Damascus, in intelligence detention facilities in Tartus and in Political Security and Military Intelligence detention facilities in Al Ladhiqiyah and Idlib. One defector stated that "people had their feet and hands bound with plastic handcuffs. They were beaten mercilessly, including 10-year-old children. Some children urinated out of fear while they were being beaten. It was very cruel."

73.   Numerous testimonies indicated that boys were subjected to sexual torture in places of detention in front of adult men.

74.   The commission received many reports on the use of schools as detention facilities and on the deployment of snipers on the roofs of schools. Several children expressed concerns that they were prevented from continuing their education.

F.   Displacement and restriction of movement

75.   The repression of protests has prompted a significant number of Syrians to flee the country. Syrian refugees number around 8,000 in Turkey, 3,400 in Lebanon and 1,000 in Jordan.[20] There are no recorded numbers for internally displaced people, but the commission received information on significant internal displacement from areas where military operations are prevalent, including in Homs.

76.   Disturbing accounts were received of Syrian security and military forces using live fire against, and sometimes killing, individuals trying to flee the country. In an incident near Idlib in August 2011, a family with children travelling in a car towards a crossing at the Turkish border came under fire from Syrian armed forces; two family members were killed and one wounded. In another incident, in September 2011, Syrian forces killed a man as he attempted to cross the border into Turkey.

77.   Numerous cases documented individuals who felt compelled to cross the border because their names appeared on lists of people wanted by the security services because of their mere participation in peaceful protests.

78.   Individuals who had succeeded in crossing the border were targeted by State forces when they later approached the border while still on the territory of the neighbouring State.

79.   In the context of such cases, the commission is furthermore gravely concerned at recent reports of Syrian armed forces laying mines near the border with Lebanon, putting those compelled to flee at grave risk of severe injury or death.

G.   Violations of economic and social rights

80.   Numerous testimonies were received regarding the obstruction and denial of medical assistance to the injured and sick. Many of the injured were prevented from receiving treatment in public hospitals in several locations, including Al Ladhiqiyah, Baniyas, Homs and Idlib. Consistent testimonies described how members of the security forces tracked down wounded protesters in both public and private hospitals. Security forces conducted

[20]   These figures relate to refugees/asylum-seekers who have registered with Governments or the Office of the United Nations High Commissioner for Refugees. The number of unregistered persons who have fled the country is likely to be significant.

raids in early June and late July in hospitals in Hama. Injured demonstrators were arrested and taken to military hospitals, where they were reportedly interrogated and tortured.

81.   Individuals suspected by the Government of being involved in setting up and operating alternative medical facilities or providing medical supplies or treatments were also subjected to arrest and torture by the security forces. According to testimonies, security forces warned the staff of private hospitals and ambulance drivers not to treat or provide assistance to injured protestors. Instead, they were ordered to transfer all such patients to either public or military hospitals. While some private hospitals complied with Government orders, others continued to provide wounded protesters with first aid and other medical services.

82.   The rights to food and to water were violated in numerous instances, particularly in cities where wide-scale military operations were conducted. For example, witnesses told to the commission that, during the attack and blockade of Dar'a, the military and security forces barred the city's residents from obtaining food and other basic necessities. Residential water tanks and water pipes were deliberately damaged by military and security forces.

83.   The commission received credible information regarding the destruction of property, including of homes and household possessions. In the context of raids, security and military forces received orders from their superiors to systematically loot homes, shops and other properties, steal money and other valuables. Motorcycles were confiscated, piled up and destroyed to prevent people from joining rallies outside their place of residence.

IV.   Violations and crimes under applicable international law

A.   International human rights law

84.   On the basis of the information and evidence collected, the commission has reached conclusions with regard to a number of serious violations of international human rights law. The major conclusions are summarized below.

1.   Impunity

85.   Accountability constitutes the basic element of justice and the rule of law. The commission expresses its grave concern over the prevailing systemic impunity for human rights violations and its entrenchment in legislation awarding immunity for State officials, in contravention of the State's international legal obligations.

2.   Excessive use of force, extrajudicial executions and other violations of the right to life

86.   Governments have an obligation to maintain public order. They bear the ultimate responsibility for protecting individuals under their jurisdiction, including those participating in public assemblies and exercising their right to freedom of expression. In the Syrian Arab Republic, the high toll of dead and injured is the result of the excessive use of force by State forces in many regions. Isolated instances of violence on the part of demonstrators do not affect their right to protection as enshrined in international human rights law.

87.   The Syrian Arab Republic has violated the right to life, as enshrined in article 6 of the International Covenant on Civil and Political Rights, through the use of excessive force by military and security forces as well as by militia, such as *Shabbiha*, acting in complicity with, or with the acquiescence of, State officials and forces.

3. Violations of the right to peaceful assembly and the right to freedom of expression

88. Efforts by the Government to control information and the right to freedom of assembly and expression lie at the heart of the current violence. Consistent eyewitness and victim accounts indicate that military and security forces have reacted excessively to peaceful demonstrations, including the use of live ammunition to quell demonstrators and extensive cases of arbitrary detention. The presidential decree on freedom of assembly issued on 21 April has not ensured respect for human rights. The commission notes with great concern the widespread harassment of human rights defenders and journalists.

89. The commission concludes that the Syrian Arab Republic has systematically violated the rights to freedom of assembly and expression as enshrined in articles 19 and 21 of the International Covenant on Civil and Political Rights.

4. Arbitrary detention and violations of the right to a fair trial

90. The commission is seriously concerned about the absence of judicial independence and the extensive use of arbitrary and incommunicado detention without criminal charges or judicial supervision. Mass arrests have regularly been made by military and security forces. Detainees were charged with broadly defined crimes such as "weakening the national sentiment", and prosecuted at random in civil or military courts. Despite the abolition of the Supreme State Security Court in April 2011, military courts continue to operate in clear violation of the right to a fair and public hearing by a competent, independent and impartial tribunal. The commission notes with concern reports indicating the practice of involuntary and enforced disappearances.

91. The commission concludes that the Syrian Arab Republic has systematically violated the right to liberty and security of a person and of fair trial standards as enshrined in articles 9, 10 and 14 of the International Covenant on Civil and Political Rights, and articles 37 and 40 of the Convention on the Rights of the Child.

5. Torture and sexual violence

92. Information received demonstrates patterns of continuous and widespread use of torture across the Syrian Arab Republic where protests have taken place. The pervasive nature, recurrence and reported readiness of Syrian authorities to use torture as a tool to instil fear indicate that State officials have condoned its practice. Information from military and security forces defectors indicates that they received orders to torture. The commission is particularly disturbed over the extensive reports of sexual violence, principally against men and boys, in places of detention.

93. The commission concludes that the extensive practices of torture indicate a State-sanctioned policy of repression, which manifestly violates the State's obligations under article 7 of the International Covenant on Civil and Political Rights, the Convention against Torture, and article 37 of the Convention on the Rights of the Child.

6. Violations of children's rights

94. The commission expresses its deepest concern over consistent reports of extensive violations of children's rights committed since the start of the uprising in March, including killings of children during demonstrations and widespread practices of arbitrary detention, torture and ill-treatment, in particular of boys. Children were subjected to the same conditions and abuses in detention as adults. The commission concludes that the State has fundamentally failed its obligations under the Convention on the Rights of the Child, article 24 of the International Covenant on Civil and Political Rights, and the Convention against Torture.

7. Violations of the right to freedom of movement

95.   The right to freedom of movement is provided for under article 12 of the International Covenant on Civil and Political Rights. This right encompasses both the freedom of movement inside the country of residence and the freedom to leave one's country. The Syrian Arab Republic has taken measures to restrict the right to leave the country to seek protection and has deliberately targeted and killed people at or near border crossings.

8. Violations of economic and social rights

96.   Restrictions imposed by the State on the treatment of injured protesters constitute serious violations of the right to health and the right to access medical assistance guaranteed under article 12 of the International Covenant on Economic, Social and Cultural Rights. Other rights, such as the right to an adequate standard of living and the rights to food, to water (art. 11) and to education (art. 13), have been infringed upon in the context of wide-scale military operations and blockades in several locations.

B.   International humanitarian law

97.   The commission is concerned that the armed violence in the Syrian Arab Republic risks rising to the level of an "internal armed conflict" under international law. Should this occur, international humanitarian law would apply. The commission recalls that the International Court of Justice has established that human rights law continues to apply in armed conflict, with the law of armed conflict applying as *lex specialis* in relation to the conduct of hostilities.

98.   According to the Appeals Chamber of the International Criminal Tribunal for the Former Yugoslavia, an armed conflict exists when there is a resort to armed force between States or protracted armed violence between governmental authorities and organized armed groups, or between such groups within a State. The Trial Chamber in *Tadić* and subsequent cases interpreted the test for internal armed conflict as consisting of two criteria: the intensity of the conflict, and the organization of the parties to the conflict, as a way to distinguish armed conflict from banditry, unorganized and short-lived insurrections or terrorist activities, which do not fall within the scope of international humanitarian law.

99.   The commission was unable to verify the level of the intensity of combat between Syrian armed forces and other armed groups. Similarly, it has been unable to confirm the level of organization of such armed groups as the Free Syrian Army. For the purposes of the present report, therefore, the commission will not apply international humanitarian law to the events in the Syrian Arab Republic since March 2011.

100.   Nevertheless, crimes against humanity may occur irrespective of the existence of an armed conflict and the application of international humanitarian law. The commission describes below its reasons for concluding that members of the Syrian military and security forces have committed crimes against humanity in 2011.

C.   International criminal law

101.   According to article 7 of the Rome Statute of the International Criminal Court, "crimes against humanity" include acts such as murder, torture and unlawful imprisonment when committed as part of a widespread or systematic attack directed against any civilian

population, with knowledge of the attack. Crimes against humanity have five elements: there must have been an attack;[21] the attack must have been directed against the civilian population;[22] the attack must be widespread or systematic;[23] the acts of the perpetrator must form part of the attack;[24] and the perpetrator must know that there is an attack directed against the civilian population.[25]

102.   The commission received numerous, credible and consistent first-hand reports about widespread and systematic violations of the human rights of civilians in the Syrian Arab Republic since March 2011. The scale of these attacks against civilians in cities and villages across the country, their repetitive nature, the levels of excessive force used consistently by units of the armed forces and diverse security forces, the coordinated nature of these attacks and the evidence that many attacks were conducted on the orders of high-ranking military officers all lead the commission to conclude that the attacks were apparently conducted pursuant to a policy of the State.

103.   The above conclusion finds support in diverse sources of information. Multiple witnesses indicated that, on different days and in different locations, officers at the level of Colonel and Brigadier General issued orders to their subordinate units to open fire on protesters, beat demonstrators and fire at civilian homes. The commission received credible evidence that it is unlikely that the officers issued these orders independently given that the Syrian military forces are professional forces subject to military discipline. The commission therefore believes that orders to shoot and otherwise mistreat civilians originated from policies and directives issued at the highest levels of the armed forces and the Government.

104.   Security forces and the military made concerted efforts to control access to information about the protests. Prior to operations to stop civilian demonstrations, military commanders told their units, falsely, that they were going to fight "terrorists", "armed gangs" or Israelis. Television sets in barracks and soldiers' cellular telephones were confiscated. Journalists who attempted to report on the protests were arrested, detained, tortured and interrogated about the activities of their colleagues. People who filmed attempts by security forces to stop demonstrations were targeted for arrest. Different pretexts were used to create the impression that the civilian protesters were "terrorists" or "armed gangs": for example, in the Saqba suburb of Damascus, security forces circled behind protesters and fired towards the soldiers deployed there to create the impression that the soldiers were being fired upon. These efforts to control and distort available information about events reflect the existence of a plan or policy to conceal the truth.

105.   Witness testimonies revealed extensive degrees of coordination among diverse security and military forces during operations to stop protests. Members of security forces were often stationed behind soldiers or inside tanks to ensure that soldiers followed orders to shoot at protesters. On several occasions, soldiers who disobeyed these orders were shot themselves by the security forces or by army snipers. In addition, members of the *Shabbiha*

---

[21]   *Prosecutor v. Momčilo Perišić*, Judgement, Case No. IT-04-81-T, 6 September 2011, paras. 81-82.

[22]   *Prosecutor v. Jean-Pierre Bemba Gombo*, decision pursuant to article 61 (7) (a) and (b) of the Rome Statute on the charge of *Prosecutor v. Jean-Pierre Bemba Gombo*, Case No. ICC -01/05-01/08, 15 June 2009, para. 77.

[23]   *Prosecutor v. Jean-Pierre Bemba Gombo*, Decision Pursuant to Article 61 (7) (a) and (b), paras. 81 and 83; *Prosecutor v. Germain Katanga and Mathieu Ngudjolo Chui*, decision on the confirmation of charges, paras. 396 - 397.

[24]   Perišić Judgement, para. 87, citing Kunarac Appeal Judgement, paras. 85, 99 – 100; and *Prosecutor v. Mile Mrksic and Veselin Sljivancanin*, Appeal Judgement, Case No. IT-95-13/1-A, 5 May 2009, para. 41.

[25]   *Prosecutor v. Germain Katanga and Mathieu Ngudjolo Chui*, decision on the confirmation of charges, para. 401; and *Prosecutor v. Bemba*, decision on the confirmation of charges, para. 88.

paramilitary groups were often present during operations to quash demonstrations and assisted in efforts to repress protests. When soldiers detained demonstrators, they would turn them over to units of the security forces who transported the protestors to detention centres. This degree of coordination between military and security forces could only be possible under the direction of the highest levels of the Government and the military.

106. Information provided to the commission illustrates the extensive resources that the Government and armed forces has devoted to efforts to control protests. In addition to regular military units armed with automatic weapons, the military deployed snipers, Special Forces units, tanks, armoured personnel carriers and intelligence units during operations to end demonstrations. To sustain these operations, the State had to provide sufficient weapons, ammunition, tank shells, uniforms, transport vehicles, fuel, communications equipment and food. Similar material was required to sustain the different security forces deployed. The commission believes that expenditure of such large quantities of State resources would only be possible pursuant to the policies and directives of the Government.

107. The sheer scale and consistent pattern of attacks by military and security forces on civilians and civilian neighbourhoods and the widespread destruction of property could only be possible with the approval or complicity of the State.

108. According to international law, when certain crimes are committed as part of a widespread or systematic attack against civilians and the perpetrators know that their conduct is part of this attack, such offences constitute crimes against humanity. The commission is thus gravely concerned that crimes against humanity of murder,[26] torture,[27] rape[28] or other forms of sexual violence of comparable gravity,[29] imprisonment or other severe deprivation of liberty,[30] enforced disappearances of persons[31] and other inhumane acts of a similar character[32] have occurred in different locations in the country since March 2011, including, but not limited to, Damascus, Dar'a, Duma, Hama, Homs, Idlib and along the borders.

V. Responsibility

A. State responsibility

109. The Syrian Arab Republic has failed its obligations under international human rights law. Every internationally wrongful act of a State incurs the international responsibility of that State.[33] Similarly, customary international law provides that a State is responsible for all acts committed by members of its military and security forces.[34] The State is therefore responsible for wrongful acts, including crimes against humanity, committed by members of its military and security forces as documented in the present report.

---

[26] Rome Statute of the International Criminal Court, Elements of Crimes, art. 7 (1) (a).

[27] Ibid., art. 7 (1) (f).

[28] Ibid., art. 7 (1) (g) 1.

[29] Ibid., art. 7 (1) (g) 6.

[30] Ibid., art. 7 (1) (e).

[31] Ibid., art. 7 (1) (i).

[32] Ibid., art. 7 (1) (k).

[33] *Official Records of the General Assembly, Fifty-sixth Session, Supplement No. 10* (A/56/10), chap. IV, sect. E, art. 1.

[34] Ibid., commentary to article 7.

110. The prohibition of crimes against humanity is a *jus cogens* or peremptory rule, and the punishment of such crimes is obligatory pursuant to the general principles of international law.[35] Furthermore, crimes against humanity are the culmination of violations of fundamental human rights, such as the right to life and the prohibition of torture or other forms of inhuman and degrading treatment.[36] According to the principles of State responsibility in international law, the Syrian Arab Republic bears responsibility for these crimes and violations, as well as the duty to ensure that individual perpetrators are punished and that victims receive reparation.[37]

B. Individual responsibility for crimes against humanity

111. The principle of individual criminal responsibility for international crimes is well established in customary international law.[38] According to article 27 of the Rome Statute of the International Criminal Court, which the Syrian Arab Republic has signed but not ratified, the Statute applies equally to all persons, without any distinction based on official capacity. In this context, Syrian laws afford extensive immunities, in most cases, for crimes committed by Government agents at all levels during the exercise of their duties. Although the Independent Special Legal Commission was established in recent months to investigate events, the State still has not provided the commission with any details of investigations or prosecutions under way by this mechanism.

VI. Recommendations

112. **The independent international commission of inquiry recommends that the Government of the Syrian Arab Republic:**

(a) **Put an immediate end to gross human rights violations;**

(b) **Initiate prompt, independent and impartial investigations under both domestic and international law to end impunity, ensure accountability and bring perpetrators to justice;**

(c) **Pending investigations, suspend from the military and the security forces all alleged perpetrators of serious human rights violations;**

(d) **Ratify the Rome Statute of the International Criminal Court and introduce domestic legislation consistent with it;**

(e) **Release immediately all persons arbitrarily detained and provide international monitoring bodies and the International Committee of the Red Cross with access to all places of detention;**

(f) **Allow immediate and full access for the commission and outside observers, and other United Nations human rights monitoring bodies;**

---

[35] *Case of Almonacid-Arellano et al v. Chile,* Inter-American Court of Human Rights, Judgement of September 26, 2006, (Preliminary Objections, Merits, Reparations and Costs*),* para. 99. See also *Official Records of the General Assembly* (see footnote 34), Art. 26.

[36] *Almonacid-Arellano et al. v. Chile*, para. 111.

[37] See the Preamble to the Rome Statute of the International Criminal Court: "Recalling that it is the duty of every State to exercise its criminal jurisdiction over those responsible for international crimes."

[38] *Prosecutor v. Tharcisse Muvunyi*, Judgement, Case No. ICTR-00-55-T, 12 September 2006, para. 459.

(g)   Grant immediate access to affected areas and provide international organizations, United Nations specialized agencies and non-governmental organizations with full cooperation for the purpose of protecting the population and providing humanitarian assistance;

(h)   Ensure full access for media and allow both national and international journalists to cover the events in the country without harassment or intimidation;

(i)   Abolish legislation granting military and security forces immunity, and expedite the revision of relevant legislation and policies applicable to security forces, in accordance with international standards;

(j)   Support hospitals and clinics to ensure provision of adequate health care, including for those injured in the unrest;

(k)   Establish a mechanism to investigate cases of disappearances by allowing relatives of disappeared persons to report the details of their cases, and to ensure appropriate investigation;

(l)   Establish a reparation fund for victims of serious human rights violations, including killings, enforced disappearances, torture and other cruel, inhuman or degrading treatment or punishment, arbitrary detention and destruction of property;

(m)   Implement political and legal reforms announced in 2011 ensuring the respect of human rights;

(n)   Respect human rights defenders and ensure that there are no reprisals against persons who have cooperated with the commission;

(o)   Facilitate the voluntary return of Syrian refugees.

113.   The commission recommends that opposition groups ensure respect for and act in accordance with international human rights law.

114.   The commission recommends that the Human Rights Council:

(a)   Establish the mandate of special rapporteur on the situation of human rights in the Syrian Arab Republic;

(b)   Keep the situation in the Syrian Arab Republic on its agenda, and invite the United Nations High Commissioner for Human Rights to report periodically on the human rights situation;

(c)   Take urgent steps, including through the General Assembly, the Secretary-General and the Security Council, to implement the recommendations made in the present report.

115.   The commission recommends that the High Commissioner establish a field presence in the Syrian Arab Republic with a protection and promotion mandate.

116.   The commission recommends that Member States and regional organizations, particularly the League of Arab States:

(a)   Support efforts to protect the population of the Syrian Arab Republic and to bring an immediate end to gross human rights violations, and suspend the provision of arms and other military material to all parties;

(b)   Assist the Syrian Arab Republic in addressing serious institutional weaknesses by strengthening the independence of its judiciary and reforming its security sector through bilateral and multilateral development cooperation;

(c)   Provide Syrian nationals seeking protection with refuge in accordance with the provisions of the international law governing asylum.

Annexes

Annex I

Terms of reference of the independent international commission of inquiry on the Syrian Arab Republic

Mandate

1.   In its resolution S-17/1, the Human Rights Council decided to dispatch urgently an independent, international commission of inquiry:

(a)   To investigate all alleged violations of international human rights law since March 2011 in the Syrian Arab Republic;

(b)   To establish the facts and circumstances that may amount to such violations and of the crimes perpetrated including those that may constitute crimes against humanity;

(c)   To identify, where possible, those responsible with a view to ensuring that perpetrators of violations are held accountable;

(d)   To make public the report of the commission as soon as possible, and in any case before the end of November 2011;

(e)   To present a written update to the report on the situation in the Syrian Arab Republic at the nineteenth session of the Human Rights Council, in an interactive dialogue with the participation of the United Nations High Commissioner for Human Rights.

2.   The Human Rights Council decided to transmit the report of the commission and its update to the General Assembly, and recommended that the Assembly transmit the reports to all relevant bodies of the United Nations.

Cooperation of Syrian authorities

3.   The Human Rights Council called upon the Syrian Arab Republic to cooperate fully with the commission of inquiry.

4.   In accordance with established good practices, such cooperation shall include compliance with requests of the commission for assistance in collecting the required information and testimony. The Syrian Arab Republic should, in particular, guarantee the commission:

- Freedom of movement throughout its territory

- Freedom of access to all places and establishments, including prisons and detention centres of relevance to the work of the commission

- Freedom of access to all sources of information, including documentary material and physical evidence, freedom to interview representatives of governmental and military authorities, community leaders, civil society and, in principle, any individual whose testimony is considered necessary for the fulfilment of its mandate

- Appropriate security arrangements for the personnel, documents, premises and other property of the commission

- Protection of all those who are in contact with the commission in connection with the inquiry; no such person shall, as a result of such appearance or information, suffer harassment, threats of intimidation, ill-treatment, reprisals or any other prejudicial treatment

- Privileges, immunities and facilities necessary for the independent conduct of the inquiry; in particular, the members of the commission shall enjoy the privileges and immunities accorded to experts on missions under article VI of the Convention on the Privileges and Immunities of the United Nations, and to officials, as under articles V and VII of the Convention

Cooperation with other stakeholders

5.   The commission will approach third States, including neighbouring countries, with a request for cooperation in the collection of information and testimony relevant to the mandate. The commission will also request cooperation from other relevant actors.

Composition

6.   The President of the Human Rights Council appointed the experts Paulo Pinheiro (Chairperson), Karen Abuzayd and Yakin Ertürk as members of the commission.

Secretariat

7.   The Human Rights Council requested the Secretary-General and the United Nations High Commissioner for Human Rights to provide the full administrative, technical and logistical assistance needed to enable the commission to carry out its mandate. Furthermore, the High Commissioner has been requested to report on the implementation of resolution S-17/1 to the Human Rights Council at its nineteenth session.

8.   Accordingly, the commission shall be assisted by a secretariat composed of necessary staff, including administrative, logistic and technical staff.

Annex II

Note verbale dated 29 September 2011 from the independent international commission of inquiry addressed to the Permanent Representative of the Syrian Arab Republic

The Commissioners present their compliments to the Permanent Representative of the Syrian Arab Republic to the United Nations Office at Geneva and specialized institutions in Switzerland, and refer to the Note Verbale sent to the Permanent Representative, H.E Ambassador Faysal Khabbaz Hamoui, on 23 September 2011.

The Commissioners have the honour to inform the Permanent Representative that the Commission of Inquiry will be headed by Mr. Paulo Pinheiro who will be accompanied by Commissioners Ms. Yakin Ertürk and Ms. Karen AbuZayd.

The Commission of Inquiry would like to visit the Syrian Arab Republic as part of fulfilling its mandate and in preparation of its report due by the end of November 2011. The Commissioners wish to request the agreement of the Government of the Syrian Arab Republic to travel to Syrian Arab Republic in the period between 31 October and 7 November 2011.

The Commissioners avail themselves of this opportunity to renew to the Permanent Representative of the Syrian Arab Republic assurances of their highest consideration.

D.C

Geneva, 29 September 2011

Annex III

Letter dated 12 October 2011 from the Permanent Representative of the Syrian Arab Republic addressed to the independent international commission of inquiry

12 October 2011

Dear Mr. Chalev,

In reference to your letter dated 23 September 2011, I would like to draw your attention to the fact that the government of the Syrian Arab Republic has established an Independent Special Legal Commission with a clear and open mandate to investigate in all cases pertaining to the events that took place since March 2011 in Syria.

Consequently, the Syrian Arab Republic will examine the possibility of cooperating with the International Commission of Inquiry established pursuant to Human Rights Council resolution A\HRC\17\1 as soon as the Syrian Independent Special Legal Commission concludes its work.

Yours Sincerely,

OHCHR REGISTRY

1 4 OCT. 2011

Recipients : D. Chalev

Faysal Hamoui

Ambassador, Permanent Representative

Cc/ H.E Ambassador Laura Dupuy Lasserre, President of the Human Rights Council

Annex IV

Note verbale dated 19 October 2011 from the independent international commission of inquiry addressed to the Syrian Arab Republic

The Commissioners present their compliments to the Permanent Representative of the Syrian Arab Republic to the United Nations Office at Geneva and specialized institutions in Switzerland, and refer to the Note Verbale sent to the Permanent Representative, H.E Ambassador Faysal Khabbaz Hamoui, on 29 September. They also wish to acknowledge receipt of H.E Ambassador Faysal Khabbaz Hamoui's response of 12 October 2011.

The Commissioners regret that to date, the Syrian Arab Republic has not been cooperating with the International Commission of Inquiry. The Commissioners wish to reiterate their request to visit the Syrian Arab Republic as part of fulfilling their mandate and in preparation of their report due by the end of November 2011 and the written update requested by the Human Rights Council for its 19th session.

If a visit to Syria would not be possible in the coming weeks, the Commissioners would like to invite members of the Independent Special Legal Commission and relevant Syrian officials to Geneva in the second or third week of November.

The Commissioners avail themselves of this opportunity to renew to the Permanent Representative of the Syrian Arab Republic assurances of their highest consideration.

Annex V

Letter dated 27 October 2011 from the independent international commission of inquiry addressed to the Syrian Arab Republic

Dear Mr. Ambassador,

On 14 October 2011, we received your letter informing us that the Syrian Arab Republic will examine the possibility of cooperating with the Independent International Commission of Inquiry as soon as the Syrian Independent Special Legal Commission concludes its work.

Resolution A/HRC/S-17/1 requests that the Independent International Commission of Inquiry make its report public before the end of November and we are in the process of finalising our report.

In our note verbale of 19 October 2011, we reiterated our request to visit the Syrian Arab Republic as part of fulfilling our mandate and extended an invitation to the members of the Independent Special Legal Commission and relevant Syrian officials to visit Geneva in the second or third week of November.

We regret that, to date, the Syrian Arab Republic has not agreed to receive the Independent International Commission of Inquiry. This has prevented us from establishing direct contact with the authorities of your Government, as well as civil society organisations in order to share their assessment of the events since March 2011.

We believe that by doing so, the Syrian Arab Republic misses an important opportunity to cooperate with the Human Rights Council and Member States from all regional groups that are supporting our endeavour.

We hope that Syrian Arab Republic will reconsider its decision and would like to assure you that we stand ready to conduct a mission to your country and meet relevant authorities.

Meanwhile, in view of the preparation of the report due by the end of November 2011, we would be grateful if you could provide us with responses to the questionnaire enclosed herewith by 11 November 2011.

Yours Sincerely,

Paulo Pinheiro
Chairperson

Questions for the Government of the Syrian Arab Republic from the United Nations Commission Of Inquiry

The questions in this document are organized into three general categories: 1) questions concerning respect for the right to life; 2) questions concerning the right to be free from arbitrary detention and other forms of mistreatment; and 3) questions concerning recent Legislative Decrees, the Independent Special Legal Commission and other activities of the Syrian Arab Republic. The Commission of Inquiry respectfully seeks the assistance of the Government of the Syrian Arab Republic in clarifying the questions below.

I. Questions Concerning Respect for the Right to Life

1.   Please provide the Commission of Inquiry with a list of those members of the security services and armed forces who have been killed by "terrorist groups" since March 2011 and any information in the possession of the Government of the Syrian Arab Republic concerning the circumstances of their deaths.

2.   Please provide the Commission of Inquiry with information about events that were "staged" from March 2011 to the present in order to increase political pressure on the Government of the Syrian Arab Republic and its citizens.

3.   Would the Government of the Syrian Arab Republic please answer the questions a – j below about events which occurred in Syria during 2011, including, but not limited to: the Da'ra Military Operation (1 April 2011), the Hama Great Friday Incident (22 April 2011), the Jisr al Shoughour military operation/incident (5 June 2011), the Hama military operation (31 July 2011), the Homs Military operation (throughout September 2011), the Ar Rastan military operation (3 October 2011),

    (a) Which army units, police or other security agencies were deployed at the location of the events?

    (b) Which army or police officers and/or civilian leaders gave the orders for the deployment and were responsible for its execution?

    (c) Were the deployed military/security/and/or police units instructed to use force if necessary, and, if so, on what grounds?

    (d) Was a written order with clear rules of engagement and/or use of force issued for the purpose of monitoring the protests and ensuring public order? If so, can the Commission of Inquiry please receive a copy of the order(s)?

    (e) Which kind of weapons were the military/security and/or police forces issued and authorized to use in order to ensure public order?

    (f) How many armed individuals were arrested or killed by Government forces during the events?

    (g) How many unarmed individuals were arrested or killed by Government forces in the events?

    (h) How many and what type of weapons have been seized in the operation?

    (i) Were any militia groups (including so-called "Shabiha") present at these events? If so, how did such militia groups participate in these events?

(j) Will the Government make public a record and disclose details and circumstances regarding the fatalities and casualties incurred by Government forces, armed opposition groups and civilians?

II. Questions Concerning the Right to Be Free from Arbitrary Detention and Other Forms of Mistreatment

4.   Could the Government of the Syrian Arab Republic please describe to the Commission of Inquiry what measures the Government has implemented to investigate allegations since March 2011 of torture, arbitrary arrest, and enforced disappearances by members of Government security forces, the army and/or the police, militia groups (including the so-called "Shabiha"), and prosecute those individuals responsible for these alleged crimes? Has the Government been able to disprove any such allegations and if so, which ones? Has the Government established that any of these allegations are true? If so, have any of the perpetrators been charged with a crime or disciplined?

5.   Do local authorities keep an official up-to-date register of all persons deprived of liberty, including those arrested from March 2011 onwards, in every place of detention? Does the Government of the Syrian Arab Republic maintain a similar centralized register? If so, is the information contained in these registers made available to family members, their counsel, or any other person having a legitimate interest in the information? Will the International Committee of the Red Cross be granted access to those persons who are detained? Will the Commission of Inquiry be granted access to those persons who are detained?

6.   The Commission of Inquiry understands that persons detained in the Syrian Arab Republic may challenge their detention pursuant to paragraphs 2 and 4 of Article 28 of the Constitution. During 2011, to date, how many detained persons in Syria have challenged their arrest/detention under these provisions of the Constitution? How many such challenges have been successful? Can you please provide examples?

7.   In paragraph 32 of its report to the Human Rights Council dated 2 September 2011, the Government of the Syrian Arab Republic explains that "[t]he Ministry of Justice and the Ministry of the Interior oversee a process of effective, constant, systematic and continuous monitoring of prisons and prison inspections."

8.   Can you please describe how this process has functioned during 2011? Which prisons have been monitored and inspected? What procedures occurred when these prisons were monitored and inspected? Who carried them out? How many prisoners were monitored and/or inspected? Where are the records of these procedures and inspections? May the Commission of Inquiry please be given access to these records?

9.   Could the Government of the Syrian Arab Republic please inform the Commission of Inquiry how many persons detained during the demonstrations in 2011 have applied for bail? How many have received bail?

10.   Could the Government of the Syrian Arab Republic please inform the Commission of Inquiry how many children between the ages of 10 and 18 have been arrested during the demonstrations in 2011? Where have they been detained? Are any such children still detained? May the Commission of Inquiry please be given access to them?

11.   During 2011, how many persons have been detained for longer than sixty days for violations of State Security laws? Where are these persons detained and can the Commission of Inquiry please receive a list of their names? What is the legal basis for holding these persons for longer than sixty days? Can the Commission of Inquiry please receive access to these persons?

12.   The Commission of Inquiry understands that the National Dialogue Commission met in June 2011 and made the following recommendations:

(k)   All political prisoners must be released immediately, together with prisoners of conscience who have not committed any legally punishable offence.

(l)   All those detained during the recent events should be released, if they have not already been convicted by the courts.

13.   The Commission of Inquiry would like to know how many "political prisoners" have been released since June 2011? For those "political prisoners" still detained, can the Commission of Inquiry please receive a list of their names, the place of their detention and the reasons for their detention?

14.   The Commission of Inquiry would like to know how many "prisoners of conscience" have been released since June 2011? For those "prisoners of conscience" still detained, can the Commission of Inquiry please receive a list of their names, the place of their detention and the reasons for their detention? Has the Government of the Syrian Arab Republic amended its legislation concerning the detention of "prisoners of conscience"?

III.   Questions Concerning Recent Legislative Decrees, the Independent Special Legal Commission and other Activities of the Syrian Arab Republic.

15.   What kind of fair trial guarantees are available to civilians prosecuted under "state security offenses"?

16.   Can you please provide details regarding the prosecution of military, security and law enforcement personnel involved in the use of excessive force while preventing or stopping the protests that have occurred in several cities and locations in the Syrian Arab Republic since March 2011. Does the law of the Syrian Arab Republic provide immunity from prosecution for members of the intelligence, security, police and/or armed forces who use excessive force?

17.   Could you please update the Commission of Inquiry regarding progress related to the work of the Independent Special Legal Commission established on 31 March tasked with investigating the events in Dara'a? Will the work of the Independent Special Legal Commission be extended to encompass other incidents of political unrest over the past seven months? Can the Commission of Inquiry receive access to the findings and methodology of the Judicial Commission?

18.   Were the amnesties granted by the Government Decrees No. 61 of 31 May 2011 and No. 72 of 17 July 2011 also applied to offenses related to treason and terrorism? Can you describe the practical application of these decrees? How many persons received amnesties? For what crimes or charges? How many persons requested amnesty but were rejected? If requests for amnesty were rejected, can you please describe the reasons why?

19.   Can you please clarify which specific measures have been taken to implement the lifting of the state of emergency? Would you please provide a list of prisoners whose offenses were related to breaches of "state security" during 2011? Have any of these prisoners received amnesty? For those who have not received amnesty, have they been prosecuted? Where are they detained or imprisoned?

20.   Could you please provide details on the application of the recently enacted decree No. 55 of 21 April 2011 on the use of detention without judicial review for up to seven days, renewable for up to two months? Has any suspect been apprehended, investigated, and prosecuted under this new provision?

21.   The Commission of Inquiry understands that Legislative Decree 54 of 21 April 2011, creates new procedures for authorization of peaceful protests. How many requests to make peaceful protests have been made since the enactment of law? How many such requests have been granted? Where requests have been denied, what were the reasons for the denial? Since this law was enacted, how many persons have been arrested for "the staging of unlawful demonstrations or riots?" Where are those persons detained and for how long have they been detained?

22.   In paragraph 87 of its National Report dated 2 September 2011, the Government of the Syrian Arab Republic explains that, in implementation of the "amnesty" decrees, i.e. Legislative Decree 34 of 7 March 2011, Legislative Decree 61 of 31 May 2011 and Legislative Decree 72 of 20 June 2011, 10,433 persons were released immediately from detention. Does the Government of the Syrian Arab Republic have a list of those persons, the locations of their detentions, the reasons for their detentions, and the contact details of these persons? If so, can the Commission of Inquiry have access to this information? Of these 10,433 persons released, how many of these persons were being detained for "offenses against State Security and public order?" How many persons whose cases were before the "Supreme State Security Court" when it was abolished, received amnesties?

23.   To date, during 2011, how many persons in the Syrian Arab Republic have been prosecuted for violations of articles 357, 358, 359 and 555 of the Criminal Code concerning unlawful deprivations of liberty? Can you please provide some examples of these prosecutions? How many people have been convicted for such violations? What penalties have they received?

24.   Pursuant to the Legislative Decree 34 of 7 March 2001, Legislative Decree 61 of 31 May 2011 and Legislative Decree 72 of 20 June 2011, how many members of the army, police or other government institutions were granted "amnesty" for violations of articles 357, 358, 359 and 555 of the Criminal Code? How many members of the army, police or other government institutions were granted "amnesty" for "unlawful deprivation of liberty" pursuant to Article 105 of the Code of Criminal Procedure?

26.   Could you please clarify the meaning and scope of Decree No. 14 of 1969, particularly article 16; and Decree No. 69 of 2008?

Annex VI

Note verbale dated 4 November 2011 from the independent international commission of inquiry addressed to the Syrian Arab Republic

The Commissioners present their compliments to the Permanent Representative of the Syrian Arab Republic to the United Nations Office at Geneva and specialized institutions in Switzerland, and refer to their Notes Verbales of 29 September 2011 and 19 October 2011 as well to the Chairperson's letter of 27 October 2011.

The Commissioners welcome the decision made by the Council of the League of Arab State during its extraordinary session on 2 November and sincerely hope that the agreement reached between the League of Arab State and your Government will contribute towards the protection of the lives and human rights in Syria.

The Commissioners note the commitment made by the Syrian Government to cease all violence, the withdrawal of its armed presence from cities and inhabited areas, as well as to release all those detained in relation to the recent events.

In light of these developments, the Commissioners wish to reiterate their request to visit the Syrian Arab Republic as part of fulfilling their mandate and in preparation of their report due by the end of November 2011 and the written update requested by the Human Rights Council for its 19th session. The Commissioners also wish to reiterate their invitation to the members of the national Independent Special Legal Commission and relevant Syrian officials to meet with them in Geneva in the second or third week of November.

The Commissioners avail themselves of this opportunity to renew to the Permanent Representative of the Syrian Arab Republic assurances of their highest consideration.

Annex VII

Note verbale dated 17 November 2011 from the Syrian Arab Republic addressed to the independent international commission of inquiry

N° 568/11   Geneva, 17 November 2011

The Permanent Mission of the Syrian Arab Republic to the United Nations Office and other International Organizations in Geneva presents its compliments to the Chairperson of the Independent International Commission of Inquiry pursuant to resolution A/HRC/S-17/1, and with reference to his letter of 27th October 2011 with a questionnaire enclosed, has the honour to kindly attached herewith the responses of the Government of the Syrian Arab Republic to this mentioned questionnaire.

The Permanent Mission of the Syrian Arab Republic avails itself of this opportunity to renew to the Chairperson of ht Independent International Commission of Inquiry to resolution of A/HFC/S-17/1 the assurances of its highest consideration.

M. Paulo Pinheiro
Office of High Commissioner for Human Rights
Palais Wilson

OHCHR REGISTRY

1 8 NOV. 2011

Recipients : ....D...Chaker (encl)
....
....
....

تود الحكومة السورية الإشارة إلى أن الأسئلة المذكورة أعلاه مهتمة بها اللجنة القضائية الوطنية المستقلة المشكلة بتاريخ ٢٠١١/٣/٣١، والتي توسعت صلاحيتها بتاريخ ٢٠١١/٥/١١، لتصبح مهمتها إجراء التحقيقات الفورية في جميع القضايا التي أودت بحياة مواطنين مدنيين أو عسكريين أو أمنيين، منذ بداية الأحداث في سورية، وفي كافة المحافظات، وبجميع الجرائم التي رافقت هذه الأحداث، وشكلت بدورها لجان قضائية فرعية في كل محافظة، تتبع لها مباشرة للتحقيق في كافة الأحداث الجارية بالمحافظات، والتي لا زالت تمارس مهامها الموكلة إليها، وبالتالي لا يمكن في ظل ذلك تزويد رئيس لجنة التحقيق الدولية السيد باولو بينيرو بالأجوبة التفصيلية المطلوبة، حتى انتهاء اللجنة القضائية الوطنية من تحقيقاتها، ورفع النتائج الكاملة عن تحقيقاتها. ويمكن إحاطة اللجنة حالياً بالمعلومات التالية:

– لم تتوقف قط الضغوط السياسية وغيرها على سورية لتغيير نهجها المعارض لسياسات الاحتلال والمحاولات الأمريكية وغيرها للهيمنة على المنطقة، وجعلها تدور في فلك السياسية الأمريكية، وازدادت الأحداث المنظمة والضاغطة على سورية بشكل كبير منذ بداية الأحداث في شهر آذار ٢٠١١، وعلى المستويين الإقليمي والدولي، قام الاتحاد الأوروبي بفرض العديد من العقوبات الاقتصادية والسياسية لزيادة الضغط على الحكومة والشعب في سورية للإسراع بإخضاعه للإملاءات الغربية، كما سعت دول الاتحاد بالتعاون مع الولايات المتحدة مرات عديدة لاتخاذ قرارات إدانة للحكومة السورية في مجلس الأمن، ومختلف المحافل الدولية.

– إن التساؤل عن أحداث وعمليات عسكرية زمنياً ومكانياً لا يقدم الصورة الحقيقية لما يجري في سورية، من عمليات إرهابية لمسلحين خارجين عن القانون يقومون بترويع المواطنين وإجبارهم على ترك منازلهم وممتلكاتهم

وتهجيرهم إلى مناطق ذات لون طائفي معين أو قتلهم وتشويه جثثهم لتقسيم البلد طائفياً وتشجيع الحرب الأهلية. والقوات التي تتصدى لهؤلاء الإرهابيين معنية بحفظ النظام، وتلاحق الإرهابيين المطلوبين للعدالة لإلقاء القبض عليهم وتقديمهم للقضاء لمحاكمتهم وفق القوانين النافذة، ومصادرة أسلحتهم المتنوعة التي بلغت آلاف البنادق الآلية وغيرها من الأسلحة الفردية، والقواذف والقنابل والألغام المعدة للتفجير، ومعظمها يهرب من الخارج، وكلما حاولت السلطات المختصة التوجه إلى المسلحين لتسليم أسلحتهم للعفو عنهم وتطويق الأزمة تبادر جهات خارجية بتشجيعهم على عدم تسليم أسلحتهم للاستمرار بقتل المدنيين، وكان آخر هذه المبادرات ما أدلى به الناطق الرسمي باسم الخارجية الأمريكية.

– أما بالنسبة للمشاركين في العمليات الأمنية، فهم كما وضحنا من القوات المتخصصة بحفظ النظام ومكافحة الإرهاب، وما يطلق عليهم مصطلح الشبيحة الذي يتم تداوله خارجياً، فهو غير موجود في سورية أبداً، إلا إذا كان المقصود به كل مواطن سوري يعمل لمنع هدر الدماء وتطويق الأزمة، وهؤلاء يمثلون أكثر من ٨٠% من سكان سورية.

– إن كل حادثة وفاة تتم سواءً من قوى حفظ النظام أو المدنيين أو المسلحين الإرهابيين الخارجين عن القانون يتم تسجيلها كواقعة في سجلات رسمية بمديريات الشؤون المدنية في كافة المحافظات السورية، تشرف عليها مكاتب رسمية في الدولة.

[Unofficial translation]

Letter dated 17 November 2011 from the Syrian Arab Republic to the international independent commission of inquiry

The Syrian Government would like to point out that the above-mentioned questionnaire is being considered by the Independent Special Legal Commission, which was established on 31 March 2011, and whose mandate has been expanded on 11 May 2011 to carry out immediate investigations into all cases involving the death of citizens, including civilians, military or security personnel since the beginning of the events in Syria. The mandate of the commission covers all events and crimes in all Governorates of Syria. In this regard, the commission has established sub-commissions operating under its supervision in order to carry out investigations in all the Governorates of Syria. The commission is still in the process of carrying out its mandate. Therefore, it will not be possible to provide Mr. Paulo Pinheiro with the required detailed answers before the commission has concluded and presented the full outcome of its investigations.

At this moment, it is possible to inform the commission [of inquiry] of the following:

- Political and other forms of pressure have been on-going to try and coerce Syria to reverse its stance towards policies of occupation and efforts by America and other countries to dominate the region and make it part of the sphere of influence of American policies. These pressures have increased significantly since the beginning of March 2011. At both the regional and international levels, the European Union has imposed economic and political sanctions to increase pressure on the Government and on the people of Syria in order to accelerate their submission to Western policies. European Union States together with the United States have sought resolutions condemning the Government of Syria at the UN Security Council and in other international forums.

- Questions regarding incidents, time and place of military operations cannot depict the picture of what has been really happening in Syria, in terms of terrorist operations carried out by armed outlaws who are terrorizing our citizens and forcing them to abandon their homes and properties, and eventually resulting in their displacement to areas of certain sectarian demography, or resulting in their death and the mutilation of their bodies, in order to divide the country along sectarian lines and incite civil war. The [Syrian security] forces dealing with those terrorists are tasked with maintaining public order. They chase wanted terrorists in order to arrest them and bring them to justice, in accordance with the law, and to confiscate their weapons, which include automatic rifles, small arms, launchers, bombs, landmines, the majority of which is smuggled in from abroad. Every time the authorities attempted to engage those armed individuals, requesting that they hand over their guns in return for amnesty, foreign entities stepped in and encouraged them not to turn in their arms so that they continue killing civilians. The latest of such initiatives was that expressed by the Spokesperson of the US State Department.

- As already explained above, those involved in security operations, are the [State] Public Order and Anti-Terrorism forces. Regarding the so-called *Shabbiha*, this is an expression which has been used abroad and never in Syria, unless it is meant to refer to all Syrian citizens working towards putting an end to the bloodshed and to the crisis, which would account for more than 80% of the population of Syria.

- Every death whether it is caused by Public Order forces, civilians or armed terrorist outlaws, is recorded in official registries at the Civilian Affairs Directorates in every Syrian Governorate, which are supervised by official bureaus of the Government.

Annex VIII

Map of the Syrian Arab Republic

United Nations

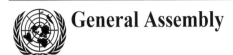

General Assembly

A/HRC/19/69

Distr.: General
22 February 2012

Original: English

DOCUMENT 2c

Human Rights Council
Nineteenth session
Agenda item 4
Human rights situations that require the Council's attention

Report of the independent international commission of inquiry on the Syrian Arab Republic· ··

Summary

The human rights situation in the Syrian Arab Republic has deteriorated significantly since November 2011, causing further suffering to the Syrian people. Widespread violence and increasingly aggravated socio-economic conditions have left many communities in a perilous state. Meeting basic needs to sustain everyday life has become increasingly difficult.

The present situation risks further radicalizing the population, deepening inter-communal tensions and eroding the fabric of society. Divisions among the international community complicate the prospects for ending the violence.

The Government has manifestly failed in its responsibility to protect its people. Since November 2011, its forces have committed more widespread, systematic and gross human rights violations. Anti-Government groups have also committed abuses, although not comparable in scale and organization to those carried out by the State.

The commission calls for an end to gross violations and related impunity, and recommends that the Office of the United Nations High Commissioner for Human Rights (OHCHR) and the Special Rapporteur on the situation of human rights in the Syrian Arab Republic continue to monitor gross human rights violations with a view to ensuring that perpetrators are held accountable. In cooperation with the Special Rapporteur, OHCHR should maintain and update the confidential database established by the commission.

---

* The annexes to the present report are reproduced as received, in the languages of submission only.
·· Late submission.

The commission also recommends the initiation of an inclusive political dialogue, bringing together the Government, the opposition and other anti-Government actors to negotiate an end to the violence, to ensure respect for human rights and to address the legitimate demands of the Syrian people. A contact group composed of States with diverse positions on the situation should be established to initiate a process leading to such a dialogue.

Reconciliation and accountability will be achieved only if there are credible consultations with the population, including women and minorities, as well as with victims. Profound political, justice and security sector reforms must also be undertaken.

Contents

I. Introduction

1.   The independent international commission of inquiry, established pursuant to Human Rights Council resolution S-17/1 to investigate all alleged violations of international human rights law since March 2011 in the Syrian Arab Republic,[1] continued to investigate alleged violations of international human rights law and sought to establish the facts and circumstances that may amount to such violations.

2.   In the present report, which builds on and should be read in conjunction with the initial report (A/HRC/S-17/2/Add.1), the commission gives an update for the period since November 2011 (sect. III). It provides an account of the ongoing suffering of the Syrian population, the widespread, systematic and gross human rights violations that State forces continue to commit, and the human rights abuses committed by anti-Government armed groups.

3.   Consistent with its mandate, the commission also endeavoured, where possible, to identify those responsible for violations and crimes perpetrated since March 2011, with a view to ensuring that perpetrators of violations, including those that may constitute crimes against humanity, are held accountable.[2] Its findings on responsibility (sect. IV) cover the period from March 2011 until mid-February 2012.

A.   Cooperation with the Government

4.   The commission regrets that the Government of the Syrian Arab Republic did not give the commission access to the country, nor did it respond positively to its requests to interview authorized Government spokespersons.

5.   The commission met with the Permanent Representative of the Syrian Arab Republic on 7 and 15 February 2012.

6.   The present report reflects relevant information provided by the Government in response to the commission's repeated and detailed requests (annexes I to XII). On 15 February 2012, the day the present report was finalized, the Permanent Representative presented the commission with documents containing detailed information on armed group attacks. The report reflects the overall content of the documents received, which comprised several hundred pages in Arabic. In addition, the commission drew on public statements of senior officials. The commission also followed the reporting of the official Syrian Arab news agency SANA.

B.   Methodology

7.   The commission endeavoured to reflect violations and abuses on all sides. The lack of access to the country, however, posed particular challenges for the documentation of abuses committed by anti-Government armed groups and opposition actors, given that most victims and witnesses of such abuses have remained in the country and the Government had not facilitated interviews with victims of armed group violence during the period under review. The opportunity to engage with communities and officials on the ground would

---

[1]   On 12 September 2011, the President of the Human Rights Council appointed three high-level experts as members of the commission: Paulo Pinheiro (Chairperson), Yakin Ertürk and Karen Koning AbuZayd.
[2]   Human Rights Council resolution S-17/1, para. 13.

also have allowed the commission to better appreciate the circumstances of human rights concerns and related human suffering.

8.   After its first report, the commission interviewed additional victims and witnesses of violations, defectors and other individuals with relevant inside knowledge. From 9 to 25 January 2012, the commission travelled to several countries to gather first-hand testimony from people who had recently fled the Syrian Arab Republic.[3] Additional interviews, including with victims and witnesses still in the country, journalists who recently visited the Syrian Arab Republic and individuals known to support the Government were conducted by telephone. After its initial report, the commission interviewed a further 136 victims and witnesses, bringing the total numbers of interviews conducted by the commission to 369.

9.   The commission also examined photographs, video recordings and available Government documents. Satellite imagery of areas where military and security forces were deployed and related reported violations occurred, corroborated a number of witness accounts. The commission took into account the report of the observer mission of the League of Arab States of 22 January 2012 and also interviewed former observers of that mission.

10.   With regard to the documentation of violations, the commission applied the standard of proof used in its first report.[4] Particular incidents are described in the report if there are reasonable grounds to believe that they occurred, namely if the commission obtained a reliable body of evidence, consistent with other information, indicating their occurrence. The incidents discussed in the report were the subject of two or more consistent and reliable witness accounts, which were often supported by additional corroborating evidence. In exceptional cases, where credible sources reported relevant incidents but the commission was unable to corroborate them through eyewitness interviews, incidents were included and the source identified. The patterns described in the report are based on multiple documented incidents that are further corroborated by verified circumstances.

11.   To obtain a general background on the situation and the diplomatic efforts to address it, the commission met with the permanent representatives of Member and observer States of the Human Rights Council from all regional groups. It also spoke with representatives of international and regional organizations, including the League of Arab States.

12.   The report reflects information received as at 15 February 2012.

13.   The commission did not apply international humanitarian law for the purposes of the report and the period covered.[5] International humanitarian law is applicable if the situation can be qualified as an armed conflict, which depends on the intensity of the violence and the level of organization of participating parties. While the commission is gravely concerned that the violence in certain areas may have reached the requisite level of intensity, it was unable to verify that the Free Syrian Army (FSA), local groups identifying themselves as such or other anti-Government armed groups had reached the necessary level of organization.[6] By the same token, the commission uses the term "FSA group" to refer to any local armed group whose members identify themselves as belonging to the FSA, without this necessarily implying that the group has been recognized by the FSA leadership or obeys the command of the FSA leadership abroad.

---

[3] Places where interviews were conducted have been withheld to protect witnesses and victims.
[4] A/HRC/S-17/2/Add.1, paras. 5-6.
[5] Ibid., paras. 97-100.
[6] Ibid., paras.106-108.

II. Context

A. Domestic political developments

14.   The Government maintains that the opposition is part of a foreign conspiracy and that Government military and security operations target terrorists. On 10 January 2012, the President affirmed that "restoration of security and fighting terrorism with an iron fist" remained its foremost priority.[7] At the same time, the Government has pressed forward with an agenda of holding elections and adopting new laws, including regarding political participation and the media. On 13 February, the President received the draft of a new Constitution and announced that it would be subjected to a referendum on 26 February. One of the stated objectives of the text would be a political system "based on political pluralism" and sets out a presidential term limit.[8] Local elections were held on 12 December 2011; according to the Government, a participation rate of 80 per cent was recorded. Parliamentary elections are announced to follow in May or June 2012. On 15 January, the President decreed the latest of four general amnesties (see also paragraph 66 below).

15.   Protests against the Government continued in many parts of the country, although they tended to be more brief and localized to avoid the security forces. Demonstrations in support of the Government were also organized in different governorates.

16.   The political opposition in the country has organized itself mainly through local coordination committees under the umbrella of the Syrian Revolutionary General Commission. The committees have taken a leading role in organizing protests and humanitarian relief. The opposition "Syrian National Council", comprising a diverse set of members ranging from the Muslim Brotherhood to secular formations and representatives of local coordination committees, sought to present itself as the legitimate representative of the Syrian people, although other opposition groups exist inside and outside the country. The Syrian National Council has rejected any political dialogue with the Government under present conditions. Serious rifts apparently remain within the Council itself, and between the Council, whose leadership largely resides abroad, and other parts of the opposition.

B. Increasing violence and polarization

17.   In recent months, the crisis has become increasingly violent and militarized. The State's campaign of violently suppressing dissent, which from the outset employed lethal force against peaceful protests, was followed by defections and the formation of anti-Government armed groups. The rise of an armed opposition led the Government to intensify its violent repression.

18.   Many among the anti-Government armed groups identify themselves as FSA and consist of defectors (mainly from the army) and an increasing number of armed civilians. The FSA leadership resides abroad and its control over the different FSA groups inside the country remains unclear. In mid-January, the FSA leadership and the Syrian National Council agreed to improve their coordination.

19.   Most FSA groups initially adopted a defensive posture. More recently, a number of FSA groups carried out offensive operations targeting checkpoints, installations of State

---

[7] http://sana.sy/eng/21/2012/01/10/393338.htm.
[8] http://sana.sy/eng/36/2012/02/16/400646.htm.

forces, police stations and Government vehicles. For example, the FSA claimed responsibility for an attack in Dar'a governorate on 15 December 2011, during which at least 27 soldiers were killed. In its report, the League of Arab States indicated that, in Homs and Dar'a, armed groups committed acts of violence against Government forces, resulting in death and injury.

20.   The activity of FSA groups resulted in the temporary withdrawal of State forces from cities or areas in the Rif Dimashq, Idlib and Homs governorates. Since December 2011, the army has attacked these areas with heavy weapons, leading to massive casualties and the destruction of homes and infrastructure (see paragraphs 38-46 below).

21.   The Government stated that other armed non-State actors not affiliated to the FSA are operating in the country, including Al-Qaida and other religious extremists. In its report, the League of Arab States also makes a distinction between the FSA and "other opposition armed groups". Numerous sources report the presence of extremist groups in the country. The commission was unable to verify information on the membership, background and operations of such groups.

22.   On 23 December 2011, 50 people were reportedly killed in two bombings next to the offices of security agencies in Damascus, which the Government attributed to Al-Qaida. No one, including Al-Qaida, claimed responsibility. In its report, the League of Arab States mentioned that its observers in Homs, Hama and Idlib reported the bombing of a civilian bus (with eight casualties), a police bus (two casualties), a train loaded with diesel fuel, an oil pipeline and small bridges. In other cases, League observers found that alleged bombings were falsely reported. On 10 February 2012, 28 people were reportedly killed and 235 injured in two large explosions at Military Intelligence and police buildings in Aleppo. The Government and other sources attributed these explosions to terrorists. On 14 February, a major pipeline near Homs exploded. The Government blamed "terrorist saboteurs", while opposition activists attributed the act to State forces shelling in the area.

23.   According to all accounts, casualties rose steeply as the violence intensified; thousands of lives have been lost.

24.   On 27 December 2011, the Government informed the commission that, according to hospital and police reports, at least 2,131 civilians had been killed in the period from 15 March to 19 December 2011. The Government added that a total of 913 soldiers and 215 police officers (1,128 people in total) were killed during the same period.[9] According to the Government, from 23 December 2011 to 10 February 2012, a further 651 members of the army and security forces were killed and 2,292 injured.[10] In addition, 519 unidentified bodies were found. On 15 February 2012, the Government provided additional figures, according to which 2,493 civilians and 1,345 soldiers and police officers had been killed in the Syrian Arab Republic in the period from 15 March 2011 to 18 January 2012.

25.   The Violations Documenting Centre, affiliated to the local coordination committees, counted 6,399 civilians and 1,680 army defectors killed in the period from 15 March 2011 to 15 February 2012.[11] The victims included 244 adult women, 115 girls and 425 boys.

---

[9]   See annex IV. In another note verbale (annex III), the Government stated that, as at 21 December 2011, a total of 2,000 police officers and soldiers had been killed. There was no indication of the methodology used to determine the secondt set of figures.

[10]   The Government provided a long list indicating the names, rank and personal details of military and security forces personnel killed, together with the date and place of death or injury.

[11]   The Centre (www.vdc-sy.org) relies on medical records, direct contacts with victims' families and information received from the Imam of the Mosque performing the burial.

December 2011 (1,046 victims), January (1,196) and the first half of February 2012 (983) have been clearly the most violent period since the unrest erupted in March 2011.

26.   The Government, on the one hand, and the opposition Syrian National Council, Syrian Revolutionary General Commission and local coordination committees, on the other, have consistently proclaimed their commitment to non-sectarianism while accusing the other side of instigating hatred. Attempts to mobilize political support have given rise to tensions and crimes with sectarian undertones, especially in Homs. On several occasions in January and February 2012, entire families – children and adults – were brutally murdered in Homs. On both sides, there is a pattern of abducting people not directly involved in the clashes for the purposes of revenge, ransom or as hostages.

27.   Minorities' fears have been used to garner their support. Most Christians, for example, feel particularly vulnerable in the light of developments in some of the other countries in the region. Sectarian allegiances have also been invoked in calls to oppose the Government. Many Syrian citizens, including intellectuals and religious leaders of different creeds, have stood up for tolerance and denounced such politicking.

C.   International context

28.   While the permanent members of the Security Council have continued to disagree on how to frame or address the crisis, regional organizations and individual States have continued to apply diplomatic pressure and introduced more sanctions. The European Union and the United States of America have hardened sanctions, in particular by imposing a boycott on the purchase of Syrian oil. Targeted sanctions have been imposed on a growing number of individuals and entities. Turkey banned transactions with the Government and its central bank, froze Government assets and imposed severe import duties on Syrian goods.

29.   On 16 November, the League of Arab States called on the Government to cease violence and protect its citizens, release detainees, withdraw its forces from the cities, provide free access to Arab and international media and accept the deployment of an observer mission. The Government's initial refusal to sign a protocol agreeing to these terms led the League to adopt sanctions, halting among other things transactions with the Syrian Central Bank and imposing a travel ban on senior officials.

30.   On 19 December, the Government signed the protocol, and on 24 December, the observer mission of the League of Arab States was deployed to the Syrian Arab Republic. After the mission filed its report, the League issued a resolution on 23 January 2012 calling for a transfer of authority from the President to his first vice-president and the formation of a national unity Government. The Government rejected this plan. Shortly afterwards, the League suspended the work of the mission, citing security concerns.

31.   On 7 February, the Minister for Foreign Affairs of the Russian Federation met with President Assad in Damascus to discuss proposals to address the crisis.

32.   On 8 February, the Secretary-General of the United Nations evoked the prospect of resuming the observer mission as a joint operation of the League of Arab States and the United Nations. On 12 February, the League adopted a resolution calling on the Security Council to authorize a joint Arab-United Nations force to "supervise the execution of a ceasefire", and urged its members to "halt all forms of diplomatic cooperation" with the Government of the Syrian Arab Republic.

33.   Most in the international community have not favoured direct military intervention to protect the Syrian people. Available information, however, points to existing or planned support for either the Government or the opposition. A number of experts have begun to

report on the presence in the country of individuals and interested parties, some perhaps supported by Governments whose intention is to assist one side or the other. Such information deserves attention in the context of the country's pivotal place in the regional and international context and concerns about the consequences of potential changes in its national and international role and relationships.

D. Socio-economic impact

34. The crisis has exacerbated pre-existing high levels of poverty and unemployment. The economy is estimated to have shrunk by 2 to 4 per cent in 2011, with a markedly higher drop expected for 2012. Tourism, which accounted for 6 to 9 per cent of gross domestic product, has collapsed. The Government has attributed economic concerns to the sanctions and armed groups sabotaging fuel supplies and civilian infrastructure, while maintaining that such concerns can be addressed through economic self-reliance initiatives.

35. Syrians, particularly day labourers and others in precarious employment situations, are feeling the impact of the downturn. In December 2011, the Minister for Labour and Social Affairs announced that the unemployment rate was in the range of 22 to 30 per cent.[12]

36. The boycott on Syrian oil exports, sanctions against the banking sector and reported capital flight have devalued the Syrian currency, spurring inflation. The Ministry of the Economy estimated that, by the end of 2011, prices for basic food items had increased by up to 37 per cent,[13] hurting the poor in particular. The Government sought to offset price increases by raising public sector salaries and extending or increasing subsidies on fuel and other essential goods.

37. People have suffered through an unusually harsh winter, while fuel for cooking and heating has become more expensive and scarce, especially in areas of unrest. Power cuts are frequent in many parts of the country.

III. Human rights situation

38. Since November 2011, the escalation of violence, owing to the intensification of armed operations, has led to an even more dire human rights situation and increased human suffering.

A. Attacks targeting residential areas and civilians

39. Starting in early November 2011, the level of violence between State forces and anti-Government armed groups increased in areas of Homs, Hama, Rif Dimashq and Idlib governorates with a strong presence of such groups. State forces withdrew from and then surrounded many of these areas. Army snipers and *Shabbiha*[14] gunmen posted at strategic points terrorized the population, targeting and killing small children, women and other unarmed civilians. Fragmentation mortar bombs were also fired into densely populated neighbourhoods.

---

[12] Sarah Abu Assali "Labour in vain", *Syria Today*. Available from http://syria-today.com/index.php/focus/17955-labour-invain.

[13] "The cost of Syria's crackdown", Al Jazeera, 15 January 2012. Available from www.aljazeera.com/programmes/insidesyria/2012/01/2012115721352136.html.

[14] A/HRC/C/S-17/2/Add.1, para. 20.

40.   After the withdrawal of League of Arab States observers in late January, the army intensified its bombardment with heavy weapons. It gave no warning to the population and unarmed civilians were given no chance to evacuate. As a result, large numbers of people, including many children, were killed. Several areas were bombarded and then stormed by State forces, which arrested, tortured and summarily executed suspected defectors and opposition activists.

41.   According to the Violations Documenting Centre, at least 787 civilians, including 53 adult women, 26 girls and 49 boys, were killed in the first two weeks of February 2012 alone. The largest number of victims died in Homs.

42.   In Idlib governorate, the army shelled the villages of Ihsim, Ibleen, Ibdita, Kasanfra and Kafar Awid in mid-December. When State forces took control of the villages, security agents pillaged houses and loaded their loot into trucks brought along to transport detainees. On 20 December, local residents discovered the bodies of 74 defectors in a deserted area between Kafar Awid and Kasanfra. Their hands had been tied behind their back and they appeared to have been summarily executed. On 21 December, State forces attacked a group of activists from Kafar Awid who had sought refuge in the village mosque. After the forces withdrew, 60 bodies were discovered in the mosque. The victims appeared to have been tortured before their execution.

43.   From 24 to 26 December 2011, the army launched a large-scale operation in Bab Amr, Homs, where an FSA group was present. Residential buildings in Bab Amr were shelled by tanks and anti-aircraft guns. League of Arab States observers, who visited on 27 December, confirmed that the area had been shelled. State snipers also shot at and killed unarmed men, women and children. On 19 January, State forces shelled Homs again, including Bab Houd and Bayada, killing civilians.

44.   On 12 January 2012, the army started shelling Zabadani, Rif Dimashq, causing civilian casualties. Armed clashes with an FSA group lasted for six days and ended with the military redeploying to the outskirts of the city and imposing a blockade.

45.   On 24 January, tanks and snipers surrounded and shelled Bab Qebli neighbourhood in Hama, where an FSA group had been present. FSA members had apparently withdrawn upon the approach of the army, but many opposition activists remained in the neighbourhood. The next day, soldiers raided the neighbourhood, arresting many and looting homes. On 26 and 27 January, State forces conducted a similar operation in the Al Hamidieh neighbourhood in Hama. After the operations in Bab Qebli and Al Hamidieh, the handcuffed bodies of persons who had apparently been executed were dumped in Hama.

46.   On 3 February 2012, in an escalation of violence, State forces in Homs began shelling densely populated areas in Khaldieh with heavy weapons. The presence of snipers prevented civilians from fleeing. On 6 February, the same type of operation was extended to Bab Amr, which the Government shelled and attacked with rockets.

B.   Attacks on the political opposition, human rights defenders and the media

47.   The crackdown on peaceful protesters and raids on neighbourhoods suspected of supporting the opposition continued. The commission received additional accounts of military, security forces and *Shabbiha* using live ammunition against unarmed protesters. Defectors indicated that soldiers continued to receive "shoot to kill" orders. The Government also carried out reprisals in response to opposition calls for strikes. Participants in strikes on 11 December 2011 in Rif Dimashq and on 24 January 2012 in Hama were attacked by State forces.

48.   During their deployment from 24 December 2011 to 20 January 2012, League of Arab States observers witnessed several peaceful opposition demonstrations, which were held without State interference. The observers considered that their presence may have dissuaded State forces from using violence to disperse demonstrators. The observers also noted that citizens in Homs and Dar'a pleaded with them not to leave, which the observers attributed to a possible fear of reprisals.

49.   In a televised interview broadcast on 7 December 2011, the President stated that the military and security forces had received "no command to kill or be brutal", while acknowledging that some members of the State forces had gone "too far".

50.   The Government informed the commission that armed groups were killing or forcibly displacing individuals who resisted calls to participate in demonstrations or strikes. The commission documented cases of opposition activists threatening shopkeepers who refused to join strikes. The commission also found cases of anti-Government armed groups executing suspected *Shabbiha* (see also paragraphs 114 and 115 below).

51.   On 28 August 2011, the Government issued a new media law (Decree No. 108/2011), which sets out a number of basic rights relating to freedom of expression and information for journalists and citizens.[15] includes broad prohibitions, including a ban on publishing any news related to the armed forces not actually issued by the forces themselves. It leaves untouched the vaguely defined criminal offences described in articles 285 to 287 of the Penal Code that have long been used to punish and silence critical journalists, human rights defenders and political dissidents. In November, the Government established a national media council to implement the media law, and appointed a former deputy Minister for Information to head it. On 8 February 2012, the President issued a decree on organizing Internet communications and combating cybercrime, which sets out broad offences that restrict freedom of expression on the Internet.

52.   In practice, freedom of expression and information has continued to be severely restricted. The Government systematically uses censorship and the arbitrary denial of media licenses to control the media. Journalists and bloggers who have expressed dissenting views have been harassed, dismissed from Government jobs, arbitrarily arrested and detained.

53.   Activists and human rights defenders have continued to mobilize through the Internet and social media. "Citizen journalists" have filmed human rights violations by the military and security forces and posted them on the Internet. Others have conveyed their dissent through cultural expressions, such as satirical puppet plays broadcast over the Internet. In response, the Government has tried to block or slow down Internet access in restive cities at different times, destroyed computer equipment during raids and hacked into private e-mail and social media accounts.

54.   Pro- and anti-Government hackers have fought for control of cyberspace and, in some cases, spread disinformation. According to testimony received, these include the "virtual Syrian army", an online network that disseminates news supporting the Government and tries to sabotage opposition sites. A member of this group told the commission that the group neither worked for the Government nor engaged in illegal activities, but sought only to provide a balanced picture of the unrest.

55.   Syrian journalists covering the crisis and related violations remained at risk. The Committee to Protect Journalists and Reporters without Borders reported on three killings of Syrian journalists, two of which were attributed to State forces. On 19 November 2011,

---

[15] "President al-Assad issues legislative decree on media law", SANA, 29 August 2011. Available from www.sana.sy/eng/361/2011/08/29/366490.htm.

cameraman Ferzat Jarban was arrested by security agents while filming an anti-Government protest in Alqaseer (Homs governorate); he was found dead the next day, his eyes gouged out. On 29 December, citizen journalist Basil Al-Sayed was shot dead by State security forces while he was filming the violent crackdown on a demonstration in Homs. On 30 December, Shukri Ahmed Ratib Abu Burghul, a radio show host and censor for a Government newspaper, was shot dead by unknown gunmen in Damascus.

56. In late December 2011, in accordance with the League of Arab States protocol, the Government recommenced issuing short-term visas to selected foreign journalists. Their movements within the country were often restricted and their contacts monitored by Government officials accompanying them.

57. On 11 January 2012, a shell exploded near a group of journalists covering demonstrations in Homs. French journalist Gilles Jacquier and several Syrians were killed. The Government and the FSA exchanged accusations over responsibility for the incident. The Government stated that it had launched an inquiry.

C. Arbitrary arrests, torture, abductions and enforced disappearances

58. The Government has continued to arbitrarily arrest and detain suspected protesters, opposition activists, human rights defenders and deserters. Arbitrary arrests typically were not formally acknowledged and suspects were often held incommunicado without their families being notified about their arrest or whereabouts.

59. Arbitrary arrests across the country followed similar patterns. During protests, military and security forces would often encircle the protesters. Those arrested, including the wounded among them, would be transported in Government buses and trucks to detention centres operated by security agencies, sometimes after being temporarily held in facilities such as sports stadiums or schools. In addition, soldiers and security agents often carried out arrests at checkpoints on the basis of lists of wanted persons prepared by the local security branch.

60. More large-scale raids were conducted, especially in areas where defectors are presumed to be hiding or in areas perceived as being sympathetic to the protesters. The regular army normally cordoned off the area before security forces or elite army units, sometimes accompanied by *Shabbiha,* carried out house-to-house searches. In such raids, women were targeted for arbitrary arrest and detention, in many cases also to force male relatives to turn themselves in. Many women also emphasized the traumatic invasion of their privacy when security forces raided their houses, typically at night, and vandalized or looted their personal possessions.

61. The commission received additional testimonies from persons who, long after their family members were arrested, had received no information from the authorities or through informal channels about where their family members were and whether they were still alive. The commission remains concerned about such cases of enforced disappearance.[16]

62. Torture in places of detention continued. Victims and witnesses provided credible and consistent accounts of places and methods of torture. A list of 38 detention locations in 12 cities, where the commission documented cases of torture since March 2011, is annexed to the present report (annex XIII).

63. Security agencies continued to systematically arrest wounded patients in State hospitals and to interrogate them, often using torture, about their supposed participation in

---

[16] A/HRC/S-17/2/Add.1, para. 59.

opposition demonstrations or armed activities. The commission documented evidence that sections of Homs Military Hospital and Al Ladhiqiyah State Hospital had been transformed into torture centres. Security agents, in some cases joined by medical staff, chained seriously injured patients to their beds, electrocuted them, beat wounded parts of their body or denied them medical attention and water. Medical personnel who did not collaborate faced reprisals.

64.   The above campaign has created a climate of fear. Doctors operated clandestinely on patients facing arrest and hospitals did not keep operated patients for post-surgical care. Some women chose to give birth in unsafe conditions rather than go to a State hospital. In many places of unrest, civilians set up clandestine field hospitals with volunteer practitioners, rudimentary equipment and medical supplies smuggled from abroad, donated by concerned citizens or diverted from State hospitals.

65.   The commission received frequent accounts of security officials threatening men with the rape of female relatives.

66.   On 19 January 2012, the Government informed the League of Arab States observers that it had released 3,569 detainees under the amnesty declared on 15 January. The observers were able to verify the release of 1,669 detainees under the said amnesty.

67.   Given the large number of arbitrary arrests and the fact that most arrests and releases have occurred outside formal procedures, it is difficult to determine with any degree of certainty how many people remain in detention. The commission has requested the Government to provide pertinent figures.

68.   According to the Violations Documenting Centre, which gathers the names of detainees and the place and date of their arrest from families and local coordination committees, more than 18,000 detainees, including more than 200 women and girls and more than 400 boys, remained in detention at 15 February 2012.

69.   Armed groups, including FSA groups, carried out abductions. In some instances, victims were killed or tortured.

70.   The Government informed the commission that, between 15 March and 19 December 2011, 666 civilians, 70 soldiers and 164 police officers were abducted. According to the Government, between 23 December 2011 and 10 February 2012 a further 506 military and security personnel were abducted.

D.   Deprivation of economic and social rights

71.   While the population at large suffers as a result of the economic impact of the crisis and related sanctions (see paragraphs 34-36 above), communities in restive areas face particularly serious humanitarian concerns. There, formal economic activity and public services are collapsing and such essential supplies as fuel for cooking and heating, medical supplies and, in areas under blockade, increasingly also food, have become scarce. With men in hiding, arrested or killed, many women find themselves having to cope with a range of additional responsibilities in providing and caring for their families.

72.   According to estimates, 70,000 people have been arbitrarily displaced within the country. More than 20,000 Syrians found themselves in a precarious situation as refugees in other countries.

73.   The military and security forces continued to impose blockades on areas with a significant presence of anti-Government armed groups, including in Homs, Hama, Idlib and Rif Dimashq. Medicine, food and other essential supplies were not allowed to pass. State forces arbitrarily arrested and assaulted individuals who tried to bring in such supplies. The

Government also withheld fuel rations and the electricity supply to punish communities and families whose members had participated in anti-Government demonstrations.

74.   The Syrian Arab Red Crescent has provided humanitarian relief to part of the affected population in an increasingly difficult environment. According to the International Federation of Red Cross and Red Crescent Societies, the Secretary-General of the Syrian Arab Red Crescent, Dr. Abd-al-Razzaq Jbeiro, was shot and killed on 25 January 2012 on the main Aleppo–Damascus highway while traveling in a vehicle clearly marked with the Red Crescent emblem.

75.   Local coordination committees and individual Syrians have established community support mechanisms. International humanitarian actors have not been given the direct humanitarian access necessary to assess and address comprehensively the basic humanitarian needs that have arisen since March 2011.

76.   The Government provided information on attacks by armed groups on medical facilities. Between 15 March 2011 and 9 February 2012, the Government counted 17 attacks on hospitals and 48 on medical centres. A total of 15 medical staff members were killed, 27 were injured and 119 medical vehicles damaged.

77.   The commission documented several cases in which injured patients at State hospitals were forced to falsely state on camera that their injuries had resulted from attacks by armed groups.

E.   Violations of children's rights

78.   As the violence intensified, children continued to be the victims. The State authorities made no visible efforts to protect children's rights. According to a reliable source, more than 500 children have been killed since March 2011, with the highest number of children killed in December 2011 (80 deaths) and January 2012 (72). The largest group were adolescents aged between 16 and 18 years. Snipers and other State forces killed or wounded children, including those aged 10 years and younger. Many children were killed when the army shelled residential areas in Homs and other cities in January and February 2012.

79.   Children continued to be arbitrarily arrested and tortured while in detention. According to former detainees interviewed by the commission, children were treated in the same way as adults, in blatant disregard of their age. They were kept in the same cells and subject to the same methods of torture as adults.

80.   Injured children did not benefit from adequate medical treatment, given that hospitals and health clinics were not safely accessible and because adults accompanying them risked arrest. Many children are traumatized and need psychosocial support as a result of witnessing atrocities.

81.   Children's education was disrupted by the violence, movement restrictions imposed by the Government and opposition strikes and boycotts of schools. The commission also received information on how the Government used teenage children to participate in staged pro-Government demonstrations, leading many parents to keep them out of school when demonstrations were scheduled.

82.   On 10 January 2012, the President announced that school enrolment had dropped by half. He added that 30 teachers and university professors had been killed by anti-Government armed groups, and that more than 1,000 schools had been vandalized, burned or destroyed. The commission requested to be provided with details. On 15 February, the Government provided the commission with information on physical damage and looting concerning 866 schools in the governorates of Idlib (240 incidents), Dar'a (151), Damascus

(131), Homs (127), Rif Dimashq (63), Alhasak (47), Deir el-Zour (45), Tartus (19), Halab (18), Al Ladhiqiyah (12), Hama (10 and Ar Raqqah (30). The Government also highlighted that nine school directors had stones thrown at them and two had been shot and injured.

IV. Responsibility for crimes against humanity, gross violations and abuses

83.　The commission documented a widespread and systematic pattern of gross violations committed by State forces – in conditions of impunity – since March 2011. It also found instances of gross abuses committed by anti-Government armed groups. Consistent with its mandate, the commission endeavoured, where possible, to identify those responsible with a view to ensuring that perpetrators of violations, including those that may constitute crimes against humanity, are held accountable.

84.　On 31 March 2011, the Government established the National Independent Legal Commission, composed of four judges, to carry out comprehensive investigations into crimes committed in the context of the crisis. The commission enquired the Government and the Commission itself about its powers, functions and preliminary results. On 23 January 2012, the Government informed the commission that the National Independent Legal Commission and its branches in the different governorates were investigating more than 4,070 cases and that it would inform the commission about the outcome of these investigations upon their conclusion.

85.　In a speech on10 January 2012, President Assad claimed that a limited number of people working for the State had been arrested for murder and other crimes. The Government did not respond to the commission's request to provide more details on the number of arrests or the outcome of the criminal investigations pertaining to them. The Government also provided none of the requested information on any cases in which immunity from prosecution that members of the military and security forces enjoy under Decrees Nos. 14/1969 and 69/2008 had been lifted.

86.　The commission was unable to identify any case of a successful prosecution of any military or security force commanders or civilian superiors bearing responsibility for any of the crimes against humanity or other gross human rights violations in the Syrian Arab Republic since March 2011.

87.　Following a further review of its evidence, including information collected since November 2011, the commission is satisfied that a reliable body of evidence exists that, consistent with other verified circumstances, provides reasonable grounds to believe that particular individuals, including commanding officers and officials at the highest levels of Government, bear responsibility for crimes against humanity and other gross human rights violations. The commission has deposited with the United Nations High Commissioner for Human Rights a sealed envelope containing the names of these people, which might assist future credible investigations by competent authorities. The commission also identified particular army units, security agencies and their branch offices for which there are reasonable grounds to believe that they carried out gross human rights violations. FSA groups, for which the commission documented human rights abuses, are also listed.

88.　Furthermore, the commission has deposited with the High Commissioner a comprehensive database containing all evidence collected, which may be disclosed to competent authorities carrying out credible investigations, subject to witness protection and confidentiality concerns.

A.   State authorities

1.   State policies and directives

89.   The evidence collected since its first report affirms the commission's conviction that gross human rights violations were conducted pursuant to a policy of the State, and that orders to commit such violations originated from policies and directives issued at the highest levels of the armed forces and the Government.[17] This follows from the nature of the operations involving gross violations and information the commission obtained regarding the planning and implementation process.

90.   The commission interviewed individuals with inside knowledge of the planning process. It received reliable accounts that the National Security Bureau[18] of the Baath Party National Command was used to translate policy directives from a higher level into joint strategic plans underlying operations. These plans directed State forces and agencies with regard to their expected contributions to operations. On the basis of the Bureau's plans and directives, security agency directors passed orders on to their branch offices in the governorates. Orders to the army passed through the military chain of command.

91.   At the local level, military and security forces, civilian authorities and Baath Party officials coordinated operations through local security committees, which were usually dominated by the local representatives of security agencies and commanders of army units deployed in the area. On several occasions, senior security officials were deployed from the capital to coordinate operations involving crimes against humanity and other gross violations.

92.   Most crimes against humanity and gross human rights violations were carried out in complex operations that involved the entire security apparatus, and therefore would have required superior directives. The four major intelligence and security agencies with direct reporting lines to the Presidency – Military Intelligence, Air Force Intelligence, the General Intelligence Directorate and the Political Security Directorate – were at the heart of almost all operations. Most divisions of the Syrian Arab Army, and on some occasions also Syrian Arab Navy units and Air Force defence troops, participated in operations that were conducted in their areas of deployment. However, as the crisis has evolved, the elite army units closest to the leadership – the Special Forces, the Republican Guard and the Fourth Division – have played an increasingly prominent role, the latter two especially in Damascus and its suburbs.

93.   State officials, aided by certain businessmen with links to the security apparatus, also paid, armed and informally organized the groups of de facto agents known as *Shabbiha*. In a number of operations, the commission documented how *Shabbiha* members were strategically employed to commit crimes against humanity and other gross violations. In other cases, their participation was difficult to verify, as many operations also involved plain-clothed security agents.

94.   For many operations, reinforcements were sent from the capital, including on some occasions Special Forces transported by Air Force helicopters. In many cases, State officials carefully organized operations so that units were disassembled into their sub-units, which were then deployed to different places, where they would be regrouped with members of other units and members of the security forces prior to the start of operations. Testimony from defectors indicates that this strategy was employed to break bonds of trust

---

[17]   See A/HRC/S-17/2/Add.1, paras. 102 and 103.

[18]   Membership of the Bureau includes, but is not limited to, the heads of the four main intelligence and security agencies, the Deputy National Secretary of the Baath Party and the Minister for the Interior.

within the unit and to prevent collective disobedience or desertion when orders to commit crimes were received.

95.   The commission observed that large-scale operations conducted in different governorates – such as raids on neighbourhoods or attacks on larger demonstrations (see paragraphs 59 and 60 above) – often involved a similar modus operandi and related patterns of violations, which suggests that they were based on uniform directives from the State. Over the last three months of the period under review in particular, the army conducted a number of similar large-scale operations in at least four governorates, in which it surrounded entire neighbourhoods where anti-Government armed groups were present, then shelled these residential areas with heavy weapons, with complete disregard for potential civilian casualties.

96.   The most intense of these operations, conducted in Hama and Homs, were carried out after the Minister for Foreign Affairs publicly stated, on 24 January 2012, that a "security solution was imposed by necessity which has become obvious with the existence of the armed militias of the so-called 'Free Army' and other armed groups not affiliated to it that commit crimes."[19] The declaration was followed by a statement by the Minister for the Interior, on 29 January, who stressed that "the Internal Security Forces' keenness on continuing efforts to purify the Syrian land from all outlaws to achieve justice and restore stability and security to Syria."[20]

2.   Individual responsibility for violations

97.   In examining specific operations, the commission received credible and consistent evidence identifying high- and mid-ranking members of the armed forces who ordered their subordinates to shoot at unarmed protestors, kill soldiers who refused to obey such orders, arrest persons without cause, mistreat detained persons and attack civilian neighbourhoods with indiscriminate tank and machine-gun fire. In some cases, they gave explicit orders to commit crimes, in others they used more general terms (e.g. "use any force necessary") that, in the circumstances, left no room for interpretation. The commission verified that, in some locations, individual army officers ordered the indiscriminate shelling of civilian neighbourhoods in urban areas such as Hama, Al Ladhiqiyah, Dar'a and Homs.

98.   Individual officers in the armed forces and Government security forces personally killed, unlawfully imprisoned, tortured, or committed other inhumane acts against innocent civilians. Officers shot unarmed protestors, including children, as well as medical doctors, ambulance drivers and mourners at funerals in cities such as Al Ladhiqiyah, Dar'a, Saida (Dar'a governorate), Zabadani and Jobar (Rif Dimashq governorate) and Almastoumah (Idlib governorate).

99.   Army officers and members of the security forces also aided and abetted attacks against civilians; for example, commanders of Government security forces routinely placed their units behind conscripts to ensure that the soldiers would fire at demonstrators. On several occasions, security forces shot conscripts who disobeyed orders to shoot protestors. Furthermore, military officers and commanders of security forces often stationed their units at checkpoints and other strategic locations in urban areas so that other units could attack neighbourhoods to loot homes and arrest residents. In addition, security force commanders

[19] "Al-Moallem: the observers' report didn't please those plotting against Syria: the solution is Syrian and based on the people's interests", SANA, 24 January 2012. Available from www.sana.sy/eng/21/2012/01/24/396268.htm.
[20] "Interior Ministry honors families of martyrs", SANA, 29 January 2012. Available from www.sana.sy/eng/21/2012/01/29/397129.htm.

managed detention centres throughout the country where prisoners were subjected to torture, sexual assaults and other inhumane acts.

3. Command and superior responsibility

100. A number of military commanders and civilian superiors may reasonably be suspected of responsibility for crimes against humanity because of their knowing failure to take all necessary and reasonable measures within their power to prevent or repress the commission of relevant crimes by their subordinates or to submit the matter to the competent authorities.

101. During the past year, soldiers and members of security forces who refused to obey manifestly unlawful orders to commit crimes against humanity frequently were subjected to severe punishment, including execution, a vivid illustration of the level of control that commanders hold over their subordinates. The broad and repetitive nature of these crimes and the availability of public reports on such crimes by international media broadcasting in Arabic, United Nations human rights mechanisms and the observer mission of the League of Arab States all indicate that military commanders and civilian superiors at the highest levels must have had knowledge of such events. On 7 December 2011, in a televised interview, the President himself referred to the findings made by the present commission in its first report.

102. Notwithstanding this knowledge about crimes, no serious effort was made to prevent and repress them. As discussed above, the commission is not aware of any successful prosecutions; indeed, the commission documented how some officers who directly participated in crimes against humanity were promoted or commended. The commission's evidence also demonstrates a consistent and continuing effort by the Government, the military and the security forces to conceal the facts about crimes. State officials often forced families of those killed by State forces to sign declarations attributing responsibility to armed groups before they would allow the body of the person killed to be released. Where such false declarations were signed, branch offices of the National Independent Legal Commission refused to carry out investigations. The commission of inquiry also found that pro-Government media were used to cover up violations or falsely attribute them to anti-Government armed groups.

103. Structural obstacles, including the immunity from prosecution enjoyed by members of the State forces, and the dependence of the judiciary on the presidency and the Baath Party have fostered impunity.[21]

104. Under the present legal framework and circumstances, it appears that the judiciary lacks the capacity to effectively address crimes against humanity committed on the basis of State policy.

B. Anti-Government armed groups, including Free Syrian Army groups

105. By all accounts, anti-Government armed groups, especially FSA groups, have become much more active since November 2011. The commission assumes to have described only part of the spectrum of anti-Government armed groups that have emerged and their activities.

---

[21] A/HRC/S.17/2/Add.1, paras. 21 and 22.

1. Free Syrian Army policies and lack of central control

106.   The commission carefully reviewed the information gathered on the operations and activities to date of FSA groups. In this regard, the commission notes that, at a minimum, human rights obligations constituting peremptory international law (*ius cogens*) bind States, individuals and non-State collective entities, including armed groups. Acts violating *ius cogens* – for instance, torture or enforced disappearances – can never be justified.

107.   FSA leaders abroad also assured the commission that the FSA was committed to conducting its operations in accordance with human rights and international law. They requested guidance in shaping rules of engagement consistent with this undertaking. The FSA leadership indicated to the commission that commanders in the field currently made their own rules of engagement in accordance with the training received in the Syrian Armed Forces.

108.   The commission was unable to ascertain the extent to which the FSA leadership abroad commanded and controlled the various FSA groups operating in the Syrian Arab Republic. It received conflicting accounts from inside the country. Some local groups seem to recognize the leadership, yet may not communicate with it regularly or receive specific orders from it. Others merely adopt the name "FSA" to underscore their revolutionary aspirations, their army background or the fact that they are not *Shabbiha*. The commission also received information about Syrian civilians reinforcing anti-Government armed groups, which increases problems of effective control even at the level of local FSA groups. The FSA leadership abroad indicated to the commission that groups on the ground did not receive orders from it. The leadership saw its role as facilitating coordination between different FSA groups and ensuring its media outreach.

109.   As the commission was unable to verify the existence of a functioning chain of command or a superior/subordinate relationship between the highest leadership of the FSA and local units, it was unable to determine individual responsibility of FSA leaders abroad. Rather, the commission's findings pertain to violations perpetrated by FSA groups in different locations within the country.

2. Abuses by Free Syrian Army groups and other armed groups

110.   The Government, in public statements and communications to the commission, repeatedly stated that anti-Government armed groups, in particular FSA groups, had committed gross abuses of human rights. In its note verbale addressed to the commission dated 23 January 2012 (annex XI), the Government referred to "acts of kidnapping, killing, mutilation, forced and involuntary disappearance and violations of the right to life committed by armed groups against Syrian citizens, including women, children and personnel of the army and security forces". It also mentioned "the killing and forced displacement of anyone who did not comply with the orders of armed groups to participate in protests, strikes, civil disobedience or did not subscribe to their terrorist agenda." SANA has alleged such incidents in its daily reporting.

111.   The commission repeatedly invited the Government to provide information on specific cases. On 15 February 2012, the Government provided a list of specific incidents, providing the date, place and details on "armed actions by terrorist armed gangs" for the period from 23 December 2011 to 10 February 2012. The lists details attacks in all 14 governorates on military and security forces and civilian targets such as schools, universities, factories and warehouses. In the category of attacks on public and State property, 212 incidents are detailed; another 162 incidents concerned bombings or attempted bombings, and 85 incidents involved attacks on installations of the State forces and the police.

112. In its report, the League of Arab States referred to bombing of buildings, trains carrying fuel, vehicles carrying diesel oil and explosions targeting the police, members of the media and fuel pipelines. Without further disaggregating responsibility, the League concluded that some of the attacks had been carried out by the FSA, and others by other anti-Government armed groups.

113. The commission documented instances of gross human rights abuses committed by members of various FSA groups.

114. In Homs, FSA members were found to have tortured and executed suspected *Shabbiha* members in retaliation for abuses committed by *Shabbiha* or plain-clothed security officials posing as them. In late January 2012, in Karm Al-Zeitun, FSA members and others lynched a man suspected of working with the State security forces, and paraded his body on a pick-up truck through the streets.

115. In late December 2011, FSA members in Bab Amr captured two suspected *Shabbiha* members following an exchange of fire. The two men were beaten by the local population. In this instance, FSA members pulled the men away from the angry mob and took them for interrogation to an undisclosed location.

116. In November 2011, in Bab Amr, armed group members abducted a foreign media worker and mistreated him for several hours before releasing him.

117. There were also reports of FSA members in Homs taking security agents, their family members or foreign nationals of certain countries hostage to obtain the release of people detained by State forces. The FSA leadership acknowledged in a written exchange with the commission that FSA groups had indeed abducted foreign nationals, but described those captured as foreign fighters.

118. Some armed civilians in Homs, including armed civilians belonging to the FSA, sought to exact blood revenge for abuses by killing family members of security personnel or *Shabbiha*. The FSA leadership in Homs and also the local coordination committee denounced such collective reprisals and tried to contain them.

119. Credible reports indicated that members of FSA groups in other locations had tortured or summarily executed captured members of the armed forces or security forces. In mid-November 2011, members of the FSA near Talbiseh tortured a member of Military Intelligence during an interrogation. The captured man was beaten, whipped with a cable and threatened with a knife. In late November 2011, a FSA group from Rif Dimashq captured, tortured and killed a member of the security forces.

120. The commission highlights the fact that FSA members, including local commanders that have command responsibility, may incur criminal responsibility under international law.

V. Conclusions and recommendations

121. **The grave and ongoing human rights crisis in the Syrian Arab Republic is the consequence of a combination of factors, including a State that has failed to respond to the legitimate political, economic and social demands of its people and its position in the highly complex geopolitics of the region.**

122. **The response of the security apparatus to what started as peaceful dissent soon led to armed clashes. One year later, the Syrian Arab Republic is on the brink of an internal armed conflict. Diverging agendas within a deeply divided international community complicate the prospects for ending the violence.**

123. The socio-economic situation in the country has deteriorated, leaving the vast majority of the population in a state of disarray. Meeting basic needs to sustain everyday life has become increasingly difficult for the population at large. In this respect, the commission of inquiry does not support the imposition of economic sanctions that would have negative impact on the human rights of the population, in particular of vulnerable groups.

124. The continuation of the crisis carries the risk of radicalizing the population, deepening inter-communal tensions and eroding the fabric of society.

125. The commission remains convinced that the only possible solution to end the violence is an inclusive dialogue leading to a negotiated settlement that effectively ensures the human rights of all people in the country.

126. The Government has manifestly failed in its responsibility to protect the population; its forces have committed widespread, systematic and gross human rights violations, amounting to crimes against humanity, with the apparent knowledge and consent of the highest levels of the State. Anti-Government armed groups have also committed abuses, although not comparable in scale and organization with those carried out by the State.

127. In accordance with international law, the responsibility to investigate, prosecute and punish international crimes and other gross violations rests first and foremost with the State. The crimes against humanity and other gross violations documented in the commission's reports have been committed, however, within a system of impunity. Profound structural reforms in the political, justice and security sectors are necessary to break the culture of impunity and to deliver justice to the victims.

128. Reconciliation and accountability should be based on broad, inclusive and credible consultations involving all Syrian people and situated within the framework of international law. International justice mechanisms could be used to support and complement national efforts.

129. In the meantime, thorough monitoring of the situation of human rights needs to be continued and evidence of international crimes and other gross violations systematically collected to facilitate the process of holding those responsible for such acts accountable.

130. The commission makes the recommendations below to immediately end the violence and to initiate a longer process to achieve reform, reconciliation and accountability.

A. Ending violence

131. The commission calls for an urgent, inclusive political dialogue, bringing together the Government, opposition and anti-Government actors to negotiate an end to the violence, to ensure respect for human rights and to address the legitimate demands of the Syrian people. A contact group composed of States with diverse positions on the situation in the Syrian Arab Republic should be established to initiate a process leading to such a political dialogue. An international peace conference should be convened as soon as possible to facilitate this process.

132. The commission recommends that the Government implement the recommendations issued in its first report,[22] and that it also:

(a) Ensure that all people in detention are informed promptly of the reasons for their detention and any charges against them, and allowed prompt and regular access to a lawyer of their choice and visits by their families, who should also be notified about their status and location;

(b) Conduct fair trials for deserters and armed group members, and ensure that no evidence obtained by torture is relied on;

(c) Take all feasible measures to locate and identify persons who died during the unrest and determine the fate of disappeared persons;

(d) Deploy civilian police, instead of the army or security forces, to control and protect protests by unarmed civilians, and provide them with training and non-lethal equipment to control crowds in compliance with international standards;

(e) Publish a list of all places currently being used as detention facilities, together with information on the agency or unit responsible for their supervision;

(f) Publish the rules of engagement guiding army and security force operations against anti-Government armed groups.

133. The commission renews its recommendation that all armed groups ensure respect for and act in accordance with international human rights law. Armed groups, in particular the FSA and its local groups, should:

(a) Adopt and publicly announce rules of conduct that are in accordance with international human rights law and other applicable international standards, including those reflected in the Declaration of Minimum Humanitarian Standards;[23]

(b) Publicly pledge not to torture or execute captured soldiers, *Shabbiha* members or civilians, not to target people who take no part in the clashes, and not to take hostages, whether civilian or military;

(c) Instruct FSA members to abide by these commitments and hold perpetrators of abuses within their ranks accountable;

(d) Take care to minimize the risk of civilians coming under Government fire or facing reprisals as a result of the deployment of FSA members in specific places;

(e) Provide relevant humanitarian and human rights institutions with all available information on the fate of persons it has captured, and give such actors full and unimpeded access to detainees.

134. The commission recommends that the United Nations include a strong human rights component in any international mission deployed to the Syrian Arab Republic, with the mandate and capacity to monitor effectively any human rights violations, including those involving violence against women, children and minorities.

135. The commission recommends that OHCHR and the future Special Rapporteur on the situation of human rights in the Syrian Arab Republic continue to identify, where possible, those responsible for international crimes with a view to ensure that perpetrators are held accountable. OHCHR, in cooperation with the Special

---

[22] A/HRC/17-2/Add.1, para. 112.
[23] E/CN.4/1995/116.

Rapporteur, should maintain and update the confidential database established by the commission.

B. Reconciliation, accountability and reparation

136. The commission recommends that the Syrian Arab Republic carry out profound political, justice and security sector reforms. These should include the removal of legal and institutional obstacles to the independence of the judiciary; the abolition of immunities from prosecution enjoyed by members of the military and security forces; a credible vetting process to remove officers involved in gross human rights violations from the military and security forces; a comprehensive reform of the Penal Code; the ratification of the Rome Statute of the International Criminal Court; and the adoption of domestic legislation consistent with it.

137. The Syrian people, on the basis of broad, inclusive and credible consultations, should determine, within the framework provided by international law, the process and mechanisms to achieve reconciliation, truth and accountability for gross violations occurring since March 2011, as well as reparations and effective remedies for the victims. Women, minorities and victims groups should be adequately represented.

138. The process should provide for reparation and effective remedies for victims and their families. The international community should contribute to make adequate reparation possible.

139. The commission recommends that the Syrian Arab Republic seek technical assistance with regard to reform and consultation processes and related training for policymakers, judges, prosecutors and security sector officials from the United Nations, in particular OHCHR. To facilitate the process to achieve reconciliation and accountability, the international community should consider implementing the jurisdiction of suitable international justice mechanisms.

Annexes

Annex I

Note verbale dated 13 December 2011 addressed to the Permanent Representative of the Syrian Arab Republic

NATIONS UNIES

HAUT COMMISSARIAT AUX DROITS DE L'HOMME

UNITED NATIONS

HIGH COMMISSIONER FOR HUMAN RIGHTS

Tel: 41-22-9179101

Independent International Commission of Inquiry pursuant to resolution A/HRC/S-17/1

The Independent International Commission of Inquiry on the Syrian Arab Republic presents its compliments to the Permanent Representative of the Syrian Arab Republic to the United Nations Office at Geneva and specialized institutions in Switzerland, and refers to its notes verbales of 29 September 2011, 19 October 2011 and 4 November 2011, as well to the Chairperson's letter of 27 October 2011. The Commission also takes note of the letter dated 12 October 2011 from the Permanent Representative of the Syrian Arab Republic and the note verbale dated 17 November 2011 from the Syrian Arab Republic addressed to the Independent International Commission of Inquiry.

In its report, transmitted to the Syrian Arab Republic and the President of the Human Rights Council on 28 November 2011, the Commission strove to reflect the position of the Government of the Syrian Arab Republic, including existing policies and announced reforms expressed in public pronouncements and media reports. The Commission believes that a visit to the country would have allowed the Commission to interact directly with Government officials and to ascertain the circumstances of the reported killing of members of the military and security forces. The Commission remains eager to reach out to their families and to wounded soldiers, as well as to suffering civilians across Syrian communities. It also looks forward to the opportunity of meeting the members of the National Independent Special Legal Commission and learning about its work and findings.

In this context, the Commission wishes to reiterate its request to visit the Syrian Arab Republic as part of fulfilling its mandate and in preparation of the written update requested by the Human Rights Council for its 19th session. The Commission looks forward to the results of the 12 December 2011 local elections and to interact with newly elected officials.

The Commission avails itself of this opportunity to renew to the Permanent Representative of the Syrian Arab Republic assurances of its highest consideration.

13 December 2011

Annex II

Note verbale dated 21 December 2011 from the Permanent Representative of the Syrian Arab Republic addressed to the commission

MISSION PERMANENTE

DE LA

RÉPUBLIQUE ARABE SYRIENNE

GENÈVE

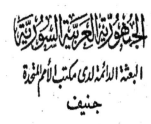

21 December, 2011

598/11

The Permanent Mission of the Syrian Arab Republic to the United Nations Office and other International Organizations in Geneva presents its compliments to The Office of the High Commissioner for Human Rights, and in reference to the Note Verbal of the Independent International Commission of Inquiry pursuant to resolution A/HRC/S-17/1 dated 13/12/2011; has the honour to attach herewith the respond of the Syrian Arab Republic Government to the request of the Commission to visit Syria.

The Permanent Mission of the Syrian Arab Republic avails itself of this opportunity to renew to The Office of the High Commissioner for Human Rights the assurances of its highest consideration.

OHCHR REGISTRY

2 2 DEC 2011

Recipients :..M.E.N.A...............

....

....

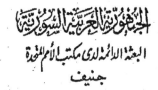

MISSION PERMANENTE
DE LA
RÉPUBLIQUE ARABE SYRIENNE
GENÈVE

Mr. Chairperson and Members of the Independent International Commission of Inquiry pursuant to resolution A/HRC/S-17/1

We received your Note Verbal dated 13/12/2011, which reiterates the request of the commission to visit the Syrian Arab Republic "as part of fulfilling its mandate and in preparation of the written update" to its report published on 13/11/2011, in which you politicized the human rights situation in Syria in an unprofessional, selective and subjective manner, where you undertook what you called "investigations" in a way that lacks the simplest basis of professional investigation, and consigns with the agenda of certain countries aiming to destroy Syria, and to intervene militarily in Syria under the pretext of "protecting the civilians".

You have grossly exceeded your mandate by holding the Syrian Government fully accountable for what has been going on in Syria, while you have given a blind eye to the violations of human rights committed by the terrorist groups, and you have refrained from referring to millions of dollars funneled to these groups in the form of money, weapons, and media and logistical support, aiming to ruin Syria and kill its people.

Syria has fully cooperated with you, despite the fact that it has not approved of the resolution establishing your committee, and has provided you with numerous documents and documented information regarding the real situation in Syria.

367

However, you have ignored everything you have received from Syria and you were content only with certain references to them in your report, calling them "allegations" or annexes.

Syria has reiterated that it has formed an independent, impartial and honest judicial Investigation Commission with wide powers to investigate all the crimes committed in the context of the recent events. The Judicial Commission is working continuously to prove the truth for the sake of comforting the souls of the victims and to punish the perpetrators. We have repeatedly clarified that this Commission has not concluded its work yet, and that the Syrian government does not want to anticipate its work and to present non-objective or politically motivated results as did the International Commission of Inquiry in its report. Furthermore, we have reiterated our readiness to consider cooperation with the international commission of inquiry after the Syrian investigation committee has reached concrete results. However, you chose to refuse this and instead turned to listening to whom you call witnesses from international and regional organizations and journalists and NGOs, and those whom you call "defectors from the military and security services". You have interviewed 223 "witnesses" as mentioned in your report, which leads us here to ask you: Have you called upon any of the martyr Sari Saoud's family members to listen to their testimony? Or have you listened to the testimony of the "deceased" Zainab, whom you have added to the list of "civilians killed by the security forces" and those you described as "Al Shabiha" based on media reports, which later turned out to be alive? Or have you listened to the testimony of any of the family members of the martyr General Abdo Kheder Tallawi's who was killed along with his three children in cold blood and whose bodies were mutilated? And why have you refused all of the documented information you received from Syria regarding the case of the child Hamza Al Khatib and preferred instead certain false media reports in order to form serious accusations against Syria of committing crimes against humanity.

You have relied upon interviews with politicians, journalists, and persons who have interest in destroying Syria, as well as non-Syrian citizens, some of whom are from countries that are involved in the events causing the deaths of Syrians on a daily basis. Some of those are directly contributing to the fabrications of stories against Syria, and others have Syrian blood on their hands. You have shut your ears to the voices of the real victims. How do you claim impartiality and objectivity while you have never met any of the above mentioned victims and many others who have suffered from the scourge of terrorism in Syria?

Hundreds of terrorists have publically admitted that they killed protestors and that they were involved in looting, killing, mutilating bodies, and fabricating stories in return of money they received from some neighboring countries. Those people described the killings of whoever did not protest with them or cooperated in ruining Syria. They also proudly spoke of the burnings, mutilations of bodies, and rape.

You have ignored all of our confirmed information as well as the confirmed information of a number of news agencies upon which you relied in your investigations pertaining to the existence of armed groups killing innocent people and targeting the army, security, intellectuals and scientists in Syria. With the aim to draw the attention to the non peaceful nature of the events in Syria, we have previously informed the office of the High Commissioner for Human Rights on 22/06/2011 of the death of more than /260/ martyrs from the army and security forces in armed attacks. This number grew to /600/ martyrs by 20/08/2011, and then /1100/ by 19/10/2011. The total number of martyrs has now surpassed /2000/ members of the security forces and the Syrian Army, this while you still refuse to believe or listen to the fact that terrorist acts are being committed in Syria. Is there no place for these facts in your report?

We did not find any indication to the destruction of railways, oil pipelines, as well as the burning of schools, hospitals and official establishments, nor any reference to the destruction of the infrastructure and the ruining of the economy. Do the victims of these violations not deserve your attention?

Does the terrorizing of civilians and forcing them to abandon their homes and properties, and rending them displaced in areas of a certain sectarian color, and killing them and mutilating their bodies to divide the country on a sectarian basis - in a clear violation of their right to life, and a violation of the prevention of extrajudicial killing as well as the violation of the freedom of religion and belief, does it not deserve any attention from you considering that you have been mandated to investigate these violations? And we ask here: do you plan to call for any non-politicized action to address these issues other than the call for military intervention in Syria?

How can the Commission confirm that crimes against humanity have been committed without having followed the simplest rules of professional and objective investigation in collecting evidence? Unfortunately the International Commission of Inquiry chose to describe everything that it has received concerning these gross violations of human rights in Syria as allegations, while it considered everything all the allegations made by journalists and representatives of NGOs as confirmed and documented information, even though this information is not linked in any way with evidence. The Commission was deliberately selective in using information regardless of its source and credibility, in a clear breach of the basic principles of impartiality, objectiveness and professionalism implemented in any investigation process. The report lacks professionalism in its preparation and precision in the information and method, and has used erroneous and fabricated information to launch serious accusations and in making recommendations that go in the direction towards intensifying the campaign waged by certain countries against Syria. Therefore, this report cannot be considered separate from this campaign.

The Commission has fully exceeded its mandate, and surpassed its original mission of investigating violations of International Human Rights Law free from double standards and politicization. The Commission immersed itself in the campaign against Syria in a clear violation of its mandate and the resolution establishing it.

The Commission failed to abide by one of the most important objectives of the United Nations which is the obligation to refrain from the threat or use of force against the territorial integrity or political independence of any state. The Commission's report was completely politicized and selective, and lacks professionalism and the simplest rules of International Law and Rules of International Human Rights Law, but also the Charter of the United Nations. It has become clear that one cannot build on this report in any future action against Syria, and raises serious questions about the credibility of the Commission.

Syria has previously underlined, and also reiterates today that the only solution to this crises is national dialogue. Unfortunately, the commission has failed to call for any form of national dialogue, and preferred to violate the Human Rights of the Syrian citizens, first and foremost the right of life, by calling for foreign armies to intervene in Syria.

Syria has chosen the path of reform and fulfilling the demands of its people, and to investigate the events in an impartial and honest manner. Syria also has chosen the path of dialogue. We expect the Commission to contribute to the achievement of these goals, and to participate in helping Syrians to move peacefully through dialogue towards a better future, and not through calling for the intervention of foreign armies under the pretext of the Protection of Civilians.

We call upon you to listen to the voice of righteousness, justice and objectivity, and to reflect the truth as it comes from the voices of those who know it and live it, and not through allegations of people living thousands of miles from Syria and who are implicated in acts of killings and terrorizing Syrians. We also call upon you not to follow the calls for foreign intervention in Syria and ask you to restore your true role in investigating human rights violations, and to support reform and dialogue plans in Syria in order to overcome this crisis which is draining precious Syrian blood to the benefit of foreign agendas that do not help in protecting and promoting human rights.

In light of the above, and in light of: your lack of commitment to the principles of professional, non-politicized and non-selective investigation; your lack of concern to expose the reality and the violations of victims' rights committed by terrorists groups against Syrians; and your satisfaction with exposing the mere of what you receive from the Syrian authorities and describing it as "allegations" or adding them in "annexes"; we do not see at the present time any benefit in any request to visit Syria. We await seeing a real change in the direction of working towards revealing the truth according to real testimonies of real witnesses and victims of human rights violations. Only then you will find all our doors open for you in Syria.

Kindly accept our highest considerations.

nnex III

Note verbale dated 27 December 2011 from the Permanent Representative of the Syrian Arab Republic addressed to the President of the Human Rights Council

MISSION PERMANENTE
DE LA
RÉPUBLIQUE ARABE SYRIENNE
GENÈVE

الجمهورية العربية السورية
البعثة الدائمة لدى مكتب الأم المتحدة
جنيف

OHCHR REGISTRY

2 7 DEC 2011
Recipients : ....H.R.Consil.
....
....

N° 611 / 11

Geneva, 27ᵗʰ December 2011

The Permanent Mission of the Syrian Arab Republic to the United Nations Office and other International Organizations in Geneva presents its compliments to The Office of the High Commissioner for Human Rights, and following all the Mission's communications regarding the recent events in the Syrian Arab Republic, has the honour to forward to H.E Ms. Laura Dupuy Lasserre, President of the Human Rights Council the attached official statistics of the documented acts of killing, kidnapping, looting, and car theft that took place in the Syrian Arab Republic between 15/03/2011 and 19/12/2011.

The Permanent Mission of the Syrian Arab Republic kindly requests the publication of the above mentioned document, in all official languages of the UN, as official documents of the Human Rights Council.

The Permanent Mission of the Syrian Arab Republic avails itself of this opportunity to renew to the President of the Human Rights Council, the assurances of its highest consideration.

H.E Ms. Laura Dupuy Lasserre
President of the Human Rights
The Office of the High Commisioner for Human Rights
Palais des Nations
1211 — Geneva 10

إحصائيات بحوادث (القتل والخطف والسلب وسرقة السيارات) في القطر منذ بداية الأحداث وحتى تاريخ ٢٠١١/١٢/١٩م

أولاً . حوادث القتل الواقعة على المدنيين والعسكريين والشرطة، وفقاً لتقارير المشافي، والضبوط المنظمة من قبل الوحدات الشرطية، وبلغ عددها /٣٢٥٩/ موزعة على الشكل التالي :

١. حوادث القتل الواقعة على المدنيين :

المحافظة	دمشق	ريف دمشق	درعا	السويداء	القنيطرة	حمص	حماة	طرطوس	اللاذقية	إدلب	حلب	الرقة	دير الزور	الحسكة	المجموع
العدد	٨٥	١٥٣	٣٤١	–	–	٨٢٩	٢٨٠	٢٢	١٢٤	٢٤٣	١٠	–	٤٢	٢	٢١٣١

علماً أن هناك عدد غير معروف من القتلى المدنيين خلال الأحداث لم يتم التعرف على عددهم نظراً لعدم إمكانية الوصول إلى جثثهم، أو تنظيم ضبوط بمقتلهم بسبب دفنهم فوراً من قبل ذويهم دون الإعلام عن وفاتهم، أو دفن بعضهم من قبل المسلحين حتى لا يتم التعرف عليهم.

٢. حوادث القتل الواقعة على العسكريين :

(الشهداء من الجيش ٩١٣) وفقاً لقائمة وزارة الدفاع المرسلة لمكتب الأمن القومي حتى تاريخ ٢٠١١/١٢/١٨م .

٣. حوادث القتل الواقعة على الشرطة (الشهداء من الشرطة ٢١٥):

المحافظة	دمشق	ريف دمشق	درعا	السويداء	القنيطرة	حمص	حماة	طرطوس	اللاذقية	إدلب	حلب	الرقة	دير الزور	الحسكة	المجموع
العدد	٣	١٥	٢٢	–	–	٨٣	٥٥	–	١	٢٩	–	–	٦	١	٢١٥

ثانياً : حوادث السلب بالعنف الواقعة على الأشخاص أو الآليات، ويبلغ عددها /١٦٦٣/ حادثة موزعة على الشكل التالي :

١. حوادث السلب بالعنف الواقعة على الأشخاص:

المحافظة	دمشق	ريف دمشق	درعا	السويداء	القنيطرة	حمص	حماة	طرطوس	اللاذقية	إدلب	حلب	الرقة	دير الزور	الحسكة	المجموع
العدد	٥	٢١	١٩	١٨	–	٩٩	٧٨	٢	٨	١١١	٣٠	٤	٢٣	١٠	٤٦٨

٢. حوادث السلب بالعنف الواقعة على الآليات ، وفقاً لما ورد في التقارير المرفقة :

المحافظة	دمشق	ريف دمشق	درعا	السويداء	القنيطرة	حمص	حماة	طرطوس	اللاذقية	إدلب	حلب	الرقة	دير الزور	الحسكة	المجموع
العدد	١٠	٥٥	–	–	–	١٠٧	٣٠٨	٦	–	٦٦١	٤٤	٣	١	–	١١٩٥

ثالثاً : حوادث الخطف الواقعة على المدنيين والعسكريين والشرطة، وفقاً لما تم التبليغ عنه، والنتيجة التي آلت إليه عملية الخطف، ويبلغ عددهم /٩٠٠/ حادثة موزعة على الشكل التالي :

١ . حوادث خطف المدنيين:

المحافظة	إجمالي المخطوفين	النتيجة المترتبة على الخطف					
		قتل بعد الخطف	ترك بفدية	ترك بدون فدية	ترك بعد ساعات	تحرير	مجهول المصير
دمشق	٨	ــ	ــ	٤	١	ــ	٣
ريف دمشق	٢٥	٣	٢	١٦	ــ	ــ	٤
درعا	٣	١	ــ	٢	ــ	ــ	ــ
السويداء	ــ	ــ	ــ	ــ	ــ	ــ	ــ
القنيطرة	ــ	ــ	ــ	ــ	ــ	ــ	ــ
حمص	٣٨٨	٧٣	٢	٢١٩	٨	٦	٨٠
حماة	١٢٩	١٠	١٠	٥٩	ــ	١	٤٩
طرطوس	ــ	ــ	ــ	ــ	ــ	ــ	ــ
اللاذقية	٤	ــ	ــ	٤	ــ	ــ	ــ
إدلب	٩٩	٩	٥	٧١	ــ	ــ	١٤
حلب	٧	ــ	٣	٣	ــ	ــ	١
الرقة	ــ	ــ	ــ	ــ	ــ	ــ	ــ
دير الزور	ــ	ــ	ــ	ــ	ــ	ــ	ــ
الحسكة	٣	ــ	ــ	٢	ــ	ــ	١
المجموع	٦٣٢	٩٢	٢٢	٣٨٠	٩	٧	١٥٣

٢ . حوادث خطف العسكريين ، وفقاً لما ورد في التقارير المرفقة :

المحافظة	إجمالي المخطوفين	قتل بعد الخطف	ترك بفدية	ترك بدون فدية	ترك بعد معليه	تحرير	هروب	مجهول المصير
ريف دمشق	ــ	ــ	ــ	ــ	ــ	ــ	ــ	ــ
درعا	٢	ــ	١ مقابل /١٤٠٠/ طلقة	ــ	٨ سلب سلاحه	ــ	ــ	ــ
السويداء	ــ	ــ	ــ	ــ	ــ	ــ	ــ	ــ
القنيطرة	ــ	ــ	ــ	ــ	ــ	ــ	ــ	ــ
حمص	١٧	٣	ــ	١	ــ	٣	ــ	١٠
حماه	٢٤	١	ــ	٢	ــ	ــ	ــ	٢١
طرطوس	ــ	ــ	ــ	ــ	ــ	ــ	ــ	ــ
اللاذقية	ــ	ــ	ــ	ــ	ــ	ــ	ــ	ــ
إدلب	٢٢	١	١	٣	ــ	ــ	ــ	١٧
حلب	١	١	ــ	ــ	ــ	ــ	ــ	ــ
الرقة	ــ	ــ	ــ	ــ	ــ	ــ	ــ	ــ
دير الزور	٤	ــ	ــ	٣	ــ	ــ	ــ	١
الحسكة	ــ	ــ	ــ	ــ	ــ	ــ	ــ	ــ
المجموع	٧٠	٥	٣	٩	١	٣	ــ	٤٩

٣. حوادث خطف الشرطة ، وفقاً لما ورد في التقارير المرفقة :

المحافظة	عدد المخطوفين الإجمالي	قتل بعد الخطف	ترك بفدية	ترك بدون فدية	ترك بعد تسليمه	تجريد	هروب	مجهول المصير
ريف دمشق	٢	—	١	—	—	—	—	١
درعا	٨	٢	—	٢	طلب معلوماتهما	١	١	—
السويداء	—	—	—	—	—	—	—	—
القنيطرة	—	—	—	—	—	—	—	—
حمص	١٥	٤	—	٧	—	—	—	٤
حماة	٧٢	٤	—	٣١	—	—	—	٣٧
دمشق	١	—	—	١	—	—	—	—
طرطوس	—	—	—	—	—	—	—	—
اللاذقية	١	—	—	١	—	—	—	—
إدلب	٣١	٦	—	١٣	—	—	—	١٢
حلب	٣٠	—	—	٢٩	—	—	—	١
الرقة	—	—	—	—	—	—	—	—
دير الزور	٤	—	—	١	—	—	٣	—
الحسكة	—	—	—	—	—	—	—	—
المجموع	١٦٤	١٦	١	٨٥	٢	١	٤	١٥٥

رابعاً ـ السيارات المسروقة في المحافظات، ويبلغ عددها /٨٨٨/ سيارة موزعة على الشكل التالي :

١. السيارات الشرطية :

المحافظة											
العدد	—	—	—	٥	—	٤	—	—	—	—	—

٢. السيارات الحكومية :

المحافظة	دمشق		درعا		السويداء	القنيطرة	حمص	حماة	اللاذقية	طرطوس		الرقة	الحسكة	المجموع
العدد	—	٣	٢	—	—	٤١	١٢٧	١	—	١١٧	٤	—	١	٢٩٥

٣. السيارات المدنية :

المحافظة														المجموع
العدد	٤٧	٧٧	٨	—	—	١١٧	١١٨	٩	—	١٥٩	٢٦	١	٢١	٥٨٣

ـ ربطاً ملف تفصيلي.

(Unofficial translation)

Statistics of Acts of Killing, Kidnapping, Looting and Car Theft from 15/3/2011 - 19/12/2011

Source: letter from the Permanent Mission of the Syrian Arab Republic dated 27/12/2011

1. Killing incidents of civilians, military personnel and policemen according to hospital reports and policing units

Province	Total	Hassakah	Deir Al Zour	Al Raqah	Aleppo	Idlib	Al Ladhiqiyah	Tartus	Hamah	Homs	Al Qunaytirah	Al Suwayda	Draa	Rif Dimashq	Damascus
Killings of civilians[a]	2,131	2	42	–	10	234	124	22	280	829	–	–	341	153	85
Killing of policemen	215	1	6	–	–	29	1	–	55	83	–	–	22	15	3
Killing of soldiers (based on information provided by the Office of National Security as of 18.12.2011)	913														
Total	**3,259**														

[a] The list is not exhaustive because the State could not physically reach all bodies, or because they were buried by family members or armed groups

2. Looting

Province	Total	Hassakah	Deir Al Zour	Al Raqah	Aleppo	Idlib	Al Ladhiqiyah	Tartus	Hamah	Homs	Al Qunaytirah	Al Suwayda	Draa	Rif Dimashq	Damascus
Civilians	468	10	23	4	30	111	8	2	78	99	–	18	19	61	5
Vehicles	1,195	–	1	3	44	661	–	6	308	107	–	–	–	55	10
Total	**1,663**														

Kidnapping incidents: Civilians, military personnel and policemen and the result

Kidnapped civilians	Total	Killing after kidnapping	Released after ransom	Released without ransom	Released after looting	Liberation	unknown destiny
Damascus	8	–	–	4	1	–	3
Rif Dimashq	25	3	2	16	–	–	4
Draa	3	1	–	2	–	–	–
Al Suwayda	–	–	–	–	–	–	–
Al Qunaytirah	–	–	–	–	–	–	–
Homs	388	73	2	219	8	6	80
Hamah	129	10	10	59	–	1	49
Tartus	–	–	–	–	–	–	–
Al Ladhiqiyah	4	–	–	4	–	–	–
Idlib	99	9	5	71	–	–	14
Aleppo	7	–	3	3	–	–	1
Al Raqa	–	–	–	–	–	–	–
Deir Al Zour	–	–	–	–	–	–	–
Hassakah	3	–	–	2	–	–	1
Total	**666**	**96**	**22**	**380**	**9**	**7**	**152**

Kidnapped military personnel	Total	Killing after kidnapping	Released after ransom	Released without ransom	Released after looting	Liberation	Escaped	unknown destiny
Rif Dimashq	–	–	–	–	–	–	–	–
Dar'a	2	–	1 (1,400 bullets)	1 (weapon)		–	–	–
Al Suwayda	–	–	–	–	–	–	–	–
Al Qunaytirah	–	–	–	–	–	–	–	–
Homs	17	3	–	1	–	3	–	10
Hamah	24	1	–	2	–	–	–	21
Tartus	–	–	–	–	–	–	–	–
Al Ladhiqiyah	–	–	–	–	–	–	–	–
Idlib	22	1	1	3	–	–	–	17
Aleppo	1	–	1	–	–	–	–	–
Al Raqa	–	–	–	–	–	–	–	–
Deir el-Zour	4	–	–	3	–	–	–	1
Hassakah	–	–	–	–	–	–	–	–
Total	**70**	**5**	**3**	**9**	**1**	**3**	**–**	**49**

Kidnapped policemen	Total	Killing after kidnapping	Released after ransom	Released without ransom	Released after looting	Liberation	Escaped	unknown destiny
Rif Dimashq	2	–	1	–	–	–	–	1
Dar'a	8	2	–	2	2 (guns)	1	1	–
Al Suwayda	–	–	–	–	–	–	–	–
Al Qunaytirah	–	–	–	–	–	–	–	–
Homs	15	4	–	7	–	–	–	4
Hamah	72	4	–	31	–	–	–	37
Damascus	1	–	–	1	–	–	–	–
Tartus	–	–	–	–	–	–	–	–
Al Ladhiqiyah	1	–	–	1	–	–	–	–
Idlib	31	6	–	13	–	–	–	12
Aleppo	30	–	–	29	–	–	–	1
Al Raqa	–	–	–	–	–	–	–	–
Deir el-Zour	4	–	–	1	–	–	3	–
Hassakah	–	–	–	–	–	–	–	–
Total	164	16	1	85	2	1	4	55

Total kidnappings

Total kidnapping incidents	*900*

Car theft

Police car	*9*
Government car	296
Civil car	583
Total	**888**

Annex IV

Note verbale dated 28 December 2011 addressed to the Permanent Representative of the Syrian Arab Republic

NATIONS UNIES
HAUT COMMISSARIAT AUX DROITS DE L'HOMME

UNITED NATIONS
HIGH COMMISSIONER FOR HUMAN RIGHTS

Tel: 41-22-9179101

Independent International Commission of Inquiry pursuant to resolution A/HRC/S-17/1

The Independent International Commission of Inquiry on the Syrian Arab Republic presents its compliments to the Permanent Representative of the Syrian Arab Republic to the United Nations Office at Geneva and specialized institutions in Switzerland, and refers to its note verbale of 13 December 2011 and the response dated 21 December 2011 from the Syrian Arab Republic Government.

The Commission wishes to recall that the Human Rights Council, in its resolution S-17/1 of 23 August, mandated the Commission to (i) investigate all alleged violations of international human rights law since March 2011 in the Syrian Arab Republic, (ii) to establish the facts and circumstances that may amount to such violations and of the crimes perpetrated and, (iii) where possible, to identify those responsible with a view of ensuring that perpetrators of violations, including those that may constitute crimes against humanity, are held accountable. The Human Rights Council requested the Commission to make its report public before the end of November 2011 and to present a written update to the Council at its nineteenth session, in March 2012. It also requested the full cooperation of the Syrian Arab Republic.

In order to fulfil its mandate, the Commission collected first-hand information through interviews with victims and witnesses of events in the Syrian Arab Republic. The Commission undertook 223 interviews with Syrians who left the country after the unrest began. Among those interviewed 69 % were civilian victims and witnesses, 25% were defectors from the military and security forces and 6% were other sources. The standard of proof was met when the Commission obtained a reliable body of evidence, consistent with other information, indicating the occurrence of a particular incident or event. The Commission ensured that all its interlocutors had the opportunity and time to consider the Commission's request for interviews and either accept it or reject it.

In addition, a public call was made to all interested persons and organizations to submit relevant information and documentation that would help the Commission implement its mandate. It held meetings with Member States from all regional groups, regional organizations, including the League of Arab States and the Organization of Islamic Cooperation, non-governmental organizations, human rights defenders, journalists and experts. Reports, scholarly analyses and media accounts, including Syrian official sources such as SANA, as well as audio and visual material, were also duly considered.

Prior to the release of its report S-17/2/Add.1 dated 28 November 2011, the Commission requested access to the Syrian Arab Republic in its notes verbales dated 29 September, 19 October, 27 October and 4 November 2011. In its letter dated 27 October 2011, the Commission reiterated its invitation to the members of the national Independent Special

1

Legal Commission and relevant Syrian officials to visit Geneva in November. A questionnaire was annexed to the letter with a view of engaging the Government of the Syrian Arab Republic in a dialogue. The Commission stressed that the deadline for the submission of its report to the Human Rights Council was before the end of November.

Despite these numerous attempts, to date, the Commission has not received from the Syrian Arab Republic Government any cooperation, documents or substantive information related to the events since March 2011. No access to the Syrian Arab Republic was granted to the Commission. No Syrian officials met with the Commission even when on official visit to Geneva in the context of the Universal Periodic Review. No answers were provided by the Government on the detailed questionnaire sent by the Commission. No information was provided concerning the work of the national Independent Special Legal Commission.

The only correspondence from the Government of the Syrian Arab Republic received by the Commission prior to the release of its report were two letters dated 12 October and 17 November 2011. In those letters, attached as Annex III and VII to the Commission's report, the Government expressed its position that it would examine the possibility of cooperating with the commission once its own commission had concluded its work and this despite the deadline of the public release of the Commission's report by end-November.

While the Commission deeply regrets not having had access to the Syrian Arab Republic and despite the lack of cooperation by the Syrian Arab Republic, the Commission's report of 28 November and more specifically paragraphs 30, 31, 32, 33, 34, 37, 38, 40 and 51, strove to reflect the position of the Government of the Syrian Arab Republic, including existing policies and announced reforms expressed in public pronouncements and media reports.

As stated in its report, the Commission is aware of acts of violence committed by demonstrators, army defectors or opponents of the Government. It also referred to 1,100 members of State forces who had been killed by terrorists and armed gangs according to official statements. The Commission did not receive from the Government any information about the cases of Sari Saud, General Abdo Kheder Tallawi and his children as well as the case of Hamza Al Khatib. The Commission would have welcomed the Government's cooperation in facilitating contacts with the families of killed or wounded military and security personnel, as well as other victims. No offer of such good offices was made. Neither did the Government provide any information about the public confessions of hundreds of terrorists that the Government refers to.

The Commission continues to believe that a visit to the country would have allowed the Commission to interact directly with Government officials and to ascertain the circumstances of the reported killing of members of the military and security forces. The Commission remains eager to reach out to their families and to wounded soldiers, as well as to suffering civilians across Syrian communities. In its report, the Commission recommended that opposition groups ensure respect for and act in accordance with international human rights law and that Member States suspend the provision of arms and other military material to all parties.

The Commission refutes any accusation of politicisation, selectivity and non-objectivity. The Commission has shown extreme diligence in maintaining its independence from all Member States and organisations. At no point has the Commission advocated, implied or referred to any use of force or foreign intervention. It has submitted its report to the Human Rights

Council asking the Government of the Syrian Arab Republic, the Human Rights Council, Member States, regional organisations and non-State actors to ensure the implementation of the recommendations contained in the report led by the sole and only purpose of protecting the Syrian population. In its resolution S-17/1, the Human Rights Council decided to transmit the report of the commission and its update to the General Assembly, and recommended that the Assembly transmit the reports to all relevant bodies of the United Nations.

The Commission hopes that cooperation and dialogue could be established for the second phase of its work which will result in a written update to the Human Rights Council on 12 March 2012. Due to United Nations reporting requirements, the Commission should submit its written update by mid-February. Therefore, an open dialogue with the Government of the Syrian Arab Republic including a visit to the country and provision of relevant information should take place not later than mid-January. The Commission looks forward to the opportunity of meeting Syrian officials and the members of the National Independent Special Legal Commission.

The Commission avails itself of this opportunity to renew to the Permanent Representative of the Syrian Arab Republic assurances of its highest consideration.

28 December 2011

Annex V

Letter dated 18 January 2012 from the commission addressed to the President of the Syrian Arab Republic

NATIONS UNIES		UNITED NATIONS
HAUT COMMISSARIAT AUX DROITS DE L'HOMME		HIGH COMMISSIONER FOR HUMAN RIGHTS

Tel: 41-22-9179101

Independent International Commission of Inquiry pursuant to resolution A/HRC/17/1

Geneva, 17 January 2012

The Independent International Commission of Inquiry established pursuant to resolution S-17/1 of the Human Rights Council, presents its compliments to the Permanent Mission of the Syrian Arab Republic to the United Nations in Geneva and has the honour to transmit a letter addressed to H.E. Mr. Basher AL-ASSAD, President of the Syrian Arab Republic.

The Commission avails itself of the opportunity to extend the assurances of its highest consideration to the Permanent Mission of the Syrian Arab Republic.

NATIONS UNIES
HAUT COMMISSARIAT AUX DROITS DE L'HOMME

UNITED NATIONS
HIGH COMMISSIONER FOR HUMAN RIGHTS

Tel: 41-22-9179101

Independent International Commission of Inquiry pursuant to resolution A/HRC/S-17/1

17 January 2012

Excellency,

We have the honour to address you in our capacity as the Independent International Commission of Inquiry on the Syrian Arab Republic.

The Human Rights Council of the United Nations, in its resolution S-17/1 of 23 August 2011, mandated the Commission to (i) investigate all alleged violations of international human rights law since March 2011 in the Syrian Arab Republic, (ii) to establish the facts and circumstances that may amount to such violations and of the crimes perpetrated and, (iii) where possible, to identify those responsible with a view of ensuring that perpetrators of violations, including those that may constitute crimes against humanity, are held accountable.

The Commission expresses its gratitude to Your Excellency's Government for the information provided by your note verbale of 27 December 2011. We also applaud your Excellency's decision to accept the deployment of the Observer Mission established pursuant to the Plan of Action agreed between the League of Arab States and Your Excellency's Government and hope that this decision will be followed by further cooperation with United Nations mechanisms, including this Commission.

We were encouraged to take note of reports that Your Excellency had issued an amnesty under Decree 10/2012 in relation to events since March 2011. We would be grateful to receive a copy of the decree as well as information on how many people have applied for amnesty under this or other amnesty decrees issued since March 2011, how many people have been released from detention as a result of the amnesty and how many continue to be detained.

In addition, the Commission respectfully seeks more information on several important issues that Your Excellency addressed in your comprehensive speech of 10 January 2012.

The speech made reference to acts of terrorism, sabotage and murder and the theft, looting and destruction of public and private property, including the deaths of about 30 teachers and university professors and the vandalisation, burning and destruction of over a thousand schools. In this context, it was asserted that perpetrators had received money, arms and other support from foreign sources. We would be grateful for a list of specific acts of this nature and their victims; available information on the alleged perpetrators and legal action taken against them; and any evidence that the alleged acts were carried out with foreign support. Furthermore, we would be interested in continuing to receive figures on how many unarmed civilians, active members of the

State security forces, military defectors and other armed opponents have been killed in relation to the events that have taken place since March 2011.

We appreciate that Your Excellency emphasized that there is no order at any level of the State to shoot at any citizen. The speech acknowledged individual mistakes and notes that a limited number of people working for the State have been arrested in relation to murder and other crimes. We would be grateful to receive a list of state officials arrested in connection with such crimes, detailing what rank they held, what crimes they were prosecuted for, who the victims were and what reparation was provided to victims or their families. In this respect, we would also be interested to find out more about the mandate, composition and achievements of the Independent Special Legal Commission established by the Government to investigate all cases pertaining to the events that had taken place since March 2011. Furthermore, we respectfully request information on steps ordered by Your Excellency's Government to prevent future wrongdoings, in line with your command responsibility.

In the course of your speech, Your Excellency reiterated your commitment to advance reforms. In respect of our mandate, we would be particularly interested to receive copies of the Media, Political Parties and Anti-Corruption laws that were passed as well as information about the implementation of these laws. Furthermore, we would be interested to finding out more about the constitutional amendments that are to be approved in the upcoming referendum and the envisaged legislative elections.

Finally, Your Excellency also made references to economic sanctions taken against Syria and citizens being deprived of cooking gas, heating fuel and medicine. In this context, the Commission would be interested to receive more detailed information on the impact sanctions imposed against Syria have had on the living conditions and economic and social rights of the population, including the most vulnerable groups.

In the impartial pursuit of our mandate, we remain committed to seek the cooperation of the Government and undertake to reflect the information provided in our updated report to the 19th session of the Human Rights Council. To ensure that information provided by your Excellency's Government is fully reflected in the report, which will be finalized in mid-February, we would be grateful for a response at your earliest convenience. We also take this occasion to reiterate our request to carry out a visit to Syria to obtain a first-hand impression of the situation on the ground. Meanwhile, we remain open to engage in a direct, constructive dialogue with any representatives Your Excellency chooses to designate.

Please accept, Excellency, the assurances of our highest consideration.

Paulo Pinheiro
Chairperson

Annex VI

Letter dated 23 January 2012 from the commission addressed to the Minister for Justice of the Syrian Arab Republic

NATIONS UNIES
HAUT COMMISSARIAT AUX DROITS DE L'HOMME

UNITED NATIONS
HIGH COMMISSIONER FOR HUMAN RIGHTS

Tel: 41-22-9179101

Independent International Commission of Inquiry pursuant to resolution A/HRC/S-17/1

23 January 2012

The Independent International Commission of Inquiry established pursuant to resolution S-17/1 of the Human Rights Council, presents its compliments to the Permanent Mission of the Syrian Arab Republic to the United Nations Office in Geneva and specialized institutions in Switzerland and has the honour to transmit a letter addressed to Judge Tayseer Qala Awwad, Minister of Justice in Damascus.

The Commission avails itself of the opportunity to extend the assurances of its highest consideration to the Permanent Mission of the Syrian Arab Republic to the United Nations Office in Geneva and specialized institutions in Switzerland.

NATIONS UNIES
HAUT COMMISSARIAT AUX DROITS DE L'HOMME

UNITED NATIONS
HIGH COMMISSIONER FOR HUMAN RIGHTS

Tel: 41-22-9179101

Independent International Commission of Inquiry pursuant to resolution A/HRC/S-17/1

23 January 2012

Your Excellency,

I am writing on behalf of the Independent International Commission of Inquiry on the Syrian Arab Republic to respectfully request your assistance and good offices in the fulfilment of the Commission's mandate.

The United Nations Human Rights Council, in its resolution S-17/1, mandated the Commission to investigate all alleged violations of international human rights law since March 2011 in the Syrian Arab Republic, to establish the facts and circumstances that may amount to such violations and of the crimes perpetrated and, where possible, to identify those responsible with a view of ensuring that perpetrators of violations, including those that may constitute crimes against humanity, are held accountable.

In accordance with its mandate, the Commission respectfully requests information about dissidents who have been brought before criminal courts since March 2011 for offences related to disruption of public order and/or to their conduct during demonstrations. We also remain eager to learn about your cooperation with the Independent Special Legal Commission established by the Syrian Government to investigate all cases pertaining to the events that have taken place since March 2011. The Commission looks forward to reviewing any document or statistics that the Ministry of Justice could provide related to the inquiry mandated by the United Nations Human Rights Council.

The Commission would appreciate collaboration with the Ministry of Justice which would enhance the reach of its findings.

Yours Sincerely,

Paulo Pinheiro
Chairperson

Judge Tayseer Qala Awwad
Minister of Justice
Damascus, Syrian Arab Republic

NATIONS UNIES
HAUT COMMISSARIAT AUX DROITS DE L'HOMME

UNITED NATIONS
HIGH COMMISSIONER FOR HUMAN RIGHTS

لجنة التحقيق الدولية المستقلة بشأن الجمهورية العربية السورية

هاتف: 9179101-22-41+

السيد الوزير

القاضي تيسير قلا عواد

وزير العدل

حكومة الجمهورية العربية السورية

۲۳ كانون الثاني ۲۰۱۲

معالي الوزير،

أكتب إليكم نيابةً عن لجنة التحقيق الدولية المستقلة بشأن الجمهورية العربية السورية لطلب مساعدتكم بهدف تنفيذ المهام المنوطة بها اللجنة حسب ولايتها، وكما أمل أن تتيحوا لنا مساعيكم الحميدة عند الحاجة.

قام مجلس حقوق الإنسان التابع للأمم المتحدة بتكليف اللجنة، في قراره د إ – ۱/۱۷، بالتحقيق في جميع الانتهاكات المزعومة للقانون الدولي لحقوق الإنسان منذ شهر آذار/ مارس ۲۰۱۱ في الجمهورية العربية السورية، للوقوف على الحقائق والظروف التي قد ترقى إلى هذه الانتهاكات، وفي الجرائم التي ارتكبت، من أجل تحديد المسؤولين عنها، حيثما أمكن، بغية ضمان مساءلة مرتكبي هذه الانتهاكات، بما فيها الانتهاكات التي قد تشكل جرائم ضد الإنسانية.

وفقاً لولاية لجنة التحقيق الدولية المستقلة بشأن الجمهورية العربية السورية، نلتمس من سيادتكم تزويدنا بمعلومات بخصوص المعارضين الذين مثلوا أمام المحاكم الجنائية منذ شهر آذار/ مارس ۲۰۱۱ بتهم متعلقة بالإخلال بالنظام العام و / أو بسلوك المحتجين خلال المظاهرات. اللجنة حريصة أيضاً على معرفة ما هو نوع التعاون بين وزير العدل واللجنة القضائية الخاصة المستقلة التي أنشأتها حكومة الجمهورية العربية السورية للتحقيق في جميع الحالات المتصلة بالأحداث التي وقعت منذ شهر آذار/مارس ۲۰۱۱. وكما تأمل اللجنة الدولية المستقلة بشأن الجمهورية العربية السورية ان تقوم وزارة العدل بتزويدها بأية وثائق او إحصائيات تخص مهمة التحقيق المكلفة بها اللجنة من قبل مجلس حقوق الإنسان.

في الختام تود لجنة التحقيق الدولية المستقلة بشأن الجمهورية العربية السورية ان توجه فائق التقدير الى وزارة العدل في الجمهورية العربية السورية لتعاونها مع اللجنة بغية تنفيذ مهامها.

مع فائق الاحترام والتقدير،

باولو بنهيرو

رئيس لجنة التحقيق الدولية المستقلة بشأن الجمهورية العربية السورية

Annex VII

Letter dated 23 January 2012 from the commission addressed to the Minister for the Interior of the Syrian Arab Republic

NATIONS UNIES
HAUT COMMISSARIAT AUX DROITS DE L'HOMME

UNITED NATIONS
HIGH COMMISSIONER FOR HUMAN RIGHTS

Tel: 41-22-9179101

Independent International Commission of Inquiry pursuant to resolution A/HRC/S-17/1

23 January 2012

The Independent International Commission of Inquiry established pursuant to resolution S-17/1 of the Human Rights Council, presents its compliments to the Permanent Mission of the Syrian Arab Republic to the United Nations Office in Geneva and specialized institutions in Switzerland and has the honour to transmit a letter addressed to Major General Mohammad Ibrahim AL-Shaar, Minister of Interior in Damascus.

The Commission avails itself of the opportunity to extend the assurances of its highest consideration to the Permanent Mission of the Syrian Arab Republic to the United Nations Office in Geneva and specialized institutions in Switzerland.

NATIONS UNIES
HAUT COMMISSARIAT AUX DROITS DE L'HOMME

UNITED NATIONS
HIGH COMMISSIONER FOR HUMAN RIGHTS

Tel: 41-22-9179101

Independent International Commission of Inquiry pursuant to resolution A/HRC/S-17/1

23 January 2012

Your Excellency,

I am writing on behalf of the Independent International Commission of Inquiry on the Syrian Arab Republic to respectfully request your assistance and good offices in the fulfilment of the Commission's mandate.

The United Nations Human Rights Council, in its resolution S-17/1, mandated the Commission to investigate all alleged violations of international human rights law since March 2011 in the Syrian Arab Republic, to establish the facts and circumstances that may amount to such violations and of the crimes perpetrated and, where possible, to identify those responsible with a view of ensuring that perpetrators of violations, including those that may constitute crimes against humanity, are held accountable.

In accordance with its mandate, the Commission respectfully requests information concerning dissidents who have been arrested and detained since March 2011 for offences related to disruption of public order and/or to their conduct during demonstrations. We remain eager to learn whether investigations by the Ministry of Interior have taken place to ascertain specific responsibilities of individuals, as well as the number of persons who have been detained and the nature of the charges brought against such offenders. The Commission looks forward to reviewing any document or statistics that the Ministry of Interior could provide relating to the inquiry mandated by the United Nations Human Rights Council.

The Commission would appreciate collaboration with the Ministry of Interior which would enhance the reach of its findings.

Yours Sincerely,

Paulo Pinheiro

Chairperson

Major General Mohammad Ibrahim Al-Shaar
Minister of Interior
Damascus, Syrian Arab Republic

NATIONS UNIES
HAUT COMMISSARIAT AUX DROITS DE L'HOMME

UNITED NATIONS
HIGH COMMISSIONER FOR HUMAN RIGHTS

لجنة التحقيق الدولية المستقلة بشأن الجمهورية العربية السورية

هاتف: 9179101-22-41+

السيد الوزير

اللواء محمد ابراهيم الشعار

وزير الداخلية

حكومة الجمهورية العربية السورية

٢٣ كانون الثاني٢٠١٢

معالي الوزير،

أكتب إليكم نيابةً عن لجنة التحقيق الدولية المستقلة بشأن الجمهورية العربية السورية لطلب مساعدتكم بهدف تنفيذ المهام المنوطة بها اللجنة حسب ولايتها، وكما أمل أن تتيحوا لنا مساعيكم الحميدة عند الحاجة.

قام مجلس حقوق الإنسان التابع للأمم المتحدة بتكليف اللجنة، في قراره د إ – ١/١٧، بالتحقيق في جميع الانتهاكات المزعومة للقانون الدولي لحقوق الإنسان منذ شهر آذار/ مارس ٢٠١١ في الجمهورية العربية السورية، للوقوف على الحقائق والظروف التي قد ترقى إلى هذه الانتهاكات، وفي الجرائم التي ارتكبت، من أجل تحديد المسؤولين عنها، حيثُما أمكن، بغية ضمان مساءلة مرتكبي هذه الانتهاكات، بما فيها الانتهاكات التي قد تشكل جرائم ضد الإنسانية.

وفقاً لولاية لجنة التحقيق الدولية المستقلة بشأن الجمهورية العربية السورية، نلتمس من سيادتكم تزويدنا بأسماء المعارضين الذين اعتقلوا واحتجزوا منذ شهر آذار/ مارس ٢٠١١ بتهم متعلقة بالإخلال بالنظام العام و / أو بسلوك المحتجين خلال المظاهرات. اللجنة حريصة على معرفة ما إذا كانت التحقيقات التي أجرتها وزارة الداخلية قد اجريت لتحديد المسؤولية عن الأحداث. كما نود أن تحيطونا علماً بعدد المحتجزين من المتظاهرين، وطبيعة التهم الموجهة اليهم. وكما تأمل اللجنة الدولية المستقلة بشأن الجمهورية العربية السورية ان تقوم وزارة الداخلية بتزويدها بأية وثائق او إحصائيات تخص مهمة التحقيق المكلفة بها اللجنة من قبل مجلس حقوق الإنسان.

في الختام تود لجنة التحقيق الدولية المستقلة بشأن الجمهورية العربية السورية ان توجهه فائق التقدير الى وزارة الداخلية في الجمهورية العربية السورية لتعاونها مع اللجنة بغية تنفيذ مهامها.

مع فائق الاحترام والتقدير،

باولو بنهيرو

رئيس لجنة التحقيق الدولية المستقلة بشأن الجمهورية العربية السورية

Annex VIII

Letter dated 23 January 2012 from the commission to the Minister for Defence of the Syrian Arab Republic

NATIONS UNIES
HAUT COMMISSARIAT AUX DROITS DE L'HOMME

UNITED NATIONS
HIGH COMMISSIONER FOR HUMAN RIGHTS

Tel: 41-22-9179101

Independent International Commission of Inquiry pursuant to resolution A/HRC/S-17/1

23 January 2012

The Independent International Commission of Inquiry established pursuant to resolution S-17/1 of the Human Rights Council, presents its compliments to the Permanent Mission of the Syrian Arab Republic to the United Nations Office in Geneva and specialized institutions in Switzerland and has the honour to transmit a letter addressed to General Dawoud Rajiha, Minister of Defense in Damascus.

The Commission avails itself of the opportunity to extend the assurances of its highest consideration to the Permanent Mission of the Syrian Arab Republic to the United Nations Office in Geneva and specialized institutions in Switzerland.

NATIONS UNIES
HAUT COMMISSARIAT AUX DROITS DE L'HOMME

UNITED NATIONS
HIGH COMMISSIONER FOR HUMAN RIGHTS

Tel: 41-22-9179101

Independent International Commission of Inquiry pursuant to resolution A/HRC/S-17/1

23 January 2012

Your Excellency,

I am writing on behalf of the Independent International Commission of Inquiry on the Syrian Arab Republic to respectfully request your assistance and good offices in the fulfilment of the Commission's mandate.

The United Nations Human Rights Council, in its resolution S-17/1, mandated the Commission to investigate all alleged violations of international human rights law since March 2011 in the Syrian Arab Republic, to establish the facts and circumstances that may amount to such violations and of the crimes perpetrated and, where possible, to identify those responsible with a view of ensuring that perpetrators of violations, including those that may constitute crimes against humanity, are held accountable.

In accordance with its mandate, the Commission respectfully requests information concerning the names, ranks and number of killed and wounded among the military and security forces since March 2011, as well as the circumstances that have led to deaths and injuries. We would be grateful for your good offices to be allowed to contact the families of those members of the armed and security forces who were killed or injured since March 20011. The Commission looks forward to reviewing any document or statistics that the Ministry of Defence could provide relating to the inquiry mandated by the United Nations Human Rights Council.

The Commission would appreciate collaboration with the Ministry of Defence which would enhance the reach of its findings.

Yours Sincerely,

Paulo Pinheiro

Chairperson

Gen. Dawoud Rajiha
Minister of Defense
Damascus, Syrian Arab Republic

LAW AND WAR IN SYRIA

NATIONS UNIES
HAUT COMMISSARIAT AUX DROITS DE L'HOMME

UNITED NATIONS
HIGH COMMISSIONER FOR HUMAN RIGHTS

لجنة التحقيق الدولية المستقلة بشأن الجمهورية العربية السورية

هاتف: 9179101-22-41+

السيد الوزير

العماد أول داود عبدالله راجحة

وزير الدفاع

حكومة الجمهورية العربية السورية

٢٣ كانون الثاني ٢٠١٢

معالي الوزير،

أكتب إليكم نيابةً عن لجنة التحقيق الدولية المستقلة بشأن الجمهورية العربية السورية لطلب مساعدتكم بهدف تنفيذ المهام المنوطة بها اللجنة حسب ولايتها، وكما أمل أن تتيحوا لنا مساعيكم الحميدة عند الحاجة.

قام مجلس حقوق الإنسان التابع للأمم المتحدة بتكليف اللجنة، في قراره د إ – ١/١٧، بالتحقيق في جميع الانتهاكات المزعومة للقانون الدولي لحقوق الإنسان منذ شهر آذار/ مارس ٢٠١١ في الجمهورية العربية السورية، للوقوف على الحقائق والظروف التي قد ترقى إلى هذه الانتهاكات، وفي الجرائم التي ارتكبت، من أجل تحديد المسؤولين عنها، حيثما أمكن، بغية ضمان مساءلة مرتكبي هذه الانتهاكات، بما فيها الانتهاكات التي قد تشكل جرائم ضد الإنسانية.

وفقاً لولاية لجنة التحقيق الدولية المستقلة بشأن الجمهورية العربية السورية، نلتمس من سيادتكم تزويدنا بمعلومات بخصوص عدد وأسماء ورتب أفراد قوات الأمن والجيش في الجمهورية العربية السورية الذين قتلوا أو اصيبوا، بما في ذلك الظروف التي اودت بحياتهم او اصابتهم. و تقدر اللجنة بامتنان مساعيكم الحميدة بالسماح لنا بالتواصل مع عائلات أفراد قوات الأمن والجيش الذين قتلوا او جرحوا منذ شهر آذار/مارس ٢٠١١. وكما تأمل اللجنة الدولية المستقلة بشأن الجمهورية العربية السورية ان تقوم وزارة الدفاع بتزويدها بأية وثائق او إحصائيات تخص مهمة التحقيق المكلفة بها اللجنة من قبل مجلس حقوق الإنسان.

في الختام تود لجنة التحقيق الدولية المستقلة بشأن الجمهورية العربية السورية ان توجهه فائق التقدير الى وزارة الدفاع في الجمهورية العربية السورية لتعاونها مع اللجنة بغية تنفيذ مهامها.

مع فائق الاحترام والتقدير،

باولو بنهيرو

رئيس لجنة التحقيق الدولية المستقلة بشأن الجمهورية العربية السورية

Annex IX

Letter dated 23 January 2012 from the commission addressed to the President of the People's Assembly of the Syrian Arab Republic

NATIONS UNIES
HAUT COMMISSARIAT AUX DROITS DE L'HOMME

UNITED NATIONS
HIGH COMMISSIONER FOR HUMAN RIGHTS

Tel: 41-22-9179101

Independent International Commission of Inquiry pursuant to resolution A/HRC/S-17/1

23 January 2012

The Independent International Commission of Inquiry established pursuant to resolution S-17/1 of the Human Rights Council, presents its compliments to the Permanent Mission of the Syrian Arab Republic to the United Nations Office in Geneva and specialized institutions in Switzerland and has the honour to transmit a letter addressed to H.E. Mr. Mahmoud Al-Abrash, Chairperson of the Peoples' Assembly in Damascus.

The Commission avails itself of the opportunity to extend the assurances of its highest consideration to the Permanent Mission of the Syrian Arab Republic to the United Nations Office in Geneva and specialized institutions in Switzerland.

NATIONS UNIES
HAUT COMMISSARIAT AUX DROITS DE L'HOMME

UNITED NATIONS
HIGH COMMISSIONER FOR HUMAN RIGHTS

Tel: 41-22-9179101

Independent International Commission of Inquiry pursuant to resolution A/HRC/S-17/1

23 January 2012

Your Excellency,

I am writing on behalf of the Independent International Commission of Inquiry on the Syrian Arab Republic to respectfully request your assistance and good offices in the fulfilment of the Commission's mandate.

The United Nations Human Rights Council, in its resolution S-17/1, mandated the Commission to investigate all alleged violations of international human rights law since March 2011 in the Syrian Arab Republic, to establish the facts and circumstances that may amount to such violations and of the crimes perpetrated and, where possible, to identify those responsible with a view of ensuring that perpetrators of violations, including those that may constitute crimes against humanity, are held accountable.

In accordance with its mandate, the Commission respectfully requests information concerning the role of the Peoples' Assembly in monitoring the events since March 2011 as well as the impact of existing and new legislation in this regard. We remain eager to learn how the Permanent Committee on National Security and the Permanent Committee on Constitutional Affairs responded to the legislative changes resulting from the unrest in the Syrian Arab Republic since March 2011 and how they gather information regarding the implementation of the reforms announced by the Government. The Commission looks forward to reviewing any document or statistics that the Peoples' Assembly could provide relating to the inquiry mandated by the United Nations Human Rights Council.

The Commission would appreciate collaboration with the Peoples' Assembly which would enhance the reach of its findings.

Yours Sincerely,

Paulo Pinheiro
Chairperson

H.E. Mr. Mahmoud Al-Abrash
Chairperson
Peoples' Assembly
Damascus, Syrian Arab Republic

NATIONS UNIES
HAUT COMMISSARIAT AUX DROITS DE L'HOMME

UNITED NATIONS
HIGH COMMISSIONER FOR HUMAN RIGHTS

لجنة التحقيق الدولية المستقلة بشأن الجمهورية العربية السورية

هاتف: 9179101-22-41+

السيد الدكتور محمد الأبرش

رئيس مجلس الشعب السوري

الجمهورية العربية السورية

٢٣ كانون الثاني ٢٠١٢

معالي رئيس مجلس الشعب السوري،

أكتب إليكم نيابةً عن لجنة التحقيق الدولية المستقلة بشأن الجمهورية العربية السورية لطلب مساعدتكم بهدف تنفيذ المهام المنوطة بها اللجنة حسب ولايتها، وكما أمل أن تتيحوا لنا مساعيكم الحميدة عند الحاجة.

كما تعلمون قام المجلس الدولي لحقوق الإنسان بتكليف اللجنة، في قراره د إ – ١/١٧، بالتحقيق في جميع الانتهاكات المزعومة للقانون الدولي لحقوق الإنسان منذ شهر آذار/ مارس ٢٠١١ في الجمهورية العربية السورية، للوقوف على الحقائق والظروف التي قد ترقى إلى هذه الانتهاكات، وفي الجرائم التي ارتكبت، من أجل تحديد المسؤولين عنها، حيثما أمكن، بغية ضمان مساءلة مرتكبي هذه الانتهاكات، بما فيها الانتهاكات التي قد تشكل جرائم ضد الإنسانية.

وفقاً لولاية لجنة التحقيق الدولية المستقلة بشأن الجمهورية العربية السورية، نلتمس من سيادتكم تزويدنا بمعلومات حول دور مجلس الشعب السوري في مراقبة أعمال العنف المتصلة بالأحداث التي وقعت منذ شهر اذار/مارس ٢٠١١. كما نود أن تحيطونا علماً بأثر التشريعات القائمة والتشريعات الجديدة في هذا الصدد. اللجنة حريصة أيضاً على معرفة دور لجنة الأمن القومي ولجنة الشؤون الدستورية واستجابتهن للتحديات الناجمة عن الأحداث منذ شهر اذار/مارس٢٠١١، بما في ذلك كيفية جمعهن المعلومات حول تنفيذ الإصلاحات التي قامت حكومة الجمهورية العربية السورية بإعلانها في هذا الصدد. وكما تأمل اللجنة الدولية المستقلة بشأن الجمهورية العربية السورية ان يقوم مجلس الشعب السوري بتزويدها بأية وثائق او إحصائيات ذات صلة بمهمة التحقيق المكلفة بها اللجنة من قبل مجلس حقوق الإنسان.

في الختام تود لجنة التحقيق الدولية المستقلة بشأن الجمهورية العربية السورية ان توجه فائق التقدير الى مجلس الشعب السوري لتعاونه مع اللجنة بغية تنفيذ مهامها.

مع فائق الاحترام والتقدير،

باولو بنهيرو

A/HRC/19/69

Annex X

Letter dated 23 January 2012 from the commission addressed to the Chairman of the National Independent Legal Commission

NATIONS UNIES   UNITED NATIONS
HAUT COMMISSARIAT AUX DROITS DE L'HOMME   HIGH COMMISSIONER FOR HUMAN RIGHTS

Tél: 41-22-9179101

Independent International Commission of Inquiry pursuant to resolution A/HRC/S-17/1

23 January 2012

The Independent International Commission of Inquiry established pursuant to resolution S-17/1 of the Human Rights Council, presents its compliments to the Permanent Mission of the Syrian Arab Republic to the United Nations Office in Geneva and specialized institutions in Switzerland and has the honour to transmit a letter addressed to Judge Muhammad Deeb Al-Muqatrin, Chairman of the Independent Special Legal Commission in Damascus.

The Commission avails itself of the opportunity to extend the assurances of its highest consideration to the Permanent Mission of the Syrian Arab Republic to the United Nations Office in Geneva and specialized institutions in Switzerland.

NATIONS UNIES
HAUT COMMISSARIAT AUX DROITS DE L'HOMME

UNITED NATIONS
HIGH COMMISSIONER FOR HUMAN RIGHTS

Tel: 41-22-9179101

Independent International Commission of Inquiry pursuant to resolution A/HRC/S-17/1

23 January 2012

Your Excellency,

I am writing on behalf of the Independent International Commission of Inquiry on the Syrian Arab Republic to respectfully request your assistance and good offices in the fulfilment of the Commission's mandate.

The United Nations Human Rights Council, in its resolution S-17/1, mandated the Commission to investigate all alleged violations of international human rights law since March 2011 in the Syrian Arab Republic, to establish the facts and circumstances that may amount to such violations and of the crimes perpetrated and, where possible, to identify those responsible with a view of ensuring that perpetrators of violations, including those that may constitute crimes against humanity, are held accountable.

In accordance with its mandate, the Commission respectfully requests a copy of the mandate of the Independent Special Legal Commission established by the Government of the Syrian Arab Republic. In addition, the Commission of Inquiry would be grateful to receive information concerning dissidents as well as members of the armed forces and Government security forces who the Special Legal Commission has investigated since its creation in March 2011. We remain eager to learn whether investigations by your Commission have taken place to ascertain specific responsibilities of individuals, as well as the number of persons who have been detained as a result of the work of your Commission and the nature of the charges brought against such offenders. The Commission looks forward to reviewing any document or statistics that the Special Legal Commission could provide relating to the inquiry mandated by the United Nations Human Rights Council.

The Commission would appreciate collaboration with the Independent Special Legal Commission which would enhance the reach of its findings.

Yours Sincerely,

Paulo Pinheiro

Chairperson

Judge Muhammad Deeb Al-Muqatrin
Chairman
Independent Special Legal Commission
Damascus, Syrian Arab Republic

NATIONS UNIES
HAUT COMMISSARIAT AUX DROITS DE L'HOMME

UNITED NATIONS
HIGH COMMISSIONER FOR HUMAN RIGHTS

لجنة التحقيق الدولية المستقلة بشأن الجمهورية العربية السورية

هاتف: 41-22-9179101+

السيد القاضي محمد ديب المقطرن
رئيس اللجنة القضائية الخاصة المستقلة
بشأن الجمهورية العربية السورية

٢٣ كانون الثاني ٢٠١٢

حضرة السيد القاضي محمد ديب المقطرن المحترّم،

أكتب إليكم نيابةً عن لجنة التحقيق الدولية المستقلة بشأن الجمهورية العربية السورية لطلب مساعدتكم بهدف تنفيذ المهام المنوطة بها اللجنة حسب ولايتها، وكما أمل أن تتيحوا لنا مساعيكم الحميدة عند الحاجة.

قام مجلس حقوق الإنسان التابع للأمم المتحدة بتكليف اللجنة، في قراره د إ – ١/١٧، بالتحقيق في جميع الانتهاكات المزعومة للقانون الدولي لحقوق الإنسان منذ شهر آذار/ مارس ٢٠١١ في الجمهورية العربية السورية، للوقوف على الحقائق والظروف التي قد ترقى إلى هذه الانتهاكات، وفي الجرائم التي ارتكبت، من أجل تحديد المسؤولين عنها، حيثما أمكن، بغية ضمان مساءلة مرتكبي هذه الانتهاكات، بما فيها الانتهاكات التي قد تشكل جرائم ضد الإنسانية.

وفقاً لولاية لجنة التحقيق الدولية المستقلة بشأن الجمهورية العربية السورية، نلتمس من سيادتكم تزويدنا بنسخة من كتاب تفويض اللجنة القضائية الخاصة المستقلة التي أنشأتها حكومة الجمهورية العربية السورية للتحقيق في جميع الحالات المتصلة بالأحداث التي وقعت منذ شهر آذار/مارس٢٠١١. لجنة التحقيق الدولية المستقلة بشأن الجمهورية العربية السورية حريصة ايضاً على الحصول على معلومات بخصوص المعارضين وافراد قوات الأمن والقوات المسلحة الذي تم التحقيق معهم منذ انشاء اللجنة القضائية الخاصة. وكما نود معرفة ما إذا اجريت هذه التحقيقات بغية تحديد مسؤولية الأفراد، فضلاً عن عدد الأشخاص الذي تم اعتقالهم نتيجة التحقيقات وطبيعة التهم الموجهة اليهم. وتأمل اللجنة الدولية المستقلة بشأن الجمهورية العربية السورية ان تقوم اللجنة القضائية الخاصة بتزويدها بأية وثائق او إحصائيات تخص مهمة التحقيق المكلفة بها اللجنة الدولية من قبل مجلس حقوق الإنسان.

في الختام تود لجنة التحقيق الدولية المستقلة بشأن الجمهورية العربية السورية ان توجه فائق التقدير الى اللجنة القضائية لتعاونها مع اللجنة الدولية بغية تنفيذ مهامها.

مع فائق الاحترام والتقدير،

باولو بنهيرو
رئيس لجنة التحقيق الدولية المستقلة بشأن الجمهورية العربية السورية

Annex XI

Note verbale dated 23 January 2012 from the Permanent Representative of the Syrian Arab Republic addressed to the commission

MISSION PERMANENTE
DE LA
RÉPUBLIQUE ARABE SYRIENNE
GENÈVE

الجمهورية العربية السورية
البعثة الدائمة لدى مكتب الأمم المتحدة
جنيف

27/12

23 January, 2012

The Permanent Mission of the Syrian Arab Republic to the United Nations Office and other International Organizations in Geneva presents its compliments to The Office of the High Commissioner for Human Rights, and in reference to the letter of the Independent International Commission of Inquiry dated 28/12/2011, has the honour to attach herewith the official response of the Government of the Syrian Arab Republic to the above mentioned letter.

The Permanent Mission of the Syrian Arab Republic avails itself of this opportunity to renew to The Office of the High Commissioner for Human Rights the assurances of its highest consideration.

OHCHR REGISTRY

2 3 JAN 2012

Recipients ........M.E.N.A..........
........D.C..................

Office of the High Commissioner for Human Rights
Palais Wilson

Rue de Lausanne 72 (3e étage), 1202 Genève   Tel: +41 22 715 45 60   Fax: +41 22 738 42 75

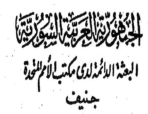

MISSION PERMANENTE
DE LA
RÉPUBLIQUE ARABE SYRIENNE
GENÈVE

1- The Syrian Arab Republic has always welcomed cooperation and dialogue with all UN Human Rights mechanisms that enjoy objectivity, impartiality and non politicization. Syria Is always ready to pursue its dialogue and cooperation within these international norms. Nevertheless, and as Syria has pointed out in previous communications, the International Commission of Inquiry has failed at its very first test. And as Syria had expected, the Commission's Report was written beforehand, therefore it does not deserve examination because it was based on false information and predetermined ideas. For the same above mentioned reasons, the Syrian Arab Republic refuses the allegations included in the International Commission of inquiry letter dated 28/12/2011.

2- The Syrian Arab Republic had clearly expressed in several communications its position regarding the cooperation with the Commission, and based the matter of this cooperation upon the work of the National Independent legal Commission (the Syrian Investigation Commission). It is known that the Syrian Legal Commission and its branches in the different Syrian Governorates are investigating more than /4070/ cases, and they are working exhaustively in investigating these cases in line with the principles of justice, honesty, impartiality and objectivity, and without predetermined assumptions. The International Commission of Inquiry will be informed with the outcomes of these investigations when they are concluded.

3- The government of the Syrian Arab republic refuses the claims of the Commission that the Syrian Government did not provide information about the victims of the violations of human rights committed by the armed terrorist groups, and uses such claims as an excuse to ignore the victims of these violations. The Commission distanced itself from objectivity and professional investigation rules when it limited its report to the allegations presented by hostile parties to the Syrian Arab Republic with well-known motives.

4- The Human Rights Council has mandated the International Commission of Inquiry in its resolution S-17/1 "to establish the facts and circumstances that may amount" to violations of human rights. Hence, the Commission is requested to comply with its duties in this regards, as impartiality and professionalism oblige the Commission to seek the truth. The dangerous method adopted by the Commission in dealing with information it receives contradicts with its mandate.

5- The Government of the Syrian Arab Republic provided the High Commissioner of Human Rights with a considerable amount of information about victims of Human Rights violations committed by the armed terrorist groups against army and security forces and civilians. The Syrian government reiterates its will to keep the Commission and the High Commissioner of Human rights informed with the facts and cases of such violations.

6- As the Commission had been busy working on presenting evidence to support its pre assumptions in order to accuse the Syrian Government of committing violations of Human Rights, it neglected its duty in illustrating the stance of the International Human Rights Law regarding acts of kidnapping, killing, mutilation, forced and involuntarily disappearance, and the violation of the Right of Life committed by the armed groups against the Syrian citizens, including women, children, and personnel of the army and the security forces, in addition to depriving the Syrian People from the right to "Freedom from Fear" as expressed in the preamble of the Universal Declaration of Human Rights. The Commission did not make reference to the killing and forced displacement of anyone who did not comply with the orders of the armed groups to participate in protests, strikes, civil disobedience or who do not subscribe to their terrorist agenda, which contradicts with the right of freedom of expression. Furthermore, the Commission did not refer to the killing and targeting of members of certain religious groups, and to the incitement of hatred against them which also violates the right of the Freedom of Religion and Beliefs. Thus, the Syrian Arab Republic is still waiting for the commission to correct its errors in this regard.

7- The Government of the Syrian Arab Republic, is still waiting for the Commission to clarify its position on the attacks that targeted oil pipelines, electricity stations fuel lines, bridges as well as the suicide attacks. Would the Commission ignore these facts in its report, while it waits for the Syrian Government to provide such information?

8- The Commission admitted in its letter the acts of violence committed by "demonstrators and defectors and government opponents". However, the Commission merely called upon these groups to "assure their commitment to respect Human Rights", which indicates that the Commission is convinced that these groups commit themselves to International Human Rights Law, and it only asks these groups to reiterate their commitment to it, which means that the Commission does not admit the violations committed by these groups.

9- The recommendations of the Commission's report did not include any suggestions to hold these groups accountable for the terrorist acts they executed, and did not indicate the crimes against humanity they committed. The Commission did not call for the accountability of the armed groups, even though it admitted their presence, which reflects the Commission's selectivity when it limited its accusations to the Syrian Authorities. This also proves that the report is merely based on the Commission's pre-assumptions.

10- In this regard, we would like to refer to the various public statements made by high officials in certain countries which certifies the existence of armed groups in Syria. These statements called upon these groups to lay down their arms and engage in the dialogue called for by the Syrian Government to stop the bloodshed of all Syrians. However, all these calls did not find their way to the Commission's report, despite the fact that such statements were made during the preparation period of the report. Furthermore, the Commission did not include in its report any recommendation that calls for stopping the incitement against the Syrian Arab Republic, which reconfirm the Commission's selectivity.

11- The Government of the Syrian Arab Republic is deeply concerned by the Commission's lack of professionalism, and is also concerned about the methodology adopted by the commission in its investigations, which led it to claim its ignorance of the attacks, kidnapping, torture, killings, mutilations and destructions carried out by the terrorist groups against the Syrian law enforcement personnel, their families and their homes. The Commission instead made serious accusations against these personnel in a non-objective and unprofessional manner. The Syrian Arab Republic considers these accusations to be totally false, and fully rejects them, for the Syrian Arab Army and the security forces are fulfilling their duty by protecting the Syrian People from the armed groups' terrorism and their violations of Human Rights.

12- Another evidence on the politicization and selectivity of the report is the Commission's use of false information in its report under the title

"Political Background", and its listing of indications that seek to divide the Syrian society on a confessional basis, whereas it refrained from exposing related information and facts, such as Syria being a secular state enjoying a unique reality of coexistence and tolerance between all components of the Syrian society, especially that theses political facts are essential in reflecting the dangerous agenda of the terrorist groups which aim to destroy the civil peace and social structure in the Syrian Arab republic. The approach adopted by the Commission works in favour of those who seek to trigger a Civil War in Syria, by exonerating them from rejected and condemned acts of confessional incitement.

13- The Commission claims that it did not call for any international intervention in the Syrian Arab Republic. However, its recommendations reflect the opposite: the Commission had recommended immediate steps through the Security Council to implement its recommendations. The important question raised here is: what was the aim of the Commission when it called for the transmission of its report to the Security Council had it not been the foreign military intervention as was the outcome of the transmission of other countries' files to the Security Council - leading to the killing of more than 50.000 Libyan Citizens. Furthermore, the call of the Commission to support "efforts to protect the population of the Syrian Arab Republic" without specifying such efforts leaves the door open for the military intervention under the pretext of "protecting the civilians".

14- In this context, and considering that the Commission claims that its will is to protect the Syrian People, why did it not recommends the call for national dialogue - as it is the optimum solution to solve all issues in accordance with the Charter of the United Nations - and chose instead to support efforts to punish the Syrian People, and efforts for foreign intervention?

15- The Syrian Arab Republic had wished that the report's recommendations would have included the support of the reforms undertaken by the Syrian Government to fulfil its people's demands, and the call for the international community to offer all the support to these reforms, instead of portraying them as allegations, despite the fact that these reforms will promote the political, economic, social and cultural Rights of the Syrian People.

16- The Syrian Arab Republic also asks the Commission whether its call to support the efforts of the League of Arab States includes the boycott of Syria and the siege and the starvation of the Syrian People? Does this conform with the Commission's claim that its aim is the protection of the Syrian People?

17- The Syrian Arab Republic regrets once again the Commission's neglect of all information provided by Syria in response to the questions previously sent by the Commission, and that the Commission presented part of this information as "allegations", while it presented the allegations and fabrications of other parties against the Syrian Arab Republic as facts, which proves that the report of the Commission is non-credible.

Annex XII

Note verbale dated 2 February 2012 from the commission addressed to the Permanent Representative of the Syrian Arab Republic

NATIONS UNIES
HAUT COMMISSARIAT AUX DROITS DE L'HOMME

UNITED NATIONS
HIGH COMMISSIONER FOR HUMAN RIGHTS

Tel: 41-22-9179101

Independent International Commission of Inquiry pursuant to resolution A/HRC/S-17/1

2 February 2012

The Independent International Commission of Inquiry established pursuant to resolution S-17/1 of the Human Rights Council presents its compliments to the Permanent Representative of the Syrian Arab Republic to the United Nations in Geneva and has the honour to acknowledge receipt of your note verbale dated 23 January 2012.

With respect to the criticisms of the Commission's first report contained in your note, the Commission wishes to assure your Government that we remain very firmly committed to reflecting violations and abuses on all sides, including acts committed by armed groups to which you refer.

We recall in this regard our requests for information on abuses by non-state armed groups mentioned in our communications to you of 27 October 2011, 28 December 2011 and 18 January 2012, and we would appreciate your undertaking to keep us informed about such violations. As indicated earlier, the Commission would be grateful to receive information on specific cases involving such violations and their victims, as well as available information on the alleged perpetrators and any legal action taken against them.

To reach our crucial objective of reflecting all violations and abuses, we respectfully reaffirm that only detailed information on specific cases will enable us to include the issues your Government would like to see reflected in our forthcoming report due for submission mid-February in preparation for presentation at the Human Rights Council in March.

The Commission recalls that we have received a one page table from you on 27 December 2011, but there is no description of the methodology used or of the events underlying the figures. We regret we have not yet received from your Government detailed information or data that can be followed up or used in our report.

The Commission takes note that the National Independent Legal commission is investigating more the 4,070 cases. This is the only specific item conveyed in your note verbale. We reiterate our deep interest in receiving more information about the mandate, composition and achievements of the NILC. In particular, we would like to be informed of which investigations carried out so far have led to arrests and indictments of those responsible for the violations.

The Commission would be grateful for a response at your earliest convenience to ensure that the information provided can be reflected in our report, to be finalized, as mentioned above, mid-February 2012.

The Commission takes this occasion to recall our request to visit the Syrian Arab Republic, so that we may obtain a first-hand impression of the situation on the ground and interview victims of abuses on all sides. Meanwhile, we remain open to engage in a direct, constructive dialogue with any representative(s) your Government chooses to designate.

We assure you that such a visit will have an essential impact, particularly at this present juncture, on our report, since nothing can substitute for direct and effective contact with your Government and the Syrian communities. The Commission does not take sides, and we assure you that we are concerned both by the consequences of the intensification of violence experienced recently by civilians and by members of the armed and security forces.

The main objective of the Commission is the wellbeing of all Syrians. Direct access to these communities will allow them to express their views and perceptions, and to describe their hardships and needs. A direct dialogue with members of your Government and its institutions would help clarify any questions or assessments that have arisen over the course of our inquiry. We are eager to share with your Government our methodology in full transparency. We are ready to discuss the terms of reference for such a visit with your representative in Geneva.

We understand that independent non-government organizations have recently had free access to your country, while we have not been able to visit. We assure you and your Government of the independence of our Commission and of its impartial and objective engagement with the subject matter of our inquiry. If our Commission is given the opportunity to come to your country, we will be open to discuss all aspects of our first report tabled at the Human Rights Council on 2 December 2011. We can only repeat our insistence that a direct exchange would contribute significantly to the preparation of our second report.

The Commission avails itself of the opportunity to extend the assurances of its highest consideration to the Permanent Mission of the Syrian Arab Republic. Dc

Annex XIII

Detention locations for which the commission documented cases of torture and ill-treatment (since March 2011)

City	Type	Detention center
Aleppo	Security Forces	Political Security Branch
Banias	Security Forces	Military Security Branch
	Security Forces	Political Security Branch
Damascus	Military Prison	Sednaya Military Prison
	Police	Criminal Security Branch
	Prison	Adra Central Prison
	Security Forces	Air Force Intelligence Branch in Bab Tuma
	Security Forces	Air Force Intelligence Branch in Harastah
	Security Forces	Palestine Branch
	Security Forces	State Security Branch in Kafar Sussa
	Security Forces	State Security Branch in Duma
Dar'a	Police	Criminal Security Branch
	Prison	Gharez Central Prison
	Security Forces	Air Force Intelligence Branch
	Security Forces	Military Security Branch
	Security Forces	Political Security Branch
	Security Forces	State Security Branch
Hama	Security Forces	State Security Branch
Homs	Prison	Central Prison
	Security Forces	Air Force Intelligence Branch
	Security Forces	State Hospital
Idlib	Prison	Central Prison
	Security Forces	Detention facility
	Security Forces	Military Security Branch
Jisr Al Shughour	Security Forces	Military Security Branch
	Security Forces	Political Security Branch
Al Ladhiqiyah	Security Forces	Military Security Branch

City	Type	Detention center
	Security Forces	Political Security Branch
	Security Forces	State Hospital
Rif Dimashq	Security Forces	Air Force Intelligence Branch
	Security Forces	Military Security Branch
	Security Forces	Military Security Branch
	Security Forces	State Security Branch
Tadmur	Military Prison	Tadmur Military Prison
Tartus	Security Forces	Intelligence detention centre
	Security Forces	Military Security Branch
	Security Forces	Political Security Branch
	Security Forces	State security branch

Annex XIV

Map of the Syrian Arab Republic

A/HRC/20/CRP.1

Distr.: Restricted
26 June 2012

English only

DOCUMENT 2d

Human Rights Council
Twentieth session
Agenda item 4
Human rights situations that require the Council's attention

Oral Update of the Independent International Commission of Inquiry on the Syrian Arab Republic

I. Introduction

1.   The Independent International Commission of Inquiry (CoI) submits this Update pursuant to Human Rights Council resolution 19/22 of 23 March 2012. The Update describes the findings of the CoI based on investigations into alleged human rights violations in the Syrian Arab Republic that have taken place since the CoI previous report dated 22 February 2012 (A/HRC/19/69). On 1 June 2012, the Human Rights Council in special session adopted resolution A/HRC/RES/S-19/1 further mandating the CoI to urgently conduct a special inquiry into the events in Al-Houla.

2.   The findings reported are based on three investigative missions conducted in March and in April, and on a third one that began in May and continues at the time of writing. It builds upon two previous Periodic Updates, one released on 16 April and the other on 24 May. It includes information gathered through 15 June 2012. The CoI conducted 383 interviews, of which 50 were with women and 11 with children. The protection and safety of interviewees is of paramount importance. Consequently, names and other identifying features of those interviewed are not included in the Update.

3.   In rendering its findings, the CoI has adopted an inclusive approach to information gathering, accepting submissions from a wide range of sources, including the Government of the Syrian Arab Republic and those groups and organizations opposing it. The collected materials, which include photographs, videos, satellite imagery, interviews and documentary evidence, are carefully examined for reliability and credibility. Incidents are included in the Update only when corroborated to a level where the CoI found it had reasonable grounds to believe that events occurred as described. As the CoI continues investigating, it is updating the confidential list of identified perpetrators, which it will hand over to the High Commissioner once the mandate of the Commission ends.

4.   The CoI Chair is grateful to the Syrian authorities for enabling a visit to Damascus on 23–25 June, which provided him an opportunity to explain in person to the members of the Government the nature of the Commission's work as well as the modalities necessary for it to be successful. While there, he met with the Deputy Foreign Minister, the Deputy Justice Minister and other officials, including the Head of the National Independent Legal Commission established by the Government to investigate crimes committed in the context of the crisis since March 2011. He also met with staff of the UN Supervision Mission in Syria (UNSMIS), members of the diplomatic community and civil society. He met as well with the Syrian Orthodox Patriarch in Damascus and 20 families from Damascus and Homs governorates whose relatives were killed allegedly due to their allegiance to the Government. The visit allowed him to discuss the Al-Houla investigation with the authorities and to come to an understanding as to how the CoI would deploy effectively in the Syrian Arab Republic for the purposes of carrying out investigations. He hopes that the visit will pave the way for the CoI to begin its work in earnest in the Syrian Arab Republic, thereby fulfilling its mandate.

Context

5.   Since its establishment in September 2011, the CoI has consistently expressed its concern about the deteriorating human rights situation in the Syrian Arab Republic. Gross violations of human rights are occurring regularly, in the context of increasingly militarized fighting which – in some areas – bears the characteristics of a non-international armed conflict. Whereas the Government had initially responded to demonstrations with police units and security forces, the violence soon shifted to fighting between its army together with what appear to be pro-Government militias and numerous, armed anti-Government

fighters. The rapid rise in violence occurs in inverse proportion to the respect for international human rights norms.

6.   The CoI remains concerned by the displacement of civilian populations, both within the Syrian Arab Republic and across its international borders – numbers of refugees now reaching 92,000; the pillaging and burning of homes; the tightly controlled security environment resulting in restrictions on the fundamental freedoms of movement, speech and association; and the systematic denial, in some areas, of the basic requirements of human life such as food, water and medical care. OCHA reports that 1.5 million people need humanitarian assistance in Syria.

Political Developments

7.   Throughout the reporting period, efforts to reach a political solution have been undermined by further escalation of violence. The League of Arab States (LAS) initiative withdrew in February 2012. The departure of the LAS monitors took place against a backdrop of rapidly escalating violence, especially in the city of Homs, where heavy artillery was used in shelling entire residential areas, resulting in significant civilian casualties. On 29 February 2012, Government troops entered Baba Amr neighbourhood and the anti-Government armed groups withdrew. This did not put an end to violence in Homs. In March 2012, the CoI recorded massacres in several neighborhoods of the city.

8.   Alongside the upturn in violence, diplomatic efforts to negotiate a peaceful resolution to the crisis gathered pace. On 23 February 2012, the UN and the LAS jointly named former Secretary-General of the United Nations, Kofi Annan, as Joint Special Envoy (JSE) on the Syrian crisis. On 16 March 2012, the JSE announced a "six point plan"[1] to stop violence and start a political process. The 12 April 2012 announcement of a cease-fire was swiftly followed by the arrival of the UN Supervision Mission in Syria (UNSMIS) led by Major-General Robert Mood. The arrival of UNSMIS led initially to a decrease in violence in some areas and an opening to the possibility of a Syria-led negotiation process.

9.   Meanwhile the Syrian authorities proceeded with two political initiatives, which aimed at reform. The first was the referendum on a new constitution on 26 February 2012, followed by parliamentary elections on 7 May 2012. Official election sources declared participation levels of 51% of the electorate. These political steps were viewed by neither the Syrian opposition nor the anti-Government armed groups as inclusive or sufficient.

10.   By May 2012, violence was once again escalating. Armed clashes began to be reported daily between pro-Government forces and anti-Government armed groups throughout the country, many resulting in civilian deaths and injuries. Killings took place

---

[1] Excerpts of the JSE's six-point plan:
(1) commit to work with the Envoy in an inclusive Syrian-led political process to address the legitimate aspirations and concerns of the Syrian people;
(2) commit to stop the fighting and achieve urgently an effective United Nations supervised cessation of armed violence in all its forms . . . the Syrian government should immediately cease troop movements towards, and end the use of heavy weapons in population centres, and begin pullback of military concentrations in and around population centres. . . Similar commitments would be sought by the Envoy from the opposition and all relevant elements to stop the violence;
(3) ensure timely provision of humanitarian assistance to all areas affected by the fighting;
(4) intensify the pace and scale of release of arbitrarily detained persons;
(5) ensure freedom of movement throughout the country for journalists and a non-discriminatory visa policy for them;
(6) respect freedom of association and the right to demonstrate peacefully as legally guaranteed

on what appeared to be mainly sectarian grounds. Where previously victims were targeted on the basis of their being pro- or anti-Government, the CoI has recorded a growing number of incidents where victims appear to have been targeted because of their religious affiliation.

11.   The 7 June 2012 speech of the JSE to the UN articulated the difficulties faced by those making diplomatic efforts. The JSE urged the international community to take action to prevent the situation in the country from further deterioration. The obstacles faced by UNSMIS reflected a lack of common ground among the parties to the conflict. These challenges were exacerbated by significant differences among States.

Military and security situation

12.   Despite the commitment to a 'cessation of armed violence', military engagements have escalated dramatically over the reporting period and have extended to other regions and levels not previously involved. The situation on the ground is dangerously and quickly deteriorating.

13.   The Syrian Government forces have intensified their military operations against areas presumed to be strongholds of anti-Government armed groups or those supporting them. Government forces continued to use machine guns, artillery and tanks in shelling restive neighbourhoods and localities while increasingly employing aviation assets in attacks against anti-Government armed group strongholds. Heavy military equipment including tanks, armoured personnel carriers (APC), mounted machine guns and artillery continued to be deployed and used in different localities. Meanwhile, a small but steady flow of defections, coupled with cases documented by the CoI where the army has abandoned its checkpoints in Homs governorate, indicate that the regular forces are exhibiting a certain fatigue.

14.   Helicopter gunships and artillery have been used in the shelling of entire neighbourhoods believed to be anti-Government, even during the presence of observers, as occurred in Dayr Al-Zawr and Aleppo in May 2012. This reveals the increasing difficulty of the Government to preserve its hold over large areas through the deployment of military and security forces. The inability to hold territory equally explains the army's shift in strategy from static permanent positions to attacking the anti-Government armed forces and then making tactical withdrawals.

15.   Defections from different army and security forces continued during the reporting period throughout the Syrian Arab Republic, sometimes costing the lives of the defecting soldiers and often leading to retaliatory operations against their families or communities by the Government forces.

16.   The anti-Government armed groups, including those affiliated to the "Free Syrian Army" (FSA), continued to engage with the Government forces through direct combat, the use of Improvised Explosive Devices (IEDs) and attacks on military/security facilities. The Homs neighbourhoods of Khaldieh, Al-Qusour, Bab S'baa and the city of Al-Qusayr have effectively become battlefields between the FSA and Government forces, causing thousands of inhabitants to flee. While the CoI has not noted the use of new or more sophisticated weaponry by anti-Government armed groups, their operations in some locations are improving in efficiency and organisation. These groups appear to have spread throughout the country, expanding their activities to new areas, and clashing simultaneously with Government forces on multiple fronts. Their increasing capacity to access and make use of available weapons has been demonstrated in recent weeks.

17.   In Damascus, Homs, Hama, Idlib and Aleppo governorates, these groups have effectively challenged the Government authority. For example, the Government forces'

control of the country's borders has been regularly undermined. Cross border movements of refugees as well as of anti-Government fighters appear to be more frequent and fluid.

18.   The CoI has noted the increased use by anti-Government armed groups of IEDs against army and security convoys, patrols and facilities such as military buildings and checkpoints. In, at least, one case, this has led to collateral damage among civilians and their properties. According to reliable sources, anti-Government armed groups have also been using IEDs in assassinations, targeting Government officials and individuals from the army and security forces.

19.   New anti-Government groups, bolstered by defections, have emerged. Several newly created groups, such as Ahrar Al-Sham and Al-Islam Brigades, have not announced an affiliation to the FSA. Most of these groups declare their objective to be the protection of civilians from attacks by the military and security forces. The CoI, however, has documented cases where groups are involved in criminal/opportunist activities such as kidnappings and abductions for ransom.

II.   The CoI Findings

Casualties

20.   The CoI has recorded numerous casualties resulting from incidents across the country. In line with its methodology, the CoI reports the deaths only of those persons about which it has first-hand information through individual interviews that its investigators conducted. In the CoI figures, no distinction is made between civilians and fighters. Injured persons are not included in the count of casualties. The CoI, through 383 interviews of victims and witnesses of events since its February 2012 report to 15 June 2012, was able to confirm 435 deaths.

21.   Information provided by the Syrian Government concerning the number of deaths as a result of the unrest, indicates that by 27 April 2012 some 6143 Syrian citizens had been killed. This number includes 3211 civilians, 478 public order officers, 2088 military personnel, 204 women and 56 children. Another 106 people were assassinated according to the Government. The Syrian Government supplemented these figures, according to which 804 persons were killed (both armed forces and civilians) in the period between 7 May and 4 June 2012. The CoI is not in a position to confirm these figures.

22.   Other entities, in particular non-Governmental organizations, are also counting casualties by employing a variety of methods. The number reported by these groups ranges from 13,000 to 17,000. These figures could not be confirmed by the CoI.

Special inquiry into Al-Houla

Introduction

23.   On 25 May 2012, amidst armed confrontations between Government and anti-Government armed forces in the town of Taldou, Homs Governorate, more than 100 people were allegedly killed. Although some were victims of armed clashes, the significant majority were reported to be women and children who had been deliberately killed in their homes.

24.   In resolution A/HRC/RES/S-19/1 the Human Rights Council directed the CoI

    "to urgently conduct a comprehensive, independent and unfettered special inquiry, consistent with international standards, into the events in el-Houleh, and if possible

to publicly identify those who appear responsible for these atrocities, and to preserve the evidence of crimes for possible future criminal prosecutions or a future justice process, with a view to hold to account those responsible; and also requests the commission to provide a full report of the findings of its special inquiry to the Human Rights Council at its twentieth session, and to coordinate, as appropriate, with relevant UN mechanisms."

25.   Al-Houla refers to a group of towns located approximately 30 kilometers northwest of Homs. Its three main towns - Tal Addahab, Kafr Laha and Taldou - have a population exceeding 100,000 of which the majority is Sunni Muslim. The towns are ringed by Shia villages to the southeast, and Alawi villages to the southwest and the north. Government forces are present in Al-Houla with permanent security force installations, including police and military intelligence services. A number of fortified checkpoints were set up during the crisis (see annexed Maps).

Government's account of the events

26.   Immediately after the incident the Government of the Syrian Arab Republic announced the formation of a National Commission of Inquiry (inquiry), including membership from the Ministries of Defense, Interior and Justice. The General Command of the Armed Forces appointed Brigadier General Jamal Qassem Al-Suleiman to lead the inquiry. On 4 June the CoI addressed a Note Verbale to the Permanent Mission of the Syrian Arab Republic requesting access to the country and a copy of the results of the inquiry. On 6 June the CoI received a report containing the preliminary results. There is no information when the final report will be available.

27.   The Government's inquiry found that the Syrian Army defended itself from an attack by what it deemed 'terrorists' (the term used in the Note Verbale), and that a number of its soldiers were killed in the clashes. The report acknowledged the deaths of civilians and describes the victims as peaceful families who had refused to rise up against the State or participate in demonstrations. It further suggested as a motive for the Al-Sayed family killings that they were allied with Abdelmuti Mashlab, a new member of the Syrian Parliament, and their political loyalties were thus, presumably, pro-Government.

28.   The victims were reportedly killed by terrorists numbering between 600–800, who had entered Al-Houla previously from the villages of Al-Rastan, Sa'an, Bourj Qaei and Samae'leen, among other locations. The terrorists were said to have gathered in Taldou, launched the attack on security forces and while that attack was taking place a part of the group, or a separate group, went to the crime scenes and perpetrated the murders.

29.   The Government inquiry further found that the number of deceased people claimed in media reports of the incident were inflated because they included also members of terrorist groups who had been killed fighting Government forces. The Government inquiry also found that the evidence of close proximity killings exculpated the military as the victims could, thus, not have been killed in shelling – as was initially claimed. The report included testimony from two eye-witnesses who appeared to have been in the vicinity of the armed groups at various points during the events and whose testimony is consistent with the Government's version.

30.   The report does not describe the methodology employed in the inquiry, for example, the number of witnesses interviewed or how and where the Government inquiry interviewed the witnesses.   The inquiry's preliminary report states that the two eyewitnesses were "from the region," and that their identities were kept confidential for fear of reprisal. There is no indication of any other evidentiary material collected for the inquiry, whether it examined video or photographic evidence or whether it attempted to visit the scene of the crime, find and interview injured persons or secure medical records.

The report does not indicate that testimony was collected from military personnel who would have been involved in the fighting or present on the day the events occurred.

Findings

31.   The CoI was unable to visit the site of the killing as it has yet to be afforded access to the country. This fact substantially hampered the investigation, and its findings should be viewed in that light.

32.   The CoI conducted its investigation by interviewing witnesses either by telephone/skype, or in person if they had fled the country. It collected and reviewed materials from a variety of sources, both governmental and non-governmental. The CoI reviewed satellite imagery taken prior to and after the incident, as well as other photographs and videos.

33.   The CoI also took note of the engagement by various UN human rights mechanisms following the allegations concerning the Al-Houla events. On 30 May 2012 the Committee against Torture expressed its grave concern over the tragic events. On 31 May 2012, the Committee on the Rights of the Child deplored the possible deliberate targeting of children. Both statements were transmitted to the President of the Human Rights Council (HRC) on 1 June 2012. On the part of Special Procedures, a statement on behalf of all mandate-holders was delivered at the 19th Special Session of HRC on 1 June 2012, condemning a series of attacks on residential areas in Syria, in particular the massacre of civilians in Al-Houla.

34.   The evidence collected by the CoI indicates that in the 24-hour period beginning at noon on 25 May 2012, at least 100 people were killed in the town of Taldou. Shortly after the Friday prayers, a demonstration took place near the town center. The protestors appear to have been fired upon or shelled by Government forces. Either in retaliation, or in a pre-meditated attack, anti-Government armed groups, including the FSA present in Taldou, fired upon the security forces checkpoints, probably overrunning one or two of them. Several people were killed in these clashes or as a result of the shelling. According to multiple accounts, shelling by Government forces continued throughout the day. The CoI was able to verify shelling damage to buildings by comparing satellite images from the morning of 25 and the morning of 26 May. Much of the damage appeared to be caused by mortars, including large caliber mortars, heavy machine guns or light artillery.

35.   In the late afternoon and evening of 25 May, at a minimum 50 civilians were killed, the bulk of those were members of the Abdulrazzak family. Another 13–15 members of the Al-Sayed family were killed later, probably after dark, although the precise timing for either killing could not be determined by the CoI. The CoI received information that members of other families may have been killed, but the CoI was unable to verify these assertions. The list of names of the deceased was not consistent among various sources.

36.   The victims were predominantly women and children, and most appear to have been killed in their homes. Evidence indicates they died by gunshots fired at close range to the upper body. The killings reportedly occurred in, at least, two locations. The first is on Saad Road (*Tariq Al-Sad*) which lies at the south-west edge of Taldou (Map 2: A) where many members of the Abdulrazzak family were killed. The second location is on Main Street (Al-Raeesi), approximately 1000 meters below the clock tower roundabout (Map 2: B), where members of the Al-Sayed family were killed.

37.   On 25 May there were Government checkpoints along Main street: one in the very heart of Taldou at the clock tower roundabout (Map 1: CP 1), possibly another one at the

Military intelligence building,[2] a mobile one between *Qaws* (the "Arches," at the original entrance to Taldou) and the National Hospital (Map 1: CP 2). The hospital was itself a military post, having been taken over by the army several months earlier (Map: Army post 1). Another military position established at the Water Company, described by both the opposition and the Government to be just outside the southwest entrance of the city (Map: Army post 2) – appears to be in an elevated location, providing a clear view over the town of Taldou, including Saad Road. The (direct) distance from the Water Company location to Saad Road crime scene is 1.3 km. According to accounts collected and based on satellite imagery, the river cuts access between Main Street where the army checkpoints are located and Saad Road. There were no visible checkpoints on Saad Road itself.

Saad Road killings (Abdulrazzak family and others)

38.   By most accounts the killings on Saad Road occurred between 16:00 and 18:00 hrs on 25 May. The Abdulrazzak family lived in the last set of houses on Saad Road in the direction of the dam. Apparently multiple families lived in each house. The location is 500 meters away from the closest Government checkpoint known as *Qaws*, near the National Hospital. There is, however, a small river running between the locations so they are not directly accessible one to the other - except perhaps by foot across the riverbed.

39.   Interviewees who arrived at the Abdulrazzak compound described the scene inside the houses as horrific, with groups of women, boys and girls huddled together in the corner of living rooms. Most victims appeared to have been killed at close range; their upper bodies exhibited wounds consistent with the use of firearms. Blood was visible on the walls, indicating many were standing when shot. Witnesses described bodies of men, women and children outside the homes and on the street.

40.   Accounts collected from those who told the CoI they were among the first to arrive at the scene described the use of sharp objects in the killing of the Abdulrazzak family. Multiple interviewees described stab wounds and the apparent use of axes or similar (*satour*). One person early on the scene described to the CoI a bloody knife allegedly found in one house. Another described multiple knives found, one knife bearing the inscription *"We will sacrifice ourselves for you Hussein"* - which is a Shia slogan. The CoI viewed a video of a knife with such an inscription, although it could not verify its authenticity. Other witnesses stated that all victims had been shot, apart from those killed in the shelling. Video and documentary evidence available to the CoI was inconclusive on this point.

41.   Multiple accounts indicated that the homes had been ransacked and valuables stolen in the course of the killing. There appears to have been, at least, one survivor from the Abdulrazzak home, although the CoI was unable to interview this person.

42.   Accounts varied as to who was in control of the southern portion of the village of Taldou and specifically the street where the Abdulrazzak family's house is located. Opposition forces may have been in control of parts of the city, mostly in the north.

43.   The CoI determined that neither the anti-Government armed groups nor the security forces could fully control access to Saad Road to the exclusion of the other. The Government forces' deployment on the military positions did not equate to control of Saad Road and that, in any event, it is possible that one or all checkpoints were engaged in fighting at the time of the Abdulrazzak killings. It is important to note, however, that movement of vehicles or military equipment, explosions or armed clashes would likely have been detectable by the Water Company position. Access for any sizable group would

---

[2]   The Commission understands the Military Intelligence building to be the "detachment" referred to in the Government report (see map).

have been practically impossible, especially if they arrived in vehicles, without Government forces being aware.

44.   Accounts varied as to the location from where the perpetrators entered and how they exited Saad Road. To the extent verifiable from accounts and satellite imagery, there were no checkpoints anywhere on the street. Both pro- and anti-Government forces could have accessed the crime scenes. Opposition activists managed to reach the site of the Abdulrazzak killings in broad daylight - while the clashes and shelling were reportedly ongoing. This fact indicates that routes to the Abdulrazzak crime scene were not closed to them. Anti-Government forces could also have accessed the scenes through fields, or in small numbers. While the National Hospital checkpoint is 500 meters away, the CoI was unable to determine whether that checkpoint remained actively manned at the time of the crimes, and even if manned, whether it would have been in the position to stop a small group of armed persons from accessing the Abdulrazzak homes. The checkpoint was, however, manned by Government troops at the time the UN observers arrived the morning of 26 May 2012.

45.   Some sources told the CoI that the perpetrators entered from the road leading to the south towards the dam and eventually to the neighbouring Alawite villages, including Fullah. There was testimony collected that described two white mini-buses arriving and departing from that direction. The lack of a checkpoint on this route was asserted as proof of government complicity. Other accounts described the perpetrators as working together with the army, and coming and going from the direction of the government checkpoints either at the National Hospital or the Water Company, on the southeast side of the village. To access Saad Road from there by road, the perpetrators would have had to go either through Taldou itself, including areas controlled by anti-Government armed groups, or make a detour to the Alawite villages on the other side of the reservoir, and return the same way. They might also have accessed on foot, by crossing the riverbed.

Main Street killing (Al-Sayed family and others)

46.   The CoI was able to garner little evidence of the Main Street killings, save for the location. Accounts as to the time of the incident were inconsistent, although it appears to have been sometime after 11pm. The victims' homes are situated in close proximity to the National Hospital and thus, 75 - 100 meters from a security forces checkpoint at *Qaws*. There is an alleged survivor, a young boy, and the CoI was able to interview him via skype. The CoI also considered video evidence posted by anti-Government groups of the boy being interviewed by others. In both interviews he blamed the killings on *Shabbiha* and soldiers of the Syrian army. In one interview the survivor stated that the perpetrators arrived together in tanks. The CoI took note of the age of the boy and duly considered his suggestibility.

47.   Access to the Al-Sayed family/Main Street location, if it did occur in the middle of the night, would have been possible for either pro- or anti-Government elements. Complicity of the checkpoint staff would have been all that was required for access by pro-Government forces. Even then, anyone with knowledge of Taldou could have found other routes of access by avoiding the checkpoints under the cloak of darkness. Evidence indicates that the checkpoints were sufficiently close to the crime scenes that the noises emanating therefrom (gunbursts and screams) would likely have alerted those manning the checkpoint. Thus, the CoI determined that the location of the checkpoints, although not determinative as to the perpetrators' accessing the crime scene, made it likely that those manning the pro-Government checkpoints were aware.

Alleged perpetrators

48.   The CoI considered the information available to it on the killings in Al-Houla in an impartial manner and considered carefully the prevailing views on the party responsible, determining that three were most likely in light of the evidence. First, that the perpetrators were *Shabbiha* or other local militia from neighbouring villages, possibly operating together with, or with the acquiescence of, the Government security forces; second, that the perpetrators were anti-Government forces seeking to escalate the conflict while punishing those that failed to support – or who actively opposed - the rebellion; or third, foreign groups with unknown affiliation.

49.   With the available evidence, the CoI could not rule out any of these possibilities.

50.   The Government had superior equipment. Evidence available indicates they had deployed APCs, tanks and/or self-propelled anti-aircraft guns and mortars in Taldou and the surroundings. The Government clearly had the capacity to shell any location on Saad Road and indeed the entire town – and, in fact, did so. The CoI determined that the clocktower checkpoint was overrun at some point, but there was no indication or evidence that the elevated post, the Water Company, was ever overrun, nor was the National Hospital. The vantage point of the Water Company should have been clear onto the Abdulrazzak and the Al-Sayed family sites. That said, it is unlikely that those positioned at the Water Company could have discerned between a farmer with a rake and a fighter carrying a gun, unless viewing through a sniper scope or similar. The same cannot be said for the National Hospital checkpoint which, if actively manned, could easily have made such a determination. Moreover, there is no indication that the Government attempted the next day to secure the crime scene, which had already been disturbed by the removal of the bodies.

51.   Government positions at the National Hospital and the Water Company appear to have had a clear line of site to the Abdulrazzak and Al-Sayed homes making access for perpetrators not aligned with the Government difficult. Government shelling will have caused a number of the deaths, and controlling the timing and location of the impact would also have made it easier to control access to the crime scenes. Finally, the manner in which these killings took place resembles those previously and repeatedly documented to have been committed by the Government, including in this report (see section, Violations by the Syrian Government, Unlawful killings).

52.   The village as a whole and the particular neighbourhoods in question appeared aligned to the opposition more than the Government. Leaving the sectarian aspect aside, the CoI found that the victims from the Abdulrazzak and the Al-Sayed sites were taken to areas controlled by the opposition and it was opposition groups who first arrived to the scene, cared for the wounded, prepared the deceased for burial, and were present in large numbers during the funeral. The Commission has testimony indicating that those who fled the area, fled to anti-Government controlled parts of town. Still, without further investigation, the CoI could not determine whether these specific families had loyalties one way or the other. There appears to have been a retired member of the security forces, and perhaps even one active member, among the deceased. Some information, including a video viewed by the Commission, indicated that, at least, one of the deceased children was wearing a bracelet bearing the Syrian National Flag. The video could not be verified. Nor could the CoI establish whether the Al-Sayed family and the Mashlab family (new member of parliament) were, in fact, associated.

53.   The Commission determined that while the anti-Government forces could access the Abdulrazzak crime scene despite the superior firing position of the Government, it would have been difficult (although not impossible) for them to access the Al-Sayed family site. Thus, while the CoI could not rule out the possibility of anti-Government fighters being responsible for the killing, it was considered unlikely.

54.   The CoI could not rule out the possibility of the involvement of foreign groups with unknown affiliation. The CoI received information that the anti-Government armed groups in Taldou on that day received "support from other groups from neighboring areas." Testimony was also collected that described the perpetrators as having shaved heads and long beards – descriptions which have been applied both to foreign groups and the *Shabbiha* in other contexts.   This information could not be corroborated by the Commission.

55.   The CoI is unable to determine the identity of the perpetrators at this time; nevertheless the CoI considers that forces loyal to the Government may have been responsible for many of the deaths. The investigation will continue until the end of the CoI mandate.

Perspectives on the continuation of the Al-Houla special inquiry

56.   The CoI reiterates that for it to conduct a thorough investigation, access to the territory of the Syrian Arab Republic is required.   The killings in Al-Houla, like other alleged violations recorded by the CoI, require independent, impartial investigation which the CoI exists to provide.

57.   International human rights law places the onus for protecting citizens squarely on the Government. Irrespective of the perpetrator of this crime, it is the State that bears primary responsibility for investigating it, bringing a case to an independent judicial body and ultimately providing justice to the victims.

58.   The CoI considers that the investigation undertaken so far by the Government falls short of applicable international standards. The 'UN Principles on the Effective Prevention and Investigation of Extra-legal, Arbitrary and Summary Executions' require that the inquiry be independent, thorough, prompt and impartial. Three of these four requirements have not been met. The CoI recognizes that the report it received was "preliminary," and it expects to be provided with the final version when available.[3]

59.   In the course of a further investigation, the CoI recommends: interviewing the military personnel present in Taldou; conducting crime scene examinations, including forensic and ballistic studies of available evidence; interviewing potential eyewitnesses on Saad Road and those who were wounded but survived the killings and any other eyewitnesses; examining the photos, medical records and death certificates of the deceased, if any, to verify cause/circumstances of death, age and gender. The investigation should extend to the town of Kafr Laha, and to the neighboring villages of Fullah and Ghur Gharbiye, at a minimum.

60.   It is of the utmost importance that any remaining evidence of this crime be preserved. The location must be secured to the extent possible and any available evidence brought under the control of an independent judicial or investigative body. The CoI, in line with the mandate given by the Human Rights Council, is recording and safeguarding all evidence it obtains – accounts, videos, photos, satellite imagery, etc. – bearing in mind its possible use by a future justice mechanism.

---

[3] Under these guidelines, members of a National Commissions of Inquiry "shall be chosen for their recognized impartiality, competence and independence as individuals. In particular, they shall be independent of any institution, agency or person that may be the subject of the inquiry. The commission shall have the authority to obtain all information necessary to the inquiry and shall conduct the inquiry as provided for under these Principles." Principles on the Effective Prevention and Investigation of Extra-legal, Arbitrary and Summary Executions, 24 May 1989, Art 11

A/HRC/20/CRP.1

61.   The CoI will update these findings and conclusions in its Final Report, due for delivery to the Human Rights Council at its 21st Session in September 2012, and will also deliver an amended, confidential list of suspected perpetrators.

Violations by the Syrian Government Forces

62.   In the increasingly militarized context described above, human rights violations are occurring across the country on an alarming scale during military operations against locations believed to be hosting defectors and/or those perceived as affiliated with anti-Government armed groups, including the "Free Syrian Army" (FSA).   Demonstrations, with or without "armed protection," continue to be a trigger for a heavy-handed government response, as do anti-Government armed groups' attacks on military bases, outposts and checkpoints. Other violations noted by the CoI have less clear impetus. Some appeared to have sectarian undertones while still others appeared to be reprisals, including collective punishment.

Unlawful Killings

63.   The Commission continues to receive reports of unlawful killings taking place during the shelling of towns and villages perceived as being anti-Government strongholds, and in the military operations which follow. Interviews were conducted with civilians, defectors and members of anti-Government armed fighting groups present in camps in the bordering countries. Since the Commission has not yet been afforded access to the Syrian Arab Republic, it has not been able to carry out investigations at the scenes of the alleged crimes.   Therefore, its ability to independently verify the accounts received has been limited.

64.   Over the reporting period a clear pattern to such violations has been identified. In an effort to quell a demonstration or to seize wanted persons, military and security forces attacked neighbourhoods, villages and towns across the Syrian Arab Republic. Attacks were often preceded by a blockade of main roads with checkpoints fortified by tanks, armoured personnel carriers and machine guns. Military and security forces would then reportedly begin to indiscriminately shell the encircled location. More precise shelling appeared to have been employed in some cases. The more recent deployment of helicopter gunships and heavy artillery during the shelling reflects the increasing militarization of the engagements.

65.   After shelling, military and security forces would enter, often positioning snipers on rooftops as they advanced. Once inside the area, the forces would begin house-to-house searches. Statements received by the Commission indicate that in many instances forces were accompanied by pro-Government militias, also known as *Shabbiha*. If the inhabitants anticipated the raid, those fearing reprisals would flee, usually evacuating women, children and the elderly at the same time. Young men were especially vulnerable to targeting as their age and sex were alone sufficient for them to be considered suspects. If the inhabitants were caught without warning, or they decided to remain in their homes, they would be exposed to shelling, sniper fire and searches. The military and security forces would generally leave the area in the evenings. Inhabitants who had fled would subsequently return to bury the dead and to assess the damage to their houses and other property.

66.   Unlawful killings as a result of indiscriminate shelling by the Government's military and security forces were documented in Atarib on 14 February; Ain Larouz on 5 March; Sermin on 22 March; Taftanaz on 4 April; Kili on 6 April; and El Haffe on 4 and 5 June 2012. The Commission notes the intense and prolonged indiscriminate shelling of the city of Homs, and in particular the neighbourhood of Baba Amr, where many civilians, including young children, were among those killed and injured. Also killed, on 22 February

2012, were journalist, Marie Colvin and photographer, Remi Ochlik. The shelling ceased temporarily on 1 March 2012 when anti-Government armed groups withdrew, but since late May 2012, the indiscriminate, periodic bombardment of Homs has resumed.

67.   There have been multiple consistent reports of unlawful killings, in the form of extra-judicial executions, during house searches. There are clear indications that some individuals were targeted as it was believed that their relatives were members of anti-Government armed groups or defectors. In Abdita, on 21 February 2012, the army reportedly entered the house of family members of known FSA members, took them into neighbouring fields, questioned them about a recent IED attack and executed them if they did not receive a response they considered adequate. Independent eyewitnesses told the Commission of 15 persons killed with gunshot wounds to the head, many with their hands tied behind their backs. Relatives of the FSA leader Riad al-Assad were among those allegedly summarily executed. Eight of the victims were from Abdita, while the others were from the neighbouring villages of Mashoum and Bsamas. In Sermin on 23 March 2012, three young men, said to be family members of a well-known lieutenant from the 15th Division Special Forces who had defected, were reportedly taken outside during a house search conducted by the army and shot in the front-yard, in the presence of their family.

68.   In many instances, it was less clear whether specific individuals or families had been targeted, beyond living in an area under attack by the Government's military and security forces. Extra-judicial executions were documented in Ain Larouz between 4 and 12 March; Sermin on 23 March; Taftanaz on 4 April; Kili on 6 April; Bashiriya on 8 April and in Tal Rifat on a date unknown in April 2012. In some particularly grave incidents, reports were received of large-scale executions. In Taftanaz, multiple executions were recorded occurring during the 4 April 2012 searches. Estimates of those unlawfully killed range from 84 to 110 people, many of them from a branch of the Ghazal family. Some bodies were reportedly found with gunshot wounds to the head and chest, including some that had been blindfolded with hands tied behind their backs. In Tal Rifat, 52 people were reportedly executed by the 4th Division of the Syrian army during the April 2012 attack. The Commission is not in a position to verify these figures.

69.   The Commission notes the relatively high incidence of extra-judicial executions which took place in various neighbourhoods of the city of Homs since March 2012. On 11 and 12 March 2012, the neighbourhood of Karm al-Zeytoun reportedly came under an attack by what was described as *Shabbiha* protected by the army. Multiple families were killed in their homes, apparently by knives or other sharp instruments. Estimates of casualties, unverified by the Commission, ranged from 35 to 80. In the Sultaniya neighbourhood, on a date unknown in March 2012, Syrian military and security forces and *Shabbiha* reportedly removed adult men from their houses, before lining them up and shooting them. Multiple interviews have consistently detailed extra-judicial executions taking place in the Shammas neighbourhood on 15 May 2012. Residents described members of the "security forces" and *Shabbiha* entering the neighbourhood, shooting into the air and commencing house-to-house searches. One of those interviewed stated that she saw young men, blindfolded and handcuffed, taken into a building after which shots were fired. Another interviewee indicated that, on the following day he found 23 bodies, including the local imam, in a building near the mosque. Most had bullet wounds to the head.

70.   The Commission has noted an increasing incidence of the burning of bodies following execution. Of the executions in Taftanaz taking place on 4 April 2012, the charred bodies of two adults and five young children were later discovered in the family house. In Kili on 6 April 2012, according to multiple eyewitnesses interviewed independently, elements of the security forces arrested two brothers, handcuffed and executed them and then burnt the bodies.

71.   Some casualties occurred when civilians, having ventured out of their homes, were shot by snipers. Civilians were reportedly killed by sniper fire in Ain Larouz between 9–12 March 2012, in Atarib in February, March and April 2012 and in Homs in March and April 2012. The Commission notes with concern the high number of children killed by snipers, in proportion to the total number killed. Those interviewed have also reported executions of, at least, six civilians by members of the security forces and *Shabbiha* at checkpoints placed in and around Atarib in February and March 2012.

72.   State security forces continued to use lethal force against anti-Government demonstrations. The Commission collected consistent testimony from defectors who told of orders they received to use live fire on demonstrators. The Commission recognises that many such protests were accompanied by armed groups, who have described their role as providing protection for the demonstrators. In some cases armed opposition fighters admitted they went to the mosques where many protests start after Friday prayers. In other cases anti-Government armed groups positioned themselves around the protesters or at the main entry points to the town to guard against the arrival of military and security forces. The resulting clashes often resulted in civilian casualties.

73.   On 9 May 2012, a demonstration of around 200-300 students took place on Aleppo University campus. Shortly after political security, air force intelligence, army and some *Shabbiha* elements reportedly surrounded the campus, the number of student protesters grew to over a thousand. Government forces fired tear gas at the students and live ammunition in the air. They then entered the campus and, in an operation that lasted most of the night, began arresting students, ultimately detaining approximately 200. During the raid they allegedly threw one student from the fourth floor. According to sources interviewed by the Commission, between two and five students were killed.

Arbitrary arrest and detention

74.   The Commission continues to receive first-hand accounts of arbitrary arrest and detention, predominantly of men and boys. Government forces reportedly arrested those identified previously by local informers as supporters and/or family members of anti-Government armed groups, or organisers of anti-Government protests or simply protestors. The Commission has, however, received reports of the arbitrary arrests of those injured in shelling, and in one instance, a road accident. From the interrogations which followed, it was apparent that merely being injured was deemed to be evidence of involvement in fighting. The Commission has also received reports of civilians being arrested during house-to-house searches by Government forces. Where people were arrested, their families were provided with no information about where their relatives were being held and on what charges.

75.   The Commission noted that a number of those interviewed had been transferred to multiple different facilities and interrogated by what they perceived to be different intelligence agencies. Questioning during interrogations, according to testimonies received, appeared to revolve around reasons for protesting, involvement of the detainee or his or her family members in anti-Government armed groups and, in the case of a few detainees who were members of the Government forces, about alleged plans to defect. Two of those interviewed had been transferred for separate interrogations at over ten different locations, including Military Security buildings in Halab, Idlib, Homs, Halab and Damascus.

76.   Nearly all of those interviewed had not been formally charged with any offences, and they received neither defense counsel nor family visits. In the days prior to release, the majority indicated that they had been made to sign or thumbprint a document, the contents of which they were unaware. The Commission has received reports that some of those detained were brought before a judge and then released. The Commission also interviewed one former member of the judiciary who indicated that security agencies produced

detainees who showed signs of abuse, including open wounds. The interviewee indicated that security agents would not permit questioning in their absence and, on one occasion, held the judge at gunpoint. Several detainees stated that the judges did not question them about their injuries and the presence of security units in the courtroom intimidated them.

Torture and other forms of ill-treatment

77.   The majority of detainees interviewed by the Commission stated that they had been tortured or ill-treated during their interrogation. Methods of torture documented by the Commission were consistent across the country. They included mock executions; electric shocks applied to sensitive parts of the body, including genitals; cigarettes burns; and beating with electric cables, whips, metal and wooden sticks and rifle butts. There were multiple reports of detainees being beaten about the head and on the soles of the feet. The Commission also received reports of detainees being placed into prolonged stress positions (*shabeh*) and the use of vehicle tires to hold hands and feet in uncomfortable positions (*dulab*) while beatings were administered. In many of the interviews, scars and wounds, consistent with their accounts, were still visible.

78.   The Commission further notes that several forms of torture and ill-treatment meted out to detainees would not have resulted in physical scarring. Reports received also detail detainees being forcibly shaved, made to imitate dogs and to declare that "there is no God but Bashar" while in a position of supplication.

79.   Detainees indicated that they had been held for extended periods, ranging from a week to as long as five months. The majority described being held in over-crowded cells in unhygienic conditions, with inadequate food and water. The Commission received information it could not corroborate on the denial of medication and medical treatment. One detainee stated that a man, held in his cell in the Idlib military security building in early 2012, died having not received medication for his diabetes. Another, held in the Kafr Sousa military security branch in Damascus, stated that a fellow detainee was left with a broken leg in his cell. Many of those interviewed have difficulty recalling dates and, in some cases, months.

Violations of children's rights

80.   Children continue to suffer in the context of the on-going events in the Syrian Arab Republic. They are frequently among those killed and injured during attacks on protests and the bombardment of towns and villages. During an attack on Taftanaz in April 2012, there were five people under 18 among the deceased. Additionally, specific reports of children being killed by snipers came out of Atarib in February 2012 as well as in two separate villages in Idlib in January and March 2012. In areas where anti-Government armed groups hold sway, boys older than 14 years are reportedly targeted as members of such groups. Children, including boys as young as 10 years of age, detained by State forces, have reported that they are tortured to admit that older male relatives are members or supporters of anti-Government armed groups.

81.   Wounded children have been unable to seek treatment due to fears of being perceived as anti-Government armed groups supporters or for fear of being beaten in health facilities. Children have died due to a lack of adequate health care during Government blockades. Some, including those injured as a result of torture, have been denied medical care.

82.   Accounts were recorded that primary and secondary schools have been targeted by State forces. In March 2012, a school in Atarib, Aleppo governorate, was occupied with tanks on its grounds and snipers positioned on its roof. In the same month, another school in a nearby village was burnt down, allegedly because its headmaster was rumored to be

associated with anti-Government armed groups. In early April 2012, a village school in Hama governorate was occupied by State forces, which used it as a command post, again putting snipers on its roof.

Sexual violence

83.   The CoI recognises the difficulties in collecting evidence in cases of sexual violence in the Syrian Arab Republic due to cultural, social and religious beliefs related to marriage and sexuality. This includes a victim's understandable reluctance to disclose information due to the trauma, shame and stigma linked to sexual assault. Regarding one incident, the CoI was informed that the rape victim had subsequently been killed by her brother-in-law to "preserve the honour of the family". The silence surrounding rape and other forms of sexual violence appears to have existed prior to the conflict as well.

84.   Nevertheless, interviews collected by the CoI indicate that crimes of sexual violence – against men, women and children – have continued to take place in the Syrian Arab Republic during the reporting period. The CoI conducted 23 interviews relating to allegations of sexual violence in this period, including with one victim. Information collected thus far indicates that rape and other forms of sexual violence occurred in two distinct circumstances. The first is during the searches of houses as Government forces entered towns and villages; the second, during interrogations in detention.

85.   Following the Government forces' move into the Baba Amr neighbourhood of Homs in February 2012, and the commencement of house searches, the CoI received multiple reports of rape and sexual assaults taking place. In one incident, an interviewee stated that 40-50 men stormed into the family house, destroying and stealing property as the search took place. In his testimony, he described being forced to watch as his wife and two of his daughters were raped by three of the men involved. Afterwards, he stated, he, too, was raped while his family was made to watch.

86.   In a separate incident, a soldier with the Syrian army described seeing three of his colleagues sexually assault a 15-year-old girl during a house search in Zabadani in February 2012. According to the interviewee, he attempted to prevent the assault but he was threatened and beaten by the other soldiers, so he fled. The CoI also received corroborated reports of women being forced at gunpoint to walk naked in the streets of the Karm al-Zeytoun neighbourhood of Homs, again in February 2012.

87.   The CoI heard from an eye-witness a report on the gang-rape of a female activist during an interrogation at the military security building in Dara'a in late May 2012. The victim was reportedly found unconscious in the streets of Dara'a two days later. The eyewitness also reported being a victim of a sexual assault during the same interrogation. The CoI has received multiple, uncorroborated reports of incidences of rape and sexual assault of men and women while detained.

88.   The fear of rape and sexual assault has restricted the freedom of movement of women and young girls and has adversely affected the right to education of female students. One girl told the CoI that, since 24 April 2012, female students in Latakia governate were not attending school due to fear of such assaults. It was also apparent to the CoI that many of the women interviewed who had sought refuge in neighbouring countries had done so because they feared sexual assault. The CoI also notes the lack of medical or psychological services available to victims who suffer sexual violence.

Abuses committed by anti-Government armed groups

89.   Although the international human rights legal regime operates primarily vis-à-vis states, the CoI has received reports of abuses of human rights in the Syrian Arab Republic

committed by anti-Government armed groups, many of which claim affiliation with the FSA. Lack of access to the country has hindered investigations of abuses committed by these groups.

Unlawful killings

90.   The CoI has received multiple reports of the extra-judicial executions of members of the army and security forces, *Shabbiha*, foreign fighters, suspected informers and/or collaborators, captured by anti-Government armed groups. Two such incidents occurred in Homs in April 2012. In corroborated statements taken from anti-Government fighters, the CoI recorded instances where members of Government forces perceived to have committed crimes – for example, by participating in the shelling of civilian areas – were executed on capture. A defector who fought in the ranks of Al Farouk Brigade, which is affiliated to the FSA, in Homs city stated that members of the Government forces, including those he claimed were three Iranian snipers, were summarily executed after they apparently confessed.   One anti-Government armed group fighter also admitted that he and his associates had killed Government soldiers when the captives refused to join them.

91.   In June 2012 an FSA fighter told the CoI that his unit was currently holding four senior officers for exchange. Lower level soldiers were reportedly tried by a court applying Sharia law, according to the fighter. Multiple FSA soldiers interviewed told the CoI they had never heard of international humanitarian or human rights law. One soldier stated that he believed the creed "an eye for an eye", which he described as being part of Sharia law, supersedes international standards. Another FSA soldier told the CoI that Alawite soldiers are normally killed immediately upon capture, while soldiers from other sects are offered the chance to join the FSA, and if they refuse to join, they are released to their relatives. Other soldiers have said Alawites are more valuable in prisoner exchanges, and can be traded for multiple Sunnis.

92.   One FSA member told the CoI that the number of "female informers" was on the rise. He insisted they were not raped when captured. They were, however, immediately executed.

93.   The anti-Government armed groups are reportedly developing mechanisms for trying captured members of the security forces. The CoI documented several accounts of captives being judged by military commanders as well as community and religious leaders (a Shura Council). The CoI has been unable to obtain a consistent account of a trial process or the extent of any adherence to fair trial standards. Punishment is generally execution for anyone found guilty, although for "small crimes" some captives might be released. In some locations, such as Jabal al Zawiya and Deir Sinbal, makeshift prisons have reportedly been set up.

Use of Improvised Explosive Devices

94.   The CoI has taken note of an increased use of IEDs by anti-Government armed groups. Interviewees described how, in April 2012, they had put nails inside pipes with explosive powder and a fuse. Others described the use of gas and fertilizer to create homemade bombs. Information provided by the Government, but not corroborated by the CoI, indicated that some 736 explosive devices have exploded or were dismantled during the month of May 2012 alone.

Torture and other forms of ill-treatment

95.   The CoI has received information indicating that Syrian security forces or their alleged supporters caught by the anti-Government armed groups have confessed under torture. Many of the video recordings of alleged incidents show those captured with signs

of physical abuse, including bruising and bleeding. Two Iranians, held in late January 2012 and released in late April 2012, later made public statements about physical abuse suffered, including the breaking of bones, during their captivity. A defector who joined the FSA recently also reported that the group used torture, which has in some instances led to the death of the captive. Methods employed by the FSA include beating with electrical cables and holding a captive's head under water.

Abductions

96.   The CoI has recorded instances of anti-Government armed groups abducting civilians and members of the Government forces. The apparent motivation is to enable prisoner exchanges, but one fighter told the CoI that they sometimes call families and seek ransom to purchase weapons. The CoI recorded examples in Homs in April, 2012, and in Idlib, in March 2012.

Abuse of children's rights

97.   The CoI received corroborated evidence that anti-Government armed groups have been using children as medical porters, messengers and cooks for field units, and for delivery of medical supplies to field hospitals. In May 2012, CoI staff met many children involved in these activities who were regularly traversing the Turkish/Syria border. Four of them had been injured by sniper fire on a mission to Hama in mid-March 2012.

Other crimes by anti-Government groups

98.   The CoI received information from the Government with respect to serious crimes allegedly perpetrated by the opposition armed groups, including kidnapping, looting and vehicle theft. According to this information, some 2,491 civilians and security forces personnel were either kidnapped or have disappeared since the beginning of the unrest until 15 March 2012, while another 776 persons (either civilian or security forces personnel) were reportedly kidnapped between 7 May and 4 June 2012. Over the same period, the Syrian Government registered 88 cases of attempted weapons smuggling from neighbouring countries, including Lebanon, Turkey, Iraq and Jordan. The CoI could not corroborate this information, although it is clear that the anti-Government groups possess weapons and ammunition. Some anti-Government fighters have described to the CoI that they buy or steal their weapons from the Syrian army.

99.   The Government provided the CoI with information concerning damage and financial loss to the country's infrastructure, including damage caused to the Ministry of Transportation, its employees and its facilities (exceeding SP 3824 million; until the end of February), financial losses caused to the electricity sector (some SP 334 million in the period 1 to 17 April 2012), as well as financial losses caused to the irrigation sector (USD 51.5 million in the period March 2011 to April 2012). The Government placed the responsibility for these losses on the anti-Government armed groups. However the CoI was not in a position to verify this information.

Abuses by unknown perpetrators

Attacks on the UN monitors

100.   Where international humanitarian law is applicable, attacks on personnel or objects involved in humanitarian assistance or peacekeeping missions constitute a war crime.[4] The

---

[4]   Rome Statute of the International Criminal Court, Art. 8(2)(e)(iii).

CoI has noted an increasing hostility towards the UN presence in Syria, which is apparently emanating from both sides. In the period leading up to this report, a series of attacks, primarily gunfire, were directed at UN observers' convoys. On 12 June, the convoy headed to Al-Haffe was stopped by alleged pro-Government protestors and was later fired upon by unknown gunmen. On 16 June UNSMIS stopped its patrols due to safety concerns.

Attacks on religious buildings

101. The Commission notes with concern reports that an armed group has occupied a Greek-Catholic church in Al Qusayr, Homs, attacking clergy and turning the building into a base for its operations. The Commission's investigations are on-going.

Explosions

102. In the period preceding this Update, the Syrian Arab Republic suffered a series of large explosions in which scores of civilians were killed. The explosions appear to be by suicide bombers or by explosives hidden in vehicles and detonated remotely. The CoI has compiled the list below based on open sources it deems credible and whose information is consistent with other material on hand, including interviews conducted by the CoI:

- 14 June 2012, a car bomb exploded near the Sayyidah Zaynab shrine in a Damascus suburb injuring 11 people[5];

- 10 May 2012, two large explosions in Damascus' Qazaz neighborhood killed 55 people;

- 9 May 2012, an explosion as a UN convoy passed near Dar'a wounded six soldiers of the Syrian Government escort troops;

- 30 April 2012, twin explosions near daybreak close to a government compound in the city of Idlib killed 20 people, most of them from the security services;

- 27 April 2012, a bomb near a mosque of Al-Meidan neighborhood of Damascus killed 11 people;

- 18 March 2012, a car bomb killed three people in Aleppo; and

- 17 March 2012, two bombs apparently aimed at an intelligence service office and a police headquarters killed 27 people in Damascus.

103. The CoI was not able to ascertain those responsible for these criminal acts.

III. Conclusions

104. In the reporting period, the human rights situation in the Syrian Arab Republic has deteriorated rapidly. Gross violations of human rights are occurring in the context of increasingly militarised fighting. In some areas the fighting bears the characteristics of a non-international armed conflict. The violence has shifted dramatically from confrontations between protesters and the Government's security apparatus to fighting between its army – together with what appear to be pro-Government militias - and numerous anti-Government armed groups.

---

[5] On the day when this report was finalized, the CoI received a DVD from the Permanent Mission of the Syrian Arab Republic, containing a video recording of a confession by one of the alleged perpetrators.

105.   The situation on the ground has dramatically changed in the last three months as the hostilities by anti-Government armed groups each day take on more clearly the contours of an insurrection. As a result of the estimated flow of new weapons and ammunitions, both to the Government forces and to the anti-Government armed groups, the situation risks becoming more aggravated in the coming months. The international community must not fail to implement a concerted effort to put an end to the violence.

106.   The CoI considers it has reasonable grounds to believe that Government forces and *Shabbiha* have perpetrated unlawful killings, arbitrary arrests and detention and torture and other forms of ill-treatment, as detailed above. Particularly affected are children who continue to suffer in the context of the on-going events in the Syrian Arab Republic. Despite, the difficulties in collecting evidence of sexual violence, interviews conducted by the Commission indicated that Government forces and *Shabbiha* have committed acts of sexual violence against men, women and children during the reporting period.

107.   The CoI considers it has reasonable grounds to believe that anti-Government armed groups have extra-judicially executed captured members of the Government forces, *Shabbiha*, foreign fighters, supporters of the Government, suspected informers and/or collaborators. The Commission also found that anti-Government armed groups have tortured captured members of the Syrian security forces and/or their alleged supporters and abducted civilians and members of Government forces, usually to facilitate prisoner exchanges. The CoI is especially concerned by reports that anti-Government armed groups have been using children as medical porters, messengers and cooks, exposing them to risk of death and injury.

108.   There have been a number of incidents, including attacks on United Nations staff operating inside the Syrian Arab Republic, attacks on religious buildings and the series of explosions, as described above, where the CoI was unable to determine the perpetrators. The CoI investigations are on-going.

109.   The CoI, in accordance with its mandate, continues to document human rights violations committed by all parties without distinction. The CoI hopes that its work will help a future independent, impartial judicial body to ensure the accountability of those responsible for the violations recorded in its Reports and Updates.

110.   The cessation of hostilities is of paramount importance. Through hundreds of interviews, it is apparent that it is the civilian population, from various communities, who are suffering in this conflict, many losing their lives in the spiral of violence.

111.   The CoI firmly believes that the Joint Special Envoy's Six-Point Plan, supported by UNSMIS, offers the best framework for a resolution of the conflict. The CoI, cognizant of the rapidly deteriorating human rights situation, reaffirms its belief that the further militarization of the crisis will be catastrophic for the people and the territory of the Syrian Arab Republic and also for the entire region. As stated in its previous reports, the Commission's view remains that the best solution is one of a negotiated settlement involving an inclusive dialogue among the parties.

Annex

Maps

Map 1 – Al-Houla area

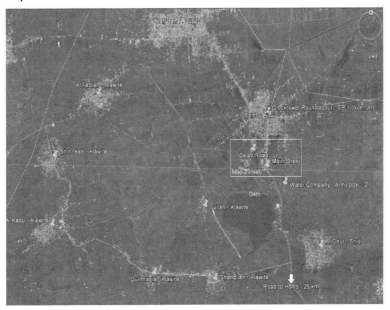

Map 2 – Inset from Map 1 – South Taldou

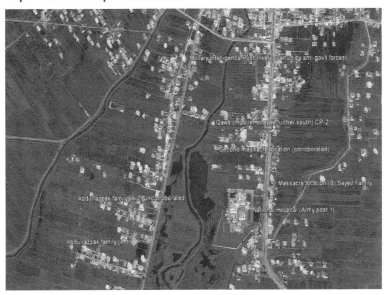

United Nations

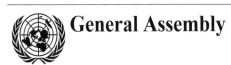

General Assembly

A/HRC/21/50

Distr.: General
16 August 2012

Original: English

Human Rights Council
Twenty-first session
Agenda item 4
Human rights situations that require the Council's attention

Report of the independent international commission of inquiry on the Syrian Arab Republic*

Summary

The situation of human rights in the Syrian Arab Republic has deteriorated significantly since 15 February 2012. Armed violence increased in intensity and spread to new areas. Active hostilities raged between Government forces (and the *Shabbiha*) and anti-Government armed groups. Sporadic clashes between the armed actors evolved into continuous combat, involving more brutal tactics and new military capabilities on both sides. The level of armed violence varied throughout the country.

During the reporting period, the commission of inquiry determined that the intensity and duration of the conflict, combined with the increased organizational capabilities of anti-Government armed groups, had met the legal threshold for a non-international armed conflict. The commission therefore applied both international humanitarian law and international human rights law in its assessment of the actions of the parties to the hostilities.

The commission found reasonable grounds to believe that Government forces and the *Shabbiha* had committed the crimes against humanity of murder and of torture, war crimes and gross violations of international human rights law and international humanitarian law, including unlawful killing, torture, arbitrary arrest and detention, sexual violence, indiscriminate attack, pillaging and destruction of property. The commission found that Government forces and *Shabbiha* members were responsible for the killings in Al-Houla.

The commission confirms its previous finding that violations were committed pursuant to State policy. Large-scale operations conducted in different governorates, their similar modus operandi, their complexity and integrated military-security apparatus indicate the involvement at the highest levels of the armed and security forces and the Government. The *Shabbiha* were identified as perpetrators of many of the crimes described in the present report. Although the nature, composition and hierarchy of the *Shabbiha*

---

* The annexes to the present report are reproduced as received, in the language of submission only.

remains unclear, credible information led to the conclusion that they acted in concert with Government forces.

The commission found reasonable grounds to believe that war crimes, including murder, extrajudicial execution and torture, had been perpetrated by organized anti-Government armed groups. Although not a party to the Geneva Conventions, these groups must abide by the principles of international humanitarian law. The violations and abuses committed by anti-Government armed groups did not reach the gravity, frequency and scale of those committed by Government forces and the *Shabbiha*.

Both groups violated the rights of children.

The commission is unaware of efforts meeting international standards made by either the Government or anti-Government armed groups to prevent or punish the crimes documented in the present report.

The lack of access significantly hampered the commission's ability to fulfil its mandate. Its access to Government officials and to members of the armed and security forces was negligible. Importantly, victims and witnesses inside the country could not be interviewed in person.

A confidential list of individuals and units believed to be responsible for crimes against humanity, breaches of international humanitarian law and gross human rights violations will be submitted to the United Nations High Commissioner for Human Rights at the close of the commission's current mandate, in September 2012.

The commission reiterates that the best solution is a negotiated settlement involving an inclusive and meaningful dialogue among all parties, leading to a political transition that reflects the legitimate aspirations of all segments of Syrian society, including ethnic and religious minorities.

Contents

I. Introduction

1.   The present report is submitted pursuant to Human Rights Council resolution 19/22 of 23 March 2012, in which the Council extended the mandate of the independent international commission of inquiry on the Syrian Arab Republic established by the Council in its resolution S-17/1 of 22 August 2011.

2.   In the present report, the commission[1] sets out its findings based on investigations conducted up until 20 July 2012. The report builds upon the commission's periodic updates released on 16 April and 24 May 2012, as well as the oral update presented by the commission to the Human Rights Council on 27 June 2012 (A/HRC/20/CRP.1). It also updates the findings of the commission's special inquiry into the events in Al-Houla, mandated by the Council in its resolution S-19/1 of 1 June 2012.

3.   The present report should be read in conjunction with the commission's previous reports (A/HRC/S-17/2/Add.1 and A/HRC/19/69) with regard to the interpretation of its mandate and working methods, as well as its factual and legal findings concerning the events in the Syrian Arab Republic between March 2011 and 15 February 2012.

A.   Challenges

4.   The commission faced a number of challenges. It was given a broad mandate — geographically, temporally and materially — to investigate all allegations of human rights violations committed in the country since March 2011. This meant conducting investigations in the context of a rapidly changing situation, which evolved into armed conflict.

5.   Lack of physical access to the country also significantly hampered the commission's ability to fulfil its mandate. In particular, its access to Government officials and to members of the armed and security forces was negligible. Importantly, victims and witnesses inside the country, especially those allegedly abused by anti-Government armed groups, could not be interviewed in person.

6.   The commission filed repeated requests to visit the country, including through notes verbales and letters dated 2 and 16 April, 1, 10 and 29 May, and 22 June 2012 (annex I), and meetings with the Permanent Representative of the Syrian Arab Republic in Geneva on 26 and 30 April and 18 and 21 June 2012. These efforts enabled the Chairperson to visit Damascus from 23 to 25 June to discuss with the authorities the commission's work, including the Al-Houla investigation. Details of the visit were reported by the commission in its oral update (A/HRC/20/CRP.1). The Government has yet to allow for in situ investigation by the commission.

7.   During the commission's mandate, the Government shared a number of documents, including reports of investigations conducted by national authorities, as well as lists of casualties. Such information is reflected in the present report, where relevant.

B.   Methodology

8.   The commission sought to adapt its methodology in view of the above challenges. While continuing efforts to reflect violations and abuses of human rights, irrespective of the

---

[1]   The Commissioners are Paulo Sergio Pinheiro (Chairperson) and Karen Koning AbuZayd.

alleged perpetrator, the commission focused on the most serious allegations. It was mindful of the protection of victims and witnesses, concerns that lie at the heart of the methodology of human rights investigations.

9. Owing to the lack of access to the Syrian Arab Republic, the commission continued to deploy to the region to collect first-hand accounts from those who had left the country. Starting on 15 February, the commission conducted 693 interviews in the field and from Geneva, including by Skype and telephone with victims and witnesses inside the country. This brought the total number of interviews conducted by the commission to 1,062 since its establishment in September 2011.

10. The commission also examined photographs, video recordings, satellite imagery and additional material, such as forensic and medical records. It continued to review reports from Government and non-governmental (both international and Syrian opposition) sources, academic analyses, media accounts (including Syrian news outlets), as well as United Nations reports, including from human rights bodies and mechanisms.

11. The commission applied the standard of proof used in previous reports, namely "reasonable grounds to believe". The commission relied mainly on first-hand accounts to corroborate incidents.

12. In its previous reports, the commission did not apply international humanitarian law. During the present reporting period, the commission determined that the intensity and duration of the conflict, combined with the increased organizational capabilities of anti-Government armed groups, had met the legal threshold for a non-international armed conflict. With this determination, the commission applied international humanitarian law in its assessment of the actions of the parties during hostilities (see also annex II).

13. The commission continued its engagement with representatives of Member States, United Nations bodies and other international and regional organizations. The commission is grateful to all those who cooperated with it in the fulfilment of its mandate, first and foremost the victims of and witnesses to human rights violations and abuses.

II. Context

A. Political background

14. Efforts to find a solution to the crisis in the Syrian Arab Republic continued throughout the reporting period. The Government launched several political and governance reforms, while the United Nations and the League of Arab States appointed a joint special envoy, Kofi Annan, on 23 February 2012. These efforts brought little progress, given the escalating violence and the significant deterioration in the situation on the ground.

15. The reform initiatives included a referendum on a new Constitution, held on 26 February 2012, parliamentary elections, held on 7 May, and the appointment of a new Government, on 23 June. These events were opportunities for introducing political pluralism and a democratic political process. They were not, however, viewed as inclusive enough to satisfy the growing dissident movement within the country or the exiled opposition.

16. President Bashar Al Assad did not succeed in engaging the opposition in a meaningful dialogue. The elections were boycotted by the opposition, and their outcome preserved the supremacy of the Baath party in Parliament as well as in the new Government, thus failing to bring emerging political forces into governance institutions. This development further antagonized segments of the population and opposition groups.

17.   The efforts of the international community channelled through the joint special envoy resulted in the presentation of a six-point plan on 10 March 2012. The plan outlined steps to bring about a cessation of violence by all parties and a commitment to a political process. The ceasefire came into effect on 12 April, followed by the deployment by the Security Council of the United Nations Supervision Mission in the Syrian Arab Republic (UNSMIS) on 21 April for an initial period of 90 days to monitor the plan's implementation. The arrival of UNSMIS observers had an initial positive impact on the ground, and levels of violence decreased in April. Thereafter, however, military operations intensified to such a level that, by 15 June, UNSMIS had to suspend its activities temporarily. On 20 July, the mandate of UNSMIS was extended for a final period of 30 days. Further renewal was conditional on the cessation of the use of heavy weapons and a reduction in violence by all sides.

18.   Opposition groups represented in the Syrian National Council refused to engage with President Assad, calling for him to leave power. Both the Syrian National Council and the Free Syrian Army (FSA) accepted the six-point plan, including the ceasefire. In March, an agreement was signed by the Council and the FSA to cooperate on channelling funds to the FSA via a liaison office within the Council; it was not implemented, however, and each group continued to operate independently.

19.   Positions varied in the international community on how to deal with the conflict. Some States demanded the immediate departure of the President; others focused on preventing any form of outside intervention. Others continued to provide military supplies to the Government. Still others called for funding, and provided communication and material support to anti-Government armed groups. The alleged presence of foreign advisers was also a point of contention among States, as was the use of sanctions. The uncertain international context undermined the efforts of the joint special envoy to achieve a political solution to the conflict.

20.   On 30 June 2012, the joint special envoy convened a meeting of an action group consisting of the United Nations, the League of Arab States and the European Union, as well as countries with an influence over the parties to the conflict, including the five Permanent Members of the Security Council. In a communiqué, the Action Group renewed a commitment to the six-point plan and set out principles and guidelines for a Syrian-led political transition. Opposition groups criticized the proposed transition for leaving the door open for President Assad to be part of a transitional Government. In a meeting held in Cairo on 2 and 3 July under the auspices of the League of Arab States, the Syrian opposition issued a common vision of a political transition and a national pact establishing justice, democracy and pluralism as the constitutional foundations of the future Syria. However, they were unable to agree on the election of a body that would represent them at the international level.

B.   Military situation[2]

21.   During the reporting period, the security situation deteriorated significantly, with armed violence increasing in intensity and spreading to new areas. Active hostilities increased between Government forces (and pro-Government militia) and anti-Government armed groups. Sporadic clashes between the armed actors evolved into continuous combat, involving more brutal tactics and new military capabilities on both sides. Levels of armed violence varied throughout the country.

---

[2] See also annex III.

22. The Government increasingly deployed its troops and heavy equipment in operations against areas perceived to be supporting opposition groups. All army divisions and security services engaged in military operations. Typically, such operations began with the cordoning off of a targeted area with checkpoints, then shelling as a prelude to incursions by ground forces to dislodge insurgents and their supporters. Shelling was also used in the context of direct clashes and in operations to quell demonstrations. Air assets also fired on fighters and unarmed demonstrators in localities under the influence of armed groups.

23. Government forces directed their main efforts towards the control of major cities such as Damascus, Aleppo, Homs and Hama. Attacks on areas allegedly infiltrated by anti-Government armed groups had the unintended effect of increasing the support of local populations for those groups. During many operations, large numbers of fighters and civilians were killed.

24. Pro-Government militia, including *Shabbiha*, reportedly acted alongside Government forces in security and military operations. Their precise nature, strength and relationship with the Government remains unclear.

25. The army faced increased attrition in personnel and equipment owing to combat operations, defections and casualties. Defections affected the troops psychologically, fuelling a crisis of confidence within the ranks and encouraging further defections. The Government also had difficulties in drafting new recruits, as many of those called up for mandatory military service refused to report.

26. Anti-Government armed groups expanded their activities throughout the country, clashing with Government forces on multiple fronts simultaneously. At the time of writing, they were involved in sustained armed confrontations inside the capital, while establishing sanctuaries throughout the rest of the country. Accounts indicated that there were foreign fighters in the ranks of some armed groups.

27. The FSA took measures to address the apparent deficiencies in its overall effective command structure. In some governorates, the FSA created local military councils that claimed leadership over groups fighting in those areas. Many groups claimed affiliation with the FSA, while other groups are emerging without a pronounced affiliation with it.

28. Anti-Government armed groups engaged with the Government forces through direct clashes, ambushes and raids. While investigations did not confirm the use of more sophisticated weaponry by anti-Government armed groups, their access to and capacity to effectively use available weapons improved. They appeared to have access to increased funding and logistical support.

29. The commission noted the increased and effective use of improvised explosive devices against the convoys, patrols and facilities of Government forces. They were also used to target members of military and security forces and Government officials.

30. Several radical Islamic armed groups have emerged in the country. The most important is the Al-Nusrah Front for the People of the Levant, a group allegedly linked with Al-Qaida, which claimed responsibility for several attacks, including suicide bombings against Government forces and senior officials.

31. There are also self-defence groups in several localities. Some of these groups emerged in villages populated by allegedly pro-Government minorities.

C.   Socioeconomic and humanitarian situation

32.   The crisis precipitated a rapid decline in the State's economy. It has exacerbated pre-existing levels of poverty and unemployment driven by a decade-long drought in rural agricultural areas, which led to the displacement of farmers to cities, and growing resentment against those who were, or appeared to be, enjoying the economic benefits distributed by the Government. According to the International Monetary Fund, the economy of the Syrian Arab Republic will contract significantly in 2012, primarily because of sanctions. The sharp drop in economic growth has been accompanied by alarming indicators, such as the devaluation of the Syrian pound, which has lost 30 per cent of its value since the onset of events, and inflation that soared to over 50 per cent.[3]

33.   The militarization of the conflict deepened the humanitarian crisis. Thousands of Syrians have been internally displaced or have fled to neighboring countries. At the time of writing, the United Nations High Commissioner for Refugees (UNHCR) estimated that 1.5 million people had been internally displaced. The Syrian population is increasingly turning to the Syrian Arab Red Crescent, the World Food Programme and other organizations for help.[4] By July, there were 114,208 Syrians registered as refugees, receiving assistance in four neighbouring countries (42,682 in Turkey, 34,050 in Jordan, 29,986 in Lebanon and 7,490 in Iraq).[5] Refugees inside the Syrian Arab Republic, including some 500,000 Palestinians and more than 103,000 registered Iraqi refugees,[6] are also affected by the situation. UNCHR reported that more than 13,000 Iraqi refugees left the Syrian Arab Republic in the first half of 2012, most returning to Iraq.[7]

34.   On 16 July, the commission received information from the Government of the Syrian Arab Republic stating that it had been subjected "to more than 60 packages of illegal unilateral coercive sanctions by the United States of America, the European Union, the League of Arab States, Turkey, Switzerland, Canada, Australia, Japan and others". In the Government's view, these sanctions, which target economic, financial and agricultural life in the country, amount to collective punishment against the Syrian people. The Government particularly deplored the sanctions imposed on the import of oil products, including domestic gas and fuel oil, which severely affected the livelihood of ordinary Syrians. The negative consequences of sanctions, including those on public and private banking systems, oil exports and the import of medical supplies, were also denounced.

35.   Accounts from interviewees demonstrated that entire communities are suffering from a lack of food, fuel, water, electricity and medical supplies. Shortages are especially acute in areas such as Homs, Idlib, Dar'a and Hama. People forced by the hostilities to leave their homes are in urgent need of shelter. According to the Office for the Coordination of Humanitarian Affairs, the number of people in urgent need of assistance has risen sharply, from an estimated 1 to 1.5 million people,[8] and continues to rise steadily.

36.   The fourth meeting of the Syrian Humanitarian Forum, held on 16 July 2012, concluded that the deteriorating humanitarian situation was a matter of grave concern to the

---

[3]   Matthew Epstein and Ahmed Saeed, "'Smart' sanctions take toll on Syria", *Financial Times*, 18 July 2012.

[4]   UNCHR, "UNHCR gravely concerned about dramatic escalation of Syria exodus", 20 July 2012, available from www.unhcr.org/50094bdcb.htm.

[5]   See UNHCR, Syria Regional Refugee Response, data.unhcr.org/syrianrefugees/regional.php.

[6]   The Government of the Syrian Arab Republic estimates that the number of Iraqi refugees in the country stands at more than 1 million.

[7]   OCHA, Humanitarian Bulletin, Syria, No. 3, 5 July 2012.

[8]   OCHA, Humanitarian Bulletin, Middle East and North Africa, No. 2, May–June 2012.

international community. The security situation has hindered the capacity of aid workers to assist the population in need. The two humanitarian assistance appeals for refugees in neighboring countries and the internally displaced persons and others in need inside the Syrian Arab Republic are only funded to 20 per cent.[9]

III. Findings

37.   While the commission focused on most serious violations of human rights, it wishes to note the overall deteriorating human rights situation. In addition to the right to life and the right to liberty and personal security, other fundamental human rights continue to be violated. Increased violence has further restricted the freedoms of expression, association and peaceful assembly, which had initially sparked the March 2011 uprising. The Syrian population is generally deprived of basic economic, social and cultural rights. As it noted in previous reports, the commission remains gravely concerned at the prevailing climate of impunity for violations of human rights law.

A. Casualties

38.   Information provided by the Government indicates that, as at 9 July 2012, 7,928 people, including Government forces and civilians, had been killed as a result of the unrest.

39.   Other entities, in particular Syrian non-governmental organizations and opposition groups, including local coordinating committees, the Centre for Documentation of Violations in Syria, the Syrian Network for Human Rights and the Syrian Observatory for Human Rights, are also counting casualties by employing a variety of methods. The numbers they report range from 17,000 to 22,000. The commission was unable to confirm these figures.

40.   The commission recorded numerous casualties resulting from incidents across the country. It reports the deaths only of those persons about which it has first-hand information through interviews conducted by its investigators. In the commission's figures, no distinction is made between civilians and fighters. Injured persons are not included. The commission, through interviews of victims and witnesses of events from 15 February to 20 July, confirmed 840 deaths.

B. Special inquiry into Al-Houla

41.   The commission delivered its preliminary findings (A/HRC/20/CRP.1) to the Human Rights Council on 27 June 2012, based on evidence gathered up until 22 June. In its report, the commission concluded that the Government was responsible for the deaths of civilians as a result of shelling the Al-Houla area and, particularly, Taldou village. It also found that the Government's investigation fell short of international human rights standards. With regard to the deliberate killing of civilians, the commission was unable to determine the identity of the perpetrators. Nevertheless, it considered that forces loyal to the Government were likely to have been responsible for many of the deaths.

42.   Access to the country was not granted despite specific requests addressed to the Government in a note verbale dated 4 June 2012 (annex I) and in person by the chairperson

---

[9] "Critical funding shortage threatens humanitarian response for Syria – UN official", UN News Centre, 16 July 2012.

during his visit to Damascus on 24 and 25 June. The Government has not delivered a final report on its own inquiry, nor has it indicated when the report might be forthcoming.

43.   The commission conducted eight additional interviews, including with six witnesses from the Taldou area, two of whom were survivors. It examined other materials, including video recordings and satellite imagery. It also reviewed analyses from other sources.

44.   Forty-seven interviews from various sources were considered by the commission. Interviews were consistent in their depiction of events and their description of the perpetrators as Government forces and *Shabbiha*. Apart from the two witnesses in the Government report, no other account supported the Government's version of events. The commission carefully reviewed the two witnesses' testimony as set out in that report, and judged their accounts as unreliable owing to a number of inconsistencies (see also annex IV). Accounts of other witnesses interviewed by different investigators remained consistent, including those collected from children, despite the fact that they were conducted over an extended period of time.

45.   In its oral update to the Human Rights Council, the commission determined that anti-Government armed groups, Government forces and *Shabbiha* could have had access to the two crime scenes: the first, the seven Abdulrazzak family homes on Saad Road (Tariq Al-Sad) and the second, the two Al-Sayed family homes on Main Street (Al-Shar'i Al-Raisi), across from the National Hospital.[10] The commission has since determined that the checkpoint at Al-Qaws, which is closest to the Al-Sayed house on Main Street, remained in Government control on the day of the incident. The front line between the opposition and Government forces was north of the checkpoint. The commission, therefore, concluded that it was highly unlikely that an anti-Government armed group would have had access to the Al-Sayed family house on the day of the killings.

46.   Regarding the Abdulrazzak site, where more than 60 people were killed, the commission considered that a large number of perpetrators would have been required to carry out the crime. The commission found, through satellite imagery and corroborated accounts, that the movement of vehicles or weapons, as well as the size of the group, would have been easily detectable by Government forces stationed at the Water Authority position. The commission therefore believes that access to the scene was not possible for any sizeable anti-Government armed group.

47.   The National Hospital had been occupied by the army for several months when the incidents took place. Although it was accessible by foot from both crime scenes, no one — whether injured or fleeing the crime scenes — sought refuge there for treatment or protection. As far as the commission could determine, all the injured and their relatives, as well as people from nearby houses, fled to opposition-controlled areas. None of the injured sought medical attention in the National Hospital. The Government report depicted the loyalties of the Al-Sayed family as pro-Government, but surviving family members fled to opposition-controlled areas of Taldou, choosing not to seek assistance from nearby Government forces.

48.   The commission remains of the view that the Government has failed in its legal obligation to investigate the murders in Al-Houla of 25 May 2012.

49.   On the basis of available evidence, the commission concluded that the elements of the war crime of murder have been met. The killing of multiple civilians, including women and children, was deliberate and connected to the ongoing armed conflict. There are

---

[10] See A/HRC/20/CRP.1, para. 44 and annex.

reasonable grounds to believe that the perpetrators of the crime, at both the Abdulrazzak and Al-Sayed family locations, were Government forces and *Shabbiha* members.

50.   There are also reasonable grounds to believe that these acts were part of a series of attacks directed against civilians, and as such, formed part of the conclusion (see section C below) that crimes against humanity were perpetrated by the Government and *Shabbiha*.

C.   Unlawful killing[11]

51.   Cases of attacks on civilians, murder and extrajudicial executions rose sharply during the reporting period. The commission conducted some 300 interviews as it investigated incidents alleging the unlawful killing of civilians and *hors de combat* fighters. The incidents that occurred in the contexts described below were corroborated by multiple accounts.[12] While both parties to the conflict perpetrated unlawful killings, the gravity, frequency and scale of the violations committed by Government forces and *Shabbiha* was, according to information available, well in excess of those committed by anti-Government armed groups.

1.   Government forces and *Shabbiha*

52.   Most unlawful killings occurred in the context of attacks against the strongholds of anti-Government armed groups. According to the most prominent pattern, attacks began with a blockade of the area and shelling,[13] followed by an assault by ground forces, including special forces and *Shabbiha*. Snipers were used extensively.[14] On securing the area, Government forces undertook house-to-house searches. Defectors, activists and fighting-age men were systematically sought out during these operations. Wounded or captured anti-Government fighters were executed. In some cases, family members of fighters, defectors and activists, as well as others who appeared to have been randomly selected, were also executed.

53.   This pattern was recorded in, inter alia, Tremseh, Al Qubeir, Al-Houla, Kili, Tal Rifat, Taftanaz, Sarmin, Ain Larouz, Atarib, Abdita, Homs and Al Qusayr.

54.   Excessive force continued to be used against demonstrators exercising their right to peaceful protest in Al Qamishli in March, and in Damascus, Aleppo and Jabal Al Zawiya in April.

55.   The commission finds that the cases of unlawful killing described in the present report provide reasonable grounds to believe that the Government forces and *Shabbiha* violated provisions of international human rights law protecting the right to life. Furthermore, many of the same killings met the elements of the war crime of murder under international criminal law.[15]

56.   Attacks were frequently directed against civilians and civilian objects. Although the Government's stated aim was to attack "terrorists", the attacks were directed at

---

[11]   See also annex II, paras. 30–42.

[12]   For a full account of the unlawful killings investigated by the commission, see annex V.

[13]   For more information on shelling, see annex VI.

[14]   Snipers regularly accompanied forces during ground assaults and were responsible for a significant number of civilian deaths. The commission recorded 35 instances of civilians shot by snipers. Dozens of interviewees described the detrimental psychological and social effects of the presence of snipers in their neighborhood. People feared leaving their houses and, when shelling started, feared staying at home.

[15]   Rome statute, art. 8 (2) (c) (i) – 1. See also annex II, paras. 30–42.

neighbourhoods, towns and regions with civilian populations (see annex VI). The commission therefore concludes that there are reasonable grounds to believe that the war crime of attacking civilians was perpetrated in many instances.

57.   There are also reasonable grounds to believe that the documented incidents constituted the crime against humanity of murder. In towns and villages where there was a pattern of blockade, shelling, ground assault and house-to-house searches, the conditions for a widespread or systematic attack against a predominately civilian population were met. The scale of the attacks, their repetitive nature, the level of excessive force consistently used, the indiscriminate nature of the shelling and the coordinated nature of the attacks led the commission to conclude that they had been conducted pursuant to State policy.

2.   Anti-Government armed groups

58.   Despite its limited access to victims of anti-Government armed groups, the commission was able to document cases of killing by anti-Government fighters of captured Government soldiers, *Shabbiha* and informers who admitted taking part in military attacks (see annex V). While the human rights legal regime differs with regard to such non-State actors as anti-Government armed groups, international humanitarian law applies equally to all parties to a conflict.

59.   The commission considered corroborated evidence of killing *hors de combat* soldiers and *Shabbiha*. In Al Qusayr, Bab Amr, Qaldiya and elsewhere, the commission noted that persons captured by anti-Government armed groups on occasion faced a quasi-judicial process prior to their execution. A consistent account of the trial process has not been forthcoming, nor has information on the extent of adherence to fair trial standards. Executing a prisoner without affording fundamental judicial guarantees is a war crime.

60.   The commission concluded that information on executions perpetrated by anti-Government armed groups — with or without a "trial" — constituted reasonable grounds to believe that the war crimes of murder or of sentencing or execution without due process had been committed on several occasions. The commission was not able to corroborate alleged attacks directed against individual civilians not participating in hostilities or against a civilian population.

3.   Unknown perpetrators

61.   The commission found that scores of civilians had been killed in nine explosions between March and July by unknown perpetrators.[16] The explosions appeared to have been caused by suicide bombers or by improvised explosive devices, including vehicle-borne ones.

62.   While the above-mentioned acts may be linked to non-international armed conflict and thus assessed under international humanitarian law, lack of access to the crime scenes combined with an absence of information on the perpetrators hampered the commission's ability to make such an assessment. These are nevertheless domestic crimes prosecutable under the Syrian criminal code. The Government is obliged to ensure that an investigation is conducted impartially, promptly, effectively and independently, in accordance with its international human rights obligations.

---

[16] See annex V, para. 55.

D.   Arbitrary detention and enforced disappearance[17]

63.   The commission interviewed 25 people who alleged to have been arbitrarily arrested and unlawfully detained. A further five interviews were conducted with defectors claiming to have observed arbitrary arrests and detentions while in active service.

64.   According to the Government, more than 10,000 people have been released since February 2011, pursuant to 4 amnesties, including 275 people released on 10 July 2012. In his report on the implementation of Security Council resolution 2043 (2012) (S/2012/523), the Secretary-General noted that UNSMIS had observed the release of 468 detainees in Dar'a, Damascus, Hama, Idlib and Deir el-Zour on 31 May and 14 June 2012.

65.   Official statistics on the number of detainees and detention centres have yet to be provided by the Government. As at 25 June, UNSMIS had received and cross-checked information on 2,185 detainees and 97 places of detention across the country. Syrian non-governmental organizations put the number of those currently detained as high as 26,000. The commission was unable to confirm the number of those arrested and detained.

66.   Most arrests were made in four situations: those believed to be planning to defect or who had refused to follow orders (usually to open fire on civilians); during house searches; at checkpoints; and protesters, either at or subsequent to protests. In a few cases, people were arrested randomly in areas where there were no active hostilities. Four of those so reported were women. Two were children, a boy of 14 and a girl of 9.

67.   No interviewee was offered or received legal counsel. With one exception, no interviewee received a family visit. Only two interviewees, arrested on suspicion of planning to defect, were formally charged with an offence.

68.   Many claimed that, prior to release, they were made to sign or thumbprint a document, the contents of which were unknown to them. Three detainees were brought before a judge and then released. In one unverified incident, the interviewee stated that, although the judge had ordered his release, he had remained in detention for another 3 months. Also interviewed was a former judge who stated that security agents prohibited questioning unless they were present and, on one occasion, held the judge at gunpoint.

69.   The duration of detention of interviewees ranged from a few hours to 5 months. Most of those interviewed were held for 60 days or fewer.

70.   The commission considers that domestic legislation in the Syrian Arab Republic (see annex II) fails to meet its obligations under article 9 of the International Covenant on Civil and Political Rights to ensure that those arrested and detained on criminal charges appear "promptly before a judge or other officer authorized by law to exercise judicial power".

71.   There are reasonable grounds to believe that Government forces arbitrarily arrested and detained individuals. Of particular concern are the detention of individuals without charge, the failure to provide detainees with legal counsel or family visits and the absence in most cases of any form of judicial review.

72.   Regarding enforced disappearance, families of those arrested were not informed at the time of arrest or at any point thereafter of the place of detention of their relatives. In most cases, families were unaware of their relatives' place of detention.

---

[17] See also annex VII.

73.   Where the Government refuses to acknowledge the arrest and detention or to disclose the fate of the person concerned, the crime of enforced disappearance has been committed.

E.   Torture and other forms of ill-treatment[18]

1.   Government forces and *Shabbiha*

74.   Starting on 15 February 2012, the commission interviewed 81 people regarding allegations of torture and other forms of cruel, inhuman or degrading treatment. Fifty-nine interviews concerned events within the reporting period. The commission was unable to visit detention centres to interview detainees or to observe detention conditions.

75.   Thirty of the above-mentioned 59 stated that they had been arrested and/or detained by Government forces or *Shabbiha*. All but one reported suffering physical violence during detention. Nineteen other interviewees reported witnessing detainees being tortured or ill-treated; this included 10 individuals who had worked in detention centres or at checkpoints before defecting. Where possible, the commission observed the wounds or scars of alleged victims.

76.   While most had been held in official detention centres, six stated that they had been detained in unofficial facilities, such as civilian houses, prior to being transferred to an official centre. In unofficial centres, interviewees reported abuse by soldiers and *Shabbiha*. A further nine interviewees stated that they had been beaten or assaulted during house searches or at checkpoints, or had witnessed the assault of others. None of the nine was subsequently detained.

77.   Reported methods of torture were consistent across the country. Interviewees described being severely beaten about the head and body with electric cables, whips, metal and wooden sticks and rifle butts, burned with cigarettes, kicked, or subjected to electric shocks applied to sensitive parts of the body, including the genitals. Six interviewees reported having lost consciousness during interrogation.

78.   Multiple reports were received about detainees being beaten on the soles of the feet (*falaqa*). Common practices included keeping detainees in prolonged stress positions, including hanging from walls or ceilings by their wrists (*shabeh*) or hanging by their wrists tied behind their backs. Other methods comprised forcing detainees to bend over and put their head, neck and legs through a tyre while beatings were administered (*dulab*); and tying detainees to a board with their head unsupported and either stretching them or folding the board in half. Some detainees were subjected to rape and other forms of sexual violence.[19] On many interviewees, scars and wounds consistent with their accounts were visible.

79.   Several forms of torture and ill-treatment meted out did not result in physical evidence. Detainees were forcibly shaved, made to imitate dogs and declare that "there is no God but Bashar". Other interviewees stated that they were forced to undress and remain naked for prolonged periods. Three interviewees stated that they were threatened with execution. One reported being present when another detainee was threatened with sexual assault; another stated that interrogators threatened to arrest and rape female relatives.

80.   Six interviewees were moved to multiple detention facilities, among different intelligence agencies. One interviewee reported having been moved to 10 different centres

---

[18]   See also annex VIII.
[19]   See also annex IX.

across four governorates in five months. Another interviewee was transferred to four different locations in Dar'a and Damascus, again during five months. Where there were multiple transfers, interviewees suffered physical violence in each location.

81. The majority of detainees described being held in small, overcrowded cells. Two interviewees reported that cells were so overcrowded that it was impossible to sit or lie down. All but one reported that food and water were inadequate. One interviewee stated that, having been without water for a week, he had to drink his own urine. Several interviewees stated that their cells had no toilet. Four interviewees described cells infested with insects and lice. The commission was unable to corroborate reports of the denial of medication and medical treatment.

82. The commission recorded accounts that, if verified, would amount to a breach of the Standard Minimum Rules for the Treatment of Prisoners (see annex II).

83. The commission confirms its previous finding that torture and other forms of cruel, inhuman or degrading treatment were committed by Government forces and *Shabbiha*, in violation of the State's obligations under international humanitarian law and international human rights law.

84. The commission determined that severe pain was inflicted upon persons in official and unofficial detention centres, during house searches and at checkpoints. It also found that torture was inflicted to punish, to humiliate or to extract information. Much of the physical violence described by interviewees has been found to constitute torture by various international tribunals (see annex II).

85. The commission found reasonable grounds to believe that torture was perpetrated as part of a widespread attack directed against civilians by Government forces and *Shabbiha* who had knowledge of the attack. It concludes that torture as a crime against humanity and as a war crime was committed by Government forces and *Shabbiha* members. Members of security forces, in particular military and air force intelligence, appear to be primarily responsible for torture and ill-treatment. The commission noted the involvement of *Shabbiha* members in acts of torture in unofficial detention centres in Homs in February and March.

86. The commission found that conduct such as forcibly shaving detainees and forcing them to imitate dogs constitutes cruel, inhuman or degrading treatment. Similarly, the conditions of detention as described in interviews constitute cruel, inhuman or degrading treatment of detainees.

2. **Anti-Government armed groups**

87. Fifteen interviews were conducted about the treatment of members of Government forces and *Shabbiha* members by anti-Government armed groups. All interviewees claimed to be members of these armed groups and detailed the capture, interrogation and either release or execution of those detained. Three interviewees stated that captured Government fighters and *Shabbiha* members were tortured during interrogation prior to execution.

88. The commission found reasonable grounds to believe that torture and other forms of ill-treatment were committed by anti-Government armed groups during interrogation of captured members of Government forces and the *Shabbiha*. It determines that severe pain was inflicted to punish, to humiliate or to extract information.

89. The commission determines, however, that the acts of torture were not committed as part of either a widespread or systematic attack on a civilian population; therefore, they do not constitute crimes against humanity, but may be prosecutable as war crimes.

F.   Indiscriminate attacks

90.   To comply with international humanitarian law, those ordering and carrying out attacks must ensure that they distinguish between civilian and military targets.[20] Accounts indicated that Government forces on occasion directed shelling to target small opposition strongholds. In many attacks, however, those firing projectiles did not distinguish between civilian and military targets. In most of the cases investigated, shelling preceded an assault by ground forces; it was also used against demonstrations. In some cases, it was used against anti-Government armed groups where the military was unwilling to risk equipment and troops.

91.   Most deaths in Bab Amr during the military operation that began in February 2012 were caused by extensive and indiscriminate shelling by Government forces of primarily civilian infrastructure and residential areas. The city of Al Qusayr suffered indiscriminate attacks between February and May; one credible source told the commission, "I witnessed what people call indiscriminate shelling – the Syrian army just spreads mortar fire across an entire neighbourhood." On 5 June, Government forces began an assault on Al Haffe by cordoning off the town and then shelling with tanks, mortars and helicopter gunships.

92.   Additional corroborated accounts of indiscriminate shelling were recorded in Atarib, on 14 February; Ain Larouz, on 5 March; Sermin, on 22 March; Taftanaz, on 4 April; Kili, on 6 April; Al-Houla, on 25 May, and 12 and 13 June; Akko, on 9 June; Salma, on 11 June; and Jobar, on various dates in late June.

93.   The commission took note of video evidence from Hama governorate in July indicating the use of cluster munitions. The material could not be corroborated. Although the Syrian Arab Republic is not a party to the Convention on Cluster Munitions, the commission notes that such weapons are inherently indiscriminate when employed in residential areas or areas frequented by civilians.

94.   On the basis of its findings, the commission determined that the legal threshold for an indiscriminate attack as a violation of customary international humanitarian law was reached. Government forces fired shells into areas inhabited by civilians while failing to direct them at a specific military objective.

95.   Moreover, the attacks, especially shelling, caused incidental loss of civilian life and injury to civilians, as well as damage to civilian objects. There are reasonable grounds to believe that the damage was excessive when compared to the anticipated military advantage.

G.   Sexual violence[21]

96.   Forty-three interviews were conducted on incidents of sexual violence, against men, women and children, committed by Government forces and the *Shabbiha* since February 2012. Interviewees included two female and three male victims of rape. Also interviewed were five eyewitnesses of rape, three of whom were also victims. Seven interviewees were defectors who stated that rape and sexual assault had been committed by soldiers and the *Shabbiha*.

97.   There were difficulties in collecting evidence of sexual violence owing to cultural, social and religious beliefs surrounding marriage and sexuality.

---

[20]   See annex II, paras. 30–42.

[21]   See also annex IX.

98.   Accounts indicated that rape and other forms of sexual violence had been committed in two circumstances. The first was during house searches and at checkpoints by Government forces and *Shabbiha*; the second, in detention. In addition, in Homs, between late February and April, there were several reports of abduction and rape of women, and corroborated accounts of women forced to walk naked in the streets of Karm-Al Zeitoun in February.

99.   Fifteen interviewees described incidents of sexual violence committed during house searches and at checkpoints during military operations in Homs between February and May, and in Al Haffe in June. Five interviewees detailed incidents of sexual violence in Zabadani in late February and in various locations in Hama governorate in April. The attacks were reportedly perpetrated by soldiers and *Shabbiha*.

100.   The commission continued to receive reports of rape and sexual assault in detention centres, committed usually as part of torture and/or ill-treatment. Multiple reports were received of male detainees receiving electric shocks to their genitals during interrogations.

101.   The commission finds reasonable grounds to believe rape and sexual assault were perpetrated against men, women and children by Government forces and *Shabbiha* members. Rape and sexual assault were also part of torture in official and unofficial detention centres.

102.   Having previously determined that military operations such as those in Homs in February and March and in Al Haffe in June were part of a widespread or systematic attack against a civilian population, the commission finds that the rapes committed during these attacks, made with knowledge of the attacks, could be prosecuted as crimes against humanity.

H.   Violations of children's rights[22]

103.   The commission conducted 168 interviews concerning alleged violations of children's rights. Of these, 30 interviewees were under the age of 18. In interviews, the adverse psychological and social impact of the violence on children was evident.

1.   Government forces and *Shabbiha*

104.   The commission recorded the killing of 125 children, mainly boys, after 15 February 2012.

105.   Children were killed and injured during the shelling of towns and villages. During a visit to a hospital in Turkey, the commission saw a 2-year-old girl, severely injured in the June shelling of Azaz. There were also multiple reports of children killed and wounded by snipers.

106.   Children were also killed during attacks on protests, such as the attack in Menaq village on 15 March, and in attacks on villages believed to be harbouring defectors or anti-Government armed groups. There were multiple accounts of children killed during military ground operations and house searches (see annex V). Forty-one children were among those killed in Al-Houla on 25 May. Some were killed during shelling, but most appeared to have been shot at close range.

107.   There were reports of the arbitrary arrest and detention of children. Children described having been beaten, whipped with electrical cables, burned with cigarettes and

---

[22] See also annex X.

subjected to electrical shocks to the genitals. There were multiple reports of detained minors held in the same cells as adults.

108.   The commission received reports of the rape and sexual assault of girls under the age of 18 (see annex VII).

109.   No evidence of Government forces formally conscripting or enlisting children under the age of 18 was received. However, three incidents were documented in which Government forces used children as hostages or as human shields.

110.   Schools in various locations across the Syrian Arab Republic were looted, vandalized and burned in response to student protests. Various accounts described their use by Government forces and *Shabbiha* members as military staging grounds, temporary bases and sniper posts (see paragraphs 116–125 below).

111.   Reports also indicated that injured people, including children, feared to seek medical treatment at public hospitals. Many children were brought to field clinics that could treat only minor injuries.

112.   Evidence gathered indicated that children's rights continue to be violated by Government forces and the *Shabbiha*. The legal conclusions reached in annexes IV, V, VII, VIII and IX apply.

113.   The detention of adults and children together is in breach of the Government's obligations under the Convention on the Rights of the Child, unless a separation breaches the right of families to be housed together.

2.   Anti-Government armed groups

114.   Eleven interviewees, including four minors, discussed the use of children by anti-Government armed groups. All stated that anti-Government armed groups, including the FSA, used children in support roles, such as assisting medical evacuations or as couriers. Five interviewees stated that the anti-Government armed groups used children under the age of 18 — and in one account, under 15 — as fighters.

115.   The commission considers that there is currently insufficient information to find that anti-Government armed groups used children under the age of 15 to participate actively in hostilities. It notes with concern, however, the reports that children under 18 are fighting and performing auxiliary roles for anti-Government armed groups.

I.   Attacks on protected persons and objects

116.   The conflict in the Syrian Arab Republic has generated thousands of casualties. Hospitals and clinics have been caught up in hostilities. Field clinics have been deliberately targeted. Civilian objects, such as schools, municipal buildings and hospitals, are routinely occupied by Government forces seeking to establish a presence. Underground field clinics are poorly equipped, unsterile and lack basic tools, medical supplies and blood. The Syrian Arab Red Crescent is also active in providing for the medical and humanitarian needs of the conflict-affected.

117.   International humanitarian law not only prohibits attacks on civilians and civilian objects but also requires their protection.[23] The commission collected video materials and

---

[23] This protection remains in place unless the protected persons or objects take part in hostile acts. See annex II, paras. 30–42.

conducted 12 interviews about attacks on protected persons or objects, in particular schools and medical facilities.

118.   The commission recorded multiple incidents of attacks on field hospitals. During an intense shelling period, the Bab Amr field hospital was hit and partially destroyed. In Al Qusayr, in late February, a field clinic was attacked by a helicopter. One witness stated that, in February, the Yousef al-Atmeh school building in Jisr Al Shughour, used as a field clinic by local residents, was bombed by security forces.

119.   Members of the Syrian Arab Red Crescent were victims of attacks. Five staff members have been killed since the beginning of the crisis, the latest on 10 July in Deir el-Zour. In May, while evacuating two injured persons in A'zaz, a Red Crescent ambulance was shot at by military snipers and two medics were injured; all of them were wearing Red Crescent uniforms. On the same day, the Red Crescent office in A'zaz was shelled and burned. The director was arrested and held for 20 days.

120.   On 24 April, in Duma, five ambulances belonging to the Syrian Arab Red Crescent were caught in crossfire. One doctor was killed and four Red Crescent staff members were injured.

121.   Government forces continued to occupy public hospitals in several localities. In May, the military placed tanks, armed vehicles and troops inside the compound and snipers on the roof of the national hospital in A'zaz and Al Qusayr. The same occurred in Al Haffe in June.

122.   Government forces occupied schools and other civilian buildings, transforming them into military staging grounds, temporary bases and sniper posts. For instance, in March, a girl from Atarib described the use of two schools as barracks for Government forces, with tanks at the school gates and snipers posted on the rooftops. The school in Al Qusayr was similarly occupied in May. One interviewee stated that, on 11 March, he was shot at by a sniper from the rooftop of the local school in Jondia.

123.   The commission finds reasonable grounds to believe that Government forces acted in violation of international humanitarian law by targeting members of the Syrian Arab Red Crescent. These acts may also be prosecutable as a war crime. Furthermore, by positioning its military assets, which are legitimate targets of enemy forces, inside civilian objects, Government forces are violating the international humanitarian law principle of distinction. Government forces have also violated international humanitarian law by deliberately shelling field clinics.

124.   The Government's occupation of hospitals and schools infringes the rights to education and health.

125.   The commission was unable to corroborate allegations of anti-Government groups targeting civilians or civilian objects.

J.   Pillaging and destruction of property[24]

1.   Government forces and *Shabbiha*

126.   The commission received corroborated reports of the pillaging, destruction and burning of property by Government forces and *Shabbiha* members during its military operations. Where such acts occurred during house searches, the commission documented

---

[24]   See also annex XI.

dozens of cases of looting of property, including of money, vehicles, jewellery and electrical goods.

127. Those interviewed indicated that searches, and thus the pillaging, burning and destruction of property, targeted groups and individuals who appeared to be defectors, members of anti-Government armed groups, demonstrators, and family members of the aforementioned. In particular, family members of defectors described how their homes, farms and shops were burned. In some instances, the looting, burning and destruction of property appeared to be directed at entire communities rather than at specific individuals.

128. According to soldiers who later defected, the looting and burning of property of opposition activists and defectors was intended to, inter alia, impose financial constraints on them and their activities. Government soldiers and *Shabbiha* also benefited from these acts financially, conducting them with complete impunity.

129. There are reasonable grounds to believe that Government forces and *Shabbiha* members committed the war crime of pillage. The commission also determined that Government forces and *Shabbiha* members engaged in the destruction and burning of property during house searches.

2. Anti-Government armed groups

130. The commission received no reports of the pillaging or destruction of property by anti-Government armed groups, but lack of access to Syrian Arab Republic hampered investigations. The Government provided information relating to crimes allegedly perpetrated by anti-Government armed groups, including looting and vehicle theft, which the commission was unable to corroborate. Consequently, the commission was unable to reach any findings regarding the alleged pillaging, burning and destruction of property by anti-Government armed groups.

IV. Responsibility

131. The commission finds reasonable grounds to believe that crimes against humanity, breaches of international humanitarian law and gross human rights violations have been committed in the Syrian Arab Republic. The commission endeavoured, where possible, to identify individuals in leadership positions who may be responsible. In March, the commission handed over to the United Nations High Commissioner for Human Rights confidential lists of suspected individuals and units.[25] Further lists will be provided at the close of its current mandate, in September 2012.

A. State responsibility

132. The evidence collected confirmed the commission's previous finding that violations had been committed pursuant to State policy. Large-scale operations conducted in different governorates, their similar modus operandi, their complexity and integrated military/security apparatus indicate involvement at the highest levels of the armed and security forces and the Government.

133. Eyewitnesses consistently identified the *Shabbiha* as perpetrators of many of the crimes described in the present report. Although the nature, composition, hierarchy and structure of this group remains opaque, credible information led to the conclusion that

---

[25] A/HRC/19/69, para. 87.

Shabbiha members acted with the acquiescence of, in concert with or at the behest of Government forces. International human rights law recognizes the responsibility of States that commit violations through proxies.

B. Responsibility of anti-Government armed groups

134.   Although not a State party to the Geneva Conventions, organized armed groups must nevertheless abide by the principles of international humanitarian law.[26] During non-international armed conflicts, serious violations of international humanitarian law committed by members of such groups are prosecutable as war crimes. Non-State actors may also bear responsibility for gross abuses of human rights, in particular those that amount to international crimes.[27] The commission identified such violations, including murder, extrajudicial execution and torture, perpetrated by members of anti-Government groups.

C. Individual responsibility

135.   Whether members of Government forces or anti-Government groups, those who intentionally commit the crimes identified in the present report bear responsibility. In addition, those who order these crimes to be committed (or plan, instigate, incite, aid or abet) are also liable. The commission received consistent evidence that mid- and high-ranking members of Government forces were directly involved in illegal acts. Defectors stated that commanders ordered their subordinates to shoot civilians and *hors de combat* fighters, and to torture and mistreat detainees. Orders were often enforced at gunpoint, and anyone hesitating to comply risked arrest or summary execution. Evidence showed that widespread looting and destruction of property occurred with the acquiescence of commanders.

136.   Leadership within anti-Government armed groups was also implicated in the war crimes and human rights abuses detailed in the present report. Local commanders either ordered the execution of captured members of Government forces and the *Shabbiha* or killed them themselves.

D. Command responsibility

137.   Military commanders and civilian superiors bear responsibility for crimes against humanity and war crimes if they fail to take reasonable measures within their power to prevent or repress the commission of these crimes or to submit the matter to the competent authorities. These measures must be implemented with respect to subordinates over whom they exercise effective command and control.

138.   Extensive coverage of events, including the likely occurrence of violations and crimes, led the commission to conclude that military commanders and civilian superiors at the highest levels of Government must have known about such events.

139.   The same applied to abuses and crimes committed by anti-Government armed groups. Local-level commanders acknowledged some of the acts described in interviews.

---

[26]   See annex II, paras. 11–13.
[27]   See annex II, paras. 8–10.

140.   The commission is unaware of efforts that meet international standards made by either the Government or anti-Government armed groups to prevent or punish crimes documented in the present report.

141.   The Government's National Independent Legal Commission has reportedly been investigating some allegations of violations.[28] The Government also set up a special inquiry into the events of Al-Houla. The investigation reports received on Tremseh, Al Qubeir and Al-Houla were considered by the commission. The commission was unable to identify any case of successful prosecution of any military or security force commanders or civilian superiors who bore responsibility for crimes against humanity, war crimes or gross human rights violations committed since March 2011.

142.   No credible information has been received about anti-Government armed groups investigating, prosecuting and punishing members of their groups alleged to have committed crimes and abuses identified.

V.   Conclusions and recommendations

143.   **The human rights crisis has escalated significantly in the context of unrestrained hostilities, which have evolved into a non-international armed conflict. The civilian population across all communities bears the brunt of this conflict, thousands having lost their lives in the spiral of violence.**

144.   **The socioeconomic and humanitarian situation has further deteriorated, leaving the majority of the population in a state of disarray. The commission maintains that sanctions result in a denial of the most basic human rights of the Syrian people.**

145.   **The commission concludes that there are reasonable grounds to believe that Government forces and the *Shabbiha* committed crimes against humanity, war crimes and violations of international human rights law and international humanitarian law. There are also reasonable grounds to believe that anti-Government armed groups committed war crimes and abuses of international human rights law and international humanitarian law. Both parties violated the rights of children.**

146.   **Human rights violations and abuses must be thoroughly investigated. Evidence of violations and abuses, including international crimes, must be systematically collected to facilitate the process of holding perpetrators accountable. Access must be accorded to the commission so that it may investigate such violations impartially and in situ.**

147.   **The commission believes that the large-scale operations during which the most serious violations were committed were conducted with the knowledge, or at the behest, of the highest levels of Government. Responsibility therefore rests with those who either ordered or planned the acts or, in the case of those in effective command and control, those who failed to prevent or punish the perpetrators. The consistent identification of the *Shabbiha* as perpetrators of many of the crimes does not relieve the Government of its responsibility, as international law recognizes the responsibility of States that commit violations through proxies.**

---

[28]   On 25 June, the commission chairperson met the head of the National Independent Legal Commission in Damascus. The Commission is represented in the capital and governorates. It reportedly received 6,500 complaints, most of which refer to deaths and missing persons, levelled against the army, police and anti-Government armed groups.

148. The commission identified violations of international humanitarian law and international human rights law committed by members of anti-Government groups. Those who either ordered or planned the acts, or in the case of those in effective command and control, failed to prevent or punish perpetrators, bear responsibility.

149. The increased militarization of the conflict is disastrous for the Syrian people and could provoke tragic consequences for the entire region. A sustained cessation of hostilities by all parties remains of paramount importance to end the violence and gross human rights violations and abuses.

150. The commission reiterates that the best solution continues to be a negotiated settlement involving an inclusive and meaningful dialogue among all parties, leading to a political transition that reflects the legitimate aspirations of all segments of Syrian society, including ethnic and religious minorities.

151. Considering the catastrophic threats to the Syrian polity and people, as well as to the stability of the region, the commission renews the recommendations made in its previous reports, and emphasizes those that follow.

152. With regard to the international community:

(a) Countries with influence over the parties to the Syrian conflict, in particular the permanent members of the Security Council, should work in concert to put pressure on the parties to end the violence and to initiate all-inclusive negotiations for a sustainable political transition process in the country;

(b) The continued presence of the United Nations in the country is essential for the effective implementation of the ceasefire and to support the Syrian people in initiating broad, inclusive and credible consultations to achieve reconciliation, accountability and reparation within the framework of international law.

153. The commission recommends that the Government of the Syrian Arab Republic:

(a) Investigate all violations of international human rights law and international humanitarian law as set out in the present report to ensure that those responsible are held to account, in accordance with due process, and that victims are afforded access to justice and reparation;

(b) Release immediately all persons arbitrarily detained, publish a list of all detention facilities and ensure that conditions of detention comply with applicable law;

(c) Abide by the rules of armed conflict and distribute the rules of engagement guiding army and security forces operations;

(d) Grant the international community immediate access to the affected areas to provide humanitarian assistance to all those in need.

154. The commission recommends that anti-Government armed groups:

(a) Adopt, publicly announce and abide by rules of conduct that are in line with international human rights law and international humanitarian law standards, and hold perpetrators of abuses to account;

(b) Provide relevant humanitarian and human rights institutions with information on the fate of persons captured, and to give access to detainees.

155. The commission recommends that the Office of the High Commissioner consolidate a presence in the region to strengthen efforts to promote and protect human rights in the Syrian Arab Republic.

156.   The commission recommends that the Human Rights Council transmit the present report to the Secretary-General for the attention of the Security Council so that appropriate action may be taken in view of the gravity of the violations, abuses and crimes perpetrated by Government forces and the *Shabbiha*, and by anti-Government groups, documented herein.

Annexes

Annex I

[Arabic/English only]

Correspondence with the Government of the Syrian Arab Republic

NATIONS UNIES
HAUT COMMISSARIAT AUX DROITS DE L'HOMME

UNITED NATIONS
HIGH COMMISSIONER FOR HUMAN RIGHTS

Tel: 41-22-9179101

Independent International Commission of Inquiry pursuant to resolution A/HRC/S-17/1

The Independent International Commission of Inquiry established pursuant to resolution S-17/1 of the Human Rights Council presents its compliments to the Permanent Representative of the Syrian Arab Republic to the United Nations in Geneva.

As the Permanent Representative will be aware, the mandate of the Commission has been extended for another six months based on resolution A/HRC/19/L.38/Rev.1. As members of the Commission embark on this phase, they wish to reiterate their commitment to full engagement with his Government and their intention to reflect the perspective of all parties in the context of the current crisis. They wish to note again, and in the spirit of this engagement, that the Commission's second report included, to the extent possible, the information sent to it by the Government. The information in the documents provided and from the Permanent Representative's letters has appeared either in the body of the text or attached as an Annex to the report.

As Commissioners Karen Abuzayd and Paulo Sergio Pinheiro pursue their work, they refer again to the importance of having direct access, including to be able to assess alleged violations committed against members of the security forces and the army in Syria. The Commissioners strive to reflect facts impartially and without bias. Their presence on the ground would enhance their ability to understand the Government's position and corroborate further the documents it has provided thus far. As stated in the recommendations in their last report, they call for inclusive national dialogue as a meaningful and peaceful exit from the current impasse. They also noted the potentially harmful and counterproductive impact of economic sanctions.

In this context, the Commissioners kindly request access for the Commission to the Syrian Arab Republic to engage further with all parties and ascertain facts on the ground. They stand ready to provide the Permanent Representative with any information or details in this regard.

The Commission avails itself of this opportunity to renew to the Permanent Representative of the Syrian Arab Republic assurances of its highest consideration.

Geneva, 2 April 2012

S.B

NATIONS UNIES
HAUT COMMISSARIAT AUX DROITS DE L'HOMME

UNITED NATIONS
HIGH COMMISSIONER FOR HUMAN RIGHTS

Tel: 41-22-9179101

Independent International Commission of Inquiry established pursuant to resolution A/HRC/S-17/1

and extended through resolution A/HRC/Res/19/22

16 April 2012

Excellency,

I am writing on behalf of the Independent International Commission of Inquiry on the Syrian Arab Republic established by the United Nations Human Rights Council pursuant to resolution S-17/1 and extended for another six months by resolution A/HRC/Res/19/22 adopted on 23 March 2012.

As the Commission begins the next phase of its work, we respectfully seek your assistance in the fulfilment of the Commission's mandate. In this regard, we wish to reassure you of our commitment to full engagement with Your Excellency's Government and our intention to reflect in our reports the perspective of all parties in the context of the current crisis, as we had done so in the Commission's last report submitted to the Human Rights Council in February 2012.

In that report, the Commission endeavoured to reflect, to the extent possible, the information sent to us by the Government authorities, which appeared either in the main body of the report or attached as an Annex. Guided by the principles of independence and impartiality, the Commission strives to reflect facts without any bias. The Commission's reporting is victim-centered, as we do not make any distinction among the victims, as such the Commission was the first body to investigate and report on human rights violations by armed opposition groups.

As stated in the recommendations in our last report, we call for an inclusive national dialogue and a negotiated settlement as a meaningful and peaceful exit from the current impasse. The recommendations also refer to the dangers of militarisation and the potentially harmful and counterproductive impact of economic sanctions on the Syrian people.

H.E. Mr. Walid al-Moallem

Minister of Foreign and Expatriates Affairs

Damascus, Syrian Arab Republic
...../...

As the Commission pursues its work, we reiterate the importance of having direct access to the country, and renew our request to visit the Syrian Arab Republic with a view to be able to see the human rights situation first-hand, to engage further with all parties, to ascertain facts on the ground, and to assess the allegations of human rights violations, including those committed against members of the security forces and the army in the Syrian Arab Republic.

The Commission's presence on the ground would be essential in enhancing its ability to understand the Government's position and corroborate further the documents it has provided thus far. In this regard, we hope that the ceasefire process, if sustained, will contribute to a better promotion and protection of human rights of all communities in your country.

In the coming six months, the Commission intends to do periodic updates on such violations, in addition to the oral report to the Human Rights Council in June and the written updated report in September, as mandated by resolution A/HRC/Res/19/22. The Commission stands ready to bring on board the perspectives of the Government in the context of such periodic reporting.

The Commission would very much appreciate your support in giving a positive consideration of our request to visit your country.

Please accept, Excellency, the assurances of our highest consideration.

Paulo Sergio Pinheiro
Chairperson

Mission Permanente
De La
République Arabe Syrienne
Genève

OHCHR REGISTRY

2 7 APR 2012

Recipients: HCNA
HC esarcep.

N°233/12

Geneva, 27th April 2012

The Permanent Mission of the Syrian Arab Republic to the United Nations Office and other International Organizations in Geneva presents its compliments to the Secretariat of the High Commissioner for Human Rights, and with reference to the letter addressed by the President of the International Commission of Inquiry to the Minister of Foreign Affairs in the Syrian Arab Republic, on 16 April 2012, has the honour to attach, herewith, the position of the Syrian Government (in Arabic) regarding the above-mentioned letter.

The Permanent Mission of the Syrian Arab Republic avails itself of this opportunity to renew to the Secretariat of the High Commissioner for Human Rights the assurances of its highest consideration.

Annex: ment.

Secretariat of the High Commissioner
for Human Rights

Rue des Pâquis 52
Palais Wilson
1201 Genève

MISSION PERMANENTE
DE LA
RÉPUBLIQUE ARABE SYRIENNE
GENÈVE

التاريخ: ٢٣/٢ /٢٠١٢/٠٤   الرقم: ٢٠١٢/233

تهدي بعثة الجمهورية العربية السورية الدائمة المعتمدة لدى مكتـب الأمم المتحدة والمنظمات الدولية الأخرى في جنيف أطيب تحياتها إلى مكتب المفوضة السامية لحقوق الإنسان؛

وبالإشارة إلى رسالة رئيس لجنة التحقيق الدولية الموجهة إلى السـيد وزير الخارجية والمغتربين في الجمهورية العربية السـورية، والمؤرخـة ٢٠١٢/٤/١٦، تتشرف بعثة الجمهورية العربية السورية بإعلام المفوضيـة السامية بما يلي:

١– لقد تعاملت الجمهورية العربية السورية مع الأمـم المتحدة بمصداقية وشفافية كاملة، وعرضت لها ما يتعرض له الشعب السوري من انتهاكات لحقوق الإنسان على أيدي المجموعات الإرهابية المسلحة، في الوقت الذي كانت فيه دول عديدة ترفض الاستماع لأي حديث عن وجـود أجنـدات خارجية وإرهاب مسلح في سورية يُمارس بشكل يزداد بشاعة يوماً بعـد يوم، بل وكان البعض يهزأ من هذا الكلام. ومن المحزن بشكل كبيـر أن يكون دم /٦١٤٣/ مواطن سوري هو جزء من الثمن الذي يدفعه الشعب السوري حتى يبدأ العالم بالاعتراف بحقيقة أن المسـألة ليسـت مطالـب شعبية ينبغي على كل حكومة تلبيتها، وإنما هي مخططات لتدمير دولـة بأكملها بمواقفها الخارجية، وذلك باستخدام العنف وارتكـاب انتهاكـات جسيمة وممنهجة لحقوق الإنسان من قبل المجموعات الإرهابية المسلحة،

ومموليهم وداعميهم الذين يسعون بكافة الطرق لمنع أي كان من معرفـة الجرائم ضد الإنسانية التي يرتكبونها.

٢- لقد أثبتت الأحداث صحة كل ما كانت سورية تصرح به أو تقدمـه مـن معلومات وبيانات، بما في ذلك ما أعلنته عن وجود عمليـات التضـليل الإعلامي ضد سورية. لقد آن الأوان لتـدارك الأخطـاء والعـودة إلـى الانحياز إلى ضحايا انتهاكات حقوق الإنسان، والتخلي عـن الاتهامـات الخطيرة التي لا تستند إلى أية حقائق، ما هدفها سوى استجرار التـدخل الأجنبي إلى سورية، بما في ذلك اتهامات ارتكاب السـلطات السـورية لجرائم ضد الإنسانية، وتحميل السلطات السورية، وعلى أعلى المستويات مسؤولية هذه الجرائم المزعومة.

٣- لقد خسرت سورية حتى الآن /٣٢١١/ مدني استشـهدوا ضـحية للقتـل خارج القانون الذي ارتكبته المجموعات الإرهابية المسلحة. كما قتلت هذه المجموعات، وأيضاً خارج نطاق القانون، /٤٧٨/ من رجال حفظ النظام، و /٢٠٨٨/ عسكرياً، بالإضافة إلى /٢٠٤/ سيدة و /٥٦/ طفـلاً. كمـا قامت هذه المجموعات باستهداف واغتيال /١٠٦/ من خيـرة الخبـرات العلمية ورجال الدين والقانون الذين لم يقبلوا الانضمام إلـى تحركـاتهم. فيما يتم تدبير عمليات تفجيرات ضد السكان قبل جلسات مجلـس الأمـن الدولي أو مجلس حقوق الإنسان للمتاجرة بالدم السوري من أجل بعـض الأسطر في بيانات عدائية رخيصة. لقد أصبحت الأمم المتحدة وأجهزتها مطالبة بعدم القبول بأن تكون أداة لتدمير الدول وقتل الشعوب كما حصل في مناطق أخرى في العالم، ترتكب فيها انتهاكات جسيمة لحقوق الإنسان تفوق ما تم إدعاءه واتخاذه ذريعة لتدمير تلك الدول.

٤- لقد شارك رئيس لجنة التحقيق الدولية في اجتماع لأعداء الشعب السوري في اسطنبول في بداية شهر نيسان/أبريل ٢٠١٢، وقد انعقد هذا الاجتماع خارج نطاق الشرعية الدولية وخارج نطاق الأمم المتحدة للالتفاف على الشرعية الدولية والتقدم بالأجندات المعادية لسورية على حساب أمنها وأمن شعبها واستقرارها. لقد أرسلت مشاركة رئيس اللجنة في الاجتماع رسالة خطيرة في انضمامه لهؤلاء وانحيازه لأطراف لا تريد السلام لسورية، الأمر الذي يجعل اللجنة تبتعد عن الحيادية والاستقلالية في تعاطيها مع الأوضاع في سورية.

٥- أصدرت لجنة التحقيق الدولية بياناً صحفياً بتاريخ ٢٠١٢/٤/١٦ تطرقت فيه إلى عدة مسائل تقع خارج نطاق ولايتها بشكل كامل:

أ- فلا ولاية للجنة في الخوض في عمل المراقبين الدوليين في سورية، إن هذا الأمر غير مرتبط بعمل اللجنة ومن المستغرب تدخلها فيه.

ب- أكدت اللجنة في بيانها على استخدام الأسلحة الثقيلة في بعض المناطق واعتقالات في مناطق أخرى، وذلك باستناد إلى ما قالت أنه "تحقيقاتها الميدانية". ومن غير المفهوم ما هو المقصود بالتحقيقات الميدانية وهي لم تدخل المناطق التي تتحدث عنها؟ إن الحديث بهذه الطريقة يسعى لإعطاء النتائج غير الصحيحة للجنة مصداقية لا تتحلى بها.

ج- اعتبرت اللجنة أن المحاسبة ضرورية باعتبارها مكوناً أساسياً "لمرحلة انتقالية تؤدي إلى دولة قائمة على مبادئ سيادة القانون والديمقراطية وحقوق الإنسان". إن الجمهورية العربية السورية ترفض أي تدخل في خيارات شعبها. إن هذا الحديث يُعتبر تدخلاً

سافراً في الشؤون الداخلية لسورية، ويدل مرة أخرى على تسـييس عمل اللجنة. وليس للجنة حق في وضع تصور لمستقبل دولة عريقة مثل سورية أو رأيها في خيارات الشعب السوري المتحضر والواعي لمستقبله.

د- أعربت اللجنة عن قلقها على مصير "النازحين واللاجئين السوريين"، وأثنت على الدول المستضيفة للاجئين السوريين، في الوقت الذي لم يسمعها أحد تصدر بياناً أو حتى تُشير إلى جهود سورية الجبارة في استضافة ما يزيد على مليون ونصف من مختلف دول المنطقة وجدوا في سورية الملاذ الآمن وبلد الخير والأمــان. لقـد تحملـت سورية حكومةً وشعباً أعباء كبيرة في اقتسام لقمـة العـيش معهـم وتأمين فضاء الحماية اللازم لهم وبما يفوق أي التزامـات مطلوبـة منها بموجب تعهداتها الدولية. والجدير بالذكر أن هؤلاء الضيوف لم يسعوا لمغادرة سورية في هذه الظروف، فقد وجدوا في سورية ما لا يجدونه في أي من دول المنطقة، حتى في هذه الظروف الصـعبة، وهم يُدركون أن سورية تبذل جهوداً إضافية لحمايتهم مـع الشـعب السوري من إرهاب المجموعات المسلحة، الأمر الذي يثير الكثيــر من إشارات الاستفهام حول حقيقة من يُسمون باللاجئين السـوريين، والأهداف السياسية والعسكرية لبعض الدول المستضيفة لهم.

٦- كانت لجنة التحقيق الدولية التقت في جنيف عدداً ممن أسـمتهم "ضـحايا انتهاكات حقوق الإنسان"، كما أنها طلبت في رسالتها إلـى الجمهوريـة العربية السورية المؤرخة ٢٠١٢/١٢/٢٨ تسهيل الاتصالات بالعـائلات القتلى والجرحى من أفراد الجيش والأمـن، بالإضافة إلـى الضحايا

الآخرين، إن الموضوعية والحيادية في عمل اللجنـة، يسـتدعيان لقـاء ضحايا انتهاكات حقوق الإنسان التي قامت بها المجموعـات الإرهابيــة المسلحة. والجمهورية العربية السورية مستعدة لتقـديم لـوائح بأسـماء المواطنين السوريين الذين تعرضوا لاعتداءات وانتهاكـات حقـوقهم أو حقوق أقربائهم على أيدي هذه المجموعات، وترى أنه من المفيد استقبالهم في جنيف، كما فعلت في أواخر العام الماضي لتجميع شــهادات معاديــة لسورية وتمثل وجهة نظر تصب في الحملة التي تتعرض لها سورية.

٧- تؤكد الجمهورية العربية السورية على أنها شكلت لجنة تحقيـق وظنيـة نزيهة ومحايدة ومستقلة للتحقيق في شكاوى ارتكاب أعمال عنـف فـي الأحداث الأخيرة، وهذه اللجنة مستمرة في عملها.

تغتنم بعثة الجمهورية العربية السورية هذه المناسبة لتعرب لمكتـب المفوضية السامية لحقوق الإنسان عن فائق اعتبارها وتقديرها.

إلى مكتب المفوضية السامية لحقوق الإنسان – جنيف

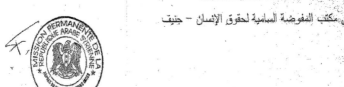

NATIONS UNIES
HAUT COMMISSARIAT AUX DROITS DE
L'HOMME

UNITED NATIONS
HIGH COMMISSIONER FOR
HUMAN RIGHTS

Tel: 41-22-9179101

Independent International Commission of Inquiry established pursuant to resolution A/HRC/S-17/1

and extended through resolution A/HRC/Res/19/22

1 May 2012

Excellency,

On behalf of the Independent International Commission of Inquiry on the Syrian Arab Republic established by the United Nations Human Rights Council pursuant to resolution S-17/1 and extended by resolution A/HRC/Res/19/22, I wish to acknowledge with thanks a Note Verbale No. 233/12 from the Permanent Mission of the Syrian Arab Republic to the United Nations Office in Geneva and specialized institutions in Switzerland, dated 27 April 2012, relaying a position of the Syrian Government in response to my letter addressed to Your Excellency on 16 April 2012.

Noting with appreciation the detailed comments provided in the Note Verbale, the Commission wishes to elaborate in more detail on some of the key points therein. Before doing so, I wish to take this opportunity to clarify that the Office of the High Commissioner for Human Rights (OHCHR), whom the Note Verbale was addressed, provides the Commission of Inquiry with the necessary secretariat support, but the Commission itself is independent from OHCHR and reports only to the Human Rights Council that has created its mandate.

Moving on to the specific points raised in the Note Verbale, I wish to share with you the following observations:

1- As stated in the Commission's last report and our previous communications to the Syrian Government, the Commission is guided by the principles of independence, impartiality and objectivity, and as such, it strives to reflect the information sent to us by the Government authorities, to the fullest extent possible, keeping in line with the established methodology of fact-finding and reporting. The Commission has dealt with the information about the victims of human rights abuses committed by the armed opposition with compassion, and it was the Commission that was first to report on such incidents, in support of all victims of such human rights violations.

2- On behalf of the Commission, I would like to reassure you of the Commission's full commitment to pursuing the implementation of its mandate and reporting thereunder in the most objective way, based on the factually accurate information, subject to its ability to collect and verify such information from all sources, in particular from those from within Syria.

H.E. Mr. Walid al-Moallem

Minister of Foreign and Expatriates Affairs

Damascus, Syrian Arab Republic   ..../...

1

3- The Commission has noted with appreciation the detailed information about civilian casualties resulting from acts of armed groups, which will be reflected in its next report.

4- The Commission would like to assure that it is in its mandate to follow all meetings and discussions linked to the on-going events in Syria. Here, we would like to assure that our presence in the Istanbul meeting of April 2012 did not amount to participation, but only to observation. The presence of the Commission in this meeting did not mean that we have compromised our neutrality and independence. Nor did our participation carry in it any political undertone - as it is suggested in your letter - by taking sides in a conflict or joining them. The aim of the Commission in its presence in the mentioned meeting was for information purposes, so that we are introduced to the evolution of the position of member states regarding the evolution of the situation in Syria.

5- With respect to paragraph 5 of your letter referring to the CoI's 16 April 2012 press statement, the CoI takes note that the agreement reached between the Syrian Arab Republic and the opposition forces to permit the deployment of international observers is not part of the mandate of the CoI. Nevertheless, it is clear that human rights violations are occurring in the context of the on-going armed confrontations - such violations being the direct subject of the mandate - and the Commission wished to express its optimism that such violations would cease with the implementation of the plan.

In point 5(b) the letter refers to the Commission's description of "heavy weaponry" and to "field investigations" undertaken. It is of course correct that the Syrian government has not afforded access to the CoI's investigators to date. Thus, the "field investigations" refer to the deployment of investigators to the region and elsewhere (except Syria) where they have conducted interviews and investigative activities with a broad spectrum of interlocutors. The methodology of the CoI is, whenever possible, to gather its own first hand observations, ideally from site visits to the locations of alleged violations. When that is impossible due to a lack of access, the second most favourable option is to take testimonies and witness statements from those who themselves saw the events in question first hand. Supporting documents and materials are also collected whenever possible. The CoI attempts to corroborate the accounts it receives with other sources, and it includes in its reports and public statements only those events which it 'reasonably suspects' to have occurred. In the case of the mentioned heavy weaponry, the CoI had credible and corroborated accounts that came from interviews gathered in the field.[1] It is the objective of the CoI to include in the future, accounts that come also from "the field" in the Syrian Arab Republic, a development which will only improve the CoI's assessment of the human rights situation.

I refer with respect to Paragraph 5(c) of your letter and the reference to the CoI's statement about the need to ensure accountability for violations "as a fundamental component in a transitional period leading to a State founded on the principles of rule of law, democracy and human rights." Read carefully, the CoI's statement does not refer to the founding of a new state, and the CoI would never imply such an outcome. Instead, in mentioning "transition" the text refers to the reforms that are already underway and that are planned in your country's ongoing efforts to bolster the principles of rule of law, democracy and human rights. The mentioned principles are those which can be found in numerous texts, declarations, and conventions to which the Syrian Arab Republic has previously ascribed and which can be readily described as the common aspirations of humankind. I referred to a "transition" away from the violence currently affecting Syria in which the principles of rule of law and democracy have fallen victim.

To achieve this, it is indeed my position as Chair of the Commission CoI, and presumably also that of the Syrian Arab Republic and all the members of the HRC, that those responsible for the serious

---

[1] The term "field" is frequently used in the human rights arena to describe locations that are not the "headquarters," or otherwise associated with a desk and computer.

human rights violations – irrespective of who perpetrated them – must be held accountable. It is a core function of the CoI's mandate to identify such persons.

In paragraph 5(d) of your letter you have noted the CoI's reference to "Syrian displaced and refugees." It is correct that the CoI has not mentioned those refugees to whom the Syrian Arab Republic is host. The CoI understands its mandate to be limited to the circumstances arising out of the hostilities within Syria.

To the point that those refugees Syria is hosting have not sought to flee, accurate as that may be, it does not detract from the notion that civilians are fleeing Syria in large numbers. The definition of 'refugee' is well-settled in international law and applies equally to those Syria is hosting as well as to those escaping the country. The CoI is aware that not all individuals purporting to be refugees meet the definition in fact, however, the testimonies the CoI has collected, and corroborated, have convinced it that families settled in the camps in Syria's neighbouring countries are legitimately refugees. In support, the CoI would refer to the UNHCR statements on this matter where some 61,000 individuals are reportedly registered as refugees.[2] The key point is that refugees must be allowed to return, in favourable conditions, to their homes.

6- The Commission is doing all its possible to gather information on human rights violations in Syria, and verify their validity. The Commission appreciates the openness of the Syrian Arab Republic to transparency and its willingness to share information, data, and eye-witness account, to help us carry out our mission. The Commission thanks the permanent Mission of Syrian Arab Republic for sharing detailed data on the victims of police and army personnel during violent events since March 2011, information which is reflected in our reports. The Commission is encouraged about the readiness of the Syrian Government to further this collaboration, and the most efficient way would be to provide access to the Commission to interview the witnesses of the Syrian victims, whether of civilian, public order, or military personnel, and have direct access to the areas of events themselves. Such an access would provide the Commission with objective and precise information about the human rights situation in the Syrian Arab Republic.

7 - With respect to point 7 of your letter, the CoI is keen to meet with the Syrian Commission and to discuss their findings. In advance, we would welcome receiving information concerning the Commission's membership, their Terms of Reference, and their methodology, as well as an anticipated date on which they anticipate completing their investigations.

8- Furthermore, as indicated in my previous letter, in the coming six months, the Commission intends to do periodic updates on human rights violations, in addition to the oral report to the Human Rights Council in June and the written updated report in September, as mandated by resolution A/HRC/Res/19/22. Keeping in line with this calendar, if the Commission were to be given access to Syria, the mission would have to be undertaken by the end of May, at the latest, in order for its findings to be reflected in the Commission's oral report to the Human Rights Council in June.

The Commission would very much appreciate your support in giving a positive consideration of our request to visit your country.

Please accept, Excellency, the assurances of our highest consideration.

Paulo Sergio Pinheiro

Chairperson

---

[2] http://www.unhcr.org/4f9137529.html

3

NATIONS UNIES
HAUT COMMISSARIAT AUX DROITS DE L'HOMME

UNITED NATIONS
HIGH COMMISSIONER FOR HUMAN RIGHTS

Tel: 41-22-9179101

Independent International Commission of Inquiry pursuant to resolution A/HRC/S-17/1

and extended through resolution A/HRC/Res/19/22

The Independent International Commission of Inquiry on the Syrian Arab Republic established pursuant to Human Rights Council resolution S-17/1 and extended through resolution A/HRC/19/22 presents its compliments to the Permanent Representative of the Syrian Arab Republic to the United Nations Office in Geneva and specialized institutions in Switzerland.

Further to its earlier Note Verbales of 2 April 2012, and of 16 April and 1 May 2012, transmitting letters addressed to H.E. Mr. Walid al-Moallem, the Minister of Foreign and Expatriates Affairs of Syria, the Commission of Inquiry wishes to recall that it is the body that, through the Human Rights Council mandate, credibly addresses the international community regarding the overall human rights situation in Syria in an impartial, objective and balanced manner. As previously mentioned, the Commission does not make any distinction among victims from any of the parties to the present unrest.

In order for the Commission to fully implement its mandate, it is essential for the Commission to have access to Syria to enable it to - more adequately and rigorously than outside the country - ascertain facts on the ground, based on first-hand information within the country and from the Syrian government.

As the Commission's next oral report is due for presentation to the Human Rights Council on 27 June 2012, the Commission's visit, if granted, as hoped by the Commission, would need to be undertaken by the end of May, at the latest, for its findings to be fairly reflected in its oral report.

The Commission avails itself of this opportunity to extend assurances of its highest consideration to the Permanent Representative of the Syrian Arab Republic to the United Nations Office in Geneva and specialized institutions in Switzerland.

Geneva, 10 May 2012

NATIONS UNIES
HAUT COMMISSARIAT AUX
DROITS DE L'HOMME

UNITED NATIONS
HIGH COMMISSIONER FOR
HUMAN RIGHTS

Tel: 41-22-9179101

Independent International Commission of Inquiry established pursuant to resolution A/HRC/S-17/1
and extended through resolution A/HRC/Res/19/22

The Independent International Commission of Inquiry on the Syrian Arab Republic established pursuant to Human Rights Council resolution S-17/1 and extended through resolution A/HRC/19/22 presents its compliments to the Permanent Representative of the Syrian Arab Republic to the United Nations Office in Geneva and specialized institutions in Switzerland.

The Commission thanks the Syrian Arab Republic for the prompt response to its Note Verbale of 24 May 2012 and acknowledges receipt, again with appreciation, of the Note Verbale, dated 25 May 2012, relaying additional information concerning criminal activity from 12 April to 23 May, 2012.

The Commission seeks to clarify that it has just released a "Periodic Update," as it is mandated to do under resolution A/HRC/19/22, para 15. The Human Rights Council requested the Commission "to conduct and continuously update a mapping exercise of gross violations of human rights since March 2011, including an assessment of casualty figures, and to publish it periodically."

Separately, on 27 June 2012, the Commission will provide an "Oral Update" to the Human Rights Council during its 20th Session. It is in the Oral Update that the Commission anticipates being able to make use of the information recently provided by the Syrian Arab Republic. The Commission takes this opportunity to reiterate that only by visiting the Syrian Arab Republic can the Commission properly investigate and corroborate the incidents and crimes about which your government has informed. Should the Syrian Arab Republic concur with a visit from the Commission, said visit must be completed prior to 15 June 2012 for the information to be considered in the Oral Update.

Finally, the Commission recalls that its final report will be submitted to the Human Rights Council during its 21st Session in September. In the interim, additional "Periodic Updates" will be issued as appropriate.

1

The Commission avails itself of this opportunity to extend assurances of its highest consideration to the Permanent Representative of the Syrian Arab Republic to the United Nations Office in Geneva and specialized institutions in Switzerland.

Geneva, 29 May 2012

2

Tel: 41-22-9179101

Independent International Commission of Inquiry pursuant to resolution A/HRC/S-17/1

and extended through resolution A/HRC/Res/19/22

The Independent International Commission of Inquiry on the Syrian Arab Republic established pursuant to Human Rights Council resolution S-17/1 and extended through resolution A/HRC/19/22 presents its compliments to the Permanent Representative of the Syrian Arab Republic to the United Nations Office in Geneva and specialized institutions in Switzerland.

Further to paragraph 8 of resolution A/HRC/S-19/L.1,' adopted on 1 June 2012, the Human Rights Council requested the Commission to urgently conduct a comprehensive, independent, and unfettered special inquiry, consistent with international standards, into the events in Al-Houla. The Commission is also requested to provide a full report of the findings of its special inquiry to the Human Rights Council at its 20th session, and to coordinate, as appropriate, with relevant UN mechanisms.

In furtherance of this mandate, paragraph 9 of the same resolution calls upon the Syrian authorities to accord the Commission full and unhindered access to Syria to enable it to conduct the special inquiry.

According to the tentative programme of work of the 20th session of the Human Rights Council, the Commission is expected to present its oral report on Wednesday, 27 June 2012. With this date in mind, the Commission, including the two Commissioners and its team of human rights investigators and forensic and military experts, stands ready to carry out an investigative mission to Syria, as soon as possible. The mission would need to be completed by Friday, 22 June, at the very latest, in order for its findings to be included in the presentation to the Human Rights Council.

The Commission has taken note of the Note Verbale from the Permanent Mission of the Syrian Arab Republic, dated 30 May 2012, containing information regarding the massacre of civilians in Al-Houla. Furthermore, the Commission noted media announcements on 31

May 2012 relating the results of a three-day investigation into the massacre, appointed by the Syrian government. In this regard, as a first step in the context of its special inquiry, the Commission would appreciate receiving a copy of the full report on the findings of the national investigation, along with an opportunity to meet with its members. In conducting the special inquiry, the Commission will also coordinate with UNSMIS and other relevant UN human rights mechanisms, as appropriate.

The Commission wishes to reassure the Permanent Representative of its full commitment to conducting its work in accordance with the highest international standards of objectivity, impartiality and independence.

The Commission avails itself of this opportunity to extend assurances of its highest consideration to the Permanent Representative of the Syrian Arab Republic to the United Nations Office in Geneva and specialized institutions in Switzerland.

Geneva, 4 June 2012

NATIONS UNIES
HAUT COMMISSARIAT AUX
DROITS DE L'HOMME

UNITED NATIONS
HIGH COMMISSIONER FOR
HUMAN RIGHTS

Tel: 41-22-9179101

Independent International Commission of Inquiry established pursuant to resolution A/HRC/S-17/1

and extended through resolution A/HRC/Res/19/22

22 June 2012

Excellency,

I thank you very much for enabling my visit to Damascus. I am particularly grateful for the opportunity to explain in person to members of the Government the nature of the Commission's work as well as the modalities necessary for it to be successful.

Your Excellency will no doubt be aware that I will be delivering an Oral Update on behalf of the Commission of Inquiry on Syria to the Human Rights Council on 27 June 2012, with special attention paid to the Al-Houla incident. Our final report, which is to be submitted to the 21st Session of the Council in September, needs to be completed by 6 August 2012.

I very much hope that this visit to Damascus will pave the way for our team to begin its work in earnest in the Syria, and thereby fulfil its mandate. However, I will only be able to include the results of future investigations if we can complete our mission there by 25 July 2012. Therefore, as time is of the essence, I am hopeful that during this visit we can build an understanding as how my colleagues and I would be able to deploy effectively in your country.

Please accept, Excellency, the assurances of our highest consideration.

Paulo Sergio Pinheiro

Chairperson

H.E. Mr. Walid al-Moallem

Minister of Foreign and Expatriates Affairs

Damascus, Syrian Arab Republic

NATIONS UNIES
HAUT COMMISSARIAT AUX DROITS DE
L'HOMME

UNITED NATIONS
HIGH COMMISSIONER FOR
HUMAN RIGHTS

Tel: 41-22-9179101.

Independent International Commission of Inquiry established pursuant to resolution A/HRC/S-17/1
and extended through resolution A/HRC/Res/19/22

The Independent International Commission of Inquiry on the Syrian Arab Republic established pursuant to Human Rights Council resolution S-17/1 and extended through resolution A/HRC/19/22 presents its compliments to the Permanent Representative of the Syrian Arab Republic to the United Nations Office in Geneva and specialized institutions in Switzerland.

We hereby acknowledge with appreciation receipt of your Nota Verbale No. 330/12, dated 25 June 2012, relaying the contents of a DVD to the Commission. We have viewed the disk with interest and have taken note of the testimonies of the two eyewitnesses therein. We have also noted that the female of these witnesses was interviewed by a Russian journalist; on ANNA Television, in June.

The Commission would like to arrange interviews with both witnesses, as well as any additional eyewitnesses that the Government of the Syrian Arab Republic recommends. We would hope to include the results of those interviews in our final report to the Human Rights Council to be delivered in September 2012. In the event you agree with this proposal, we can then discuss the modalities of the interviews. To be included in the final report we would need to conduct them by 26 July 2012.

The Commission avails itself of this opportunity to extend assurances of its highest consideration to the Permanent Representative of the Syrian Arab Republic to the United Nations Office in Geneva and specialized institutions in Switzerland.

Geneva, 13 July 2012

1

Annex II

[*English only*]

Applicable law

I. Background

1.   Whether during peacetime or periods of armed conflict, a substantial body of international law will be in operation. The sources comprise primarily treaties ratified by the country in question. Customary international law (CIL) is also applicable. In its first report submitted in November 2011, the Commission identified the Syrian Arab Republic's legal obligations under international human rights law (IHRL).[1] At that time, although violent clashes were occurring, the Syrian Arab Republic was in a state of peace and has not sought to derogate from any applicable treaty provisions.

2.   In its second report submitted in February 2012, the commission expressed its concern that the violence in the Syrian Arab Republic had reached the requisite level of intensity to trigger the applicability of International Humanitarian Law (IHL). However, because it could not verify whether the FSA, or its associated groups, had reached the necessary level of organization, the commission determined that it could not apply IHL.

3.   During the period covered by this third report, the commission has determined that the intensity and duration of the conflict, combined with the increased organizational capabilities of the FSA,[2] do, in fact, meet the legal threshold for a non-international armed conflict.[3] With this determination, the commission applied IHL, including Common Article 3, in its assessment of the actions of the parties during hostilities.

4.   As described below, egregious violations of human rights, customary or humanitarian law can give rise to individual criminal responsibility under international criminal law (ICL).

II. Regimes in effect

5.   The onset of IHL applicability does not replace existing obligations under IHRL; both regimes remain in force and are generally considered as complementary and mutually reinforcing. Where both IHL and IHRL apply, and can be applied consistently, parties to a conflict are obliged to do so. In situations where IHL and IHRL are both applicable, but cannot be applied consistently, the principle of *lex specialis* applies.[4]

---

[1] A/HRC/S-17/2/Add.1 paras. 23–26.

[2] See annex III.

[3] This view is supported by the ICRC, among others. See "the Syrian Arab Republic in civil war, Red Cross says," 15 July 2012, Available from http://www.bbc.co.uk/news/world-middle-east-18849362. President Assad himself described the Syrian Arab Republic as being in a state of war in a statement on 26 June 2012, see "the Syrian Arab Republic in a State of War, says Bashar al-Assad," 26 July 2012. Available from http://www.bbc.co.uk/news/world-middle-east-18598533.

[4] See *Legality of the Threat or Use of Nuclear Weapons, Advisory Opinion, I.C.J. Reports 1996*. The International Court of Justice ruled that IHL is *lex specialis* vis-à-vis IHRL during armed conflicts. Thus, the parties must abide by the legal regime which has a more specific provision on point. The

6.   Gross violations of either regime expose the perpetrator to criminal liability at the international level. Courts in any country can employ the principle of universal jurisdiction to try such cases. The definitional elements of international criminal law (ICL), have recently been bolstered with the adoption of the Rome Statute and the creation of the International Criminal Court (ICC), discussed below.

7.   The specific applicability of each regime is discussed below.

III. International human rights law

8.   At all times relevant to this report the Syrian Arab Republic was a party to the major United Nations human rights treaties and a number of optional protocols.[5] The Government did not declare a state of emergency nor otherwise seek to derogate from any of the aforementioned obligations which consequently remained in effect throughout the conflict, irrespective of the applicability of other legal regimes.[6]

9.   All branches of the Syrian government were therefore bound to respect, protect, promote and fulfill the human rights of all persons within its jurisdiction. The obligation included the right to afford an effective remedy to those whose rights were violated (including the provision of reparations) and to investigate and bring to justice perpetrators of particular violations.[7] The Syrian Arab Republic was also bound by relevant rules of IHRL which form a part of customary international law.

---

analysis is fact specific and therefore each regime may apply, exclusive of the other, in specific circumstances. The Human Rights Committee generally concurs with this view as set out in the General Comment 31 to the ICCPR. "The Covenant applies also in situations of armed conflict to which the rules of international humanitarian law are applicable. While, in respect of certain Covenant rights, more specific rules of international humanitarian law may be specially relevant for the purposes of the interpretation of Covenant rights, both spheres of law are complementary, not mutually exclusive."

[5]   The International Covenants on Civil and Political Rights and on Economic, Social and Cultural Rights were ratified by the Syrian Arab Republic in 1969, the same year it ratified the Convention on the Elimination of All Forms of Racial Discrimination. The Syrian Arab Republic is also party to the Convention on the Elimination of Discrimination against Women which it ratified in 2003, the Convention on the Prevention and Punishment of the Crime of Genocide in 1955, the Convention against Torture and other Cruel, Inhuman or Degrading Treatment and Punishment in 2004 and the Convention on the Rights of Child in 1993. The Syrian Arab Republic ratified the Optional Protocol to the Convention on the Rights of Child on the involvement of children in armed conflict in 2003. The Syrian Arab Republic has not ratified the Convention on the Non-applicability of Statutory Limitations to War Crimes and Crimes against Humanity.

[6]   *Legal Consequences of the Construction of a Wall in the Occupied Palestinian Territory, Advisory Opinion, I.C.J. Reports 2004*, p. 178, paras. 105–106, "[t]he protection offered by human rights conventions does not cease in case of armed conflict." See also *Nuclear Weapons case*, statements concerning IHL as *lex specialis*, at p. 240, para. 25.

[7]   See Human Rights Committee, General Comment No. 31 on The Nature of the General Legal Obligation Imposed on State Parties to the Covenant (2004), paras. 15–19. In this General Comment, the Human Rights Committee considered that the duty to bring perpetrators to justice attaches in particular to violations that are criminal under domestic or international law, torture and similar cruel, inhuman and degrading treatment, summary and arbitrary killing and enforced disappearance. See also the *Basic Principles and Guidelines on the Right to a Remedy and Reparation for Victims of Gross Violations of International Human Rights Law and Serious Violations of International Humanitarian Law*, adopted by the General Assembly in December 2005, and the *Updated Set of Principles for the Protection and Promotion of Human Rights through Action to Combat Impunity* (which were recognised in a consensus resolution of the UN Commission on Human Rights in 2005).

10.   *Non-state actors and IHRL:* Non-state actors cannot formally become parties to international human rights treaties. They must nevertheless respect the fundamental human rights of persons forming customary international law (CIL), in areas where such actors exercise *de facto* control.[8] The commission therefore examined allegations of human rights violations committed by the Syrian Government as well as abuses of customary international human rights norms perpetrated by the anti-Government armed groups.

IV.   International humanitarian law

11.   International humanitarian law (IHL), also known as the law of armed conflict, is binding on all parties to a conflict.[9] Its applicability is triggered whenever hostilities meet the threshold criteria of "armed conflict," and applies irrespective of whether any party involved has in fact declared war. IHL comprises the four Geneva Conventions of 12 August 1949 as well as its Protocols I and II and an array of other instruments and customary principles that protect those most vulnerable to the effects of armed conflict.[10]

12.   The Syrian Arab Republic is a party to the Geneva Conventions and its Protocol I, as well as to several other IHL instruments concerning weaponry and mercenaries.[11] The Syrian Arab Republic has not, however, ratified Protocol II to the Geneva Conventions which is specifically applicable during non-international armed conflict. A number of provisions of customary IHL nevertheless apply to non-international armed conflict and must be respected when the armed conflict threshold is met. The commission took note that a non-international armed conflict developed in the Syrian Arab Republic during February 2012 which triggered the applicability of Common Article 3 of the Geneva Conventions as well as customary law relevant to non-international armed conflict.

13.   As the Security Council underlined in its resolution 1325 (2011), it is important for all States to apply fully the relevant norms of IHL and IHRL to women and girls, and to take special measures to protect women and girls from gender-based violence during armed conflict.[12]

---

[8]   For a more expansive view of the application of IHRL, see Andrew Clapham, *Human Rights Obligations of Non-State Actors* (Oxford, Oxford University Press, 2006). To similar effect, see UN Secretary-General, *Report of the Secretary-General's Panel of Experts on Accountability in Sri Lanka*, 31 March 2011, para. 188, available from: http://www.un.org/News/dh/infocus/ Sri_Lanka/POE_Report_Full.pdf.

[9]   As the Special Court for Sierra Leone held, "it is well settled that all parties to an armed conflict, whether States or non-State actors, are bound by international humanitarian law, even though only States may become parties to international treaties." See *Prosecutor v. Sam Hinga Norman*, case SCSL-2004-14-AR72(E), (31 May 2004), para. 22. Common Article 3 of the Geneva Conventions itself states that "each party ... shall be bound." (emphasis added).

[10]   One repository of the principles of customary IHL can be accessed in *Customary International Humanitarian Law* (3 vols.), by Jean-Marie Henckaerts and Louise Doswald-Beck for the International Committee of the Red Cross, (Cambridge, Cambridge University Press, 2005) (*ICRC Study*).

[11]   The Syrian Arab Republic is a party to the following treaties: The Protocol for the Prohibition of the Use of Asphyxiating, Poisonous or other Gases, and of Bacteriological Methods of Warfare (1925); the Convention for the Amelioration of the Condition of the Wounded and Sick in Armies in the Field (1929); the Convention for the Protection of Cultural Property in the Event of Armed Conflict(1954) and its Protocol(1954); the International Convention against the Recruitment, Use, Financing and Training of Mercenaries (1989).

[12]   See also S/RES/1820.

V. International criminal law

14.   International criminal law provides the means of enforcement at the international level of penalties for grave violations of customary law, IHRL and serious violations of IHL which are recognized as attracting individual liability. As noted, the ICC tries persons accused of such crimes, namely genocide, crimes against humanity, aggression and war crimes.[13] The Rome Statute had been joined by 121 countries as of July 2012.[14] Although the Syrian Arab Republic has signed the text, it has not yet become a party. Pursuant to its Article 13 (b), the Security Council can refer the situation of the Syrian Arab Republic to the ICC Prosecutor for investigation. At the time of writing, no such referral has been made.

15.   *War crimes:* A complete listing of which actions constitute war crimes under the Rome Statute is contained within its Article 8. In the context of non-international armed conflict, this comprises serious violations of Common Article 3 and Protocol II, as well as other serious violations of international law.

16.   *Crimes against humanity:* Crimes against humanity are those crimes which "shock the conscience of humanity". Under the Rome Statute, crimes against humanity occur where certain acts are undertaken as part of a widespread or systematic attack against a civilian population where the perpetrator has knowledge of the attack.[15] The elements of crimes against humanity are well established in international criminal law:[16]

1.   There must be one or more attacks;

2.   The acts of the perpetrator must be part of the attack(s);

3.   The attack(s) must be directed against any civilian population;

4.   The attack(s) must be widespread or systematic;

5.   The perpetrator must know that his or her acts constitute part of a pattern of widespread or systematic crimes directed against a civilian population and know that his or her acts fit into such a pattern.

The underlying "acts" — or crimes — referred to in the above paragraph (2) have been enumerated in the Rome Statute.[17] The list includes a number of the violations described elsewhere in this report, for example, unlawful killings;[18] enforced disappearances;[19] torture

---

[13]   See William Schabas, *The International Criminal Court: A Commentary on the Rome Statute* (Oxford, Oxford University Press, 2010), Otto Triffterer, *Commentary on the Rome Statute of the International Criminal Court: Observers' Notes, Article by Article* 2nd ed., (Oxford, Hart Publishing, 2008) and M. Cherif Bassiouni, *International Criminal Law* (3 vols.) 3rd ed., (Boston, Martinus Nijhoff, 2008).

[14]   See http://www.icc-cpi.int.

[15]   Article 7, Rome Statute. See M. Cherif Bassiouni, *Crimes Against Humanity: Historical Evolution and Contemporary Practice* (Cambridge, Cambridge University Press, 2011).

[16]   The "Elements of Crimes" applied to cases at the International Criminal Court, Available from http://www.icc-cpi.int. See also *Prosecutor v. Kunarac et al.*, IT-96-23-T & IT-96-23/1-T, Judgement, Trial Chamber, 22 February 2001.

[17]   The list in the Statute includes murder, extermination, enslavement, forcible transfer of population, imprisonment, torture, rape, sexual slavery, enforced prostitution, forced pregnancy, enforced sterilization, sexual violence, persecution, enforced disappearance, apartheid and other inhumane acts. See Article 7 (1) (a–k).

[18]   Listed as murder under Article 7 (1) (a) of the Rome statute. See annex V.

[19]   Article 7 (1) (h) of the Rome statute. See annex VII.

and other cruel, inhuman and degrading treatment;[20] and/or rape,[21] and therefore their elements are not repeated here.

17.   *Widespread or systematic:* Widespread has long been defined as encompassing "the large scale nature of the attack, which should be massive, frequent, carried out collectively with considerable seriousness and directed against a multiplicity of victims".[22] As such, the element of "widespread" refers both to the large-scale nature of the attack and the number of resultant victims. The assessment is neither exclusively quantitative nor geographical, but must be carried out on the basis of the individual facts. Accordingly, a widespread attack may be the "cumulative effect of a series of inhumane acts or the singular effect of an inhumane act of extraordinary magnitude".[23]

18.   In contrast, the term "systematic" refers to:

> the "organised nature of the acts of violence and the improbability of their random occurrence" (citations omitted). An attack's systematic nature can "often be expressed through patterns of crimes, in the sense of non-accidental repetition of similar criminal conduct on a regular basis". The Chamber notes that the "systematic" element has been defined by the ICTR as (i) being thoroughly organised, (ii) following a regular pattern, (iii) on the basis of a common policy, and (iv) involving substantial public or private resources (citations omitted), whilst the ICTY has determined that the element requires (i) a political objective or plan, (ii) large-scale or continuous commission of crimes which are linked, (iii) use of significant public or private resources, and (iv) the implication of high-level political and/or military authorities.[24]

19.   It is important to note that crimes against humanity need not be both widespread and systematic. The test is disjunctive, and therefore reaching either element suffices.

VI.   Customary international law

20.   Customary International Law is made up of norms of (inter)state behaviour that have developed over time and that have become binding among states in their international relations. Treaties are often the codification of CIL norms. CIL is an inseparable component of both IHL and IHRL. The relationship between those two legal regimes and CIL can be expressed in terms of specific crimes or violations, for example, those set out in the Rome Statute. CIL is identified by legal scholars, courts, military law experts, and, for example, the ICRC.[25] CIL contains a number of core precepts such as distinction of civilians, prohibition on indiscriminate attacks, that feasible precautions are undertaken, the principle of humanity (no unnecessary suffering), and imperative military necessity.

---

[20] See annex VIII.

[21] See annex IX.

[22] ICC Pre-Trial Chamber, Situation in the Republic of Kenya, Decision Pursuant to Article 15 of the Rome Statute on the Authorization of an Investigation into the Situation in the Republic of Kenya, ICC-01/09-19, 31 March 2010, para. 95 (citations omitted).

[23] ICTY, *Dusko Tadic* Judgment, 7 May 1997, para. 648.

[24] ICC Pre-Trial Chamber, Situation in the Republic of Kenya, Decision Pursuant to Article 15 of the Rome Statute on the Authorization of an Investigation into the Situation in the Republic of Kenya, ICC-01/09-19, 31 March 2010, para. 96.

[25] See for example the ICRC Study (supra fn 46). In that extensive study, the ICRC identified 161 customary international humanitarian legal norms.

VII. State obligations to investigate, prosecute, punish and provide reparations

21.   Customary law, IHL and IHRL obligate states to investigate allegations of serious violations of their respective regimes and, when appropriate, prosecute suspected perpetrators and compensate the victims. The UN General Assembly expressed the obligation in the clearest of terms when it declared in the "Basic Principles on the Right to Remedy,"

> *"In cases of gross violations of international human rights law and serious violations of international humanitarian law constituting crimes under international law, States have the duty to investigate and, if there is sufficient evidence, the duty to submit to prosecution the person allegedly responsible for the violations and, if found guilty, the duty to punish her or him."*[26]

22.   The obligation is founded in part on Article 2 of the International Covenant on Civil and Political Rights (ICCPR),[27] wherein an effective remedy is required. The obligation to investigate is specifically confirmed in the interpretation given that provision by the Human Rights Committee.[28]

23.   The obligation is slightly different for internal armed conflicts under IHL. There, the obligation to investigate war crimes and prosecute the suspects is a matter of customary law.[29] The notion has been reaffirmed on several occasions by the UN Security Council specifically in relation to the conflicts in Afghanistan, Burundi, Democratic Republic of the Congo, Kosovo and Rwanda.[30] In a resolution on impunity adopted without a vote in 2002, the UN Commission on Human Rights recognized that perpetrators of war crimes should be prosecuted or extradited.[31] The commission has similarly adopted resolutions — most of them without a vote — requiring the investigation and prosecution of persons alleged to have violated IHL in the internal armed conflicts in Sierra Leone, Chechnya, Rwanda, Sudan, Burundi and the former Yugoslavia. It is now broadly regarded as a customary international legal obligation to investigate and punish alleged perpetrators of IHL violations – in either international or non-international armed conflicts.[32]

24.   It is thus beyond doubt that each instance of alleged gross human rights violation, and all "serious" IHL violations — perpetrated by individuals on either side of the conflict in the Syrian Arab Republic — must be investigated, and, if appropriate, prosecuted. A

---

[26]   See Supra, fn 43, *Basic Principles and Guidelines on the Right to a Remedy and Reparation for Victims of Gross Violations of International Human Rights Law and Serious Violations of International Humanitarian Law*, UNGA Resolution 60/147, 16 Dec. 2005, Art. 4.

[27]   Article 2 of ICCPR requires a State party to respect and ensure to all individuals within its territory and subject to its jurisdiction the rights recognized in it and also to ensure an effective remedy for any person whose rights have been violated.

[28]   General Comment 31, para. 8.

[29]   Unlike in internal conflicts, the obligation in international armed conflicts rests not only with customary law, but also with the "grave breaches regime," set out in the four Geneva Conventions. See Article 49 of the First Geneva Convention, Article 50 of the Second Geneva Convention, article 129 of the Third Geneva Convention and article 146 of the Fourth Geneva Convention. The 'grave breaches regime' contains a specific list of crimes that, whenever violated, oblige the state to 'try or extradite' the suspected perpetrator. The International Humanitarian Fact Finding Commission, http://www.ihffc.org/, was set up for the purpose of conducting such investigations.

[30]   UN Security Council, Res.978 (§558), Res.1193 (§559) and Res.1199 (§560); UN Security Council, Statements by the President (§§561–569).

[31]   UN Commission on Human Rights, Res.2002/79 (§589).

[32]   See ICRC's Customary IHL Rule 158.

final point to be made concerns the nature of the investigation that must be conducted to satisfy this obligation. The UN has developed guidelines for such investigations and they center around four universal principles: independence, effectiveness, promptness and impartiality.[33] These four principles lie at the heart of human rights protection and are binding on UN members in that they have been relied upon and further developed in the jurisprudence of UN-backed international courts and also have been agreed upon by the States represented within the relevant United Nations bodies.

VIII. State responsibility

25.   Every internationally wrongful act of a State incurs the international responsibility of that State.[34] Similarly, customary international law provides that a State is responsible for all acts committed by members of its military and security forces.[35] The State is therefore responsible for wrongful acts, including crimes against humanity, committed by members of its military and security forces.

26.   The prohibition of crimes against humanity is a *jus cogens* or peremptory rule, and the punishment of such crimes is obligatory pursuant to the general principles of international law.[36] Furthermore, crimes against humanity are the culmination of violations of fundamental human rights, such as the right to life and the prohibition of torture or other forms of inhuman and degrading treatment.[37] According to the principles of State responsibility in international law, the Syrian Arab Republic bears responsibility for these crimes and violations, and bears the duty to ensure that individual perpetrators are punished and that victims receive reparation.[38]

IX. Individual responsibility

27.   The principle of individual criminal responsibility for international crimes is well established in customary international law.[39] According to article 27 of the Rome Statute of the International Criminal Court, which the Syrian Arab Republic has signed but not ratified, the Statute applies equally to all persons, without any distinction based on official capacity. In this context, Syrian laws afford extensive immunities, in most cases, for crimes

---

[33] *Principles on the Effective Prevention and Investigation of Extra-Legal, Arbitrary and Summary Executions* (Economic and Social Council resolution 1989/65;text available at: http://www1.umn. edu/humanrts/instree/i7pepi.htm) and *the Principles on the Effective Investigation and Documentation of Torture and Other Cruel, Inhuman or Degrading Treatment or Punishment* (General Assembly resolution 55/89, 2000; text available at: http://www2.ohchr.org/english/law/ investigation.htm). Note that the investigation need not be conducted by a court or even a judicial body. Administrative investigations, where appropriate, may equally comply with the four principles.

[34] *Official Records of the General Assembly, Fifty-sixth Session, Supplement No. 10* (A/56/10), chap. IV, sect. E, art. 1.

[35] Ibid., commentary to article 7.

[36] Case of *Almonacid-Arellano et al v. Chile*, Inter-American Court of Human Rights, Judgement of September 26, 2006, (Preliminary Objections, Merits, Reparations and Costs), para. 99. See also Official Records of the General Assembly (see footnote 33), Art. 26.

[37] *Almonacid-Arellano et al. v. Chile*, para. 111.

[38] See the Preamble to the Rome Statute of the International Criminal Court: "Recalling that it is the duty of every State to exercise its criminal jurisdiction over those responsible for international crimes."

[39] *Prosecutor v. Tharcisse Muvunyi*, Judgement, Case No. ICTR-00-55-T, 12 September 2006, para. 459.

committed by Government agents at all levels during the exercise of their duties. Although the Independent Special Legal Commission was established in recent months to investigate events, the State still has not provided the commission with any details of investigations or prosecutions under way by this mechanism.

X. Elements of specific violations

A. Excessive use of force

28. Excessive use of force by law enforcement officials (whether police or military or other members of State security forces) impinges on fundamental human rights guarantees, including the right to life (Article 6 ICCPR) and security of persons (Article 9 ICCPR). International standards such as the Code of Conduct for Law Enforcement Officials (*Code of Conduct*) and the *Basic Principles on the Use of Force and Firearms by Law Enforcement Officials (Basic Principals)* provide further guidance for public order officials operating in potentially violent circumstances. Non-violent means are to be used as far as possible before resorting to the use of force (principle of "necessity"), and any use of force must be limited to that which is proportionate to the seriousness of the offence and the legitimate objective to be achieved (principle of "proportionality"). Firearms are to be used only in self-defence or in defence of others against imminent threat of death or serious injury; to prevent a particularly serious crime involving grave threat to life; or to arrest a person posing such a threat and who is resisting efforts to stop the threat or to prevent that person's escape. Before using firearms, law enforcement officials must identify themselves as law enforcement officials and give a clear warning that firearms will be used. Further, sufficient time must be provided for the warning to be observed, unless this would unduly create a risk of death or serious harm to the officer or other persons or would be clearly inappropriate or pointless in the circumstances.[40]

29. IHL contains provisions similarly constraining the use of force under its requirement for proportionality in attack.[41] War-time attacks, even when carefully planned, frequently result in the loss of life or injury to civilians and damage to civilian objects. Under the rule requiring proportionality, a party is required to forego any offensive where the incidental damage expected "is excessive in relation to the concrete and direct military advantage anticipated". Thus, where the military advantage is outweighed by the damage or death to civilians and their objects, the attack is forbidden. This rule applies despite the recognition that incidental injury to civilians, so–called "collateral damage", may occur even when an attack is lawful.

B. Unlawful killing

1. Arbitrary deprivation of life

30. IHRL strictly prohibits taking life arbitrarily, a restriction that bars state actors from killing a person outside a legitimate and legal basis for doing so. Those legitimate bases are twofold. First, when a fully-fledged judicial process in line with international standards has been followed. Second, in the most narrow of circumstances, where a person's life is under imminent threat.

---

[40] See Article 3 of the *Code of Conduct.* See generally the *Basic Principles*.
[41] ICRC Study Rule 14.

31.   Moreover, a state-sponsored deprivation of life will be arbitrary in the legal sense unless it is both necessary and proportionate. Therefore, when a state actor employs lethal force it must be in order to protect life (i.e., it must be proportionate) and there must also be no other means available, such as capture or incapacitation, to curtail that threat to life (i.e., it must be necessary). Only under these limited circumstances is the resort to lethal force by the State legal.

32.   The noted IHRL standards differ to a degree from those applicable to fighters/combatants during an armed conflict under IHL. For example, one would not expect soldiers to warn their enemies before an attack. So long as all applicable IHL, CIL and IHRL requirements are met, killing an enemy fighter during an armed conflict is not illegal. The converse is also true: fighters/combatants causing another person's death, even that of the enemy, during armed conflict can be unlawful when the applicable law is breached (see below).

2.   Murder as a war crime

33.   In specific circumstances, killing another person during an armed conflict is murder (also known as "wilful killing" when committed in the course of an international armed conflict). The crime of murder is a recognized offense under customary law and has been codified in the Rome Statute. In non-international armed conflict, the elements comprising the war crime of murder are as follows:

(i)   The perpetrator killed one or more persons;

(ii)   Such person or persons were either *hors de combat*, or were civilians, medical personnel, or religious personnel taking no active part in the hostilities;

(iii)   The perpetrator was aware of the factual circumstances that established this status;

(iv)   The conduct took place in the context of and was associated with an armed conflict not of an international character;

(v)   The perpetrator was aware of factual circumstances that established the existence of an armed conflict.

34.   Thus, murder is committed upon the intentional killing of a protected person in the context of an armed conflict when the perpetrator is aware of the circumstances of the victim and the conflict itself. Interpretations given by the international courts to the elements of murder largely mirror those of traditional criminal law. For example, even where the perpetrator does not directly kill the victim at his own hand, the act(s) of the perpetrator must at least be a "substantial cause of the death" of the victim. Premeditation does not appear as a required element.

35.   Murder can also be prosecuted as a crime against humanity when it is perpetrated in the context of a widespread or systematic attack against any civilian population - whether conducted in a time of war or peace. The mental element of murder as a crime against humanity not only includes the intent to cause someone's death but also the knowledge of the act being part of a widespread or systematic attack against any civilian population.

3.   Attacks on protected persons and objects; Indiscriminate attacks

36.   IHL prohibits the intentional targeting of civilians in both international and non-international armed conflicts. Violations of this provision are prosecutable in ICL,

including at the ICC.[42] Parties to a conflict have an obligation to distinguish at all times between those taking part in hostilities and the civilian population, and they must direct attacks only against military objectives. Referred to as the "principle of distinction", the International Court of Justice in its Advisory Opinion of 8 July 1996 on the Legality of the Threat or Use of Nuclear Weapons, recognised this principle as "intransgressible" in customary international law.

37. Attacks on places where both civilians and combatants may be found are prohibited if they are not directed at a specific military objective, or if they use methods or means of combat which cannot be directed at a specific military objective. It is prohibited to launch an attack which may be expected to cause incidental loss of civilian life, injury to civilians, and/or damage to civilian objects which would be excessive in relation to the anticipated concrete and direct military advantage.

38. Customary IHL establishes that all "parties to the conflict must take all feasible precautions to protect the civilian population and civilian objects under their control against the effects of attacks". Each party to the conflict must, to the extent feasible, avoid locating military objectives within or near densely populated areas. Each party to the conflict must, to the extent feasible, remove civilian persons and objects under its control from the vicinity of military objectives.

39. Attacking, destroying, removing or otherwise rendering useless objects which are indispensable to the survival of the civilian population is prohibited. Sieges must still allow for vital foodstuffs and other essential supplies to be delivered to the civilian population.

40. Medical personnel as well as hospitals, medical units and transport must be respected and protected in all circumstances. Medical personnel, units and transport lose their protection if they are being used, outside their humanitarian function, to commit acts harmful to the enemy.

41. IHL also incorporates specific protections for objects. It is prohibited to commit an act of hostility directed against places of worship which constitute the cultural or spiritual heritage of peoples.

42. The Rome Statute sets out a number of war crimes which correspond to these breaches of IHL guarantees. They include the crime of intentionally attacking civilians, and intentionally attacking civilian buildings dedicated to religion, education, art, science or charitable purposes, historic monuments, hospitals and places where the sick and wounded are collected.[43]

C. Arbitrary arrest and unlawful detention

43. Article 9 of the ICCPR prohibits arbitrary arrest or detention of individuals. It provides that "no one shall be deprived of liberty except on such grounds in accordance with such procedures as are established by law". Persons arrested are to be informed at the time of arrest of the reasons for the arrest and promptly informed of any charges.[44] Anyone arrested or detained on a criminal charge is to be brought promptly before a judge or other officer authorized by law to exercise judicial power and is entitled to trial within a reasonable period or release.[45] Persons have a right to take proceedings before a court for the purposes of reviewing the lawfulness of detention and to be released if the detention is

---

[42] Rome Statute, Art. 8 (2) (e) (i)–(iv).
[43] Rome Statute, Art. 8 (2) (e) (iv).
[44] Article 9 (2) ICCPR.
[45] Article 9 (3) ICCPR.

unlawful.[46] The term "arbitrary" needs to be considered in terms of appropriateness, proportionality and reasonableness.[47] Lawfulness of detention is to be considered as both lawfulness under domestic law and lawfulness under international law.[48]

44.   The commission therefore notes the conditions of detention provided for in the Syrian Arab Republic's domestic law. Article 4 of the State of Emergency Act (SEA) authorises the Military Governor to impose, through oral or written orders, "restrictions on the rights of people to the freedom of assembly, residence, transport, and movement, and to arrest suspected people or those threatening public security on a temporary basis, and to authorize investigations of persons and places at any time, and to allow any person to perform any task".[49] This provision has provided grounds for the arrest of peaceful demonstrators.

45.   The SEA also provides for the detention of suspects for "crimes committed against State security and public order" and "crimes committed against public authorities".[50] The commission observes that these crimes do not appear to be further defined in the Syrian Arab Republic's domestic laws. The SEA also permits the security forces to hold suspects in preventive detention without judicial oversight for indefinite periods.

46.   The commission observes that in April 2011, the Syrian Arab Republic's Code of Criminal Procedure — which previously required suspects to be brought before a judicial authority within 24 hours of arrest or else be released[51] — was amended to allow suspects to be held for up to seven days, pending investigation and the interrogation of suspects for certain crimes. This period is renewable up to a maximum of 60 days.[52]

D.   Enforced disappearance

47.   While the Syrian Arab Republic is not a party to the specialized convention concerning enforced disappearances,[53] it is a party to the ICCPR, provisions of which are infringed by enforced disappearance. Such action violates a person's right to recognition as a person before the law,[54] to liberty and security and freedom from arbitrary detention, including the right to be brought promptly before a judge or other official for review of the lawfulness of detention. Disappearance may also be associated with torture and other forms of cruel, inhuman or degrading treatment and extrajudicial execution, in violation of the right to life, prohibition on torture and other forms of cruel, inhuman or degrading treatment.[55]

---

[46] The ICCPR also provides for a right of compensation for unlawful arrest or detention.

[47] *A. v. Australia*, Human Rights Committee, communication No. 560/1993, CCPR/C/59/D/560/1993, para. 9.2. In considering unlawful remand, the Committee has also highlighted that factors of inappropriateness, injustice and lack of predictability that may render arbitrary an otherwise lawful detention; see *Van Alphen v. The Netherlands*, Human Rights Committee, communication No.305/1988, CCPR/C/39/D/305/1988.

[48] See for instance, *A. v Australia*, Human Rights Committee, communication No. 560/1993, CCPR/C/59/D/560/1993, para.9.5.

[49] While the state of emergency was lifted on 21 April 2011, the Government did not abolish the SEA, which remains in force under Syrian domestic law.

[50] State of Emergency Act, art. 6.

[51] Code of Criminal Procedure, Law No. 112 of 1950 as amended, arts. 104 (1) and (2).

[52] Legislative Decree No. 55/2011, amending article 17 of the Code of Criminal Procedure.

[53] International Convention on the Protection of all Persons from Enforced Disappearance, 2006.

[54] Article 9 ICCPR.

[55] The Human Rights Committee in its General Comment No 20 (1992), para. 11, on Article 7 of the ICCPR, recognized that safeguards against torture included having provisions against incommunicado

48. Under IHL, persons taking no active part in the hostilities are entitled to be treated humanely.[56] Customary IHL rules also include a prohibition on arbitrary deprivation of liberty[57] and require parties to the conflict to keep a register of persons deprived of their liberty,[58] respect detainees' family life, to permit detainees to receive visitors, especially near relatives to the degree practicable and allow correspondence between detainees and their families.

49. Parties to a conflict must take all feasible measure to account for persons reported missing as a result of the conflict and efforts must be made to provide family members with any information the Party has on their fate. The practice of enforced disappearance also may be a gateway to other violations such as torture, murder or extra judicial executions. The combined effect of particular IHL obligations leads to the conclusion that the practice of disappearance is prohibited by customary IHL.

50. Furthermore, "imprisonment or other severe deprivation of liberty in violation of fundamental rules of international law" and enforced disappearance are acts recognized in the Rome Statute as potentially giving rise to a crime against humanity if committed as part of a widespread or systematic attack against any civilian population, with knowledge of the attack.[59] Integral to the finding of a crime of "enforced disappearance" is a refusal to acknowledge the arrest, detention or abduction, or to give information on the fate or whereabouts of such person or persons.[60]

E. Torture and other forms of ill-treatment

51. Under IHRL, there is a clear prohibition on torture and other forms of cruel, inhuman or degrading treatment in Article 7 of the ICCPR. The Convention Against Torture and other Cruel, Inhuman or Degrading Treatment or Punishment (CAT) provides a fuller definition: "torture" means any act by which severe pain or suffering, whether physical or mental, is intentionally inflicted on a person for such purposes as obtaining from him or a third person information or a confession, punishing him for an act he or a third person has committed or is suspected of having committed, or intimidating or coercing him or a third person, or for any reason based on discrimination of any kind, when such pain or suffering is inflicted by or at the instigation of or with the consent or acquiescence of a public official or other person acting in an official capacity.

52. Torture during armed conflict is both a violation of IHL and a breach of international criminal law. Torture must not be balanced against national security interests or even the protection of other human rights. No limitations are permitted on the prohibition of torture. International humanitarian law explicitly prohibits the torture and cruel treatment of persons taking no active part in hostilities (including members of armed forces who have laid down their arms or been rendered *hors de combat*). Such conduct constitutes a war crime.

---

detention, granting detainees suitable access to persons such as doctors, lawyers and family members, ensuring detainees are held in places that are officially recognized as places of detention and for their names and places of detention, as well as for the names of persons responsible for their detention, to be kept in registers readily available and accessible to those concerned, including relatives and friends.

[56] Article 4 (1) AP II, Common Article 3 of the four Geneva Conventions of 1949.
[57] ICRC Study, Rule 99.
[58] ICRC Study, Rule 123.
[59] Rome Statute, Art. 7 (1) (i).
[60] ICC Elements of Crimes, Article 7 (1) (i).

53.   Torture can form part of a crime against humanity. The ICC's Elements of Crimes set out the following elements for the crime of torture during armed conflict:

(i)   The perpetrator inflicted severe physical or mental pain or suffering upon one or more persons;

(ii)   The perpetrator inflicted the pain or suffering for such purposes as:

(1)   Obtaining information or a confession;

(2)   Punishment;

(3)   Intimidation or coercion;

(4)   Or for any reason based on discrimination of any kind.

54.   The definition, both under CAT and under the ICC's Elements of Crimes, provides that "severe" pain must be inflicted. International tribunals and human rights bodies have, to date, found the following acts constituted torture: kicking, hitting, beating (including beating on the soles of the feet), flogging, shaking violently, inflicting electric shocks, burning, subjecting the victim to "water treatment", extended hanging from hand and/or leg chains and suffocation/asphyxiation. Mental torture has been found to have occurred where the perpetrator threatened the victim with death or simulates an execution, while having the means to carry it out. These acts have been held to constitute torture irrespective of any subjectively experienced pain of the victim.

55.   In its General Comment, the Committee Against Torture emphasised that an obligation on all state authorities exists in respect of torture. Any official who has reasonable grounds to believe that acts of torture or ill-treatment are being committed is obliged to prevent, investigate, prosecute and punish. Otherwise, the State bears responsibility and its officials will be individually considered as complicit or otherwise responsible "for acquiescing in such impermissible acts". Investigations should be conducted in accordance with the Principles on the Effective Investigation and Documentation of Torture and Other Cruel, Inhuman or Degrading Treatment or Punishment.

56.   All persons detained in connection with an armed conflict must be treated humanely. At the end of armed conflict, persons deprived of their liberty enjoy the protection afforded under Articles 5 and 6 of Protocol II, or at a minimum such protections as are recognized as customary law, until their release.

57.   The United Nations has developed a comprehensive set of standards to be enforced in places of detention. The underlying principles, based in IHL and IHRL, are humane treatment and non-discrimination. Particularly relevant is Protection Principle 7 which requires that all maltreatment of detainees be investigated and punished.

58.   The commission notes that according to the 2012 Syrian Constitution, "[n]o one may be subjected to torture or to degrading treatment and the law shall define the punishment for any person who commits such acts".[61] Further, Article 391 of the Syrian Criminal Code stipulates that: "Anyone who batters a person with a degree of force that is not permitted by law in order to extract a confession to, or information about, an offence shall be subject to a penalty of from three months to three years in prison".[62] These provisions do not, however, further define the crime of torture.

---

[61] Syrian Constitution, Article 53.
[62] Law No. 148/1949 of the Syrian Criminal Code.

F. Rape and sexual violence

59.   Rape violates the prohibition on torture and cruel, inhuman or degrading treatment and also impairs other human rights including the right to the highest attainable standard of physical and mental health under the International Covenant on Economic, Social and Cultural Rights (ICESCR). It is also expressly prohibited in armed conflict. Common article 3 to the Geneva Conventions also prohibits "violence to life and person, in particular … cruel treatment and torture" and "outrages upon personal dignity, in particular, humiliating and degrading treatment". Rape constitutes a war crime under the Rome Statute as well as potentially constituting a crime against humanity if it is part of a widespread or systematic attack on civilians. The elements of the crime of rape in non-international armed conflicts in the Rome Statute are as follows:

(i)   The perpetrator invaded the body of a person by conduct resulting in penetration, however slight, of any part of the body of the victim or of the perpetrator with a sexual organ, or of the anal or genital opening of the victim with any object or any other part of the body;

(ii)   The invasion was committed by force, or by threat of force or coercion, such as that caused by fear of violence, duress, detention, psychological oppression or abuse of power, against such person or another person, or by taking advantage of a coercive environment, or the invasion was committed against a person incapable of giving genuine consent;

(iii)   The conduct took place in the context of and was associated with an armed conflict not of an international character;

(iv)   The perpetrator was aware of factual circumstances that established the existence of an armed conflict.

60.   The Security Council has urged parties to armed conflict to protect women and children from sexual violence. Its resolution 1325 (2000) calls on all parties to the conflict to take special measures to protect women and girls from rape and others forms of sexual abuse and its resolution 1820 (2008) stresses that "sexual violence, when used or commissioned as a tactic of war in order to deliberately target civilians or as part of a widespread or systematic attack against civilian populations, can significantly exacerbate situations of armed conflict".

61.   Sexual violence can meet the definition of torture and has been prosecuted as such.

G. Children and armed conflict

62.   The Convention on the Rights of the Child (CRC) generally defines a child as any person under the age of 18. However, with respect to armed conflict, the Convention draws its language from the Protocols to the Geneva Conventions, and consequently sets the lower age of 15 as the minimum for recruitment or participation in armed forces.

63.   The Optional Protocol, which the Syrian Arab Republic adopted in 2003, without reservation, sets 18 as the minimum age for direct participation in hostilities, for recruitment into armed groups and for compulsory recruitment by governments.

64.   Under the Rome Statute, it is a war crime to use, conscript or enlist children under the age of 15 years into armed forces or use them to participate actively in hostilities.[63]

---

[63] Rome Statute, Art. 8 (2) (e) (vii).

65.   Active participation in hostilities does not solely denote children's direct participation in combat but encompasses activities linked to combat such as scouting, spying, sabotage, and the use of children as decoys, couriers, or at military checkpoints. Also prohibited is the use of children in "direct" support functions such as carrying supplies to the front line.

66.   The commission notes that international law requires that child detainees must be separated from adults, unless to do so would involve a violation of the right of families to be housed together. The requirement to incarcerate child and adult detainees separately is set forth in the CRC.[64]

H.   Pillaging

67.   By definition pillage (or plunder) is theft within the context of, and in connection with, an armed conflict. Under the Rome Statute, pillage is "the forcible taking of private property by an invading or conquering army from the enemy's subjects".[65] The Elements of Crimes of the ICC specify that the appropriation must be done for private or personal use. The prohibition of pillage is a long-standing rule of customary and treaty-based international law. It constitutes a war crime to pillage a town or place, even when taken by assault.

I.   Destruction of personal property

68.   International human rights law protects an individual's home from interference by the State. Article 17 of the ICCPR prohibits arbitrary or unlawful interference with a person's home or correspondence. The Human Rights Committee has interpreted this provision to mean that no interference can take place except in cases envisaged by the law, and that law must comport with the objectives of the ICCPR.[66] Article 11 of the ICESCR commits States Parties to providing everyone "an adequate standard of living for himself and his family, including housing, and to the continuous improvement of living conditions".

---

[64]   See CRC Art. 37 (c).
[65]   Rome Statute, Art. 8 (2) (e) (v).
[66]   General Comment 16, Art. 3.

Annex III

[English only]

Military situation

1.   During this reporting period, the military situation has deteriorated significantly with armed violence gaining in intensity and spreading to new areas. While events in the Syrian Arab Republic were once viewed as an excessive use of force against peaceful demonstrators, the dynamics of the crisis have shifted dramatically. Active hostilities between Government forces (and pro-Government militia) and anti-Government armed groups took place across broad sections of the country. Sporadic clashes between the armed actors have evolved into continuous combat, involving more brutal tactics and new military capabilities by both sides. Levels of armed violence vary throughout the country.

I.   Government forces and pro-Government militia

2.   As the Syrian Government attempts to re-establish its authority in areas which have fallen, or are at risk of falling, under the *de facto* control of anti-Government armed groups, it has increasingly engaged its military troops and heavy equipment, such as tanks and helicopters, in operations against areas perceived to be in support of the armed groups.

3.   All army divisions and security services have engaged in military operations that varied in terms of used capabilities, tactics and scale according to the confronted armed group's size, capabilities and degree of influence and support. Military operations consistently begin with Government forces deploying reinforcements to establish checkpoints around the periphery of a targeted area. This differs from the previous approach which focused on establishing checkpoints within the area. Defections among deployed soldiers and repeated attacks on isolated checkpoints by anti-Government armed groups were reportedly behind this tactical shift. Once the area has been cordoned, artillery and tank units — increasingly joined by helicopters — conduct shelling before ground forces raid the area to dislodge the insurgents. Security forces and pro-Government militia, including *Shabbiha*, have reportedly been involved in these final clearing operations, which often involve house-to-house searches.

4.   The use of heavy fire assets, such as artillery and helicopters, which earlier had been limited to certain areas such as Homs city and Zabadani, in Rif Dimashq, has been extended to all restive provinces. While previously mortars and artillery shelling had been used as a prelude to incursions by ground forces, they are regularly employed in the context of clashes, when quelling demonstrations, and when Government forces are unable to regain control of a contested area. The use of air assets, once limited to observation and transportation purposes, was also extended to fire support; as attack helicopters were used to shell localities under the control of anti-Government armed groups.

5.   In the face of rising insurgency, Government forces directed their main efforts towards the control of major population centres such as Damascus, Aleppo, Homs and Hama. They targeted suburban towns and neighbourhoods of these major localities which were perceived to have been infiltrated by anti-Government armed groups. Their attacks on such areas had the unintended effect of increasing the local populations' support for those groups. Simultaneously, operations with heavy artillery and helicopters shelling were conducted to neutralize the anti-Government armed groups' influence in key countryside towns located along main lines of communication such as in Sahl Al-Ghab between Hama

and Idlib governorates, and the Northern Aleppo countryside. During many of these operations, large numbers of fighters and civilians were killed.

6.   According to testimonies received by the commission, *Shabbiha*, continues to act alongside Government forces in security and military operations. With the increased militarization of the crisis, *Shabbiha* has supported army units by conducting raids and clearing operations once Government forces re-established control of targeted localities. Nevertheless, the composition, strength, and level of involvement of this militia remain opaque. The role of Syrian authorities in supporting this militia could not be ascertained with a sufficient degree of certainty. In part, this difficulty stems from the diverse use of the term "*Shabbiha*". Many of those interviewed by the commission use the term to refer to any armed individual dressed in civilian clothes or in mixed civilian and military clothes. Others report that, in some areas, the *Shabbiha* are composed of civilians of neighbouring villages predominantly populated by Alawites. Some interviewees claim that *Shabbiha* are organised, trained and paid by central or regional authorities, while others have stated they are local volunteers, with loyalties to the Government arising from ethnicity and/or a fear of the consequences of the fall of Government on them and their families. While it is evident that *Shabbiha* act in concert with Government forces, their precise nature and the relationship between the *Shabbiha* and the Government remains unclear.

7.   Government forces faced increased attrition in personnel and equipment due to combat operations, defections and casualties. While the number and level of defections are not yet having an operational impact, they had a psychological effect on the troops, thus fuelling a crisis of confidence within the ranks and encouraging further defections. Defections continued steadily but reach their peaks particularly in the aftermath of military operations. The Government also faced difficulties in drafting new recruits; as those called in for mandatory military service refuse to report. This situation forced the leadership to extend the conscription of those already serving in the ranks which, in turn, has created frustration and further defections among them.

II.   Anti-Government armed groups

8.   During the reporting period, anti-Government armed groups continued to engage with Government forces through direct clashes and ambushes, the use of Improvised Explosive Devices (IEDs) and raids on military/security facilities.

9.   Despite the apparent absence of an overall effective command structure, the FSA continued to "represent" the main anti-Government armed group with a significant number of groups claiming affiliation to it. The FSA has created Local Military Councils in specific governorates which claim leadership over fighting groups operating in each of those areas. High-ranking defectors within the FSA have also announced the creation of a new command structure, namely the Joint Military Command of the Syrian Revolution, in charge of organizing and unifying all armed groups, coordinating military activities with political partners and managing security and stability in the transitional period.

10.   Anti-Government armed groups vary in terms of capabilities, composition and tactics. At one end of the spectrum, there are small groups operating at the local level, mainly composed of civilians and defectors from the area, and often eluding direct confrontations with Government forces by temporarily withdrawing from their villages during army raids. Such groups mainly use IEDs attacks, overnight raids and low scale ambushes on small military units and facilities. On the other end, there are increasingly larger groups that have succeeded in integrating a number of smaller groups, and which are able to control some territory, directly confront army units in urban environment for days and conduct coordinated attacks on army positions and large convoys. The longer these

groups have been able to control territories, the better they were then able to regroup and organize in the event of being ousted. Many groups claim affiliation to the FSA, while some others reject it but increasingly coordinate their actions, and support each other with fighters and equipment. Accounts indicate the existence of foreign fighters in the ranks of some armed groups. The commission has not, however, been able to determine their significance.

11.   Anti-Government armed groups expanded their presence and activities throughout the country, clashing simultaneously with Government forces on multiple fronts. While Homs governorate was for months the main open battlefield between anti-Government armed groups and Government forces, military confrontations have spread to several other cities and regions, including Rif Dimashq, Aleppo and Deir el-Zour. At the time of writing, they are reportedly involved in sustained armed confrontations inside the capital, while establishing sanctuaries throughout the rest of the country.

12.   By July 2012, anti-Government armed groups had extended their influence to further areas in Homs, Dar'a, Sahl Al Ghab in northern Hama, Idlib countryside, Deir el-Zour and north and west of Aleppo as a result of their increased ability to coordinate their operations at the provincial level. Anti-Government armed groups have also expanded the eastern front in Deir el-Zour, requiring the Syrian forces to re-deploy key units from the Damascus area, geographically stretching State forces and forcing the regime to deploy its strongest military units.

13.   Anti-Government armed groups have increased their attacks on key infrastructure, such as oil installations and electrical plants. They have seriously undermined Government forces' control of the country's borders, leading most recently to their temporary control of some border crossing points. Cross-border movements of refugees as well as of anti-Government fighters appears to be more frequent, dense and fluid, although crossing the border through official crossing points remains a perilous trip in some areas.

14.   During the reporting period, investigations have not confirmed the use of more sophisticated weaponry by anti-Government armed groups. However, their capacity to access and effectively use available weapons has improved. Anti-Government armed groups appeared to have increasing access to more funding and logistical support, such as ammunition and small arms. Some anti-Government armed groups also possess mortars and anti-tank missiles, reportedly looted during seizure of army positions. The level of destruction lately observed on destroyed government equipment indicates the use of new military capabilities such as anti-tank weapons.

15.   The Commission has noted the increased and more efficient use of IEDs by anti-Government armed groups against army and security convoys, patrols and facilities. This asset has also been used to target members of military and security forces and Government officials; causing in many cases collateral damage among civilians and their properties.

III.   Other actors

16.   Several radical Islamic armed groups have emerged in the country. The most significant of those is the Al-Nusrah Front for the People of the Levant, an alleged Al Qaeda-linked group that has claimed responsibility for several attacks, including suicide bombings against Syrian Government forces and officials. The attacks that took place throughout the country, including in the cities of Damascus, Aleppo, Deir el-Zour, and Idlib, have targeted members of the Government, police, military, intelligence and the *Shabbiha*. The attacks consisted of suicide bombings, ambushes, assassinations, car bombings and IED attacks. The group has identified its leader as the Syrian national Sheikh Abu Muhammad al Julani. In addition to the Al Nusrah Front, other groups announced as

operating within the country include Syrian Al Baraa Ibn Malik Martyrdom Brigade in Homs and the Abdullah Azzam Brigades, a regional al Qaeda affiliate.

17.   The Commission noted the emergence of self-defence groups in several localities. Some of these groups emerged in villages populated by allegedly pro-government minorities that are not necessarily part of the *Shabbiha* militia.

Annex IV

[English only]

Special inquiry into Al-Houla

I.   Background

1.   Mandated to conduct a special inquiry into the events in Al-Houla of 25 May 2012, the commission delivered its preliminary findings to the Human Rights Council on 27 June (A/HRC/20/CRP.1), based on the evidence and materials gathered through 22 June.[a] The initial report found the Government responsible for the deaths of civilians as a result of shelling Al-Houla area and particularly the Taldou village. It also found that the Government had failed to properly conduct an investigation into the events in Al-Houla in accordance with international human rights standards. While the commission did not rule out the responsibility of other potential perpetrators in the killing of the Abdulrazzak and Al-Sayed families,[b] it concluded that it was unlikely that opposition forces were implicated.

2.   The commission has since continued its investigation focusing on identifying the perpetrators. Access to the country was not granted despite specific requests to the Syrian Arab Republic via *Note Verbale* dated 4 June 2012 (annex XI) and in person by the Chairperson during his visit to Damascus 24–25 June 2012. Moreover, the commission had not received a response to a request dated 13 July to interview two specific witnesses whose testimony had appeared in the Government report and who had been interviewed by both Syrian and Russian journalists (annex XI).[c] Although the Syrian Government provided the preliminary report of its own commission of inquiry on 7 June, it has not delivered a final report, nor indicated when such a report might be forthcoming.

3.   In its continued investigation the commission examined additional satellite imagery and interviewed a further eight witnesses, six of which were from the area of Taldou by telephone, including two survivors. It gathered several other witness accounts, video material and analysis from other sources, always giving due regard to their reliability and authenticity.

4.   As noted, the Government's report stated that the Syrian Army had defended itself from an attack by what it deemed "terrorists", and that a number of soldiers were killed in the clashes. The report acknowledged the deaths of civilians and described the Abdulrazzak family as peaceful and stated that it had refused to rise up against the State or participate in demonstrations – suggesting they were attacked by anti-government groups for their failure to support the rebellion. The motive provided for the Al-Sayed family killings was their

---

[a]   This report is to be read together with the Commission's first report, see A/HRC/20/CRP.1, 27 June 2012.

[b]   The anti-Government activists and many victims and witnesses blamed the killings on Government forces working in concert with *Shabbiha* from neighbouring villages. The Government in its report blamed the 600–700 "terrorists" for the killings. The commission also considered the possibility that foreign groups were involved.

[c]   On 3 August, the commission received a call from the Geneva Mission of the Syrian Arab Republic offering to arrange interviews with the two witnesses. By the deadline for submission of this report the interviews had not taken place.

familial ties to Abdelmuti Mashlab, a new member of parliament, and existing feuds with some members of the armed groups.

II. Findings from further investigation

A. Consistency of accounts

5.   More than forty separate interviews were considered by the commission. All interviewees were consistent in their portrayal of the events and their description of the perpetrators as Government forces and *Shabbiha*. Apart from the two witnesses in the Government report, no other account supported the Government's version of events. As noted, the commission's request to interview those two witnesses was not fulfilled. The commission, nevertheless, carefully reviewed their testimony as set out in the Government report and interviews they gave to other sources, and deemed their accounts to be unreliable as they contained a number of inconsistencies.[d] Not making the witnesses available to the commission meant that those inconsistencies could not be further explored. Separately, a high-ranking defector that the commission deemed credible reported that, prior to his defection, he was asked to help manufacture evidence supporting the Government's version of events.

6.   At the same time, accounts of other witnesses interviewed by the commission remained consistent over time, including those collected from children, despite the fact that they were conducted by different interviewers.[e] The commission found it highly unlikely that the dozens of people interviewed in Taldou could be taking part in an extensive fabrication over such an extended period.

7.   Consequently, the commission found the version of events received from the Government to be uncorroborated and insufficient when compared to the larger body of evidence collected from other sources. Besides the Government's report, little evidence was collected suggesting that anyone other than Government forces and *Shabbiha* committed the killings.[f]

---

[d]   As examples: 1. They failed to describe the location of the main incident, specifically the Abdulrazzak family home; 2. The witness purported to know that in the northern part of the town "terrorists" were distributing ammunition to each other, but elsewhere the witness described her presence as being in the centre near the clock tower or further south during the same time frame; 3-. The witness also stated that the "terrorists" included "strangers who don't belong to our village," and was able to remember their names individually while the village has 30,000 people, and the whole area of Al-Houla's population is more than 100,000. It is unclear how she could be so certain of terrorist individual identities\names in the described context; 4. The witness said she saw the burning at the hospital area "when we passed by." The area around the hospital was in government hands throughout, so it is unclear when and how she was able to reach the given location given the circumstances of the day; 5. She suggested that the armed groups were in fact mentioning the real first names of the groups' leaders over their radio communications. The commission finds this lacking credibility; 6. The witness described the Al-Sayed family as having been shot from across the street when all other evidence, including by UNSMIS visiting the scene, indicate the victims died from gunshots at close range.

[e]   UNSMIS, international human rights NGOs, journalists and the CoI have all conducted interviews during the course of their investigations into the events.

[f]   The commission examined the version of events reported in the Frankfurter Allgemeine Zeitung (FAZ), 7 June 2012, by Rainer Hermann, and by journalist Marat Musin, on Anna news and Russia Today, 2 June 2012, (Available at http://www.youtube.com/watch?v=pyi-tJ_0PPg) both of which blamed the killings on anti-Government armed groups. The commission found these reports relied

B. Location and access

8.   The commission's earlier report determined that both the anti- and pro-Government forces could have accessed the two crime scenes – the first scene being the seven Abdulrazzak family homes on Dam Street (*Tariq al-Sad*) and the second being the two Al-Sayed family homes on Main Street (*Al-Shar'i Al-Raisi*), across the street from the National Hospital (see map). The commission has since determined that the checkpoint at *Al-Qaws* remained in Government hands at the end of the day the incident occurred. The checkpoint demarcated the new front line between the opposition and Government forces. The commission concluded that Al-Sayed house was adjacent to the National Hospital and lying south of *Al-Qaws* checkpoint and that the crime scene remained in Government-controlled territory the entire time. Indeed, when UNSMIS arrived the next day and negotiated the handover of the bodies from the site (see the report of the Secretary-General to the Security Council, S/2012/523, 27 May 2012), Government soldiers were on duty at the checkpoint and in control of the crime scene.

9.   In a related finding, the commission ruled out the theory proffered by the Government that the target of the killing was in fact the newly elected Member of Parliament from Taldou, Abdelmuti Mashlab. According to the Government report,

> The first targets of this massacre were relatives of the People's Assembly member Abd Al-Moa'ti Mashlab. What was required was to take revenge, because he challenged them when he submitted his candidacy to the People's Assembly and managed to be elected as a member. This indeed happened before things went out of control and the massacre extended to slaughter other families.[8]

10.   The "other families" are those of Mashlab's distant relatives, namely the Al-Sayed family. The commission determined that the Mashlab household was in opposition-controlled areas of the town at the time of the attack. Thus it would have been accessible to an anti-Government armed group seeking to mete out such a punishment, yet the house remained untouched. Both Al-Sayed family homes, conversely, were readily accessible to Government forces or local militias, but the same access would have been extremely risky if not impossible for anti-Government groups.

11.   At the Abdulrazzak crime scene, where over 60 persons were killed, the commission considered it likely that a large number of perpetrators would have been necessary to carry out the crime. The killings occurred in broad daylight. Testimony received indicated that the perpetrators arrived both by foot and in vehicles, and that some arrived with pickups with machine guns mounted on top, in addition to a number of cars and minivans. The commission found that the movement of vehicles or weapons, as well as the size of the group, would have been detectable by Government forces at the Water Authority position. At the same time, access to the scene for any sizable group of anti-Government armed men would have been practically impossible, especially if they arrived in vehicles as multiple eyewitnesses attested.

12.   Opposition members did manage to access the scene and remove the bodies later that evening and apparently did so using vehicles. However, they were apparently shot at by Government forces and had to abandon their efforts until the following morning.

---

primarily on the same two witnesses as the Government's report and not on additional investigation or witnesses in Al-Houla. Moreover, these reports asserted that the Abdulrazzak family had converted to Shiism. The commission confirmed that all members of both families were Sunni and that no one in either family had converted.

[8]   *Note Verbale*, 281/2012 of 7 June 2012, p.3 (unofficial translation).

C. Loyalties

13. The National Hospital had been occupied by the army for several months prior to the incidents. Although it was accessible by foot from both crime scenes, no one — whether injured or fleeing the crime scenes — sought refuge there. As far as the commission could determine, all injured and surviving family members, as well as people from nearby houses, fled to opposition-controlled areas. Moreover, as mentioned in the commission's previous report, it was anti-Government activists who arrived at the area first, took care of the deceased and assisted in treating the wounded and organized their burial. The commission saw no indication that pro-Government entities attempted to do the same, namely to secure the crime scenes or to recover the wounded and deceased after news of the events broke – at either site.

14. The Government report depicted the loyalties of the Al-Sayed family as pro-Government. Muawia Al-Sayed, who was killed alongside his son and young daughter that day, was a retired colonel in the security forces. His son Ahmad was still on active duty, but had been home on extended sick leave. The commission found it compelling that their family members, who survived, fled to opposition-controlled areas of Taldou and chose not to seek assistance from the Government forces nearby. From there, they requested that UNSMIS facilitate the handing over of the bodies to their location. Moreover, testimonies from surviving members of those families clearly describe Government forces and *Shabbiha*, as the perpetrators.

III. Conclusion

15. The continued investigation since its preliminary report of 27 June 2012, has supplemented the commission's initial understanding of the events in Al-Houla. On the basis of available evidence, the commission has a reasonable basis to believe that the perpetrators of the deliberate killing of civilians, at both the Abdulrazzak and Al-Sayed family locations, were aligned to the Government. It rests this conclusion on its understanding of access to the crime sites, the loyalties of the victims, the security layout in the area including the position of the government's water authority checkpoint and the consistent testimonies of victims and witnesses with direct knowledge of the events. This conclusion is bolstered by the lack of credible information supporting other possibilities.

16. The commission remains of the view that the Government has manifestly failed in its obligation to properly investigate the murders that took place in Al-Houla on 25 May 2012.

A/HRC/21/50

Map 1 – Al-Houla area

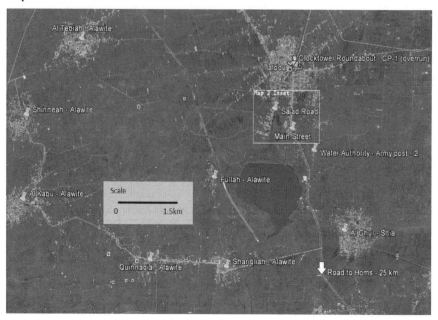

Map 2 – Inset from Map 1 – South Taldou

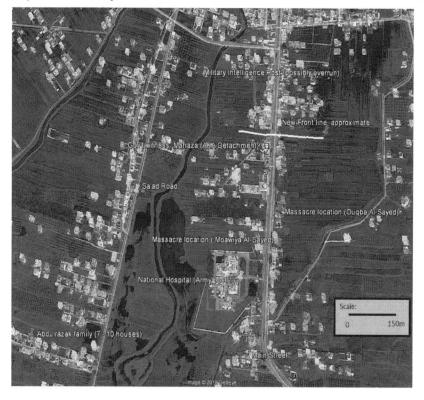

Annex V

[*English only*]

Unlawful killing

1.   The commission conducted more than 300 interviews relating to the unlawful killing of civilians and *hors de combat* fighters in more than 30 separate incidents. The bulk of the interviews — 285 — related to killings perpetrated by Government forces and *Shabbiha*. These killings occurred in the contexts set out below. The frequency of such violations has increased considerably during the reporting period. Concerning anti-Government armed groups, 15 interviewees provided information on the unlawful killing of captured members of Government forces and *Shabbiha*.

2.   Under IHRL Government forces may take the life of a citizen only when doing so is both necessary and proportionate.[a] It is manifestly illegal to kill a person that has been arrested or disarmed and thus poses no threat.[b] When the threshold of armed conflict is reached in a country and IHL is in effect, the applicable rules differ to a degree,[c] but the underlying principles remain. Purposefully killing a civilian[d] or *hors de combat* fighter,[e] without first affording them a judicial process meeting international standards is a war crime.

I. Government forces and *Shabbiha*

3.   Many forms of unlawful killing took place in the context of attacks against anti-Government armed group strongholds. The most prominent pattern began with a blockade, then shelling, use of snipers, and an assault by ground forces including *Shabbiha* followed by house searches. Defectors, activists or fighting aged men were systematically sought out during these operations. Wounded or captured Anti-Government fighters (i.e. *hors de combat*) were executed. In some cases, family members of fighters, defectors and activists as well as others who appeared to be randomly selected, were also executed.

4.   Snipers regularly accompanied attacking forces during ground assaults and were responsible for a significant number of the civilian deaths. The commission recorded 35 instances of civilians shot by sniper fire over the reporting period.[f]

5.   The following cases are emblematic of this pattern. Updates on previously reported incidents are also included below.

---

[a] See annex II, paras. 30–42.
[b] The only exception to this proscription is when the person has been sentenced to death by a lawfully constituted tribunal that provided all fundamental judicial guarantees.
[c] See annex II.
[d] Use of the terms 'civilians' in this section refers to those not taking direct part in hostilities. See ICRC Study, Rule 6.
[e] Much like in IHRL, the principle of proportionality is in effect during armed conflict. It prohibits the incidental deaths of civilians that are excessive in relation to the concrete and direct military advantage anticipated. See annex I (Applicable law). See also ICRC Study, Rule 14.
[f] Dozens of interviewees described the detrimental psychological and social effects of the presences of snipers in the neighbourhood. People feared leaving their houses, but when shelling started they feared staying home. Routine tasks such as shopping, going to work or playing outside became life threatening.

Tremseh (Hama), 12 July 2012

6.   On 12 July 2012, in the early morning, FSA positions in Tremseh came under attack by Government forces using shelling, ground troops and helicopter gunships. Prior to the offensive, Government forces had cordoned the town with checkpoints. Reports from credible sources suggest that *Shabbiha* deployed together with the army.

7.   The motive for the assault appears to have been a Government intervention to root out armed groups that had been involved in a series of tit-for-tat kidnappings with *Shabbiha*, reportedly from the neighbouring Alawi town of Safsafiah.

8.   Initial reports indicated that the attack began with cutting supplies of electricity, water and mobile-telephone services. Shelling began around 5:00 am. Helicopter gunships supported the Government ground forces, which entered the town at 8:00 am. Together they inflicted heavy losses on the anti-Government forces.

9.   Individuals attempting to flee were shot in fields on the outskirts of the town, though the commission could not determine whether they were civilians or fighters. The assault continued throughout the day, ultimately ending with Government forces retaking control of Tremseh. They withdrew around 8:00 pm.

10.   UNSMIS observers attempting to reach Tremseh on 12 July were stopped outside the town by Government forces. When UNSMIS reached the village on 13 July, they reported that civilian objects, including over 50 homes and a school, were affected. They also observed "pools of blood and brain matter ... in a number of homes". UNSMIS interviewed 27 villagers who gave consistent accounts of extrajudicial executions of men arrested by Government forces.

> *According to those interviewed, the army was conducting house to house searches asking for men and their ID cards. They alleged that after checking their identification, numerous were killed.*

11.   Other uncorroborated reports blamed rebels for the civilian deaths in this incident. The commission viewed video material purportedly from Tremseh, broadcast on Russian television, of two FSA members captured by the army confessing to having killed civilians in the town. The commission could not assess whether these confessions were obtained voluntarily.

Al-Qubeir (Hama), 6 June 2012

12.   Al-Qubeir is a predominantly Sunni village 20 km northwest of Hama. Although emptied as a result of fighting at the time of writing, it had consisted of approximately 25 houses with no more than 150 residents, most of them from the al-Yatim family. The commission examined a testimony from an eyewitness (defector), as well as reports from other credible sources with direct knowledge of the 6 June events. The Government provided the commission with a report of its findings in a *Note Verbale*, dated 19 June 2012.[g]

13.   The Al-Qubeir area had reportedly been experiencing ethnic tensions since the beginning of the conflict.[h] In the days leading up to the incident a resident of Al-Qubeir had

---

[g] Regarding the Government's report, the commission viewed video material wherein one member of the Government's commission who compiled the report on Al-Qubeir was announcing his defection. Therein he implied that the judiciary had been co-opted into covering up the misdeeds of Government forces and aligned forces. The video could not be authenticated.

[h] A journalist who visited Al-Qubeir shortly after the incident and who interviewed a person who had come back to retrieve some items, reported his interviewee as saying, "Many young men from the

an altercation with Alawi members of the neighboring village of Al-Twaime. Anticipating reprisal, the villager requested support from members of the FSA, including seven defectors from the nearby village of Grejis. According to the Government, when they arrived at the village, the FSA elements shot at some of the men in Al-Twaime. The men from Al-Twaime alerted Government security forces.

14.   From evidence collected, it appears that after shelling the houses where the anti-Government forces were holed up, ground forces moved in. They were supported by the *Shabbiha* who also deployed in the area. An eye-witness stated that many people were killed and injured in the shelling. The injured were reportedly executed by the *Shabbiha*, and their bodies burned in the houses. Video footage taken during the visit of UNSMIS monitors shows bullet holes on an interior wall of a house, accompanied by blood splattering, suggestive of deliberate killing. The number of deceased has not been confirmed and varies from the Government's account of 40, a figure that includes both killed and missing, to 78, a figure put forward by anti-Government activists. Under both accounts, at least two women and four children were among those killed.

15.   In its report the Government described how it deployed to the village with security forces in response to a request from villagers seeking protection from "terrorists". It mentioned the use of RPGs and light arms in its assault on Al-Qubeir. According to the Government's inquiry, initially its forces were repelled and at least one officer was killed, while several more were wounded. Reinforcements were brought in and, according to the report, "shelled also the places where the terrorists were stationed with RPG shells". The clash ended on the same day at about 8:00 pm and resulted in the deaths of a number of terrorists". According to the report, security forces attacked only the house of Alman Al Yatim where allegedly the "terrorists" were located.

16.   The report also states that the bodies of some women and children were examined by a forensic pathologist who determined that they had been killed by gunfire at close range prior to the arrival of the security forces in the village – the implication being that the perpetrators were the "terrorists".

17.   It is likely that many people died as a result of shelling. Some clearly died from gunshot wounds. However, some of these individuals may have been directly participating in the hostilities, which means targeting them would not be illegal under international law.

18.   The commission found that a reasonable suspicion exists that unlawful killing of civilians or *hors de combat* fighters occurred at the hands of pro-Government forces, including *Shabbiha* from neighboring villages. This conclusion is based on the following factors: the eyewitness account; the Government's report and other materials gathered indicating that residents of Al-Qubeir were feuding with their Alawi neighbors, providing a motive for reprisals; and the FSA and defectors having been invited to Al-Qubeir by villagers seeking their protection.

Al-Houla (Homs), 25 May 2012

See A/HRC/21/50, paras. 41–50.

Kili, Idlib governorate, 6 April 2012

19.   The commission interviewed six men and two women who gave accounts of extra-judicial killings in raids on the village of Kili in early April. Security forces entered this

---

Alawite villages around Al-Qubeir have died fighting for Assad against the rebels. They wanted revenge, and so they took it out on the nearest Sunni village."

town of approximately 15,000 inhabitants following an anti-Government demonstration. The eyewitnesses described in detail how the security forces entered the town after an extensive bout of shelling, arrested two brothers, Moustapha Qarsoum and 'Adil Qarsoum, executed them and then burnt the two bodies. The shelling of Kili resulted in at least eight additional civilian deaths. Many houses of perceived opposition collaborators were burned.

Tal Rifat (Aleppo), 5 April 2012

20.   The commission conducted 18 interviews with five women and 13 men who had knowledge of the events in Tal Rifat on 5 April. During a demonstration that turned violent, protestors captured four members of the security forces. The four were held for ransom, with their captors threatening to kill them unless the security forces, who had surrounded the city, withdrew. The Government forces complied, and the four were released. Immediately afterwards, the 4th Division of the Syrian army raided Tal Rifat. The village was cordoned in advance. Many of the inhabitants who supported the anti-Government armed groups had already fled. One family, the Sakrans, that was openly pro-Government, and had a member working in the military security, stayed behind, as did a small number of anti-Government fighters.

21.   At the end of the hostilities at least 52 corpses were discovered, including members of the Sakran family who had been burned in their home. At least seven of the anti-Government fighters who had stayed behind were also found dead. One testimony presented evidence suggesting three people had been executed standing against a wall. Hundreds of homes were looted and burned, reportedly as punishment for the villagers who were accused of having captured the security force personnel and harbouring members of anti-Government armed groups.

Taftanaz (Idlib), 3–4 April 2012

22.   The commission conducted 16 interviews with persons having direct knowledge of the events of 3 April 2012 in Taftanaz, including fighters and civilians. Interviewees stated that the Syrian army launched an intensive attack on the town which had been the scene of several anti-Government protests. Multiple reports indicated that shelling from two directions commenced at 7:00 am and continued for several hours while tanks formed a cordon around the town. As civilians attempted to flee, they came under attack by helicopter gunships. The commission recorded at least six civilian casualties resulting from the shelling and gunship attacks. At the time, many men from the town reportedly took up arms and engaged the Syrian army in battle, slowing their progress into Taftanaz. The commission received reports of tanks being destroyed by anti-Government forces, the latter of which were using mosque loudspeakers to direct and motivate their fighters. Two mosques were allegedly destroyed by the Syrian army.

23.   In the early hours of 4 April 2012, anti-Government forces reportedly made a tactical withdrawal from Taftanaz, leaving the way free for Government forces together with *Shabbiha* to enter Taftanaz and to conduct house searches. The commission recorded multiple executions occurring during these searches. In one case, the bodies of two adults and five young children were found burnt in a house. Some bodies were reportedly found with gunshot wounds to the head and chest. Some of those bodies were also found blindfolded with hands tied behind their backs. Casualty estimates range from 84 to 110 people, many of them from the extended Ghazal family. Over 500 houses were reportedly looted and then burnt. According to reports received between 30 and 40 people are missing, presumed to have been arrested and detained by the Government forces during the raids.

Sarmin (Idlib), 22–23 March 2012

24.   According to six witnesses, the army began shelling the town of Sarmin in the early hours of 22 March 2012. Sarmin had been the scene of anti-Government protests and the base of dozens of defectors and other members of anti-Government armed groups. Most of the civilian population and members of anti-Government armed groups fled before the attack. During the shelling, which, according to witnesses was falling in random locations, 18 people were killed. The army entered Sarmin on 23 March 2012 and, in line with established practice, commenced house searches. Snipers were positioned on rooftops. The commission received reports of men being shot either during searches or while on the street. In one corroborated account, three men, all in their 20s, were taken outside during a house search and shot in the front-yard in the presence of their families. The victims were family members of a well-known lieutenant from the 15th Division Special Forces who had defected. Reports from credible sources describe approximately 300 people arrested during the search operation, of which 10 were killed shortly afterwards. Some were later released; others were reportedly still held at the time of writing.

Ain Larouz (Idlib), 4–12 March 2012

25.   On 4 March 2012, four officers defected from an army base in Aranba and hid in the nearby village of Ain Larouz. Shortly after sunset, military and security forces raided the village looking for the four defectors. They searched houses, burned shops and vehicles and mistreated residents. They detained approximately 35 persons, including two women and a 10-year-old girl. Security forces were reported to have announced over the mosque loudspeakers a warning with a deadline for the people to hand over the defectors or else they would execute the captives and burn down the village. Following the threats most villagers fled.

26.   Five days later, on 9 March, the army blockaded the roads and began to shell the village after positioning snipers on rooftops. According to four witnesses, several persons who tried to flee were shot, either by snipers or by pursuing ground forces. Although the defecting officers were not found, the army released most captives three days later, save for four persons - believed to be relatives of the officers – whose bodies were found outside the city a few days later.

Yabroud (Rif Dimashq), 4 March 2012

27.   A defector recalled how, on 4 March, he deployed to Yabroud village to take part in an operation. Upon arrival, he joined a battalion of tanks and six buses of security and *Shabbiha* elements. He and the others were ordered to raid the village after it was shelled. An informer accompanied them in the village and pointed out the houses of activists and defectors.

28.   A group of people had fled towards a neighbouring mountainous area, but were still visible to the soldiers. The commanding officer, after consulting his superiors, went back inside a tank and fired a round at the group of approximately 60 people, apparently killing dozens. The commission could not verify the profile of this group, which may have included members of anti-Government armed groups.

Atarib (Aleppo), February–April 2012

29.   The commission conducted 17 interviews with persons with direct knowledge of the events in Atarib in February and in April 2012. The town had been the scene of several anti-Government protests. In the early afternoon of 14 February 2012, Government forces and FSA fighters clashed in Jabal Karmin, three kilometres from Atarib. On the evening of the same day, Government forces attacked Atarib. The town was reportedly shelled by

tanks located on its perimeter, resulting in the death of eight people. Ground forces are said to have entered the town, positioning snipers on the rooftops of public buildings, including at least one school. The commission received multiple, consistent reports of civilians, in particular children, being shot and killed by sniper fire in February during those events, but also in March and April 2012.

Homs, Feb–May 2012

30. Government forces launched a large-scale military attack on the neighbourhood of Bab Amr in Homs city on 2 February 2012, using mortar shells, missiles and tank shells. Although Bab Amr had been targeted on previous occasions, the sustained intensity of this attack was unprecedented. The neighbourhood was considered a hotbed of anti-Government armed groups, particularly the FSA, which had a strong presence there until 2 March, the date on which Government forces reclaimed control of the neighbourhood after 27 days of sustained shelling.

31. During the same period the FSA engaged in limited skirmishes with Government forces on the outskirts of Bab Amr, especially in the nearby Insha'at neighbourhood. Despite its lesser military capacities, the FSA was able to push Government forces back in some of the areas.

32. Government forces deployed to most access points in the area, thus severely restricting movement. At the time of writing, Bab Amr remained under the control of Government forces and was suffering a shortage of food and medical care. Much of the population fled the neighbourhood to surrounding villages and other neighbourhoods, including Khaldieh, Shammas and Al Ghouta, during the intense shelling periods throughout February 2012.

33. The commission recorded a high incidence of extra-judicial executions of civilians in various neighborhoods of the city of Homs since March 2012. Multiple accounts were received of the killing of the entire Sabbouh family in Bab Amr on 5 March. On 11 and 12 March 2012, the neighbourhood of Karm al-Zeytoun reportedly came under an attack by what was described as *Shabbiha* protected by the army. Multiple families were killed in their homes, apparently by knives or other sharp instruments. Estimates of casualties, unverified by the commission, ranged from 35 to 80 in that attack.

34. The commission found that *hors de combat* fighters were similarly killed. One man interviewed by the commission stated that he assisted in the burial of 15 bodies of fighting aged men that appeared to have been executed. Syrian security forces and *Shabbiha* reportedly removed adult men from houses in the neighbourhood of Sultaniya, before lining them up and shooting them.

35. Multiple, consistent reports have been received about extra-judicial executions of civilians in the Shammas neighbourhood in Homs on 15 May 2012. Shammas is approximately three kilometres from the Baba Amr neighbourhood. Residents describe members of the security forces and *Shabbiha* entering the area and shooting into the air before commencing house searches. One of those interviewed explained that the building opposite her house was abandoned and that security had broken in, transforming it into a "slaughter house". She described how approximately every 15 minutes security forces would bring in a man handcuffed and blindfolded and that she would hear a shot shortly afterwards. The first man that was shot was dumped in the street. Another interviewee indicated that the following day he found 23 bodies, including the local imam, in a building near the mosque. Most had bullet wounds to the head.

36. Civilians were also killed, reportedly by sniper fire, in Homs, especially in the neighborhood of Bab Amr and Khaldiya, in March and April 2012. In these cases the

commission documented that the bodies of people killed by snipers were often left where they fell, as no one risked retrieving them.[i]

Al-Qusayr (Homs), Feb 2012[j]

37.   Four interviewees described the city of Al-Qusayr being pinned down under sniper fire in February 2012. One male resident interviewed by the commission was hit on his way back from taking his wife and daughter to the doctor. He had stopped along the road to help some people to restart their car and was hit from behind. The bullet hit a nerve paralysing his left leg.

Abdita (Idlib), 21 February 2012

38.   Four women and 17 men having direct knowledge of the events in Abdita on 21 February 2012 were interviewed by the commission. Their testimonies described in detail the army's blockade of the entrances to the village that day and how they conducted house searches, apparently looking for persons implicated in an IED attack. In one well-documented instance, the army entered the house known for hosting FSA members, took the men out to a neighbouring field, asked them about the IED and shot them when they did not receive an adequate response. One of the three survived and was interviewed by the commission. Another eyewitness stated that 15 persons, out of a total of 30 who died in the clashes that day, died from wounds that suggested execution. Relatives of the FSA leader Riad al-Assad, who is originally from Abdita, were apparently among those summarily executed.

Legal conclusions

39.   The commission finds that the individual instances of killing described above provide reasonable grounds to believe that Government forces and *Shabbiha* violated IHRL provisions protecting the right to life. Furthermore, many of the same killings met the definitional requirements of the war crime of murder.[k]

40.   Additionally, the evidence indicated that many attacks were directed against civilians and civilian objects.[l] Although the Government's stated aim was to attack "terrorists", the attacks were directed at neighborhoods, towns and regions with civilian populations. The commission therefore concludes that there are reasonable grounds to believe that the war crime of attacking civilians has been perpetrated in many instances.

41.   There are reasonable grounds to believe that the documented incidents also constituted the crime against humanity of murder. In those towns and villages where there was a pattern of blockade, shelling, ground assault and house-to-house searches, the element of a widespread or systematic attack against a civilian population was met. The scale of the attacks, their repetitive nature, the level of excessive force consistently used, the indiscriminate nature of the shelling and the coordinated nature of the attacks led the commission to conclude that they were conducted pursuant to State policy.

---

[i]   A more detailed discussion of the attack on Homs has been set out above.
[j]   A more detailed discussion of the events in Al-Qusayr has been set out in annex VI.
[k]   Rome statute, Art. 8 (2) (c) (i). See also annex II.
[l]   See ICRC Customary IHL Study, Rule 1. Rome statute, Art. 8 (2) (e) (i).

II. Anti-Government armed groups

42.   The commission documented instances of anti-Government forces killing captured members of the Government forces and *Shabbiha* and suspected informers. While the human rights legal regime differs with respect to non-state actors such as the anti-Government armed groups, IHL applies equally to all parties in a conflict. Thus, killing protected persons or enemy soldiers who are *hors de combat* is illegal and can attract individual criminal responsibility.[m]

43.   Members of anti-Government armed groups have admitted killing Government soldiers after capture when the captives refused to join them or if they were deemed to have "blood on their hands". The commission documented incidents involving anti-Government armed groups — specifically the FSA — primarily in Homs, including the Bab Amr and Khaldiyah neighborhoods during the February 2012 siege, and in Al-Qusayr in June 2012.

44.   Despite its limited access to victims of anti-Government armed groups, the commission documented anti-Government fighters having killed captured Government soldiers and *Shabbiha* who had admitted, probably under duress, to taking part in shelling or military attacks.

Homs Governorate, June 2012

45.   In Qusayr, the FSA commanders decided to attack the municipality to dislodge Government snipers. The attack succeeded and the FSA captured 22 Government soldiers. One interviewee told the CoI that the detainees were judged by a judicial committee. Some were released to join their families. Some were executed as they were found guilty.

46.   In early June 2012, FSA fighters attacked a garrison near Talbisah. Apparently in coordination with Government forces soldiers inside, the FSA overran the location, took the ammunition and weapons and left with a number of defecting soldiers. According to an eyewitness who was in the army at the time, but who later defected, two Alawite soldiers were executed during the raid. He and others found their bodies inside.

47.   A defector who fought in the ranks of the FSA-affiliated Al Farouk Brigade in Homs city stated that members of the Government forces, including those he claimed were three Iranian snipers, were summarily executed after they apparently confessed to killing Syrians.

Aleppo governorate, June 2012

48.   The commission viewed video footage that portrayed the bodies of approximately 20 men, allegedly *Shabbiha*, who had been killed by the anti-Government fighters in Aleppo governorate in mid-June.

49.   The commission interviewed 10 FSA soldiers who had never heard of IHL or IHRL. One FSA fighter told the commission:

> *"We do not leave them alone until we kill them. Either they finish us or we finish them. We do not let them go and continue to kill people. We do not take prisoners, no one comes out alive. If he manages to escape he will come back to kill me."*

50.   Another FSA fighter interviewed stated that when senior military officers are captured they are exchanged for detained members of anti-Government armed groups. However, if the FSA captures an ordinary officer or soldier, "they are interrogated and submitted to trial where Sharia law is applied". The interviewee provided information on

---

[m] See annex II.

the composition and functioning of such a court in Tal Rifat. Its members are apparently educated and from diverse backgrounds. For example, some are lawyers, religious leaders and others known for their integrity. The soldier had never heard of IHL and related his view that, "[IHL] is not better than Sharia law where everyone is punished for what he has done by the same means, an eye for an eye".

51.   The commission has taken note of an increased use of IEDs by anti-Government armed groups. Interviewees described how, in April 2012, they had put nails inside pipes with explosive powder and a fuse. Others described the use of gas and fertilizer to create homemade bombs. Information provided by the Government, but not corroborated by the commission, indicated that some 1149 explosive devices have exploded or were dismantled during between May and July 2012.

Legal conclusions

52.   The commission considered the corroborated evidence of killing *hors de combat* Government soldiers and *Shabbiha*. In Qusayr, Bab Amr, Kaldiyeh and elsewhere the commission noted that persons captured by the FSA on occasion faced a quasi-judicial process prior to their execution. A consistent account of the trial process has not been forthcoming, nor has information on the extent of adherence to fair trial standards. Common Article three of the Geneva Conventions, recognized as customary IHL, prohibits such executions unless the accused has been afforded "all the judicial guarantees which are recognized as indispensable by civilized peoples" These guarantees include, inter alia, the presumption of innocence, an impartial tribunal, the ability to mount a defense and examine opposing witnesses, and especially in capital cases, the ability to appeal the judgment. Executing a prisoner without affording fundamental judicial guarantees is a war crime.

53.   The commission concluded that the information in its possession on executions perpetrated by anti-Government armed groups — with or without a "trial" — gave rise to reasonable grounds to believe that the war crime of murder had been committed on multiple occasions. The commission could not corroborate alleged attacks directed against individual civilians not participating in hostilities or against a civilian population.

III.   Unknown perpetrators

54.   The commission noted four incidents where attacks were committed by as yet unknown perpetrators. They are as follows:

(i)   In the period leading up to this report, a series of attacks, primarily gunfire, was directed at UN observers' convoys. On 12 June 2012, a convoy headed to Al-Haffe was stopped by alleged pro-Government protestors and was later fired upon by unknown gunmen. On 16 June 2012, UNSMIS stopped its patrols due to safety concerns;

(ii)   Thirteen factory workers were killed on 31 May 2012 near the village of al-Buwaida al-Sharqiya, between Qusayr and the city of Homs. The men were allegedly taken by *Shabbiha*, who arrested, robbed and then killed them. A female eyewitness was with them, but was set free;

(iii)   UNSMIS confirmed on 30 May 2012 the discovery of 13 men's bodies near the eastern city of Deir el-Zour. Their hands were tied behind their backs, and some were shot in the head. The bodies were discovered by locals in the area of Assukar, 50km east of Deir el-Zour;

iv.   Journalists from Ikhbariya TV were reportedly killed in an attack on their premises in the town of Drousha south of Damascus on 27 June 2012.

IV. Explosions

55.   Between March and July 2012, there have been a series of large explosions in which scores of civilians were killed. The explosions appear to be by suicide bombers or by explosives hidden in vehicles and detonated remotely. The commission has compiled the list below based on open sources it deems credible and where the information is consistent with other material on hand, including interviews conducted by the commission:

(i)   18 July 2012, bombing at Syria's national security building in Damascus killed the Minister of Defense and other senior Government security officials;

(ii)   30 June 2012, a car Bomb targeted a funeral procession in Zamalka, Damascus;

(iii)   14 June 2012, a car bomb exploded near the Sayyidah Zaynab shrine in a Damascus suburb injuring 11 people;

(iv)   19 May 2012, a car bomb exploded in the parking lot of a military compound in Deir el-Zour;

(v)   10 May 2012, two large car bombs exploded near the Military Intelligence branch in Damascus' Qazaz neighborhood killing 55 people;

(vi)   30 April 2012, twin explosions near daybreak close to a government compound in the city of Idlib killed 20 people, most of them from the security services;

(vii)   27 April 2012, a bomb near a mosque of Al-Meidan neighborhood of Damascus killed 11 people;

(viii)   18 March 2012, a car bomb killed three people in Aleppo; and

(ix)   17 March 2012, two bombs apparently aimed at an intelligence service office and a police headquarters killed 27 people in Damascus.

Legal conclusions

56.   While these acts may be linked to the non-international armed conflict and thus assessed under the applicable IHL rubric, lack of access to the crime scenes combined with an absence of information on the perpetrators hampered the commission's ability to render such an assessment. They are nevertheless domestic crimes prosecutable under the Syrian criminal code. The Government is obliged to ensure an investigation is conducted impartially, promptly, effectively and independently in line with its international human rights obligations.

Annex VI

[*English only*]

Indiscriminate attacks[a]

I.   Homs Governorate

Bab Amr neighbourhood, February–May 2012

1.   The majority of deaths in Bab Amr during the military operation that began in February 2012 was caused by extensive and indiscriminate shelling by Government forces on primarily civilian infrastructure and residential areas. Targets affected by the shelling included schools, state hospitals, field hospitals, shops, mosques, houses and apartment buildings, and storage facilities. While the FSA was active in the neighbourhood, either through military activity or relief efforts, shelling was the primary cause of death and injury among children, women and elderly.

2.   Most of the shelling was indiscriminate, even though in some of the cases it seemed to target specific locations. On 22 February 2012, at least two shells struck on the Bab Amr Media office, killing many of its occupants, including two foreign journalists. In another incident in early February a number of shells fell on the only operational field hospital in Bab Amr, causing the death of many of the patients and medical staff. An intense period of shelling caused significant destruction to the neighbourhood infrastructure and forced the residents to flee.

Al Qusayr, February–July 2012

3.   The city of Al-Qusayr is located a few kilometres southwest of Homs city in a mountainous region along the Syrian-Lebanese border, in the Western part of the country. Its strategic relevance derives from its location, as well as the demographic makeup of its citizenry which consists of a majority of Sunni Muslims, 10 percent Christians and a few hundred Alawites.

4.   Large numbers of its residents have joined the anti-Government protests which have spread across the country since February 2011. Al-Qusayr has been theatre to some of the heaviest clashes between the Government forces on the one hand, and the FSA and other anti-Government armed groups on the other. The city was initially placed under blockade by the Syrian army in November 2011. The period since has been continuously marred by varied measures of violence which persist at the time of writing.

5.   Since February 2012, Al-Qusayr experienced heavy armed confrontations between Government forces and anti-Government armed groups for the control of the city – particularly for the control of the Municipality building, which was used by Government forces as a base to launch attacks in the city, the market area and the main hospital.

6.   The commission interviewed 10 persons who provided accounts of alleged crimes committed in Al-Qusayr. Information gathered by first-hand witnesses indicate that the city came under heavy shelling during the period mid-February to mid-July 2012, with peaks in late March–early April 2012 and the first two weeks of June 2012.

---

[a]   See annex II, paras. 30–42.

7.   Witnesses have alleged that in early to mid-June 2012, the army in conjunction with security forces and pro-Government militias went on an offensive, indiscriminately attacking civilians and fighters alike in most of Al-Qusayr, particularly Arjoun, Abu Huri, Baasatin and generally West Qusayr. Accounts show that the Syrian forces resorted to a range of weapons, including missiles, shells and rifle grenades, striking residential areas and resulting in the loss of life and heavy injury. They also caused damage to private homes and public infrastructure.

8.   In early May after visiting Al-Qusayr, a credible source told the commission, "*I witnessed what people generally call random shelling – the Syrian army just spreads mortar fire across an entire neighbourhood. It's sometimes preventive while they put up checkpoints. While we were there we were shelled from relatively close in, and it wasn't their heaviest ammunition. Plus there were a few rocket attacks, mortar and tanks.*"

9.   Several witnesses — including children and women — suffered from shrapnel wounds as a result of shells exploding within a few meters' range. The majority of witnesses who suffered serious injuries as a result of the shelling were civilians at home or in the streets. Several people suffered gunshot wounds at the hands of snipers positioned on top of buildings in Baasatin and West Qusayr.

II.   Hama Governorate

Tremseh, 12 July 2012

10.   Shelling in Tremseh was at times aimed at specific military objectives, while at other times appeared indiscriminate. UNSMIS reported that Government forces appeared to be targeting fighters and activists with their weaponry. However the same report stated that, "a doctor and his children were killed when a mortar shell hit their home".[b]

III.   Latakya Governorate

Salma, 11 June 2012

11.   Salma is located on a strategically important road towards the border on Turkey. Anti-Government fighters repelled an attack by Government forces on 11 June. Thereafter, the Syrian army repeatedly shelled the village, using helicopter gunships, mortars and artillery. Reports suggested that the shelling did not target specific locations harboring FSA fighters, but was indiscriminate.

Al Haffe, 4–12 June 2012

12.   On 5 June 2012 Government forces began an assault on the town of Al-Haffe, Latakya governorate. Prior to the offensive, the town experienced an escalation of anti-government protests and was home to a small but increasing number of defectors. There was a protest on 4 July which, although non-violent, was clearly calling for the ouster of the Assad Government.

13.   Al-Haffe town, whose population of 10,000 is primarily Sunni, is surrounded by Alawi villages. The FSA had a presence in the area numbering as many as 600, apparently based in the nearby village of Dofeel. Government police and military intelligence are normally present in the village and were there at the time of the assault.

---

[b]   See annex V for more details on the events in Tremseh on 12 July.

14.   The commission conducted over 30 interviews with persons who fled the fighting in Al-Haffe. Many of these interviews were with people who had just been injured and evacuated. They described in detail what had been the pattern during several such offensives.

15.   Attacks began with cordoning off and then shelling, first the village of Dofeel and then later Al-Haffe itself. Both tanks and helicopter gunships were involved. The security forces present in Al-Haffe placed snipers on top of several buildings. Consistent reports stated that shooting was also coming from neighbouring villages, although the commission could not determine whether this was from Government or local militias.

16.   While the target was likely FSA positions in both areas, the shells randomly struck civilian objects such as homes, schools and mosques. Civilians were confined in their houses, while electricity and water were cut off and food supplies dwindled. At least eight civilians, including three children, were killed when a shell hit their home. Several other houses were destroyed.

17.   Injured residents were unable to seek medical treatment at the State hospital on the outskirts of Al-Haffe which was occupied by Government forces who positioned snipers on the roof. A field clinic was set up, and according to medical personnel working there, the majority of the casualties — including both killed and injured — was fighting age men. Still, there were women and children brought to the hospital who had injuries caused both from shelling and from machine gun or sniper fire.

18.   The FSA apparently held off the initial assault, inflicting heavy losses on the Government forces. One eyewitness — an FSA fighter — reported seeing Government ground forces entering the village in the early afternoon on 5 June who were forced to retreat after encountering stiff resistance. This led to increased shelling and attacks from helicopters.

19.   Around 16:00 on 5 June the FSA surrounded the Finance building from which military security forces had been firing. After an intense battle, the FSA overran the building, allegedly capturing several Government officers. The latter were reportedly set free, although the commission was unable to verify the assertion.

20.   Over the course of the following eight days, fighting continued in and around Al-Haffe. The FSA ultimately withdrew after evacuating nearly all the remaining civilian population. According to numerous corroborated accounts, the army together with *Shabbiha* entered the village on 13 June. Eyewitness accounts portrayed a campaign of burning and pillaging of the houses of suspected anti-Government supporters. UNSMIS observers, who were allowed into the town only on 15 July, noted that many public buildings were looted and burned.

IV.   Other incidents documented

21.   Additional corroborated accounts of indiscriminate shelling were recorded in Atarib (Aleppo) 14 February; Ain Larouz (Idlib) 5 March; Sermin (Idlib) 22 March; Taftanaz (Idlib) 4 April; Kili (Idlib) 6 April; Al-Houla (Homs) 25 May, and 12 and 13 June; Al-Haffe (Latakya) 4 and 5 June 2012; Akko (Hama) 9 June; Salma (Latakya) 11 June; and Jobar (Idlib) multiple dates in late June.

22.   The commission also reviewed videos of shelling in the following locations which appeared to be indiscriminate, although neither the authenticity of the videos nor the target of the attack could be verified: Talbiseh, 17 June; Zafarana, 21 June; Lajat (Dar'a), 25 June; Jalama, 12 July; Abaled, 17 July; and Hayam, 21 July.

V. Cluster munitions

23.   The Commission took note of video evidence emanating from Hama governorate in July 2012 indicating the use of cluster munitions. The photographs and video of bomblets could not be corroborated. The use of anti-personnel mortar munitions was recorded in Zabadani, Damascus governorate, on 12 April. Corroborated accounts described the shells exploding just above ground to maximize human casualties. Although the Syrian Arab Republic is not a party to the Convention on Cluster Munitions, the commission notes that such weapons are inherently indiscriminate when employed in residential areas or areas frequented by civilians.

VI. Legal conclusions

24.   Based on its findings the commission determined that the legal threshold for indiscriminate attack as a violation of customary IHL has been met. Government forces fired shells into areas inhabited by civilians while failing to direct them at a specific military objective.

25.   Moreover, the attacks, especially shelling, caused incidental loss of civilian life and injury to civilians, as well as damage to civilian objects, which in the view of the commission were excessive when compared to the anticipated military advantage.

Annex VII

[*English only*]

Arbitrary detention and enforced disappearance

1.   The commission continued to receive first-hand accounts of arbitrary arrest and detention, predominantly of men and boys. During this reporting period, 25 people were interviewed who alleged that they had been arbitrarily arrested and unlawfully detained by Government forces and *Shabbiha*. A further five interviews were conducted with defectors who stated that, while in active service, they had observed arbitrary arrests and detentions.

2.   According to information received from the Government, over 10,000 people have been released since February 2011, pursuant to four amnesties, including 275 detainees released on 10 July 2012. The Report of the Secretary-General on the implementation of Security Council resolution 2043 (2012), noted that UNSMIS had observed the release of 183 detainees in Dar'a and Damascus on 31 May 2012, and 285 detainees in Damascus, Dar'a, Hama, Idlib and Deir el-Zour on 14 June 2012.

3.   Official statistics on the number of detainees as well as the number of detention centres have yet to be provided by the Government. The Commission noted that, as of 25 June 2012, UNSMIS had received and cross-checked information on 2,185 detainees and 97 places of detention across the Syrian Arab Republic. Syrian NGOs have put the number of those currently detained as high as 26,000.

4.   Given the current lack of access to the country, the commission is not able to independently confirm numbers of those arrested and detained during the reporting period.

I. Findings

5.   The majority of arrests occurred in four contexts: arrests of those believed to be planning to defect or who had otherwise refused to follow orders (usually to open fire on civilians); arrests of persons in house searches; arrests of persons at checkpoints; and arrests of protesters, either at or immediately subsequent to the protests. A minority of cases were reported where people were arrested randomly in the street in areas where there were no active hostilities at the time. Four of those so arrested and detained were women. Two were children, a boy of 14 and a girl of nine.

6.   Eight of those interviewed were members of the Government forces at the time of arrest. Six of these stated that they had been arrested on suspicion of planning to defect. Two others stated their arrests had been a consequence of their refusing orders to fire on civilians in Idlib (February 2012) and in Homs (May 2012) respectively. Of those arrested on suspicion of planning to defect, one stated that he had been found to be in contact with anti-Government armed groups. Most, stated that they were not informed of the basis for the suspicions. One noted that he had been arrested as part of a mass arrest of 60 Sunni soldiers in Aleppo in April 2012. Three of those arrested were detained for over two months with one moved among eight different detention facilities.

7.   According to testimonies received, arrests made during house searches, were conducted by military and security forces. The commission received corroborated accounts of arrests taking places during house searches in the towns of Ibdita (Idlib) in February 2012 and of Ar-Rastan (Homs) in March 2012. House searches appeared to target specific wanted persons. As described in multiple interviews, individuals were sought because of

their defections from the Government forces or their involvement in protests. Also targeted were doctors who had treated protesters or members of the anti-Government armed groups. In at least three instances where the wanted individual could not be located, security forces arrested and detained members of his or her family instead. Two interviewees reported having been arrested and detained on multiple occasions. In three cases, interviewees stated that they had been initially held in temporary detention centres — in one case, a former fitness centre in Ar-Rastan — before being either released or moved to official detention centres.

8.   Individuals were also reportedly arrested, and in one case detained, at checkpoints in Homs, Al Ladhiqiyah, Idlib, Aleppo, Dar'a and Damacus governorates. Lists of wanted persons were allegedly circulated to checkpoints. Those arrested at checkpoints stated that they were targeted either for being defectors or for having organised or taken part in protests. In one instance, which could not be verified, an interviewee reported being arrested and detained in Tartus in March 2012 as injuries that he had suffered during a previous detention were viewed by Government forces as evidence of involvement in fighting.

9.   Reports continue to be received of people being arrested — by security forces and *Shabbiha* — during and immediately following protests. According to interviews, arrests took place following protests in the cities of Idlib in March and April 2012, and Dar'a and Damascus in April 2012. One interviewee, a 14-year-old boy, stated that he and several other adolescents were arrested after a protest in Idlib city in March 2012. The commission was unable to verify this account, but notes that another interviewee, who worked in a detention centre in Damascus until June 2012, reported that minors were arrested and detained following protests.

10.   A number of others interviewed were arrested in the street in areas where there were no active hostilities at the time. Those arrested reportedly included five females, including a nine year old girl. Additionally, a young man was allegedly arrested in Aleppo in April 2012, having been found carrying a large amount of foreign currency, which was viewed as evidence of support to anti-Government armed groups. None of those arrested in these circumstances were taken to official detention centres, but instead were reportedly held in unofficial centres, set up in buildings close to their place of arrest. None of these incidents could be verified.

12.   Only two of those interviewed, both arrested on suspicion of planning to defect, had been formally charged with any offence. No interviewee had been offered or received the benefit of legal counsel. Only one had received a family visit, with the majority unsure if their family were aware of the location of their detention.

13.   In the days prior to release, many said that they had been made to sign or thumbprint a document, the contents of which were unknown to them. Three of those detained were reportedly brought before a judge and then released. In one unverified incident, the interviewee reported that the judge had ordered his release, but he had remained in detention for another 3 months. Also interviewed was a former member of the judiciary who indicated that security agencies brought to his court detainees who showed signs of abuse, including open wounds. He said that security agents did not permit questioning unless they were present and, on one occasion, held the judge at gunpoint. Several detainees stated that the judges did not question them about their injuries and that the presence of security units in the courtroom intimidated them.

14.   The lengths of detention of those interviewed ranged from a few hours to approximately 5 months. The majority of those interviewed were held for 60 days or less by Government forces.

II. Legal conclusions

15.   The commission considers that Syria's domestic legislation fails to meet the country's obligations under Article 9 of the ICCPR to ensure that those arrested and detained on criminal charges appear "promptly before a judge or other officer authorized by law to exercise judicial power".

16.   There are reasonable grounds to believe that Government forces and *Shabbiha* have continued to arbitrarily arrest and detain individuals during this reporting period. Particular concerns are the holding of individuals without charge; the failure to provide detainees with legal counsel or family visits and the absence in the vast majority of cases reported of any form of judicial review of the detentions.

17.   With respect to the crime of enforced disappearance, the families of those arrested were not informed, at the time of arrest or at any point thereafter, of the places of detention of their relatives. With the exception of one detainee, no other detainees interviewed had been afforded family visits.

18.   The majority of the families of those detained have not, according to their testimonies, made attempts to obtain information about their relatives' places of detention. The reasons for this are said to be twofold: fear that contact with the Government, including at the time of the arrest, would prompt further arrests; and the fact that, in some instances, on-going hostilities made going to official detention centres difficult, if not impossible.

19.   Where the Government has refused to acknowledge the arrest and detention or to disclose the fate or whereabouts of the person concerned, the commission finds that there are reasonable grounds to believe that the crime of enforced disappearance has occurred.

Annex VIII

[*English only*]

Torture and other forms of ill-treatment

I.   Government forces and *Shabbiha*

1.   The commission continues to receive reports of the use of torture and other forms of cruel, inhuman or degrading treatment, occurring most often in the context of interrogations by the Government's intelligence agencies. Since 15 February 2012, the commission has interviewed 81 people regarding allegations of torture and ill-treatment. Fifty nine of these interviews related to events within the reporting period.

2.   Due to its lack of access, the commission has not been able to visit detention centres to interview detainees, those responsible for the detention centres or to observe detention conditions.

A.   Findings

3.   Thirty of the 59 individuals interviewed about events in this reporting period stated they had been arrested and/or detained by individuals from Government forces and *Shabbiha*. All but one of this group reported suffering physical violence during their detention. Nineteen others reported being present while others were tortured or otherwise ill-treated. This number includes ten individuals who had worked in detention centres or at checkpoints and who have since defected. The commission has not been able to verify the accounts received. Where possible, the commission observed the wounds/scars of alleged victims.

4.   As set out in annex V (Arbitrary detention and enforced disappearance), most of those detained following arrest were taken to official detention centres. According to interviewees, interrogations in these centres were carried out under the auspices of the Syrian Arab Republic's four principal intelligence agencies: Military Intelligence, Air Force Intelligence, General Security Directorate and the Political Security Directorate. The majority of those interviewed indicated that they had been interrogated by members of Military and/or Air Force Intelligence. All four intelligences agencies have central offices in Damascus as well as a network of regional, city and local sub-offices across the country. They appear to operate independently of each other. Questioning during interrogations reportedly revolved around reasons for protesting, involvement of the detainee or his or her family members in anti-Government armed groups and, in the case of detainees who were members of the Government forces, about alleged plans to defect.

5.   Several interviewees could not, however, confirm which agencies conducted the interrogations and, in some instances, the precise location of their interrogations. Reported reasons for this included being blindfolded during transport in and out of detention facilities, being blindfolded during interrogations, being transferred between different facilities and undergoing multiple interrogations.

6.   While the majority of those held were detained in official detention centres, six interviewees reported that they were also held in unofficial detention facilities, such as civilian houses, usually as a prelude to being transferred to an official centre. Four of the six — one of whom was a woman — were detained in late February/early March 2012 in

various neighbourhoods of Homs city. While held in unofficial centres, interviewees reported abuse by members of the army and by *Shabbiha*.

7.   In a further nine cases, interviewees stated that they were beaten or otherwise assaulted during house searches or at checkpoints or witnessed the assault of others. While most interviewees were adult men, one was a young woman living in a village in Homs governorate in April 2012. She stated that she had been beaten by soldiers when she placed herself between them and her elder brother. In none of these cases were the victims subsequently detained.

B.   Reports of torture and other forms of ill-treatment in official detention centres

8.   Reported methods of torture were consistent across the country. Interviewees described severe beatings about the head and body with electric cables, whips, metal and wooden sticks, and rifle butts; being burnt with cigarettes; being kicked; and being subjected to electric shocks applied to sensitive parts of the body, including the genitals. Six of those interviewed reported losing consciousness at points during their interrogations.

9.   The commission also received multiple reports of detainees being beaten on the soles of the feet (*falaqa*). Common practices described included the placing of detainees into prolonged stress positions, including hanging from walls or ceilings by their wrists (*shabah*) and hanging by wrists tied behind their backs. Other methods reported were forcing detainees to bend at the waist and place their head, neck and legs through a car tire while beatings were administered (*dulab*); tying the detainees to a flat board with their head unsupported and either stretching them (as on a rack) or folding the board in half (the "flying carpet"). As detailed in annex VIII (Sexual violence), some detainees reportedly suffered rape and other forms of sexual violence in the course of their detention. For many interviewees, scars and wounds, consistent with their accounts, were still visible.

10.   Several forms of torture and other forms of cruel, inhuman or degrading treatment meted out to detainees did not result in physical evidence. Reports detailed detainees being forcibly shaved, made to imitate dogs and to declare "there is no God but Bashar". Other interviewees stated that they had been forced to strip and remain naked for prolonged periods. Three of those interviewed stated that they had been threatened with execution. One said he had been present when another detainee was threatened with sexual assault; another stated that his interrogators had threatened to arrest and rape female relatives.

11.   One female interviewee stated that she, along with her nine year old sister, were arrested in May 2012 and taken to a Military Intelligence branch in Dar'a governorate. She reported that her father was suspected of supporting the anti-Government armed groups. During the interrogation, which she stated was conducted by female interrogators, the interviewee was reportedly tied to a chair, had her breasts grabbed, being slapped and had her headscarf removed. She and her sister were released within a week. She stated that her sister had also been beaten while in detention.

12.   Another interviewee, a 14-year-old boy who said he had taken part in protests in Idlib, reported that he had been arrested and detained in the Military Intelligence branch in Idlib in March 2012. He stated that he had received electric shocks and been beaten with a pipe during this interrogation.

13.   Six of those interviewed had been moved among multiple detention facilities, run by different intelligence agencies. One interviewee reported being moved among ten different detention centres across four governorates in a five month period. Another interviewee was transferred among four different locations in Dar'a and Damascus, again over a five month

period. Where there have been multiple transfers, interviewees stated that they had suffered physical violence in each location.

C. Reports of torture and other forms of ill-treatment in unofficial detention centres

14.   Six interviewees reported being held in unofficial detention centres. In various locations in Homs governorate during late February and March 2012, three interviews were reportedly taken to houses or, in one case, a fitness centre and being held there. Two of those interviewed stated that they had been taken from their houses by members of the army during house searches. The third stated she and two other women, all veiled, were removed from a bus by *Shabbiha*. In all three cases, the interviewees stated they had been beaten while detained. In two of these cases, the perpetrators were reportedly members of the *Shabbiha*.

15.   In another case, an interviewee stated that he had been stopped by unidentified individuals in Aleppo in April 2012. When searched, he stated he was found to be in possession of a quantity of foreign currency which was viewed as evidence of support of anti-Government armed groups. He was then reportedly taken to a building in Aleppo where he was beaten with electric wire, given electric shocks and interrogated. After a week he was taken to a different area of Aleppo and released. The commission has not been able to verify this account.

16.   In two cases, the interviewees were former members of the army. One reported being arrested on suspicion of planning to defect and was held at a military barracks in Idlib governorate where he was given electric shocks, hung from the ceiling by his arms and beaten about his body and on the soles of his feet. The second interviewee worked at a military airport in Hama governorate which, he stated, had been converted into a makeshift detention centre where detainees were being assaulted. The commission has not been able to verify these accounts.

D. Reports of torture and other forms of ill-treatment during house searches and at checkpoints

17.   Nine of those interviewed reported being beaten or witnessing others being beaten during house searches or at checkpoints. There were corroborated reports of adult men being beaten by members of the army during house searches in Ibdita in late February 2012 and in Homs city in March 2012. Other, unverified, reports of individuals being beaten during house searches were received in respect of events in Idlib city (April and May 2012), Baniyas (April 2012), and Talf Rif'at (April 2012).

18.   One interviewee reported being removed from his vehicle and beaten at a checkpoint near the Lebanese border, when photographs of demonstrations were discovered on his mobile phone. Another interviewee, a former member of the army, stated that he was present at a checkpoint in Idlib governorate in April 2012 when six men, including two defectors, were brought to the checkpoint where they were severely beaten with sticks and batons. The commission has not been able to verify these accounts.

E. Conditions of detention

19.   The majority of detainees described being held in small, over-crowded cells. Two interviewees reported that the cells were so overcrowded that it was impossible to sit or lie down. All but one reported being given inadequate food and water. One interviewee stated

that, having been without water for a week, he drank his own urine to survive. Health conditions in detention were reportedly poor. Several interviewees stated that their cells were not equipped with toilets. Four interviewees described cells infested with insects, including lice.

20.   The commission received information it could not corroborate on the denial of medication and medical treatment. One detainee stated that a man, held in his cell in the Idlib military intelligence building in early 2012, died, having not received medication for his diabetes. Another, held in the Kafr Susah military intelligence branch in Damascus, stated that a fellow detainee was left with a broken leg in his cell.

21.   Five of those interviewed said they had been held for longer than two months. Two had been held for approximately five months. During this time, none reported receiving legal visits. Only one interviewee said he had received a family visit, a single visit from his wife.

22.   As noted above, lack of access has rendered the commission unable to inspect detention centres. The commission has recorded accounts that, if verified, would amount to the breach of the Standard Minimum Rules for the Treatment of Prisoners, details of which are provided in annex I (Applicable law).

F.   Legal conclusions

23.   The commission confirms its previous finding that torture and other forms of cruel, inhuman or degrading treatment have been committed by Government forces and *Shabbiha*. This is in violation of the Syrian Arab Republic's obligations under international human rights and humanitarian law.

24.   The commission determines that severe pain was inflicted upon persons in official and unofficial detention centres, during house searches and at checkpoints. The Commission further finds that torture was inflicted to punish, humiliate or to extract information from detainees. Much of the physical violence described by interviewees – including kicking, hitting, beating (including beating on the soles of the feet), flogging, inflicting electric shocks, burning, extended hanging from hand and/or leg chains and threatening the victim with execution in circumstances where the interrogators had the power to carry out this threat – have been found to constitute torture by various international tribunals.[a]

25.   The commission finds there are reasonable grounds to believe that torture has been perpetrated as part of a widespread attack directed against a civilian population by Government forces and *Shabbiha*, with knowledge of the attack. It, therefore, concludes that torture as a crime against humanity has been committed by Government forces and *Shabbiha*. On the basis of interviews conducted, members of the intelligence agencies, in particular Military and Air Force Intelligence appear to be primarily responsible for torture and ill-treatment. The commission notes the involvement of *Shabbiha* in acts of torture in unofficial detention centres in Homs city in February and March 2012.

26.   The commission further finds that conduct such as forcibly shaving detainees and forcing them to imitate dogs constitutes cruel, inhuman or degrading treatment. Similarly, the conditions of detention as described in interviews conducted would, if verified, constitute the cruel, inhuman or degrading treatment of those detained.

---

[a]   See annex I (Applicable law).

II. Anti-Government armed groups

27. The commission conducted 15 interviews relating to the treatment of members of Government forces and *Shabbiha* by anti-Government armed groups. All interviewees claimed to be members of these armed groups.

28. All 15 interviews detail the capture, interrogation and either release or execution of those detained.[b] Interviewees stated that those captured were offered the chance to join anti-Government forces. Those that did not were reportedly either executed or were used as part of an exchange for captured anti-Government fighters.

29. One individual, a member of an anti-Government armed group in Idlib governorate, stated that those who did not wish to join the anti-Government forces were imprisoned. Two other anti-Government fighters stated that makeshift detention centres had been set up in the Bab Amr and El Khaldiyah neighbourhoods in Homs. The commission also notes that the majority of those interviewed claimed that those who refused to join the anti-Government armed groups were executed, in part because the groups had no means of housing and providing for prisoners.

30. Three of those interviewed stated that captured Government fighters and *Shabbiha* were tortured as part of an interrogation which took place before execution. One interviewee admitted that captured members of Government forces were beaten with electric wire and were threatened with drowning, with their heads forced in and out of water.

31. The commission has also received information indicating that Syrian security forces and/or their alleged supporters caught by the anti-Government armed groups have confessed under torture. Many of the video recordings of alleged incidents show those captured with signs of physical abuse, including bruising and bleeding. Two Iranians, held in late January 2012 and released in late April 2012, later made public statements about physical abuse suffered, including the breaking of bones, during their captivity. The commission could not verify those video recordings.

Legal conclusions

32. The commission finds there are reasonable grounds to believe that torture and other forms of cruel, inhuman or degrading treatment have been committed by anti-Government armed groups during interrogations of captured members of Government forces and *Shabbiha*. The commission determines that severe pain was inflicted to punish, humiliate or to extract information from detainees.

33. The commission determines, however, that the acts of torture were not committed as part of either a widespread or systematic attack on a civilian population. Therefore, they do not constitute crimes against humanity but may be prosecutable as war crimes.

---

[b] See annex V.

Annex IX

[*English only*]

Sexual violence

I.   Government forces and *Shabbiha*

1.   The commission conducted 43 interviews detailing incidents of sexual violence — against men, women and children — committed by Government forces and *Shabbiha* since February 2012. These interviews included two female and three male victims of rape. Also interviewed were five eyewitnesses of rape (one of whom was also a victim). Additionally, seven of those interviewed were former members of the army, now defected, who stated that rapes and other forms of sexual assault, committed by soldiers and *Shabbiha*, took place during the Government forces' ground operations as described below.

2.   There are difficulties in collecting evidence in cases of sexual violence in Syria due to cultural, social and religious beliefs surrounding marriage and sexuality. Victims' reluctance to disclose information stem from the trauma, shame and stigma linked to sexual assault. There are also serious consequences for female victims' lives and marriages. In one incident, the commission was informed that a female rape victim was subsequently killed by her brother-in-law to "preserve the honour of the family". Another interviewee stated another female rape victim had later killed herself. Several interviewees stated that female rape victims had been abandoned by their husbands and consequently struggled to survive. All victims and/or members of their families interviewed suffered psychological trauma. Many broke down during the interview.

3.   The fear of rape and sexual assault also restricted the freedom of movement of women and young girls. Many of the women interviewed sought refuge in neighbouring countries in part because they feared sexual assault.

A.   Findings

4.   Information collected indicates that rape and other forms of sexual violence occurred in two distinct circumstances. The first is during the searches of houses and at checkpoints as Government forces and *Shabbiha* entered towns and villages; the second, in detention. In a minority of cases, all occurring in Homs city between late February and April 2012, there were reports of the abduction and rape of women, and corroborated accounts of women being forced to walk naked in the street.

Sexual violence during house searches and at checkpoints

5.   Fifteen of the interviewees alleged incidents of sexual violence committed during house searches and at checkpoints during the military operations in Homs between late February and May 2012, and in Al-Haffe in early June 2012. Five interviewees detailed incidents of sexual violence in Zabadani in late February 2012 and in various locations in Hama and Idlib governorates in April and May 2012. The sexual violence was reportedly perpetrated by soldiers and *Shabbiha*.

Homs city (Homs), February–May 2012

6.   Eleven of those interviewed, including two of the victims, detailed rapes and sexual assault perpetrated by Government forces and *Shabbiha* during military operations in Homs. Four interviewees were themselves members of the Government forces in Homs during the military operations.

7.   One victim, a man living with his family in Bab Amr, stated that in late February/early March 2012, 40-50 men wearing military clothes burst into his house at 5:00 am. He described being forced to watch the gang rape of his wife and two elder daughters, 14 and 11 years old, before then being raped himself, with his family being made to watch:

> *The men raped [my two daughters] and my wife, forcing them onto the ground to do so. They raped them at the same time. When they began to rape my daughters, they forced me to raise my head and watch. You cannot imagine what that felt like, as a man to sit there and watch them do that. They raped each of them three times. Then they forced me out of the chair and ordered me onto the ground. They raped me as well and ordered my wife and children to watch. The men were jeering and said, "Look at your father." They destroyed me.*

8.   The same interviewee stated that as the family fled the city with other residents of Bab Amr, the group was stopped at a checkpoint where soldiers detained eight girls. The girls were later released and, according to the interviewee, confirmed that they had been raped.

9.   One of the defectors stated that he was deployed to Homs city in February 2012 and was given orders to shoot anything that moved. He said that commanders ordered them to tie up the men, tell them not to kill them, but to make them watch while they sexually assaulted their wives and daughters. The interviewee was present when members of the army raped women during the February 2012 military operations in Homs city.

10.   Another interviewee spoke about the rape of his wife by members of the Syrian army during ground operations in Homs city in May 2012. He stated that his family fled their home during the shelling. His wife who had returned to check on their house was stopped by five soldiers, including one lieutenant, and reportedly raped by each of them.

11.   Two residents of Karm-el-Zeytoun described soldiers and *Shabbiha* entering houses in March 2012 and raping females inside. One resident stated she witnessed soldiers raping and then executing a 16 year-old girl. A third interviewee, a young man, stated that 13 soldiers together with a number of *Shabbiha* entered his house in Karm-el-Zeytoun, looted it and detained him in a nearby house. He stated that while detained he heard women screaming in an adjoining room and believed they were being raped.

12.   Another soldier stated that he defected shortly after a gang rape of women by *Shabbiha* in Ar-Rastan in March 2012. He described being part of a group of soldiers ordered to surround a house while *Shabbiha* entered, after which he could hear women shouting to leave them alone and screaming that they would prefer to be killed. Two other defectors said that they heard colleagues bragging about committing rapes during the military operations in Bab Amr in late February 2012.

Al-Haffe (Latakia), early June 2012

13.   Four interviewees, including one victim, described rape occurring during military operations on, or in the days following 5 June 2012.

14.   A female victim stated that she was in her house with three children when "heavily armed *Shabbihas*" broke in and demanded, at gunpoint, that she undress. She was accused of providing food and support to the anti-Government armed groups before being dragged

into the street and raped there by one of the men. She stated that other women were abducted and later raped by *Shabbiha*. She stated that her marriage had fallen apart following the rape.

15. Another interviewee stated that he had been an eyewitness to the rape of several women by intelligence agents in a house in Al-Haffe in early June 2012. Two other interviewees, both resident in Al-Haffe during June 2012, stated that *Shabbiha* were entering houses and raping women. One person detailed the public rape of women in the streets of Shier neighbourhood of Al-Haffe.

Zabadani (*Rif Dimashq*), late February 2012

16. Two defectors stated that soldiers perpetrated rape during house searches in Zabadani in February 2012. One stated he was part of a contingent of soldiers that entered a house in order to loot it. When inside the house, the soldiers reportedly tied up the men and began to assault a 15-year-old girl. The interviewee, having been beaten by his colleagues, remained outside the house while the rape took place. Another defector stated that he heard his senior officers boasting about raping women during the February raid on Zabadani.

Hama, Idlib and Aleppo governorates, April–May 2012

17. Two interviewees detailed rapes occurring in various locations in Hama governorate in April and May 2012. One, a defector, stated that he had been deployed to Hama in April 2012 and was part of a contingent of soldiers undertaking house searches. He described the systematic looting of houses and stated that some soldiers and accompanying *Shabbiha* were raping women and girls who were found in the houses. He stated that some victims were killed after the rape.

18. Another interviewee stated that he collected bodies after the army and *Shabbiha* attacked Tamanaa in Idlib governorate on 12 May 2012. Among the bodies he noted one of a woman who had been eviscerated and who had a knife sticking out of her vagina.

19. The Commission also received reports of rapes and other serious sexual assaults taking place in Atarib (February 2012), Tal Rifat (April 2012) and Idlib city (April 2012).

B.   Sexual violence in detention centres

20. The commission continues to receive reports of rape and sexual assault in detention centres, committed usually as part of a course of torture and/or ill-treatment. Two male members of the same family, detained from January to March 2012 at the offices of the Political Security in Damascus, described intelligence agents forcing them to rape each other.

21. Three interviewees stated that women were raped in detention centres in Latakia (March 2012), in Hama (March 2012) and in Dar'a (May 2012). In all instances the women were suspected of supporting the anti-Government armed groups, being involved in protests or of being family members of those involved in the armed groups or protests. In the latter incident, a woman reported that she had been arrested and brought to the Military Intelligence offices in Dar'a in late May 2012 where she was interrogated by female agents. She stated that in the course of her interrogation, the agents attempted to remove her clothes and beat her. She stated she witnessed the gang rape of one of her friends who had attended protests in Dara'a, and who was being held in the same detention centre.

22. As detailed in Annex VI (Torture), many reports were received of male detainees having electric shocks applied to their genitals during interrogations.

C.   Abduction and rape of women

23.   The commission received reports of women being abducted from the streets of Homs city in April 2012. One woman, whose husband was a member of an anti-Government armed group, was reportedly abducted along with six other women (including a 14 year old girl) in early April 2012 in Karm-el-Zeytoun by ten men, dressed in black. She stated that she and other women were placed in a van and blindfolded while being transported. They were taken to a place that looked "like a storage room". There she saw 20 naked women with injuries to their bodies. She and the other six women were raped while the men shouted at them, "*You want freedom, this is your freedom.*"

24.   The interviewee remained in the room with the other women and girls for ten days, during which time they were vaginally and anally raped on multiple occasions. She stated that the other women were from various neighbourhoods of Homs city, including Baba Amr, Bab Sbaa and El Khaldiyah. The women were released, allegedly, as part of a prisoner exchange between the *Shabbiha* and the FSA. Following her release, she was abandoned by her husband.

25.   Another woman interviewed described being pulled off a bus by *Shabbiha* at a checkpoint in Bab Sbaa in April 2012. She and two other veiled women were reportedly detained while other, unveiled women were allowed back on the bus. She stated that she and the two other women were severely beaten before being taken to a house where there were eight other women from Al-Houla who were naked and injured. She stated that she and one other woman were "rescued" by a *Shabbiha* who knew them. She was not aware of what happened to the third woman.

D.   Women forced to walk naked in the streets

26.   The commission also received corroborated reports of women being forced at gunpoint to walk naked in the streets of the Karm-el-Zeytoun neighbourhood of Homs, again in February 2012.

E.   Legal conclusions

27.   The Commission finds that there are reasonable grounds to believe rape has been perpetrated against men, women and children by members of Government forces and *Shabbiha*. The rape and sexual violence was committed in connection to the armed conflict and could be prosecuted as a war crime. Rape and sexual assault also formed part of torture in both official and unofficial detention centres in violation of IHRL and IHL.

28.   Having previously identified the military operations in Homs city in February and March 2012 and in Al-Haffe in June 2012 as part of a widespread or systematic attack against a civilian population, the commission finds that the rapes which occurred during this attack, made with knowledge of the attacks, could be prosecuted as crimes against humanity.

II.   Anti-Government armed groups

29.   The commission has not received any reports of rape or other forms of sexual assault perpetrated by members of the anti-Government armed groups. Lack of access to the country has further complicated the investigation of alleged incidents of sexual violence by all parties to the conflict.

Annex X

[*English only*]

Violation of children's rights

1.   The commission conducted 168 interviews in which violations of children's rights were alleged. Of these, 30 interviewees were under 18 years of age.

2.   In the commission's interviews with children and their care-givers the adverse psychological and social impact of the continued violence was evident. Many of the children interviewed had been injured during the violence and/or saw the death or injury of parents, relatives or friends. Some children displayed signs of high stress, either mirroring that of the (often sole) caregiver or due to events the child had experienced him or herself. Some children recounted that they were "sad", while others explained that they were angry and wanted to "take revenge" for those who killed their family or community members. Many complained of sleeplessness and anxiety, or lack of ability to concentrate, all signs of Post-Traumatic Stress Disorder.

I.   Government forces and *Shabbiha*

A.   Killing and injuring of children

3.   The commission recorded the death of 125 children killed during the reporting period. The majority are male.

4.   The commission recorded the killing and injuring of children during the shelling of Atarib (Aleppo) in February; Bab Amr neighbourhood of Homs city between February and May; Al-Qusayr (Homs) between February and July; Sermin (Idlib) on 22 March; Kafar Zeita (Hama) in late March; Taftanaz (Idlib) on 4 April; Al-Houla (Homs) on 25 May; El Haffe (Latakia) between 4 and 12 June; Salma (Latakia) on 11 June; Azaz (Aleppo) in late June; and in Tremseh (Hama) on 12 July. During a visit to a hospital in Turkey, the commission saw, and met with the family of a two year old girl, injured in the June shelling of Azaz.

5.   As noted in annex V, when Government ground forces moved into towns and villages, usually following shelling, snipers were often positioned on roofs and other raised positions. There were multiple reports of children being killed and wounded by sniper fire. In Atarib (Aleppo) in February, a 10 year old boy, playing in front of his family home, was reportedly shot dead by a sniper positioned on top of a nearby police building. Another interviewee from Atarib stated that he had seen a child shot in the chest by a sniper in February. Another 14 year old boy was injured in Atarib in the same month when he was shot in the legs by a sniper, while on his way to buy food at a local market. The commission received further reports of children shot by snipers in Bab Amr in February, March and May; Taftanaz on 3 April; Aleppo in late April; Anadan village (Aleppo) in late April; and Al-Haffe on 4–6 June.

6.   Children were also killed during attacks on protests — as reportedly occurred in Menaq village (Aleppo) on 15 March — and in attacks on villages believed to be harbouring defectors or members of anti-Government armed groups. One defector asserted that children were also targeted for killing or arrest to pressure their parents to cease their protest activities. He stated that, "... *If someone is an activist we will arrest any member of*

his or her family to pressure them to turn themselves in. Worse than that is the dual beating and imprisonment of a father and his son in order to break the adult. It is very carefully thought out."

7.   There are multiple reports of children killed during military ground operations and house searches. As described more fully in annex V, Government forces and *Shabbiha* conducted a military operation in the village of Ain Larouz to look for defectors. On 4 March, Government forces detained 35 people, including two boys of 14 and 16 years and a 10 year old girl. On 12 March, all but four were released. Bodies of the two boys along with two adults were discovered lying just outside the village.

8.   Interviewees recounted the killing of children in Atarib in February; Bab Amr in March; Karm-el-Zeytoun in March; Tal Rifat (Aleppo) in early April; Taftanaz in early May and in Al Qubeir (Hama) in June. These children were killed with members of their families during military ground operations in the named towns and villages.

9.   Children were also amongst the victims killed in Al-Houla on 25 May. UN observers found at least 108 bodies, 41 of them children. Some had been killed by shrapnel during shelling, but most appeared to have been shot at close range.

B.   Children in detention

10.   Multiple reports of arrests and detentions of children were received. Children were detained during or immediately following protests or during ground operations and house searches. In two cases, children appear to have been arrested, along with older family members, because of familial links to fighters in anti-government armed groups.

11.   Children interviewed by the commission described being beaten, blindfolded, subjected to prolonged stress positions, whipped with electrical cables, scarred by cigarette burns and, in two recorded cases, subjected to electrical shocks to the genitals.

12.   One 15 year old boy said he was arrested in March by security and plain clothes officers after protesting, and taken to a Political Security office in Dara'a in March. He stated, *"There were lots of young men, children and adolescents and also older people. I was standing and the officer stood in front of me and hit me across the face. They put electricity on my temples and my stomach ... They asked us, 'Where are the weapons!' ... They used lots of electricity. It felt like five hours and went on until morning, I think. There were kids as young as 10 with me in the cell ..."* He was released five days later only after signing a confession *"... stating that we were terrible boys and had done many things wrong...I also had to sign a blank paper."*

13.   A 14-year-old boy stated that he was arrested during a demonstration in Idlib in March. He had been taken with 12 others to the Military Intelligence branch in Idlib where he was beaten with a pipe and given electric shocks. Another interviewee stated that her 17 year old son had been arrested by *Shabbiha* in Blin (Idlib) after participating in protests in late February. She stated that he had been taken to detention where he was beaten, subjected to electric shocks and made to "kneel and pray for Bashar al-Assad".

14.   Eight detainees, including two minors, stated that minors and adults were held in the same cells. This was said to have occurred in the cells of Aleppo central prison; the Political Security office in Dara'a; the Military Intelligence office in Idlib and Adra central prison which was under the control of Air Force Intelligence. One adult detainee, held in an unknown location in Damascus, stated he was held in a small overcrowded room with adult and child detainees, the youngest of who appeared to be 13 years old. Child detainees reported enduring the same conditions of detention as described in annex VIII.

C. Sexual violence

15.   As noted in annex IX, the commission received a report of the gang rape of two young girls, aged 11 and 14 years, by men in military clothes, in Bab Amr in late February/early March. The girls' father was forced to watch the rape. His daughters were reportedly then forced to watch the rape of their father. A resident of Karm-el-Zeytoun (Homs) stated she had witnessed soldiers raping a 16-year-old girl during military ground operations in March. A defector stated that he had been present at the sexual assault of a 15 year old girl in Zabadani by soldiers during a house search in February.

D. Recruitment and use of children

16.   No evidence of Government forces formally conscripting or enlisting children under the age of 18 years has been received.

17.   However, the commission documented at least three separate incidents in which Government forces reportedly used children as young as eight as hostages and as human shields. Two interviewees stated that on 21 February in Abdita (Idlib), soldiers forced women and children to walk with them as they moved around the town. When the soldiers withdrew, reportedly three families, including a number of children, were forced to walk alongside a moving tank. The families were released once the soldiers reached the outskirts of the town. Another interviewee stated that, in Taftanaz on 3 April, women and children were reportedly removed from their houses by soldiers and forced to walk in front of a tank as it moved through the town. In Ain Larouz in March, an interviewee stated that several dozen children, boys and girls ranging between the ages of eight and 13 years, were forcibly taken from their homes. These children were then reportedly placed by soldiers and *Shabbiha* in front of the windows of buses carrying military personnel into the raid on the village.

E. Attacks on schools and hospitals

18.   Schools in various locations across Syria have been looted, vandalized and burned by Government forces in response to student protests. A teacher from the village of Abdita (Idlib) testified that since January schools have effectively been closed in the entire region due to fears of imminent military attack. Many schools had been the site of protests and were therefore targeted by Government forces. The interviewee described how, in February, in response to anti-Government protests, the military fired at Abdita School, broke into the classrooms, destroyed school materials and placed graffiti slogans on the walls, all variants of the slogan, "Al Assad or no one else".

19.   As detailed in section III.I of the report of the commission of inquiry (A/HRC/21/50), multiple accounts were received concerning the use of schools by Government forces (most often the army and intelligence services) and *Shabbiha*, as military staging grounds, temporary bases and sniper posts. Several interviewees also stated that the intelligence forces and the *Shabbiha* had installed gun emplacements on the roofs of schools while students were attending classes. The attack on schools has disrupted, and in many cases, curtailed children's ability to access education.

20.   Aside from the military operations that prevented civilians from accessing hospitals over lengthy periods of time, reports also indicated that injured persons, including children and their families, failed to seek medical treatment out of fear of attack by the Government for suspected association with anti-Government armed groups. Many children who were injured were not able to receive hospital care and were taken to private or "underground"

field clinics that could treat only the most rudimentary injuries. A nurse from Idlib stated she had treated dozens of women and children in her home during attacks in early March, and that two children died because there was no appropriate equipment and because she was not skilled enough to stop the bleeding of severe wounds.

21.   The fear of arrest and torture by Government agents in hospitals denied basic healthcare to both children and women. With a few exceptions, field clinics could do more than stabilize those in frontline communities who were severely wounded. These patients then had to endure days of hardship under precarious circumstances en route to seeking health care in neighbouring countries. Testimonies point to the fact that many children could not tolerate the stress of these transfers and died either before they could be transferred or on the road to the border.

F.   Legal conclusions

22.   Evidence gathered clearly indicates that violations of children's rights by Government forces and *Shabbiha* have continued during this reporting period.

23.   The legal conclusions of annexes IV (special inquiry into Al-Houla), V (unlawful killing), VII (arbitrary detentions and enforced disappearances), VIII (torture), IX (sexual violence) apply, in respect of the treatment of children by Government forces and *Shabbiha*.

24.   There are multiple reports of minors being held in the same cells as adults, in breach of the Government's obligations under the Convention on the Rights of the Child.

II.   Anti-Government armed groups

25.   Eleven interviewees, including four minors, spoke about the use of children by anti-Government armed groups. All stated that anti-Government armed groups, including the FSA, used children to work in support roles such as assisting in medical evacuations or as messengers or porters. Five of those interviewed said the anti-Government armed groups used children under the age of 18 — and in one account, below the age of 15 — as fighters.

26.   A 17-year-old interviewee stated that he worked in a FSA medical evacuation team in Hama governorate. He said it was FSA policy that "only at 17 could a gun be used, mostly for guard duty and no active fighting". Three other interviewees, including two minors, stated that they had seen or were aware of 17 year olds actively fighting for the anti-Government armed groups. One said that his 17 year old brother was "*a member of the FSA Al Khatib battalion [and] went to the second floor of a house [in Taftanaz, Idlib governorate, in April] with a Kalashnikov and shot four soldiers*". Another interviewee stated he saw two fighters, approximately 15 years old, fighting with the FSA-affiliated Al Farouk or Bab Amr battalions in Homs city in June.

27.   Another interviewee spoke about the killing of a 17 year old boy — who was reportedly fighting with the FSA — during armed clashes with Government forces in March in Idlib governorate.

28.   A 14 year old boy stated that he was given and used a weapon while fighting with the FSA for two days in Idlib in March.

29.   There is significant evidence of anti-Government armed groups' use of children in auxiliary roles. One 17 year old interviewee worked as part of a FSA medical evacuation team, taking injured persons mainly from the Hama governorate into Turkey. He stated that in his team there were "about 15 boys under the age of 15 years", and that the youngest in

his group was 14. The same interviewee stated that boys between the ages of 15 and 17 also performed duties including delivering messages between FSA units, cooking for units in the field and delivering medical supplies to field hospitals in front line units. He stated that no girls fought or worked as auxiliary support to the anti-Government armed groups.

30.   Two other interviewees, both minors, stated that anti-Government armed groups used children aged 15 years and above to assist in the loading of ammunition.

31.   The use of children as part of medical evacuation teams and as couriers has exposed them to hostilities. One interviewee stated that one minor, who had been part of a medical evacuation team, was shot and killed by a sniper while attempting to evacuate a woman and two young men from Hama city.

32.   In a separate incident in March, the commission was informed about four boys, under 18 who were injured by sniper fire trying to evacuate injured from Helfaya. According to the same interviewee, three boys, one 15 year old and two 17 year olds, were captured by Government forces while working as part of a medical evacuation team in Hama city.

33.   A 16 year old boy who was shot by a sniper outside of Homs while evacuating a wounded girl, explained that he was volunteering to assist the FSA with medical evacuations *"... because it is all they [FSA] will allow me to do... How can I do nothing when they kill my family and my community?"*

34.   The commission received assurances from Colonel Riad al-Asaad that an FSA policy not to use children in combat is in place. There is evidence to suggest, however, that this policy is not uniformly being adhered to by the FSA and other anti-Government armed groups. It is also unclear whether the understanding of "in combat" by the anti-Government armed groups encompasses the auxiliary roles described above.

Legal conclusions

35.   As the anti-Government armed groups are not State parties, they are not bound under the Optional Protocol, which sets 18 as the minimum age for direct participation in hostilities, recruitment into armed groups and compulsory recruitment by Governments.

36.   The commission observes, however, that the conduct of anti-Government armed groups, as a party to an armed conflict, is within the jurisdiction of the International Criminal Court which has made "conscripting or enlisting children under the age of fifteen years into armed forces or groups or using them to participate actively in hostilities" a war crime. The term "participate" covers both direct participation in combat and also active participation in military activities linked to combat, for example scouting, spying, sabotage and the use of children as decoys, couriers or at military checkpoints. Use of children in a direct support function such as acting as bearers to take supplies to the front line, or activities at the front line itself, would be included.

37.   The commission considers that there is currently insufficient information to reach a finding that anti-Government armed groups have been using children under the age of 15 to participate actively in hostilities. It notes with concern, however, reports that children under the age of 18 are fighting and performing auxiliary roles for anti-Government armed groups.

Annex XI

[*English only*]

Pillaging and destruction of property

I. Government forces and *Shabbiha*

1.   The commission corroborated reports of pillaging, destruction and burning of property by Government forces and *Shabbiha* during their military operations. Such acts occurred in two contexts: first as a consequence of the shelling of towns and villages and second during the searches for defectors and members of armed groups and their supporters that took place during ground operations. The former context is discussed in annex VI (indiscriminate attacks). In the latter context, the commission interviewed 43 witnesses who described Government forces burning, destroying and pillaging their property in the wake of searches.

2.   Interviewees stated that the pillaging and destruction were targeted against groups and individuals who appeared to be defectors; members of anti-Government armed groups; demonstrators and family members of the aforementioned. In particular, family members of defectors described how their homes, farms and shops were burned following the defection of their relatives. In some instances the looting, burning and destruction of property appeared to be directed at entire communities rather than specific individuals.

3.   According to soldiers who later defected, the looting and burning of property of opposition activists and defectors was intended, inter alia, to impose financial constraints on them and on their activities. Government soldiers and *Shabbiha* also benefited from these acts financially, conducting them with complete impunity. They were viewed as a form of reward for their allegiance to the Government. One defector told the commission:

> I never got direct orders to [pillage/destroy], but it was every man's understanding that he was allowed to do everything he wanted without being held accountable for that. Not only that, but also when someone is seen not to be active in doing these things, he will be questioned about his loyalty to the regime and his relation with the oppositions.

4.   In Idlib in March 2012, instances were recorded of looting followed by burning of homes after which the army and local militias sold the looted goods. One defector told the commission of his looting prior to his defections:

> "Just go and get a TV, something for yourself, there is no FSA here... It [the military base] was like a flea market. Anything you want you can find there, including gold. Nothing was left in the houses... [We] swapped things and sold them to each other."

5.   Twelve different witnesses described the deliberate burning and looting of homes and the purposeful destruction of personal property in various neighbourhoods of Homs. Five witnesses reported the burning of more than 100 houses during the attack on Anadan (Aleppo) in March and again in April 2012. Other witnesses put the number of houses burned at over 300.

6.   One defector stated that he was ordered to shell and then to raid the village of Yabrud (Rif Dimashq) in March 2012. He had at his disposal six buses of Government forces together with tanks. A local government informer, whose face was covered,

accompanied them during this operation. The informer guided them toward houses of activists and defectors. Whenever the informer pointed out the house of a defector, FSA fighter or opposition activist, the soldiers would loot and burn it.

7.   Demonstrations occurred regularly in the village of Marayane (Idlib), one of which took place on 11 April 2012. A defector stated that on 12 April, he was with Government forces when they raided Marayane (Idlib) using T72 tanks, BMPs and 14.5 mm machine guns. Before entering the village his forces began shelling randomly in an effort to "weaken the enemy." Once inside the village, they burned more than 100 houses. He recalled specifically shelling two houses, ensuring they were razed to the ground. One belonged to the headmaster of the high school, while the other to an agricultural engineer. The defector presumed, but could not confirm, that the two men were suspected anti-Government fighters. The rest of the houses were looted by the soldiers and then shelled or burned.

8.   Another interviewee stated that in Mare'e (Aleppo) on 10 April 2012, Government forces burned 386 houses and some two hundred shops burned during the search operations. He added that all residents fled when they knew that military and security forces were about to raid their village. When people returned, they saw painted on the walls, "from here Al-Assad forces passed; if you return, we will return," and "there is no God but Bashar al-Assad".

9.   Thirteen individual accounts described widespread looting and destruction of property in Tal Rifat (Aleppo), Bayda and Jabal-az-Zawiyah (Idlib) in April 2012. When Government forces departed these villages after the attack, the inhabitants returned to find the electricity cut, crops destroyed, livestock killed, mosques and schools destroyed, money stolen and houses emptied of their furniture, jewellery, clothes and appliances. Shops had been looted completely and then destroyed either by burning or by shelling. Vehicles had been either stolen or destroyed.

10.   Corroborated evidence was collected of pillaging, deliberate destruction and burning of property by pro-Government forces in Bab Amr (Homs), end of April 2012; Ablin (Idlib), 16 June 2012; Ibdita (Idlib), 21 February 2012; Jisr-esh-Shughour (Idlib), March 2012; Al Atarib (Aleppo), 15 February 2012; Taftanaz (Idlib) 4 and 5 April 2012; Sermin (Idlib), 22 March 2012; Azaz (Aleppo), April 2012; Dar'a, June 2012; Hama, end of May and beginning of June 2012; al-Haffah (al-Ladhiqiyah), 13 June 2012; and Anadan (Aleppo), 7 April 2012.

Legal conclusions

11.   There are reasonable grounds to believe that Government forces and *Shabbiha* committed the war crime of pillage. The commission also determined that Government forces and *Shabbiha* engaged in the destruction and burning of property during house searches.

II.   Anti-Government armed groups

12.   The commission received no reports of pillaging or destruction of property by anti-Government armed groups, but lack of access to Syria hampered investigations in this regard. The Government provided information about crimes allegedly perpetrated by anti-Government armed groups, including looting and vehicle theft, which the commission was unable to corroborate. Consequently, the commission has been unable to reach any findings with regard to the alleged pillaging, burning and destruction of property by anti-Government armed groups.

Annex XII

[English only]

Map of the Syrian Arab Republic

NATIONS UNIES
HAUT COMMISSARIAT AUX
DROITS DE L'HOMME

UNITED NATIONS
HIGH COMMISSIONER FOR
HUMAN RIGHTS

Tel: +41-22-917 9989   Fax +41-22-917 9007

Independent International Commission of Inquiry on the Syrian Arab Republic

established pursuant to United Nations Human Rights Council Resolutions S-17/1, 19/22 and 21/26

20 December 2012

Periodic Update

I.   Introduction

1.   The unrelenting violence in Syria has resulted in thousands of deaths, untold thousands of wounded, detained and disappeared, and physical destruction on a massive scale. Hundreds of thousands have fled their homes and those that remain struggle to secure basic necessities. World heritage sites have been damaged or destroyed, as have entire neighbourhoods. Civilians have borne the brunt of escalating armed confrontations as the front lines between Government forces and the armed opposition have moved deeper into urban areas. The patterns of international human rights and humanitarian law violations that were noted in previous reports have continued unabated, alongside a proliferation of both anti- and pro-Government armed entities.

2.   On 28 September 2012 the Human Rights Council (HRC) extended the mandate of the Independent International Commission of Inquiry on the Syrian Arab Republic (the Commission), requesting it to investigate all massacres and continue to update its mapping exercise of gross violations of human rights since March 2011. The HRC also requested the Commission to investigate allegations of war crimes and crimes against humanity. Updates of the Commission's findings with respect to such violations are to be released periodically.

3.   This periodic update covers the period 28 September to 16 December 2012.

II. Military situation

4.   The Syrian conflict has been marked by a continuous but unequal escalation of armed violence throughout the country. Levels of violence have varied geographically due to the interplay of a number of factors: the strategic importance of a particular area, the deployment and strength of Government forces, the

sectarian composition of the local population and anti-Government armed groups' organisation and access to logistical support.

5. In the southern governorates of Dara'a, al-Suweida and al-Qunayterah, Government forces remain in control of main localities. This is due to the heavy presence of army units and security services, together with the existence of relatively disorganised and poorly armed anti-Government groups in these areas. In comparison to groups based in the north-west, armed groups in the southern governorates have struggled to establish themselves and are able only to briefly attack isolated checkpoints and individuals. In these areas, the army is still able to set up checkpoints and conduct targeted raids inside restive towns.

6. Reports from northern and central provinces describe a different reality, with anti-Government armed groups exercising control over large swathes of territory. Armed groups in governorates such as Idlib, Latakia and Aleppo have been able to coordinate effectively, both with each other and with unified local military councils. Further, they are equipped with increasingly efficient military assets allowing them to mount a serious challenge to the Government forces' authority.

7. Violence has increased dramatically in and around major cities, in particular Damascus and Aleppo, where anti-Government fighters have advanced to neighbourhoods close to the cities' centres. Anti-Government armed groups were also reported in governorates such as al-Raqqah and al-Hasakah where they have clashed with army units, provoking shelling and artillery attacks.

8. Mounting tensions have led to armed clashes between different armed groups along a sectarian divide (see Section III). Such incidents took place in mixed communities or where armed groups had attempted to take hold of areas predominantly inhabited by pro-Government minority communities. Some minority communities, notably the Alawites and Christians, have formed armed self-defence groups to protect their neighbourhoods from anti-Government fighters by establishing checkpoints around these areas. Some of those local groups, known as Popular Committees, are said to have participated alongside Government forces in military operations in Damascus countryside in Tadamon and Said al-Zeinab neighbourhoods. Interviewees alleged that the Government provided arms and uniforms to these groups.

9. During the last two months, anti-Government armed groups have reached strategic regions and were able to challenge state forces control of sensitive infrastructure such as oil fields, major highways, airports and military camps. The armed groups have increasing access to weaponry, though those in the south tend to be less well-armed. Most anti-Government armed groups are equipped with individual light weapons and small arms, typical to any insurgency, including Rocket Propelled

2

538

Grenades (RPGs) of different calibres and types. The larger armed groups possess mortars, heavy machine guns and heavy anti-aircraft machine guns. A few have obtained anti-tank and anti-aircraft missiles. The quality and quantity of such missiles appear to be limited but would be sufficient to affect Government forces use of air assets. While significant quantities of arms were taken from army camps, weapons and ammunition have also been smuggled in from neighbouring countries.

10. Interviews with fighters, including some defectors, indicate that newly formed armed opposition groups are less likely to attach themselves to the Free Syrian Army (FSA). Many operate independently from existing groups or are affiliated to Islamist groups such as Jabhat al-Nusra. Foreign fighters, many of whom also have links to other extremist groups, are present in Idlib, Latakia and Aleppo governorates. Multiple interviewees noted that while these groups are independent of the FSA, they coordinate attacks with them.

11. Government forces, along with supporting militia, have tried to adapt their deployment, tactics and capabilities to those of the armed groups. They are focussing now on securing control of main cities – particularly Aleppo and Damascus – while limiting their actions in the countryside to shelling and aerial attacks. There are fewer accounts of Government forces engaging in ground actions. Rather they continue shelling areas under anti-Government armed group control, endangering civilians who remain in these areas. Interviewees stated that joint pro-Government forces are conducting house-to-house searches in neighbourhoods used by the opposition such as Daraya in Damascus countryside and Mashari'a al-Arbaeen in Hama city. Government forces continue to besiege opposition strongholds in the central region of the country and reinforce borders with Lebanon and Jordan in an attempt to limit flows of weapons and people.

III. Increased sectarianism

12. The risk of the Syrian conflict devolving from peaceful protests seeking political reform to a confrontation between ethnic and religious groups has been ever present. As battles between Government forces and anti-Government armed groups approach the end of their second year, the conflict has become overtly sectarian in nature.

13. In recent months, there has been a clear shift in how interviewees portray the conflict. In describing the shelling of a village in Latakia governorate by Government forces, one interviewee stressed that the shelling came from positions in "Alawite villages". Another interviewee, describing ground attacks in Bosra in the southern Dara'a governorate, stated that tensions between the Shia and Sunni communities in the town were "escalating", with violence becoming increasingly inevitable.

3

14. The country's other minority groups, such as the Armenians, Christians, Druze, Palestinians, Kurds and Turkmen (see Section IV), have been drawn into the conflict. However, the sectarian lines fall most sharply between Syria's Alawite community, from which most of the Government's senior political and military figures hail, and the country's majority Sunni community who are broadly (but not uniformly) in support of the anti-Government armed groups.

15. Attacks and reprisals (and fears thereof) have led to communities arming themselves, and being armed by parties to the conflict. One interviewee, a Turkman living in Latakia, captured the situation succinctly: "it is too dangerous to live beside neighbours who are armed and [consider you to be a rebel], while you yourself remain unarmed".

16. Government forces and militias aligned with the Government have attacked Sunni civilians. One interviewee, present in Bosra in late October, described "members of the Shia militia", whom she recognised from the neighbourhood, conducting house searches. She stated that the militia told her that "they would kill all Sunnis in the region and that the area belonged to them". Another interviewee stated that he regularly witnessed Sunni commuters being pulled out of their cars and beaten at army checkpoints along the main highway between Dara'a and Damascus.

17. The Commission has received credible reports of anti-Government armed groups attacking Alawites and other pro-Government minority communities. One interviewee, an FSA fighter in Latakia, detailed how, upon capturing Government forces, the Sunni captives were imprisoned while Alawites were immediately executed. On 30 October, a bomb exploded near an important Shia shrine outside of Damascus, killing and injuring several people. On 6 November, a car bomb exploded in the Alawite neighbourhood of Hai al-Wuroud in the north-west of Damascus, reportedly killing ten people.

18. Most of the foreign fighters filtering into Syria to join the anti-Government armed groups (or to fight independently alongside them) are Sunnis hailing from countries in the Middle East and North Africa. The increasingly sectarian nature of the conflict provides one motivation for other actors to enter into the conflict. The Lebanese Shia group Hezbollah has confirmed that its members are in Syria fighting on behalf of the Government. There have also been reports, still under investigation, of Iraqi Shias coming to fight in Syria. Iran confirmed on 14 September that members of its Revolutionary Guards are in Syria providing "intellectual and advisory support".

19. One expatriate interlocutor working inside Syria described a "low intensity sectarian conflict" taking place alongside the fight against the Government. The

4

dangers are evident. Entire communities are at risk of being forced out of the country or of being killed inside the country. With communities believing – not without cause – that they face an existential threat, the need for a negotiated settlement is more urgent than ever.

IV. Minority groups in the conflict

20. Feeling threatened and under attack, ethnic and religious minority groups have increasingly aligned themselves with parties to the conflict, deepening sectarian divides.

21. Syria's Armenian Orthodox, other Christian, and Druze communities have sought protection by aligning themselves with the Government, with the consequence that they have come under attack from anti-Government armed groups.

22. The Armenian Orthodox community resides mainly in Aleppo governorate. On 16 September, ten passengers on a bus travelling from Beirut to Aleppo were kidnapped. All ten were Christian, with seven being Armenian Orthodox. Their whereabouts remain unknown. On the same day, the Saint Kevork Armenian Church in Aleppo was heavily damaged. Syrians of Armenian descent have sought refuge in Armenia.

23. Christian communities are spread throughout Syria, with the largest communities, prior to the conflict, living in Aleppo, Damascus and Homs governorates. Homs city had been home to approximately 80,000 Christians, most of whom have now fled reportedly to Damascus, with some then making their way to Beirut. It is estimated that only a few hundred remain. An interviewee, speaking about recent events in al-Suweida governorate, confirmed that the Sunni and Druze communities had clashed, leaving several dead. On 29 October, a car bomb exploded outside a bakery in Jaramana, a predominantly Christian and Druze neighbourhood in Damascus.

24. Half a million Palestinian refugees live in Syria. A third reside in the Yarmouk refugee camp in Damascus. Divisions within the community hardened after February 2012, when Hamas broke with the Government. Reports reviewed by the Commission indicate that Palestinians in Yarmouk are being armed by both the Government and the anti-Government armed groups.

25. On 5 November, approximately 20 Palestinians were killed and over 70 injured during a mortar attack on Yarmouk. Both the Government forces and the anti-Government armed groups have accused each other of firing the mortars. On the same day, the body of Mohammed Rafeh, a prominent Syrian-born Palestinian who had been outspoken in his support of President Assad, was returned to his family

5

bearing gunshots to the head and upper body. A group named "Ahfad al-Siddiqi" claimed responsibility for the killing.

26. Following airstrikes on Yarmouk on 16 December, which reportedly killed and injured dozens of residents, damaged a mosque and left the camp devastated, the Palestinian Liberation Organization (PLO) denounced the Assad Government. The Popular Front for the Liberation of Palestine – General Command continues to support the Government.

27. The Kurds, who live predominantly in the north-eastern al-Hasakah governorate, have remained relatively autonomous due to their fighting ability and independent supply lines. They have clashed with Government forces and anti-Government armed groups over control of territory. Hostilities flared between Kurdish militias and the anti-Government armed groups on 25 October in Aleppo, following the armed groups' attempt to enter the Kurdish-held Sheikh Maqsud neighbourhood. Fighting continued until 5 November, when a truce was signed. On 19 November, anti-Government armed groups attacked a Kurdish militia checkpoint in Ras al-Ayn, leaving six rebels dead. An anti-Government sniper also assassinated Abed Khalil, the president of the local Kurdish council. Four Kurdish fighters were later executed after being captured by anti-Government fighters.

28. Turkmen militias fight as part of the anti-Government armed groups in Latakia governorate. Several Turkmen civilians have emphasised the discrimination their community suffered under the Government. Interviewees also emphasised that the decision to bear arms was influenced in part by the creation of Alawite militias in surrounding villages, and the fact that Turkmen were being harassed at checkpoints and during house searches.

V. Violations of international human rights and humanitarian law

Unlawful killing and 'massacres'

29. In addition to investigating summary executions and violations of the right to life generally, under its extended mandate the Commission is also investigating massacres.

30. Investigations continue regarding reports that pro-Government forces are unlawfully killing armed and unarmed persons suspected of opposing the Government. Accounts from Latakia indicate that *Shabbiha* arrest and torture, including torturing to death, suspected opposition members. Incidents in Asfira (September) and al-Basit (August) fitting this pattern are under investigation.

31. Although fewer credible accounts were received of Government soldiers executing captives, incidents of direct targeting of civilians by aerial bombardment, including

6

"barrel bombs," rocket attacks and machine gun fire have risen significantly. The Commission recorded a large number of incidents in several governorates where multiple civilian casualties resulted from shelling by Government forces. The evidence in many of these cases indicates that Government forces take insufficient precautions to avoid incidental loss of civilian life and that their attacks are disproportionate to the concrete and direct military advantage anticipated. Investigations are on-going as to whether these attacks are indiscriminate and violate the law of armed conflict.

32. Consistent accounts of summary executions by anti-Government armed groups continue to be collected. Unlawful executions of captured Government soldiers in Aleppo (10 September), Sabouk (2 November) and Ras al-Ayn (29 November), where the unarmed captives were gathered together and then gunned down, are under investigation. Investigations indicate that in some instances captured enemy fighters are brought before a Sharia council (*al-Lajana al-Shariah*) prior to their execution. Neither the substantive nor procedural framework of these councils could be ascertained, with one interviewee positing that, "only those with blood on their hands" are executed. It is a war crime to sentence or execute a person who has been captured, has surrendered, is injured or is otherwise *hors de combat*, without due process.

33. The use of snipers has become a pronounced feature of the urban insurgency fought by both Government and anti-Government armed groups, positioned in strategic areas to freeze the frontlines and hinder movement. Civilians caught in between are exposed, vulnerable to the constant risk of being hit by snipers. Several interviews describe civilians, particularly in Aleppo city, being killed by sniper fire. There are also recorded accounts of women and children victims with injuries that indicate they were shot by snipers while going about their daily routine. Several credible accounts concern civilian victims in Latakia who came under sniper fire while collecting milk in the morning. One woman was hit adjusting the television antenna on the roof of her house. Similar accounts were recorded elsewhere.

Torture

34. Considerable evidence has been collected regarding the use of torture, particularly in Government-run detention centres in Damascus. The testimony of interviewees indicates a consistent and systematic pattern of torture during which individuals are beaten and subjected to electric shocks while held in overcrowded, underground cells. One victim who had been detained in Harasta Intelligence Branch outside of Damascus for 30 days, had his genitals electrocuted on multiple occasions. Another interviewee, a former guard of Harasta prison, described how his superiors encouraged the ill-treatment of detainees. Testimony was also gathered indicating that children were held in Harasta Intelligence Branch in the same detention areas and conditions as adults and were also tortured.

7

35.   An interviewee, arrested in August while distributing bread in one of the northern governorates, was handed over to Military Security, who beat him, asking "where are you taking this bread? Were you taking it to the FSA?" After five days of torture and detention without food or water, the interviewee reported, "I couldn't move my leg or stand up, I reached the point where I wished I could die." The interviewee was transferred through a prison in Homs and then to Military Security Branch 215 in Damascus where for two weeks he was kept in an underground cell of 4 by 5 metres with 60 other detainees. Multiple accounts have been collected of torture occurring in Military Security Branch 215, including the use of torture methods such as hanging from the ceiling by wrists (*shabeh*) and beaten inside a tyre (*dulab*). The consistency among the various accounts lends them significant credibility.

36.   In Latakia, interviewees described a pattern of *shabbiha* conduct. In manning checkpoints to majority-Alawite villages, *shabbiha* often arrest, harass and torture individuals suspected of cooperating with the opposition, detain them or hand them over to Air Force and Military Security Intelligence organs.

37.   Accounts were also received of torture by anti-Government armed groups, documenting an FSA-administered detention centre in Sahara, Aleppo where detainees were tortured and killed. In Seida al-Zeinab in Damascus, FSA members reportedly captured, interrogated and beat a suspected Hezbollah member.

Attacks on protected objects

38.   Increasing attacks on cultural property as well as the use of protected objects for military purposes by all parties to the conflict have been recorded. Available information indicates that Syria's six World Heritage sites have been damaged in the fighting. In Aleppo, the historic souk was burned (1 October), the Umayyad mosque was significantly damaged (14 October), and the Saint Kevork Church (29 October) was damaged by arsonists. The doors of the Aleppo Citadel were also damaged in August, while looters have broken into one of the world's best-preserved Crusader castles, Krak des Chevaliers. Artefacts in museums in Palmyra, Bosra and Homs have also been looted while ruins in the ancient city of Palmyra have been damaged.

39.   Interviewees described Government forces' shelling of state hospitals as well as field hospitals in opposition-controlled areas. Multiple interviewees described the shelling of hospitals in Aleppo governorate, in Aleppo city and the towns of Hirtan and El Bab. Dar al-Shifa, the main emergency hospital in Aleppo city, has been shelled on multiple occasions leading to its destruction. Investigations are on-going about the potential misuse of the hospitals at the time of attacks, the possible

8

presence of legitimate military targets nearby, and whether adequate warnings were given prior to attack.

40. Attacking protected objects is a war crime, while using protected objects for military purposes violates customary international humanitarian law in non-international armed conflict.

Use of cluster munitions

41. The use of cluster munitions in populated urban areas is currently under investigation. Syria is not party to the international Convention on Cluster Munitions which prohibits such use. Where the object of an attack was the civilian population or individual civilians not taking direct part in hostilities, the investigation will seek to verify the occurrence of the war crime of attacking civilians. Whether the use of cluster munitions was indiscriminate is also being assessed.

VI. Impact on the civilian population

42. Investigation into the conduct of hostilities of the parties to the conflict in Syria is on-going. Certain attacks are of particular concern, particularly those that inflict terror upon civilians seeking to obtain basic necessities.

43. The evidence collected indicates that anti-Government armed groups consistently fail to distinguish themselves from the civilian population. The obligation on each party to the conflict, under customary international law, to remove civilian persons and objects under their control from the vicinity of military objectives is particularly relevant where military objectives cannot feasibly be separated from densely populated areas. The manifest failure to make these distinctions has resulted in civilians being driven from their homes and contributed to the alarming increase of IDPs and refugees.

44. Faced with shelling and shortages of food, water and fuel, civilians have fled their homes, becoming refugees in neighbouring countries or finding themselves internally displaced. Towns and villages across Latakia, Idlib, Hama and Dara'a governorates have been effectively emptied of their populations. Entire neighbourhoods in southern and eastern Damascus, Deir al-Zour and Aleppo have been razed. The downtown of Homs city has been devastated.

45. The humanitarian situation in Syria has deteriorated rapidly during the reporting period. Many of those interviewed detailed the difficulty in obtaining food, potable water and fuel. This appears to be particularly acute in Idlib, Latakia and in northern Aleppo governorates. In Aleppo city, and among much of the north of Syria, electricity has been cut off, food is no longer readily available and access to

9

medical care or assistance is severely limited. In Idlib, an interviewee described how in addition to the shelling, the living conditions in the town of Hass had become unbearable, aggravated by a lack of fuel and domestic gas, frequent electricity and water cuts, and skyrocketing food prices of basic products such as bread. The situation in Latakia, according to multiple accounts, has become so dire that entire villages that are home to the Turkmen community have been emptied. Investigations are seeking to establish whether such shortages are deliberate and part of an intentional and concerted siege, or whether they are a direct, albeit unintended, consequence of protracted armed conflict.

46.   In certain areas, the humanitarian situation has been aggravated by widespread destruction and razing of residential areas. According to the Office for the Coordination of Humanitarian Affairs (OCHA), many internally displaced persons (IDPs) in Syria are unable to return to their homes because they have been destroyed. The onset of winter poses particular risk to such vulnerable groups. Numbers of refugees are expected to swell in the coming months to over 700,000, while there are already 2 million IDPs according to the latest OCHA figures.

VII. Conclusion

47.   The war of attrition that is being fought in Syria has brought immeasurable destruction and human suffering to the civilian population. As the conflict drags on, the parties have become ever more violent and unpredictable, which has led to their conduct increasingly being in breach of international law. The sole way to bring about an immediate cessation of the violence is through a negotiated political settlement which meets the legitimate aspirations of the Syrian people. The Commission strongly supports the mission of Mr. Lakhdar Brahimi, the Joint Special Representative of the United Nations and League of Arab States in its effort to bring the parties towards such a settlement.

10

United Nations

S/RES/1612 (2005)

 Security Council

Distr.: General
26 July 2005

Resolution 1612 (2005)

**Adopted by the Security Council at its 5235th meeting,
on 26 July 2005**

The Security Council,

Reaffirming its resolutions 1261 (1999) of 25 August 1999, 1314 (2000) of 11 August 2000, 1379 (2001) of 20 November 2001, 1460 (2003) of 30 January 2003, and 1539 (2004) of 22 April 2004, which contribute to a comprehensive framework for addressing the protection of children affected by armed conflict,

While noting the advances made for the protection of children affected by armed conflict, particularly in the areas of advocacy and the development of norms and standards, *remaining deeply concerned* over the lack of overall progress on the ground, where parties to conflict continue to violate with impunity the relevant provisions of applicable international law relating to the rights and protection of children in armed conflict,

Stressing the primary role of national Governments in providing effective protection and relief to all children affected by armed conflicts,

Recalling the responsibilities of States to end impunity and to prosecute those responsible for genocide, crimes against humanity, war crimes and other egregious crimes perpetrated against children,

Convinced that the protection of children in armed conflict should be regarded as an important aspect of any comprehensive strategy to resolve conflict,

Reiterating its primary responsibility for the maintenance of international peace and security and, in this connection, its commitment to address the widespread impact of armed conflict on children,

Stressing its determination to ensure respect for its resolutions and other international norms and standards for the protection of children affected by armed conflict,

Having considered the report of the Secretary-General of 9 February 2005 (S/2005/72) and stressing that the present resolution does not seek to make any legal determination as to whether situations which are referred to in the Secretary-General's report are or are not armed conflicts within the context of the Geneva Conventions and the Additional Protocols thereto, nor does it prejudge the legal status of the non-State parties involved in these situations,

05-43959 (E)

0543959

Gravely concerned by the documented links between the use of child soldiers in violation of applicable international law and the illicit trafficking of small arms and light weapons and stressing the need for all States to take measures to prevent and to put an end to such trafficking,

1.   *Strongly condemns* the recruitment and use of child soldiers by parties to armed conflict in violation of international obligations applicable to them and all other violations and abuses committed against children in situations of armed conflict;

2.   *Takes note* of the action plan presented by the Secretary-General relating to the establishment of a monitoring and reporting mechanism on children and armed conflict as called for in paragraph 2 of its resolution 1539 (2004) and, in this regard:

(a)   Underlines that the mechanism is to collect and provide timely, objective, accurate and reliable information on the recruitment and use of child soldiers in violation of applicable international law and on other violations and abuses committed against children affected by armed conflict, and the mechanism will report to the working group to be created in accordance with paragraph 8 of this resolution;

(b)   Underlines further that this mechanism must operate with the participation of and in cooperation with national Governments and relevant United Nations and civil society actors, including at the country level;

(c)   Stresses that all actions undertaken by United Nations entities within the framework of the monitoring and reporting mechanism must be designed to support and supplement, as appropriate, the protection and rehabilitation roles of national Governments;

(d)   Also stresses that any dialogue established under the framework of the monitoring and reporting mechanism by United Nations entities with non-State armed groups in order to ensure protection for and access to children must be conducted in the context of peace processes where they exist and the cooperation framework between the United Nations and the concerned Government;

3.   *Requests* the Secretary-General to implement without delay, the above-mentioned monitoring and reporting mechanism, beginning with its application, within existing resources, in close consultation with countries concerned, to parties in situations of armed conflict listed in the annexes to the Secretary-General's report (S/2005/72) that are on the agenda of the Security Council, and then, in close consultation with countries concerned, to apply it to parties in other situations of armed conflict listed in the annexes to the Secretary-General's report (S/2005/72), bearing in mind the discussion of the Security Council and the views expressed by Member States, in particular during the annual debate on Children and Armed Conflict, and also taking into account the findings and recommendations of an independent review on the implementation of the mechanism to be reported to the Security Council by 31 July 2006. The independent review will include:

(a)   An assessment of the overall effectiveness of the mechanism, as well as the timeliness, accuracy, objectivity and reliability of the information compiled through the mechanism;

2

(b)   Information on how effectively the mechanism is linked to the work of the Security Council and other organs of the United Nations;

(c)   Information on the relevance and clarity of the division of responsibilities;

(d)   Information on the budgetary and other resource implications for United Nations actors and voluntary funded organizations contributing to the mechanism;

(e)   Recommendations for the full implementation of the mechanism;

4.   *Stresses* that the implementation of the monitoring and reporting mechanism by the Secretary-General will be undertaken only in the context of and for the specific purpose of ensuring the protection of children affected by armed conflict and shall not thereby prejudge or imply a decision by the Security Council as to whether or not to include a situation on its agenda;

5.   *Welcomes* the initiatives taken by UNICEF and other United Nations entities to gather information on the recruitment and use of child soldiers in violation of applicable international law and on other violations and abuses committed against children in situations of armed conflict and invites the Secretary-General to take due account of these initiatives during the initial phase of implementation of the mechanism referred to in paragraph 3;

6.   *Notes* that information compiled by this mechanism, for reporting by the Secretary-General to the General Assembly and the Security Council, may be considered by other international, regional and national bodies, within their mandates and the scope of their work, in order to ensure the protection, rights and well-being of children affected by armed conflict;

7.   *Expresses* serious concern regarding the lack of progress in development and implementation of the action plans called for in paragraph 5 (a) of its resolution 1539 (2004) and, pursuant to this, calls on the parties concerned to develop and implement action plans without further delay, in close collaboration with United Nations peacekeeping missions and United Nations country teams, consistent with their respective mandates and within their capabilities; and requests the Secretary-General to provide criteria to assist in the development of such action plans;

8.   *Decides* to establish a working group of the Security Council consisting of all members of the Council to review the reports of the mechanism referred to in paragraph 3 of this resolution, to review progress in the development and implementation of the action plans mentioned in paragraph 7 of this resolution and to consider other relevant information presented to it; *decides further* that the working group shall:

(a)   Make recommendations to the Council on possible measures to promote the protection of children affected by armed conflict, including through recommendations on appropriate mandates for peacekeeping missions and recommendations with respect to the parties to the conflict;

(b)   Address requests, as appropriate, to other bodies within the United Nations system for action to support implementation of this resolution in accordance with their respective mandates;

9.   *Recalls* paragraph 5 (c) of its resolution 1539 (2004), and reaffirms its intention to consider imposing, through country-specific resolutions, targeted and

S/RES/1612 (2005)

graduated measures, such as, inter alia, a ban on the export and supply of small arms and light weapons and of other military equipment and on military assistance, against parties to situations of armed conflict which are on the Security Council's agenda and are in violation of applicable international law relating to the rights and protection of children in armed conflict;

10. *Stresses* the responsibility of United Nations peacekeeping missions and United Nations country teams, consistent with their respective mandates, to ensure effective follow-up to Security Council resolutions, ensure a coordinated response to CAAC concerns and to monitor and report to the Secretary-General;

11. *Welcomes* the efforts undertaken by United Nations peacekeeping operations to implement the Secretary-General's zero-tolerance policy on sexual exploitation and abuse and to ensure full compliance of their personnel with the United Nations code of conduct, requests the Secretary-General to continue to take all necessary action in this regard and to keep the Security Council informed, and urges troop-contributing countries to take appropriate preventive action including predeployment awareness training, and to take disciplinary action and other action to ensure full accountability in cases of misconduct involving their personnel;

12. *Decides* to continue the inclusion of specific provisions for the protection of children in the mandates of United Nations peacekeeping operations, including the deployment, on a case-by-case basis, of child-protection advisers (CPAs), and requests the Secretary-General to ensure that the need for and the number and roles of CPAs are systematically assessed during the preparation of each United Nations peacekeeping operation; welcomes the comprehensive assessment undertaken on the role and activities of CPAs with a view to drawing lessons learned and best practices;

13. *Welcomes* recent initiatives by regional and subregional organizations and arrangements for the protection of children affected by armed conflict, and encourages continued mainstreaming of child protection into their advocacy, policies and programmes; development of peer review and monitoring and reporting mechanisms; establishment, within their secretariats, of child-protection mechanisms; inclusion of child-protection staff and training in their peace and field operations; sub- and interregional initiatives to end activities harmful to children in times of conflict, in particular cross-border recruitment and abduction of children, illicit movement of small arms, and illicit trade in natural resources through the development and implementation of guidelines on children and armed conflict;

14. *Calls upon* all parties concerned to ensure that the protection, rights and well-being of children affected by armed conflict are specifically integrated into all peace processes, peace agreements and post-conflict recovery and reconstruction planning and programmes;

15. *Calls upon* all parties concerned to abide by the international obligations applicable to them relating to the protection of children affected by armed conflict as well as the concrete commitments they have made to the Special Representative of the Secretary-General for Children and Armed Conflict, to UNICEF and other United Nations agencies and to cooperate fully with the United Nations peacekeeping missions and United Nations country teams, where appropriate, in the context of the cooperation framework between the United Nations and the concerned Government, in the follow-up and implementation of these commitments;

4

S/RES/1612 (2005)

16. *Urges* Member States, United Nations entities, regional and subregional organizations and other parties concerned, to take appropriate measures to control illicit subregional and cross-border activities harmful to children, including illicit exploitation of natural resources, illicit trade in small arms, abduction of children and their use and recruitment as soldiers as well as other violations and abuses committed against children in situations of armed conflict in violation of applicable international law;

17. *Urges* all parties concerned, including Member States, United Nations entities and financial institutions, to support the development and strengthening of the capacities of national institutions and local civil society networks for advocacy, protection and rehabilitation of children affected by armed conflict to ensure the sustainability of local child-protection initiatives;

18. *Requests* that the Secretary-General direct all relevant United Nations entities to take specific measures, within existing resources, to ensure systematic mainstreaming of CAAC issues within their respective institutions, including by ensuring allocation of adequate financial and human resources towards protection of war-affected children within all relevant offices and departments and on the ground as well as to strengthen, within their respective mandates, their cooperation and coordination when addressing the protection of children in armed conflict;

19. *Reiterates* its request to the Secretary-General to ensure that, in all his reports on country-specific situations, the protection of children is included as a specific aspect of the report, and expresses its intention to give its full attention to the information provided therein when dealing with those situations on its agenda;

20. *Requests* the Secretary-General to submit a report by November 2006 on the implementation of this resolution and resolutions 1379 (2001), 1460 (2003), and 1539 (2004) which would include, inter alia:

(a) Information on compliance by parties in ending the recruitment or use of children in armed conflict in violation of applicable international law and other violations being committed against children affected by armed conflict;

(b) Information on progress made in the implementation of the monitoring and reporting mechanism mentioned in paragraph 3;

(c) Information on progress made in the development and implementation of the action plans referred to in paragraph 7 of the present resolution;

(d) Information on the assessment of the role and activities of CPAs;

21. *Decides* to remain actively seized of this matter.

5

DOCUMENT 3b

United Nations

S/RES/1882 (2009)

 Security Council

Distr.: General
4 August 2009

Resolution 1882 (2009)

Adopted by the Security Council at its 6176th meeting, on 4 August 2009

The Security Council,

Reaffirming its resolutions 1261 (1999) of 25 August 1999, 1314 (2000) of 11 August 2000, 1379 (2001) of 20 November 2001, 1460 (2003) of 30 January 2003, 1539 (2004) of 22 April 2004, and 1612 (2005) of 26 July 2005, and the Statements of its President on 24 July 2006 (S/PRST/2006/33), 28 November 2006 (S/PRST/2006/48), 12 February 2008 (S/PRST/2008/6), 17 July 2008 (S/PRST/2008/28) and 29 April 2009 (S/PRST/2009/9), which contribute to a comprehensive framework for addressing the protection of children affected by armed conflict,

Acknowledging that the implementation of its resolution 1612 (2005) has generated progress, resulting in the release and reintegration of children into their families and communities and in a more systematic dialogue between the United Nations country-level task forces and parties to the armed conflict on the implementation of time-bound action plans, *while remaining deeply concerned* over the lack of progress on the ground in some situations of concern, where parties to conflict continue to violate with impunity the relevant provisions of applicable international law relating to the rights and protection of children in armed conflict,

Stressing the primary role of national Governments in providing protection and relief to all children affected by armed conflicts,

Reiterating that all actions undertaken by United Nations entities within the framework of the monitoring and reporting mechanism must be designed to support and supplement, as appropriate, the protection and rehabilitation roles of national Governments,

Recalling the responsibilities of States to end impunity and to prosecute those responsible for genocide, crimes against humanity, war crimes and other egregious crimes perpetrated against children,

Welcoming the fact that several individuals who are alleged to have committed crimes against children in situations of armed conflict have been brought to justice by national justice systems and international justice mechanisms and mixed criminal courts and tribunals,

Convinced that the protection of children in armed conflict should be an important aspect of any comprehensive strategy to resolve conflict,

Calling on all parties to armed conflicts to comply strictly with the obligations applicable to them under international law for the protection of children in armed conflict, including those contained in the Convention on the Rights of the Child and its Optional Protocol on the involvement of Children in Armed Conflict, as well as the Geneva Conventions of 12th August 1949 and their Additional Protocols of 1977,

Reiterating its primary responsibility for the maintenance of international peace and security and, in this connection, its commitment to address the widespread impact of armed conflict on children,

Stressing its determination to ensure respect for its resolutions and other international obligations and applicable norms on the protection of children affected by armed conflict,

Having considered the report of the Secretary-General of 26 March 2009 (S/2009/158) and *stressing* that the present resolution does not seek to make any legal determination as to whether situations which are referred to in the Secretary-General's report are or are not armed conflicts within the context of the Geneva Conventions and the Additional Protocols thereto, nor does it prejudge the legal status of the non-State parties involved in these situations,

Deeply concerned that children continue to account for a considerable number of casualties resulting from killing and maiming in armed conflicts including as a result of deliberate targeting, indiscriminate and excessive use of force, indiscriminate use of landmines, cluster munitions and other weapons and use of children as human shields and *equally deeply concerned* about the high incidence and appalling levels of brutality of rape and other forms of sexual violence committed against children, in the context of and associated with armed conflict including the use or commissioning of rape and other forms of sexual violence in some situations as a tactic of war,

1. *Strongly condemns* all violations of applicable international law involving the recruitment and use of children by parties to armed conflict as well as their re-recruitment, killing and maiming, rape and other sexual violence, abductions, attacks against schools or hospitals and denial of humanitarian access by parties to armed conflict and all other violations of international law committed against children in situations of armed conflict;

2. *Reaffirms* that the monitoring and reporting mechanism will continue to be implemented in situations listed in the annexes to the reports of the Secretary-General on children and armed conflict in line with the principles set out in paragraph 2 of its resolution 1612 (2005) and that its establishment and implementation shall not prejudge or imply a decision by the Security Council as to whether or not to include a situation on its agenda;

3. *Recalls* paragraph 16 of its resolution 1379 (2001) and *requests* the Secretary-General also to include in the annexes to his reports on children and armed conflict those parties to armed conflict that engage, in contravention of applicable international law, in patterns of killing and maiming of children and/or rape and other sexual violence against children, in situations of armed conflict,

S/RES/1882 (2009)

bearing in mind all other violations and abuses against children, and notes that the present paragraph will apply to situations in accordance with the conditions set out in paragraph 16 of its resolution 1379 (2001);

4. *Invites* the Secretary-General through his Special Representative for Children and Armed Conflict to exchange appropriate information and maintain interaction from the earliest opportunity with the governments concerned regarding violations and abuses committed against children by parties which may be included in the annexes to his periodic report;

5. *While noting* that some parties to armed conflict have responded to its call upon them to prepare and implement concrete time-bound action plans to halt recruitment and use of children in violation of applicable international law;

(a) *Reiterates* its call on parties to armed conflict listed in the annexes of the Secretary-General's report on children and armed conflict that have not already done so to prepare and implement, without further delay, action plans to halt recruitment and use of children in violation of applicable international law;

(b) *Calls upon* those parties listed in the annexes of the Secretary-General's report on children and armed conflict that commit, in contravention of applicable international law, killing and maiming of children and/or rape and other sexual violence against children, in situations of armed conflict, to prepare concrete time-bound action plans to halt those violations and abuses;

(c) *Further calls* upon all parties listed in the annexes to the Secretary-General's report on children and armed conflict to address all other violations and abuses committed against children and undertake specific commitments and measures in this regard;

(d) *Urges* those parties listed in the annexes of the Secretary-General's report on children and armed conflict to implement the provisions contained in this paragraph in close cooperation with the Special Representative of the Secretary-General for Children and Armed Conflict and the United Nations country-level task forces on monitoring and reporting;

6. In this context, *encourages* Member States to devise ways, in close consultations with the United Nations country-level task force on monitoring and reporting and United Nations country teams, to facilitate the development and implementation of time-bound action plans, and the review and monitoring by the United Nations country-level task force of obligations and commitments relating to the protection of children in armed conflict;

7. *Reiterates* its determination to ensure respect for its resolutions on children and armed conflict, and in this regard:

(a) *Welcomes* the sustained activity and recommendations of its Working Group on Children and Armed Conflict as called for in paragraph 8 of its resolution 1612 (2005), and invites it to continue reporting regularly to the Security Council;

(b) *Requests* enhanced communication between the Working Group and relevant Security Council Sanctions Committees, including through the exchange of pertinent information on violations and abuses committed against children in armed conflict;

(c) *Reaffirms* its intention to take action against persistent perpetrators in line with paragraph 9 of its resolution 1612 (2005);

8. *Stresses* the responsibility of the United Nations country-level task forces on monitoring and reporting and United Nations country teams, consistent with their respective mandates, to ensure effective follow-up to Security Council resolutions on children and armed conflict, to monitor and report progress to the Secretary-General in close cooperation with his Special Representative for Children and Armed Conflict and ensure a coordinated response to issues related to children and armed conflict;

9. *Requests* the Secretary-General to include more systematically in his reports on children and armed conflict specific information regarding the implementation of the Working Group recommendations;

10. *Reiterates* its request to the Secretary-General to ensure that, in all his reports on country-specific situations, the matter of children and armed conflict is included as a specific aspect of the report, and expresses its intention to give its full attention to the information provided therein, including the implementation of relevant Security Council resolutions and of the recommendations of its Working Group on Children and Armed Conflict, when dealing with those situations on its agenda;

11. *Welcomes* the efforts of the Department of Peacekeeping Operations in mainstreaming child protection into peacekeeping missions, in line with that Department's recently adopted Child Protection Policy directive, and encourages the deployment of Child Protection Advisers to peacekeeping operations, as well as into relevant peacebuilding and political missions, and decides to continue the inclusion of specific provisions for the protection of children in such mandates;

12. *Requests* Member States, United Nations peacekeeping, peacebuilding and political missions and United Nations country teams, within their respective mandates and in close cooperation with governments of the concerned countries, to establish appropriate strategies and coordination mechanisms for information exchange and cooperation on child protection concerns, in particular cross-border issues, bearing in mind relevant conclusions by the Security Council Working Group on Children and Armed Conflict and paragraph 2 (d) of its resolution 1612 (2005);

13. *Stresses* that effective disarmament, demobilization and reintegration programmes for children, building on best practices identified by UNICEF and other relevant child protection actors, are crucial for the well-being of all children who, in contravention of applicable international law, have been recruited or used by armed forces and groups, and are a critical factor for durable peace and security, and urges national Governments and donors to ensure that these community-based programmes receive timely, sustained and adequate resources and funding;

14. *Also stresses* the importance of timely, sustained and adequate resources and funding for effective welfare programmes for all children affected by armed conflict;

15. *Calls upon* Member States, United Nations entities, including the Peacebuilding Commission and other parties concerned to ensure that the protection, rights, well-being and empowerment of children affected by armed conflict are integrated into all peace processes and that post-conflict recovery and reconstruction

S/RES/1882 (2009)

planning, programmes and strategies prioritize issues concerning children affected by armed conflict;

16. *Calls upon* concerned Member States to take decisive and immediate action against persistent perpetrators of violations and abuses committed against children in situations of armed conflict, and further calls upon them to bring to justice those responsible for such violations that are prohibited under applicable international law, including with regard to recruitment and use of children, killing and maiming and rape and other sexual violence, through national justice systems, and where applicable, international justice mechanisms and mixed criminal courts and tribunals, with a view to ending impunity for those committing crimes against children;

17. *Requests* the Secretary-General to continue to take the necessary measures including, where applicable, to bring the monitoring and reporting mechanism to its full capacity, to allow for prompt advocacy and effective response to all violations and abuses committed against children and to ensure that information collected and communicated by the mechanism is accurate, objective, reliable and verifiable;

18. *Requests* the Secretary-General to provide administrative and substantive support for the Security Council Working Group on Children and Armed Conflict taking into consideration its current workload and the need to strengthen its capacities and institutional memory;

19. *Requests* the Secretary-General to submit a report by May 2010 on the implementation of its resolutions and presidential statements on children and armed conflict, including the present resolution, which would include, inter alia:

(a) Annexed lists of parties in situations of armed conflict on the agenda of the Security Council or in other situations of concern, in accordance with paragraph 3 of the present resolution;

(b) Information on measures undertaken by parties listed in the annexes to end all violations and abuses committed against children in armed conflict;

(c) Information of progress made in the implementation of the monitoring and reporting mechanism established in its resolution 1612 (2005);

(d) Information on the criteria and procedures used for listing and de-listing parties to armed conflict in the annexes to his periodic reports, bearing in mind the views expressed by all the members of the Working Group during informal briefings to be held before the end of 2009;

20. *Decides* to remain actively seized of this matter.

DOCUMENT 3c

United Nations

S/RES/1998 (2011)

 Security Council

Distr.: General

12 July 2011

Resolution 1998 (2011)

Adopted by the Security Council at its 6581st meeting, on 12 July 2011

The Security Council,

Reaffirming its resolutions 1261 (1999) of 25 August 1999, 1314 (2000) of 11 August 2000, 1379 (2001) of 20 November 2001, 1460 (2003) of 30 January 2003, 1539 (2004) of 22 April 2004, 1612 (2005) of 26 July 2005, and 1882 (2009) of 4 August 2009, and all relevant Statements of its President, which contribute to a comprehensive framework for addressing the protection of children affected by armed conflict;

Reiterating its primary responsibility for the maintenance of international peace and security and, in this connection, its commitment to address the widespread impact of armed conflict on children;

Calling on all parties to armed conflicts to comply strictly with the obligations applicable to them under international law for the protection of children in armed conflict, including those contained in the Convention on the Rights of the Child and its Optional Protocol on the involvement of Children in armed conflict, as well as the Geneva Conventions of 12th August 1949 and their Additional Protocols of 1977;

Acknowledging that the implementation of its resolutions 1612 (2005) and 1882 (2009) has generated progress, resulting in the release and reintegration of children into their families and communities, and in a more systematic dialogue with the United Nations country-level task force and parties to the armed conflict on the implementation on time-bound action plans, while remaining deeply concerned over the lack of progress on the ground in some situations of concern where parties to conflict continue to violate with impunity the relevant provisions of applicable international law relating to the rights and protection of children in armed conflict;

Stressing the primary role of Governments in providing protection and relief to all children affected by armed conflict, and reiterating that all actions undertaken by United Nations entities within the framework of the monitoring and reporting mechanism must be designed to support and supplement, as appropriate, the protection and rehabilitation roles of national Governments;

Convinced that the protection of children in armed conflict should be an important aspect of any comprehensive strategy to resolve conflict;

11-41118 (E)

 Please recycle

S/RES/1998 (2011)

Recalling the responsibilities of States to end impunity and to prosecute those responsible for genocide, crimes against humanity, war crimes and other egregious crimes perpetrated against children;

Stressing the need for alleged perpetrators of crimes against children in situations of armed conflict to be brought to justice through national justice systems and, where applicable, international justice mechanisms and mixed criminal courts and tribunals in order to end impunity;

Noting also relevant provisions of the Rome Statute of the International Criminal Court;

Having considered the report of the Secretary-General of 11 May 2011 (A/65/820-S/2011/250) and stressing that the present resolution does not seek to make any legal determination as to whether situations which are referred to in the Secretary-General's report are or are not armed conflicts within the context of the Geneva Conventions and the Additional Protocols thereto, nor does it prejudge the legal status of the non-State parties involved in these situations;

Expressing deep concern about attacks as well as threats of attacks in contravention of applicable international law against schools and/or hospitals, and protected persons in relation to them as well as the closure of schools and hospitals in situations of armed conflict as a result of attacks and threats of attacks, and calling upon all parties to armed conflict to immediately cease such attacks and threats;

Recalling the provisions of the resolution of the General Assembly on "The right to education in emergency situations" (A/RES/64/290) related to children in armed conflict;

Noting that Article 28 of the Convention on the Rights of the Child recognizes the right of the child to education and sets forth obligations for State parties to the Convention, with a view to progressively achieving this right on the basis of equal opportunity;

1. Strongly *condemns* all violations of applicable international law involving the recruitment and use of children by parties to armed conflict, as well as their re-recruitment, killing and maiming, rape and other sexual violence, abductions, attacks against schools or hospitals and denial of humanitarian access by parties to armed conflict and all other violations of international law committed against children in situations of armed conflict;

2. *Reaffirms* that the monitoring and reporting mechanism will continue to be implemented in situations listed in annex I and annex II ("the annexes") to the reports of the Secretary-General on children and armed conflict, in line with the principles set out in paragraph 2 of its resolution 1612 (2005), and that its establishment and implementation shall not prejudge or imply a decision by the Security Council as to whether or not to include a situation on its agenda;

3. *Recalls* paragraph 16 of its resolution 1379 (2001) and requests the Secretary-General to also include in the annexes to his reports on children and armed conflict those parties to armed conflict that engage, in contravention of applicable international law;

(a) in recurrent attacks on schools and/or hospitals

S/RES/1998 (2011)

(b) in recurrent attacks or threats of attacks against protected persons in relation to schools and/or hospitals in situations of armed conflict, bearing in mind all other violations and abuses committed against children, and notes that the present paragraph will apply to situations in accordance with the conditions set out in paragraph 16 of its resolution 1379 (2001);

4. *Urges* parties to armed conflict to refrain from actions that impede children's access to education and to health services and requests the Secretary-General to continue to monitor and report, inter alia, on the military use of schools and hospitals in contravention of international humanitarian law, as well as on attacks against, and/or kidnapping of teachers and medical personnel;

5. *Invites* the Secretary General, through the Special Representative of the Secretary-General for Children and Armed Conflict, to exchange appropriate information and maintain interaction from the earliest opportunity with the governments concerned regarding violations and abuses committed against children by parties which may be included in the annexes to his periodic report;

6. While *noting* that some parties to armed conflict have responded to its call upon them to prepare and implement concrete time-bound action plans to halt recruitment and use of children in violation of applicable international law;

(a) *Reiterates* its call on parties to armed conflict listed in the annexes of the Secretary-General's report on children and armed conflict that have not already done so to prepare and implement, without further delay, action plans to halt recruitment and use of children and killing and maiming of children, in violation of applicable international law, as well as rape and other sexual violence against children;

(b) *Calls upon* those parties that have existing action plans and have since been listed for multiple violations to prepare and implement separate action plans, as appropriate, to halt the killing and maiming of children, recurrent attacks on schools and/or hospitals, recurrent attacks or threats of attacks against protected persons in relation to schools and/or hospitals, in violation of applicable international law, as well as rape and other sexual violence against children;

(c) *Calls upon* those parties listed in the annexes of the Secretary-General's report on children and armed conflict that commit, in contravention of applicable international law, recurrent attacks on schools and/or hospitals, recurrent attacks or threats of attacks against protected persons in relation to schools and/or hospitals, in situations of armed conflict, to prepare without delay, concrete time-bound action plans to halt those violations and abuses;

(d) Further *calls upon* all parties listed in the annexes of the Secretary-General's report on children and armed conflict, to address all other violations and abuses committed against children and undertake specific commitments and measures in this regard;

(e) *Urges* those parties listed in the annexes of the Secretary-General's report on children and armed conflict to implement the provisions contained in this paragraph in close cooperation with the Special Representative of the Secretary-General for Children and Armed Conflict and the United Nations country-level task forces on monitoring and reporting;

7. In this context, *encourages* Member States to devise ways, in close consultations with the United Nations country-level task force on monitoring and reporting and United Nations country teams, to facilitate the development and implementation of time-bound actions plans, and the review and monitoring by the United Nations country level task force of obligations and commitments relating to the protection of children and armed conflict;

8. *Invites* the United Nations country-level task force on monitoring and reporting to consider including in its reports the relevant information provided by the government concerned and to ensure that information collected and communicated by the mechanism is accurate, objective, reliable, and verifiable;

9. *Reiterates* its determination to ensure respect for its resolutions on children and armed conflict, and in this regard:

(a) *Welcomes* the sustained activity and recommendations of its Working Group on Children and Armed Conflict as called for in paragraph 8 of its resolution 1612 (2005), and invites it to continue reporting regularly to the Security Council;

(b) *Expresses* deep concern that certain parties persist in committing violations and abuses against children and expresses its readiness to adopt targeted and graduated measures against persistent perpetrators, taking into account the relevant provisions of its resolutions 1539 (2004), 1612 (2005) and 1882 (2009);

(c) *Requests* enhanced communication between the Working Group and relevant Security Council Sanctions Committees, including through the exchange of pertinent information on violation and abuses committed against children in armed conflict;

(d) *Encourages* its relevant Sanctions Committees to continue to invite the Special Representative of the Secretary-General for children and armed conflict to brief them on specific information pertaining to her mandate that would be relevant to the work of the committees, and encourages the Sanctions Committees to bear in mind the relevant recommendations of the Secretary-General's report on children and armed conflict and *encourages* the Special Representative of the Secretary-General to share specific information contained in the Secretary-General's reports with relevant Sanctions Committees expert groups;

(e) *Expresses* its intention, when establishing, modifying or renewing the mandate of relevant Sanctions regimes, to consider including provisions pertaining to parties to armed conflict that engage in activities in violation of applicable international law relating to the rights and protection of children in armed conflict;

10. *Encourages* Members States that wish to do so to continue to communicate relevant information to the Security Council on the implementation of its resolutions on children and armed conflict;

11. *Calls upon* Member States concerned to take decisive and immediate action against persistent perpetrators of violations and abuses committed against children in situations of armed conflict, and further calls upon them to bring to justice those responsible for such violations that are prohibited under applicable international law, including with regard to recruitment and use of children, killing and maiming, rape and other sexual violence, attacks on schools and/or hospitals, attacks or threats of attacks against protected persons in relation to schools and/or hospitals through national justice systems, and where applicable, international

S/RES/1998 (2011)

justice mechanisms and mixed criminal courts and tribunals, with a view to ending impunity for those committing crimes against children;

12. *Stresses* the responsibility of the United Nations country-level task forces on monitoring and reporting and United Nations country teams, consistent with their respective mandates, to ensure effective follow-up to Security Council resolutions on children and armed conflict, to monitor and report progress to the Secretary-General in close cooperation with his Special Representative for Children and Armed Conflict and ensure a coordinated response to issues related to children and armed conflict;

13. *Reiterates* its request to the Secretary-General to ensure that, in all his reports on country-specific situations, the matter of children and armed conflict is included as a specific aspect of the report, and expresses its intention to give its full attention to the information provided therein, including the implementation of relevant Security Council resolutions and of the recommendations of its Working Group on Children and Armed Conflict, when dealing with those situations on its agenda;

14. *Reaffirms* its decision to continue to include specific provisions for the protection of children in the mandates of all relevant United Nations peacekeeping, peacebuilding and political missions, encourages deployment of Child Protection Advisers to such missions and calls upon the Secretary-General to ensure that such advisers are recruited and deployed in line with the Council's relevant country specific resolutions and the Department of Peacekeeping Operations (DPKO) Policy Directive on Mainstreaming the Protection Rights and Wellbeing of Children by Armed Conflict;

15. *Requests* Member States, United Nations peacekeeping, peacebuilding and political missions and United Nations country teams, within their respective mandates and in close cooperation with the Governments of the countries concerned, to establish appropriate strategies and coordination mechanisms for information exchange and cooperation on child protection concerns, in particular on cross-border issues, bearing in mind relevant conclusions by the Security Council Working Group on Children and Armed Conflict and paragraph 2 (d) of its resolution 1612 (2005);

16. *Welcoming* the progress achieved by the Country Task Forces on Monitoring and Reporting and stressing that a strengthened monitoring and reporting mechanism with adequate capacities is necessary to ensure an adequate follow up on the Secretary General's recommendations and on the conclusions of the Working Group of Children and Armed Conflict, in accordance with its resolutions 1612 (2005) and 1882 (2009);

17. *Requests* the Secretary-General to continue to take the necessary measures including, where applicable, to bring the monitoring and reporting mechanism to its full capacity, to allow for prompt advocacy and effective response to all violations and abuses committed against children and to ensure that information collected and communicated by the mechanism is accurate, objective, reliable and verifiable;

18. *Stresses* that effective disarmament, demobilisation and reintegration programmes for children, building on best practices identified by UNICEF and other relevant child protection actors, including the International Labour Organization, are

crucial for the well-being of all children who, in contravention of applicable international law, have been recruited or used by armed forces and groups, are a critical factor for durable peace and security, and urges national Governments and donors to ensure that these community-based programmes receive timely, sustained and adequate resources and funding;

19. *Calls upon* Member States, United Nations entities, including the Peacebuilding Commission and other parties concerned to ensure that the protection, rights, well-being and empowerment of children affected by armed conflict are integrated into all peace processes and that post-conflict recovery and reconstruction planning, programmes and strategies prioritize issues concerning children affected by armed conflict;

20. *Invites* the Special Representative for Children and Armed Conflict to brief the Security Council on the modalities of the inclusion of parties into the annexes of the periodic report of the Secretary-General on children and armed conflict, enabling an exchange of views;

21. *Directs* its Working Group on Children and Armed Conflict, with the support of the Special Representative for Children and Armed Conflict, to consider, within one year, a broad range of options for increasing pressure on persistent perpetrators of violations and abuses committed against children in situations of armed conflict;

22. *Requests* the Secretary-General to submit a report by June 2012 on the implementation of its resolutions and presidential statements on children and armed conflict, including the present resolution, which would include, inter alia:

(a) Annexed lists of parties in situations of armed conflict on the agenda of the Security Council or in other situations, in accordance with paragraph 19 (a) of resolution 1882 (2009) and paragraph 3 of the present resolution;

(b) Information on measures undertaken by parties listed in the annexes to end all violations and abuses committed against children in situations of armed conflict;

(c) Information on progress made in the implementation of the monitoring and reporting mechanism established in its resolution 1612 (2005);

(d) Information on the criteria and procedures used for listing and de-listing parties to armed conflict in the annexes of his periodic reports, in accordance with paragraph 3 of the present resolution, bearing in mind the views expressed by all the members of the Working Group during informal briefings to be held before the end of 2011;

23. *Decides* to remain actively seized of this matter.

United Nations

 Security Council

S/RES/1973 (2011)

Distr.: General
17 March 2011

Resolution 1973 (2011)

Adopted by the Security Council at its 6498th meeting, on 17 March 2011

The Security Council,

Recalling its resolution 1970 (2011) of 26 February 2011,

Deploring the failure of the Libyan authorities to comply with resolution 1970 (2011),

Expressing grave concern at the deteriorating situation, the escalation of violence, and the heavy civilian casualties,

Reiterating the responsibility of the Libyan authorities to protect the Libyan population and *reaffirming* that parties to armed conflicts bear the primary responsibility to take all feasible steps to ensure the protection of civilians,

Condemning the gross and systematic violation of human rights, including arbitrary detentions, enforced disappearances, torture and summary executions,

Further condemning acts of violence and intimidation committed by the Libyan authorities against journalists, media professionals and associated personnel and *urging* these authorities to comply with their obligations under international humanitarian law as outlined in resolution 1738 (2006),

Considering that the widespread and systematic attacks currently taking place in the Libyan Arab Jamahiriya against the civilian population may amount to crimes against humanity,

Recalling paragraph 26 of resolution 1970 (2011) in which the Council expressed its readiness to consider taking additional appropriate measures, as necessary, to facilitate and support the return of humanitarian agencies and make available humanitarian and related assistance in the Libyan Arab Jamahiriya,

Expressing its determination to ensure the protection of civilians and civilian populated areas and the rapid and unimpeded passage of humanitarian assistance and the safety of humanitarian personnel,

Recalling the condemnation by the League of Arab States, the African Union, and the Secretary General of the Organization of the Islamic Conference of the serious violations of human rights and international humanitarian law that have been and are being committed in the Libyan Arab Jamahiriya,

Taking note of the final communiqué of the Organisation of the Islamic Conference of 8 March 2011, and the communiqué of the Peace and Security Council of the African Union of 10 March 2011 which established an ad hoc High Level Committee on Libya,

Taking note also of the decision of the Council of the League of Arab States of 12 March 2011 to call for the imposition of a no-fly zone on Libyan military aviation, and to establish safe areas in places exposed to shelling as a precautionary measure that allows the protection of the Libyan people and foreign nationals residing in the Libyan Arab Jamahiriya,

Taking note further of the Secretary-General's call on 16 March 2011 for an immediate cease-fire,

Recalling its decision to refer the situation in the Libyan Arab Jamahiriya since 15 February 2011 to the Prosecutor of the International Criminal Court, and *stressing* that those responsible for or complicit in attacks targeting the civilian population, including aerial and naval attacks, must be held to account,

Reiterating its concern at the plight of refugees and foreign workers forced to flee the violence in the Libyan Arab Jamahiriya, *welcoming* the response of neighbouring States, in particular Tunisia and Egypt, to address the needs of those refugees and foreign workers, and *calling on* the international community to support those efforts,

Deploring the continuing use of mercenaries by the Libyan authorities,

Considering that the establishment of a ban on all flights in the airspace of the Libyan Arab Jamahiriya constitutes an important element for the protection of civilians as well as the safety of the delivery of humanitarian assistance and a decisive step for the cessation of hostilities in Libya,

Expressing concern also for the safety of foreign nationals and their rights in the Libyan Arab Jamahiriya,

Welcoming the appointment by the Secretary General of his Special Envoy to Libya, Mr. Abdel-Elah Mohamed Al-Khatib and supporting his efforts to find a sustainable and peaceful solution to the crisis in the Libyan Arab Jamahiriya,

Reaffirming its strong commitment to the sovereignty, independence, territorial integrity and national unity of the Libyan Arab Jamahiriya,

Determining that the situation in the Libyan Arab Jamahiriya continues to constitute a threat to international peace and security,

Acting under Chapter VII of the Charter of the United Nations,

1.   *Demands* the immediate establishment of a cease-fire and a complete end to violence and all attacks against, and abuses of, civilians;

2.   *Stresses* the need to intensify efforts to find a solution to the crisis which responds to the legitimate demands of the Libyan people and *notes* the decisions of the Secretary-General to send his Special Envoy to Libya and of the Peace and Security Council of the African Union to send its ad hoc High Level Committee to Libya with the aim of facilitating dialogue to lead to the political reforms necessary to find a peaceful and sustainable solution;

3.   *Demands* that the Libyan authorities comply with their obligations under international law, including international humanitarian law, human rights and refugee law and take all measures to protect civilians and meet their basic needs, and to ensure the rapid and unimpeded passage of humanitarian assistance;

Protection of civilians

4.   *Authorizes* Member States that have notified the Secretary-General, acting nationally or through regional organizations or arrangements, and acting in cooperation with the Secretary-General, to take all necessary measures, notwithstanding paragraph 9 of resolution 1970 (2011), to protect civilians and civilian populated areas under threat of attack in the Libyan Arab Jamahiriya, including Benghazi, while excluding a foreign occupation force of any form on any part of Libyan territory, and *requests* the Member States concerned to inform the Secretary-General immediately of the measures they take pursuant to the authorization conferred by this paragraph which shall be immediately reported to the Security Council;

5.   *Recognizes* the important role of the League of Arab States in matters relating to the maintenance of international peace and security in the region, and bearing in mind Chapter VIII of the Charter of the United Nations, requests the Member States of the League of Arab States to cooperate with other Member States in the implementation of paragraph 4;

No Fly Zone

6.   *Decides* to establish a ban on all flights in the airspace of the Libyan Arab Jamahiriya in order to help protect civilians;

7.   *Decides further* that the ban imposed by paragraph 6 shall not apply to flights whose sole purpose is humanitarian, such as delivering or facilitating the delivery of assistance, including medical supplies, food, humanitarian workers and related assistance, or evacuating foreign nationals from the Libyan Arab Jamahiriya, nor shall it apply to flights authorised by paragraphs 4 or 8, nor other flights which are deemed necessary by States acting under the authorisation conferred in paragraph 8 to be for the benefit of the Libyan people, and that these flights shall be coordinated with any mechanism established under paragraph 8;

8.   *Authorizes* Member States that have notified the Secretary-General and the Secretary-General of the League of Arab States, acting nationally or through regional organizations or arrangements, to take all necessary measures to enforce compliance with the ban on flights imposed by paragraph 6 above, as necessary, and *requests* the States concerned in cooperation with the League of Arab States to coordinate closely with the Secretary General on the measures they are taking to implement this ban, including by establishing an appropriate mechanism for implementing the provisions of paragraphs 6 and 7 above,

9.   *Calls upon* all Member States, acting nationally or through regional organizations or arrangements, to provide assistance, including any necessary over-flight approvals, for the purposes of implementing paragraphs 4, 6, 7 and 8 above;

10.   *Requests* the Member States concerned to coordinate closely with each other and the Secretary General on the measures they are taking to implement

paragraphs 4, 6, 7 and 8 above, including practical measures for the monitoring and approval of authorised humanitarian or evacuation flights;

11. *Decides* that the Member States concerned shall inform the Secretary-General and the Secretary-General of the League of Arab States immediately of measures taken in exercise of the authority conferred by paragraph 8 above, including to supply a concept of operations;

12. *Requests* the Secretary-General to inform the Council immediately of any actions taken by the Member States concerned in exercise of the authority conferred by paragraph 8 above and to report to the Council within 7 days and every month thereafter on the implementation of this resolution, including information on any violations of the flight ban imposed by paragraph 6 above;

Enforcement of the arms embargo

13. *Decides that* paragraph 11 of resolution 1970 (2011) shall be replaced by the following paragraph : "Calls upon all Member States, in particular States of the region, acting nationally or through regional organisations or arrangements, in order to ensure strict implementation of the arms embargo established by paragraphs 9 and 10 of resolution 1970 (2011), to inspect in their territory, including seaports and airports, and on the high seas, vessels and aircraft bound to or from the Libyan Arab Jamahiriya, if the State concerned has information that provides reasonable grounds to believe that the cargo contains items the supply, sale, transfer or export of which is prohibited by paragraphs 9 or 10 of resolution 1970 (2011) as modified by this resolution, including the provision of armed mercenary personnel, *calls upon* all flag States of such vessels and aircraft to cooperate with such inspections and authorises Member States to use all measures commensurate to the specific circumstances to carry out such inspections";

14. *Requests* Member States which are taking action under paragraph 13 above on the high seas to coordinate closely with each other and the Secretary-General and *further requests* the States concerned to inform the Secretary-General and the Committee established pursuant to paragraph 24 of resolution 1970 (2011) ("the Committee") immediately of measures taken in the exercise of the authority conferred by paragraph 13 above;

15. *Requires* any Member State whether acting nationally or through regional organisations or arrangements, when it undertakes an inspection pursuant to paragraph 13 above, to submit promptly an initial written report to the Committee containing, in particular, explanation of the grounds for the inspection, the results of such inspection, and whether or not cooperation was provided, and, if prohibited items for transfer are found, further requires such Member States to submit to the Committee, at a later stage, a subsequent written report containing relevant details on the inspection, seizure, and disposal, and relevant details of the transfer, including a description of the items, their origin and intended destination, if this information is not in the initial report;

16. *Deplores* the continuing flows of mercenaries into the Libyan Arab Jamahiriya and *calls upon* all Member States to comply strictly with their obligations under paragraph 9 of resolution 1970 (2011) to prevent the provision of armed mercenary personnel to the Libyan Arab Jamahiriya;

Ban on flights

17. *Decides* that all States shall deny permission to any aircraft registered in the Libyan Arab Jamahiriya or owned or operated by Libyan nationals or companies to take off from, land in or overfly their territory unless the particular flight has been approved in advance by the Committee, or in the case of an emergency landing;

18. *Decides that* all States shall deny permission to any aircraft to take off from, land in or overfly their territory, if they have information that provides reasonable grounds to believe that the aircraft contains items the supply, sale, transfer, or export of which is prohibited by paragraphs 9 and 10 of resolution 1970 (2011) as modified by this resolution, including the provision of armed mercenary personnel, except in the case of an emergency landing;

Asset freeze

19. *Decides* that the asset freeze imposed by paragraph 17, 19, 20 and 21 of resolution 1970 (2011) shall apply to all funds, other financial assets and economic resources which are on their territories, which are owned or controlled, directly or indirectly, by the Libyan authorities, as designated by the Committee, or by individuals or entities acting on their behalf or at their direction, or by entities owned or controlled by them, as designated by the Committee, and *decides further* that all States shall ensure that any funds, financial assets or economic resources are prevented from being made available by their nationals or by any individuals or entities within their territories, to or for the benefit of the Libyan authorities, as designated by the Committee, or individuals or entities acting on their behalf or at their direction, or entities owned or controlled by them, as designated by the Committee, and directs the Committee to designate such Libyan authorities, individuals or entities within 30 days of the date of the adoption of this resolution and as appropriate thereafter;

20. *Affirms* its determination to ensure that assets frozen pursuant to paragraph 17 of resolution 1970 (2011) shall, at a later stage, as soon as possible be made available to and for the benefit of the people of the Libyan Arab Jamahiriya;

21. *Decides* that all States shall require their nationals, persons subject to their jurisdiction and firms incorporated in their territory or subject to their jurisdiction to exercise vigilance when doing business with entities incorporated in the Libyan Arab Jamahiriya or subject to its jurisdiction, and any individuals or entities acting on their behalf or at their direction, and entities owned or controlled by them, if the States have information that provides reasonable grounds to believe that such business could contribute to violence and use of force against civilians;

Designations

22. *Decides* that the individuals listed in Annex I shall be subject to the travel restrictions imposed in paragraphs 15 and 16 of resolution 1970 (2011), and *decides* further that the individuals and entities listed in Annex II shall be subject to the asset freeze imposed in paragraphs 17, 19, 20 and 21 of resolution 1970 (2011);

23. *Decides* that the measures specified in paragraphs 15, 16, 17, 19, 20 and 21 of resolution 1970 (2011) shall apply also to individuals and entities determined by the Council or the Committee to have violated the provisions of resolution 1970

(2011), particularly paragraphs 9 and 10 thereof, or to have assisted others in doing so;

Panel of Experts

24. *Requests* the Secretary-General to create for an initial period of one year, in consultation with the Committee, a group of up to eight experts ("Panel of Experts"), under the direction of the Committee to carry out the following tasks:

(a) Assist the Committee in carrying out its mandate as specified in paragraph 24 of resolution 1970 (2011) and this resolution;

(b) Gather, examine and analyse information from States, relevant United Nations bodies, regional organisations and other interested parties regarding the implementation of the measures decided in resolution 1970 (2011) and this resolution, in particular incidents of non-compliance;

(c) Make recommendations on actions the Council, or the Committee or State, may consider to improve implementation of the relevant measures;

(d) Provide to the Council an interim report on its work no later than 90 days after the Panel's appointment, and a final report to the Council no later than 30 days prior to the termination of its mandate with its findings and recommendations;

25. *Urges* all States, relevant United Nations bodies and other interested parties, to cooperate fully with the Committee and the Panel of Experts, in particular by supplying any information at their disposal on the implementation of the measures decided in resolution 1970 (2011) and this resolution, in particular incidents of non-compliance;

26. *Decides* that the mandate of the Committee as set out in paragraph 24 of resolution 1970 (2011) shall also apply to the measures decided in this resolution;

27. *Decides* that all States, including the Libyan Arab Jamahiriya, shall take the necessary measures to ensure that no claim shall lie at the instance of the Libyan authorities, or of any person or body in the Libyan Arab Jamahiriya, or of any person claiming through or for the benefit of any such person or body, in connection with any contract or other transaction where its performance was affected by reason of the measures taken by the Security Council in resolution 1970 (2011), this resolution and related resolutions;

28. *Reaffirms* its intention to keep the actions of the Libyan authorities under continuous review and underlines its readiness to review at any time the measures imposed by this resolution and resolution 1970 (2011), including by strengthening, suspending or lifting those measures, as appropriate, based on compliance by the Libyan authorities with this resolution and resolution 1970 (2011).

29. *Decides* to remain actively seized of the matter.

Libya: UNSCR proposed designations

Number	Name	Justification	Identifiers

Annex I: Travel Ban

1	QUREN SALIH QUREN AL QADHAFI	Libyan Ambassador to Chad. Has left Chad for Sabha. Involved directly in recruiting and coordinating mercenaries for the regime.	
2	Colonel AMID HUSAIN AL KUNI	Governor of Ghat (South Libya). Directly involved in recruiting mercenaries.	

Number	Name	Justification	Identifiers

Annex II: Asset Freeze

1	Dorda, Abu Zayd Umar	Position: Director, External Security Organisation	
2	Jabir, Major General Abu Bakr Yunis	Position: Defence Minister	**Title**: Major General **DOB**: --/--/1952. **POB**: Jalo, Libya
3	Matuq, Matuq Mohammed	Position: Secretary for Utilities	**DOB**: --/--/1956. **POB**: Khoms
4	Qadhafi, Mohammed Muammar	Son of Muammar Qadhafi. Closeness of association with regime	**DOB**: --/--/1970. **POB**: Tripoli, Libya
5	Qadhafi, Saadi	Commander Special Forces. Son of Muammar Qadhafi. Closeness of association with regime. Command of military units involved in repression of demonstrations	**DOB**: 25/05/1973. **POB**: Tripoli, Libya
6	Qadhafi, Saif al-Arab	Son of Muammar Qadhafi. Closeness of association with regime	**DOB**: --/--/1982. **POB**: Tripoli, Libya
7	Al-Senussi, Colonel Abdullah	Position: Director Military Intelligence	**Title**: Colonel **DOB**: --/--/1949. **POB**: Sudan

Entities

1	Central Bank of Libya	Under control of Muammar Qadhafi and his family, and potential source of funding for his regime.	

Number	Name	Justification	Identifiers
2	Libyan Investment Authority	Under control of Muammar Qadhafi and his family, and potential source of funding for his regime.	**a.k.a**: Libyan Arab Foreign Investment Company (LAFICO) **Address**: 1 Fateh Tower Office, No 99 22nd Floor, Borgaida Street, Tripoli, Libya, 1103
3	Libyan Foreign Bank	Under control of Muammar Qadhafi and his family and a potential source of funding for his regime.	
4	Libyan Africa Investment Portfolio	Under control of Muammar Qadhafi and his family, and potential source of funding for his regime.	**Address**: Jamahiriya Street, LAP Building, PO Box 91330, Tripoli, Libya
5	Libyan National Oil Corporation	Under control of Muammar Qadhafi and his family, and potential source of funding for his regime.	**Address**: Bashir Saadwi Street, Tripoli, Tarabulus, Libya

United Nations

S/RES/1970 (2011)*

 Security Council

Distr.: General
26 February 2011

DOCUMENT 4b

Resolution 1970 (2011)

Adopted by the Security Council at its 6491st meeting, on 26 February 2011

The Security Council,

Expressing grave concern at the situation in the Libyan Arab Jamahiriya and condemning the violence and use of force against civilians,

Deploring the gross and systematic violation of human rights, including the repression of peaceful demonstrators, expressing deep concern at the deaths of civilians, and rejecting unequivocally the incitement to hostility and violence against the civilian population made from the highest level of the Libyan government,

Welcoming the condemnation by the Arab League, the African Union, and the Secretary General of the Organization of the Islamic Conference of the serious violations of human rights and international humanitarian law that are being committed in the Libyan Arab Jamahiriya,

Taking note of the letter to the President of the Security Council from the Permanent Representative of the Libyan Arab Jamahiriya dated 26 February 2011,

Welcoming the Human Rights Council resolution A/HRC/RES/S-15/1 of 25 February 2011, including the decision to urgently dispatch an independent international commission of inquiry to investigate all alleged violations of international human rights law in the Libyan Arab Jamahiriya, to establish the facts and circumstances of such violations and of the crimes perpetrated, and where possible identify those responsible,

Considering that the widespread and systematic attacks currently taking place in the Libyan Arab Jamahiriya against the civilian population may amount to crimes against humanity,

Expressing concern at the plight of refugees forced to flee the violence in the Libyan Arab Jamahiriya,

Expressing concern also at the reports of shortages of medical supplies to treat the wounded,

---

* Second reissue for technical reasons (10 March 2011).

Recalling the Libyan authorities' responsibility to protect its population,

Underlining the need to respect the freedoms of peaceful assembly and of expression, including freedom of the media,

Stressing the need to hold to account those responsible for attacks, including by forces under their control, on civilians,

Recalling article 16 of the Rome Statute under which no investigation or prosecution may be commenced or proceeded with by the International Criminal Court for a period of 12 months after a Security Council request to that effect,

Expressing concern for the safety of foreign nationals and their rights in the Libyan Arab Jamahiriya,

Reaffirming its strong commitment to the sovereignty, independence, territorial integrity and national unity of the Libyan Arab Jamahiriya.

Mindful of its primary responsibility for the maintenance of international peace and security under the Charter of the United Nations,

Acting under Chapter VII of the Charter of the United Nations, and taking measures under its Article 41,

1. *Demands* an immediate end to the violence and calls for steps to fulfil the legitimate demands of the population;

2. *Urges* the Libyan authorities to:

(a) Act with the utmost restraint, respect human rights and international humanitarian law, and allow immediate access for international human rights monitors;

(b) Ensure the safety of all foreign nationals and their assets and facilitate the departure of those wishing to leave the country;

(c) Ensure the safe passage of humanitarian and medical supplies, and humanitarian agencies and workers, into the country; and

(d) Immediately lift restrictions on all forms of media;

3. *Requests* all Member States, to the extent possible, to cooperate in the evacuation of those foreign nationals wishing to leave the country;

ICC referral

4. *Decides* to refer the situation in the Libyan Arab Jamahiriya since 15 February 2011 to the Prosecutor of the International Criminal Court;

5. *Decides* that the Libyan authorities shall cooperate fully with and provide any necessary assistance to the Court and the Prosecutor pursuant to this resolution and, while recognizing that States not party to the Rome Statute have no obligation under the Statute, urges all States and concerned regional and other international organizations to cooperate fully with the Court and the Prosecutor;

6. *Decides* that nationals, current or former officials or personnel from a State outside the Libyan Arab Jamahiriya which is not a party to the Rome Statute of the International Criminal Court shall be subject to the exclusive jurisdiction of that State for all alleged acts or omissions arising out of or related to operations in the

Libyan Arab Jamahiriya established or authorized by the Council, unless such exclusive jurisdiction has been expressly waived by the State;

7.   *Invites* the Prosecutor to address the Security Council within two months of the adoption of this resolution and every six months thereafter on actions taken pursuant to this resolution;

8.   *Recognizes* that none of the expenses incurred in connection with the referral, including expenses related to investigations or prosecutions in connection with that referral, shall be borne by the United Nations and that such costs shall be borne by the parties to the Rome Statute and those States that wish to contribute voluntarily;

Arms embargo

9.   *Decides* that all Member States shall immediately take the necessary measures to prevent the direct or indirect supply, sale or transfer to the Libyan Arab Jamahiriya, from or through their territories or by their nationals, or using their flag vessels or aircraft, of arms and related materiel of all types, including weapons and ammunition, military vehicles and equipment, paramilitary equipment, and spare parts for the aforementioned, and technical assistance, training, financial or other assistance, related to military activities or the provision, maintenance or use of any arms and related materiel, including the provision of armed mercenary personnel whether or not originating in their territories, and decides further that this measure shall not apply to:

(a)   Supplies of non-lethal military equipment intended solely for humanitarian or protective use, and related technical assistance or training, as approved in advance by the Committee established pursuant to paragraph 24 below;

(b)   Protective clothing, including flak jackets and military helmets, temporarily exported to the Libyan Arab Jamahiriya by United Nations personnel, representatives of the media and humanitarian and development workers and associated personnel, for their personal use only; or

(c)   Other sales or supply of arms and related materiel, or provision of assistance or personnel, as approved in advance by the Committee;

10.   *Decides* that the Libyan Arab Jamahiriya shall cease the export of all arms and related materiel and that all Member States shall prohibit the procurement of such items from the Libyan Arab Jamahiriya by their nationals, or using their flagged vessels or aircraft, and whether or not originating in the territory of the Libyan Arab Jamahiriya;

11.   *Calls upon* all States, in particular States neighbouring the Libyan Arab Jamahiriya, to inspect, in accordance with their national authorities and legislation and consistent with international law, in particular the law of the sea and relevant international civil aviation agreements, all cargo to and from the Libyan Arab Jamahiriya, in their territory, including seaports and airports, if the State concerned has information that provides reasonable grounds to believe the cargo contains items the supply, sale, transfer, or export of which is prohibited by paragraphs 9 or 10 of this resolution for the purpose of ensuring strict implementation of those provisions;

12.   *Decides* to authorize all Member States to, and that all Member States shall, upon discovery of items prohibited by paragraph 9 or 10 of this resolution,

seize and dispose (such as through destruction, rendering inoperable, storage or transferring to a State other than the originating or destination States for disposal) items the supply, sale, transfer or export of which is prohibited by paragraphs 9 or 10 of this resolution and decides further that all Member States shall cooperate in such efforts;

13. *Requires* any Member State when it undertakes an inspection pursuant to paragraph 11 above, to submit promptly an initial written report to the Committee containing, in particular, explanation of the grounds for the inspections, the results of such inspections, and whether or not cooperation was provided, and, if prohibited items for transfer are found, further requires such Member States to submit to the Committee, at a later stage, a subsequent written report containing relevant details on the inspection, seizure, and disposal, and relevant details of the transfer, including a description of the items, their origin and intended destination, if this information is not in the initial report;

14. *Encourages* Member States to take steps to strongly discourage their nationals from travelling to the Libyan Arab Jamahiriya to participate in activities on behalf of the Libyan authorities that could reasonably contribute to the violation of human rights;

Travel ban

15. *Decides* that all Member States shall take the necessary measures to prevent the entry into or transit through their territories of individuals listed in Annex I of this resolution or designated by the Committee established pursuant to paragraph 24 below, provided that nothing in this paragraph shall oblige a State to refuse its own nationals entry into its territory;

16. *Decides* that the measures imposed by paragraph 15 above shall not apply:

(a) Where the Committee determines on a case-by-case basis that such travel is justified on the grounds of humanitarian need, including religious obligation;

(b) Where entry or transit is necessary for the fulfilment of a judicial process;

(c) Where the Committee determines on a case-by-case basis that an exemption would further the objectives of peace and national reconciliation in the Libyan Arab Jamahiriya and stability in the region; or

(d) Where a State determines on a case-by-case basis that such entry or transit is required to advance peace and stability in the Libyan Arab Jamahiriya and the States subsequently notifies the Committee within forty-eight hours after making such a determination;

Asset freeze

17. *Decides* that all Member States shall freeze without delay all funds, other financial assets and economic resources which are on their territories, which are owned or controlled, directly or indirectly, by the individuals or entities listed in annex II of this resolution or designated by the Committee established pursuant to paragraph 24 below, or by individuals or entities acting on their behalf or at their direction, or by entities owned or controlled by them, and decides further that all

Member States shall ensure that any funds, financial assets or economic resources are prevented from being made available by their nationals or by any individuals or entities within their territories, to or for the benefit of the individuals or entities listed in Annex II of this resolution or individuals designated by the Committee;

18. *Expresses* its intention to ensure that assets frozen pursuant to paragraph 17 shall at a later stage be made available to and for the benefit of the people of the Libyan Arab Jamahiriya;

19. *Decides* that the measures imposed by paragraph 17 above do not apply to funds, other financial assets or economic resources that have been determined by relevant Member States:

(a) To be necessary for basic expenses, including payment for foodstuffs, rent or mortgage, medicines and medical treatment, taxes, insurance premiums, and public utility charges or exclusively for payment of reasonable professional fees and reimbursement of incurred expenses associated with the provision of legal services in accordance with national laws, or fees or service charges, in accordance with national laws, for routine holding or maintenance of frozen funds, other financial assets and economic resources, after notification by the relevant State to the Committee of the intention to authorize, where appropriate, access to such funds, other financial assets or economic resources and in the absence of a negative decision by the Committee within five working days of such notification;

(b) To be necessary for extraordinary expenses, provided that such determination has been notified by the relevant State or Member States to the Committee and has been approved by the Committee; or

(c) To be the subject of a judicial, administrative or arbitral lien or judgment, in which case the funds, other financial assets and economic resources may be used to satisfy that lien or judgment provided that the lien or judgment was entered into prior to the date of the present resolution, is not for the benefit of a person or entity designated pursuant to paragraph 17 above, and has been notified by the relevant State or Member States to the Committee;

20. *Decides* that Member States may permit the addition to the accounts frozen pursuant to the provisions of paragraph 17 above of interests or other earnings due on those accounts or payments due under contracts, agreements or obligations that arose prior to the date on which those accounts became subject to the provisions of this resolution, provided that any such interest, other earnings and payments continue to be subject to these provisions and are frozen;

21. *Decides* that the measures in paragraph 17 above shall not prevent a designated person or entity from making payment due under a contract entered into prior to the listing of such a person or entity, provided that the relevant States have determined that the payment is not directly or indirectly received by a person or entity designated pursuant to paragraph 17 above, and after notification by the relevant States to the Committee of the intention to make or receive such payments or to authorize, where appropriate, the unfreezing of funds, other financial assets or economic resources for this purpose, 10 working days prior to such authorization;

Designation criteria

22. *Decides* that the measures contained in paragraphs 15 and 17 shall apply to the individuals and entities designated by the Committee, pursuant to paragraph 24 (b) and (c), respectively;

(a) Involved in or complicit in ordering, controlling, or otherwise directing, the commission of serious human rights abuses against persons in the Libyan Arab Jamahiriya, including by being involved in or complicit in planning, commanding, ordering or conducting attacks, in violation of international law, including aerial bombardments, on civilian populations and facilities; or

(b) Acting for or on behalf of or at the direction of individuals or entities identified in subparagraph (a).

23. *Strongly encourages* Member States to submit to the Committee names of individuals who meet the criteria set out in paragraph 22 above;

New Sanctions Committee

24. *Decides* to establish, in accordance with rule 28 of its provisional rules of procedure, a Committee of the Security Council consisting of all the members of the Council (herein "the Committee"), to undertake to following tasks:

(a) To monitor implementation of the measures imposed in paragraphs 9, 10, 15, and 17;

(b) To designate those individuals subject to the measures imposed by paragraphs 15 and to consider requests for exemptions in accordance with paragraph 16 above;

(c) To designate those individuals subject to the measures imposed by paragraph 17 above and to consider requests for exemptions in accordance with paragraphs 19 and 20 above;

(d) To establish such guidelines as may be necessary to facilitate the implementation of the measures imposed above;

(e) To report within thirty days to the Security Council on its work for the first report and thereafter to report as deemed necessary by the Committee;

(f) To encourage a dialogue between the Committee and interested Member States, in particular those in the region, including by inviting representatives of such States to meet with the Committee to discuss implementation of the measures;

(g) To seek from all States whatever information it may consider useful regarding the actions taken by them to implement effectively the measures imposed above;

(h) To examine and take appropriate action on information regarding alleged violations or non-compliance with the measures contained in this resolution;

25. *Calls upon* all Member States to report to the Committee within 120 days of the adoption of this resolution on the steps they have taken with a view to implementing effectively paragraphs 9, 10, 15 and 17 above;

Humanitarian assistance

26. *Calls upon* all Member States, working together and acting in cooperation with the Secretary General, to facilitate and support the return of humanitarian agencies and make available humanitarian and related assistance in the Libyan Arab Jamahiriya, and requests the States concerned to keep the Security Council regularly informed on the progress of actions undertaken pursuant to this paragraph, and expresses its readiness to consider taking additional appropriate measures, as necessary, to achieve this;

Commitment to review

27. *Affirms* that it shall keep the Libyan authorities' actions under continuous review and that it shall be prepared to review the appropriateness of the measures contained in this resolution, including the strengthening, modification, suspension or lifting of the measures, as may be needed at any time in light of the Libyan authorities' compliance with relevant provisions of this resolution;

28. *Decides* to remain actively seized of the matter.

Annex I

Travel ban

1. Al-Baghdadi, Dr Abdulqader Mohammed

   Passport number: B010574. Date of birth: 01/07/1950.

   Head of the Liaison Office of the Revolutionary Committees. Revolutionary Committees involved in violence against demonstrators.

2. Dibri, Abdulqader Yusef

   Date of birth: 1946. Place of birth: Houn, Libya.

   Head of Muammar Qadhafi's personal security. Responsibility for regime security. History of directing violence against dissidents.

3. Dorda, Abu Zayd Umar

   Director, External Security Organisation. Regime loyalist. Head of external intelligence agency.

4. Jabir, Major General Abu Bakr Yunis

   Date of birth: 1952. Place of birth: Jalo, Libya.

   Defence Minister. Overall responsibility for actions of armed forces.

5. Matuq, Matuq Mohammed

   Date of birth: 1956. Place of birth: Khoms.

   Secretary for Utilities. Senior member of regime. Involvement with Revolutionary Committees. Past history of involvement in suppression of dissent and violence.

6. Qadhaf Ai-dam, Sayyid Mohammed

   Date of birth: 1948. Place of birth: Sirte, Libya.

   Cousin of Muammar Qadhafi. In the 1980s, Sayyid was involved in the dissident assassination campaign and allegedly responsible for several deaths in Europe. He is also thought to have been involved in arms procurement.

7. Qadhafi, Aisha Muammar

   Date of birth: 1978. Place of birth: Tripoli, Libya.

   Daughter of Muammar Qadhafi. Closeness of association with regime.

8. Qadhafi, Hannibal Muammar

   Passport number: B/002210. Date of birth: 20/09/1975. Place of birth: Tripoli, Libya. Son of Muammar Qadhafi. Closeness of association with regime.

9. Qadhafi, Khamis Muammar

   Date of birth: 1978. Place of birth: Tripoli, Libya.

   Son of Muammar Qadhafi. Closeness of association with regime. Command of military units involved in repression of demonstrations.

10. Qadhafi, Mohammed Muammar

    Date of birth: 1970. Place of birth: Tripoli, Libya.

    Son of Muammar Qadhafi. Closeness of association with regime.

11. Qadhafi, Muammar Mohammed Abu Minyar

    Date of birth: 1942. Place of birth: Sirte, Libya.

    Leader of the Revolution, Supreme Commander of Armed Forces.
    Responsibility for ordering repression of demonstrations, human rights abuses.

12. Qadhafi, Mutassim

    Date of birth: 1976. Place of birth: Tripoli, Libya.

    National Security Adviser. Son of Muammar Qadhafi. Closeness of association
    with regime.

13. Qadhafi, Saadi

    Passport number: 014797. Date of birth: 25/05/1973. Place of birth: Tripoli,
    Libya.

    Commander Special Forces. Son of Muammar Qadhafi. Closeness of
    association with regime. Command of military units involved in repression of
    demonstrations.

14. Qadhafi, Saif al-Arab

    Date of birth: 1982. Place of birth: Tripoli, Libya.

    Son of Muammar Qadhafi. Closeness of association with regime.

15. Qadhafi, Saif al-Islam

    Passport number: B014995. Date of birth: 25/06/1972. Place of birth: Tripoli,
    Libya.

    Director, Qadhafi Foundation. Son of Muammar Qadhafi. Closeness of
    association with regime. Inflammatory public statements encouraging violence
    against demonstrators.

16. Al-Senussi, Colonel Abdullah

    Date of birth: 1949. Place of birth: Sudan.

    Director Military Intelligence. Military Intelligence involvement in
    suppression of demonstrations. Past history includes suspicion of involvement
    in Abu Selim prison massacre. Convicted in absentia for bombing of UTA
    flight. Brother-in-law of Muammar Qadhafi.

Annex II

Asset freeze

1. Qadhafi, Aisha Muammar

    Date of birth: 1978. Place of birth: Tripoli, Libya.

    Daughter of Muammar Qadhafi. Closeness of association with regime.

2. Qadhafi, Hannibal Muammar

    Passport number: B/002210. Date of birth: 20/09/1975. Place of birth: Tripoli, Libya. Son of Muammar Qadhafi. Closeness of association with regime.

3. Qadhafi, Khamis Muammar

    Date of birth: 1978. Place of birth: Tripoli, Libya.

    Son of Muammar Qadhafi. Closeness of association with regime. Command of military units involved in repression of demonstrations.

4. Qadhafi, Muammar Mohammed Abu Minyar

    Date of birth: 1942. Place of birth: Sirte, Libya.

    Leader of the Revolution, Supreme Commander of Armed Forces.
    Responsibility for ordering repression of demonstrations, human rights abuses.

5. Qadhafi, Mutassim

    Date of birth: 1976. Place of birth: Tripoli, Libya.

    National Security Adviser. Son of Muammar Qadhafi. Closeness of association with regime.

6. Qadhafi, Saif al-Islam

    Passport number: B014995. Date of birth: 25/06/1972. Place of birth: Tripoli, Libya.

    Director, Qadhafi Foundation. Son of Muammar Qadhafi. Closeness of association with regime. Inflammatory public statements encouraging violence against demonstrators.

General Assembly

Distr.: General
23 February 2012

Sixty-sixth session
Agenda item 69 (*c*)

Resolution adopted by the General Assembly

[*on the report of the Third Committee (A/66/462/Add.3)*]

66/176. Situation of human rights in the Syrian Arab Republic

The General Assembly,

Guided by the Charter of the United Nations,

Reaffirming the purposes and principles of the Charter, the Universal Declaration of Human Rights[1] and relevant international human rights treaties, including the International Covenants on Human Rights,[2]

Recalling Human Rights Council resolution S-16/1 of 29 April 2011,[3] and recalling also Human Rights Council resolution S-17/1 of 23 August 2011,[3] which established an independent international commission of inquiry to investigate all alleged violations of international human rights law since March 2011 in the Syrian Arab Republic, and regretting the lack of cooperation of the Syrian authorities with the commission of inquiry,

Welcoming all efforts made by the League of Arab States to address all aspects of the situation in the Syrian Arab Republic, and the steps undertaken by the League of Arab States to ensure the implementation of its Plan of Action, including those aimed at ending all human rights violations and all acts of violence,

Expressing concern about the continuing lack of commitment by the Syrian authorities to fully and immediately implement the Plan of Action of the League of Arab States of 2 November 2011,

Welcoming the decisions of the League of Arab States of 12 and 16 November 2011 on the developments in respect of the situation in the Syrian Arab Republic,

Expressing deep concern about the ongoing human rights violations and use of violence by the Syrian authorities against their population,

---

[1] Resolution 217 A (III).

[2] Resolution 2200 A (XXI), annex

[3] See *Official Records of the General Assembly, Sixty-sixth Session, Supplement No. 53* (A/66/53), chap. I.

Reaffirming that all States Members of the United Nations should refrain in their international relations from the threat or use of force against the territorial integrity or political independence of any State, or in any other manner inconsistent with the purposes of the United Nations,

1. *Strongly condemns* the continued grave and systematic human rights violations by the Syrian authorities, such as arbitrary executions, excessive use of force and the persecution and killing of protesters and human rights defenders, arbitrary detention, enforced disappearances, torture and ill-treatment of detainees, including children;

2. *Calls upon* the Syrian authorities to immediately put an end to all human rights violations, to protect their population and to fully comply with their obligations under international human rights law, and calls for an immediate end to all violence in the Syrian Arab Republic;

3. *Also calls upon* the Syrian authorities to implement the Plan of Action of the League of Arab States in its entirety without further delay;

4. *Invites* the Secretary-General, in accordance with his functions, to provide support, if requested, to the League of Arab States observer mission in the Syrian Arab Republic, consistent with the decisions of the League of Arab States of 12 and 16 November 2011;

5. *Calls upon* the Syrian authorities to comply with Human Rights Council resolutions S-16/1[3] and S-17/1,[3] including by cooperating fully and effectively with the independent international commission of inquiry.

89th plenary meeting
19 December 2011

United Nations

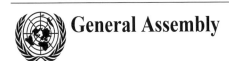
General Assembly

A/HRC/20/37

Distr.: General
22 June 2012

Original: English

Human Rights Council
Twentieth session
Agenda items 2 and 4
Annual report of the United Nations High Commissioner
for Human Rights and reports of the Office of the
High Commissioner and the Secretary-General

Human rights situations that require the Council's attention

Situation of human rights in the Syrian Arab Republic: implementation of Human Rights Council resolution 19/22[*]

Report of the Secretary-General

Summary

   The present report reflects the status of implementation of Human Rights Council resolution 19/22 of 23 March 2012. It contains information on the recent developments on the ground up until 11 May 2012, a summary of the information submitted by the Government of the Syrian Arab Republic in several notes verbales addressed to the Office of the United Nations High Commissioner for Human Rights during the reporting period, as well as information on measures and actions taken by relevant international stakeholders.

   Although a ceasefire brokered by the United Nations was announced on 12 April 2012, its implementation remained partial and fragile during the reporting period. Despite some improvements on the ground, violence and killings, including during armed clashes, through shelling and the use of explosive devices, continued throughout the Syrian Arab Republic, and the civilian population remained significantly insecure. There were credible reports of ongoing serious human rights violations.

---

[*] Late submission.

Contents

I. Introduction

1.   In its resolution 19/22, the Human Rights Council condemned in the strongest terms the sharply escalating widespread, systematic and gross violations of human rights and fundamental freedoms perpetrated by the authorities of the Syrian Arab Republic. In the resolution, the Council requested actions from the Government of the Syrian Arab Republic to put an immediate end to all violence and all human rights violations. It also requested that I present a report on the implementation of resolution 19/22 at its twentieth and twenty-first sessions. The present report, which is submitted to the Council pursuant to that request, summarizes the recent developments on the ground up until 11 May 2012 and information submitted by the Government of the Syrian Arab Republic by means of notes verbales addressed to the Office of the United Nations High Commissioner for Human Rights (OHCHR) between 2 April and 7 May 2012. The report also contains information on actions taken by relevant international stakeholders, including the Security Council, the Joint Special Envoy of the United Nations and the League of Arab States, and other United Nations entities.

II. Recent developments

2.   On 16 February 2012, the General Assembly adopted resolution 66/253, in which it endorsed the Plan of Action of the League of Arab States of 2 November 2011 and the League's decisions of 22 January and 12 February 2012. In that context, the Assembly requested me and other United Nations entities to support the efforts of the League of Arab States, including through the appointment of a special envoy to promote a peaceful solution, and through technical and material assistance. On 23 February 2012, in response to resolution 66/253, the Secretary-General of the League of Arab States and I announced the appointment of Kofi Annan as our Joint Special Envoy to help to resolve the Syrian crisis. The Security Council lent its support to the appointment in the statements made by the President of the Council on 21 March (S/PRST/2012/6) and 5 April 2012 (S/PRST/2012/10), and in resolutions 2042 and 2043 (2012) of 14 and 21 April 2012, respectively.

3.   The mandate of the Joint Special Envoy is to use his good offices to bring an end to all violence and human rights violations and to promote a peaceful solution to the Syrian crisis, working with all relevant actors of the United Nations and the League of Arab States through consultations on the political, socio-economic, security and humanitarian situation in the Syrian Arab Republic. Since his appointment, the Envoy has engaged with the Government of the Syrian Arab Republic and the Syrian opposition, as well as with regional and international stakeholders, with a view to finding a peaceful solution to the crisis.

4.   On 25 March 2012, the Government of the Syrian Arab Republic pledged to implement the six-point plan proposed by the Joint Special Envoy, which aimed at bringing an immediate end to all forms of violence by all parties, to protect civilians, obtain humanitarian access and facilitate an inclusive Syrian-led political process to address the legitimate aspirations and concerns of the Syrian people. In a communication addressed to the Envoy on 1 April 2012, the Government of the Syrian Arab Republic pledged to immediately cease troop movements, end the use of heavy weapons in population centres and begin to pull back military concentrations in and around population centres no later than 10 April 2012. Similar commitments to respect the cessation of violence were sought from anti-Government armed groups by the Envoy. While the ceasefire came into effect on 12 April 2012, it was not fully respected during the reporting period.

5.   In the framework of the six-point plan, the Government of the Syrian Arab Republic also committed itself to intensify the pace and scale of release of arbitrarily detained persons, including especially vulnerable categories of persons and persons involved in peaceful political activities, and to allow access to detention places. The Government also pledged to ensure freedom of movement throughout the country for journalists, and to ensure a non-discriminatory visa policy for them. In addition, the Government undertook to respect freedom of association and the right to peaceful assembly.

6.   It should be recalled that the Security Council, in its resolution 2043 (2012), authorized, for an initial period of 90 days, the deployment of the United Nations Supervision Mission in the Syrian Arab Republic (UNSMIS), comprising an initial deployment of up to 300 unarmed military observers as well as an appropriate civilian component, as required by the Mission to fulfil its mandate. Its mandate is to monitor the cessation of armed violence in all its forms by all parties, and to monitor and support the full implementation of the above-mentioned six-point plan. During the reporting period, a certain reduction in violence was observed in areas where UNSMIS was present.

III.   Information from the Government of the Syrian Arab Republic

7.   In its resolution 19/22, the Human Rights Council requested specific actions from the Government of the Syrian Arab Republic to address the human rights and humanitarian situation, particularly in paragraphs 3, 4, 9, 11, 12, 13, 17 and 18. On 12 April 2012, OHCHR, on my behalf, addressed a note verbale to the Permanent Mission of the Syrian Arab Republic in which it requested information on any steps taken by the Government to implement resolution 19/22. In response, on 1 May 2012, the Permanent Mission addressed a note verbale to OHCHR in which it pointed out that the Government rejected and would continue to reject resolution 19/22, arguing that it went beyond the mandate of the Council, was inconsistent with the Charter of the United Nations and did not reflect the reality on the ground. According to the Government, resolution 19/22 lacked credibility owing to the absence of reference to the grave and systematic human rights violations perpetrated by what it called "terrorist armed groups". The Government provided information on human rights violations that it attributed to "terrorist armed groups", as described below. Information on alleged violations committed by other actors was not provided.

8.   In its note verbale of 1 May 2012, the Government of the Syrian Arab Republic stated that, in accordance with its international obligations and commitments and in line with the State's sovereignty and the choices of the Syrian people, it had cooperated openly and transparently with all United Nations mechanisms, eschewing politicization and prejudgements based on "fabricated evidence" to condemn the Syrian Arab Republic. According to the Government, States seeking the "destruction" of the Syrian Arab Republic had ignored its cooperation with the United Nations. In this context, the Government considered that the information it had transmitted to OHCHR and the United Nations prior to the adoption of Human Rights Council resolution 19/22 had not been reflected in the resolution. The Government considered resolution 19/22 to be part of a campaign against the Syrian Arab Republic and, in its view, it merely reflected accounts from media outlets funded by States seeking the "destruction" of the Syrian Arab Republic.

9.   In its note verbale of 1 May 2012, the Government of the Syrian Arab Republic stated that resolution 19/22 sent a clear message to "terrorist armed groups" and their sponsors that they were allowed "to spill Syrian blood and to continue their operations". In the view of the Government, this negative and dangerous message had resulted in an escalation of terrorist operations in Damascus and the second largest city in the Syrian Arab Republic, Aleppo, in addition to other cities where, the Government stated, residents did

not obey the instructions of "terrorist armed groups". The Government also stated that intentional, widespread and gross violations that amounted to crimes against humanity committed by "terrorist armed groups" had intensified in Syrian cities. The Government deplored the fact that resolution 19/22 did not address the issue of countries that fund, arm and train "terrorist armed groups", contrary to the Charter. In this context, the Government noted that neighbouring countries were being used as a base for "terrorist armed groups", and reported that the relevant Syrian authorities had been thwarting infiltration attempts of "terrorist armed groups" into the Syrian Arab Republic on a daily basis.

10.   From 2 April to 7 May 2012, the Permanent Mission of the Syrian Arab Republic addressed several notes verbales to OHCHR, mainly on casualty figures within the national security and armed forces, as well as among civilians, reportedly as a result of acts committed by "terrorist armed groups". The Government also provided information on kidnappings and armed attacks on, and the sabotage and looting of, private and public property. The present report includes the most recent figures submitted by the Government. According to information sent by the Government, "terrorist armed groups" had committed the following violations:

(a)   **Killings**. According to the Government, more than 6,144 Syrian citizens, including civilians and members of national security forces and armed forces, had been killed. The Government also reported that 478 members of the national security and 2,091 members of the armed forces had been killed by "terrorist armed groups" between 23 March 2011 and 20 March 2012. It added that more than 100 Syrian scientists, intellectuals and athletes had been killed for refusing to join the "terrorist armed groups". The Government reported that different methods had been used by the "terrorist armed groups" to kill people from different groups: those who did not support the calls of the "terrorist armed groups" and belonged to given groups in society were shot and killed, while the "slaughter technique" was reserved for other population groups. The Government reported that dead bodies had been put on display, killings had been filmed by perpetrators and footage disseminated over the Internet;

(b)   **Kidnappings and abductions**. According to the Government, more than 1,500 citizens had been kidnapped or abducted, of whom the fate of 1,000 remained unknown. The majority of those kidnapped or abducted had been reportedly subjected to torture and detention. The Government reported that it had begun to find bodies of victims in wells, rivers and sanitation networks;

(c)   **Torture**. The Government stated that "terrorist armed groups" had kidnapped and tortured citizens in detention facilities under their control, a number of which were reportedly in areas "freed from the grip of terrorists". The Government added that instruments utilized for torture were found at these locations. According to the Government, people were killed if the requested ransom was not paid, or were executed without any request for ransom;

(d)   **Violations of freedoms of religion and belief**. The Government reported that "terrorist armed groups" had targeted and tried to expel particular communities from areas in which they have lived for generations by threatening, intimidating or killing those who refused to give up their private property. The Government also pointed out that terrorist armed groups had targeted mosques, churches and monasteries;

(e)   **Violations of freedom of opinion and expression**. The Government stated that "terrorist armed groups" had threatened, intimidated and killed those who disagreed with them or ignored their calls to participate in strikes or protests, or whom they suspected of supporting the Government, as well as journalists who, according to the Government, wrote the truth and were targeted and killed;

(f)   **Violence against women**. According to the Government, there were many cases where citizens had been held up on highways, with women raped before being shot. The Government reported on other cases where women had been kidnapped and forced to become sex slaves by "terrorist armed groups", reportedly in detention facilities under their control;

(g)   **Violence against children**. According to the Government, "terrorist armed groups" had lured several children into carrying out terrorist operations for money, and reportedly kidnapped and killed children (as in the case of a boy named "Adnan Amran", less than 9 years old, whose body was found on the rooftop of a building in Al-Ladhiqiyah). According to the Government, children had been killed to put pressure on their parents (as in the case of the son of the Grand Mufti of the Syrian Arab Republic, Saria Hassoun);

(h)   **Violations of the right to food**. According to the Government, "terrorist armed groups" had destroyed sources of staple food, olive groves and water resources relied on by farmers. In some areas, farmers had reportedly been prevented from reaching their farms and gathering their harvest;

(i)   **Violations of the right to health**. According to the Government, "terrorist armed groups" had kidnapped and killed doctors, raped nurses, shelled hospitals and stolen and destroyed medical supplies. The Government underlined the psychological suffering of Syrian citizens as a result of these acts;

(j)   **Violations of the right to education**. The Government stated that "terrorist armed groups" had deprived citizens of their right to education by preventing children and students from going to school and university in some governorates and by using schools as a base for their terrorist operations;

(k)   **Incidents of theft and sabotage**. The Government reported that there had been 1,292 incidents of looting, 2,256 cases of theft of vehicles and 2,618 cases of sabotage of private and public property from the beginning of the events to 15 March 2012. According to the Government, the financial losses of the electricity sector caused by the attacks of "terrorist armed groups" exceeded 334 million Syrian pounds during the period from 1 to 17 April 2012;

(l)   **Transportation sector**. The Government reported that "terrorist armed groups" had killed eight employees of the Ministry of Transport, and had kidnapped another 14. The fate of eight of them remained unknown. The Government added that "terrorist armed groups" deliberately targeted buses used to transport Ministry employees. The Government also added that "terrorist armed groups" had stolen the identification cards of State employees to perpetrate terrorist operations. According to the Government, damage to the Ministry of Transport up until the end of February 2012 exceeded an estimated 3.8 billion Syrian pounds as a result of attacks by "terrorist armed groups".

12.   In a note verbale dated 7 April 2012, the Government of the Syrian Arab Republic stated that it was continuing its investigations into human rights violations and would hold the perpetrators accountable. It stated that it had received more than 4,800 complaints. The Government reported that a number of commissioned officers with different ranks, including two brigadier generals, non-commissioned officers and elements of the national security and armed forces, were facing trial, and that 74 members of the public forces of order had been punished. The Government stated that it would continue to investigate all alleged human rights violations.

IV. Implementation of Human Rights Council resolution 19/22

13.   In paragraphs 3 and 4 of its resolution 19/22, the Human Rights Council strongly urged the Government of the Syrian Arab Republic to put an immediate end to violence and all human rights violations, and demanded that it meet its responsibility to protect its population. As noted above, the Government, in its note verbale of 1 May 2012, did not provide information in that regard.

14.   Despite the announcement of a ceasefire brokered by the United Nations on 12 April 2012, implementation of the ceasefire remained partial and fragile during the reporting period. Despite some improvements on the ground, the civilian population remained significantly insecure. Violence and killings, including during armed clashes, continued throughout the country. An increase in the use of explosive devices, inflicting loss of life among civilians, was also reported. Credible reports indicated that Government security and armed forces continued, unabated, to commit serious violations of human rights, including by the shelling of civilian areas and the use of lethal force against demonstrators, arbitrary arrests, torture and summary and extrajudicial execution of activists, defectors and opponents. Furthermore, ongoing violations by armed anti-Government forces continued to be reported, including cases of kidnapping and abduction, and the torture and killing of members of the security and armed forces and pro-Government elements.

15.   In paragraph 9 of resolution 19/22, the Human Rights Council urged the Government of the Syrian Arab Republic to ensure timely, safe and unhindered access for all humanitarian actors and to ensure the safe passage of humanitarian and medical supplies into the country. The Government did not provide OHCHR with information on the status of implementation of paragraph 9. In its note verbale of 1 May 2012, however, the Government stated that the Council had failed to address, in this context, the unilateral sanctions imposed on the Syrian Arab Republic or the attacks by "terrorist armed groups", which had resulted in the current livelihood crisis in the country.

16.   On the basis of a Government-led needs assessment mission conducted from 18 to 26 March 2012, the United Nations and the Organization of Islamic Cooperation estimated that, at that time, 1 million people were in need of humanitarian assistance in the Syrian Arab Republic. The scale and scope of humanitarian operations, however, remained insufficient to meet humanitarian needs, and the humanitarian capacity remained limited on the ground. Further to the needs assessment mission, the Syrian authorities and humanitarian actors agreed about the significant humanitarian needs and that civilians in affected areas needed urgent and effectively targeted aid in terms of shelter, food, health, education, livelihood, agriculture, water and sanitation. As at 8 May 2012, however, the modalities of the humanitarian response were still being discussed with the Government of the Syrian Arab Republic. As a result, civilians continued to bear the brunt of the deteriorating humanitarian situation.

17.   In paragraph 10 of resolution 19/22, the Human Rights Council invited all relevant United Nations agencies, in particular the Office of the United Nations High Commissioner for Refugees (UNHCR), to provide Syrian refugees, and the neighbouring countries hosting them, with support. In March 2012, UNHCR launched the Syria Regional Refugee Plan to address the needs for protection and assistance of refugees fleeing from the Syrian Arab Republic into neighbouring countries, namely Iraq, Jordan, Lebanon and Turkey. According to UNHCR, as at 9 May 2012, more than 67,668 refugees fleeing the Syrian Arab Republic were receiving assistance from UNHCR and the national authorities in Iraq (3,391), Jordan (15,344), Lebanon (25,922) and Turkey (23,011). The number of Syrian refugees in Turkey had reportedly decreased slightly in the previous month owing to voluntary repatriations. UNHCR had registered 55,198 persons from the Syrian Arab Republic in neighbouring countries.

18.   In paragraph 11 (*a*) of resolution 19/22, the Human Rights Council demanded that the Syrian authorities respect the demands and aspirations of the Syrian people. I took note of the parliamentarian elections held on 7 May 2012 and of the fact that the opposition boycotted the poll. As noted above, the six-point plan is aimed at facilitating an inclusive Syrian-led political process to address the legitimate aspirations and concerns of the Syrian people once fully implemented.

19.   In paragraph 11 (*b*) of resolution 19/22, the Human Rights Council also demanded that the Syrian authorities put an immediate end to all attacks on journalists and to ensure adequate protection, fully respect freedom of expression and allow independent and international media to operate. The Joint Special Envoy reported that he had been informed by the Government that more than 114 journalists had been given visas, and that international reporting from the Syrian Arab Republic had increased pursuant to the six-point plan.

20.   In paragraph 11 (*c*) of resolution 19/22, the Human Rights Council further demanded that the Syrian authorities take immediate steps to ensure the safety of foreign nationals in the Syrian Arab Republic, including refugees and diplomatic staff, and to ensure the protection of their property. The Government did not provide OHCHR with information on the status of implementation of paragraph 11 (*c*). According to media reports, some foreigners were killed while others were detained.

21.   In paragraph 11 (*d*) of resolution 19/22, the Human Rights Council demanded that the Syrian authorities lift the blockade of Homs, Dar'a and Zabadani and of all other cities under siege. The Government did not provide OHCHR with information on the implementation of paragraph 11 (*d*). Credible sources report that checkpoints controlled by Government forces and by armed anti-Government groups remained, mainly in Homs, Idlib, Dar'a and Hama.

22.   In paragraphs 12 and 13 of resolution 19/22, the Human Rights Council called upon the Government to act in accordance with the Plan of Action of the League of Arab States of 2 November 2011, and its decisions of 22 January and 12 February 2012, including to release all those detained arbitrarily following the recent incidents; to withdraw all military and armed forces from cities and towns; to guarantee the freedom of peaceful assembly; and to allow access for all relevant institutions of the League. Despite the six-point plan and the announcement of the ceasefire, reports of the use of live and lethal fire during protests continued. Furthermore, credible sources reported continued cases of arbitrary detention, including of children. In addition, other credible sources reported that the Government had not withdrawn all heavy weapons from cities.

23.   Paragraphs 14, 15, 16, 17 and 21 of resolution 19/22 concerned the mandate and work of the independent international commission of inquiry on the Syrian Arab Republic, established by the Human Rights Council in its resolution S-17/1 of 23 August 2011. Further to paragraph 14 of resolution 19/22, in which the Council extended the mandate of the commission of inquiry, the commission resumed its work and OHCHR continued to provide it with full secretariat support. The commission is to give an oral update to the Council at its twentieth session, and to present a written update report at its twenty-first session. To date, despite the fact that the Council, in paragraph 17 of resolution 19/22, called upon the Government to cooperate with the commission of inquiry, the commission has not been granted access to the country. On 26 March 2012, further to paragraph 21 of resolution 19/22, the Council transmitted the updated report of the commission of inquiry to me for appropriate action and transmission to all relevant United Nations bodies.

24.   In paragraph 18 of resolution 19/22, the Human Rights Council reiterated its call upon the Government of the Syrian Arab Republic to cooperate with the special procedures of the Council and with OHCHR, including through the establishment of a field presence.

While the Government of the Syrian Arab Republic has interacted with some special procedures, recent requests by mandate holders for visits to the country remain pending or unanswered. For instance, on 19 October 2011, the Government replied positively to a request made by the Special Rapporteur on the rights to freedom of peaceful assembly and of association to visit the Syrian Arab Republic. In its reply to the request, the Government invited the Special Rapporteur to visit at an appropriate time for both sides during the first months of 2012. A letter from the Special Rapporteur suggesting a visit in March 2012 remained, however, unanswered. On 19 April 2012, the Special Rapporteur on the human rights of internally displaced persons addressed a request to visit the Syrian Arab Republic to its Permanent Mission in Geneva.

25.   With reference to an OHCHR field presence in the Syrian Arab Republic, the Government did not address this issue in its note verbale of 1 May 2012. It should be recalled that the Ambassador of the Syrian Arab Republic, during a meeting with representatives of OHCHR on 11 January 2012, pointed out that, at the time, his Government was not yet ready to cooperate with OHCHR.

26.   In paragraph 19 of its resolution 19/22, the Human Rights Council invited me to take the measures necessary to support the efforts of the League of Arab States to achieve a peaceful solution to the situation in the Syrian Arab Republic. As noted above, the General Assembly, in its resolution 66/253, endorsed the Plan of Action of the League of Arab States of 2 November 2011, and the League's decisions of 22 January and 12 February 2012. The mandate of the Joint Special Envoy, which is based on resolution 66/253, reflects therefore all relevant decisions of the League of Arab States. The Envoy has regularly briefed the Assembly and the Security Council on his activities, and continues to provide regular reports thereon, as requested. I have also reported to the Assembly and to the Council on support for the efforts of the League of Arab States to achieve a peaceful solution to the situation in the Syrian Arab Republic consistent with the Charter of the United Nations and the League's decisions. In this context, both the Joint Special Envoy and I have called on all parties to adhere to the cessation of violence in all its forms, to cooperate with UNSMIS and to implement the six-point plan in its entirety with a view to paving the way for an inclusive Syrian-led political process to address the legitimate aspirations and concerns of the Syrian people. As I have noted previously, the efforts of the Envoy and UNSMIS are possibly the only remaining chance to stabilize the situation in the Syrian Arab Republic and to avoid a civil war.

27.   In accordance with paragraph 21 of Human Rights Council resolution 19/22, an update report on the implementation of the resolution is being prepared and will be presented to the Council at its twenty-first session.

United Nations

A/RES/60/1

 General Assembly

Distr.: General
24 October 2005

DOCUMENT 7

Sixtieth session
Agenda items 46 and 120

Resolution adopted by the General Assembly

[*without reference to a Main Committee (A/60/L.1)*]

60/1. 2005 World Summit Outcome

The General Assembly

Adopts the following 2005 World Summit Outcome:

2005 World Summit Outcome

I.   Values and principles

1.   We, Heads of State and Government, have gathered at United Nations Headquarters in New York from 14 to 16 September 2005.

2.   We reaffirm our faith in the United Nations and our commitment to the purposes and principles of the Charter of the United Nations and international law, which are indispensable foundations of a more peaceful, prosperous and just world, and reiterate our determination to foster strict respect for them.

3.   We reaffirm the United Nations Millennium Declaration,[1] which we adopted at the dawn of the twenty-first century. We recognize the valuable role of the major United Nations conferences and summits in the economic, social and related fields, including the Millennium Summit, in mobilizing the international community at the local, national, regional and global levels and in guiding the work of the United Nations.

4.   We reaffirm that our common fundamental values, including freedom, equality, solidarity, tolerance, respect for all human rights, respect for nature and shared responsibility, are essential to international relations.

5.   We are determined to establish a just and lasting peace all over the world in accordance with the purposes and principles of the Charter. We rededicate ourselves to support all efforts to uphold the sovereign equality of all States, respect their territorial integrity and political independence, to refrain in our international relations from the threat or use of force in any manner inconsistent with the purposes and principles of the United Nations, to uphold resolution of disputes by

---

[1] See resolution 55/2.

peaceful means and in conformity with the principles of justice and international law, the right to self-determination of peoples which remain under colonial domination and foreign occupation, non-interference in the internal affairs of States, respect for human rights and fundamental freedoms, respect for the equal rights of all without distinction as to race, sex, language or religion, international cooperation in solving international problems of an economic, social, cultural or humanitarian character and the fulfilment in good faith of the obligations assumed in accordance with the Charter.

6.   We reaffirm the vital importance of an effective multilateral system, in accordance with international law, in order to better address the multifaceted and interconnected challenges and threats confronting our world and to achieve progress in the areas of peace and security, development and human rights, underlining the central role of the United Nations, and commit ourselves to promoting and strengthening the effectiveness of the Organization through the implementation of its decisions and resolutions.

7.   We believe that today, more than ever before, we live in a global and interdependent world. No State can stand wholly alone. We acknowledge that collective security depends on effective cooperation, in accordance with international law, against transnational threats.

8.   We recognize that current developments and circumstances require that we urgently build consensus on major threats and challenges. We commit ourselves to translating that consensus into concrete action, including addressing the root causes of those threats and challenges with resolve and determination.

9.   We acknowledge that peace and security, development and human rights are the pillars of the United Nations system and the foundations for collective security and well-being. We recognize that development, peace and security and human rights are interlinked and mutually reinforcing.

10.   We reaffirm that development is a central goal in itself and that sustainable development in its economic, social and environmental aspects constitutes a key element of the overarching framework of United Nations activities.

11.   We acknowledge that good governance and the rule of law at the national and international levels are essential for sustained economic growth, sustainable development and the eradication of poverty and hunger.

12.   We reaffirm that gender equality and the promotion and protection of the full enjoyment of all human rights and fundamental freedoms for all are essential to advance development and peace and security. We are committed to creating a world fit for future generations, which takes into account the best interests of the child.

13.   We reaffirm the universality, indivisibility, interdependence and interrelatedness of all human rights.

14.   Acknowledging the diversity of the world, we recognize that all cultures and civilizations contribute to the enrichment of humankind. We acknowledge the importance of respect and understanding for religious and cultural diversity throughout the world. In order to promote international peace and security, we commit ourselves to advancing human welfare, freedom and progress everywhere, as well as to encouraging tolerance, respect, dialogue and cooperation among different cultures, civilizations and peoples.

15.   We pledge to enhance the relevance, effectiveness, efficiency, accountability and credibility of the United Nations system. This is our shared responsibility and interest.

16.   We therefore resolve to create a more peaceful, prosperous and democratic world and to undertake concrete measures to continue finding ways to implement the outcome of the Millennium Summit and the other major United Nations conferences and summits so as to provide multilateral solutions to problems in the four following areas:

- Development

- Peace and collective security

- Human rights and the rule of law

- Strengthening of the United Nations

II.   Development

17.   We strongly reiterate our determination to ensure the timely and full realization of the development goals and objectives agreed at the major United Nations conferences and summits, including those agreed at the Millennium Summit that are described as the Millennium Development Goals, which have helped to galvanize efforts towards poverty eradication.

18.   We emphasize the vital role played by the major United Nations conferences and summits in the economic, social and related fields in shaping a broad development vision and in identifying commonly agreed objectives, which have contributed to improving human life in different parts of the world.

19.   We reaffirm our commitment to eradicate poverty and promote sustained economic growth, sustainable development and global prosperity for all. We are encouraged by reductions in poverty in some countries in the recent past and are determined to reinforce and extend this trend to benefit people worldwide. We remain concerned, however, about the slow and uneven progress towards poverty eradication and the realization of other development goals in some regions. We commit ourselves to promoting the development of the productive sectors in developing countries to enable them to participate more effectively in and benefit from the process of globalization. We underline the need for urgent action on all sides, including more ambitious national development strategies and efforts backed by increased international support.

Global partnership for development

20.   We reaffirm our commitment to the global partnership for development set out in the Millennium Declaration,[1] the Monterrey Consensus[2] and the Johannesburg Plan of Implementation.[3]

21.   We further reaffirm our commitment to sound policies, good governance at all levels and the rule of law, and to mobilize domestic resources, attract international

---

[2] Monterrey Consensus of the International Conference on Financing for Development (*Report of the International Conference on Financing for Development, Monterrey, Mexico, 18-22 March 2002* (United Nations publication, Sales No. E.02.II.A.7), chap. I, resolution 1, annex).

[3] Plan of Implementation of the World Summit on Sustainable Development (*Report of the World Summit on Sustainable Development, Johannesburg, South Africa, 26 August-4 September 2002* (United Nations publication, Sales No. E.03.II. A.1 and corrigendum), chap I, resolution 2, annex).

flows, promote international trade as an engine for development and increase international financial and technical cooperation for development, sustainable debt financing and external debt relief and to enhance the coherence and consistency of the international monetary, financial and trading systems.

22. We reaffirm that each country must take primary responsibility for its own development and that the role of national policies and development strategies cannot be overemphasized in the achievement of sustainable development. We also recognize that national efforts should be complemented by supportive global programmes, measures and policies aimed at expanding the development opportunities of developing countries, while taking into account national conditions and ensuring respect for national ownership, strategies and sovereignty. To this end, we resolve:

(a) To adopt, by 2006, and implement comprehensive national development strategies to achieve the internationally agreed development goals and objectives, including the Millennium Development Goals;

(b) To manage public finances effectively to achieve and maintain macroeconomic stability and long-term growth and to make effective and transparent use of public funds and ensure that development assistance is used to build national capacities;

(c) To support efforts by developing countries to adopt and implement national development policies and strategies through increased development assistance, the promotion of international trade as an engine for development, the transfer of technology on mutually agreed terms, increased investment flows and wider and deeper debt relief, and to support developing countries by providing a substantial increase in aid of sufficient quality and arriving in a timely manner to assist them in achieving the internationally agreed development goals, including the Millennium Development Goals;

(d) That the increasing interdependence of national economies in a globalizing world and the emergence of rule-based regimes for international economic relations have meant that the space for national economic policy, that is, the scope for domestic policies, especially in the areas of trade, investment and industrial development, is now often framed by international disciplines, commitments and global market considerations. It is for each Government to evaluate the trade-off between the benefits of accepting international rules and commitments and the constraints posed by the loss of policy space. It is particularly important for developing countries, bearing in mind development goals and objectives, that all countries take into account the need for appropriate balance between national policy space and international disciplines and commitments;

(e) To enhance the contribution of non-governmental organizations, civil society, the private sector and other stakeholders in national development efforts, as well as in the promotion of the global partnership for development;

(f) To ensure that the United Nations funds and programmes and the specialized agencies support the efforts of developing countries through the common country assessment and United Nations Development Assistance Framework process, enhancing their support for capacity-building;

(g) To protect our natural resource base in support of development.

Financing for development

23. We reaffirm the Monterrey Consensus[2] and recognize that mobilizing financial resources for development and the effective use of those resources in developing countries and countries with economies in transition are central to a global partnership for development in support of the achievement of the internationally agreed development goals, including the Millennium Development Goals. In this regard:

(*a*) We are encouraged by recent commitments to substantial increases in official development assistance and the Organization for Economic Cooperation and Development estimate that official development assistance to all developing countries will now increase by around 50 billion United States dollars a year by 2010, while recognizing that a substantial increase in such assistance is required to achieve the internationally agreed goals, including the Millennium Development Goals, within their respective time frames;

(*b*) We welcome the increased resources that will become available as a result of the establishment of timetables by many developed countries to achieve the target of 0.7 per cent of gross national product for official development assistance by 2015 and to reach at least 0.5 per cent of gross national product for official development assistance by 2010 as well as, pursuant to the Brussels Programme of Action for the Least Developed Countries for the Decade 2001-2010,[4] 0.15 per cent to 0.20 per cent for the least developed countries no later than 2010, and urge those developed countries that have not yet done so to make concrete efforts in this regard in accordance with their commitments;

(*c*) We further welcome recent efforts and initiatives to enhance the quality of aid and to increase its impact, including the Paris Declaration on Aid Effectiveness, and resolve to take concrete, effective and timely action in implementing all agreed commitments on aid effectiveness, with clear monitoring and deadlines, including through further aligning assistance with countries' strategies, building institutional capacities, reducing transaction costs and eliminating bureaucratic procedures, making progress on untying aid, enhancing the absorptive capacity and financial management of recipient countries and strengthening the focus on development results;

(*d*) We recognize the value of developing innovative sources of financing, provided those sources do not unduly burden developing countries. In that regard, we take note with interest of the international efforts, contributions and discussions, such as the Action against Hunger and Poverty, aimed at identifying innovative and additional sources of financing for development on a public, private, domestic or external basis to increase and supplement traditional sources of financing. Some countries will implement the International Finance Facility. Some countries have launched the International Finance Facility for immunization. Some countries will implement in the near future, utilizing their national authorities, a contribution on airline tickets to enable the financing of development projects, in particular in the health sector, directly or through financing of the International Finance Facility. Other countries are considering whether and to what extent they will participate in these initiatives;

---

[4] A/CONF.191/13, chap. II.

(e)   We acknowledge the vital role the private sector can play in generating new investments, employment and financing for development;

(f)   We resolve to address the development needs of low-income developing countries by working in competent multilateral and international forums, to help them meet, inter alia, their financial, technical and technological requirements;

(g)   We resolve to continue to support the development efforts of middle-income developing countries by working, in competent multilateral and international forums and also through bilateral arrangements, on measures to help them meet, inter alia, their financial, technical and technological requirements;

(h)   We resolve to operationalize the World Solidarity Fund established by the General Assembly and invite those countries in a position to do so to make voluntary contributions to the Fund;

(i)   We recognize the need for access to financial services, in particular for the poor, including through microfinance and microcredit.

Domestic resource mobilization

24.   In our common pursuit of growth, poverty eradication and sustainable development, a critical challenge is to ensure the necessary internal conditions for mobilizing domestic savings, both public and private, sustaining adequate levels of productive investment, increasing human capacity, reducing capital flight, curbing the illicit transfer of funds and enhancing international cooperation for creating an enabling domestic environment. We undertake to support the efforts of developing countries to create a domestic enabling environment for mobilizing domestic resources. To this end, we therefore resolve:

(a)   To pursue good governance and sound macroeconomic policies at all levels and support developing countries in their efforts to put in place the policies and investments to drive sustained economic growth, promote small and medium-sized enterprises, promote employment generation and stimulate the private sector;

(b)   To reaffirm that good governance is essential for sustainable development; that sound economic policies, solid democratic institutions responsive to the needs of the people and improved infrastructure are the basis for sustained economic growth, poverty eradication and employment creation; and that freedom, peace and security, domestic stability, respect for human rights, including the right to development, the rule of law, gender equality and market-oriented policies and an overall commitment to just and democratic societies are also essential and mutually reinforcing;

(c)   To make the fight against corruption a priority at all levels and we welcome all actions taken in this regard at the national and international levels, including the adoption of policies that emphasize accountability, transparent public sector management and corporate responsibility and accountability, including efforts to return assets transferred through corruption, consistent with the United Nations Convention against Corruption.[5] We urge all States that have not done so to consider signing, ratifying and implementing the Convention;

(d)   To channel private capabilities and resources into stimulating the private sector in developing countries through actions in the public, public/private and

---

[5] Resolution 58/4, annex.

private spheres to create an enabling environment for partnership and innovation that contributes to accelerated economic development and hunger and poverty eradication;

(*e*)   To support efforts to reduce capital flight and measures to curb the illicit transfer of funds.

Investment

25.   We resolve to encourage greater direct investment, including foreign investment, in developing countries and countries with economies in transition to support their development activities and to enhance the benefits they can derive from such investments. In this regard:

(*a*)   We continue to support efforts by developing countries and countries with economies in transition to create a domestic environment conducive to attracting investments through, inter alia, achieving a transparent, stable and predictable investment climate with proper contract enforcement and respect for property rights and the rule of law and pursuing appropriate policy and regulatory frameworks that encourage business formation;

(*b*)   We will put into place policies to ensure adequate investment in a sustainable manner in health, clean water and sanitation, housing and education and in the provision of public goods and social safety nets to protect vulnerable and disadvantaged sectors of society;

(*c*)   We invite national Governments seeking to develop infrastructure projects and generate foreign direct investment to pursue strategies with the involvement of both the public and private sectors and, where appropriate, international donors;

(*d*)   We call upon international financial and banking institutions to consider enhancing the transparency of risk rating mechanisms. Sovereign risk assessments, made by the private sector should maximize the use of strict, objective and transparent parameters, which can be facilitated by high-quality data and analysis;

(*e*)   We underscore the need to sustain sufficient and stable private financial flows to developing countries and countries with economies in transition. It is important to promote measures in source and destination countries to improve transparency and the information about financial flows to developing countries, particularly countries in Africa, the least developed countries, small island developing States and landlocked developing countries. Measures that mitigate the impact of excessive volatility of short-term capital flows are important and must be considered.

Debt

26.   We emphasize the high importance of a timely, effective, comprehensive and durable solution to the debt problems of developing countries, since debt financing and relief can be an important source of capital for development. To this end:

(*a*)   We welcome the recent proposals of the Group of Eight to cancel 100 per cent of the outstanding debt of eligible heavily indebted poor countries owed to the International Monetary Fund, the International Development Association and African Development Fund and to provide additional resources to ensure that the financing capacity of the international financial institutions is not reduced;

(*b*) We emphasize that debt sustainability is essential for underpinning growth and underline the importance of debt sustainability to the efforts to achieve national development goals, including the Millennium Development Goals, recognizing the key role that debt relief can play in liberating resources that can be directed towards activities consistent with poverty eradication, sustained economic growth and sustainable development;

(*c*) We further stress the need to consider additional measures and initiatives aimed at ensuring long-term debt sustainability through increased grant-based financing, cancellation of 100 per cent of the official multilateral and bilateral debt of heavily indebted poor countries and, where appropriate, and on a case-by-case basis, to consider significant debt relief or restructuring for low- and middle-income developing countries with an unsustainable debt burden that are not part of the Heavily Indebted Poor Countries Initiative, as well as the exploration of mechanisms to comprehensively address the debt problems of those countries. Such mechanisms may include debt for sustainable development swaps or multicreditor debt swap arrangements, as appropriate. These initiatives could include further efforts by the International Monetary Fund and the World Bank to develop the debt sustainability framework for low-income countries. This should be achieved in a fashion that does not detract from official development assistance resources, while maintaining the financial integrity of the multilateral financial institutions.

Trade

27. A universal, rule-based, open, non-discriminatory and equitable multilateral trading system, as well as meaningful trade liberalization, can substantially stimulate development worldwide, benefiting countries at all stages of development. In that regard, we reaffirm our commitment to trade liberalization and to ensure that trade plays its full part in promoting economic growth, employment and development for all.

28. We are committed to efforts designed to ensure that developing countries, especially the least-developed countries, participate fully in the world trading system in order to meet their economic development needs, and reaffirm our commitment to enhanced and predictable market access for the exports of developing countries.

29. We will work towards the objective, in accordance with the Brussels Programme of Action,[4] of duty free and quota-free market access for all least developed countries' products to the markets of developed countries, as well as to the markets of developing countries in a position to do so, and support their efforts to overcome their supply-side constraints.

30. We are committed to supporting and promoting increased aid to build productive and trade capacities of developing countries and to taking further steps in that regard, while welcoming the substantial support already provided.

31. We will work to accelerate and facilitate the accession of developing countries and countries with economies in transition to the World Trade Organization consistent with its criteria, recognizing the importance of universal integration in the rules-based global trading system.

32. We will work expeditiously towards implementing the development dimensions of the Doha work programme.[6]

Commodities

33. We emphasize the need to address the impact of weak and volatile commodity prices and support the efforts of commodity-dependent countries to restructure, diversify and strengthen the competitiveness of their commodity sectors.

Quick-impact initiatives

34. Given the need to accelerate progress immediately in countries where current trends make the achievement of the internationally agreed development goals unlikely, we resolve to urgently identify and implement country-led initiatives with adequate international support, consistent with long-term national development strategies, that promise immediate and durable improvements in the lives of people and renewed hope for the achievement of the development goals. In this regard, we will take such actions as the distribution of malaria bed nets, including free distribution, where appropriate, and effective anti-malarial treatments, the expansion of local school meal programmes, using home-grown foods where possible, and the elimination of user fees for primary education and, where appropriate, health-care services.

Systemic issues and global economic decision-making

35. We reaffirm the commitment to broaden and strengthen the participation of developing countries and countries with economies in transition in international economic decision-making and norm-setting, and to that end stress the importance of continuing efforts to reform the international financial architecture, noting that enhancing the voice and participation of developing countries and countries with economies in transition in the Bretton Woods institutions remains a continuous concern.

36. We reaffirm our commitment to governance, equity and transparency in the financial, monetary and trading systems. We are also committed to open, equitable, rule-based, predictable and non-discriminatory multilateral trading and financial systems.

37. We also underscore our commitment to sound domestic financial sectors, which make a vital contribution to national development efforts, as an important component of an international financial architecture that is supportive of development.

38. We further reaffirm the need for the United Nations to play a fundamental role in the promotion of international cooperation for development and the coherence, coordination and implementation of development goals and actions agreed upon by the international community, and we resolve to strengthen coordination within the United Nations system in close cooperation with all other multilateral financial, trade and development institutions in order to support sustained economic growth, poverty eradication and sustainable development.

39. Good governance at the international level is fundamental for achieving sustainable development. In order to ensure a dynamic and enabling international

---

[6] See A/C.2/56/7, annex.

economic environment, it is important to promote global economic governance through addressing the international finance, trade, technology and investment patterns that have an impact on the development prospects of developing countries. To this effect, the international community should take all necessary and appropriate measures, including ensuring support for structural and macroeconomic reform, a comprehensive solution to the external debt problem and increasing the market access of developing countries.

South-South cooperation

40.   We recognize the achievements and great potential of South-South cooperation and encourage the promotion of such cooperation, which complements North-South cooperation as an effective contribution to development and as a means to share best practices and provide enhanced technical cooperation. In this context, we note the recent decision of the leaders of the South, adopted at the Second South Summit and contained in the Doha Declaration[7] and the Doha Plan of Action,[8] to intensify their efforts at South-South cooperation, including through the establishment of the New Asian-African Strategic Partnership and other regional cooperation mechanisms, and encourage the international community, including the international financial institutions, to support the efforts of developing countries, inter alia, through triangular cooperation. We also take note with appreciation of the launching of the third round of negotiations on the Global System of Trade Preferences among Developing Countries as an important instrument to stimulate South-South cooperation.

41.   We welcome the work of the United Nations High-Level Committee on South-South Cooperation and invite countries to consider supporting the Special Unit for South-South Cooperation within the United Nations Development Programme in order to respond effectively to the development needs of developing countries.

42.   We recognize the considerable contribution of arrangements such as the Organization of Petroleum Exporting Countries Fund initiated by a group of developing countries, as well as the potential contribution of the South Fund for Development and Humanitarian Assistance, to development activities in developing countries.

Education

43.   We emphasize the critical role of both formal and informal education in the achievement of poverty eradication and other development goals as envisaged in the Millennium Declaration,[1] in particular basic education and training for eradicating illiteracy, and strive for expanded secondary and higher education as well as vocational education and technical training, especially for girls and women, the creation of human resources and infrastructure capabilities and the empowerment of those living in poverty. In this context, we reaffirm the Dakar Framework for Action adopted at the World Education Forum in 2000[9] and recognize the importance of the United Nations Educational, Scientific and Cultural Organization strategy for the eradication of poverty, especially extreme poverty, in supporting the Education for

---

[7] A/60/111, annex I.

[8] Ibid., annex II.

[9] See United Nations Educational, Scientific and Cultural Organization, *Final Report of the World Education Forum, Dakar, Senegal, 26-28 April 2000* (Paris, 2000).

All programmes as a tool to achieve the millennium development goal of universal primary education by 2015.

44.   We reaffirm our commitment to support developing country efforts to ensure that all children have access to and complete free and compulsory primary education of good quality, to eliminate gender inequality and imbalance and to renew efforts to improve girls' education. We also commit ourselves to continuing to support the efforts of developing countries in the implementation of the Education for All initiative, including with enhanced resources of all types through the Education for All fast-track initiative in support of country-led national education plans.

45.   We commit ourselves to promoting education for peace and human development.

Rural and agricultural development

46.   We reaffirm that food security and rural and agricultural development must be adequately and urgently addressed in the context of national development and response strategies and, in this context, will enhance the contributions of indigenous and local communities, as appropriate. We are convinced that the eradication of poverty, hunger and malnutrition, particularly as they affect children, is crucial for the achievement of the Millennium Development Goals. Rural and agricultural development should be an integral part of national and international development policies. We deem it necessary to increase productive investment in rural and agricultural development to achieve food security. We commit ourselves to increasing support for agricultural development and trade capacity-building in the agricultural sector in developing countries. Support for commodity development projects, especially market-based projects, and for their preparation under the Second Account of the Common Fund for Commodities should be encouraged.

Employment

47.   We strongly support fair globalization and resolve to make the goals of full and productive employment and decent work for all, including for women and young people, a central objective of our relevant national and international policies as well as our national development strategies, including poverty reduction strategies, as part of our efforts to achieve the Millennium Development Goals. These measures should also encompass the elimination of the worst forms of child labour, as defined in International Labour Organization Convention No. 182, and forced labour. We also resolve to ensure full respect for the fundamental principles and rights at work.

Sustainable development: managing and protecting our common environment

48.   We reaffirm our commitment to achieve the goal of sustainable development, including through the implementation of Agenda 21[10] and the Johannesburg Plan of Implementation.[3] To this end, we commit ourselves to undertaking concrete actions and measures at all levels and to enhancing international cooperation, taking into account the Rio principles.[11] These efforts will also promote the integration of the

---

[10] *Report of the United Nations Conference on Environment and Development, Rio de Janeiro, 3-14 June 1992* (United Nations publication, Sales No. E.93.I.8 and corrigenda), vol. I: *Resolutions adopted by the Conference*, resolution 1, annex II.

[11] Ibid., annex I.

three components of sustainable development – economic development, social development and environmental protection – as interdependent and mutually reinforcing pillars. Poverty eradication, changing unsustainable patterns of production and consumption and protecting and managing the natural resource base of economic and social development are overarching objectives of and essential requirements for sustainable development.

49.   We will promote sustainable consumption and production patterns, with the developed countries taking the lead and all countries benefiting from the process, as called for in the Johannesburg Plan of Implementation. In that context, we support developing countries in their efforts to promote a recycling economy.

50.   We face serious and multiple challenges in tackling climate change, promoting clean energy, meeting energy needs and achieving sustainable development, and we will act with resolve and urgency in this regard.

51.   We recognize that climate change is a serious and long-term challenge that has the potential to affect every part of the globe. We emphasize the need to meet all the commitments and obligations we have undertaken in the United Nations Framework Convention on Climate Change [12] and other relevant international agreements, including, for many of us, the Kyoto Protocol.[13] The Convention is the appropriate framework for addressing future action on climate change at the global level.

52.   We reaffirm our commitment to the ultimate objective of the Convention: to stabilize greenhouse gas concentrations in the atmosphere at a level that prevents dangerous anthropogenic interference with the climate system.

53.   We acknowledge that the global nature of climate change calls for the widest possible cooperation and participation in an effective and appropriate international response, in accordance with the principles of the Convention. We are committed to moving forward the global discussion on long-term cooperative action to address climate change, in accordance with these principles. We stress the importance of the eleventh session of the Conference of the Parties to the Convention, to be held in Montreal in November 2005.

54.   We acknowledge various partnerships that are under way to advance action on clean energy and climate change, including bilateral, regional and multilateral initiatives.

55.   We are committed to taking further action through practical international cooperation, inter alia:

(*a*)   To promote innovation, clean energy and energy efficiency and conservation; improve policy, regulatory and financing frameworks; and accelerate the deployment of cleaner technologies;

(*b*)   To enhance private investment, transfer of technologies and capacity-building to developing countries, as called for in the Johannesburg Plan of Implementation, taking into account their own energy needs and priorities;

(*c*)   To assist developing countries to improve their resilience and integrate adaptation goals into their sustainable development strategies, given that adaptation to the effects of climate change due to both natural and human factors is a high

---

[12] United Nations, *Treaty Series*, vol. 1771, No. 30822.

[13] FCCC/CP/1997/7/Add.1, decision 1/CP.3, annex.

priority for all nations, particularly those most vulnerable, namely, those referred to in article 4.8 of the Convention;

(*d*)   To continue to assist developing countries, in particular small island developing States, least developed countries and African countries, including those that are particularly vulnerable to climate change, in addressing their adaptation needs relating to the adverse effects of climate change.

56.   In pursuance of our commitment to achieve sustainable development, we further resolve:

(*a*)   To promote the United Nations Decade of Education for Sustainable Development and the International Decade for Action, "Water for Life";

(*b*)   To support and strengthen the implementation of the United Nations Convention to Combat Desertification in Those Countries Experiencing Serious Drought and/or Desertification, Particularly in Africa, [14] to address causes of desertification and land degradation, as well as poverty resulting from land degradation, through, inter alia, the mobilization of adequate and predictable financial resources, the transfer of technology and capacity-building at all levels;

(*c*)   That the States parties to the Convention on Biological Diversity[15] and the Cartagena Protocol on Biosafety[16] should support the implementation of the Convention and the Protocol, as well as other biodiversity-related agreements and the Johannesburg commitment for a significant reduction in the rate of loss of biodiversity by 2010. The States parties will continue to negotiate within the framework of the Convention on Biological Diversity, bearing in mind the Bonn Guidelines, [17] an international regime to promote and safeguard the fair and equitable sharing of benefits arising out of the utilization of genetic resources. All States will fulfil commitments and significantly reduce the rate of loss of biodiversity by 2010 and continue ongoing efforts towards elaborating and negotiating an international regime on access to genetic resources and benefit-sharing;

(*d*)   To recognize that the sustainable development of indigenous peoples and their communities is crucial in our fight against hunger and poverty;

(*e*)   To reaffirm our commitment, subject to national legislation, to respect, preserve and maintain the knowledge, innovations and practices of indigenous and local communities embodying traditional lifestyles relevant to the conservation and sustainable use of biological diversity, promote their wider application with the approval and involvement of the holders of such knowledge, innovations and practices and encourage the equitable sharing of the benefits arising from their utilization;

(*f*)   To work expeditiously towards the establishment of a worldwide early warning system for all natural hazards with regional nodes, building on existing national and regional capacity such as the newly established Indian Ocean Tsunami Warning and Mitigation System;

---

[14] United Nations, *Treaty Series*, vol. 1954, No. 33480

[15] Ibid., vol. 1760, No. 30619.

[16] UNEP/CBD/ExCOP/1/3 and Corr.1, part two, annex.

[17] UNEP/CBD/COP/6/20, annex I, decision VI/24A.

(g) To fully implement the Hyogo Declaration[18] and the Hyogo Framework for Action 2005–2015[19] adopted at the World Conference on Disaster Reduction, in particular those commitments related to assistance for developing countries that are prone to natural disasters and disaster-stricken States in the transition phase towards sustainable physical, social and economic recovery, for risk-reduction activities in post-disaster recovery and for rehabilitation processes;

(h) To assist developing countries' efforts to prepare integrated water resources management and water efficiency plans as part of their national development strategies and to provide access to safe drinking water and basic sanitation in accordance with the Millennium Declaration[1] and the Johannesburg Plan of Implementation,[3] including halving by 2015 the proportion of people who are unable to reach or afford safe drinking water and who do not have access to basic sanitation;

(i) To accelerate the development and dissemination of affordable and cleaner energy efficiency and energy conservation technologies, as well as the transfer of such technologies, in particular to developing countries, on favourable terms, including on concessional and preferential terms, as mutually agreed, bearing in mind that access to energy facilitates the eradication of poverty;

(j) To strengthen the conservation, sustainable management and development of all types of forests for the benefit of current and future generations, including through enhanced international cooperation, so that trees and forests may contribute fully to the achievement of the internationally agreed development goals, including those contained in the Millennium Declaration, taking full account of the linkages between the forest sector and other sectors. We look forward to the discussions at the sixth session of the United Nations Forum on Forests;

(k) To promote the sound management of chemicals and hazardous wastes throughout their life cycle, in accordance with Agenda 21 and the Johannesburg Plan of Implementation, aiming to achieve that by 2020 chemicals are used and produced in ways that lead to the minimization of significant adverse effects on human health and the environment using transparent and science-based risk assessment and risk management procedures, by adopting and implementing a voluntary strategic approach to international management of chemicals, and to support developing countries in strengthening their capacity for the sound management of chemicals and hazardous wastes by providing technical and financial assistance, as appropriate;

(l) To improve cooperation and coordination at all levels in order to address issues related to oceans and seas in an integrated manner and promote integrated management and sustainable development of the oceans and seas;

(m) To achieve significant improvement in the lives of at least 100 million slum-dwellers by 2020, recognizing the urgent need for the provision of increased resources for affordable housing and housing-related infrastructure, prioritizing slum prevention and slum upgrading, and to encourage support for the United Nations Habitat and Human Settlements Foundation and its Slum Upgrading Facility;

---

[18] A/CONF.206/6 and Corr.1, chap. I, resolution 1.

[19] Hyogo Framework for Action 2005-2015: Building the Resilience of Nations and Communities to Disasters (A/CONF.206/6 and Corr.1, chap. I, resolution 2).

(*n*) To acknowledge the invaluable role of the Global Environment Facility in facilitating cooperation with developing countries; we look forward to a successful replenishment this year along with the successful conclusion of all outstanding commitments from the third replenishment;

(*o*) To note that cessation of the transport of radioactive materials through the regions of small island developing States is an ultimate desired goal of small island developing States and some other countries and recognize the right of freedom of navigation in accordance with international law. States should maintain dialogue and consultation, in particular under the aegis of the International Atomic Energy Agency and the International Maritime Organization, with the aim of improved mutual understanding, confidence-building and enhanced communication in relation to the safe maritime transport of radioactive materials. States involved in the transport of such materials are urged to continue to engage in dialogue with small island developing States and other States to address their concerns. These concerns include the further development and strengthening, within the appropriate forums, of international regulatory regimes to enhance safety, disclosure, liability, security and compensation in relation to such transport.

HIV/AIDS, malaria, tuberculosis and other health issues

57. We recognize that HIV/AIDS, malaria, tuberculosis and other infectious diseases pose severe risks for the entire world and serious challenges to the achievement of development goals. We acknowledge the substantial efforts and financial contributions made by the international community, while recognizing that these diseases and other emerging health challenges require a sustained international response. To this end, we commit ourselves to:

(*a*) Increasing investment, building on existing mechanisms and through partnership, to improve health systems in developing countries and those with economies in transition with the aim of providing sufficient health workers, infrastructure, management systems and supplies to achieve the health-related Millennium Development Goals by 2015;

(*b*) Implementing measures to increase the capacity of adults and adolescents to protect themselves from the risk of HIV infection;

(*c*) Fully implementing all commitments established by the Declaration of Commitment on HIV/AIDS[20] through stronger leadership, the scaling up of a comprehensive response to achieve broad multisectoral coverage for prevention, care, treatment and support, the mobilization of additional resources from national, bilateral, multilateral and private sources and the substantial funding of the Global Fund to Fight AIDS, Tuberculosis and Malaria as well as of the HIV/AIDS component of the work programmes of the United Nations system agencies and programmes engaged in the fight against HIV/AIDS;

(*d*) Developing and implementing a package for HIV prevention, treatment and care with the aim of coming as close as possible to the goal of universal access to treatment by 2010 for all those who need it, including through increased resources, and working towards the elimination of stigma and discrimination, enhanced access to affordable medicines and the reduction of vulnerability of

---

[20] Resolution S-26/2, annex.

persons affected by HIV/AIDS and other health issues, in particular orphaned and vulnerable children and older persons;

(*e*) Ensuring the full implementation of our obligations under the International Health Regulations adopted by the fifty-eighth World Health Assembly in May 2005,[21] including the need to support the Global Outbreak Alert and Response Network of the World Health Organization;

(*f*) Working actively to implement the "Three Ones" principles in all countries, including by ensuring that multiple institutions and international partners all work under one agreed HIV/AIDS framework that provides the basis for coordinating the work of all partners, with one national AIDS coordinating authority having a broad-based multisectoral mandate, and under one agreed country-level monitoring and evaluation system. We welcome and support the important recommendations of the Global Task Team on Improving AIDS Coordination among Multilateral Institutions and International Donors;

(*g*) Achieving universal access to reproductive health by 2015, as set out at the International Conference on Population and Development, integrating this goal in strategies to attain the internationally agreed development goals, including those contained in the Millennium Declaration, aimed at reducing maternal mortality, improving maternal health, reducing child mortality, promoting gender equality, combating HIV/AIDS and eradicating poverty;

(*h*) Promoting long-term funding, including public-private partnerships where appropriate, for academic and industrial research as well as for the development of new vaccines and microbicides, diagnostic kits, drugs and treatments to address major pandemics, tropical diseases and other diseases, such as avian flu and severe acute respiratory syndrome, and taking forward work on market incentives, where appropriate through such mechanisms as advance purchase commitments;

(*i*) Stressing the need to urgently address malaria and tuberculosis, in particular in the most affected countries, and welcoming the scaling up, in this regard, of bilateral and multilateral initiatives.

Gender equality and empowerment of women

58. We remain convinced that progress for women is progress for all. We reaffirm that the full and effective implementation of the goals and objectives of the Beijing Declaration and Platform for Action[22] and the outcome of the twenty-third special session of the General Assembly is an essential contribution to achieving the internationally agreed development goals, including those contained in the Millennium Declaration, and we resolve to promote gender equality and eliminate pervasive gender discrimination by:

(*a*) Eliminating gender inequalities in primary and secondary education by the earliest possible date and at all educational levels by 2015;

(*b*) Guaranteeing the free and equal right of women to own and inherit property and ensuring secure tenure of property and housing by women;

---

[21] World Health Assembly resolution 58.3.

[22] *Report of the Fourth World Conference on Women, Beijing, 4-15 September 1995* (United Nations publication, Sales No. E.96.IV.13), chap. I, resolution 1, annexes I and II.

(c) Ensuring equal access to reproductive health;

(d) Promoting women's equal access to labour markets, sustainable employment and adequate labour protection;

(e) Ensuring equal access of women to productive assets and resources, including land, credit and technology;

(f) Eliminating all forms of discrimination and violence against women and the girl child, including by ending impunity and by ensuring the protection of civilians, in particular women and the girl child, during and after armed conflicts in accordance with the obligations of States under international humanitarian law and international human rights law;

(g) Promoting increased representation of women in Government decision-making bodies, including through ensuring their equal opportunity to participate fully in the political process.

59. We recognize the importance of gender mainstreaming as a tool for achieving gender equality. To that end, we undertake to actively promote the mainstreaming of a gender perspective in the design, implementation, monitoring and evaluation of policies and programmes in all political, economic and social spheres, and further undertake to strengthen the capabilities of the United Nations system in the area of gender.

Science and technology for development

60. We recognize that science and technology, including information and communication technology, are vital for the achievement of the development goals and that international support can help developing countries to benefit from technological advancements and enhance their productive capacity. We therefore commit ourselves to:

(a) Strengthening and enhancing existing mechanisms and supporting initiatives for research and development, including through voluntary partnerships between the public and private sectors, to address the special needs of developing countries in the areas of health, agriculture, conservation, sustainable use of natural resources and environmental management, energy, forestry and the impact of climate change;

(b) Promoting and facilitating, as appropriate, access to and the development, transfer and diffusion of technologies, including environmentally sound technologies and corresponding know-how, to developing countries;

(c) Assisting developing countries in their efforts to promote and develop national strategies for human resources and science and technology, which are primary drivers of national capacity-building for development;

(d) Promoting and supporting greater efforts to develop renewable sources of energy, such as solar, wind and geothermal;

(e) Implementing policies at the national and international levels to attract both public and private investment, domestic and foreign, that enhances knowledge, transfers technology on mutually agreed terms and raises productivity;

(f) Supporting the efforts of developing countries, individually and collectively, to harness new agricultural technologies in order to increase agricultural productivity through environmentally sustainable means;

(g) Building a people-centred and inclusive information society so as to enhance digital opportunities for all people in order to help bridge the digital divide, putting the potential of information and communication technologies at the service of development and addressing new challenges of the information society by implementing the outcomes of the Geneva phase of the World Summit on the Information Society and ensuring the success of the second phase of the Summit, to be held in Tunis in November 2005; in this regard, we welcome the establishment of the Digital Solidarity Fund and encourage voluntary contributions to its financing.

Migration and development

61. We acknowledge the important nexus between international migration and development and the need to deal with the challenges and opportunities that migration presents to countries of origin, destination and transit. We recognize that international migration brings benefits as well as challenges to the global community. We look forward to the high-level dialogue of the General Assembly on international migration and development to be held in 2006, which will offer an opportunity to discuss the multidimensional aspects of international migration and development in order to identify appropriate ways and means to maximize their development benefits and minimize their negative impacts.

62. We reaffirm our resolve to take measures to ensure respect for and protection of the human rights of migrants, migrant workers and members of their families.

63. We reaffirm the need to adopt policies and undertake measures to reduce the cost of transferring migrant remittances to developing countries and welcome efforts by Governments and stakeholders in this regard.

Countries with special needs

64. We reaffirm our commitment to address the special needs of the least developed countries and urge all countries and all relevant organizations of the United Nations system, including the Bretton Woods institutions, to make concerted efforts and adopt speedy measures for meeting in a timely manner the goals and targets of the Brussels Programme of Action for the Least Developed Countries for the Decade 2001–2010.[4]

65. We recognize the special needs of and challenges faced by landlocked developing countries and therefore reaffirm our commitment to urgently address those needs and challenges through the full, timely and effective implementation of the Almaty Programme of Action: Addressing the Special Needs of Landlocked Developing Countries within a New Global Framework for Transit Transport Cooperation for Landlocked and Transit Developing Countries[23] and the São Paulo Consensus adopted at the eleventh session of the United Nations Conference on Trade and Development.[24] We encourage the work undertaken by United Nations regional commissions and organizations towards establishing a time-cost methodology for indicators to measure the progress in implementation of the Almaty Programme of Action. We also recognize the special difficulties and concerns of landlocked developing countries in their efforts to integrate their economies into the

---

[23] *Report of the International Ministerial Conference of Landlocked and Transit Developing Countries and Donor Countries and International Financial and Development Institutions on Transit Transport Cooperation, Almaty, Kazakhstan, 28 and 29 August 2003* (A/CONF.202/3), annex I.

[24] TD/412, part II.

multilateral trading system. In this regard, priority should be given to the full and timely implementation of the Almaty Declaration[25] and the Almaty Programme of Action.[23]

66. We recognize the special needs and vulnerabilities of small island developing States and reaffirm our commitment to take urgent and concrete action to address those needs and vulnerabilities through the full and effective implementation of the Mauritius Strategy adopted by the International Meeting to Review the Implementation of the Programme of Action for the Sustainable Development of Small Island Developing States,[26] the Barbados Programme of Action[27] and the outcome of the twenty-second special session of the General Assembly.[28] We further undertake to promote greater international cooperation and partnership for the implementation of the Mauritius Strategy through, inter alia, the mobilization of domestic and international resources, the promotion of international trade as an engine for development and increased international financial and technical cooperation.

67. We emphasize the need for continued, coordinated and effective international support for achieving the development goals in countries emerging from conflict and in those recovering from natural disasters.

Meeting the special needs of Africa

68. We welcome the substantial progress made by the African countries in fulfilling their commitments and emphasize the need to carry forward the implementation of the New Partnership for Africa's Development[29] to promote sustainable growth and development and deepen democracy, human rights, good governance and sound economic management and gender equality and encourage African countries, with the participation of civil society and the private sector, to continue their efforts in this regard by developing and strengthening institutions for governance and the development of the region, and also welcome the recent decisions taken by Africa's partners, including the Group of Eight and the European Union, in support of Africa's development efforts, including commitments that will lead to an increase in official development assistance to Africa of 25 billion dollars per year by 2010. We reaffirm our commitment to address the special needs of Africa, which is the only continent not on track to meet any of the goals of the Millennium Declaration by 2015, to enable it to enter the mainstream of the world economy, and resolve:

(*a*) To strengthen cooperation with the New Partnership for Africa's Development by providing coherent support for the programmes drawn up by African leaders within that framework, including by mobilizing internal and

---

[25] *Report of the International Ministerial Conference of Landlocked and Transit Developing Countries and Donor Countries and International Financial and Development Institutions on Transit Transport Cooperation, Almaty, Kazakhstan, 28 and 29 August* 2003 (A/CONF.202/3), annex II.

[26] *Report of the International Meeting to Review the Implementation of the Programme of Action for the Sustainable Development of Small Island Developing States, Port Louis, Mauritius, 10-14 January 2005* (United Nations publication, Sales No. E.05.II.A.4 and corrigendum), chap. I, resolution 1, annex II.

[27] *Report of the Global Conference on the Sustainable Development of Small Island Developing States, Bridgetown, Barbados, 25 April-6 May 1994* (United Nations publication, Sales No. E.94.I.18 and corrigenda), chap. I, resolution 1, annex I.

[28] Resolution S-22/2, annex.

[29] A/57/304, annex.

external financial resources and facilitating approval of such programmes by the multilateral financial institutions;

(*b*) To support the African commitment to ensure that by 2015 all children have access to complete, free and compulsory primary education of good quality, as well as to basic health care;

(*c*) To support the building of an international infrastructure consortium involving the African Union, the World Bank and the African Development Bank, with the New Partnership for Africa's Development as the main framework, to facilitate public and private infrastructure investment in Africa;

(*d*) To promote a comprehensive and durable solution to the external debt problems of African countries, including through the cancellation of 100 per cent of multilateral debt consistent with the recent Group of Eight proposal for the heavily indebted poor countries, and, on a case-by-case basis, where appropriate, significant debt relief, including, inter alia, cancellation or restructuring for heavily indebted African countries not part of the Heavily Indebted Poor Countries Initiative that have unsustainable debt burdens;

(*e*) To make efforts to fully integrate African countries in the international trading system, including through targeted trade capacity-building programmes;

(*f*) To support the efforts of commodity-dependent African countries to restructure, diversify and strengthen the competitiveness of their commodity sectors and decide to work towards market-based arrangements with the participation of the private sector for commodity price-risk management;

(*g*) To supplement the efforts of African countries, individually and collectively, to increase agricultural productivity, in a sustainable way, as set out in the Comprehensive Africa Agriculture Development Programme of the New Partnership for Africa's Development as part of an African "Green Revolution";

(*h*) To encourage and support the initiatives of the African Union and subregional organizations to prevent, mediate and resolve conflicts with the assistance of the United Nations, and in this regard welcomes the proposals from the Group of Eight countries to provide support for African peacekeeping;

(*i*) To provide, with the aim of an AIDS-, malaria- and tuberculosis-free generation in Africa, assistance for prevention and care and to come as close as possible to achieving the goal of universal access by 2010 to HIV/AIDS treatment in African countries, to encourage pharmaceutical companies to make drugs, including antiretroviral drugs, affordable and accessible in Africa and to ensure increased bilateral and multilateral assistance, where possible on a grant basis, to combat malaria, tuberculosis and other infectious diseases in Africa through the strengthening of health systems.

III. Peace and collective security

69. We recognize that we are facing a whole range of threats that require our urgent, collective and more determined response.

70. We also recognize that, in accordance with the Charter, addressing such threats requires cooperation among all the principal organs of the United Nations within their respective mandates.

71. We acknowledge that we are living in an interdependent and global world and that many of today's threats recognize no national boundaries, are interlinked and

must be tackled at the global, regional and national levels in accordance with the Charter and international law.

72. We therefore reaffirm our commitment to work towards a security consensus based on the recognition that many threats are interlinked, that development, peace, security and human rights are mutually reinforcing, that no State can best protect itself by acting entirely alone and that all States need an effective and efficient collective security system pursuant to the purposes and principles of the Charter.

Pacific settlement of disputes

73. We emphasize the obligation of States to settle their disputes by peaceful means in accordance with Chapter VI of the Charter, including, when appropriate, by the use of the International Court of Justice. All States should act in accordance with the Declaration on Principles of International Law concerning Friendly Relations and Cooperation among States in accordance with the Charter of the United Nations.[30]

74. We stress the importance of prevention of armed conflict in accordance with the purposes and principles of the Charter and solemnly renew our commitment to promote a culture of prevention of armed conflict as a means of effectively addressing the interconnected security and development challenges faced by peoples throughout the world, as well as to strengthen the capacity of the United Nations for the prevention of armed conflict.

75. We further stress the importance of a coherent and integrated approach to the prevention of armed conflicts and the settlement of disputes and the need for the Security Council, the General Assembly, the Economic and Social Council and the Secretary-General to coordinate their activities within their respective Charter mandates.

76. Recognizing the important role of the good offices of the Secretary-General, including in the mediation of disputes, we support the Secretary-General's efforts to strengthen his capacity in this area.

Use of force under the Charter of the United Nations

77. We reiterate the obligation of all Member States to refrain in their international relations from the threat or use of force in any manner inconsistent with the Charter. We reaffirm that the purposes and principles guiding the United Nations are, inter alia, to maintain international peace and security, to develop friendly relations among nations based on respect for the principles of equal rights and self-determination of peoples and to take other appropriate measures to strengthen universal peace, and to that end we are determined to take effective collective measures for the prevention and removal of threats to the peace and for the suppression of acts of aggression or other breaches of the peace, and to bring about by peaceful means, in conformity with the principles of justice and international law, the adjustment or settlement of international disputes or situations that might lead to a breach of the peace.

78. We reiterate the importance of promoting and strengthening the multilateral process and of addressing international challenges and problems by strictly abiding

---

[30] Resolution 2625 (XXV), annex.

by the Charter and the principles of international law, and further stress our commitment to multilateralism.

79.   We reaffirm that the relevant provisions of the Charter are sufficient to address the full range of threats to international peace and security. We further reaffirm the authority of the Security Council to mandate coercive action to maintain and restore international peace and security. We stress the importance of acting in accordance with the purposes and principles of the Charter.

80.   We also reaffirm that the Security Council has primary responsibility in the maintenance of international peace and security. We also note the role of the General Assembly relating to the maintenance of international peace and security in accordance with the relevant provisions of the Charter.

Terrorism

81.   We strongly condemn terrorism in all its forms and manifestations, committed by whomever, wherever and for whatever purposes, as it constitutes one of the most serious threats to international peace and security.

82.   We welcome the Secretary-General's identification of elements of a counter-terrorism strategy. These elements should be developed by the General Assembly without delay with a view to adopting and implementing a strategy to promote comprehensive, coordinated and consistent responses, at the national, regional and international levels, to counter terrorism, which also takes into account the conditions conducive to the spread of terrorism. In this context, we commend the various initiatives to promote dialogue, tolerance and understanding among civilizations.

83.   We stress the need to make every effort to reach an agreement on and conclude a comprehensive convention on international terrorism during the sixtieth session of the General Assembly.

84.   We acknowledge that the question of convening a high-level conference under the auspices of the United Nations to formulate an international response to terrorism in all its forms and manifestations could be considered.

85.   We recognize that international cooperation to fight terrorism must be conducted in conformity with international law, including the Charter and relevant international conventions and protocols. States must ensure that any measures taken to combat terrorism comply with their obligations under international law, in particular human rights law, refugee law and international humanitarian law.

86.   We reiterate our call upon States to refrain from organizing, financing, encouraging, providing training for or otherwise supporting terrorist activities and to take appropriate measures to ensure that their territories are not used for such activities.

87.   We acknowledge the important role played by the United Nations in combating terrorism and also stress the vital contribution of regional and bilateral cooperation, particularly at the practical level of law enforcement cooperation and technical exchange.

88.   We urge the international community, including the United Nations, to assist States in building national and regional capacity to combat terrorism. We invite the Secretary-General to submit proposals to the General Assembly and the Security Council, within their respective mandates, to strengthen the capacity of the United

Nations system to assist States in combating terrorism and to enhance the coordination of United Nations activities in this regard.

89. We stress the importance of assisting victims of terrorism and of providing them and their families with support to cope with their loss and their grief.

90. We encourage the Security Council to consider ways to strengthen its monitoring and enforcement role in counter-terrorism, including by consolidating State reporting requirements, taking into account and respecting the different mandates of its counter-terrorism subsidiary bodies. We are committed to cooperating fully with the three competent subsidiary bodies in the fulfilment of their tasks, recognizing that many States continue to require assistance in implementing relevant Security Council resolutions.

91. We support efforts for the early entry into force of the International Convention for the Suppression of Acts of Nuclear Terrorism [31] and strongly encourage States to consider becoming parties to it expeditiously and acceding without delay to the twelve other international conventions and protocols against terrorism and implementing them.

Peacekeeping

92. Recognizing that United Nations peacekeeping plays a vital role in helping parties to conflict end hostilities and commending the contribution of United Nations peacekeepers in that regard, noting improvements made in recent years in United Nations peacekeeping, including the deployment of integrated missions in complex situations, and stressing the need to mount operations with adequate capacity to counter hostilities and fulfil effectively their mandates, we urge further development of proposals for enhanced rapidly deployable capacities to reinforce peacekeeping operations in crises. We endorse the creation of an initial operating capability for a standing police capacity to provide coherent, effective and responsive start-up capability for the policing component of the United Nations peacekeeping missions and to assist existing missions through the provision of advice and expertise.

93. Recognizing the important contribution to peace and security by regional organizations as provided for under Chapter VIII of the Charter and the importance of forging predictable partnerships and arrangements between the United Nations and regional organizations, and noting in particular, given the special needs of Africa, the importance of a strong African Union:

(*a*) We support the efforts of the European Union and other regional entities to develop capacities such as for rapid deployment, standby and bridging arrangements;

(*b*) We support the development and implementation of a ten-year plan for capacity-building with the African Union.

---

[31] Resolution 59/290, annex.

94. We support implementation of the 2001 Programme of Action to Prevent, Combat and Eradicate the Illicit Trade in Small Arms and Light Weapons in All Its Aspects.[32]

95. We urge States parties to the Anti-Personnel Mine Ban Convention[33] and Amended Protocol II to the Convention on Certain Conventional Weapons[34] to fully implement their respective obligations. We call upon States in a position to do so to provide greater technical assistance to mine-affected States.

96. We underscore the importance of the recommendations of the Adviser to the Secretary-General on Sexual Exploitation and Abuse by United Nations Peacekeeping Personnel,[35] and urge that those measures adopted in the relevant General Assembly resolutions based upon the recommendations be fully implemented without delay.

Peacebuilding

97. Emphasizing the need for a coordinated, coherent and integrated approach to post-conflict peacebuilding and reconciliation with a view to achieving sustainable peace, recognizing the need for a dedicated institutional mechanism to address the special needs of countries emerging from conflict towards recovery, reintegration and reconstruction and to assist them in laying the foundation for sustainable development, and recognizing the vital role of the United Nations in that regard, we decide to establish a Peacebuilding Commission as an intergovernmental advisory body.

98. The main purpose of the Peacebuilding Commission is to bring together all relevant actors to marshal resources and to advise on and propose integrated strategies for post-conflict peacebuilding and recovery. The Commission should focus attention on the reconstruction and institution-building efforts necessary for recovery from conflict and support the development of integrated strategies in order to lay the foundation for sustainable development. In addition, it should provide recommendations and information to improve the coordination of all relevant actors within and outside the United Nations, develop best practices, help to ensure predictable financing for early recovery activities and extend the period of attention by the international community to post-conflict recovery. The Commission should act in all matters on the basis of consensus of its members.

99. The Peacebuilding Commission should make the outcome of its discussions and recommendations publicly available as United Nations documents to all relevant bodies and actors, including the international financial institutions. The Peacebuilding Commission should submit an annual report to the General Assembly.

100. The Peacebuilding Commission should meet in various configurations. Country-specific meetings of the Commission, upon invitation of the Organizational

---

[32] See *Report of the United Nations Conference on the Illicit Trade in Small Arms and Light Weapons in All Its Aspects, New York, 9-20 July 2001* (A/CONF.192/15), chap. IV, para. 24.

[33] Convention on the Prohibition of the Use, Stockpiling, Production and Transfer of Anti-personnel Mines and on Their Destruction (United Nations, *Treaty Series*, vol. 2056, No. 35597).

[34] Amended Protocol II to the Convention on Prohibitions or Restrictions on the Use of Certain Conventional Weapons Which May Be Deemed to Be Excessively Injurious or to Have Indiscriminate Effects (CCW/CONF.I/16 (Part I), annex B).

[35] A/59/710, paras. 68-93.

Committee referred to in paragraph 101 below, should include as members, in addition to members of the Organizational Committee, representatives from:

(*a*)   The country under consideration;

(*b*)   Countries in the region engaged in the post-conflict process and other countries that are involved in relief efforts and/or political dialogue, as well as relevant regional and subregional organizations;

(*c*)   The major financial, troop and civilian police contributors involved in the recovery effort;

(*d*)   The senior United Nations representative in the field and other relevant United Nations representatives;

(*e*)   Such regional and international financial institutions as may be relevant.

101. The Peacebuilding Commission should have a standing Organizational Committee, responsible for developing its procedures and organizational matters, comprising:

(*a*)   Members of the Security Council, including permanent members;

(*b*)   Members of the Economic and Social Council, elected from regional groups, giving due consideration to those countries that have experienced post-conflict recovery;

(*c*)   Top providers of assessed contributions to the United Nations budgets and voluntary contributions to the United Nations funds, programmes and agencies, including the standing Peacebuilding Fund, that are not among those selected in (*a*) or (*b*) above;

(*d*)   Top providers of military personnel and civilian police to United Nations missions that are not among those selected in (*a*), (*b*) or (*c*) above.

102. Representatives from the World Bank, the International Monetary Fund and other institutional donors should be invited to participate in all meetings of the Peacebuilding Commission in a manner suitable to their governing arrangements, in addition to a representative of the Secretary-General.

103. We request the Secretary-General to establish a multi-year standing Peacebuilding Fund for post-conflict peacebuilding, funded by voluntary contributions and taking due account of existing instruments. The objectives of the Peacebuilding Fund will include ensuring the immediate release of resources needed to launch peacebuilding activities and the availability of appropriate financing for recovery.

104. We also request the Secretary-General to establish, within the Secretariat and from within existing resources, a small peacebuilding support office staffed by qualified experts to assist and support the Peacebuilding Commission. The office should draw on the best expertise available.

105. The Peacebuilding Commission should begin its work no later than 31 December 2005.

Sanctions

106. We underscore that sanctions remain an important tool under the Charter in our efforts to maintain international peace and security without recourse to the use of force, and resolve to ensure that sanctions are carefully targeted in support of clear

objectives, to comply with sanctions established by the Security Council and to ensure that sanctions are implemented in ways that balance effectiveness to achieve the desired results against the possible adverse consequences, including socio-economic and humanitarian consequences, for populations and third States.

107. Sanctions should be implemented and monitored effectively with clear benchmarks and should be periodically reviewed, as appropriate, and remain for as limited a period as necessary to achieve their objectives and should be terminated once the objectives have been achieved.

108. We call upon the Security Council, with the support of the Secretary-General, to improve its monitoring of the implementation and effects of sanctions, to ensure that sanctions are implemented in an accountable manner, to review regularly the results of such monitoring and to develop a mechanism to address special economic problems arising from the application of sanctions in accordance with the Charter.

109. We also call upon the Security Council, with the support of the Secretary-General, to ensure that fair and clear procedures exist for placing individuals and entities on sanctions lists and for removing them, as well as for granting humanitarian exemptions.

110. We support efforts through the United Nations to strengthen State capacity to implement sanctions provisions.

Transnational crime

111. We express our grave concern at the negative effects on development, peace and security and human rights posed by transnational crime, including the smuggling of and trafficking in human beings, the world narcotic drug problem and the illicit trade in small arms and light weapons, and at the increasing vulnerability of States to such crime. We reaffirm the need to work collectively to combat transnational crime.

112. We recognize that trafficking in persons continues to pose a serious challenge to humanity and requires a concerted international response. To that end, we urge all States to devise, enforce and strengthen effective measures to combat and eliminate all forms of trafficking in persons to counter the demand for trafficked victims and to protect the victims.

113. We urge all States that have not yet done so to consider becoming parties to the relevant international conventions on organized crime and corruption and, following their entry into force, to implement them effectively, including by incorporating the provisions of those conventions into national legislation and by strengthening criminal justice systems.

114. We reaffirm our unwavering determination and commitment to overcome the world narcotic drug problem through international cooperation and national strategies to eliminate both the illicit supply of and demand for illicit drugs.

115. We resolve to strengthen the capacity of the United Nations Office on Drugs and Crime, within its existing mandates, to provide assistance to Member States in those tasks upon request.

Women in the prevention and resolution of conflicts

116. We stress the important role of women in the prevention and resolution of conflicts and in peacebuilding. We reaffirm our commitment to the full and effective implementation of Security Council resolution 1325 (2000) of 31 October 2000 on

women and peace and security. We also underline the importance of integrating a gender perspective and of women having the opportunity for equal participation and full involvement in all efforts to maintain and promote peace and security, as well as the need to increase their role in decision-making at all levels. We strongly condemn all violations of the human rights of women and girls in situations of armed conflict and the use of sexual exploitation, violence and abuse, and we commit ourselves to elaborating and implementing strategies to report on, prevent and punish gender-based violence.

Protecting children in situations of armed conflict

117. We reaffirm our commitment to promote and protect the rights and welfare of children in armed conflicts. We welcome the significant advances and innovations that have been achieved over the past several years. We welcome in particular the adoption of Security Council resolution 1612 (2005) of 26 July 2005. We call upon States to consider ratifying the Convention on the Rights of the Child[36] and the Optional Protocol to the Convention on the Rights of the Child on the involvement of children in armed conflict.[37] We also call upon States to take effective measures, as appropriate, to prevent the recruitment and use of children in armed conflict, contrary to international law, by armed forces and groups, and to prohibit and criminalize such practices.

118. We therefore call upon all States concerned to take concrete measures to ensure accountability and compliance by those responsible for grave abuses against children. We also reaffirm our commitment to ensure that children in armed conflicts receive timely and effective humanitarian assistance, including education, for their rehabilitation and reintegration into society.

IV. Human rights and the rule of law

119. We recommit ourselves to actively protecting and promoting all human rights, the rule of law and democracy and recognize that they are interlinked and mutually reinforcing and that they belong to the universal and indivisible core values and principles of the United Nations, and call upon all parts of the United Nations to promote human rights and fundamental freedoms in accordance with their mandates.

120. We reaffirm the solemn commitment of our States to fulfil their obligations to promote universal respect for and the observance and protection of all human rights and fundamental freedoms for all in accordance with the Charter, the Universal Declaration of Human Rights[38] and other instruments relating to human rights and international law. The universal nature of these rights and freedoms is beyond question.

Human rights

121. We reaffirm that all human rights are universal, indivisible, interrelated, interdependent and mutually reinforcing and that all human rights must be treated in a fair and equal manner, on the same footing and with the same emphasis. While the significance of national and regional particularities and various historical, cultural and religious backgrounds must be borne in mind, all States, regardless of their

---

[36] United Nations, *Treaty Series*, vol. 1577, No. 27531.

[37] Resolution 54/263, annex I.

[38] Resolution 217 A (III).

political, economic and cultural systems, have the duty to promote and protect all human rights and fundamental freedoms.

122. We emphasize the responsibilities of all States, in conformity with the Charter, to respect human rights and fundamental freedoms for all, without distinction of any kind as to race, colour, sex, language or religion, political or other opinion, national or social origin, property, birth or other status.

123. We resolve further to strengthen the United Nations human rights machinery with the aim of ensuring effective enjoyment by all of all human rights and civil, political, economic, social and cultural rights, including the right to development.

124. We resolve to strengthen the Office of the United Nations High Commissioner for Human Rights, taking note of the High Commissioner's plan of action, to enable it to effectively carry out its mandate to respond to the broad range of human rights challenges facing the international community, particularly in the areas of technical assistance and capacity-building, through the doubling of its regular budget resources over the next five years with a view to progressively setting a balance between regular budget and voluntary contributions to its resources, keeping in mind other priority programmes for developing countries and the recruitment of highly competent staff on a broad geographical basis and with gender balance, under the regular budget, and we support its closer cooperation with all relevant United Nations bodies, including the General Assembly, the Economic and Social Council and the Security Council.

125. We resolve to improve the effectiveness of the human rights treaty bodies, including through more timely reporting, improved and streamlined reporting procedures and technical assistance to States to enhance their reporting capacities and further enhance the implementation of their recommendations.

126. We resolve to integrate the promotion and protection of human rights into national policies and to support the further mainstreaming of human rights throughout the United Nations system, as well as closer cooperation between the Office of the United Nations High Commissioner for Human Rights and all relevant United Nations bodies.

127. We reaffirm our commitment to continue making progress in the advancement of the human rights of the world's indigenous peoples at the local, national, regional and international levels, including through consultation and collaboration with them, and to present for adoption a final draft United Nations declaration on the rights of indigenous peoples as soon as possible.

128. We recognize the need to pay special attention to the human rights of women and children and undertake to advance them in every possible way, including by bringing gender and child-protection perspectives into the human rights agenda.

129. We recognize the need for persons with disabilities to be guaranteed full enjoyment of their rights without discrimination. We also affirm the need to finalize a comprehensive draft convention on the rights of persons with disabilities.

130. We note that the promotion and protection of the rights of persons belonging to national or ethnic, religious and linguistic minorities contribute to political and social stability and peace and enrich the cultural diversity and heritage of society.

131. We support the promotion of human rights education and learning at all levels, including through the implementation of the World Programme for Human Rights Education, as appropriate, and encourage all States to develop initiatives in this regard.

Internally displaced persons

132. We recognize the Guiding Principles on Internal Displacement[39] as an important international framework for the protection of internally displaced persons and resolve to take effective measures to increase the protection of internally displaced persons.

Refugee protection and assistance

133. We commit ourselves to safeguarding the principle of refugee protection and to upholding our responsibility in resolving the plight of refugees, including through the support of efforts aimed at addressing the causes of refugee movement, bringing about the safe and sustainable return of those populations, finding durable solutions for refugees in protracted situations and preventing refugee movement from becoming a source of tension among States. We reaffirm the principle of solidarity and burden-sharing and resolve to support nations in assisting refugee populations and their host communities.

Rule of law

134. Recognizing the need for universal adherence to and implementation of the rule of law at both the national and international levels, we:

(*a*) Reaffirm our commitment to the purposes and principles of the Charter and international law and to an international order based on the rule of law and international law, which is essential for peaceful coexistence and cooperation among States;

(*b*) Support the annual treaty event;

(*c*) Encourage States that have not yet done so to consider becoming parties to all treaties that relate to the protection of civilians;

(*d*) Call upon States to continue their efforts to eradicate policies and practices that discriminate against women and to adopt laws and promote practices that protect the rights of women and promote gender equality;

(*e*) Support the idea of establishing a rule of law assistance unit within the Secretariat, in accordance with existing relevant procedures, subject to a report by the Secretary-General to the General Assembly, so as to strengthen United Nations activities to promote the rule of law, including through technical assistance and capacity-building;

(*f*) Recognize the important role of the International Court of Justice, the principal judicial organ of the United Nations, in adjudicating disputes among States and the value of its work, call upon States that have not yet done so to consider accepting the jurisdiction of the Court in accordance with its Statute and consider means of strengthening the Court's work, including by supporting the Secretary-General's Trust Fund to Assist States in the Settlement of Disputes through the International Court of Justice on a voluntary basis.

---

[39] E/CN.4/1998/53/Add.2, annex.

Democracy

135. We reaffirm that democracy is a universal value based on the freely expressed will of people to determine their own political, economic, social and cultural systems and their full participation in all aspects of their lives. We also reaffirm that while democracies share common features, there is no single model of democracy, that it does not belong to any country or region, and reaffirm the necessity of due respect for sovereignty and the right of self-determination. We stress that democracy, development and respect for all human rights and fundamental freedoms are interdependent and mutually reinforcing.

136. We renew our commitment to support democracy by strengthening countries' capacity to implement the principles and practices of democracy and resolve to strengthen the capacity of the United Nations to assist Member States upon their request. We welcome the establishment of a Democracy Fund at the United Nations. We note that the advisory board to be established should reflect diverse geographical representation. We invite the Secretary-General to help to ensure that practical arrangements for the Democracy Fund take proper account of existing United Nations activity in this field.

137. We invite interested Member States to give serious consideration to contributing to the Fund.

Responsibility to protect populations from genocide, war crimes, ethnic cleansing and crimes against humanity

138. Each individual State has the responsibility to protect its populations from genocide, war crimes, ethnic cleansing and crimes against humanity. This responsibility entails the prevention of such crimes, including their incitement, through appropriate and necessary means. We accept that responsibility and will act in accordance with it. The international community should, as appropriate, encourage and help States to exercise this responsibility and support the United Nations in establishing an early warning capability.

139. The international community, through the United Nations, also has the responsibility to use appropriate diplomatic, humanitarian and other peaceful means, in accordance with Chapters VI and VIII of the Charter, to help to protect populations from genocide, war crimes, ethnic cleansing and crimes against humanity. In this context, we are prepared to take collective action, in a timely and decisive manner, through the Security Council, in accordance with the Charter, including Chapter VII, on a case-by-case basis and in cooperation with relevant regional organizations as appropriate, should peaceful means be inadequate and national authorities are manifestly failing to protect their populations from genocide, war crimes, ethnic cleansing and crimes against humanity. We stress the need for the General Assembly to continue consideration of the responsibility to protect populations from genocide, war crimes, ethnic cleansing and crimes against humanity and its implications, bearing in mind the principles of the Charter and international law. We also intend to commit ourselves, as necessary and appropriate, to helping States build capacity to protect their populations from genocide, war crimes, ethnic cleansing and crimes against humanity and to assisting those which are under stress before crises and conflicts break out.

140. We fully support the mission of the Special Adviser of the Secretary-General on the Prevention of Genocide.

Children's rights

141. We express dismay at the increasing number of children involved in and affected by armed conflict, as well as all other forms of violence, including domestic violence, sexual abuse and exploitation and trafficking. We support cooperation policies aimed at strengthening national capacities to improve the situation of those children and to assist in their rehabilitation and reintegration into society.

142. We commit ourselves to respecting and ensuring the rights of each child without discrimination of any kind, irrespective of the race, colour, sex, language, religion, political or other opinion, national, ethnic or social origin, property, disability, birth or other status of the child or his or her parent(s) or legal guardian(s). We call upon States to consider as a priority becoming a party to the Convention on the Rights of the Child.[36]

Human security

143. We stress the right of people to live in freedom and dignity, free from poverty and despair. We recognize that all individuals, in particular vulnerable people, are entitled to freedom from fear and freedom from want, with an equal opportunity to enjoy all their rights and fully develop their human potential. To this end, we commit ourselves to discussing and defining the notion of human security in the General Assembly.

Culture of peace and initiatives on dialogue among cultures, civilizations and religions

144. We reaffirm the Declaration and Programme of Action on a Culture of Peace[40] as well as the Global Agenda for Dialogue among Civilizations and its Programme of Action[41] adopted by the General Assembly and the value of different initiatives on dialogue among cultures and civilizations, including the dialogue on interfaith cooperation. We commit ourselves to taking action to promote a culture of peace and dialogue at the local, national, regional and international levels and request the Secretary-General to explore enhancing implementation mechanisms and to follow up on those initiatives. In this regard, we also welcome the Alliance of Civilizations initiative announced by the Secretary-General on 14 July 2005.

145. We underline that sports can foster peace and development and can contribute to an atmosphere of tolerance and understanding, and we encourage discussions in the General Assembly for proposals leading to a plan of action on sport and development.

V. Strengthening the United Nations

146. We reaffirm our commitment to strengthen the United Nations with a view to enhancing its authority and efficiency, as well as its capacity to address effectively, and in accordance with the purposes and principles of the Charter, the full range of challenges of our time. We are determined to reinvigorate the intergovernmental organs of the United Nations and to adapt them to the needs of the twenty-first century.

---

[40] Resolutions 53/243 A and B.
[41] See resolution 56/6.

147. We stress that, in order to efficiently perform their respective mandates as provided under the Charter, United Nations bodies should develop good cooperation and coordination in the common endeavour of building a more effective United Nations.

148. We emphasize the need to provide the United Nations with adequate and timely resources with a view to enabling it to carry out its mandates. A reformed United Nations must be responsive to the entire membership, faithful to its founding principles and adapted to carrying out its mandate.

General Assembly

149. We reaffirm the central position of the General Assembly as the chief deliberative, policymaking and representative organ of the United Nations, as well as the role of the Assembly in the process of standard-setting and the codification of international law.

150. We welcome the measures adopted by the General Assembly with a view to strengthening its role and authority and the role and leadership of the President of the Assembly and, to that end, we call for their full and speedy implementation.

151. We call for strengthening the relationship between the General Assembly and the other principal organs to ensure better coordination on topical issues that require coordinated action by the United Nations, in accordance with their respective mandates.

Security Council

152. We reaffirm that Member States have conferred on the Security Council primary responsibility for the maintenance of international peace and security, acting on their behalf, as provided for by the Charter.

153. We support early reform of the Security Council - an essential element of our overall effort to reform the United Nations - in order to make it more broadly representative, efficient and transparent and thus to further enhance its effectiveness and the legitimacy and implementation of its decisions. We commit ourselves to continuing our efforts to achieve a decision to this end and request the General Assembly to review progress on the reform set out above by the end of 2005.

154. We recommend that the Security Council continue to adapt its working methods so as to increase the involvement of States not members of the Council in its work, as appropriate, enhance its accountability to the membership and increase the transparency of its work.

Economic and Social Council

155. We reaffirm the role that the Charter and the General Assembly have vested in the Economic and Social Council and recognize the need for a more effective Economic and Social Council as a principal body for coordination, policy review, policy dialogue and recommendations on issues of economic and social development, as well as for implementation of the international development goals agreed at the major United Nations conferences and summits, including the Millennium Development Goals. To achieve these objectives, the Council should:

(a) Promote global dialogue and partnership on global policies and trends in the economic, social, environmental and humanitarian fields. For this purpose, the Council should serve as a quality platform for high-level engagement among

Member States and with the international financial institutions, the private sector and civil society on emerging global trends, policies and action and develop its ability to respond better and more rapidly to developments in the international economic, environmental and social fields;

(*b*) Hold a biennial high-level Development Cooperation Forum to review trends in international development cooperation, including strategies, policies and financing, promote greater coherence among the development activities of different development partners and strengthen the links between the normative and operational work of the United Nations;

(*c*) Ensure follow-up of the outcomes of the major United Nations conferences and summits, including the internationally agreed development goals, and hold annual ministerial-level substantive reviews to assess progress, drawing on its functional and regional commissions and other international institutions, in accordance with their respective mandates;

(*d*) Support and complement international efforts aimed at addressing humanitarian emergencies, including natural disasters, in order to promote an improved, coordinated response from the United Nations;

(*e*) Play a major role in the overall coordination of funds, programmes and agencies, ensuring coherence among them and avoiding duplication of mandates and activities.

156. We stress that in order to fully perform the above functions, the organization of work, the agenda and the current methods of work of the Economic and Social Council should be adapted.

Human Rights Council

157. Pursuant to our commitment to further strengthen the United Nations human rights machinery, we resolve to create a Human Rights Council.

158. The Council will be responsible for promoting universal respect for the protection of all human rights and fundamental freedoms for all, without distinction of any kind and in a fair and equal manner.

159. The Council should address situations of violations of human rights, including gross and systematic violations, and make recommendations thereon. It should also promote effective coordination and the mainstreaming of human rights within the United Nations system.

160. We request the President of the General Assembly to conduct open, transparent and inclusive negotiations, to be completed as soon as possible during the sixtieth session, with the aim of establishing the mandate, modalities, functions, size, composition, membership, working methods and procedures of the Council.

Secretariat and management reform

161. We recognize that in order to effectively comply with the principles and objectives of the Charter, we need an efficient, effective and accountable Secretariat. Its staff shall act in accordance with Article 100 of the Charter, in a culture of organizational accountability, transparency and integrity. Consequently we:

(*a*) Recognize the ongoing reform measures carried out by the Secretary-General to strengthen accountability and oversight, improve management performance and transparency and reinforce ethical conduct, and invite him to report to the General Assembly on the progress made in their implementation;

(*b*) Emphasize the importance of establishing effective and efficient mechanisms for responsibility and accountability of the Secretariat;

(*c*) Urge the Secretary-General to ensure that the highest standards of efficiency, competence, and integrity shall be the paramount consideration in the employment of the staff, with due regard to the principle of equitable geographical distribution, in accordance with Article 101 of the Charter;

(*d*) Welcome the Secretary-General's efforts to ensure ethical conduct, more extensive financial disclosure for United Nations officials and enhanced protection for those who reveal wrongdoing within the Organization. We urge the Secretary-General to scrupulously apply the existing standards of conduct and develop a system-wide code of ethics for all United Nations personnel. In this regard, we request the Secretary-General to submit details on an ethics office with independent status, which he intends to create, to the General Assembly at its sixtieth session;

(*e*) Pledge to provide the United Nations with adequate resources, on a timely basis, to enable the Organization to implement its mandates and achieve its objectives, having regard to the priorities agreed by the General Assembly and the need to respect budget discipline. We stress that all Member States should meet their obligations with regard to the expenses of the Organization;

(*f*) Strongly urge the Secretary-General to make the best and most efficient use of resources in accordance with clear rules and procedures agreed by the General Assembly, in the interest of all Member States, by adopting the best management practices, including effective use of information and communication technologies, with a view to increasing efficiency and enhancing organizational capacity, concentrating on those tasks that reflect the agreed priorities of the Organization.

162. We reaffirm the role of the Secretary-General as the chief administrative officer of the Organization, in accordance with Article 97 of the Charter. We request the Secretary-General to make proposals to the General Assembly for its consideration on the conditions and measures necessary for him to carry out his managerial responsibilities effectively.

163. We commend the Secretary-General's previous and ongoing efforts to enhance the effective management of the United Nations and his commitment to update the Organization. Bearing in mind our responsibility as Member States, we emphasize the need to decide on additional reforms in order to make more efficient use of the financial and human resources available to the Organization and thus better comply with its principles, objectives and mandates. We call on the Secretary-General to submit proposals for implementing management reforms to the General Assembly for consideration and decision in the first quarter of 2006, which will include the following elements:

(*a*) We will ensure that the United Nations budgetary, financial and human resource policies, regulations and rules respond to the current needs of the Organization and enable the efficient and effective conduct of its work, and request the Secretary-General to provide an assessment and recommendations to the General Assembly for decision during the first quarter of 2006. The assessment and recommendations of the Secretary-General should take account of the measures already under way for the reform of human resources management and the budget process;

(*b*)   We resolve to strengthen and update the programme of work of the United Nations so that it responds to the contemporary requirements of Member States. To this end, the General Assembly and other relevant organs will review all mandates older than five years originating from resolutions of the General Assembly and other organs, which would be complementary to the existing periodic reviews of activities. The General Assembly and the other organs should complete and take the necessary decisions arising from this review during 2006. We request the Secretary-General to facilitate this review with analysis and recommendations, including on the opportunities for programmatic shifts that could be considered for early General Assembly consideration;

(*c*)   A detailed proposal on the framework for a one-time staff buyout to improve personnel structure and quality, including an indication of costs involved and mechanisms to ensure that it achieves its intended purpose.

164.   We recognize the urgent need to substantially improve the United Nations oversight and management processes. We emphasize the importance of ensuring the operational independence of the Office of Internal Oversight Services. Therefore:

(*a*)   The expertise, capacity and resources of the Office of Internal Oversight Services in respect of audit and investigations will be significantly strengthened as a matter of urgency;

(*b*)   We request the Secretary-General to submit an independent external evaluation of the auditing and oversight system of the United Nations, including the specialized agencies, including the roles and responsibilities of management, with due regard to the nature of the auditing and oversight bodies in question. This evaluation will take place within the context of the comprehensive review of the governance arrangements. We ask the General Assembly to adopt measures during its sixtieth session at the earliest possible stage, based on the consideration of recommendations of the evaluation and those made by the Secretary-General;

(*c*)   We recognize that additional measures are needed to enhance the independence of the oversight structures. We therefore request the Secretary-General to submit detailed proposals to the General Assembly at its sixtieth session for its early consideration on the creation of an independent oversight advisory committee, including its mandate, composition, selection process and qualification of experts;

(*d*)   We authorize the Office of Internal Oversight Services to examine the feasibility of expanding its services to provide internal oversight to United Nations agencies that request such services in such a way as to ensure that the provision of internal oversight services to the Secretariat will not be compromised.

165.   We insist on the highest standards of behaviour from all United Nations personnel and support the considerable efforts under way with respect to the implementation of the Secretary-General's policy of zero tolerance regarding sexual exploitation and abuse by United Nations personnel, both at Headquarters and in the field. We encourage the Secretary-General to submit proposals to the General Assembly leading to a comprehensive approach to victims' assistance by 31 December 2005.

166.   We encourage the Secretary-General and all decision-making bodies to take further steps in mainstreaming a gender perspective in the policies and decisions of the Organization.

167. We strongly condemn all attacks against the safety and security of personnel engaged in United Nations activities. We call upon States to consider becoming parties to the Convention on the Safety of United Nations and Associated Personnel[42] and stress the need to conclude negotiations on a protocol expanding the scope of legal protection during the sixtieth session of the General Assembly.

System-wide coherence

168. We recognize that the United Nations brings together a unique wealth of expertise and resources on global issues. We commend the extensive experience and expertise of the various development-related organizations, agencies, funds and programmes of the United Nations system in their diverse and complementary fields of activity and their important contributions to the achievement of the Millennium Development Goals and the other development objectives established by various United Nations conferences.

169. We support stronger system-wide coherence by implementing the following measures:

Policy

- Strengthening linkages between the normative work of the United Nations system and its operational activities

- Coordinating our representation on the governing boards of the various development and humanitarian agencies so as to ensure that they pursue a coherent policy in assigning mandates and allocating resources throughout the system

- Ensuring that the main horizontal policy themes, such as sustainable development, human rights and gender, are taken into account in decision-making throughout the United Nations

Operational activities

- Implementing current reforms aimed at a more effective, efficient, coherent, coordinated and better-performing United Nations country presence with a strengthened role for the senior resident official, whether special representative, resident coordinator or humanitarian coordinator, including appropriate authority, resources and accountability, and a common management, programming and monitoring framework

- Inviting the Secretary-General to launch work to further strengthen the management and coordination of United Nations operational activities so that they can make an even more effective contribution to the achievement of the internationally agreed development goals, including the Millennium Development Goals, including proposals for consideration by Member States for more tightly managed entities in the fields of development, humanitarian assistance and the environment

---

[42] United Nations, *Treaty Series*, vol. 2051, No. 35457.

Humanitarian assistance

- Upholding and respecting the humanitarian principles of humanity, neutrality, impartiality and independence and ensuring that humanitarian actors have safe and unhindered access to populations in need in conformity with the relevant provisions of international law and national laws

- Supporting the efforts of countries, in particular developing countries, to strengthen their capacities at all levels in order to prepare for and respond rapidly to natural disasters and mitigate their impact

- Strengthening the effectiveness of the United Nations humanitarian response, inter alia, by improving the timeliness and predictability of humanitarian funding, in part by improving the Central Emergency Revolving Fund

- Further developing and improving, as required, mechanisms for the use of emergency standby capacities, under the auspices of the United Nations, for a timely response to humanitarian emergencies

Environmental activities

- Recognizing the need for more efficient environmental activities in the United Nations system, with enhanced coordination, improved policy advice and guidance, strengthened scientific knowledge, assessment and cooperation, better treaty compliance, while respecting the legal autonomy of the treaties, and better integration of environmental activities in the broader sustainable development framework at the operational level, including through capacity-building, we agree to explore the possibility of a more coherent institutional framework to address this need, including a more integrated structure, building on existing institutions and internationally agreed instruments, as well as the treaty bodies and the specialized agencies

Regional organizations

170. We support a stronger relationship between the United Nations and regional and subregional organizations, pursuant to Chapter VIII of the Charter, and therefore resolve:

(*a*) To expand consultation and cooperation between the United Nations and regional and subregional organizations through formalized agreements between the respective secretariats and, as appropriate, involvement of regional organizations in the work of the Security Council;

(*b*) To ensure that regional organizations that have a capacity for the prevention of armed conflict or peacekeeping consider the option of placing such capacity in the framework of the United Nations Standby Arrangements System;

(*c*) To strengthen cooperation in the economic, social and cultural fields.

Cooperation between the United Nations and parliaments

171. We call for strengthened cooperation between the United Nations and national and regional parliaments, in particular through the Inter-Parliamentary Union, with a view to furthering all aspects of the Millennium Declaration in all fields of the work of the United Nations and ensuring the effective implementation of United Nations reform.

Participation of local authorities, the private sector and civil society, including non-governmental organizations

172. We welcome the positive contributions of the private sector and civil society, including non-governmental organizations, in the promotion and implementation of development and human rights programmes and stress the importance of their continued engagement with Governments, the United Nations and other international organizations in these key areas.

173. We welcome the dialogue between those organizations and Member States, as reflected in the first informal interactive hearings of the General Assembly with representatives of non-governmental organizations, civil society and the private sector.

174. We underline the important role of local authorities in contributing to the achievement of the internationally agreed development goals, including the Millennium Development Goals.

175. We encourage responsible business practices, such as those promoted by the Global Compact.

Charter of the United Nations

176. Considering that the Trusteeship Council no longer meets and has no remaining functions, we should delete Chapter XIII of the Charter and references to the Council in Chapter XII.

177. Taking into account General Assembly resolution 50/52 of 11 December 1995 and recalling the related discussions conducted in the General Assembly, bearing in mind the profound cause for the founding of the United Nations and looking to our common future, we resolve to delete references to "enemy States" in Articles 53, 77 and 107 of the Charter.

178. We request the Security Council to consider the composition, mandate and working methods of the Military Staff Committee.

8th plenary meeting
16 September 2005

UNITED NATIONS
PRESS RELEASE

For immediate release
(New York, 15 March 2012)

Marking a full year of violent suppression of anti-government protests in Syria, the United Nations Secretary-General's Special Advisers on the Prevention of Genocide, Francis Deng, and on the Responsibility to Protect, Edward Luck, release the following statement:

Over the past year, the Syrian Government's increasingly violent assault of its population has deepened sectarian divides and brought the country to the brink of civil war. Clearly, the Government has manifestly failed to protect the Syrian population. It has resorted to extreme violence, instead of allowing the Syrian people to freely express their opinions and make their voices heard about the fate of their country. In the name of order, it has brought chaos and the destruction of whole neighborhoods in some of the country's major cities.

The lack of unified international condemnation and response to protect the Syrian population has encouraged the Government to continue its course of action. Reports suggest that the Government has intensified its attacks in the face of Security Council paralysis, leading to a sharp increase in the number of deaths, injuries and cases of abuse and torture over recent weeks and months.

The lack of timely and decisive action by the international community has left the Syrian population to fend for itself. As a result, reports suggest that an increasing number of Syrians have taken up arms. A growing number of soldiers have reportedly chosen to defect rather than obey orders to commit crimes against civilians. As attacks by Government forces and allied militias against civilians continue, we fear that the risk of retributive acts along sectarian lines will also increase. To prevent further rounds of violence, which could have devastating effects for the country and the region, the Government must stop its attacks on the people of Syria now.

There is strong and growing evidence that crimes against humanity are being committed in Syria. We reiterate our calls for the Government of Syria to immediately end all violence against its population and for all parties, including non-state actors, to meet their obligations under international law. Violence by any party against civilian populations is unacceptable. We call on the international community, including the Security Council, to take immediate collective action, utilizing the full range of tools available under the United Nations Charter, to protect populations at risk of further atrocity crimes in Syria. The international community must act on the pledge by all Heads of State and Government at the 2005 World Summit to protect populations from genocide, war crimes, ethnic cleansing and crimes against humanity, including their incitement.

* **** *

For media queries please contact:

Office on Genocide Prevention and the Responsibility to Protect
http://www.un.org/en/preventgenocide/adviser/

Phone: +1 917-367-4961, +1 212 963-3928

Mobile: +1 646-538-3282, +1 516-849-3670
Email: mrozm@un.org
866 UN Plaza, Suite 600

**UNITED NATIONS
PRESS RELEASE**

[For immediate release]

Statement of the Special Adviser of the Secretary-General on the Prevention of Genocide on the situation in Syria

(New York, 20 December 2012) Mr. Adama Dieng, Special Adviser of the Secretary-General on the Prevention of Genocide, warned today of the increasing risk of sectarian violence in Syria.

"I am deeply concerned that entire communities risk paying the price for crimes committed by the Syrian Government," said Mr. Dieng. As the situation in Syria deteriorates further, there is a growing risk that civilian communities, including Alawite and other minorities perceived to be associated with the Government, its security forces, militias and allies could be subject to large scale reprisal attacks.

"I urge all parties to the conflict to adhere to international humanitarian and human rights law, which prohibits the targeting of individuals or groups based on religious or ethnic identity as well as attacks against civilians not taking direct part in hostilities."

"I also call on all actors to condemn hate speech that could constitute incitement to violence against communities based on their religious affiliation," stated Mr. Dieng. "Reprisal attacks, hate speech and incitement to violence against a particular community have, in the past, been precursors to serious and massive violations of human rights and international humanitarian law."

"I urge armed opposition forces to protect and respect the rights of all individuals in their custody, as well as civilians residing in territory under their control, without discrimination," stated Mr. Dieng.

"The Government of Syria is manifestly failing to protect its populations. The international community must act on the commitment made by all Heads of State and Government at the 2005 World Summit to protect populations from genocide, war crimes, ethnic cleansing and crimes against humanity, including their incitement," said Mr. Dieng.

"I also reiterate the calls of the international community for the Security Council to refer the situation in Syria to the International Criminal Court and stress the importance of taking steps now to facilitate future transitional justice processes in Syria to reduce the risk of retribution, promote reconciliation and provide all communities with a sense of justice and dignity."

* **** *

For media queries please contact:

Mallory Mroz
Office on Genocide Prevention and the Responsibility to Protect
http://www.un.org/en/preventgenocide/adviser/
Phone: +1 917-367-4961 Email: mrozm@un.org

UN General Assembly Resolution 66/253, Syria

The UN General Assembly passed this resolution on February 16, 2012. The press release states, "Strongly condemning continued widespread and systematic human rights violations by the Syrian authorities, the General Assembly today voted over-whelmingly to call on both the Government and allied forces and armed groups "to stop all violence or reprisals immediately".

Adopting an Arab-backed resolution by a recorded vote of 137 in favour to 12 against, with 17 abstentions, the Assembly expressed grave concern at the deteriorating situa-tion in Syria, and condemned a raft of violations carried out by the authorities, such as the use of force against civilians, the killing and persecution of protestors and journa-lists, and sexual violence and ill-treatment, including against children."

Prevention of armed conflict

Andorra, Australia, Bahrain, Comoros, Croatia, Denmark, Egypt, Finland, France, Greece, Hungary, Jordan, Kuwait, Libya, Montenegro, Morocco, Norway, Oman, Pa-nama, Qatar, Republic of Korea, Saudi Arabia, Somalia, Tunisia, Turkey, United Arab Emirates, United Kingdom of Great Britain and Northern Ireland, United States of America: draft resolution

The situation in the Syrian Arab Republic

The General Assembly,

Recalling its resolution 66/176 of 19 December 2011, as well as Human Rights Council resolutions S-16/1 of 29 April 2011,1 S-17/1 of 23 August 20111 and S-18/1 of 2 De-cember 2011,

Expressing grave concern at the deterioration of the situation in the Syrian Arab Re-public, in particular the ongoing human rights violations and use of violence by the Syrian authorities against its population,

Reaffirming the role of regional and subregional organizations in the maintenance of international peace and security as set out in Chapter VIII of the Charter of the United Nations,

Reaffirming also its strong commitment to the sovereignty, independence, unity and territorial integrity of the Syrian Arab Republic and to the principles of the Charter,

Reaffirming further that all States Members of the United Nations should refrain in their international relations from the threat or use of force against the territorial inte-grity or political independence of any State or in any other manner inconsistent with the purposes of the United Nations,

Welcoming the engagement of the Secretary-General and all diplomatic efforts aimed at ending the crisis,

1. Reaffirms its strong commitment to the sovereignty, independence, unity and terri-torial integrity of the Syrian Arab Republic, and stresses the need to resolve the current

political crisis in the Syrian Arab Republic peacefully;

2. Strongly condemns the continued widespread and systematic violations of human rights and fundamental freedoms by the Syrian authorities, such as the use of force against civilians, arbitrary executions, the killing and persecution of protestors, human rights defenders and journalists, arbitrary detention, enforced disappearances, interference with access to medical treatment, torture, sexual violence and ill-treatment, including against children;

3. Calls upon the Government of the Syrian Arab Republic to immediately put an end to all human rights violations and attacks against civilians, protect its population, fully comply with its obligations under applicable international law and fully implement Human Rights Council resolutions S-16/1, S-17/1 and S-18/1, as well as General Assembly resolution 66/176, including by cooperating fully with the independent international commission of inquiry;

4. Condemns all violence, irrespective of where it comes from, and calls upon all parties in the Syrian Arab Republic, including armed groups, to stop all violence or reprisals immediately, in accordance with the League of Arab States initiative;

5. Stresses again the importance of ensuring accountability and the need to end impunity and hold to account those responsible for human rights violations, including those violations that may amount to crimes against humanity;

6. Demands that the Government of the Syrian Arab Republic, in accordance with the Plan of Action of the League of Arab States of 2 November 2011 and its decisions of 22 January and 12 February 2012, without delay:
(a) Cease all violence and protect its population;
(b) Release all persons detained arbitrarily owing to the recent incidents;
(c) Withdraw all Syrian military and armed forces from cities and towns and return them to their original home barracks;
(d) Guarantee the freedom of peaceful demonstration;
(e) Allow full and unhindered access and movement for all relevant League of Arab States institutions and Arab and international media in all parts of the Syrian Arab Republic to determine the truth about the situation on the ground and monitor the incidents taking place;

7. Calls for an inclusive Syrian-led political process, conducted in an environment free from violence, fear, intimidation and extremism and aimed at effectively addressing the legitimate aspirations and concerns of the people of the Syrian Arab Republic, without prejudging the outcome;

8. Fully supports the League of Arab States decision of 22 January 2012 to facilitate a Syrian-led political transition to a democratic, pluralistic political system, in which citizens are equal regardless of their affiliations or ethnicities or beliefs, including through the commencement of a serious political dialogue between the Government of the Syrian Arab Republic and the whole spectrum of the Syrian opposition, under the auspices of the League of Arab States and in accordance with the timetable set out by the League of Arab States;

9. Calls upon all Member States to provide support to the Arab League initiative, as requested;

10. Calls upon the Syrian authorities to allow safe and unhindered access for humanitarian assistance in order to ensure the delivery of humanitarian aid to persons in need of assistance;

11. Requests, in this context, the Secretary-General and all relevant United Nations bodies to provide support to the efforts of the League of Arab States, both through good offices aimed at promoting a peaceful solution to the Syrian crisis, including through the appointment of a Special Envoy, and through technical and material assistance, in consultation with the League of Arab States;

12. Requests the Secretary-General to report on the implementation of the present resolution, in consultation with the League of Arab States, within 15 days of its adoption.